Understanding Digital Computers

Prob for wed.
Study ch. on F.F.
complete table on
P. 39 (36 on lab book)
by analyzing the
circuit on P. 38
also analyze the
circuit on P. 41
and table.

SYSTEMS 810B

Library of Congress Catalogue Card Number: 71-149774
ISBN 0-471-79065-6
Printed in the United States of America
10 9 8 7 6 5 4 3 2 1

UNDERSTANDING DIGITAL COMPUTERS

Second Edition

Paul Siegel

JOHN WILEY & SONS, INC., New York · London · Sydney · Toronto

TO MY SON, NORMAN,
AND MY DAUGHTER, DEBORAH

Preface

This textbook is a comprehensive introduction to the fundamentals of digital computer "hardware." It is about principles—not about specific commercial computers. Its objective is to convey a good understanding of how digital computers are designed and built.

The book consists of an introductory chapter and three sections. The introduction describes the digital computer and its functions. In a sense, it is a distillation of the entire volume. Hopefully, it generates an appreciation—a feel—for digital computers and a desire to learn more about them.

Sections I to III move from a theoretical discussion of arithmetic and logic to the exposition of techniques for achieving these ideas in practice. These building blocks then are combined into larger functional units from which a complete computer may be constructed. The final chapter describes a specimen computer.

The material is presented in a way that should facilitate learning. Basic ideas are discussed first, and each succeeding chapter builds on the facts and ideas considered in previous chapters. Wherever possible, new concepts are illustrated by examples. The major points of each chapter are given in a summary that includes a list of key words developed in the chapter. Each chapter also includes exercises. Most exercises are numerical in order to reinforce the specific principles learned. However, the exercises at the end of the final chapter (The Specimen Computer) are in the form of questions to encourage class discussion of the various approaches to computer organization.

The emphasis is on logic—not on electronics. (See the *Note to the Instructor* that follows.)

Although this textbook can be used fruitfully without a laboratory, it has been carefully designed to allow almost all types of commercially available laboratory blocks or units to be used with it. Section II permits coordination between logical blocks in the text and logical blocks that may be built in the laboratory. Section III points the way for a student to synthesize these logical blocks into the functional units of a digital computer. An ambitious laboratory course would encourage the student to go further and to build the specimen computer.

I gratefully acknowledge the constructive criticism of Al Meyerhoff and Ed Veitch of Burroughs Corporation, and I am especially indebted to James Maginnis, Director of the Computing Laboratory of Drexel University, for his thorough review of the first edition of this work.

PAUL SIEGEL

Note to the Instructor

The book may be used in one of three ways:

1. In a three-semester-hour junior college first course on digital computers for the prospective computer technician, engineer, scientist, or programmer who has some background in electronics.
2. In an introductory digital computer course that is combined with student laboratory work for use in computer technical schools and junior college vocational schools.
3. In a three-semester-hour survey course that is part of the curriculum of a liberal arts or liberal science college for students who are unfamiliar with electronics.

For students with no electronics background, only the first part of Chapter 5 needs to be covered. For students who possess some knowledge of electronics, the parts of the chapter set off by asterisks (which are devoted to electronics) may be included as well.

Asterisks also are used to separate the last part of Chapter 14, which covers "Advanced Concepts," from the remainder of the chapter. This part may or may not be included in the course, depending on the instructor's discretion.

For guidance in a laboratory-associated course, all examples, exercises, and other material in Sections II and III that comprise portions of the specimen computer are prefaced with an asterisk.

P.S.

Contents

CHAPTER 1
Introduction: What is a Digital Computer? 1

Digital Devices 1
Mechanical Calculating Machines 4
Electronic Calculating Machines 5
Analog versus Digital Computers 6
Fast Moron versus Slow Genius 8
Simple Hardware, Complicated Logic 10
Functional Organization of the Computer 12
Machine Language and Programming 13
Direct Man-Computer Communication 16
Summary 17
Exercises 17

section I
ARITHMETIC AND LOGIC

CHAPTER 2
Word and Number Languages 21

Language 22
Positional Number Systems 23
Translation Between Number Systems 33
Coded-Decimal Numbers 39
Negative Numbers and Complements 41
Self-Checking Codes 45
Alphanumeric Codes 46
Summary 49
Exercises 50

CHAPTER 3

Arithmetic Processes 52

Algebraic Addition 52
Multiplication 54
Division 56
Square Root 59
Binary Arithmetic 63
Location of Decimal or Binary Point 65
Checking 68
Summary 71
Exercises 72

CHAPTER 4

Machine Logic 74

Basic Elements of Formal Logic 74
Practical Logical Elements 96
Summary 99
Exercises 101

section II

BUILDING BLOCKS

CHAPTER 5

Logical Building Blocks 105

Types of Logical Building Blocks 105

* * * * * *

Semiconductor Diodes 110
Transistors 115
Electromagnetic Logical Elements 125

* * * * * *

Summary 135
Exercises 136

CHAPTER 6

Translators 140

Gates 140
Decoders 141
Encoders 145
Summary 150
Exercises 150

CHAPTER 7

Registers and Counters 152

Registers 152
Counters 164
Summary 173
Exercises 174

CHAPTER 8

Comparators and Adders 176

Binary Comparator 176
Parity Generators and Detectors 178
Complementers 182
Coincidence Adders and Subtractors 184
Accumulators 189
Summary 193
Exercises 194

CHAPTER 9

Bulk Logic 196

Bulk Storage 197
Bulk Switching 225
Bulk Storage and Switching 230
Summary 238
Exercises 239

section III

FUNCTIONAL UNITS OF A DIGITAL COMPUTER

CHAPTER 10

Machine Language and Programming 245

Basic Data Structure 245
Instruction Word 247
Data Word 250
Internal Communication 253
Machine Language 258
High-Level Language 268
Summary 273
Exercises 275

CHAPTER 11

Memory Unit 278

What is Memory? 279
Coordinate Access Memory 279

Cyclic Access Memory 286
Content Addressable Memory 290
Summary 291
Exercises 291

CHAPTER 12

Input-Output System 293

Input-Output Channel 294
External Storage Channel 295
Communication Channel 297
Data Transfer 306
Input-Output Instructions 317
Off-Line Devices 319
Summary 320
Exercises 322

CHAPTER 13

Arithmetic and Logic Unit 325

Addition 325
Algebraic Addition 329
Quantitative Comparisons 334
Multiplication 335
Division 342
Nonarithmetic Manipulation 347
Summary 349
Exercises 350

CHAPTER 14

Control Unit 352

Basic Machine Cycle 352
Modification of Instruction Sequence 362
Instruction Modification 365
Concurrency 375

* * * * * *

Advanced Concepts 378

* * * * * *

Summary 392
Exercises 394

CHAPTER 15

A Specimen Computer 397

General Description 397
Memory 402

Input-Output 406
Arithmetic 407
Control 414
Programming 421
Operation and Maintenance 429
Exercises 430

Appendix 433

Glossary 441

Bibliography 451

Index 455

Understanding Digital Computers

CHAPTER 1

Introduction: What is a digital computer?

What is a digital computer? Is it a lightning calculator which can multiply two 10-digit numbers in the time it takes a jet plane to fly 1 inch? Is it an intellectual tool that may be used to amplify the mental capabilities of managers and engineers, doctors, and teachers? Or is it a device which can make decisions and check its own work? Or a device which accepts a set of thousands of instructions and then faithfully executes them in the appropriate sequence without outside help?

The digital computer is all these and more. It is more because its complicated mechanism is composed of childishly simple, basic elements; because it applies the rules of logic to simulate many of the functions of the human brain; and because of its fantastic accuracy, reliability, and flexibility.

The basic principles of operation of the remarkable electronic digital computer are portrayed in this introductory chapter. The more prosaic details of operation are presented in the remaining chapters.

DIGITAL DEVICES

In what way is a digital computer different from the many calculating machines man has devised ever since he learned how to count? Before we can discuss the digital computer itself, we must know what is meant by a digital device.

The simplest digital device is any device which can count. The simplest of all counting devices are the ten fingers. As a matter of fact, the word "digital" is derived from the latin *digitus*, which means finger. Another simple digital device is the clock. It ticks away, or counts, little bits of time called seconds.

In ancient days, man learned to substitute beads for fingers in order to help him count. He built a counting board which consisted of several stiff wires mounted on a wooden frame, with ten sliding beads on each wire (Fig. 1*a*).

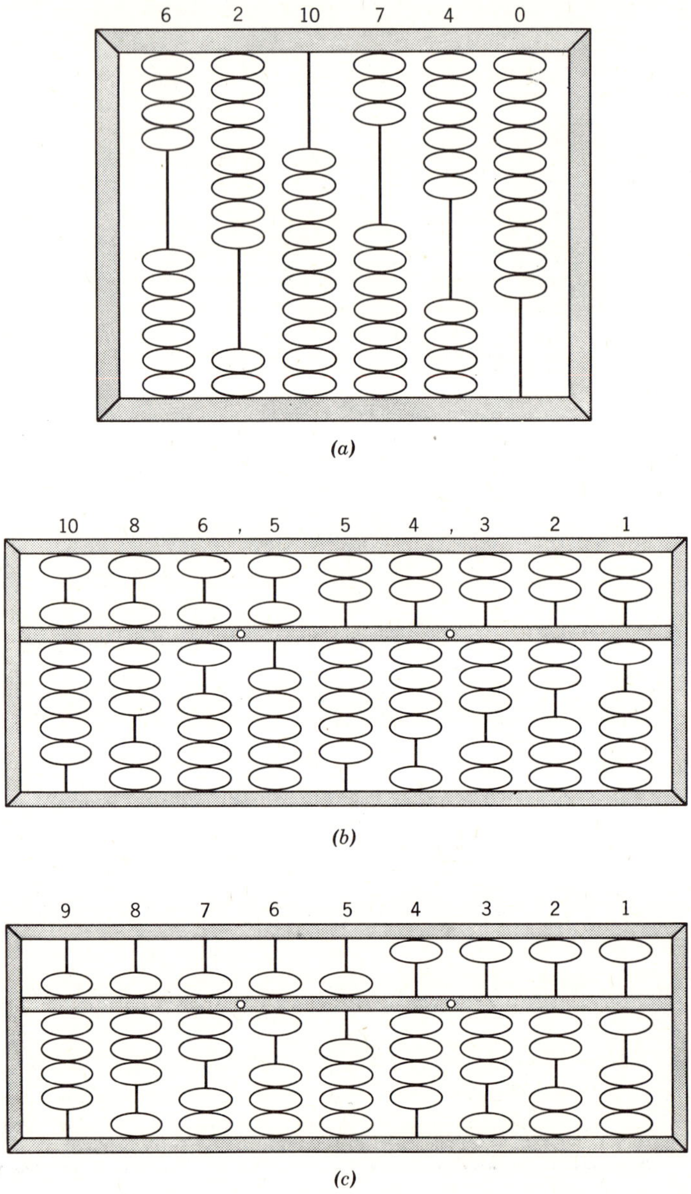

Figure 1 The counting board and the abacus. (*a*) Counting board. (*b*) Abacus—Chinese. (*c*) Abacus—Japanese.

By moving a certain number of beads toward the bottom of the board, any digit from 0 to 9 can be placed on each of the wires. Even 10 can be placed on a wire, as is shown in the figure. This 10 is interpreted as a 0 in the indicated column plus a carry of 1 to the column to its left. The counting board in the figure is storing 630,740.

The ancient Chinese simplified the counting board into the abacus (Fig. 1*b*). Instead of ten beads on each wire, the abacus has seven. Two beads are mounted above a dividing wooden member, and five beads are mounted below the wooden member. All beads are in neutral position when they are furthest from the dividing member. Each of the lower beads has a value of one; each of the upper beads has a value of five. The number 1,086,554,321 is stored in the abacus of Fig. 1*b*.

The Japanese made the abacus more efficient. They used only five beads: four 1-unit beads below the dividing member and one 5-unit bead above. The number 987,654,321 is stored in the Japanese abacus of Fig. 1*c*.

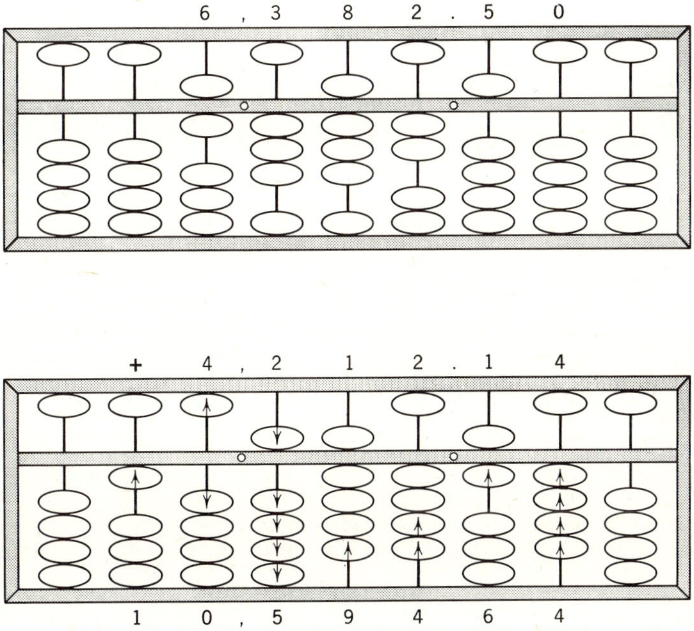

Figure 2 Addition by means of abacus.

Figure 2 illustrates how the Japanese abacus is used to add $6,382.50 and $4,212.14. First $6,382.50 are placed in the abacus as shown. The first period from the left on the dividing member is used as a comma and the second period is used as a decimal point. Four 1-unit beads are added to the rightmost column; one 1-unit bead is added to the 5-unit bead stored in column 2 (assuming that columns are numbered consecutively starting with the rightmost column as 1) ; two 1-unit beads are added to the two 1-unit beads in column 3 ; and a 1-unit bead is added to the representation for eight stored in column 4.

In the fifth column the operation is not so straightforward because two 1-unit beads must be added to the three already stored. This cannot be done since there are only four 1-unit beads to a column. So all the 1-unit beads are brought back to neutral and the 5-unit bead is brought down to the reading position. In column 6 we must add four 1-unit beads to a column where a 1-unit bead and the 5-unit bead are already stored. This is obviously impossible since there are only three 1-unit beads left in the column. So all the beads are brought to neutral and a carry is placed in column 7. The sum can be read from the abacus as $10,594.64.

By extensions of the above process, subtraction, multiplication, and division may be performed on the abacus.

MECHANICAL CALCULATING MACHINES

A great step forward in the art of adding mechanically was made by Blaise Pascal in 1642. Pascal used wheels divided into parts instead of wires holding ten beads. The ten-part wheel can be compared to the wire with the ten beads bent so the two ends meet. The wheel represents a great improvement over the bead-holding wire, especially in the production of a carry. When going from

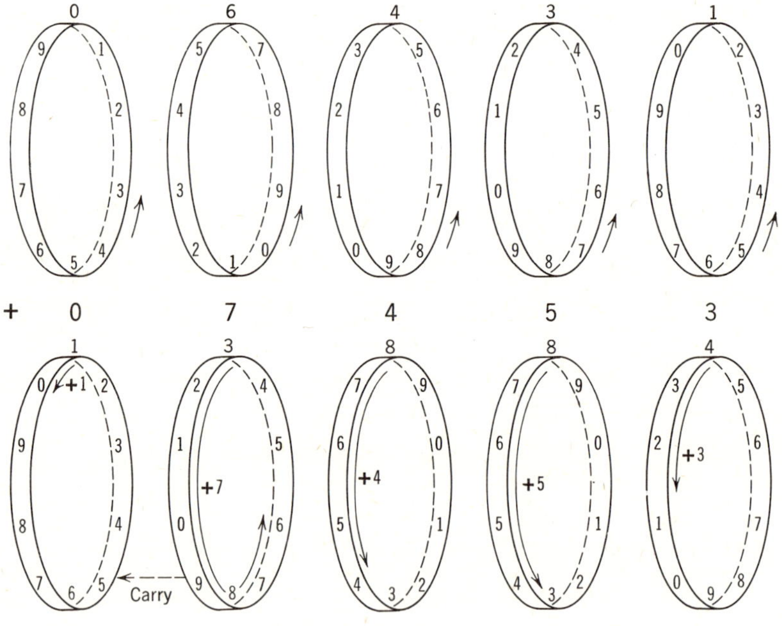

Figure 3 Adding by means of wheel calculator.

9 to 0 in any one column of the abacus, all the beads must be brought to neutral and a unit bead must be added to the column to its left. In the wheel-using machine just one turn of the wheel is all that is needed. The wheel moves to 0 and mechanical linkage is used to automatically cause a small carry movement in the wheel to its left.

Figure 3 shows 6431 stored in a wheel-using calculator. To add 7453 to this number, each wheel is caused to turn by the indicated number of wheel divisions. During the rotation of the fourth wheel from the right, the 0 division passes the reading position, causing a carry to the fifth wheel. By means of mechanical linkage, the fifth wheel moves from 0 to 1. The sum 13,884 is retained in the calculator.

Modern mechanical calculating machines also use wheels. Electric motors cause the wheels to turn at a rapid rate, yet the basic principle behind modern calculators is the same as that used by Pascal in his machine. An important achievement has been made, namely, electric power is substituted for hand power. However, the drudgery of placing individual digits into the machine is still present.

ELECTRONIC CALCULATING MACHINES

To speed up the counting process, electronic devices may be substituted for mechanical wheels. By shifting electrons from one place to another for each unit of the digit, the same counting effect can be produced as by moving a bead at a time, or turning a wheel a division at a time. A diagrammatic representation of this idea is shown in Fig. 4. Instead of a column being represented by a wheel, it is represented by a circle of ten circuits shown as boxes in this figure. Originally the 0 box in each column is energized. Upon receipt of a bit of electric energy representing a unit, electrons flow from the energized box to the next box. Each successive bit of energy causes activation

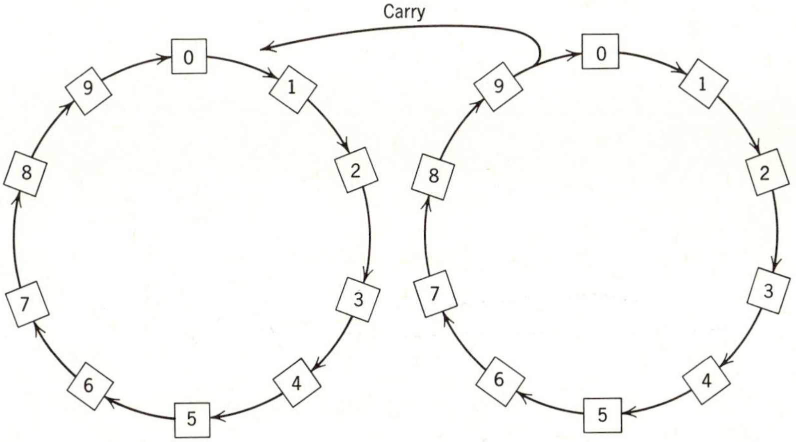

Figure 4 Counting with electrons.

of the box next in line. As with the mechanical arrangement, the pulse which causes activation of the 0 box again, also causes a carry pulse—a bit of electric energy—to be applied to the circle on the left.

In practice there is no need to put these "boxes" in a circle. It was done here only to show the analogy with mechanical wheels.

Why should a machine using moving electrons be so much faster than one using mechanical wheels? The answer to this question is very simple. The speed with which anything can be made to move depends on its weight, and the weight of an electron is practically nonexistent when compared to any mechanical gadget. Thus, with very little energy applied, electrons can be made to travel at tremendous speeds. This fact enables us to build computers which can perform millions of additions in the time it takes a comptometer operator just to touch a key on her keyboard.

With machines of such lightning speed, it becomes ridiculous to have the operator feed it one problem at a time. Therefore, a logical control was built into the computer. This logical control enables the machine to accept a complete routine of instructions at one time, and then perform each instruction in the proper sequence. As a matter of fact, as will be seen later, the logical control enables the machine to accept generalized instructions which can cause it to perform more operations than are actually fed into the machine.

The tremendous speeds at which these machines can work, and the flexibility built into them due to the logical control, make modern electronic digital computers a millionfold more powerful than mechanical calculators.

ANALOG VERSUS DIGITAL COMPUTERS

Even before the advent of the electronic digital computer, the analog computer was busy doing important jobs which could not be performed by desk calculators. For instance, instead of building a costly experimental model of an airplane and then running exhaustive wind-tunnel tests, the whole "experiment" can be performed by the analog computer. Instead of using an actual airplane, design data for an airplane are fed into the analog computer. Instead of using a wind tunnel, formulas representing the effects produced by varying flight conditions are fed into the computer. The output of the analog computer is usually a curve representing results for a complete set of conditions. Effectively, the tests are performed without any hardware. Upon completion of one "experiment," the computer is ready to perform a new "experiment."

What exactly is an analog computer? or, more fundamentally, an analog device? An analog device is any device whose operation is analogous to some physical quantity we want to measure. A thermometer is a simple analog device. It compares, or draws an analogy, between the expansion of mercury and temperature. A simple spring balance is another analog device. It compares the weight of an object with the force necessary to move a spring. Other examples are the oil-pressure gage in the car and the glass graduate used to prepare baby's formula.

If an analogy can be formed between the operation of a device and a mathematical process, this device can form the basis for an analog computer. Many physical phenomena may be used to construct analog computers. But since electrons are so mobile, most present-day analog computers perform mathematical operations with the aid of electronic circuits. Electronic circuits have been built which perform operations analogous to those of addition, subtraction, multiplication, division, and even higher mathematical operations such as integration. For instance to add 6 and 5, a 6-volt signal and a 5-volt signal are fed to an electronic adder. The circuit of the electronic adder is designed so that, under these circumstances an 11-volt signal is produced as output. Similar effects occur with the subtractor, multiplier, divider, and integrator.

Notice that in analog computers, measurement is always involved; in digital computers, numbers are used. Data in analog computers change smoothly; data in digital computers change in discrete steps. Analog computer results must be read off a scale. Results of digital computation are given by means of a representation for the digits of the number.

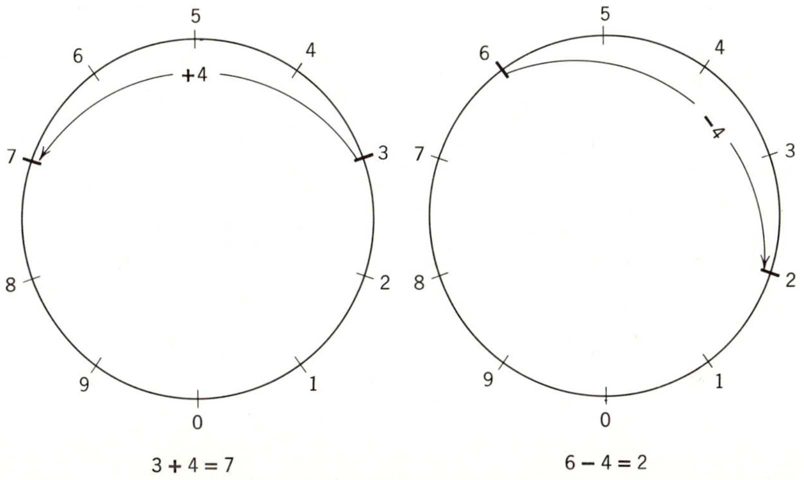

Figure 5 Difference between addition and subtraction.

There is a limit to the accuracy obtainable from an analog computer. This is so because there is a limit to the accuracy with which one can read a scale. The scale can be enlarged to increase the available accuracy. But even if this is done, the accuracy of the electronic circuits feeding the scale must be improved. Eventually the point is reached where it is difficult, if not impossible, to improve greatly the available accuracy.

However, the accuracy obtainable from a digital computer is theoretically unlimited. This is so because a separate circuit takes care of each column in a set of figures. Thus, 5 adders are needed to add a 5-digit number to another

5-digit number, and 50 adders are needed to add a 50-digit number to another 50-digit number. Theoretically, therefore, we can obtain answers accurate to any decimal place by merely providing the appropriate number of circuits.

FAST MORON VERSUS SLOW GENIUS

The digital computer is extremely fast, but it has the "brains" of a moron. Basically all the machine can do is add. If this is true, how can the computer perform problems in higher mathematics? The answer to this question is that for a respectable number of mathematical operations no matter how sophisticated they may appear, they can be shown to be related to addition.

Subtraction is the converse of addition. Addition of two digits is performed by first counting the units of one digit and then continuing to count the units of the second digit. Subtraction is performed in a similar way except that the counting for the second digit is in the opposite direction (see Fig. 5).

Multiplication is a form of repeated addition. For instance,

$$\begin{array}{r} 5 \\ \times 6 \\ \hline 30 \end{array} \quad \text{is equivalent to} \quad \begin{array}{r} 6 \\ 6 \\ 6 \\ 6 \\ 6 \\ \hline 30 \end{array}$$

Since division is the converse of multiplication, division may be considered to be an advanced form of subtraction.

Algebra is an extension of arithmetic processes. For instance, in order to find *X* in

$$2X = 8 + 4$$

both sides are divided by two, giving

$$X = \frac{8+4}{2} = \frac{12}{2} = 6$$

The answer is obtained by means of ordinary arithmetic.

Even the process of integration used in calculus can be shown to be equivalent to a series of additions. Integration is a means for finding the area included by a curve. Mathematicians have developed formulas and rules for performing integration. But finding the area included by a curve can be done in a much more simple manner.

For instance, to find the area of triangle *ABC* in Fig. 6, the length of the base (4) is multiplied by one-half the altitude (2). Another method of obtaining the same answer is to divide the triangle into four rectangles and then sum the areas of the rectangles. This gives the correct answer because the area outside

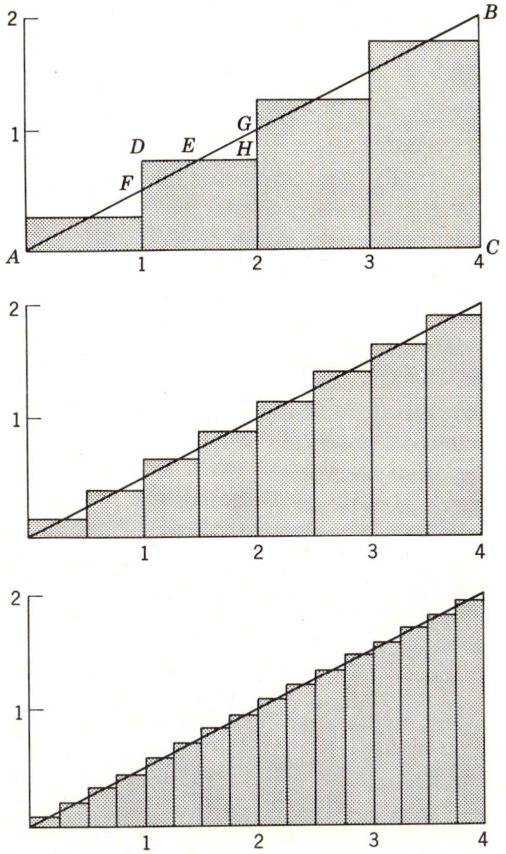

Figure 6 Obtaining area of triangle.

of the triangle which each rectangle covers is just as large as the area inside the triangle which each rectangle does not cover (triangle *DEF* is equal to triangle *EGH* in Fig. 6). Dividing the triangle into many more rectangles and summing the areas provide the same answer.

Suppose the same process is performed on the circle of Fig. 7. If the circle is divided into three rectangles and the areas of the rectangles are summed, only the *approximate* area of the circle is obtained. This is so because area *ABC* is not exactly equal to area *CDE*, and the areas bounded by *EFGH* and *E'F'G'H'* are not counterbalanced by any other area. However, if the circle is divided into more and more rectangles (Figs. 7*b* and 7*c*), the sum of the rectangle areas gets closer and closer to the true area of the circle. By dividing the circle into very many rectangles and summing their areas, an excellent approximation to the area of the circle may be obtained. This process can be used for finding the area included in any curve or sets of curves.

The mathematician—the genius—does not plod through all this work. He has developed formulas and rules which he uses similar to shorthand. With the use of this shorthand method he arrives at the correct answer quickly. The machine—the moron—does the problem the slow way by summing a large number of rectangles. But the machine is inherently so much faster that it arrives at the answer faster with the slow, stupid method than the mathematical genius with his supposedly short sophisticated method!

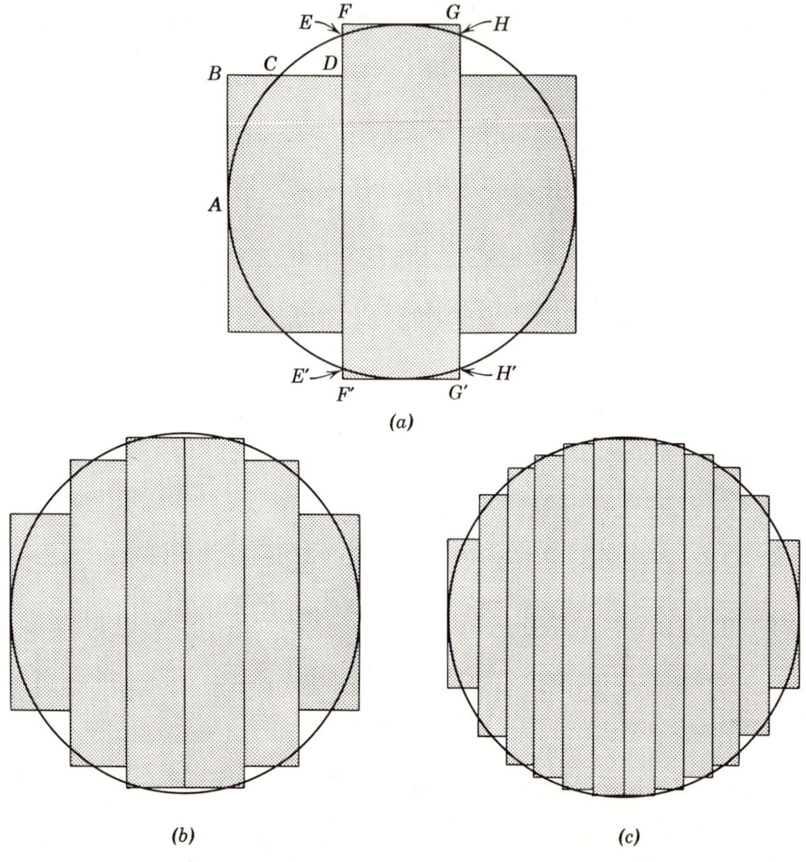

Figure 7 Obtaining area of circle.

SIMPLE HARDWARE, COMPLICATED LOGIC

The computer, then, does only additions in a sequence determined by a logical control. This seems to imply that it is a simple machine. In a sense it is, since only a handful of different types of circuits are needed to build the most awesome machine in existence. What then produces the complication? The complication is produced by the many interconnections among these few basic circuits. The method of interconnection is called logic, and the few basic circuits are called logical elements.

Of course, you are wondering how the concept of logic fits into a discussion of computers. A digital computer processes data. In that sense each part of it can be said to be communicating with or "speaking" to other parts of the machine. For this purpose the machine uses a "language." Whatever form this language may take, it must possess rules indicating how subjects are connected. These connectives are similar to connectives used in ordinary speech. Some of these grammatical connectives are "if, all, then, also, and, or not, only . . ." These connectives are the cement of the language. They indicate the relationships among the different elements of a sentence. Because they are so important for indicating relationships, they are the fundamental building blocks of logic.

These connectives not only indicate the relationships among elements of a sentence but also among propositions in a logical syllogism. Take the following syllogism for instance:

If all men have two eyes,
and you are a man,
then you have two eyes.

What are the key words? The connectives "if," "and," "then." Take another syllogism:

Freedom is possible *only* in a democracy.
Russia is *not* a democracy.
There is *no* freedom in Russia.

The important connectives within the sentences, in this case, are "only," "not," "no." The key words which connect the three statements are understood to be "if" before the first sentence, "and" before the second sentence, and "then" before the third.

Now here is the important consideration. *All the possible connectives may be reduced to only three basic ones—"and," "or," and "not"*! This idea is discussed more fully in Chapter 4. Suffice it to say here that, if a circuit could be developed for each of the three logical connectives, we would have the necessary cement for the machine language. Then we only would need circuits to store the "propositions" before and after being applied through the connective circuits. These connective and storage circuits are called logical elements.

Logical elements may take on many forms. Originally, relays and vacuum tubes were used for this purpose. But a new era dawned when the magnetic core, the transistor, and the semiconductor integrated circuit were developed. These components enabled manufacturers to reduce the size of electronic computers to the point where they became feasible for use in ordinary offices.

FUNCTIONAL ORGANIZATION OF THE COMPUTER

To repeat, the logical elements built into the computer are simple. The big problem in understanding digital computers is the logic which ties the logical elements into a unit performing arithmetic and logical operations.

Fortunately, all computer operations can be grouped into five functional categories. The method in which these five functional categories are related to one another represents the functional organization of a digital computer. By studying the functional organization, a broad view of the computer is obtained, a view which aids materially in the study of the detailed logic.

To gain an understanding of the functional organization, let us analyze what we do when confronted with a simple problem such as:

$$55 \times 35 + 67 \times 25 - \tfrac{24}{4}$$

To begin with, we pick up a pencil and record the problem on a sheet of paper. Next we decide which portion of the problem to do first. Let us assume we decide to do the first multiplication. We record the problem on another part of the paper and perform the calculation. As soon as the calculation is done, we store the product on another part of the paper. Next, we perform the second multiplication and store its product; then we do the division and store the quotient. Now we add the two products, and then subtract the quotient from the sum. The calculating steps in the precedure are summarized below.

(1)	(2)	(3)	(4)	(5)
55	67	$\frac{24}{4} = 6$	+1925	+3600
×35	×25		+1675	− 6
275	335		+3600	+3594
165	134			
+1925	+1675			

Notice, first, that we need a pencil, or a means of recording data—*input equipment*. Input equipment in computers take on various forms such as modified typewriters which produce electric pulses when the keys are depressed; magnetic-tape units which convert data stored in the form of tiny, magnetized areas on tape into electric pulses; or punched cards where data represented by holes punched in specific areas are converted into electric signals.

Second, the problem is recorded on paper. This is necessary because we can not do all parts of the problem at once. Therefore, we must have a *memory*—the paper—which retains the bits of data until we are ready to use them. In computers, memory is provided by magnetic discs which store many bits of data by magnetizing (or not magnetizing) tiny areas around many tracks; by magnetic cores which store the data by being magnetized one way or another; by vacuum tubes, relays, transistors, thin magnetic films, and a host of other devices.

Third, we must decide which operation to perform first, and then choose the data needed for that operation. In the computer this is done by the *control* circuits, according to instructions placed in the computer by the operator. Incidentally, these instructions are usually placed into the machine through the input equipment.

Fourth, the rules of addition, subtraction, multiplication, and division must be applied to obtain the answers to the individual parts of the problem. In the computer, these operations are performed by the *arithmetic* unit.

Fifth, when the problem is done, the operator records the result in a special place. If he is an accountant, he may put his answer in a ledger. This operation is called *output*. The *output* equipment in the computer often is similar to the input equipment, since they both either transfer data from the "outside world" to the computer, or vice versa. Another type of output device is the printer which is used for the preparation of reports, bills, and other forms.

To summarize, the five major functional units of a digital computer are:

1. INPUT—To insert outside data into the machine.
2. MEMORY—To store data and make it available at the appropriate time.
3. ARITHMETIC—To perform the calculations.
4. OUTPUT—To remove data from the machine to the outside.
5. CONTROL—To cause all parts of the computer to act as a team.

Figure 8 shows how the five functional units of the computer act together. A complete set of instructions plus data is usually fed through the input equipment to the memory where it is stored. Each instruction is then fed to the control unit. The control unit interprets the instructions and issues commands (dashed lines on figure) to the other functional units to cause operations to be performed on the data. Arithmetic operations are performed in the arithmetic unit, and the results are then fed back to the memory. Data may be fed from either the arithmetic unit or the memory through the ouput equipment to the outside world.

MACHINE LANGUAGE AND PROGRAMMING

The five units of the computer must communicate with each other. This they do by means of a machine language which uses a code composed of combinations of electric pulses. These pulse combinations are usually represented by ZEROS and ONES where the ONE may be a plus pulse and the ZERO a minus pulse; or the ONE may be a pulse and the ZERO a no-pulse. One possible code for the 10-decimal digits is

0	0000	5	0101
1	0001	6	0110
2	0010	7	0111
3	0011	8	1000
4	0100	9	1001

Numbers are communicated between one unit and another by means of these ONE–ZERO or pulse–no-pulse combinations. The input has the additional

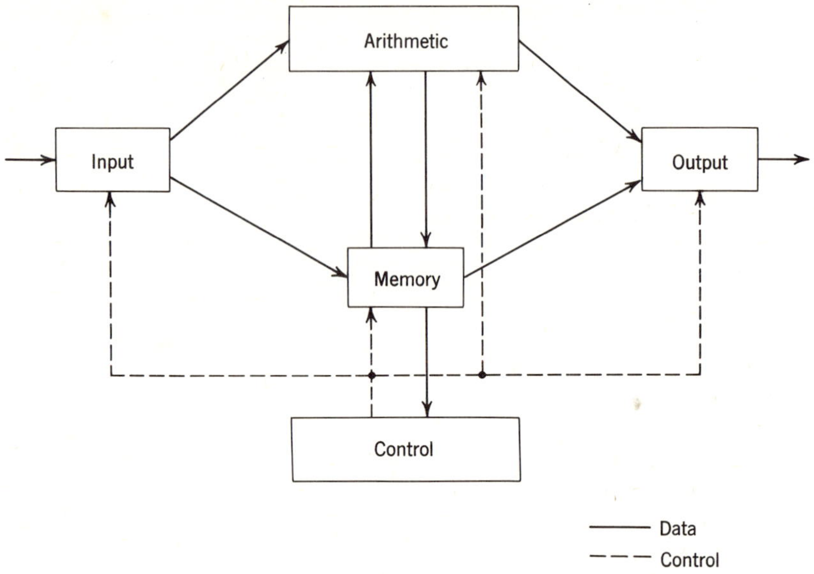

Figure 8 Functional organization of a digital computer.

job of converting information fed in by the operator into machine language. In other words, it translates from our language into the pulse–no-pulse combinations understandable to the computer. The output has the additional job of converting the pulse–no-pulse combinations into a form understandable to us, such as a line of print or a display.

In addition to data, the input translates instructions needed to perform a given problem into pulse–no-pulse combinations. These instructions are originated by a programmer whose job it is to translate a scientific or business problem presented in human language into a sequence of detailed instructions understandable to the machine.

What is involved in programming and the steps the computer goes through when it follows the program are shown in a very general way in Fig. 9. The data and the program of instructions necessary to perform the problem previously given are placed in the input system. During the first part of the execution of the problem, the control unit sends signals to the input and to the memory for the entire program to be stored in the memory. Then the control accepts each instruction in turn from the memory, interprets it, and sends the proper control signals to the other units for execution of these instructions. First it sends 55 and 35 to the arithmetic unit, and the multiplication instruction to the control for interpretation and execution. After the multiplication, the product is fed back to a designated spot in memory. Then the computer, following its program, repeats the above routine for the 67 and 25 factors and stores the product in another spot in memory. After this, the computer performs the division, $\frac{24}{4}$, and stores the quotient. Once these portions of the problem are completed, the two products are fed to the arithmetic unit and summed. Then the quotient is subtracted from the sum in the arithmetic unit and the grand total is stored in memory. The last instruction may call for a print-out of the answer. In this case, the control sends signals to memory and output for the answer to be printed.

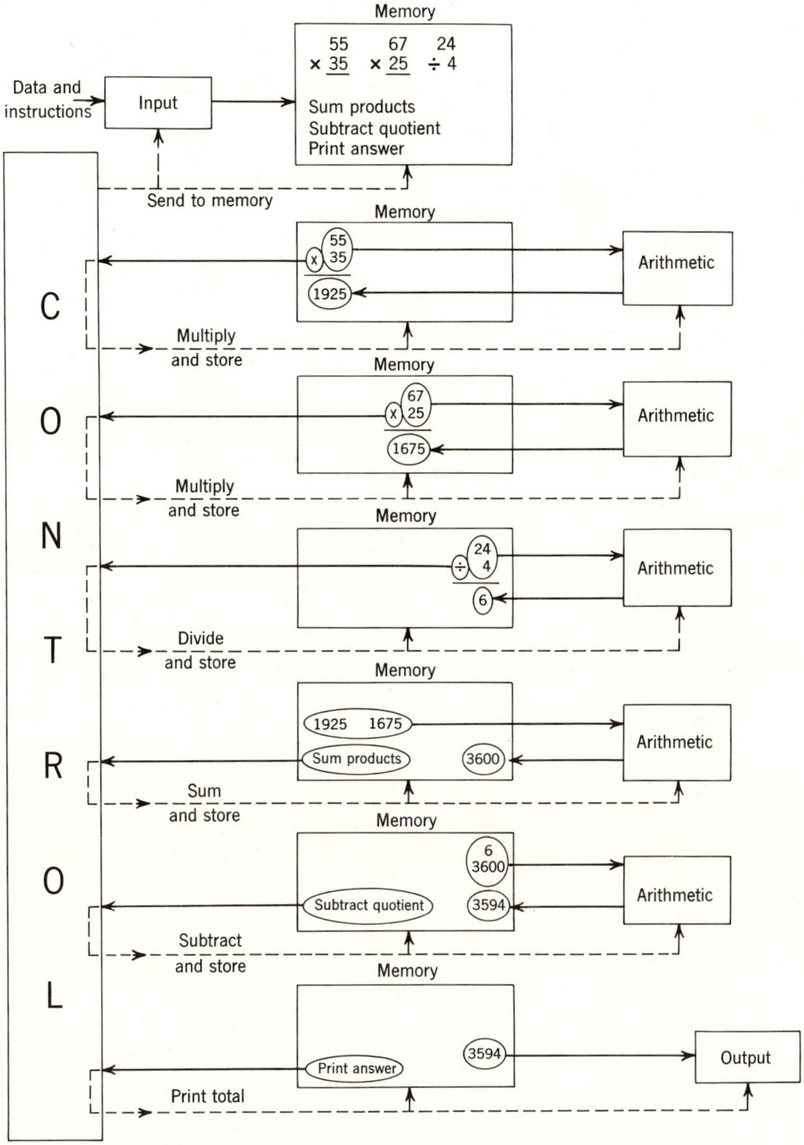

Figure 9 Execution of simple problem by computer.

It is easy to see that there are many detailed steps necessary to perform even a very simple problem. In some of the more complicated problems, the number of instructions necessary to specify the problem completely may take up about 200 pages of instructions!

Programming is tedious work. For instance, a straightforward way to cause the machine to sum 10,000 numbers would be to instruct the machine as follows:

Add the 1st number to the arithmetic contents (0 at the beginning).
Add the 2nd number to the arithmetic contents.
Add the 3rd number to the arithmetic contents.
Add the 4th number to the arithmetic contents, etc.

To accomplish this task the programmer must write 10,000 addition instructions!

But ways have been found whereby the programmer does *not* have to specify *every* instruction he wants the computer to execute. This is done by writing a generalized instruction sequence which is repeated over and over, each time with a slight modification. To see how this is done, first note that each location in memory is numbered and that the program for adding the 10,000 numbers really reads something like this:

Add the number in memory location No. 1 to the sum stored in arithmetic.
Add the number in memory location No. 2 to the sum stored in arithmetic.
Add the number in memory location No. 3 to the sum stored in arithmetic.
Add the number in memory location No. 4 to the sum stored in arithmetic, etc.

The only difference among these instruction is the number of the memory location referred to. Therefore, the routine could be written as follows:

Add the number in memory location No. 1 to the sum stored in arithmetic.
Add 1 to the memory location referred to in the addition instruction.
Repeat routine.

Of course, this is not the complete program. But enough is given to show the general idea.

DIRECT MAN-COMPUTER COMMUNICATION

Lately programming has been simplified to the point where the programmer need worry very little about the internal details of the machine. High-level programming languages, such as FORTRAN and COBOL, have been developed that allow him to enter his problems into the machine in more simple form. Of course, other programs such as compilers are needed to translate from the high-level language to the machine language the computer understands.

This process has been taken further. The general user—the clerk, engineer, or manager—who knows nothing about programming can enter his problem in a language that is a subset of English. Again, to make this possible, considerable programming must first be done by a programming specialist.

SUMMARY

1. The modern electronic digital computer executes all types of mathematical problems and logical procedures extremely fast.
2. There are five major functional units to the computer: input, memory, arithmetic, output, and control. They communicate with each other by means of a language composed of coded combinations of ONE'S and ZERO'S.
3. To execute problems on the computer, the user breaks them down into small subproblems easily expressed in a quasi-English language. Inside the computer, a program previously entered by a system programmer translates these subproblems into instructions the computer can perform.
4. The following are some of the advantages that electronic digital computers have over other mathematical machines:
   a. *Speed.* The electronic machine is faster than the mechanical one because electrons travel much faster than any mechanical object.
   b. *Accuracy.* The digital computer is capable of much greater accuracy than the analog computer. Another decimal place of accuracy can be added to a digital machine by merely inserting an extra circuit to take care of this decimal place.
   c. *Reliability.* Machine reliability is the result of the strict logic on which the computer is based; circuit standardization; and the self-checking features of the machine.
   d. *Flexibility.* This is obtained by the logical control; the use of many types of input and output equipment to communicate between the "outside world" and the computer; and the memory.

Exercises

1. What is the difference between the Chinese abacus and the Japanese abacus? What is the value of the bead above the dividing horizontal member of the Japanese abacus?
2. What is a carry? How many carries are produced when 1 is added to 999?
3. Why are electronic calculators faster than mechanical calculators?
4. What is the purpose of the control unit in the electronic computer? What is the purpose of the memory?
5. State two differences between analog and digital computers? Which can provide the greatest theoretical accuracy? What is the relationship between number of digits and accuracy?

6. Express 8×4 as a series of additions.
7. Find the quotient of $\frac{32}{4}$, using a series of subtractions.
8. Define addition in terms of counting. Define subtraction in terms of counting.
9. What is a logical element? What is the relationship between grammar and logic?
10. What are the three basic logical elements?
11. What is meant by machine language?
12. What does a programmer do?
13. Consider the following problem and break it up into a sequence of sub-problems similar to the sequence of solution that is normally followed by a computer program:

$$\frac{5 \times 20 \times 3}{7} - (8 + 6)(3 - 2)$$

section I

ARITHMETIC AND LOGIC

There are many types of digital computers. There are special-purpose computers which are built to do a specific job, and general-purpose computers which are built to do many jobs. There are fixed-program machines which sequence the computer through the same operations over and over, and computers whose programs can be modified. There are computers built for the solving of individual problems, others built for the control of physical systems, and still others for interaction with human beings in the performance of complex intellectual activities. But all the different types of computers are based on the same principles—the principles of arithmetic and logic.

In this first section of the book we discuss the principles of arithmetic and logic. In Section II these principles are used to develop building blocks; in Section III the building blocks are put together to form a specimen computer.

Section I is divided into three chapters. In the first chapter we show that number languages are similar to word languages and we develop several number languages. In the second chapter we discuss rules for performing arithmetic in several of the number languages. Since practically any calculating job can be broken down into a series of arithmetic operations, the rules of arithmetic provide a good foundation upon which to build our knowledge of computers. In the third chapter the fundamental elements needed to mechanize the rules of arithmetic are presented in the rules of logic.

CHAPTER 2

Word and number languages

Each man has his impressions of the world around him. These impressions are definitely unalike. How can anyone convey his inward impressions to another in a manner such that the second person can understand him? This can be done only by a set of symbols the meanings of which have been agreed upon by everybody. A set of such meaningful symbols put together according to commonly agreed rules is a language.

The language of ancient man was composed of pictures. The pictures were symbols and they were understood by all. But a picture can convey only subjective feeling; it is unsuitable for precise thinking.

The early picture languages developed into the ideographs of the Chinese and Japanese. The ideographs are a little less subjective, but still not quite objective enough.

Now most languages use words formed of letters. These words representing simple ideas are linked together with other words to form sentences representing more complicated ideas. The symbols used in modern languages are more abstract than the ideographs, and thus are better tools for orderly thought. But even in modern languages, words receive connotations which tarnish their usefulness for rigorous thought. This is the reason mathematicians and scientists like to use mathematical symbols for their more profound thinking.

We need language not only to communicate with our fellow men but also to communicate with ourselves, that is, to think. We can do some thinking without language. We can think of being hungry or of going fishing. But it is impossible for us to do abstract thinking without language. How would we think, "I want to go hunting next week," without a language. How would we think of "blue," "thin," "good," "better," "a mile"? We need to manipulate symbols in order to do any but the most primitive type of thinking.

LANGUAGE

Redundancy and Dependability

What are the rules of language? We usually have symbols tied together in a word. Each word consists of a different combination of symbols. The relationships among words are expressed by means of the logical rules of grammar. In order to understand a language, we must know the symbols, the rules of construction of words, and the grammar.

Because of the many relationships expressed by means of rules, not every symbol in a word, or every word in a sentence, conveys meaning or gives information. Some symbols are there only to take care of the rules. For instance, in the previous sentence why do we need to use four words, "to take care of," instead of one word, "care"? In the word "grammar," why do we need two m's? These extra symbols are called redundancies.

There is a relationship between redundancy and probability. Which would you expect to find more often in an English sentence, a t or an x? How often is t followed by h? What letter will almost inevitably follow *q*? Similarly, there are frequently occurring word combinations such as "in order," "and the," "there is," "because of," and "expect to." Because we have a good statistical idea of what symbols to expect in the above cases, these examples contain redundancies.

Redundancy is defined as the use of more symbols to encode a message than is strictly necessary.

These extra symbols, however, increase the dependability of a language. Because language rules tell us to some extent what to expect, garbled messages may be deciphered more readily. Redundancy thus makes a language easier to understand.

Brevity and Power

If redundancy increases the dependability of a language, it also makes language more cumbersome. To increase the informational efficiency of a language, we must remove redundancies—make the language tightly packed. This is the reason mathematicians use symbols instead of words to present their ideas.

There are many ways to abbreviate. One way is to designate a letter or a short group of letters to represent a larger combination of letters, for example, as in shorthand used by secretaries. St., Dr., and Mr. are other examples. Abbreviations enable us to transmit the message faster.

Another form of abbreviation—although it is never called that—is the use of one sophisticated word instead of a group of commonly known words. Some examples of this are "ambiguous" instead of "not clearly understood"; "sadist" instead of "one who likes to inflict pain on others"; "atheist" instead of "one who does not believe in God." The word "God" represents a large variety of ideas. We have many such meaningful words: democracy, thermodynamics, logic, etc. There is little redundancy in these words. We can employ them to convey information compactly. They are powerful words, used by great thinkers, but difficult to understand.

Probably the most powerful way of expressing ideas is by means of mathematical symbols. Remember the age problem:

> John is 15 years old.
> Five years ago Jack was twice as old as John.
> How old is Jack now?

To solve this problem we designate John's present age by X and Jack's present age by Y; then we express the whole problem compactly thus:

$$X = 15$$
$$Y = 2(X - 5) + 5$$

Once the problem is expressed in mathematical form, we do not care what the symbols represent. We operate with them according to definite rules. In this case we substitute the value for X into the second equation, and perform the indicated arithmetic, thus:

$$Y = 2(X - 5) + 5 = 2(15 - 5) + 5 = 2 \times 10 + 5 = 20 + 5 = 25$$

After the answer is obtained, we translate it back into English. Remembering that Y stands for Jack's present age, we draw the conclusion that Jack's present age is 25.

Mathematical symbols decrease the redundancy and greatly increase the efficiency of our thinking. But both the sender and the receiver of the message must completely understand the meaning of the symbols. The more the symbol represents, the harder it is to be sure that the meaning of the symbol will get across. Therefore, we say that brevity increases the efficiency of communication at the expense of reliability.

POSITIONAL NUMBER SYSTEMS

Words and Numbers

We have been talking for the most part about languages based on words. We do have languages based on numbers. Word languages and number languages are similar in many respects. Word languages are built from letters which are combined into words. Relationships among these words are expressed by means of the rules of grammar. Number languages are built from digits which are combined into numbers; relationships among these numbers are expressed by means of the rules of arithmetic (+, −, ×, ÷).

Some words are related to each other by rules of spelling or of grammar. But many words are unrelated. All numbers, however, are related by a scheme of counting.

Because number languages are built on a firmer foundation, they are much more reliable for reasoning than are word languages. "Twenty percent of the people are thieves" means more than "some people are thieves"; or "Joe made a grade of 90% on the examination" expresses more than "Joe is a good student." However, an attempt has been made to place word language on just as rigorous a basis by means of the algebra of logic. The algebra of logic is discussed at greater length in Chapter 4.

Table 1 summarizes the similarities between word language and number language.

table 1 SIMILARITIES BETWEEN WORD AND NUMBER LANGUAGES

Item Compared	Word Language	Number Language
Fundamental unit	letter	digit
Coded combination	word	number
Rules for forming combinations	spelling and grammar	counting
Logic of Language	grammar	arithmetic
Shorthand	abbreviations	mathematics

What is Zero?

The decimal number system is in most common use today. To appreciate the decimal number system, let us look at ancient number systems, some of which are shown in Table 2. Note that in all these systems, numbers are built up in an *additive* manner: symbols having different weights are combined to produce a sum representing the number. For instance, in the Roman system symbols I, V, X, L, C, D, M representing 1, 5, 10, 50, 100, 500, and 1000, respectively, are combined to produce:

$$\text{LXVIII} = 50 + 10 + 5 + 1 + 1 + 1 = 68$$

$$\text{MCXII} = 1000 + 100 + 10 + 1 + 1 = 1112$$

In some cases units are not added but subtracted, as in the following:

$$\text{CXLIV} = 100 - 10 + 50 - 1 + 5 = 144$$

$$\text{CMXCII} = -100 + 1000 - 10 + 100 + 1 + 1 = 992$$

It is very difficult to do arithmetic with these ancient number systems. Can you imagine trying to multiply CCCXXXIX by XLVII? These number systems are unwieldy because there is no simple way to set down the rules for counting. It is true that each symbol represents a certain value, but its relationship to the whole number depends upon the symbol before and the symbol after it. Furthermore, symbols in any relative position do not represent any particular range of numbers.

table 2 ANCIENT NUMBER SYSTEMS

Decimal	Roman	Mayan	Hieroglyphics (3400 BC)
1	I	•	∩
2	II	• •	∩ ∩
3	III	• • •	∩ ∩ ∩
4	IV	• • • •	∩ ∩ ∩ ∩
5	V	—	∩ ∩ ∩ ∩ ∩
6	VI	• over —	∩ ∩ ∩ ∩ ∩ ∩
7	VII	• • over —	∩ ∩ ∩ ∩ ∩ ∩ ∩
8	VIII	• • • over —	∩ ∩ ∩ ∩ ∩ ∩ ∩ ∩
9	IX	• • • • over —	∩ ∩ ∩ ∩ ∩ ∩ ∩ ∩ ∩
10	X	=	⋒
11	XI	• over =	⋒ ∩
12	XII	• • over =	⋒ ∩ ∩
13	XIII	• • • over =	⋒ ∩ ∩ ∩
14	XIV	• • • • over =	⋒ ∩ ∩ ∩ ∩
15	XV	≡	⋒ ∩ ∩ ∩ ∩ ∩
16	XVI	• over ≡	⋒ ∩ ∩ ∩ ∩ ∩ ∩
17	XVII	• • over ≡	⋒ ∩ ∩ ∩ ∩ ∩ ∩ ∩
18	XVIII	• • • over ≡	⋒ ∩ ∩ ∩ ∩ ∩ ∩ ∩ ∩
19	XIX	• • • • over ≡	⋒ ∩ ∩ ∩ ∩ ∩ ∩ ∩ ∩ ∩
20	XX		⋒⋒
40	XL		⋒⋒⋒⋒
100	C	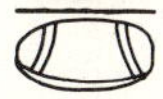	

By contrast, the decimal system is simple to use. Any schoolboy can multiply 528×44 and obtain 23232 by following simple rules, thus

$$\begin{array}{r} 528 \\ \times 44 \\ \hline 2112 \\ 2112 \\ \hline 23232 \end{array}$$

Arithmetic in the decimal system is simplified because each digit represents a number between 0 and 9 or a 10's multiple of that number; the *position* of the digit in the number determines which 10's multiple the digit represents. In other words, the multiplicand in the above example is

$$528 = 500 + 20 + 8$$

the multiplier is

$$44 = 40 + 4$$

and the product is

$$23232 = 20000 + 3000 + 200 + 30 + 2$$

Because numbers in this positional enumeration system are put together by means of simple rules, the rules of arithmetic are made simple.

Why could not the ancients use positional notation? The answer is that they did not know about zero. Zero means more than nothing. Zero is a digit which indicates position without signifying value. The number 4000 is distinguished from the number 4 by the number of zeros. In the first case, the digit 4 is in the fourth column (from the right) and in the second case the digit 4 is in the first column. These facts are apparent when we use the following notation:

$$4. = 4 \times 10^0$$

$$4000. = 4 \times 10^3$$

The exponent indicates the number of zeros to the left of the decimal point.

The zero can be used to distinguish among fractional numbers too. The difference between .4 and .00004 is that in the first case the digit 4 is in the first column to the right of the decimal point, whereas in the second case the digit 4 is in the fifth column to the right of the decimal point. These facts are summarized in the following notation:

$$.4 \quad = 4 \times 10^{-1}$$

$$.00004 = 4 \times 10^{-5}$$

The minus exponent indicates that the zeros are to the right of the decimal point.

Numbers in Exponential Form

As we have seen, the number 23232 can be expressed as

$$20000 + 3000 + 200 + 30 + 2$$

Instead of writing down all the zeros, the same numbers may be expressed in the following manner:

$$2 \times 10^4 + 3 \times 10^3 + 2 \times 10^2 + 3 \times 10^1 + 2 \times 10^0$$

For consistency, the rightmost digit is considered to be multiplied by 10^0 which is equal to 1.

Note that in this positional enumeration system the exponent represents the number of the column in which the associated digit occurs, if we count columns from right to left and label the first column zero. We call the leftmost digit the Most Significant Digit (MSD) because a change in this digit has the greatest effect upon the value of the total number. We call the rightmost digit the Least Significant Digit (LSD) because a change in this digit has the least effect upon the value of the total number.

Example

Write 1023 in exponential form:

$$1 \times 10^3 + 0 \times 10^2 + 2 \times 10^1 + 3 \times 10^0$$

In this example, the MSD is 1 and the LSD is 3.

The same idea of positional enumeration can be applied to decimal fractions. The decimal fraction 0.6217453 can be expressed as

$$6 \times 10^{-1} + 2 \times 10^{-2} + 1 \times 10^{-3} + 7 \times 10^{-4} + 4 \times 10^{-5} + 5 \times 10^{-6} + 3 \times 10^{-7}$$

The minus sign in the exponent indicates that a multiple of one-tenth rather than of 10 is taken. The leftmost digit (6) is still the MSD and the rightmost digit (3) is still the LSD.

Example

Write .53174 in exponential form

$$5 \times 10^{-1} + 3 \times 10^{-2} + 1 \times 10^{-3} + 7 \times 10^{-4} + 4 \times 10^{-5}$$

Counting Process

Let us review the decimal counting process (Table 3). We start with each column holding a zero. In the first column from the right (column 0) we go through the sequence of digits from 1 to 9 and back to 0. As we return to 0, we sequence the digit in column 1 from 0 to 1. We follow through another cycle of ten digits in column 0 and, as we return to 0 again, we sequence the digit in column 1 from 1 to 2. We go through this cycle ten times or until the digit in column 1 is switched from 9 to 0. At this point we change the digit in column 2 from 0 to 1. This process is continued *ad infinitum.* This counting process can be performed by a group of rotating wheels. The wheel at the right makes a complete revolution for each ten digits. Each of the other wheels rotates at one-tenth the speed of the wheel to its right.

Because there are ten digits in this system of counting, each column produces a multiple of ten. We recognize this fact when we speak of the units, tens, hundreds, and thousands columns. Because we use ten digits in the decimal system, we say that it has a *base* or *radix* of 10. The base is defined as the number of digits used in a positional enumeration system.

table 3 DECIMAL COUNTING

Columns:	3	2	1	0
Weight:	10^3	10^2	10^1	10^0
				0
				1
				2
				3
				.
				.
				.
				8
				9
			1 ←	0
			1	1
			1	2
			1	3
			.	.
			.	.
			.	.
			1	8
			1	9
			2 ←	0
			2	1
			2	2
			2	3
			.	.
			.	.
			.	.
			2	8
			2	9
			3 ←	0
			3	1
			3	2
			.	.
			.	.
			9	9
		1 ←	0 ←	0
		1	0	1
		1	0	2
		.	.	.
		.	.	.
		1	0	9
		1	1 ←	0
		.	.	.
		.	.	.
		1	9	9
		2 ←	0 ←	0
		.	.	.
		.	.	.
		9	9	9
	1 ←	0 ←	0 ←	0

Theoretically, we use an infinite number of columns, and we can go on counting forever. But for any physical device, there is always a finite number of columns used. The odometer of a car, for instance, has five columns (not including the one representing tenths of miles). This means that the largest number that can be represented by the ordinary odometer is 99999—one less than 100000.

What does this fact mean in practical terms? It means that if the odometer in a car reads 00500, we could not know for certain whether the car has traveled 500 or 100,500 or 200,500 miles. We say that the odometer reads numbers in modulus 100000, or 10^5 form. If it has 20 columns, it reads numbers in modulus 10^{20} form.

The modulus is a standard of measurement. It is one more than the last possible number that can be read from a practical counter. It is not the last number, but the number after it because we normally start counting with one and not with zero. If in the odometer the number 0 were used to represent the first mile, the reading of 99,999 would represent the 100,000th mile. As a matter of fact for most computer applications we do assume that zero is the first number. Reference to this point will be made later in this book.

Several Positional Number Systems

The almost universal use of the base of 10 for numbering developed only because we happen to possess ten fingers. But many bases are possible. Numbers in some of the bases used in computers are shown in Table 4.

The duodecimal system with a base of 12 consists of digits 0 to 9 of the decimal system plus two more—*A* and *B* for instance—representing the digits 10 and 11. In this system, whenever a digit in a column is sequenced from digit *B* to digit 0, the digit in the column to its left is sequenced to its next digit.

The digit in each column represents a multiple of 12; its position determines which multiple it is. For instance, 1*AB*6 is equivalent to

$$1\times(12)^3 + A\times(12)^2 + B\times(12)^1 + 6\times(12)^0$$
$$= 1\times 1728 + 10\times 144 + 11\times 12 + 6\times 1 = 3462$$

Some people believe that arithmetic is simpler in the duodecimal system. They base their contention on the fact that 10 is divisible by only two digits besides 1, i.e., 2 and 5; whereas 12 is divisible by four digits, that is, 2, 3, 4, and 6.

Example

Express the following duodecimal number in exponential form and translate to decimal:

$$1294A$$
$$1\times 12^4 + 2\times 12^3 + 9\times 12^2 + 4\times 12^1 + A\times 12^0$$
$$= 1\times 20736 + 2\times 1728 + 9\times 144 + 4\times 12 + 10\times 1$$
$$= 20736 + 3456 + 1296 + 48 + 10 = 25546$$

table 4 POSITIONAL NUMBER SYSTEMS

Decimal 10	Hexa-decimal 16	Duo-decimal 12	Octal 8	Ternary 3	Binary 2
0	0	0	0	0	0
1	1	1	1	1	1
2	2	2	2	2	10
3	3	3	3	10	11
4	4	4	4	11	100
5	5	5	5	12	101
6	6	6	6	20	110
7	7	7	7	21	111
8	8	8	10	22	1000
9	9	9	11	100	1001
10	*A*	*A*	12	101	1010
11	*B*	*B*	13	102	1011
12	*C*	10	14	110	1100
13	*D*	11	15	111	1101
14	*E*	12	16	112	1110
15	*F*	13	17	120	1111
16	10	14	20	121	10000
17	11	15	21	122	10001
18	12	16	22	200	10010
19	13	17	23	201	10011
20	14	18	24	202	10100
40	28	34	50	1111	101000
100	64	84	144	10201	1100100

The hexadecimal system has a base of 16. It consists of the ten decimal digits plus six additional symbols—*A, B, C, D, E,* and *F*—to represent the digits 10, 11, 12, 13, 14, and 15. Just as in the decimal system, a digit is worth 10 times more than a digit to its right, and in the duodecimal system a digit is worth 12 times more than a digit to its right, so in the hexadecimal system a digit is worth 16 times more than a digit to its right. Just as in the decimal system the placement of a zero to the right of the LSD multiplies the whole number by 10, and in the duodecimal system the placement of a zero to the right of the LSD multiplies the whole number by 12, so in the hexadecimal system the placement of a zero to the right of the LSD multiplies the whole number by 16.

Example

Express the following hexadecimal number in exponential form and translate to decimal:

$$235$$

$$2 \times 16^2 + 3 \times 16^1 + 5 \times 16^0$$
$$= 2 \times 256 + 3 \times 16 + 5 \times 1 = 512 + 48 + 5 = 565$$

Just as we may choose bases greater than 10, so may we choose bases less than 10. The octal system with a base of 8, the ternary system with a base of 3, and the binary system with a base of 2 are some commonly occurring schemes.

In the octal system, eight digits—0, 1, 2, 3, 4, 5, 6, and 7—are used. A number such as 6472 represents

$$6 \times 8^3 + 4 \times 8^2 + 7 \times 8^1 + 2 \times 8^0$$
$$= 6 \times 512 + 4 \times 64 + 7 \times 8 + 2 \times 1$$
$$= 3072 + 256 + 56 + 2 = 3386$$

In the ternary system, only three digits—0, 1, and 2—are used. A number such as 210112 represents

$$2 \times 3^5 + 1 \times 3^4 + 0 \times 3^3 + 1 \times 3^2 + 1 \times 3^1 + 2 \times 3^0$$
$$= 2 \times 243 + 1 \times 81 + 0 \times 27 + 1 \times 9 + 1 \times 3 + 2 \times 1$$
$$= 486 + 81 + 0 + 9 + 3 + 2$$
$$= 581$$

The digit in each column is worth three times more than a digit to its right.

In the binary system there are only two digits, 0 and 1. A number such as 100101011 is equivalent to

$$1 \times 2^8 + 0 \times 2^7 + 0 \times 2^6 + 1 \times 2^5 + 0 \times 2^4 + 1 \times 2^3 + 0 \times 2^2 + 1 \times 2^1 + 1 \times 2^0$$
$$= 1 \times 256 + 0 \times 128 + 0 \times 64 + 1 \times 32 + 0 \times 16 + 1 \times 8 + 0 \times 4 + 1 \times 2 + 1 \times 1$$
$$= 256 + 0 + 0 + 32 + 0 + 8 + 0 + 2 + 1$$
$$= 299$$

A digit in each column is worth twice as much as a digit in a column to its right. Evaluation in binary is much simpler than with any other base because no digit higher than 1 is used, and therefore no multiplication is needed.

The two digits of the binary system are called bits, which is a contraction of *bi*nary digi*ts*.

Example

Express binary 11001 in exponential form and translate into decimal.

$$1 \times 2^4 + 1 \times 2^3 + 0 \times 2^2 + 0 \times 2^1 + 1 \times 2^0$$
$$= 1 \times 16 + 1 \times 8 + 0 \times 4 + 0 \times 2 + 1 \times 1$$
$$= 16 + 8 + 0 + 0 + 1 = 25$$

Advantages of Binary Number System

It is obvious that it takes many more digits to express a number in binary than it does in decimal. As was shown before, the binary 100101011 is equivalent to decimal 299. In this case, nine bits are needed for the binary representation as contrasted with three digits for the decimal representation. But this disadvantage is outweighed by the following advantages of the binary number system:

1. The binary ONE and ZERO can represent the TRUE and FALSE of formal logic.
2. Binary numbers are easy to mechanize reliably.
3. Binary arithmetic is very simple

Each of these advantages is discussed below.

Binary ONE and ZERO can represent the TRUE and FALSE of formal logic. Formal logic deals with relationships among classes. Propositions normally state that an item is a member of a class, or that it is not a member of a class. For instance, a proposition may state that an item such as "pen" is a member of the class "black"; or that an item such as "Jack" is not a member of the class "fish." These propositions may be either true or false, and for this reason, formal logic is often called bivalued logic. The true statements may be represented by binary ONE and the false statements by binary ZERO.

Binary numbers are easy to mechanize reliably. It is much easier to develop a circuit which has only two stable states than it is to develop a circuit with ten stable states. For instance, to cause a transistor circuit to have ten stable states, we must design it so that it can conduct at ten distinct current levels. We must design it so that under steady conditions the current does not change enough to make the circuit change levels. We must design it to have equally spaced stable states; in other words, it should take just as much energy to go from one state to an adjacent state as it would to go from another state to an adjacent state.

We have no such problems designing 2-stable-state devices. Some bistable devices which have been used to store ONE'S and ZERO'S are relays which open and close; gas-discharge tubes which conduct or are cut off; magnetic materials which magnetize in one direction or the other; teletype tape in which holes represent ONE'S and no holes represent ZERO S; and flip-flops which have one leg conducting and the other leg cut off, or vice versa. In each of these devices the two states are distinct, and it is easy to flip from one to the other without ambiguity.

Binary arithmetic is very simple. To perform decimal arithmetic, we must first memorize addition and multiplication tables. We must do this also in the binary system. These tables are extremely easy, as shown in Tables 5*a* and 5*b*. The sum of 0 and 0 is 0; of 0 and 1, 1; and of 1 and 1, 0 with a 1 to carry. The multiplication of all 2-bit combinations except 1 times 1 produces a 0; 1 times 1 produces 1. Can arithmetic rules be any simpler? The simple rules of binary arithmetic are reflected in the simple circuitry needed to accomplish this arithmetic electronically.

table 5*a* ADDITION TABLE

Augend / Addend	0	1
0	0	1
1	1	0 (carry)

table 5*b* MULTIPLICATION TABLE

Multiplicand / Multiplier	0	1
0	0	0
1	0	1

TRANSLATION BETWEEN NUMBER SYSTEMS

Decimal-to-Binary Translation

The following are some methods by which numbers in the decimal system may be translated into numbers in the binary system:

1. Dividing successively by the base.
2. Multiplying successively by the base.
3. Using meaning of binary ZERO.
4. Using rule of number formation.

Each of these methods is discussed below.

Dividing successively by the base. This method is applicable to integral decimal numbers. To translate an integral decimal number into binary, divide successively by 2 and record the remainder in each case. Continue this process until the original number is reduced to 0. The first recorded remainder bit is the LSD and the last recorded remainder bit is the MSD of the number in the binary system.

Example

Translate decimal 137 into binary.

DIVIDE BY 2	QUOTIENT	REMAINDER	
137/2	68	1	LSD
68/2	34	0	
34/2	17	0	
17/2	8	1	
8/2	4	0	
4/2	2	0	
2/2	1	0	
1/2	0	1	MSD → 10001001 Binary

Multiplying successively by the base. This method is applicable to fractional decimal numbers. To translate a fractional decimal number into binary, multiply the fraction successively by 2. Each time the product becomes greater than 1, disregard the 1 and continue multiplying the fractional part of the number. For each multiplication that causes the product to become greater than 1—there is a carry to the units column—record a 1. For each multiplication that does not cause the product to become greater than 1—there is no carry to the units column—record a 0. Repeat this procedure until about three times as many binary digits as decimal digits are obtained. The first recorded bit is the MSD and the last recorded bit is the LSD of the number in binary.

Example

Translate decimal .413 into binary.

MULTIPLY BY 2	PRODUCT	CARRY TO UNITS COLUMN	
.413×2	.826	0	MSD
.826×2	1.652	1	
.652×2	1.304	1	
.304×2	.608	0	
.608×2	1.216	1	
.216×2	.432	0	0.011010011 Binary
.432×2	.864	0	
.864×2	1.728	1	
.728×2	1.456	1	LSD

Using meaning of binary ZERO. Writing a 0 to the right of the LSD of an integral binary number is the same as multiplying the whole number by 2. Writing a 0 to the left of the MSD (between the MSD and binary point) of a fractional binary number is equivalent to dividing the whole number by 2. These facts can be used to translate from decimal to binary, as is shown by the following example.

Example

Translate decimal 855.0625 to binary. The integral portion and the fractional portion are best treated separately.

The integral portion, 855, may be considered to be composed of 800+40+15. The binary equivalents of 15 and 40 may be obtained from Table 4; they are:

$$15 = 1111$$
$$40 = 101000$$

The value for 800 may be obtained by recording the value for 100 and doubling it three times:

$$100 = 1100100$$
$$200 = 11001000$$
$$400 = 110010000$$
$$800 = 1100100000$$

The value of the number is now obtained by adding the three binary equivalents thus:

$$\begin{array}{r@{\ =\ }r} 800 & 1100100000 \\ +40 & 101000 \\ \hline 840 & 1101001000 \\ +15 & 1111 \\ \hline 855 & 1101010111 \end{array}$$

The fractional part .625 is translated to binary as follows:

$$\begin{aligned} .5 &= .1 \\ .25 &= .01 \\ .125 &= .001 \\ .0625 &= .0001 \end{aligned}$$

Therefore, decimal 855.0625 equals 1101010111.0001 in binary.

Using rule of number formation. The following example illustrates this method.

Example

Express 972 in binary. This number can be expressed as

$$9 \times 10^2 + 7 \times 10^1 + 2 \times 10^0$$

If the binary equivalent to each of these numbers is obtained, and the indicated arithmetic is performed, the binary equivalent for the whole number is derived. From Table 4 we find that the following decimal numbers have the indicated binary equivalents:

9	1001
7	0111
2	0010
10	1010
100	1100100

The number 972 can therefore be expressed as

$$\begin{aligned} & 9 \times 10^2 + 7 \times 10^1 + 2 \times 10^0 \\ &= 1001 \times 1100100 + 111 \times 1010 + 10 \\ &= 1110000100 + 1000110 + 10 \\ &= 1111001100 \end{aligned}$$

Binary-to-Decimal Translation

The following are three methods which may be used to translate binary numbers into decimal numbers:

1. Using meaning of binary ZERO.
2. Dividing successively by binary equivalent of 10.
3. Assigning weights to bit positions.

The first two methods are good for translation of integers only. The third method may be used for fractional numbers as well. Each of these methods is discussed in the following.

Using meaning of binary ZERO. Start by recording a 1 for the MSD. Then double the number for each succeeding bit if it is a 0. Double the number and add 1 if the bit is a 1.

Example

Find the decimal equivalent of 10101100.

Binary number:	1	0	1	0	1	1	0	0	
Double numbers:	1	2	4	10	20	42	86	172	172 = Decimal equivalent
Add 1:			+1		+1	+1			
			5		21	43			

Dividing successively by binary equivalent of 10. The binary equivalent of decimal 10 is 1010. By dividing the given number and then successive quotients by 1010, each successive remainder translated into a decimal is a digit of the equivalent decimal number.

Example

Find the decimal equivalent of 10000100.

```
          1101
1010)10000100
       1010
       ----
        1101
        1010
        ----
         1100
         1010
         ----
           10 = 2 ——— LSD ————┐
                              │
           1                  │
1010)1101                     ↓
      1010
      ----
        11    = 3            132   Decimal
                              ↑
1010)1        = 1 ——— MSD ————┘
```

Assigning weights to bit positions. This is the most straightforward way. Remembering that each bit to the left of the binary point is worth twice the value of the bit to its right, and that each bit to the right of the binary point is worth half as much as the bit to its left, we can assign weights to all bit positions as follows:

256	128	64	32	16	8	4	2	1	·	1/2	1/4	1/8	1/16	1/32	1/64
x	x	x	x	x	x	x	x	x	·	x	x	x	x	x	x

table 6 TRANSLATING DECIMAL 540 TO BINARY, TERNARY, QUARTERNARY, AND OCTAL

Binary			Ternary			Quarternary			Octal		
Divide by Base	Quotient	Remainder	Divide by Base	Quotient	Remainder	Divide by Base	Quotient	Remainder	Divide by Base	Quotient	Remainder
540/2	270	0—LSD	540/3	180	0—LSD	540/4	135	0—LSD	540/8	67	4—LSD
270/2	135	0	180/3	60	0	135/4	33	3	67/8	8	3
135/2	67	1	60/3	20	0	33/4	8	1	8/8	1	0
67/2	33	1	20/3	6	2	8/4	2	0	1/8	0	1—MSD→1034
33/2	16	1	6/3	2	0	2/4	0	2—MSD→20130			
16/2	8	0	2/3	0	2—MSD→202000						
8/2	4	0									
4/2	2	0									
2/2	1	0									
1/2	0	1—MSD→1000011100									

To translate from binary to decimal, place the bits under the appropriate weights. Then add up all the weights in the positions in which 1's appear in the binary number.

Example

Find the decimal equivalent of 10101100.10101.

Place bits under appropriate weights:

									·					
Weights:	128	64	32	16	8	4	2	1	·	1/2	1/4	1/8	1/16	1/32
Bits:	1	0	1	0	1	1	0	0	·	1	0	1	0	1

Add weights in positions in which 1's appear:

$$128 + 32 + 8 + 4 + 1/2 + 1/8 + 1/32 = 172.6562$$

The translation can also be performed by treating the mixed number as a fraction: 1010110010101/100000.

Weights:	4096	2048	1024	512	256	128	64	32	16	8	4	2	1
Bits:	1	0	1	0	1	1	0	0	1	0	1	0	1

Numerator: 4096+1024+256+128+16+4+1 = 5525

Weights:	32	16	8	4	2	1
Bits:	1	0	0	0	0	0

Denominator: 32

Fraction: 5525/32 = 172.6562

Translation to and from Other Number Systems

One of the best methods of translating from decimal to binary is successive division (multiplication if the number is fractional) by 2, the remainder after each division being one of the bits of the resultant number. This method may be applied to translation from decimal to any number system with a base less than 10; division in each case is by the base of the number system to which we are translating. Table 6 shows how the decimal number 540 is translated into ternary, quarternary, and octal as well as binary.

One of the best methods of translating from binary to decimal is by assigning weights to bit positions, multiplying the weights by the digits in the respective positions and summarizing. This method may be applied to translation from any number system with a base less than 10 to decimal. Table 7 shows how the ternary, quaternary, and octal as well as binary equivalents of 540 are translated into decimal.

Translation from binary to octal, and vice versa, is very simple because there is a direct relationship between the binary number system and the octal number system: if the bits of a binary number are divided into groups of three, the evaluation of each group provides the equivalent octal digit. This can be seen from the table of binary-octal equivalents (Table 8). The reason for this simple relation is this: there are only eight possible combinations for each group of three bits.

table 7 TRANSLATING BINARY, TERNARY, QUARTERNARY, AND OCTAL EQUIVALENTS OF 540 TO DECIMAL

Number in binary: 1000011100

Weights:	512 256 128 64 32 16 8 4 2 1
Bits:	1 0 0 0 0 1 1 1 0 0
Bits × weights:	$1\times512+0\times256+0\times128+0\times64$ $+0\times32+1\times16+1\times8+1\times4$ $+0\times5+0\times1$
Decimal equivalent:	$512+16+8+4=540$

Number in ternary: 202000

Weights:	243 81 27 9 3 1
Digits:	2 0 2 0 0 0
Digits × weights:	$2\times243+0\times81+2\times27+0\times9+0\times3+0\times1$
Decimal equivalent:	$486+54=540$

Number in Quarternary: 20130

Weights:	256 64 16 4 1
Digits:	2 0 1 3 0
Digits × weights:	$2\times256+0\times64+1\times16+3\times4+0\times1$
Decimal equivalent:	$512+16+12=540$

Number in Octal: 1034

Weights:	512 64 8 1
Digits:	1 0 3 4
Digits × weights:	$1\times512+0\times64+3\times8+4\times1$
Decimal equivalent:	$512+24+4=540$

CODED-DECIMAL NUMBERS

The decimal number system is universally used. But the binary number system possesses a simplicity that lends itself to machine use. These two advantages are available in one system, called the coded-decimal system. Numbers in the coded-decimal system are represented by decimal digits; but each digit is encoded by means of four bits. For instance, the binary representations for the digits 0 to 9 may be used to encode each digit. In this system the number 52963 is encoded as follows:

52963 = 0101 0010 1001 0110 0011

table 8 BINARY-OCTAL EQUIVALENTS

Decimal	Binary	Octal
0	000	0
1	001	1
2	010	2
3	011	3
4	100	4
5	101	5
6	110	6
7	111	7
8	001 000	10
9	001 001	11
10	001 010	12
11	001 011	13
12	001 100	14
13	001 101	15
14	001 110	16
15	001 111	17
16	010 000	20
17	010 001	21
18	010 010	22
19	010 011	23
20	010 100	24
40	101 000	50
100	001 100 100	144

We may assign to each of the four bit positions (from right to left) the weights of 1, 2, 4, and 8; and then add the weights in positions holding 1's to evaluate each digit. The above binary-coded decimal representation may therefore be translated in the following manner:

Binary-Coded Decimal Digits	Weights 8 4 2 1	Decimal
0101	0+4+0+1	5
0010	0+0+2+0	2
1001	8+0+0+1	9
0110	0+4+2+0	6
0011	0+0+2+1	3

This type of representation is called a weighted-bit code. There are many other possible weights that can be given to each bit position to produce other coded-decimal systems. Some of these are listed in the Appendix. Values for digits in typical 4-bit codes are given in Table 9.

table 9 VALUES FOR TYPICAL 4-BIT CODES

	Weighted				Nonweighted	
Decimal	2421	8421	5421	5211	Excess-3	Excess-6
0	0000	0000	0000	0000	0011	0110
1	0001	0001	0001	0001	0100	0111
2	0010	0010	0010	0011	0101	1000
3	0011	0011	0011	0110	0110	1001
4	0100	0100	0100	0111	0111	1010
5	1011	0101	1000	1000	1000	1011
6	1100	0110	1001	1001	1001	1100
7	1101	0111	1010	1100	1010	1101
8	1110	1000	1011	1110	1011	1110
9	1111	1001	1100	1111	1100	1111

In coded-decimal systems an ambiguity may arise in the use of the word "significant." The leftmost decimal digit (5 in the above example) may be called the most significant. Similarly, the leftmost bit comprising each digit may be called the most significant. To avoid confusion, we will always use "significant" when referring to digits, and "order" when referring to the bits of a digit. The leftmost decimal digit in the above example is the MSD and the rightmost is the LSD. The first-, second-, third-, and fourth-order bits of the MSD are 1, 0, 1, and 0, respectively.

There are 16 distinct possible combinations that can be obtained by the use of 4 bits to a digit. In the 8421 system, the first ten combinations in the binary number system are chosen. It is possible, however, to choose the middle ten combinations in the group of 16. This means that the binary representations for 3 to 12 would represent decimal digits from 0 to 9. This is shown in Table 9 as "Excess-3" code. The code is called excess-3 because the coded representation is the binary number for three more than the actual decimal number it represents. For instance, the excess-3 representation for 0 is 0011, or the binary equivalent for 3.

Similarly, in the excess-6 code, each coded representation is equal to the binary number for six more than the decimal number it usually represents.

NEGATIVE NUMBERS AND COMPLEMENTS

Up to now we have been dealing only with positive numbers, that is, we counted from a reference point in a forward direction. But it is just as easy to start at the reference point and count in the opposite direction. If we assume that counting to the right is counting forward, then counting to the left is counting backward. When we count to the right, we add a one to obtain each succeeding number; when we count to the left we subtract one to obtain each succeeding number.

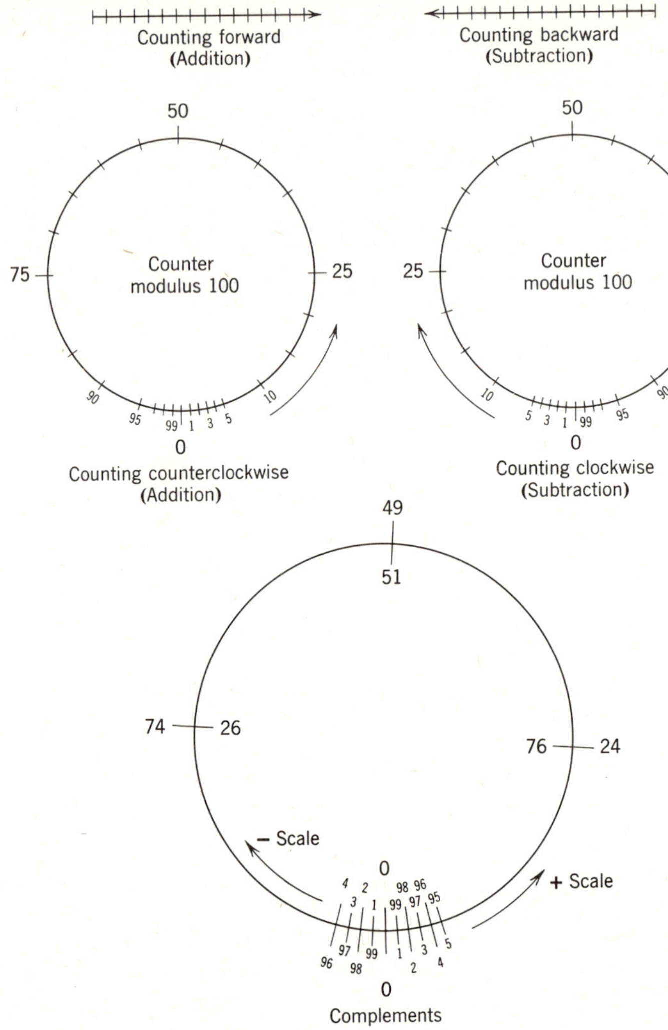

Figure 10 Principle of complements.

Because of its finite modulus, a practical counter is better represented by a circle, as shown in Fig. 10. In the circle representation, counting counterclockwise may be called forward counting, and counting clockwise may be called backward counting. If we place the positive numbers obtained through forward counting and the negative numbers obtained through backward counting side by side around the circle, the corresponding numbers are complements of each other. A complement is a number derived from a given number according to a definite rule; the complement is used to facilitate arithmetic.

The complement concept is valuable in the mechanization of subtraction. Subtraction may be performed by reversing the direction of a wheel (or some other device which behaves conceptually like a wheel). By converting negative numbers to their complements, we can convert all subtraction problems into addition problems—we can have the "wheel" always moving in the same direction.

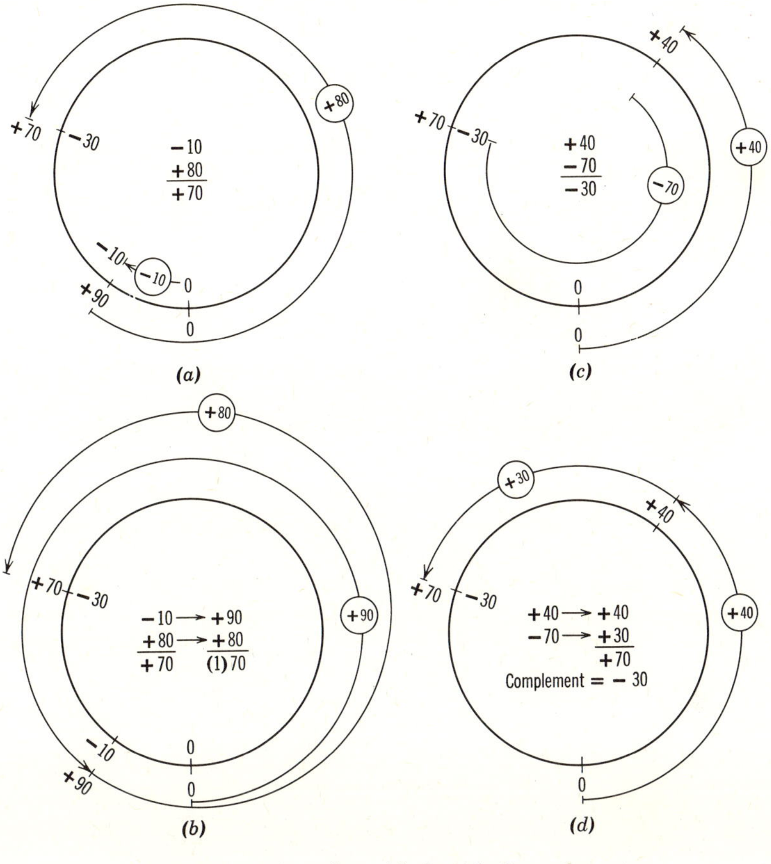

Figure 11 Subtraction with the aid of complements.

Figure 11 shows how the complement concept is applied in a counter with a modulus of 100. The numbers −10 and +80 are combined normally in Fig. 11*a* to produce +70: Starting at the reference point, we subtract 10 by ticking off ten spaces clockwise; from the resultant we trace 80 spaces counterclockwise, which brings us back to the +70 point on the wheel. Figure 11*b* shows how the same problem is solved by means of complements; here we combine the complement of −10, which is +90, with +80; we count 170 divisions from the reference point, which brings us to the +70 point on the wheel. In Figs. 11*c* and *d*, +40 and −70 are combined. In Fig. 11*c* we count 40 divisions forward and then 70 divisions backward, which brings us to the −30 spot. In Fig. 11*d* we convert −70 to +30, and count first 40 divisions and then 30 divisions counterclockwise, which brings us to the +70 or −30 spot on the wheel.

If the modulus is given in the decimal system, the complement is called the 10's complement. The 10's complement of a number is defined as that number which when added to the original number gives the modulus. For instance, the 10's complement of 642 is 358 because

$$\begin{array}{r} 642 \\ +358 \\ \hline 1000 \end{array} = \text{modulus for a 3-digit decimal number system}$$

The 10's complement of the same 642 in modulus 10^5 is 99358 because

$$\begin{array}{r} 00642 \\ +99358 \\ \hline 100000 \end{array} = \text{modulus for a 5-digit decimal number system}$$

Another way of expressing the last statement is as follows: If we count 642 times backwards from 100000, we reach number 99358.

Instead of obtaining the 10's complement by subtracting the number from the modulus, the first digit (LSD) may be subtracted from 10 and all the other digits subtracted from 9. This process gives the same result as can be seen from the following:

$$\begin{array}{r} 100000 \\ -42135 \\ \hline 57865 \end{array} \qquad \begin{array}{r} 9\;9\;9\;9\;10 \\ -4\;2\;1\;3\;\;5 \\ \hline 5\;7\;8\;6\;\;5 \end{array} \qquad \begin{array}{rl} 9\;9\;9\;9\;9 & \\ -4\;2\;1\;3\;5 & \\ \hline 5\;7\;8\;6\;4 & \text{9's complement} \\ +1 & \\ \hline 5\;7\;8\;6\;5 & \text{10's complement} \end{array}$$

Instead of obtaining the 10's complement directly, we may subtract each digit from 9 to obtain the 9's complement, and then add 1 to convert it into the 10's complement. The 10's complement is always equal to the 9's complement plus 1.

Example

Find the 10's complement of 263 in a 4-digit number system.

$$\begin{array}{rl} 9\;9\;9\;9 & \\ -\;\;2\;6\;3 & \\ \hline 9\;7\;3\;6 & \text{9's complement} \\ +1 & \\ \hline 9\;7\;3\;7 & \text{10's complement} \end{array}$$

In the binary number system, the 2's and 1's complements are analogous to the 10's and 9's complements respectively. The 2's complement is defined as that binary number which must be added to the original binary number to obtain the modulus. The 1's complement is defined to be one less than the 2's complement. The following example shows the relationships between the 2's and 1's complements:

Example

Find the 2's complement of 10101 in a 5-bit modulus system.

```
 100000      1 1 1 1 10      1 1 1 1 1
-10101      -1 0 1 0  1     -1 0 1 0 1
------      ----------      ----------
  01011      0 1 0 1  1      0 1 0 1 0    1's Complement
                                    +1
                            ----------
                             0 1 0 1 1    2's Complement
```

Note that in the binary number system, the 1's complement can be obtained by simply interchanging all 0's with 1's and all 1's with 0's.

SELF-CHECKING CODES

Four bits can be combined in 16 different ways. Since only ten of these combinations are used in a coded-decimal system, six combinations are extra or redundant. This redundancy increases the reliability of the code because the machine can be made to detect the six forbidden combinations. The forbidden combinations in the 8421 system, for instance, are 1010, 1011, 1100, 1101, 1110, and 1111. If one of these combinations occurs, we know that the machine has made an error. By introducing at the appropriate point in the machine a device which can detect any of these six forbidden combinations, we have an automatic means of detecting machine errors.

But the detection of forbidden combinations does not detect *all* errors. Suppose the number 1000 is transmitted and the machine causes the second-order bit to invert, thus transmitting 1010. Since this is a forbidden combination, the machine can detect it. But suppose the *first*-order bit is inverted and 1001 is transmitted. This is not a forbidden combination—it is the representation for 9—and it may go undetected.

If we increase the redundancy further by introducing another bit to each coded combination, we could develop a system which could discover an error due to the change of any of the bits in the coded combination. To do this, we would have to make this bit related to the others. One way of doing this would be to form the rule that the sum of all the ONE bits in each 5-bit combination must always be odd. On the basis of this rule, the check bit (as the fifth-order bit is called) for the 8421 code is as follows:

Decimal \ Weight \ Order of Bit	5 Check	4 8	3 4	2 2	1 1
0	1	0	0	0	0
1	0	0	0	0	1
2	0	0	0	1	0
3	1	0	0	1	1
4	0	0	1	0	0
5	1	0	1	0	1
6	1	0	1	1	0
7	0	0	1	1	1
8	0	1	0	0	0
9	1	1	0	0	1

If a bit in any of these combinations should change, the sum of the ONE'S would no longer be odd but even. The machine could be made to detect this. This system of checking is called *parity checking.*

This binary-coded decimal system with an added check bit is called a self-checking code. Other self-checking codes are shown in the Appendix.

ALPHANUMERIC CODES

In addition to the 10 digits, computers can process the 26 letters of the alphabet as well as many editing marks. Obviously, 4-bit codes are not enough. Neither, it would seem, are 5 bits, since 5 bits can provide only 32 combinations. However, teletype transmission uses only 5-bit codes. It gets around this apparent impasse by using the same codes for the 26 letters as it does for the digits and editing marks. To avoid confusion, one of the unused combinations is used to signal that the message which follows consists of alphabetic data; or, if receiving alphabetic data, the special code signals that the following data consists of digits and editing marks. The teletype code is shown in Table 10.

To take care of all alphanumeric characters without the above subterfuge, 6 bits are required. One such code, the Transcode, is shown in Table 11.

Because of the additional requirement for distinguishing between upper- and lowercase letters and characters for communication control, 8-bit character combinations have become standard. There are two such standards: the Extended Binary Coded Decimal Interchange Code (EBCDIC), and the United States of America Standard Code for Information Interchange (USASCII). Digits and characters for the two codes are shown in the Appendix.

table 10 TELETYPE CODES

Letters \ Order of Bit	5	4	3	2	1	Figures and Editing Marks
A	0	0	0	1	1	–
B	1	1	0	0	1	?
C	0	1	1	1	0	:
D	0	1	0	0	1	$
E	0	0	0	0	1	3
F	0	1	1	0	1	!
G	1	1	0	1	0	&
H	1	0	1	0	0	£
I	0	0	1	1	0	8
J	0	1	0	1	1	'
K	0	1	1	1	1	(
L	1	0	0	1	0	)
M	1	1	1	0	0	.
N	0	1	1	0	0	,
O	1	1	0	0	0	9
P	1	0	1	1	0	0
Q	1	0	1	1	1	1
R	0	1	0	1	0	4
S	0	0	1	0	1	Bell
T	1	0	0	0	0	5
U	0	0	1	1	1	7
V	1	1	1	1	0	;
W	1	0	0	1	1	2
X	1	1	1	0	1	/
Y	1	0	1	0	1	6
Z	1	0	0	0	1	"
"Switch to Letters"	1	1	1	1	1	
	1	1	0	1	1	"Switch to Figures"

table 11 SIX-BIT TRANSCODE

Character \ Order of Bits	6	5	4	3	2	1
0	1	1	0	0	0	0
1	1	1	0	0	0	1
2	1	1	0	0	1	0
3	1	1	0	0	1	1
4	1	1	0	1	0	0
5	1	1	0	1	0	1
6	1	1	0	1	1	0
7	1	1	0	1	1	1
8	1	1	1	0	0	0
9	1	1	1	0	0	1
A	0	0	0	0	0	1
B	0	0	0	0	1	0
C	0	0	0	0	1	1
D	0	0	0	1	0	0
E	0	0	0	1	0	1
F	0	0	0	1	1	0
G	0	0	0	1	1	1
H	0	0	1	0	0	0
I	0	0	1	0	0	1
J	0	1	0	0	0	1
K	0	1	0	0	1	0
L	0	1	0	0	1	1
M	0	1	0	1	0	0
N	0	1	0	1	0	1
O	0	1	0	1	1	0
P	0	1	0	1	1	1
Q	0	1	1	0	0	0
R	0	1	1	0	0	1
S	1	0	0	0	1	0
T	1	0	0	0	1	1
U	1	0	0	1	0	0
V	1	0	0	1	0	1
W	1	0	0	1	1	0
X	1	0	0	1	1	1
Y	1	0	1	0	0	0
Z	1	0	1	0	0	1

SUMMARY

1. The more redundant the language, the greater its reliability. The less redundant the language, the more powerful it is as an instrument for rigorous thought.
2. Ancient number systems were additive; present-day number systems are positional. The invention of zero made the positional notation possible. When numbers are written in exponential form, a positive exponent indicates the number of digits between the most significant digit and the decimal point to the right; a minus exponent indicates the number of digits to the right of the decimal point.
3. The binary number system with two digits (ZERO and ONE) is especially useful because of its similarity to bivalued logic, the ease with which it can be mechanized, and the resultant simplicity of binary arithmetic.
4. Integral (fractional) decimal numbers may be converted to numbers in a base less than 10 by a technique of dividing (multiplying) successively by the base. Numbers in systems having bases of less than 10 may be converted to decimal by multiplying each digit by a weight assigned to the digit position in question, and summarizing; the weights are multiples of the base of the number system from which the numbers are being converted.
5. There is a special relationship between binary and octal numbers. If bits of a binary number are grouped into threes, the decimal value of each 3-bit combination provides the octal equivalent of the binary number.
6. Four bits may be used to encode a decimal digit. By weighting each bit differently, several such encoding schemes can be produced. By using six bits, letters of the alphabet, editing marks as well as digits may be encoded. EBCDIC and USASCII codes consist of 8-bit combinations.
7. Addition is the process of counting two numbers in the same direction. Subtraction is the process of first counting one number in one direction, then counting the other number in the opposite direction. Negative numbers may be replaced by complements to convert subtraction problems into addition problems.
8. Checking is facilitated by redundancies. Any coded-decimal system may be converted to a self-checking code by the inclusion of a checking bit.
9. *Definitions to Remember*

   Digit. A symbol representing one of the elements in a positional number system.

   Bit. One of the two elements used in the binary number system. Also one of the two elements used in coded-decimal systems.

   Base or Radix. Number of digits (or bits) to a number system.

   Modulus. One more than the maximum number attainable in any practical counter.

   Significance. Rank of digit position in a number.

   Least Significant Digit (LSD). The rightmost digit of a number.

   Most Significant Digit (MSD). The leftmost digit of a number.

   Binary-Coded Decimal Notation. A decimal number system in which each digit is represented by a group of bits.

Order. Rank of bits in a coded-decimal digit.

Complement:

10's—The number which must be added to the given number to obtain the modulus in the decimal system.

9's—One less than the 10's complement.

2's—The number which must be added to the given number to obtain the modulus in the binary system.

1's—One less than the 2's complement.

Redundancy. The use of more symbols to encode a message than are strictly necessary.

Parity Check. Comparison of the sum of 1 bits in a coded representation to see if it is odd or even.

Forbidden Combination Check. A check which tests for occurrence of a nonpermissible code combination.

Self-Checking Code. A code in which it is easy to check each character because of a redundancy in each character.

Binary. Involving the integer 2.

Octal Notation. A system for representing numbers in the radix of 8.

Exercises

1. Write the following decimal numbers in exponential form:
   a. 43275 b. 0.2574 c. 154.673 d. 0.0023 e. 1003.005
2. Complete Table 4 for decimal digits 21 to 39.
3. Express the following numbers in exponential form and translate them into decimal form:
   a. Binary 1100101 d. Hexadecimal 3509
   b. Ternary 102120 e. Octal 7630
   c. Duodecimal 29*A* f. Hexadecimal *ABC*
4. Express the following binary numbers in octal form:
   a. 111000 b. 11101 c. 1110101 d. 1010101
5. Write addition and multiplication tables (similar to Tables 5*a* and 5*b*) for ternary numbers.
6. Write addition table for octal numbers.
7. Translate the following decimal numbers into binary by dividing successively by the base:
   a. 754 b. 346 c. 159 d. 333 e. 6001
8. Translate the following decimal fractions into binary by multiplying successively by the base:
   a. 0.563 b. 0.274 c. 0.896 d. 0.03
9. Translate the following decimal numbers into binary by using the meaning of binary ZERO and the values in Table 4:
   a. 355.5 b. 718.25 c. 60.125 d. 94.03125

10. Translate the following decimal numbers into binary by using the rule of number formation and the values in Table 4:
a. 43 b. 75 c. 364 d. 1357

11. Translate the following binary numbers into decimal by using the meaning of binary ZERO:
a. 10101 b. 11100 c. 10000 d. 11111

12. Translate the following binary numbers into decimal by dividing succesively by the binary equivalent of 10:
a. 10101011 b. 11001100 c. 11110000 d. 10000001

13. Translate the following binary numbers into decimal by assigning weights to bit positions:
a. 1000011100 c. 11.00011001
b. 11110.00001 d. 1000011100.11110

14. Translate the following decimal numbers into ternary, quarternary, and octal:
a. 64 b. 32 c. 346 d. 675

15. Write the following numbers in 5421 code; in 2421 code; in excess-3 code:
a. 69 b. 86 c. 105 d. 500

16. Find the 9's and 10's complement of the following decimal numbers:
a. 250 b. 643 c. 915 d. 362 in modulus 10^6

17. Find the 1's and 2's complements of the following binary numbers:
a. 1010 b. 101011 c. 11111 d. 101 in modulus 2^6

18. Find values of the odd parity bits for digits 0 to 9 in the 5421 coded decimal system. Prepare a table similar to the one shown on page 45

CHAPTER 3

Arithmetic processes

Almost all practical mathematical operations may be converted into arithmetic operations; and all arithmetic operations are extensions of the operation of addition. This means that if we can build a device which can add, we can, with a few modifications, convert it to a device which can also subtract, multiply, divide, take the square root, and integrate; and by proper programming, we can even cause it to perform problems in higher mathematics.

Before building this adding device, we review the rules of algebraic addition, and then go through several methods for multiplying, dividing, and taking the square root in the decimal system. This is followed by methods of performing the same arithmetic operations in binary and in coded-decimal systems.

ALGEBRAIC ADDITION

Algebraic addition refers to the summation of numbers some of which are positive and some of which are negative. There are several methods for algebraic addition in the decimal system. The addition may be performed by using the numbers given, or it may be done after the negative numbers are converted into their 10's or 9's complements. Variations of these techniques are possible. Some of the common methods of algebraic addition are discussed in the following.

Using Absolute Values

The rules of algebraic addition of absolute decimal numbers are simple and straightforward.

1. To add two numbers whose signs are alike—both plus or both minus—add the numbers and give the sum the sign of either number.

Example

+372	−372	Augend
+198	−198	Addend
+570	−570	Sum

2. To add algebraically two numbers whose signs are unlike—plus and minus or minus and plus—subtract the numerically smaller number from the numerically larger number and give the sum the sign of the numerically larger number.

Example

+372	−372	Augend
−198	+198	Addend
+174	−174	Sum

Using 10's Complement

Algebraic addition of two terms whose signs are unlike may be performed in the following manner. All negative numbers may be replaced by their 10's complements and the terms added. The treatment of the sum depends upon whether or not a decimal carry is produced from the most significant position.

1. If a decimal carry occurs, ignore the carry and make the sign plus.

Example

```
+372——————————————→372
−198——10's complement→802
+174               (1) 174——————————→+174 = Sum
```

2. If no decimal carry occurs, take the 10's complement of the tentative sum and make the sign negative:

Example

```
−372——10's complement→628
+198——————————————→198
−174                   826——10's complement→−174 = Sum
```

Note that, if we change the sign of the number every time we complement, we automatically arrive at the correct sign of the answer. This is logical because when we take the complement we count in the opposite direction from that in which we have been counting before.

Using the 9's Complement

A similar set of rules applies for determining the sum of two unlike numbers when algebraic addition is performed with the aid of the 9's rather than the 10's complements. Again we take the complement of the negative term and add. The sum is treated in one of two ways depending upon whether or not a decimal carry is produced from the most significant position:

1. If a decimal carry occurs, add this 1 to the LSD of the tentative sum (end-around carry), and make the sign of the sum positive.

Example

```
+372——————————————→372
−198——9's complement→801
−174               (1) 173
                         1    End-around carry
                       174——————————→+174 = Sum
```

2. If no decimal carry occurs, take the 9's complement of the tentative sum and make the sign of the sum negative.

Example

```
+198──────────────────────→198
−372───9's complement──→627
────                    ───
−174                    825───9's complement──→ −174 = Sum
```

Adding the end-around carry when working with the 9's complement is equivalent to taking the 10's complement of the addend originally, because the 10's complement of a number is one more than the 9's complement of the number.

MULTIPLICATION

Pencil-and-Paper Multiplication

Every schoolboy knows the following method of multiplying 728 by 451:

728	Multiplicand
×451	Multiplier
728	First partial product
3640	Second partial product
2912	Third partial product
328328	Product

Why do we indent the second partial product (3640) one digit position to the left? and the third partial product another digit position to the left? The answer is as follows. When we multiply 728 by the least significant digit of the multiplier (1), what we are actually doing is this:

$$\begin{array}{ccc} 700 & 20 & 8 \\ \times 1 & \times 1 & \times 1 \\ \hline 700 + & 20 + & 8 \end{array} = 728 = \text{First partial product}$$

When we multiply 728 by the second digit (5), we are not really multiplying by 5 but by 50:

$$\begin{array}{ccc} 700 & 20 & 8 \\ \times 50 & \times 50 & \times 50 \\ \hline 35000 + & 1000 + & 400 \end{array} = 36400 = \text{Second partial product}$$

We put the second partial product down as 3640, but indented to the left one place, making it equivalent to 36400. In the same way when we multiply 728 by 4, we are not really multiplying by 4 but by 400:

$$\begin{array}{ccc} 700 & 20 & 8 \\ \times 400 & \times 400 & \times 400 \\ \hline 280000 + & 8000 + & 3200 \end{array} = 291200 = \text{Third partial product}$$

We put the third partial product down as 2912, but shifted one digit position to the left of the second partial product, making it equivalent to 291200.

Right- and Left-Hand Component Method

When multiplying pairs of digits in the pencil-and-paper method, we may obtain a carry; this carry must be added to the result of the multiplication of the next pair of digits. To avoid complication which such a routine may cause in a machine, the product of each digit pair may be separated into a right-hand or product digit, and a left-hand or carry digit. These digits are part of the left- and right-hand components respectively. The right- and left-hand components are summed separately. The sum of the left-hand components is then shifted one place to the left and added to the sum of the right-hand components to obtain the product.

Example

$$
\begin{array}{lrrl}
 & & 728 & \\
 & & \times 451 & \\
\cline{3-3}
 & 000 & 728 & \\
\text{Left-hand components} & 314 & 500 & \text{Right-hand components} \\
 & 203 & 882 & \\
\cline{2-3}
\text{Left-hand sum} & 23440 & 93928 & \text{Right-hand sum} \\
 & & 23440 & \text{Left-hand sum, shifted left} \\
\cline{3-3}
 & & 328328 & \text{Product}
\end{array}
$$

Multiplication by Repeated Addition

By storing the multiplication table in the machine's memory, it is possible to adapt the pencil-and-paper method of multiplication to machine computation. To avoid occupying such valuable storage space, multiplication in most present-day machines is performed by a process of repeated addition. Very little extra storage is needed because the additions are performed by the same adder used for straightforward addition.

The method of repeated addition is based upon the meaning of multiplication. The multiplication symbol tells us to add the multiplicand to itself the number of times specified by the multiplier. For instance, 8 times 4 means that we should add four 8's together to get 32.

Example

$$
\begin{array}{rlclcl}
728 = & 728 & & 728 & & 728 \\
\times 451 & \times 4 \times 10^2 & & \times 5 \times 10^1 & & \times 1 \times 10^0 \\
\hline
 & 2912 \times 10^2 & & 3640 \times 10^1 & & 728 \times 10^0 \\
 & 728 & & 728 & & 728 \\
 & 728 & & 728 & & \\
= & 728 & + & 728 & + & \\
 & 728 & & 728 & & \\
 & & & 728 & & \\
\hline
 & 2912 \times 10^2 & + & 3640 \times 10^1 & + & 728 \times 10^0 \\
= & 291200 & + & 36400 & + & 728 \\
= & 328328 & & & &
\end{array}
$$

The following summation is equivalent to the above steps:

```
     728   ×1
    728 ⎫
    728 ⎪
    728 ⎬ ×5
    728 ⎪
    728 ⎭
   728  ⎫
   728  ⎪
   728  ⎬ ×4
   728  ⎭
 ------
 328328
```

The latter summation is easy to adapt to machine computation because only addition and shifting of digits are required.

DIVISION

Pencil-and-Paper Division

The following is an example of the pencil-and-paper method of division:

Example

```
               1241   Quotient
Divisor  365)452980   Dividend
             365
             ---
             879      First intermediate remainder
             730
             ----
             1498     Second intermediate remainder
             1460
             ----
              380     Third intermediate remainder
              365
              ---
               15     Remainder
```

If the understood zeros are filled in, the example looks like this:

```
       1241
 365)452980
     365000
     ------
      87980
      73000
      -----
      14980
      14600
      -----
        380
        365
        ---
         15
```

Whereas in multiplication the multiplicand is shifted one place to the left before adding it to the previous partial product to form a new one, in division each successive intermediate remainder is formed by shifting the divisor one place to the right before subtracting it from the previous remainder.

Division by Repeated Subtraction

The pencil-and-paper method of division is hard to mechanize because of the comparisons and trial-quotient digits needed. A more easily mechanized way of performing division uses a system of repeated subtraction. In this method the divisor is repeatedly subtracted from the dividend until an intermediate remainder is obtained which admits of no further subtraction (without obtaining a negative result). The number of subtractions performed is the value of the MSD of the quotient. Next, the divisor is shifted one place to the right and the subtractions are repeated. The number of subtractions required to produce a remainder which admits of no further subtractions determines the next most significant digit of the quotient. This procedure is repeated until the required decimal places have been obtained.

Example

```
                                   QUOTIENT DIGIT
365)452980
    365000——1 substraction         1——MSD——┐
    ------                                 │
     87980                                 │
     36500\                                │
     -----  \                              │
     51480   >2 subtractions       2       │
     36500  /                              │
     -----                                 │
     14980                                 │
      3650\                                │
     -----  \                              │
     11330   \                             │
      3650\   \                            │
     -----  \  \                           │
      7680    >4 subtractions      4       │
      3650  /  /                           │
     -----    /                            ↓
      4030   /                         1241 = Quotient
      3650 /                                 ↑
     -----                                   │
       380                                   │
       365——1 subtractions         1——LSD————┘
      ----
        15
```

Restoring Method of Division

From the standpoint of the machine, division by repeated subtraction has one flaw: the machine cannot tell by looking at it whether an intermediate remainder admits of further subtraction or not. To get around this objection we make the machine repeatedly subtract the divisor until a *negative* intermediate remainder is obtained. The negative remainder indicates that the divisor was subtracted one more time than necessary. Therefore, as soon as a negative intermediate remainder is detected, the divisor is added to it to restore it to the correct intermediate remainder. This is why this method is called the restoring method of division. After the first intermediate remainder is developed, the divisor is shifted to the right one place, and the next series of subtractions is performed.

Example

			QUOTIENT DIGIT
	365)452980		
Subtract	365000		
	087980	2 subtractions	1—MSD
Subtract	365000		
	−722980		
Add to restore	365000		
	087980		
Shift and subtract	36500		
	51480		
Subtract	36500	3 subtractions	2
	14980		
Subtract	36500		
	−78480		
Add to restore	36500		
	14980		
Shift and subtract	3650		
	11330		
Subtract	3650		
	7680		
Subtract	3650	5 subtractions	4
	4030		
Subtract	3650		
	0380		
Subtract	3650		
	−6730		
Add to restore	3650		1241 = Quotient
	0380		
Shift and subtract	365		
	015	2 subtractions	1—LSD
Subtract	365		
	−650		
Add to restore	365		
	015		

Note that the quotient digit in each case is one less than the number of subtractions required to yield a negative intermediate remainder.

SQUARE ROOT

Three methods of obtaining the square root are discussed here: the pencil-and-paper method, the subtractive method, and the approximation method.

Pencil-and-Paper Method

The pencil-and-paper method of obtaining the square root of a number can be illustrated best by an example.

Example

	3 7	Square root
	√13 69	Square
	9	
Trial divisor	67) 4 69	First intermediate remainder
	4 69	

Note that before any calculation is performed the digits of the number whose square root is to be obtained are grouped in pairs. The most significant digit of the square root is then obtained by a process of trial and error: we look for a digit whose square is as close as possible to 13 without being greater than 13. After subtracting the square of 3—which is 9—from 13 and then bringing down the next pair of digits (69), we double 3 and record the 6 with a space to its right as a trial divisor. Again, by a process of trial and error, we seek a digit which can be placed to the right of the 3 above the square root sign and also to the right of the 6 in the trial divisor. This digit—in this case 7—must be so chosen that when it is multiplied by the trial divisor—in this case 67—we will get a number smaller than or equal to the intermediate remainder 469.

Subtractive Process

This method is easy to mechanize because it depends upon a simple rule and the steps in the rule are very much alike. The method is based upon an unusual relationship which is shown in Table 12.

table 12 RELATIONSHIP BETWEEN EQUIVALENT SERIES OF ODD TERMS AND SQUARE ROOTS

Square	Equivalent Series	Square Root (Number of Terms)
1	1	1
4	1 + 3	2
9	1 + 3 + 5	3
16	1 + 3 + 5 + 7	4
25	1 + 3 + 5 + 7 + 9	5
36	1 + 3 + 5 + 7 + 9 + 11	6
49	1 + 3 + 5 + 7 + 9 + 11 + 13	7

The number of terms combined is equal in every case to the square root of the number in question. This relationship has been proved to be universally true. This principle may be applied in practice, as shown by the following examples.

Example

Find the square root of 25

	25
Subtract	1
	24
Subtract	3
	21
Subtract	5
	16
Subtract	7
	9
Subtract	9
	0

5 subtractions ; the square root is 5

Example

	$\sqrt{13\ 83.\ 84}$	SQUARE ROOT DIGIT
Subtract	1	
	12	
Subtract	3	3 subtractions 3—MSD
	9	
Subtract	5	
	4 83	
Add 1 to last subtrahend (5) and shift; Repeat odd series in units position		
Subtract	61	
	4 22	
Subtract	63	
	3 59	
Subtract	65	
	2 94	
Subtract	67	7 subtractions 7
	2 27	
Subtract	69	
	1 58	
Subtract	71	
	87	
Subtract	73	
	14 84	
Add 1 to last subtrahend (73) and shift; Repeat odd series in units position		37.2 = Square root
Subtract	7 41	
	7 43	2 subtractions 2—LSD
Subtract	7 43	
	00	

When the number whose square root is to be found consists of more than two digits, the digits are marked off into groups of two, just as is done in the pencil-and-paper method. The odd numbers 1, 3, 5, etc., are subtracted successively from the most significant pair of digits until a remainder is reached from which the next digit in the series cannot be subtracted without producing a negative term. The number of subtractions performed is the MSD of the square root. The next pair of digits of the square is brought down. Then a 1 is added to the last subtrahend used; with this digit as the 10's digit and the series 1, 3, etc., as the units digits, we subtract successively again until a remainder is produced from which the next digit cannot be subtracted without producing a negative number. The number of subtractions performed is the second significant digit of the square root. The next pair of digits of the square is brought down, a 1 is added to the LSD of the last subtrahend, and with the series 1, 3, etc., placed to the right of this number, we again subtract successively to obtain the next digit in the square root.

Instead of subtracting, we may add complements. A machine can easily execute this process by performing a series of additions and shifts; a counter can keep track of the number of additions performed.

Approximation Formula

The square root of a number may be obtained by means of the following approximation formula:

$$y_{i+1} = y_i + .5\left(\frac{a}{y_i} - y_i\right)$$

New square root = previous square root

$$+ \text{half}\left(\frac{\text{square}}{\text{previous square root}} - \text{previous square root}\right)$$

At first a guess of the square root is made, and this value is substituted for the "previous square root" in the above formula. The calculated "new square root" is then substituted for the previous square root, and the formula is applied once more. This procedure is repeated, and each time the new square root becomes closer and closer to the actual value of the square root.

Example

Find $\sqrt{64}$; $a = 64$; first guess for $y_i = y_0 = 2$.

First approximation

$$y_1 = y_0 + .5\left(\frac{a}{y_0} - y_0\right)$$

$$y_1 = 2 + .5(\tfrac{64}{2} - 2) = 2 + .5(30) = 17$$

Second approximation

$$y_2 = y_1 + .5\left(\frac{a}{y_1} - y_1\right)$$

$$y_2 = 17 + .5(\tfrac{64}{17} - 17) = 17 + .5(-13.235) = 10.382$$

Third approximation

$$y_3 = y_2 + .5\left(\frac{a}{y_2} - y_2\right)$$

$$y_3 = 10.382 + .5\left(\frac{64}{10.382} - 10.382\right) = 10.382 + .5(-4.218) = 8.273$$

Fourth approximation

$$y_4 = y_3 + .5\left(\frac{a}{y_3} - y_3\right)$$

$$y_4 = 8.273 + .5\left(\frac{64}{8.273} - 8.273\right) = 8.273 + .5(-.5370) = 8.004$$

Fifth approximation

$$y_5 = y_4 + .5\left(\frac{a}{y_4} - y_4\right)$$

$$y_5 = 8.004 + .5\left(\frac{64}{8.004} - 8.004\right) = 8.004 + .5(-.008) = 8$$

Sixth approximation

$$y_6 = y_5 + .5\left(\frac{a}{y_5} - y_5\right)$$

$$y_6 = 8 + .5(\tfrac{64}{8} - 8) = 8 + .5(0) = 8$$

This procedure for finding the square root is not usually built into a computer. Any computer which can add, subtract, multiply, and divide may be programmed to perform this operation.

BINARY ARITHMETIC

The rules of binary addition are similar to those for decimal addition, except that a binary carry instead of a decimal carry is obtained.

Example

```
   1 1 0 1
   1 1 0 0
   1          Carry
  ---------
 1 1 0 0 1
```

The subtraction required as part of the algebraic addition of binary numbers of unlike signs is similar to decimal subtraction. When subtracting a larger bit (1) from a smaller bit (0), borrows are used as in decimal subtraction.

Example

```
 1 0 1 0
 0 1 0 1
 1   1      Borrow
 -------
 0 1 0 1
```

Subtraction by the use of complements is made easy since the 1's complement of a number is obtained by converting all 0's to 1's and all 1's to 0's.

Example

```
+1010─────────────────────────→1010
-0101───1's complement───→1010
                                1 1     Carry
                               ─────
                              ┌10100
                              └───→1    End-around carry
                               ─────
                                0101──────────────→+0101 = Sum
```

Example

```
+1011─────────────────────────→1011
-1100───1's complement───→0011
                                 11     Carry
                                ────
                                1110─1's complement→ -0001 = Sum
```

In multiplication we either write the multiplicand or zero as a partial product depending upon whether the multiplier bit is 1 or 0. Then the partial products are summed.

Example

```
    1101
    1011
    ────
    1101
   1101
  0000
 1101
────────
10001111
```

Division is similarly straightforward because each quotient bit is either 1 or 0. If the portion of the dividend compared is less than the divisor, the quotient bit must be 0; if it is greater, the quotient bit must be 1.

Example

```
            1101
1110)10111010
     1110
     ─────
     10010
      1110
      ────
      1001
      0000
      ─────
      10010
       1110
       ────
        100
```

LOCATION OF DECIMAL OR BINARY POINT

The decimal point separates the digits which represent powers of ten on the left from digits which represent powers of tenths on the right. The binary point separates bits which represent powers of two on the left from bits which represent powers of a half on the right.

Before addition can be performed, the decimal or binary points must be aligned.

Example

```
654127.    .654127    654.127
   312.    .312         3.12
-------    -------    -------
654439.    .966127    657.247
```

Example

```
110011.     .110011    110.111
   111.     .111         1.11
-------    --------   --------
111010.    1.101011   1000.001
```

In multiplication, the rules for locating the decimal (binary) point in the product are as follows:

1. Count the number of places from the right to where the decimal (binary) point appears in the multiplicand.
2. Count the number of places from the right to where the decimal (binary) point appears in the multiplier.
3. Add the two numbers. The sum is the number of places from the right where the decimal (binary) point should be placed in the product.

Example

```
                    NO OF PLACES POINT IS FROM RIGHT
 65.4                       1
 ×.31                      +2
 ----                      --
  654
1962
------
20.274                      3
```

Example

```
                        NO OF PLACES POINT IS FROM RIGHT
110110.11                           2
     ×.111                         +3
----------                         --
  11011011
 11011011
11011011
------------
101111.11101                        5
```

In division the rule for determining the decimal (binary) point depends upon the relative values of the divisor digits and of an equivalent number of digits at the most significant end of the dividend. If the value of the divisor digits is greater than the value of an equivalent number of digits at the most significant end of the dividend, do the following:

1. Count the number of places from the left to where the decimal (binary) point appears in the dividend.
2. Count the number of places from the left to where the decimal (binary) point appears in the divisor.
3. Subtract the latter from the former. The difference is the number of places from the left where the decimal (binary) point should be placed in the quotient.

Example

Dividend	324.0	Divisor digits
Divisor	4886	greater

$$4886.\overline{)324.000} \quad \text{quotient } .0x$$

	NO OF PLACES POINT IS FROM LEFT
Dividend	3
Divisor	−4
Quotient	−1

Minus one means that the point is not one place to the right of the most significant nonzero digit but one place to the left of it.

Example

Dividend	101010.	Divisor digits
Divisor	1110	greater

$$1110.\overline{)101010.000} \quad \text{quotient } 1x.xxx$$

	NO OF PLACES POINT IS FROM LEFT
Dividend	6
Divisor	−4
Quotient	2

If the value of the divisor digits is smaller than the value of an equivalent number of digits in the dividend, the subtraction is performed as before, but this time the remainder *plus one* is the number of places the point in the quotient is from the left.

Example

Dividend	488648.	Divisor digits
Divisor	244	smaller

$$244.\overline{)488648.000} \quad \text{quotient } xxxx.$$

	NO OF PLACES POINT IS FROM LEFT
Dividend	6
Divisor	−3
	3
	+1
Quotient	4

Example

Dividend	11.000	}	Divisor digits	
Divisor	10 101		Smaller	
				NO OF PLACES POINT IS FROM LEFT
	.00x			
	10101.)11.0000		Dividend	2
			Divisor	−5
				−3
				+1
			Quotient	−2

The decimal (binary) point need not be moved directly. We may express numbers with the aid of the base and exponent as follows:

$$3000. = .3 \times 10^4$$

$$.00324 = .324 \times 10^{-2}$$

$$654.127 = .654127 \times 10^3$$

The decimal (binary) point may be located indirectly by properly changing the exponent of the base. The rules for dealing with the exponents are as follows.

To add two numbers follow these rules.

1. Make both exponents the same.
2. Add the significant digits.
3. The new sum consists of the sum of the significant digits multiplied by the base to the common exponent.

Example

$$\begin{array}{r} 654.127 \\ 3.120 \\ \hline 657.247 \end{array} \begin{array}{c} = \\ = \\ = \end{array} \begin{array}{l} .654127 \times 10^3 \\ .00312 \quad \times 10^3 \\ \hline .657247 \times 10^3 \end{array}$$

Example

$$\begin{array}{r} 11101.101 \\ .0011 \\ \hline 11101.1101 \end{array} \begin{array}{c} = \\ = \\ = \end{array} \begin{array}{l} .11101101 \quad \times 2^5 \\ .000000011 \times 2^5 \\ \hline .111011101 \times 2^5 \end{array}$$

Multiplication is fairly easy. Multiply the digits in the ordinary way, but add the exponents.

Example

$$\begin{array}{r} 65.4 \\ \times .31 \\ \hline 654 \\ 1962 \\ \hline 20.274 \end{array} \begin{array}{c} = \\ = \\ \\ \\ \\ = \end{array} \begin{array}{r} .654 \times 10^2 \\ .31 \quad \times 10^0 \\ \hline 654 \\ 1962 \\ \hline .20274 \times 10^2 \end{array}$$

Example

$$\begin{array}{rcl} 11.011 & = & .11011 \times 2^{2} \\ \times .011 & = & \times .11 \quad \times 2^{-1} \\ \hline 11011 & & 11011 \\ 11011 & & 11011 \\ \hline 1.010001 & = & .101001 \times 2^{1} \end{array}$$

In division the digits are divided normally but the exponent of the divisor is subtracted from the exponent of the dividend.

Example

$$\frac{488648}{200} = 2443$$

$$\begin{array}{rcl} 488648 & = & .488648 \times 10^{6} \\ 200 & = & .200 \quad \times 10^{3} \\ \hline \dfrac{.488648}{.200} & = & 2.443 \quad \times 10^{3} \end{array}$$

Example

$$\frac{10101.010}{10.1} = 1000.1$$

$$\begin{array}{rcl} 10101.010 & = & .10101010 \times 2^{5} \\ 10.1 & = & .101 \quad \times 2^{2} \\ \hline \dfrac{.10101010}{.101} & = & 1.0001 \quad \times 2^{3} \end{array}$$

CHECKING

The forbidden combination check, the parity check, and other types of redundancy checks are based on the rules of the language. It is also possible to perform checking based on arithmetic. Several arithmetic checking schemes utilized by computers are discussed in the following.

Duplication

We all do this type of checking, especially when adding columns of digits. We repeat the addition. If the sum obtained the second time is the same as the sum obtained the first time, we assume the addition is correct. If the second sum is different from the first sum, we assume we made an error. This procedure is applicable to any arithmetic operation.

Inverse Arithmetic

An arithmetic operation may be checked by performing its inverse. Subtraction is the inverse of addition, division is the inverse of multiplication, and taking the square root is the inverse of squaring. The method is obvious from the following examples.

Example

SUBTRACTION		CHECK BY ADDITION	
7	Minuend	3	Difference
−4	Subtrahend	+4	Subtrahend
3	Difference	7	Minuend

Example

DIVISION

$$\begin{matrix}\text{Dividend} \\ \text{Divisor}\end{matrix} \quad \frac{100}{5} = 20 \text{ Quotient}$$

CHECK BY MULTIPLICATION	
20	Quotient
×5	Divisor
100	Dividend

Example

SQUARE ROOT		CHECK BY SQUARING	
5	Square root	5	Square root
		×5	Square root
25	Square	25	Square

Casting Out 9's and 7's

Casting out 9's is a checking scheme which has been used by bookkeepers for years. In this scheme every number taking part in an arithmetic operation is divided by 9; the remainder is therefore a number in modulus 9. This remainder is called the Residue Modulus Nine or RMN.

Example

Find RMN of 236.

$$\frac{236}{9} = 26\tfrac{2}{9} \qquad \text{RMN} = 2$$

Example

Find RMN of 421.

$$\frac{421}{9} = 46\tfrac{7}{9} \qquad \text{RMN} = 7$$

Checking is accomplished by performing the same operations on the RMN's as are performed on the numbers. The following rules apply to the RMN'S:

1. To check addition, add the RMN's of the numbers. The result should be equal to the RMN of the sum.

Example

NUMBERS		RMN	
2534		5	
+1273		+4	
3807	RMN of sum =	0	= Sum of RMN's

Note that in the modulus 9 scheme, the digit after 8 is not 9, but 0.

2. To check subtraction, subtract the RMN's of the numbers. The result should be equal to the RMN of the difference.

Example

NUMBERS		RMN	
2534		5	
−1273		−4	
1261	RMN of difference =	1	= Difference of RMN's

3. To check multiplication, multiply the RMN's of the numbers. The result should be equal to the RMN of the product.

Example

NUMBERS		RMN	
253		1	
×75		×3	
18975	RMN of product =	3	= Product of RMN's

4. To check division, multiply the RMN of the quotient by the RMN of the divisor and add the RMN of the remainder. The result should be the RMN of the dividend.

Example

$$\frac{6479}{21} = 308\tfrac{11}{21}$$

NUMBERS		RMN	
308	Quotient	2	
×21	Divisor	×3	
6468		6	
+11	Remainder	+2	
6479	RMN of dividend =	8	= (RMN of quotient) × (RMN of divisor) + RMN of remainder

Binary numbers may be checked by a scheme of casting out 7's. To obtain the Residue Modulus Seven (RMS) of a binary number, the number is divided by binary 7 or 111; the remainder is the RMS.

Example

Find the RMS of 1010110.

```
          1 100
111)1 010 110
    111
    011 110
     11 1
         010 = RMS
```

The rules for checking in the RMS system are similar to those used in the RMN system.

Example of Addition

NUMBERS		RMS	
1 010 110		010	
+010 111		010	
1 101 101	RMS of sum =	100	= Sum of RMS's

SUMMARY

1. In algebraic addition, if the signs are the same, the terms are added normally. If the signs of the augend and addend are different, the complement of the negative term is added to the absolute value of the other operand.
   a. If a carry is produced from the most significant digit position, it is ignored if the 10's or 2's complement has been taken; an end-around carry is performed if the 9's or 1's complement has been taken. The result is positive.
   b. If no carry is produced, the complement—10's, 9's, 2's, or 1's—of the sum is taken. The result is negative.
2. Most systems of multiplication are based upon the pencil-and-paper method. In the left-and-right-hand component method, the product of each pair of digits is divided into two components: left and right; then the components are summarized separately and combined to give the product. In the method of repeated addition, the multiplicand is repeatedly added a number of times as determined by the multiplier digits. Each successive group of additions is shifted one position to the left.
3. Division is usually performed by a system of repeated subtraction. In the restoring method, each group of subtractions is taken to the point where the remainder changes sign, then an addition is performed to restore the remainder. At that point the divisor is shifted right, and the next series of subtractions is performed, etc.
4. Arithmetic in binary is very simple because of the simple addition and multiplication tables.

5. Arithmetic may be checked by a system of casting out 9's or 7's. RMN or RMS of each factor is obtained by dividing by 9 or 7. The RMN and RMS are used as follows:

   a. The sum of the RMN (RMS) of two numbers is equal to the RMN (RMS) of the sum.
   b. The difference of the RMN (RMS) of two numbers is equal to the RMN (RMS) of the difference.
   c. The product of the RMN (RMS) of two numbers is equal to the RMN (RMS) of the product.
   d. If the RMN (RMS) of the quotient is multiplied by the RMN (RMS) of the divisor and added to the RMN (RMS) of the remainder, the result should be the RMN (RMS) of the dividend.

Exercises

1. Add algebraically the following and check results by inverse arithmetic:

a.	b.	c.	d.
+463	+574	−627	−246
−265	−986	+483	+861

2. Repeat the algebraic additions of problem 1, using the 10's complement to represent negative numbers.
3. Repeat the algebraic additions of problem 1, using the 9's complement to represent negative numbers.
4. Perform the following multiplications using the Right- and Left-hand Component Method and check the results by inverse arithmetic:
   a. 647×235 c. 62.5×1.24
   b. 355×840 d. .504×1.10
5. Perform the multiplications of problem 4, using the Multiplication by Repeated Addition Method.
6. Perform the following divisions by the Method of Repeated Subtraction and check the results by means of inverse arithmetic:
   a. 650/25 b. 463.748/6.24
7. Repeat problem 6 using the Restoring Method of Division.
8. Using the subtractive process, find the square root of the following:
   a. 81 b. 2564 c. 3956.41
9. Using the approximation formula with a first guess of 5, find the square root of:
   a. 100 b. 225 c. 560
10. Algebraically add the following by using the 1's complement to represent negative numbers:

a.	b.	c.	d.
+1100	+1001	−100.11	−111.
−0101	−1101	+ .1011	+110.01

11. Repeat problem 10, using the 2's complement.
12. Multiply the following binary numbers:
   a. 111×111 b. 1001×1110 c. .110110×110.01

13. Divide the following binary numbers:
a. 1110/101 b. 1001/10.1011

14. Perform the following arithmetic operations and check the results by the Method of Casting Out 9's:
a. 350+256 b. 690−530 c. 625×29 d. 54673/62

15. Perform the following arithmetic operations and check the results by the Method of Casting out 7's:
a. 1110+111 b. 101010−1011 c. 1101×11 d. 111000/101

16. Adding 4980 to a quantity once after which the 4980 is shifted right once and subtracted from the sum 6 times, is equivalent to adding 498 to the original quantity how many times?

CHAPTER 4
Machine logic

Logic is the cement of language. Formal logic is the cement holding the propositions of syllogisms together. In the more general case formal logic applies to the relationships among classes. By using letters of the alphabet to designate bivalued classes and symbols to represent logical connectives, an algebra of logic can be developed.

This logical algebra can be applied to mechanize the rules of arithmetic (or anything else) in the following way. The conditions of the problem are summarized in what is known as a truth table. From this truth table are found the algebraic equation or equations expressing the relationships among all the classes of the problem. This equation or set of equations is then converted to a logical block diagram, which is essentially a plan for the construction of the device.

But there is more to the plan of a practical device than what can be specified by the rules of algebra of logic. In the computer propositions are represented by signals, and amplifiers are needed to maintain the strength of these signals. In formal logic time is not considered; in practical machine logic time is a very important element, and its consideration leads to the use of storage devices. Practical machine logic therefore consists of amplifiers and storage elements in addition to elements representing the fundamental logical connectives.

BASIC ELEMENTS OF FORMAL LOGIC

Graphical Logic

Logic deals with relationships among classes. For instance:

All men who go to college have a high IQ.
Jack is a man who is attending college.
Therefore, Jack has a high IQ.

The above is a syllogism having three classes: Jack, men who attend college, and men with high IQ. This simple syllogism may therefore be expressed graphically as shown in Fig. 12. The illustration shows that class *A*, or Jack, is a member of class *B*, or the class of men attending college, which in turn is a member of *U*, the universal class consisting of all men with high IQ.

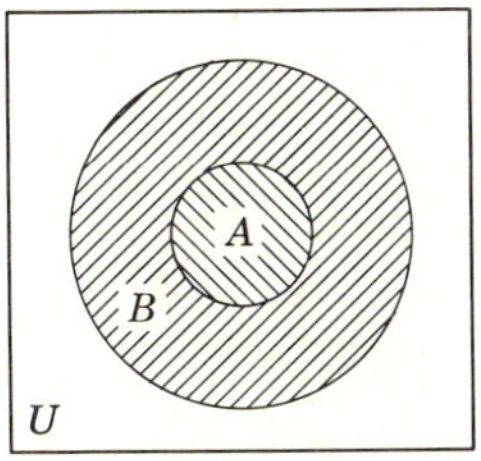

U = Universal class of men with high IQ
B = Class of men attending college
A = Jack

Figure 12 Graphical representation of syllogism.

If only one property such as college attendance is considered, the universal class may be divided into two classes: those who attend and those who do not attend—class *A* and class Not-*A*. If two properties of the universal class—such as college attendance (*A*) and wearing of gray hats (*B*)—are considered, then several classes are obtained as shown in the illustration. By combining the fundamental classes *A*, Not-*A*, *B*, and Not-*B*, by means of the AND connectives we obtain:

1. *A* and Not-*B*—The class of men who attend college and who do not wear gray hats.
2. Not-*A* and *B*—The class of men who do not attend college and who wear gray hats.
3. *A* and *B*—The class of men who attend college and who wear gray hats.
4. Not-*A* and Not-*B*—The class of men who do not attend college and of men who do not wear gray hats.

These classes are shown in Fig. 13*a*. *A* and Not-*B* is represented by the portion of the *A* circle to the left of the *B* circle boundary; Not-*A* and *B* is represented by the portion of the *B* circle to the right of the *A* circle boundary; *A* and *B* is represented by the cross-hatched portion; Not-*A* and Not-*B* is represented by the area outside the *A* and *B* circles.

Note that the AND connective is restrictive: as a rule, there are fewer members in a class containing an AND element than there are in any of the fundamental classes.

Combining the fundamental classes by means of an OR connective we obtain:

1. *A* or *B*—The class of men who attend college or of men who wear gray hats.

2. Not-*A* and *B*—The class of men who do not attend college and who wear gray hats.
3. Not-*A* or *B*—The class of men who do not go to college or of men who wear gray hats.
4. Not-*A* or Not-*B*—The class of men who are not attending college or of men who are not wearing gray hats.

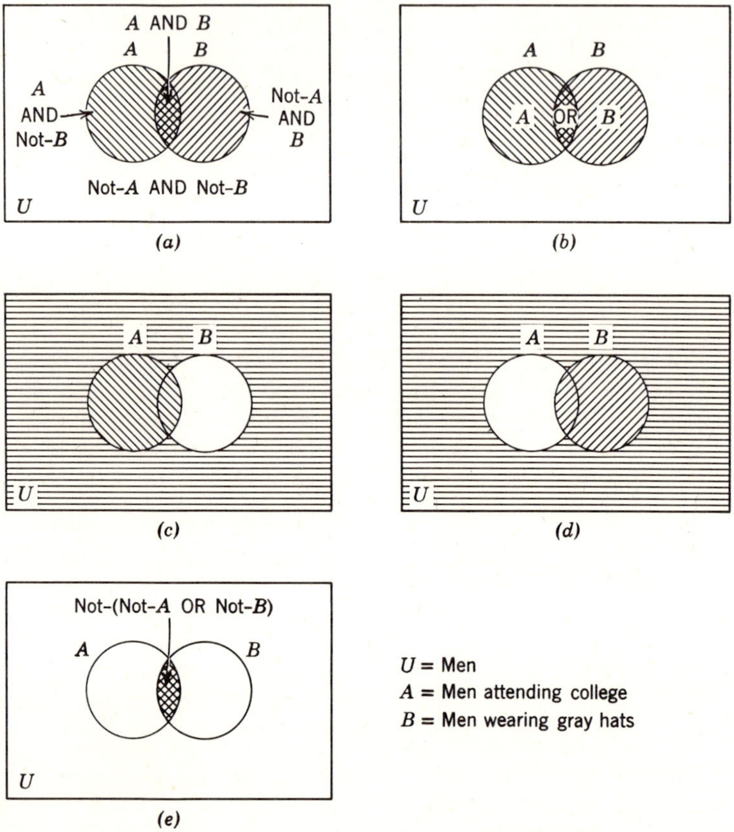

Figure 13 Graphical logic—2 classes. (*a*) AND relationships. (*b*) *A* or *B*. (*c*) *A* or Not-*B*. (*d*) Not-*A* or *B*. (*e*) Not-*A* or Not-*B* (vacant area).

These classes are shown in Fig. 13*b* to 13*e*. *A* or *B* is represented by the area covered by both circles (Fig. 13*b*); *A* or Not-*B* is represented by the entire area outside the blank portion of *B* in Fig. 13*c*; Not-*A* or *B* is represented by the entire area outside the blank portion of *A* in Fig. 13*d*; Not-*A* or Not-*B* is represented by everything outside the crosshatched area in Fig. 13*e*.

Notice that the OR relation used here is the INCLUSIVE OR as distinguished from the EXCLUSIVE OR. The difference between the two can be seen from the following interpretations of *A* or *B*:

A or *B* (INCLUSIVE OR)—*A* or *B* or both *A* and *B*.
A or *B* (EXCLUSIVE OR)—*A* or *B*, but not both *A* and *B*.

In this book, OR refers to INCLUSIVE OR, unless specifically stated otherwise.

If three properties of the universal class—such as *A*, *B*, and *C*—are considered, then eight possible AND combinations may be obtained as shown in Fig. 14; and eight possible OR combinations may be obtained as shown in Fig. 15.

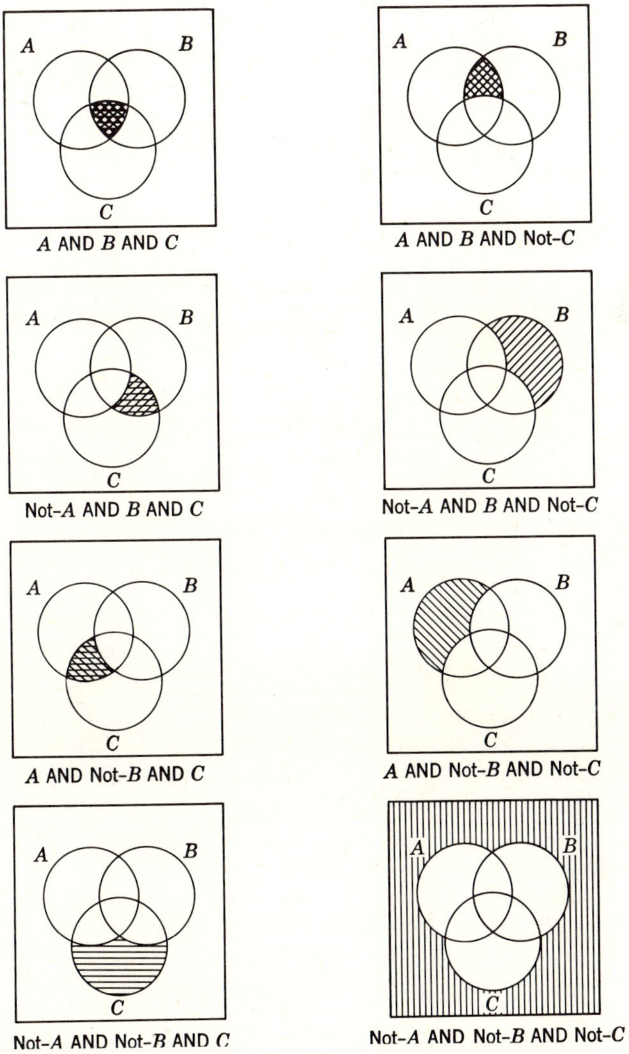

Figure 14 Graphical logic—3 classes—AND combination.

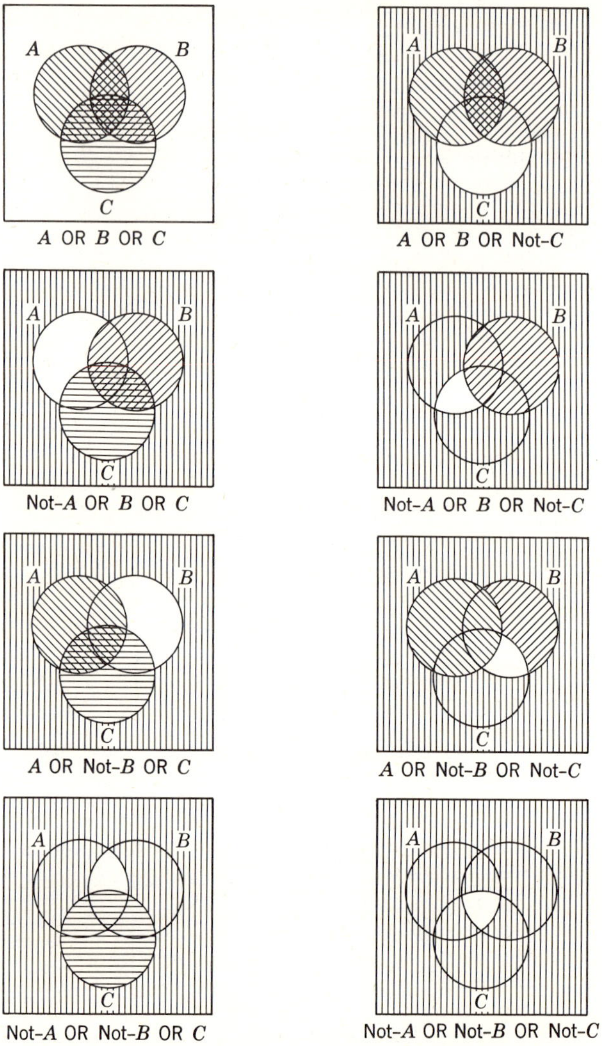

Figure 15 Graphical logic—3 classes—OR combinations.

Mathematical Logic

From the above graphical presentation it appears that relationships among classes may be presented by means of three logical functions:

AND, OR, and NOT

The more fundamental classes there are, the more difficult it is to express the many logical relationships graphically. But the same ideas may be expressed easily mathematically, as the following equalities show:

$$A \text{ AND } B \text{ AND } C = A \cdot B \cdot C$$
$$A \text{ OR } B \text{ OR } C = A + B + C$$
$$\text{Not-}A = \bar{A}$$

Example

Express the following mathematically.

1. A and B, or A and $C = A \cdot B + A \cdot C$
2. A and B, or $C = A \cdot B + C$
3. A and Not-B, or B and Not-$C = A \cdot \bar{B} + B \cdot \bar{C}$
4. A or B, and B or $C = (A+B) \cdot (B+C)$

With the aid of the above symbols, we may form logical expressions and operate on them mathematically. However, a few simple identities and laws must first be presented. The following are some identities involving AND, OR, and NOT functions:

$A \cdot 0 = 0$ A class with no members (0) can not intersect a class with members (A).

$U \cdot A = A$ Members of class A and of the universal class are the same only in class A.

$A \cdot \bar{A} = 0$ It is impossible for a class to intersect its complement.

$A + A = A$ Class A or class A equals class A.

$0 + A = A$ The class composed of members of the empty class or of class A is class A.

$U + A = U$ The class composed of members of the universal class or of class A is the universal class.

$A + \bar{A} = U$ The universal class consists of members of a class or of members of the complement of this class.

$\bar{\bar{A}} = A$ The complement of the complement of a class is the same as the class itself.

In addition to the above identities, there are three laws which all logical expressions follow. These laws are illustrated by means of examples as follows:

1. *The commutative law:*

$$A + B = B + A$$
$$A \cdot B = B \cdot A$$

2. *The associative law:*

$$A + (B + C) = (A + B) + C$$
$$A \cdot (B \cdot C) = (A \cdot B) \cdot C$$

3. *The distributive law:*

$$A \cdot (B + C) = (A \cdot B) + (A \cdot C)$$
$$A + (B \cdot C) = (A + B) \cdot (A + C)$$

These laws are similar to those used in ordinary arithmetic—all except the last one: $2+(3 \times 4)$ is not equal to $(2+3) \times (2+4)$.

The distributive law may be used to simplify expressions, as the following examples show.

Example

Simplify the following by factoring.

1. $(A \cdot \bar{B}) + (A \cdot C) = A \cdot (\bar{B} + C)$
2. $(A \cdot B \cdot \bar{C}) + (\bar{A} \cdot B \cdot \bar{C}) = B \cdot \bar{C}(A + \bar{A}) = B \cdot \bar{C}$
3. $(A + \bar{B}) \cdot (\bar{B} + C) = \bar{B} + (A \cdot C)$
4. $(A + B + C) \cdot (C + \bar{D} + E) = C + (A + B) \cdot (\bar{D} + E)$

Logical Relationships

There are other logical functions besides AND, OR, and NOT. But all other connectives can be shown to be made up of combinations of these three logical functions. Several such functions are discussed.

1. EXCLUSIVE OR—The EXCLUSIVE OR may be expressed as "*A* or else *B*." This phrase is interpreted to mean *A* or *B* but not both *A* and *B*, or mathematically,

$$(A + B) \cdot (\overline{A \cdot B})$$

2. IF AND ONLY IF—"*A* if and only if *B*" means that, if we have *A*, we also have *B*, but if we do not have *A*, we also do not have *B*, or mathematically,

$$(A \cdot B) + (\bar{A} \cdot \bar{B})$$

3. IF, THEN—"If *A* then *B*" means that, if we have *A*, we must have *B* too, but if we do not have *A*, we may or may not have *B*, or mathematically,

$$(A \cdot B) + (\bar{A} \cdot B) + (\bar{A} \cdot \bar{B})$$

4. INHIBIT—"*A* is inhibited by *B*" means that *A* occurs providing *B* is not present, or Not-*B is* present; mathematically this is expressed as

$$A \cdot \bar{B}$$

Not even the three functions AND, OR, and NOT are independent of each other. There is a relationship among these three which can be developed from the graphs shown in Fig. 16. The upper left-hand graph shows that the area within the bold curve is equal to $A+B$. This means that everything outside this area is $(\overline{A+B})$. The upper right-hand graph shows the same areas in terms of the AND function. Everything outside circle *A* is Not-*A* (horizontal hatching); everything outside circle *B* is Not-*B* (vertical hatching); everything outside both circles is $\bar{A} \cdot \bar{B}$. Thus we arrive at the conclusion that

$$(\overline{A + B}) = \bar{A} \cdot \bar{B}$$

Similarly for the lower graphs. In the lower left-hand graph the horizontal hatching represents $\bar{A}$ and the vertical hatching represents $\bar{B}$. The entire area

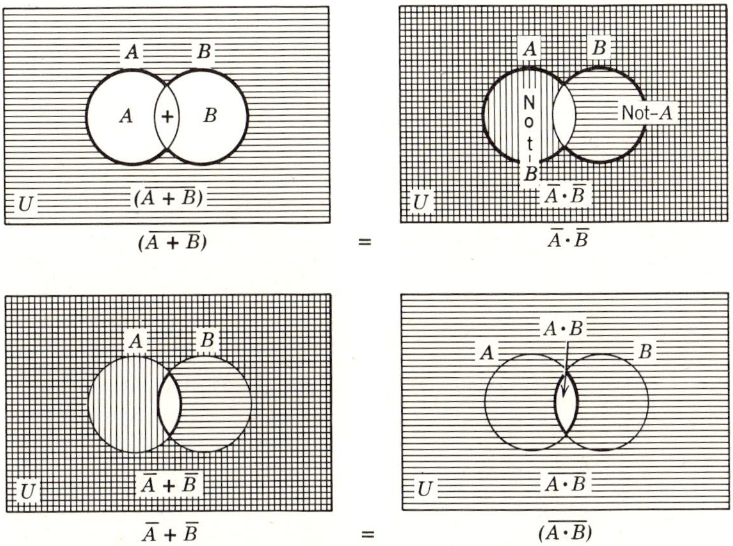

Figure 16 Relationships between AND and OR functions.

outside the bold center curve is, therefore, $\bar{A}+\bar{B}$. The lower right-hand graph shows the same area as being $\overline{A\cdot B}$. Thus we arrive at the conclusion that

$$\overline{(A\cdot B)} = \bar{A}+\bar{B}$$

From the above two relationships we arrive at the following rule:

To obtain the inverse of a function, replace all AND's with OR's and all OR's with AND's, and invert the terms.

$\overline{(A+B)} = \bar{A}\cdot\bar{B}$ = INVERTED OR = NOR

$\overline{(A\cdot B)} = \bar{A}+\bar{B}$ = INVERTED AND = NAND

$\overline{(A\cdot\bar{B})} = \bar{A}+B$ = INVERTED INHIBIT

As will be shown in Section II, the inverted functions occur often, especially in circuits which use amplifiers that invert the phase of the signal.

Examples

Convert the following AND functions into OR functions:

1. $\overline{(A\cdot B\cdot C)} = \bar{A}+\bar{B}+\bar{C}$
2. $\overline{(A\cdot\bar{B}\cdot C)} = \bar{A}+B+\bar{C}$
3. $(\bar{A}\cdot B\cdot C) = \overline{(A+\bar{B}+\bar{C})}$

Examples

Convert the following OR functions into AND functions:

1. $\overline{(A+B+C)} = \bar{A}\cdot\bar{B}\cdot\bar{C}$
2. $\overline{(A+B+\bar{C})} = \bar{A}\cdot\bar{B}\cdot C$
3. $(\bar{A}+\bar{B}+\bar{C}) = \overline{(A\cdot B\cdot C)}$

Examples

Convert the following combinatorial functions to equivalent functions.

1. $\overline{(\bar{A}\cdot B)+(A\cdot \bar{B})} = \overline{(\bar{A}\cdot B)}\cdot\overline{(A\cdot \bar{B})}$
$= (A+\bar{B})\cdot(\bar{A}+B)$

2. $\overline{(A+B)\cdot(\bar{A}+\bar{B})} = \overline{(A+B)}+\overline{(\bar{A}+\bar{B})}$
$= (\bar{A}\cdot\bar{B})+(A\cdot B)$

3. $A\cdot B+\bar{A}\cdot\bar{B} = (\overline{\overline{(A\cdot B)}\cdot\overline{(\bar{A}\cdot\bar{B})}})$

Converting each parenthetical expression produces

$$(\overline{(\bar{A}+\bar{B})\cdot(A+B)})$$

By expanding terms this becomes equal to

$$\overline{\bar{A}\cdot A+\bar{A}\cdot B+\bar{B}\cdot A+\bar{B}\cdot B}$$

Since $\bar{A}\cdot A$ and $\bar{B}\cdot B$ are both equal to zero, this reduces to

$$\overline{\bar{A}\cdot B+\bar{B}\cdot A}$$
$$= \overline{(\bar{A}\cdot B)}\cdot\overline{(\bar{B}\cdot A)}$$
$$= (A+\bar{B})\cdot(B+\bar{A})$$

4. $\bar{A}\cdot B+A\cdot\bar{B} = \overline{\overline{(\bar{A}\cdot B)}\cdot\overline{(A\cdot\bar{B})}}$

Converting each parenthetical expression produces

$$\overline{(A+\bar{B})\cdot(\bar{A}+B)}$$

By expanding terms this becomes equal to

$$\overline{A\cdot\bar{A}+A\cdot B+\bar{A}\cdot\bar{B}+B\cdot\bar{B}}$$

Since $A\cdot\bar{A}$ and $B\cdot\bar{B}$ are both equal to zero, this reduces to

$$\overline{A\cdot B+\bar{A}\cdot\bar{B}}$$
$$= \overline{(A\cdot B)}\cdot\overline{(\bar{A}\cdot\bar{B})}$$
$$= (\bar{A}+\bar{B})\cdot(A+B)$$

Truth Tables

To apply the rules of the algebra of logic to a problem, we make use of a truth table. A truth table is a statement of all the conditions of a problem in tabular form. To facilitate the formation of this table, follow the convention that ONE stands for the YES and ZERO stands for the NO of a proposition. Stated differently, a ONE indicates the presence of a certain class, A, and ZERO represents the presence of the opposite class, $\bar{A}$. From the truth table it is easy to develop the logical expressions stating all the conditions in algebraic terms.

To understand fully the meaning of a truth table, let us write one which represents the operation of a binary comparator. A binary comparator is a device which looks at two bits and produces the answer to the following question: "Are the two bits unlike?" A ONE output indicates "Yes, they are unlike"; a ZERO output indicates "No, they are not unlike, they are alike." If the input bits are labeled A and B, and the output bit K, then the conditions of the problem are summarized in Table 13.

table 13 TRUTH TABLE FOR BINARY COMPARATOR

Bit (A)	Bit (B)	Comparator Output (K)
0	0	0
0	1	1
1	0	1
1	1	0

To find the logical equation for the binary comparator, we ask ourselves "Under what conditions does the comparator produce a ONE?" The answer is given on lines two and three: when A equals ZERO and B equals ONE or $\bar{A} \cdot B$; or when A equals ONE and B equals ZERO or $A \cdot \bar{B}$. Therefore, the algebraic expression for the binary comparator is

$$K = (\bar{A} \cdot B) + (A \cdot \bar{B})$$

Now let us find the equation for a half-adder from its truth table. A half-adder is a binary adder that has two inputs, augend and addend. It is called a half-adder because it does only half the job of addition; a full adder adds three bits, the augend, addend, and carry from the last bit position. The half-adder addition table is presented in Table 14.

table 14 TRUTH TABLE FOR HALF-ADDER

Augend (A)	Addend (B)	Sum (S)	Carry (C)
0	0	0	0
0	1	1	0
1	0	1	0
1	1	0	1

To express the operation of a half-adder, we need two equations: one for the sum and one for the carry. From the table we see that the sum is ONE under the same conditions as for the binary comparator. Therefore the sum is

$$S = (\bar{A} \cdot B) + (A \cdot \bar{B})$$

The table also shows that a carry is produced or C = ONE only when both A and B are ONE, or

$$C = A \cdot B$$

Since the equation for the 2-bit sum represents roughly one half the job performed by the half-adder, a circuit which performs this operation is often called a quarter-adder. Now, we know that

$$S = K = (\bar{A} \cdot B) + (A \cdot \bar{B})$$

From the previous example we know that

$$(\bar{A} \cdot B) + (A \cdot \bar{B}) = (A + B) \cdot (\bar{A} + \bar{B})$$

We also know that

$$(\bar{A} + \bar{B}) = (\overline{A \cdot B})$$

The equation for the 2-bit sum then reduces to

$$S = K = (A + B) \cdot (\overline{A \cdot B})$$

which is exactly the same as the equation for the exclusive OR function. Therefore, the binary comparator, quarter-adder, and EXCLUSIVE OR are all one and the same.

The truth table for a full 3-input binary adder is given in Table 15.

table 15 TRUTH TABLE FOR BINARY ADDER

Augend (A)	Addend (B)	Previous Carry (C')	Sum (S)	Carry (C)
0	0	0	0	0
0	0	1	1	0
0	1	0	1	0
0	1	1	0	1
1	0	0	1	0
1	0	1	0	1
1	1	0	0	1
1	1	1	1	1

There are eight lines to this table, since these three variables may be combined in eight ways. The associated sum and carry bits are shown for each combination. The second, third, fifth, and eighth lines indicate separate conditions under which the sum S is equal to ONE. Therefore,

$$S = (\bar{A} \cdot \bar{B} \cdot C') + (\bar{A} \cdot B \cdot \bar{C}') + (A \cdot \bar{B} \cdot \bar{C}') + (A \cdot B \cdot C')$$

or S equals ONE when the three inputs are

0, 0 and 1 *or* 0, 1 and 0 *or* 1, 0 and 0 *or* 1, 1 and 1

The fourth, sixth, seventh, and eighth lines indicate alternative conditions under which the carry C is equal to ONE. Therefore,

$$C = (\bar{A} \cdot B \cdot C') + (A \cdot \bar{B} \cdot C') + (A \cdot B \cdot \bar{C}') + (A \cdot B \cdot C')$$

or C equals ONE when the three inputs are

0, 1 and 1 *or* 1, 0 and 1 *or* 1, 1 and 0 *or* 1, 1 and 1

Example

Prove that $S = (\bar{A} \cdot \bar{B} \cdot C') + (\bar{A} \cdot B \cdot \bar{C}') + (A \cdot \bar{B} \cdot \bar{C}') + (A \cdot B \cdot C')$ is equivalent to $S = C'(\overline{\bar{A} \cdot B + A \cdot \bar{B}}) + \bar{C}'(\bar{A} \cdot B + A \cdot \bar{B})$

Factoring

$$S = C'(\bar{A} \cdot \bar{B} + A \cdot B) + \bar{C}'(\bar{A} \cdot B + A \cdot \bar{B})$$

From the previous example we know that

$$\bar{A} \cdot \bar{B} + A \cdot B = (\overline{\bar{A} \cdot B + A \cdot \bar{B}})$$

Therefore

$$S = C'(\overline{\bar{A} \cdot B + A \cdot \bar{B}}) + \bar{C}'(\bar{A} \cdot B + A \cdot \bar{B})$$

Example

Prove that $C = (\bar{A} \cdot B \cdot C') + (A \cdot \bar{B} \cdot C') + (A \cdot B \cdot \bar{C}') + (A \cdot B \cdot C')$ is equivalent to $C = C'(\bar{A} \cdot B + A \cdot \bar{B}) + A \cdot B$

Factoring

$$C = C'(\bar{A} \cdot B + A \cdot \bar{B}) + A \cdot B\,(C' + \bar{C}')$$

Since $C' + \bar{C}'$ is equal to the universal class U, the above expression reduces to

$$C = C'(\bar{A} \cdot B + A \cdot \bar{B}) + A \cdot B$$

Next let us find the 9's complements of numbers in the 5421 system. Table 16 is a summary of all the conditions that must be met. The 9's complement of each number represented by the four bits in the left-hand column is given by the number represented by the four bits in the right-hand column and vice versa.

To find the logical expressions summarizing the information in this table we determine the conditions in the left-hand columns under which a ONE appears in each of the four right-hand columns. Four logical expressions are needed, one for each bit position.

table 16 TRUTH TABLE FOR 5421 COMPLEMENTER

Number					Complement				
Order of Bit / Weight / Decimal	A_4 5	A_3 4	A_2 2	A_1 1	A'_4 5	A'_3 4	A'_2 2	A'_1 1	Order of Bit / Weight / Decimal
0	0	0	0	0	1	1	0	0	9
1	0	0	0	1	1	0	1	1	8
2	0	0	1	0	1	0	1	0	7
3	0	0	1	1	1	0	0	1	6
4	0	1	0	0	1	0	0	0	5

From the truth table we see that A'_1 is equal to ONE whenever A_1 is equal to ONE, and at no other time. Therefore,

$$A'_1 = A_1$$

A'_2 is equal to ONE on lines two and three. On these two lines on the left side we note that the bits in the first two orders are either ZERO and ONE or ONE and ZERO. Expressed algebraically,

$$A'_2 = \bar{A}_2 \cdot A_1 + A_2 \cdot \bar{A}_1$$

A'_3 is equal to ONE on line one. On this line bits A_1, A_2, A_3, and A_4 are all ZERO. Therefore,

$$A'_3 = \bar{A}_4 \cdot \bar{A}_3 \cdot \bar{A}_2 \cdot \bar{A}_1$$

If $\bar{A}_4$ is removed from this expression, we still have a unique expression for A'_3. The $\bar{A}_4$ is thus redundant, and it is enough to state

$$A'_3 = \bar{A}_3 \cdot \bar{A}_2 \cdot \bar{A}_1$$

Lastly, A'_4 is equal to ONE whenever A_4 is equal to ZERO or

$$A'_4 = \bar{A}_4$$

The four logical equations derived above express all the conditions necessary to produce a 9's complement for all numbers between 0 and 4. The same equations hold for the complementation of numbers between 5 and 9, as can readily be seen by inspecting the truth table.

Veitch Diagrams

Relationships among classes may be shown by means of rectangles instead of circles. When this is done, the resultant diagrams are called Veitch diagrams. The Veitch diagram may be drawn to show the relationship among any number of classes, although for practical reasons it is rarely used for more than 6. The Veitch diagram is an excellent tool for the simplification of logical expressions.

Figure 17 shows a Veitch diagram for 2 variables. Notice that, instead of 2 circles meeting in the middle, we have two rectangles meeting at one corner. Hatching is used only to show relationships. Any of the 4 possible AND functions is designated by a 1 in the appropriate box.

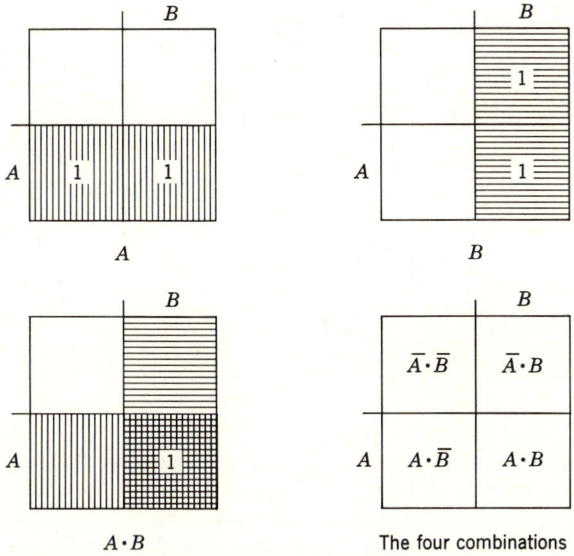

Figure 17 Veitch diagrams—2 variables.

In Fig. 18 is shown a Veitch diagram with the 8 possible AND combination for 3 variables. Notice that in this case *A*, *B*, and *C*, respectively, are represented by a 1 in each of 4 squares; that $A{\cdot}B$, $A{\cdot}C$, and $B{\cdot}C$, respectively, are represented by a 1 in each of only 2 squares; and that $A{\cdot}B{\cdot}C$ is represented by a 1 in only 1 square.

In Fig. 19 is shown a Veitch diagram with the 16 possible AND combinations for 4 variables. Here function *A* is represented by a 1 in 8 squares; function $A{\cdot}B$ by a 1 in 4 squares; function $A{\cdot}B{\cdot}C$ by a 1 in 2 squares; and function $A{\cdot}B{\cdot}C{\cdot}D$ by a 1 in only 1 square.

There is a lot of symmetry in Veitch diagrams. For instance, in the diagram for *A* in Fig. 19, one half the boxes labeled 1 are in state *B*, the other one half in state $\bar{B}$; one half are in state *C*, the other one half in state $\bar{C}$; one half are in state *D*, the other one half in state $\bar{D}$. In the diagram for $A{\cdot}B$, one half the boxes labeled 1 are in state *C*, the other one half in state $\bar{C}$; one half in state *D*, the other one half in state $\bar{D}$. In the diagram for $A{\cdot}B{\cdot}C$, one half the boxes labeled 1 are in state *D*, the other one half in state $\bar{D}$.

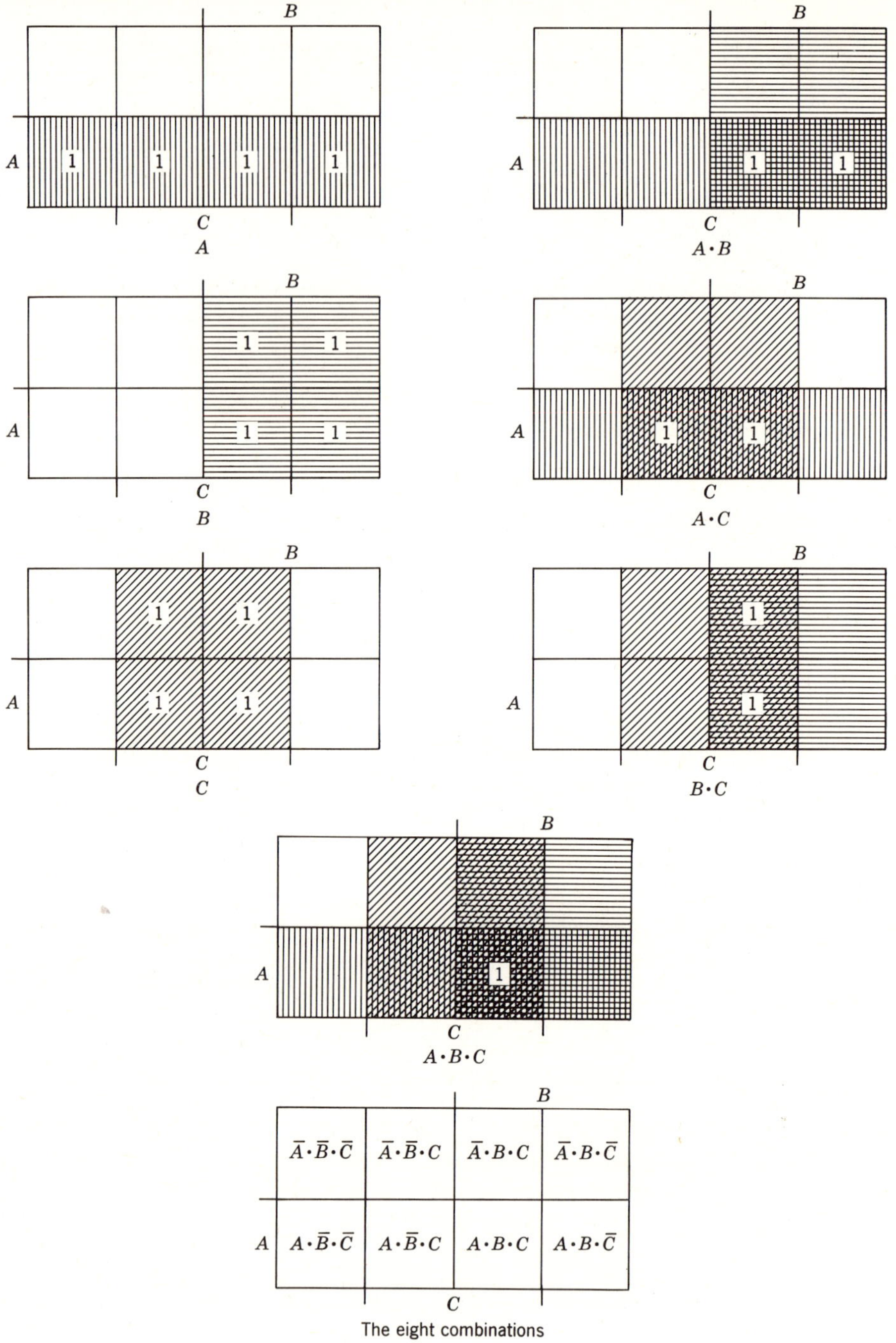

Figure 18 Veitch diagrams—3 variables.

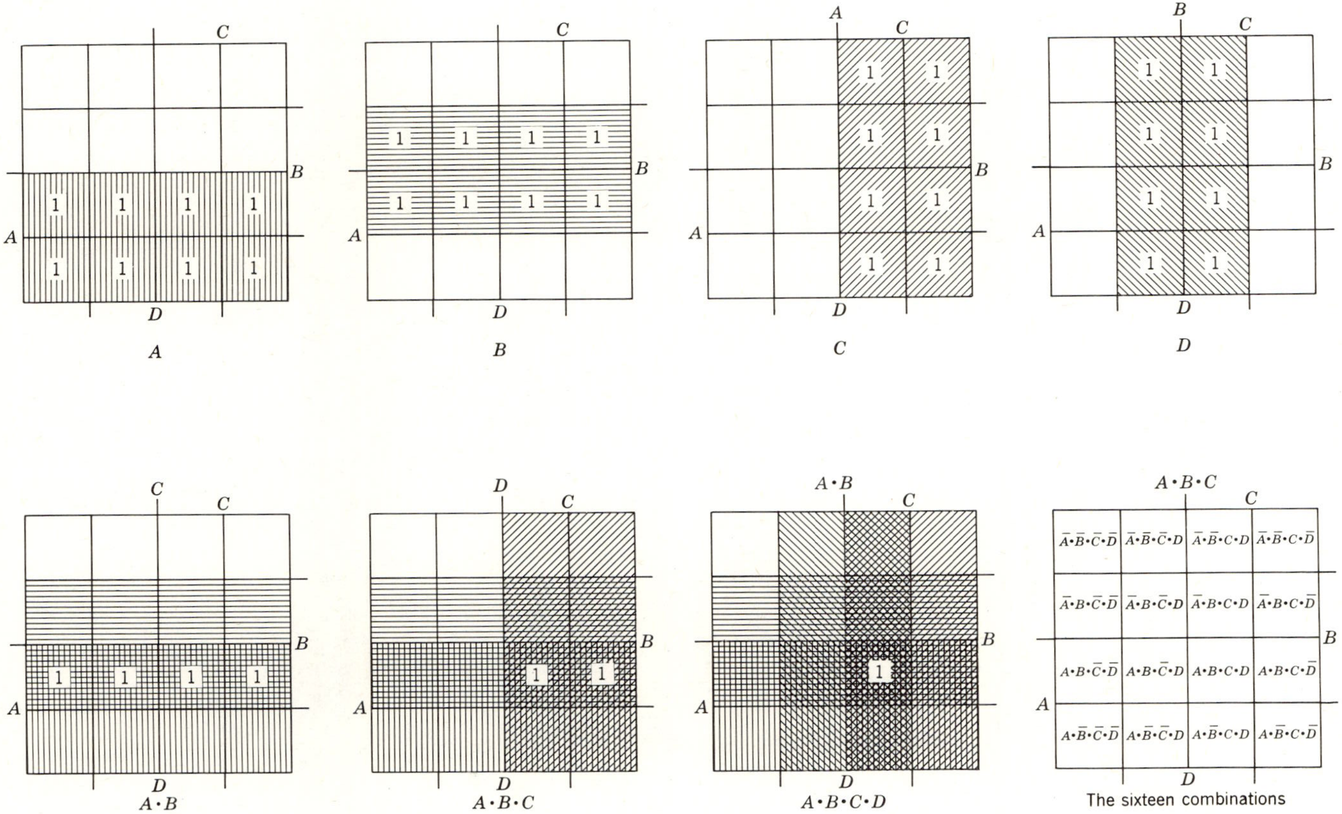

Figure 19 Veitch diagrams—4 variables.

It is this symmetry that makes the Veitch diagram such a useful device for simplifying logical expressions. Figure 20 and the following examples illustrate how Veitch diagrams are used.

Examples

Simplify the following expressions by means of a Veitch diagram and compare the result to that obtained mathematically:

1. $$X = A \cdot B + A \cdot B \cdot C + A \cdot B \cdot C \cdot D$$

Figure 20*a* shows that $A \cdot B \cdot C \cdot D$ is embedded within $A \cdot B \cdot C$, which, in turn, is embedded within $A \cdot B$. Therefore

$$X = A \cdot B$$

Mathematically

$$\begin{aligned} X &= A \cdot B + A \cdot B \cdot C + A \cdot B \cdot C \cdot D \\ &= A \cdot B (1 + C + C \cdot D) \end{aligned}$$

Since 1 (representing the universal class) plus anything equals 1

$$X = A \cdot B$$

2. $$X = A \cdot B \cdot \bar{C} \cdot \bar{D} + A \cdot \bar{B} \cdot \bar{C} \cdot \bar{D} + A \cdot B \cdot \bar{C} \cdot D + A \cdot \bar{B} \cdot \bar{C} \cdot D + A \cdot \bar{B} \cdot C \cdot D + A \cdot \bar{B} \cdot C \cdot \bar{D}$$

If a 1 is placed in each square as determined by each term in the equation, the pattern of 1's shown in Fig. 20*b* is obtained. These squares may be divided into the two groupings shown, making

$$X = A \cdot \bar{B} + A \cdot \bar{C}$$

Mathematically

$$X = A \cdot B \cdot \bar{C} \cdot \bar{D} + A \cdot \bar{B} \cdot \bar{C} \cdot \bar{D} + A \cdot B \cdot \bar{C} \cdot D + A \cdot \bar{B} \cdot \bar{C} \cdot D + A \cdot \bar{B} \cdot C \cdot D + A \cdot \bar{B} \cdot C \cdot \bar{D}$$

Factoring

$$\begin{aligned} X &= A \cdot (B \cdot \bar{C} \cdot \bar{D} + \bar{B} \cdot \bar{C} \cdot \bar{D} + B \cdot \bar{C} \cdot D + \bar{B} \cdot \bar{C} \cdot D + \bar{B} \cdot C \cdot D + \bar{B} \cdot C \cdot \bar{D}) \\ &= A \cdot (B \cdot (\bar{C} \cdot \bar{D} + \bar{C} \cdot D) + \bar{B} \cdot (\bar{C} \cdot \bar{D} + \bar{C} \cdot D + C \cdot D + C \cdot \bar{D})) \\ &= A \cdot (B \cdot (\bar{C} \cdot (\bar{D} + D)) + \bar{B} \cdot (\bar{C} \cdot (\bar{D} + D) + C \cdot (D + \bar{D}))) \end{aligned}$$

Since $\bar{D} + D = 1$

$$X = A \cdot (\bar{B} + B \cdot \bar{C}) = A \cdot \bar{B} + A \cdot B \cdot \bar{C}$$

Notice that $A \cdot B \cdot \bar{C}$ is represented by the diagonally hatched area in Fig. 20*b*.

The above equation may be simplified further:

$$\bar{B} + B \cdot \bar{C} = \overline{B \cdot (\overline{B \cdot \bar{C}})}$$

Simplifying the contents of the parentheses gives for the right side

$$\overline{B \cdot (\bar{B} + C)}$$

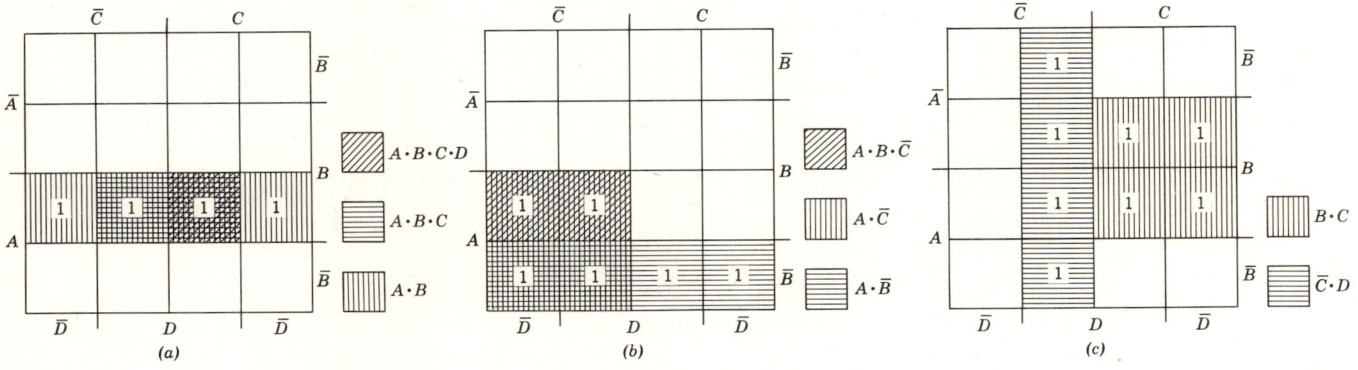

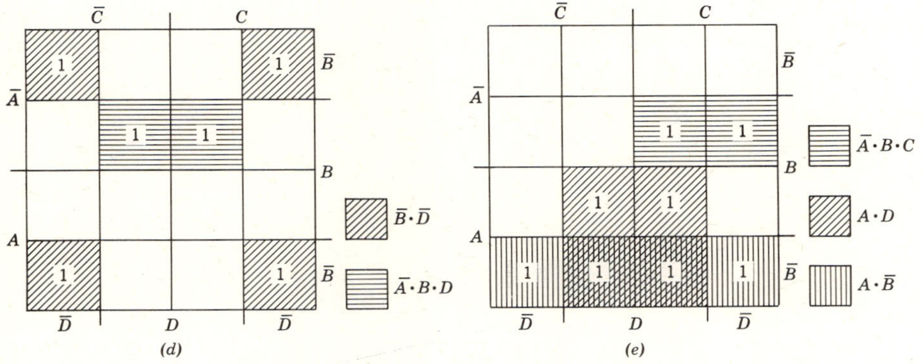

Figure 20 Logical simplification with Veitch diagrams.

(*a*) $X = A\cdot B + A\cdot B\cdot C + A\cdot B\cdot C\cdot D = A\,B.$

(*b*) $X = A\cdot B\cdot \bar{C}\cdot \bar{D} + A\cdot B\cdot \bar{C}\cdot D + A\cdot \bar{B}\cdot \bar{C}\cdot \bar{D} + A\cdot \bar{B}\cdot \bar{C}\cdot D + A\cdot \bar{B}\cdot \bar{C}\cdot D + A\cdot \bar{B}\cdot C\cdot D = A\cdot \bar{B} + A\cdot \bar{C}.$

(*c*) $X = \bar{A}\cdot \bar{B}\cdot \bar{C}\cdot D + \bar{A}\cdot B\cdot \bar{C}\cdot D + A\cdot B\cdot \bar{C}\cdot D + A\cdot \bar{B}\cdot \bar{C}\cdot D + \bar{A}\cdot B\cdot C\cdot D + A\cdot B\cdot C\cdot D + \bar{A}\cdot B\cdot C\cdot \bar{D} + A\cdot B\cdot C\cdot \bar{D} = B\cdot C + \bar{C}\cdot D.$

(*d*) $X = \bar{A}\cdot \bar{B}\cdot \bar{C}\cdot \bar{D} + A\cdot \bar{B}\cdot \bar{C}\cdot D + \bar{A}\cdot B\cdot \bar{C}\cdot D + \bar{A}\cdot B\cdot C\cdot D + \bar{A}\cdot \bar{B}\cdot C\cdot \bar{D} + A\cdot \bar{B}\cdot C\cdot \bar{D} = \bar{B}\cdot \bar{D} + \bar{A}\cdot B\cdot D.$

(*e*) $X = \bar{A}\cdot B\cdot C\cdot \bar{D} + B\cdot C\cdot D + A\cdot B\cdot D + A\cdot \bar{B}\cdot D + A\cdot \bar{B} = \bar{A}\cdot B\cdot C + A\cdot D + A\cdot \bar{B}.$

Combining terms under the bar gives

$$\overline{B\cdot\bar{B}+B\cdot C}=\overline{B\cdot C}$$

which reduces to

$$\bar{B}+\bar{C}$$

Therefore

$$X=A\cdot(\bar{B}+\bar{C})=A\cdot\bar{B}+A\cdot\bar{C}$$

3. $$X=\bar{A}\cdot\bar{B}\cdot\bar{C}\cdot D+\bar{A}\cdot B\cdot\bar{C}\cdot D+A\cdot B\cdot\bar{C}\cdot D+A\cdot\bar{B}\cdot\bar{C}\cdot D \\ +\bar{A}\cdot B\cdot C\cdot D+A\cdot B\cdot C\cdot D+\bar{A}\cdot B\cdot C\cdot\bar{D}+A\cdot B\cdot C\cdot\bar{D}$$

If a 1 is placed in each square as determined by each term in the equation, the pattern of 1's shown in Fig. 20*c* is obtained. The two broad groupings in which these squares may be divided are shown, making

$$X=B\cdot C+\bar{C}\cdot D$$

Mathematically

$$X=\bar{A}\cdot\bar{B}\cdot\bar{C}\cdot D+\bar{A}\cdot B\cdot\bar{C}\cdot D+A\cdot B\cdot\bar{C}\cdot D+A\cdot\bar{B}\cdot\bar{C}\cdot D \\ +\bar{A}\cdot B\cdot C\cdot D+A\cdot B\cdot C\cdot D+\bar{A}\cdot B\cdot C\cdot\bar{D}+A\cdot B\cdot C\cdot\bar{D}$$

Factoring

$$X=\bar{C}\cdot D\cdot(\bar{A}\cdot\bar{B}+\bar{A}\cdot B+A\cdot B+A\cdot\bar{B})+B\cdot C(\bar{A}\cdot D+\bar{A}\cdot\bar{D}+A\cdot D+A\cdot\bar{D}) \\ =\bar{C}\cdot D(\bar{A}(\bar{B}+B)+A(B+\bar{B}))+B\cdot C(\bar{A}(D+\bar{D})+A(D+\bar{D}))$$

Since $B+\bar{B}=D+\bar{D}=A+\bar{A}=1$,

$$X=\bar{C}\cdot D+B\cdot C$$

4. $$X=\bar{A}\cdot\bar{B}\cdot\bar{C}\cdot\bar{D}+A\cdot\bar{B}\cdot\bar{C}\cdot\bar{D}+\bar{A}\cdot B\cdot\bar{C}\cdot D+\bar{A}\cdot B\cdot C\cdot D+\bar{A}\cdot\bar{B}\cdot C\cdot\bar{D}+A\cdot\bar{B}\cdot C\cdot\bar{D}$$

The pattern of 1's is shown in Fig. 20*d*. Two broad groupings are found making

$$X=\bar{B}\cdot\bar{D}+\bar{A}\cdot B\cdot D$$

Mathematically

$$X=\bar{A}\cdot\bar{B}\cdot\bar{C}\cdot\bar{D}+A\cdot\bar{B}\cdot\bar{C}\cdot\bar{D}+\bar{A}\cdot B\cdot\bar{C}\cdot D+\bar{A}\cdot B\cdot C\cdot D+\bar{A}\cdot\bar{B}\cdot C\cdot\bar{D}+A\cdot\bar{B}\cdot C\cdot\bar{D}$$

Factoring

$$X=\bar{B}\cdot\bar{D}(\bar{A}\cdot\bar{C}+\bar{A}\cdot C+A\cdot\bar{C}+A\cdot C)+\bar{A}\cdot B\cdot D(C+\bar{C})$$

Since $\bar{C}+C=\bar{A}+A=1$,

$$X=\bar{B}\cdot\bar{D}+\bar{A}\cdot B\cdot D$$

5. $$X=\bar{A}\cdot B\cdot C\cdot\bar{D}+B\cdot C\cdot D+A\cdot B\cdot D+A\cdot\bar{B}\cdot D+A\cdot\bar{B}$$

The pattern of 1's is shown in Fig. 20*e*. Three broad groupings are found making

$$X=\bar{A}\cdot B\cdot C+A\cdot D+A\cdot\bar{B}$$

Mathematically

$$X=\bar{A}\cdot B\cdot C\cdot\bar{D}+B\cdot C\cdot D+A\cdot B\cdot D+A\cdot\bar{B}\cdot D+A\cdot\bar{B}$$

Multiplying the 2nd term by $(A+\bar{A})$ gives

$$X=\bar{A}\cdot B\cdot C\cdot\bar{D}+\bar{A}\cdot B\cdot C\cdot D+A\cdot B\cdot C\cdot D+A\cdot B\cdot D+A\cdot\bar{B}\cdot D+A\cdot\bar{B}$$

Factoring

$$X=\bar{A}\cdot B\cdot C(\bar{D}+D)+A\cdot D(B\cdot C+B+\bar{B})+A\cdot\bar{B}$$

Since $\bar{D}+D=\bar{B}+B=1$

$$X=\bar{A}\cdot B\cdot C+A\cdot D(1+B\cdot C)+A\cdot\bar{B}$$
$$=\bar{A}\cdot B\cdot C+A\cdot D+A\cdot\bar{B}$$

Logical Block Diagrams

Logical expressions relate symbols representing classes by means of AND, OR and NOT functions. These mathematical expressions may be represented by means of equivalent AND, OR, and NOT blocks in a logical block diagram. As will be seen in Section II, several physical devices are available which correspond closely in their operations to these logical blocks. Thus, the logical block diagram is a plan from which the actual hardware may be designed and built.

Figure 21 shows the relationships among several logical blocks and their associated truth tables and logical expressions. The first three blocks are primary: the most complicated logical expressions may be built from them. The INHIBIT function $A\cdot\bar{B}$ may be represented by a NOT block which converts B to $\bar{B}$ and an AND block which combines A and $\bar{B}$. These two blocks are equivalent to the one block shown. The circle at the end of input line B represents an inhibit signal: whenever B is present, it inhibits the flow of signal A.

The INVERTED OR or NOR may be drawn in two ways. In the first diagram both A and B are inverted and then fed to an AND block; this produces $\bar{A}\cdot\bar{B}$. In the second diagram, A and B are ORed and then fed through an inverter; this produces $\overline{A+B}$. Both block diagrams are equivalent and may be represented compactly by the diagram on the right.

The INVERTED AND or NAND may similarly be drawn in two ways. In the first diagram, A and B are individually inverted and then fed through an OR to produce $\bar{A}+\bar{B}$. In the second diagram, A and B are ANDed and then inverted to produce $\overline{A\cdot B}$. Both block diagrams are equivalent and may be represented compactly by the diagram on the right.

With the aid of these fundamental logical blocks we can convert any logical expression into a logical block diagram. The binary comparator, quarter-adder, or EXCLUSIVE OR is shown in block diagram form in Fig. 22. By substituting for A and B, in turn, each of the four combinations shown and following the signals through, it can be seen that this block diagram does perform everything required of it by the truth table.

A	B	$A \cdot B$
0	0	0
0	1	0
1	0	0
1	1	1

A	B	$A + B$
0	0	0
0	1	1
1	0	1
1	1	1

A	$\bar{A}$
0	1
1	0

A	B	$A \cdot \bar{B}$
0	0	0
0	1	0
1	0	1
1	1	0

A	B	$\overline{A + B}$
0	0	1
0	1	0
1	0	0
1	1	0

A	B	$\overline{A \cdot B}$
0	0	1
0	1	1
1	0	1
1	1	0

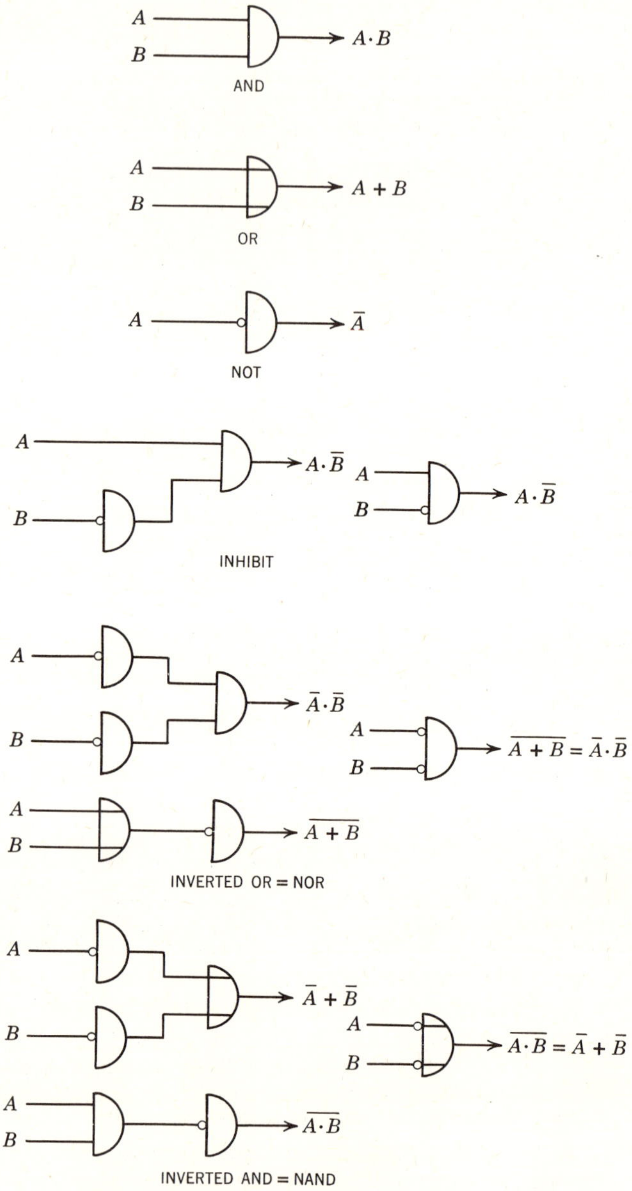

Figure 21 Fundamental logical blocks.

A	B	K
0	0	0
0	1	1
1	0	1
1	1	0

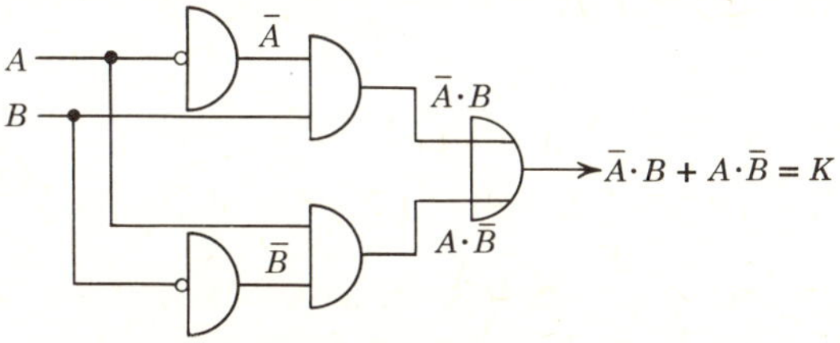

Figure 22 Binary Comparator.

The block diagram of the half-adder (Fig. 23) illustrates why the following expression for the sum

$$S = (A + B) \cdot (\overline{A \cdot B})$$

is preferable to

$$S = (\bar{A} \cdot B) + (A \cdot \bar{B})$$

In the former, the carry ($C = A \cdot B$) is produced as part of the formation of the sum. Therefore, there is a saving in the number of logical blocks needed.

A	B	S	C
0	0	0	0
0	1	1	0
1	0	1	0
1	1	0	1

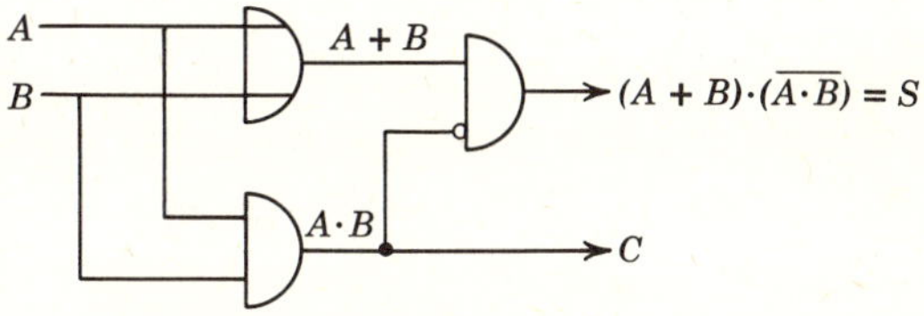

Figure 23 Half-adder.

Figure 24 shows how two half-adders may be combined to form a full binary adder. One half-adder adds the augend and addend to produce a partial sum and carry. The other half-adder adds the partial sum and the previous carry to produce the sum and a carry. The carries from both half-adders are combined in an OR block to produce a carry which is applied to the addition of bits in the following bit position.

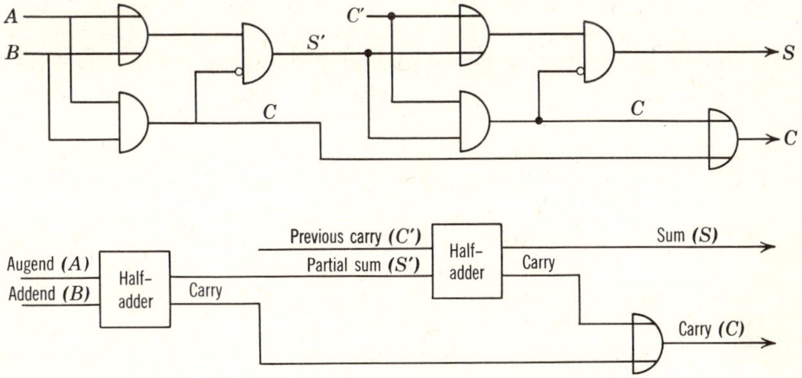

Figure 24 Binary adder composed of two half-adders.

If we proceed in a straightforward manner to develop a 3-input adder, we develop the truth table shown in Fig. 25. From the resultant algebraic expressions, we form the block diagram shown. Although it looks entirely different from the block diagram in Fig. 24, the two are equivalent in function.

Figure 26 shows the block diagram for the 5421 complementer.

PRACTICAL LOGICAL ELEMENTS

In a practical machine, propositions or classes are represented by signals. As these signals progress from one stage to the next, they lose energy. Amplifiers restore this energy.

If a signal is produced now but must be applied to a certain circuit a little later, the signal waits in a storage device.

Amplification

There are in general two types of amplifiers: those that invert the polarity of the input signal and those that do not. The first is called an inverting amplifier and the second is called simply an amplifier. The amplifier and inverting amplifier blocks are shown in Fig. 27. Amplifiers are also used in memories and to drive external devices.

Storage

Storage may be represented in block diagrams in several ways. Some of the more common blocks are the time delay, the storage cell, and the flip-flop. Time delay implies that the signal is delayed for a definite amount of time before being applied to another point in the circuit, whereas a storage cell holds a bit for an indefinite time, until called for. Logical blocks representing delay and the storage cell are shown in Fig. 27.

Also shown in Fig. 27 are several flip-flops. The *R–S* flip-flop is a versatile storage cell. It has two input lines labeled "set" and "reset"; and two output lines labeled ONE and ZERO. A signal applied to the set line produces a continuous ONE output. A signal applied to the reset line removes the information from the ONE output line and causes the ZERO output line to produce a continuous signal. In the first instance, the flip-flop is set; in the second case it is reset. The flip-flop remains in one of these two stable states until a signal flips the flip-flop to the opposite state. But in either state, the two output lines produce signals that are out of phase with each other. This means that the flip-flop produces a signal and its complement simultaneously.

Observe from the truth table that in the *R–S* flip-flop a ONE applied simultaneously to the set and reset inputs is not allowed. In the *J–K* flip-flop, however, this condition is allowed. Here, *J* stands for set and *K* for reset. When *J* and *K* occur simultaneously the state of the flip-flop changes regardless of its state before the advent of the two signals.

A	B	C'	S	C
0	0	0	0	0
0	0	1	1	0
0	1	0	1	0
0	1	1	0	1
1	0	0	1	0
1	0	1	0	1
1	1	0	0	1
1	1	1	1	1

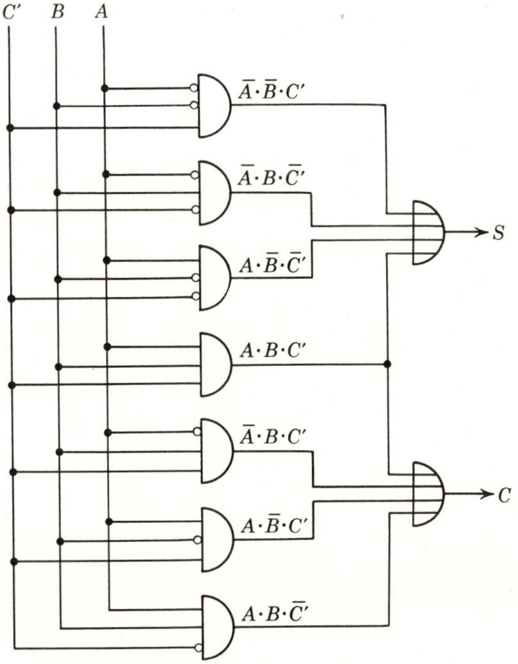

Figure 25 Binary adder.

A_4	A_3	A_2	A_1	A'_4	A'_3	A'_2	A'_1
0	0	0	0	1	1	0	0
0	0	0	1	1	0	1	1
0	0	1	0	1	0	1	0
0	0	1	1	1	0	0	1
0	1	0	0	1	0	0	0

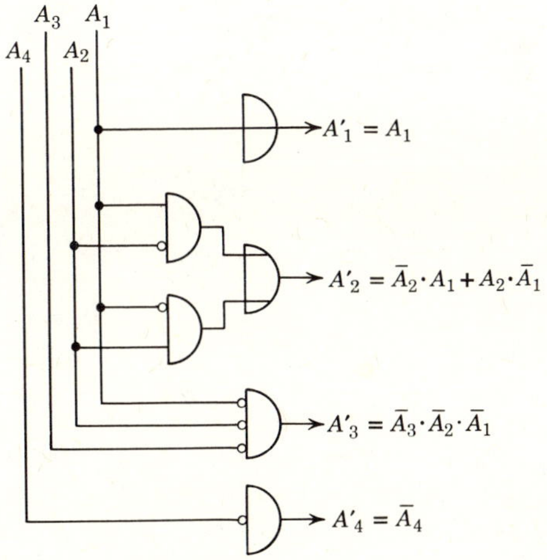

Figure 26 5421 Complementer.

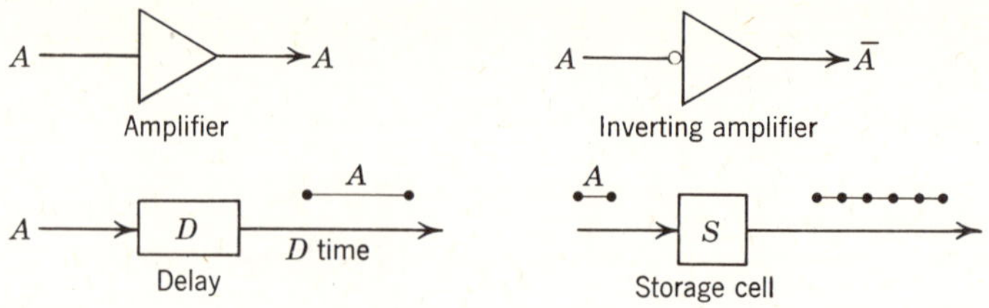

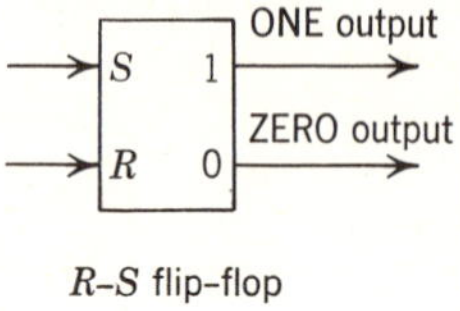

R	S	ONE Output at t	at t + 1
0	0	0	0
0	0	1	1
0	1	0	1
0	1	1	1
1	0	0	0
1	0	1	0
1	1	0	–
1	1	1	–

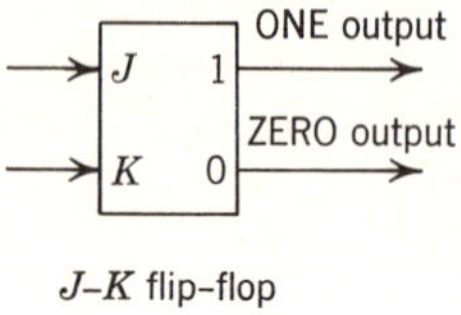

J	K	ONE Output at t	at t + 1
0	0	0	0
0	0	1	1
0	1	0	1
0	1	1	1
1	0	0	0
1	0	1	0
1	1	0	1
1	1	1	0

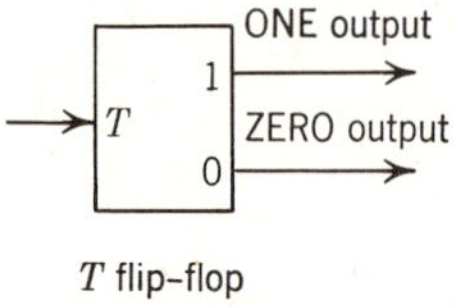

T	ONE Output at t	at t + 1
0	0	0
0	1	1
1	0	1
1	1	0

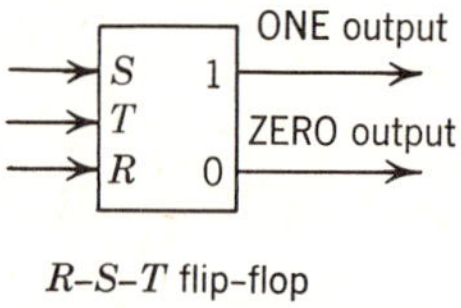

R	S	T	ONE Output at t	at t + 1
0	0	0	0	0
0	0	0	1	1
0	0	1	0	1
0	0	1	1	0
0	1	0	0	1
0	1	0	1	1
1	0	0	0	0
1	0	0	1	0

Figure 27 **Amplifying and storage elements.**

Another type of flip-flop is the trigger or *T* flip-flop. Whenever a ONE pulse is applied to *T*, the state of the flip-flop changes. The *R–S–T* flip-flop combines the features of the *R–S* and of the *T* flip-flop.

Examples of Practical Logic

As a rough indication of the value of these practical logical elements the adder (composed of two half-adders) and the binary comparator are redrawn in Fig. 28. Part *a* shows the use of the amplifiers and delay elements. As the signal passes through each block, it deteriorates. Therefore, after every few basic logical blocks, the signal is fed through an amplifier as shown. If signals *A*, *B*, and *C′* occur at the same time, and if it is assumed that it takes a finite time for a signal to pass through each logical element—as it must—then the signal *C′* reaches A_3 before *S′* does. Time delay D_1 is inserted to make sure that both signals are applied to A_3 at the same time. Similarly, the carry *C* from A_1 is delayed by D_2 to make sure it is applied to the next stage (0_3) at the same time as the output of A_3.

Part b shows the use of $R–S$ flip-flops in a binary comparator. A_1 produces an output signal only when flip-flop $FF1$ is reset and flip-flop $FF2$ is set. A_2 produces an output signal only when $FF1$ is set and $FF2$ is reset. The output of 0_1 is, therefore,

$$K = (A \cdot \bar{B}) + (\bar{A} \cdot B)$$

The output K remains indefinitely at either ONE or ZERO until $FF1$ or $FF2$ reverses states.

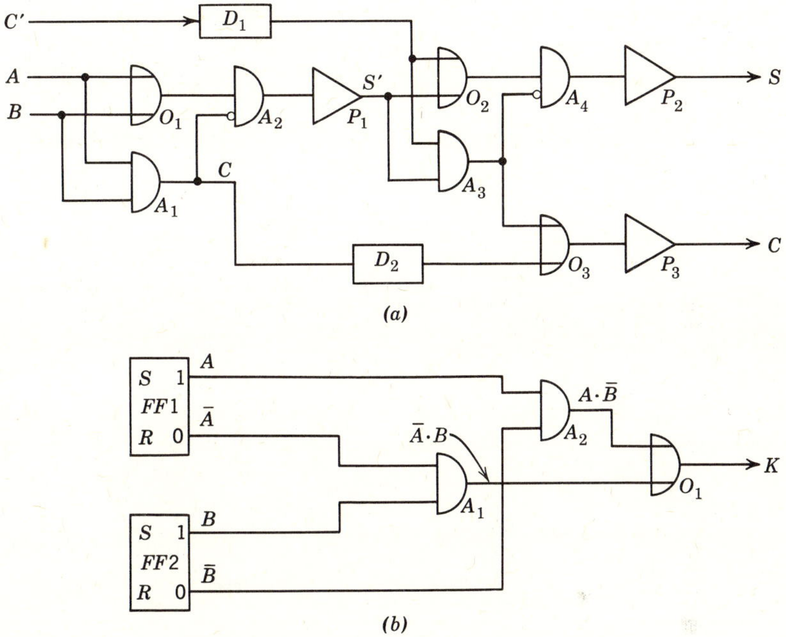

Figure 28 Use of amplifying and storage elements. (*a*) Binary adder. (*b*) Comparator.

SUMMARY

1. There are three basic logical elements: AND, OR, and NOT. But for practical machine logic, five more logical elements must be included: amplifier, inverting amplifier, time delay, storage cell, and flip-flop.
2. The three fundamental logical elements may be manipulated according to simple algebraic rules. Amplifying and storage elements are kept track of with the aid of logical block diagrams.
3. To develop a device to perform a certain job, a truth table is drawn from which logical algebraic expressions are derived. The algebraic expressions

table 17 SUMMARY OF LOGICAL RULES

Name	Block	Type Output or Conditions Under Which Output Produced
(a) Fundamental Elements		
AND	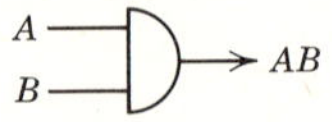	Only if A and B signals present
OR	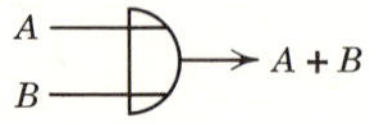	If either signal A or B or both present
NOT	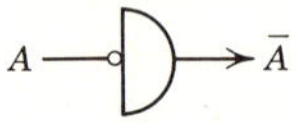	If no signal at input
Amplifier	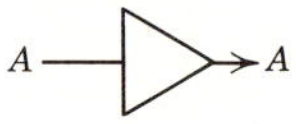	Amplified signal
Inverting amplifier	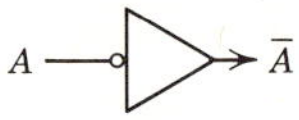	Amplified signal out of phase with input
Delay	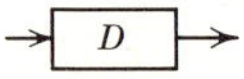	Delayed in time by an amount D
Storage cell	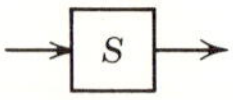	Store bit for indefinite time
Flip-flop	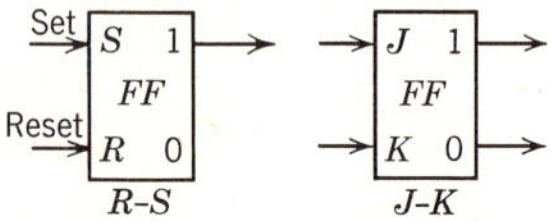	Set pulse (S or J) turns on ONE output Reset pulse (R or K) turns on ZERO output
Flip-flop	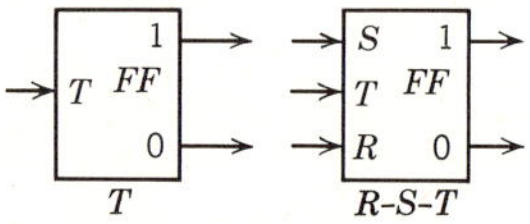	T pulse switches state of flip-flop
(b) Combinatorial Elements		
INHIBIT	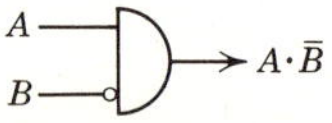	If A is present and B is not present
INVERTED AND (NAND)	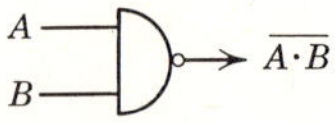 $\overline{A \cdot B}$	Complement of AND circuit
INVERTED OR (NOR)	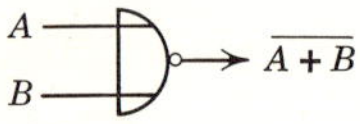 $\overline{A + B}$	Complement of OR circuit

(c) Laws

Commutative: $A + B = B + A$

$A \cdot B = B \cdot A$

Associative: $A + (B + C) = (A + B) + C$

$A \cdot (B \cdot C) = (A \cdot B) \cdot C$

Distributive: $A \cdot (B + C) = (A \cdot B) + (A \cdot C)$

$A + (B \cdot C) = (A + B) \cdot (A + C)$

(d) Identities

$$A \cdot 0 = 0$$
$$U \cdot A = A$$
$$A \cdot \bar{A} = 0$$
$$A + A = A$$
$$0 + A = A$$
$$U + A = U$$
$$A + \bar{A} = U$$
$$\bar{\bar{A}} = A$$

(e) Important Relations

$$(\overline{A + B}) = \bar{A} \cdot \bar{B}$$
$$(\overline{A \cdot B}) = \bar{A} + \bar{B}$$
$$(\bar{A} \cdot B) + (A \cdot \bar{B}) = (\bar{A} + \bar{B}) \cdot (A + B)$$
$$(\bar{A} \cdot \bar{B}) + (A \cdot B) = (A + \bar{B}) \cdot (\bar{A} + B)$$

are converted to block diagrams, to which then are added amplifying and storage blocks. The final logical block diagram is a plan for the construction of the device.

4. Some of the more important blocks, algebraic laws, identities, and relationships are summarized in Table 17.

5. *Definitions to Remember*

Exclusive or = Binary Comparator = Quarter-Adder. A device which compares two bits. If the two bits are alike, a ZERO output is produced. If the two bits are unlike, a ONE output is produced.

Truth Table. A statement of all conditions of a problem in tabular form.

Half-Adder. A device which produces the binary sum and carry of two bits. (The sum portion may be obtained by a quarter adder.)

Binary Adder. A device which produces the binary sum and carry when the augend, addend, and carry from previous bit position are applied.

Exercises

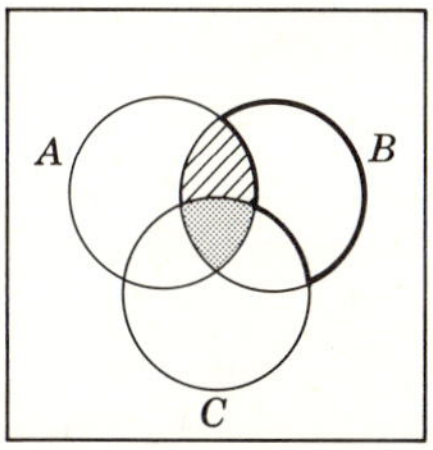

1. In the following diagram, where circles A, B, and C represent different classes, what is the logical expression for:
   a. The center solid area?
   b. The hatched area?
   c. The area enclosed by the bold curves?
2. Are the following relationships true or false:
   a. $A \cdot \bar{A} = 0$?
   b. $A + \bar{A} = 0$?
   c. $U \cdot A = A$?
   d. $\bar{\bar{\bar{A}}} = A$?
   e. $\overline{A + O} = 0$?
   f. $\overline{A + \bar{A}} = 0$?
   g. $A + B = B + A + 0$?
   h. $A \cdot (B + C) = (A \cdot B) + C$?
   i. $(\bar{A} \cdot \bar{B}) + (A \cdot B) = (\bar{A} \cdot B) + (A \cdot \bar{B})$?
   j. $(\bar{A} + \bar{B}) \cdot (A + B) = (\bar{A} \cdot B) + (A \cdot \bar{B})$?
   k. $\bar{A} \cdot (B + (C \cdot A)) = \bar{A} \cdot B$?
3. Write the truth table for a 9's complementer in the Excess-6 code.
4. Form the logical equations representing the truth table developed in problem 3.
5. Draw a logical block diagram representing the logical equations developed in problem 4.
6. If $A = 1$, $B = 0$, and $C' = 1$, what is the value at the output of each of the logical blocks shown in the binary adder in Fig. 25?
7. If 2 positive pulses representing ONES are simultaneously fed to an AND circuit and one pulse has a duration of 1 μs and the other a duration of 1.5 μs, what is the duration of the output positive pulse? (Assume the beginning of both pulses occur at the same time.)

8. If a positive 2 μs pulse appears at the input of an inverting amplifier, what appears at the output?

9. Convert the following AND function to equivalent OR functions:

   a. $\overline{(A \cdot \bar{B} \cdot C \cdot \bar{D})}$
   b. $(\bar{A} \cdot B \cdot C)$

10. Convert the following OR functions to AND functions:

   a. $A+B+C+D$
   b. $\overline{(\bar{A}+B)}$

11. Simplify the following:

   a. $(A \cdot \bar{B})+(\bar{A} \cdot B)$
   b. $(A+B) \cdot (\bar{A}+\bar{B})$
   c. $(A \cdot B)+(A \cdot \bar{C})$

12. Simplify by means of a Veitch diagram:

   a. $Y=\bar{A} \cdot \bar{B} \cdot \bar{C} \cdot \bar{D}+\bar{A} \cdot \bar{B} \cdot C \cdot \bar{D}+\bar{A} \cdot \bar{B} \cdot C \cdot D+\bar{A} \cdot B \cdot \bar{C} \cdot \bar{D}+\bar{A} \cdot B \cdot \bar{C} \cdot D$
   $+\bar{A} \cdot B \cdot C \cdot \bar{D}+A \cdot \bar{B} \cdot \bar{C} \cdot \bar{D}+A \cdot \bar{B} \cdot C \cdot \bar{D}+A \cdot \bar{B} \cdot C \cdot D$
   b. $Y=\bar{A} \cdot \bar{B} \cdot C \cdot D+\bar{A} \cdot B \cdot \bar{C} \cdot \bar{D}+\bar{A} \cdot B \cdot C \cdot D$
   c. $Y=A \cdot B \cdot \bar{C}+\bar{A} \cdot B \cdot C \cdot +A \cdot \bar{B} \cdot \bar{C}+\bar{A} \cdot \bar{B} \cdot C$

13. Negate the following expressions:

   a. $\bar{A} \cdot \bar{B}$
   b. $(A+B) \cdot (C+\bar{D})$
   c. $(A \cdot B)+\bar{C}$
   d. $((A+\bar{B}) \cdot C) \cdot (\bar{D} \cdot E)$

section II

BUILDING BLOCKS

A digital computer may be considered to be composed of a specified combination of building blocks. This section develops the building block structure on two levels. On the first level are the hardware realizations of the basic logical, amplification, and storage functions—logical building blocks. On the second level are the logical building blocks combined into larger entities—functional building blocks.

In Chapter 5, logical building-block systems are described: the first section presents the major types in terms of easily understood mechanical and relay circuits; the remaining sections present diode, transistor, and electromagnetic techniques of implementation. Chapters 6 to 8 describe major functional building blocks in terms of logical block diagrams. Chapter 9 describes bulk techniques for the fabrication of functional building blocks.

CHAPTER 5

Logical building blocks

Logical building blocks may be described in two ways: (1) by block diagram and (2) by circuit diagram. The first presents the logic and the second the method of implementation. Although our main concern is with logic, it is difficult to comprehend what a logical component does without understanding the implementation. For this reason, we use mechanical and relay circuits as a means for describing the basic logical building blocks. This discussion comprises the first section of this chapter.

In the remaining sections we concentrate on circuits and methods of implementation.

TYPES OF LOGICAL BUILDING BLOCKS

Three major types of logical functions are executed by logical building blocks. They are switching, amplification, and storage. In some types of logical building blocks, each of these functions is executed by a different block. In others, the same block may be used for a combination of two or more of the above functions.

Switching Circuits

The fundamental elements of logical algebra may be expressed practically by means of switches (see Fig. 29). If the switches are wired in series, then all switches—*A and B and C*—must be turned on to light the lamp. This is an AND circuit. If the switches are wired in parallel, then the turning on of either switch *A or B or C or* any combination of switches causes the lamp to light. This is an OR circuit. If a normally closed switch keeps the lamp lit except when the switch is depressed, then the circuit is a NOT circuit.

In this arrangement, depressing the switch represents the input signal, and a voltage or current flow lighting the lamp represents the output signal of the switching circuit. It would be much more satisfactory from the point

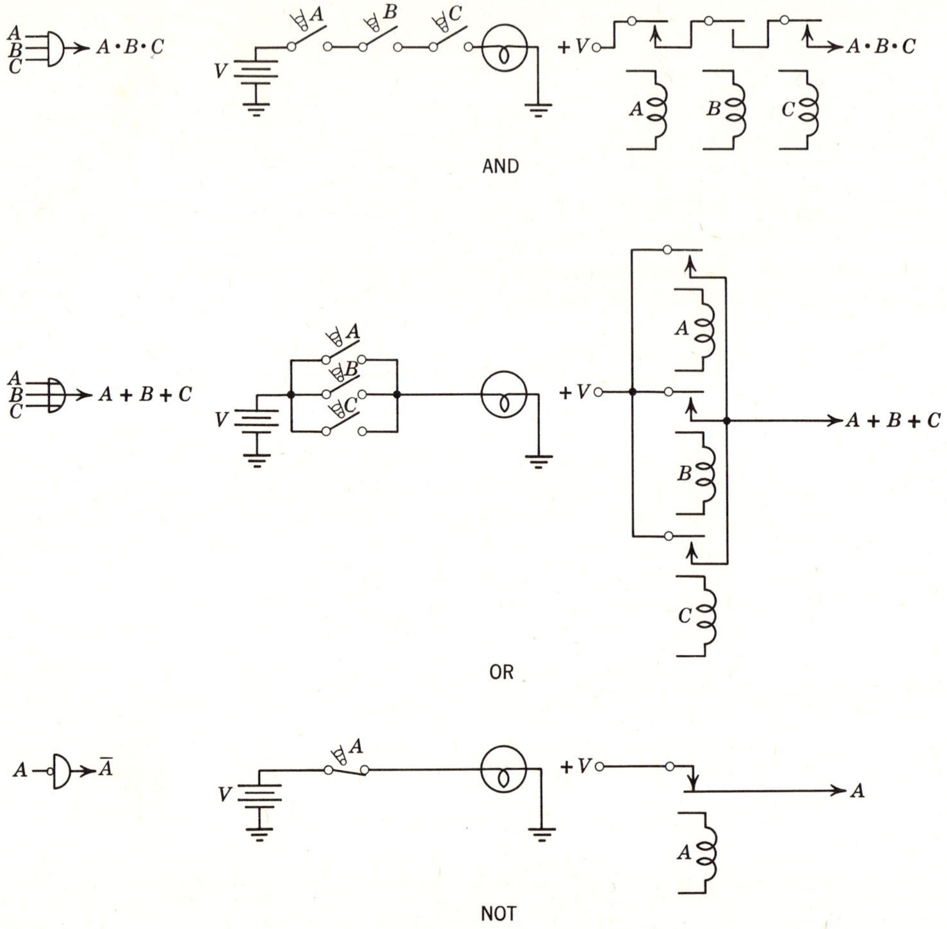

Figure 29 Switching circuits.

of view of mechanization to have the input and output signals alike. This is easily accomplished by substituting relays for switches, as shown in Fig. 29. Here voltage (or current) signals activate the relay coils, and voltage (or current) signals are produced at the output lines. The output of each relay switching circuit, may therefore be fed to another switching circuit.

Example

Draw a logical block diagram and the equivalent relay circuit to represent the following expression:

$$A \cdot B \cdot C + D \cdot E \cdot F$$

See Fig. 30 for the solution.

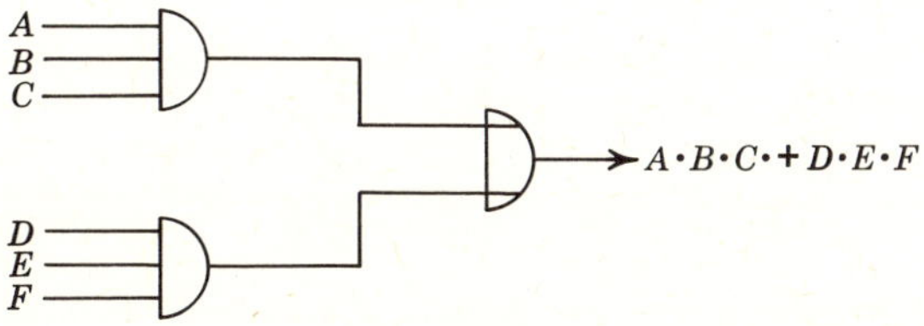

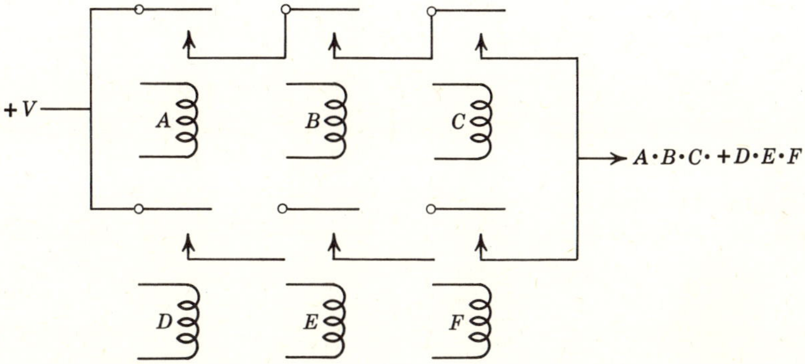

Figure 30 Graphical representation for $A \cdot B \cdot C + D \cdot E \cdot F$. (*a*) Logical block diagram. (*b*) Relay schematic.

Example

Draw a logical block diagram and the equivalent relay circuit to represent the following expression:

$$\bar{A} \cdot B \cdot \bar{C} + \bar{B} \cdot C$$

See Fig. 31 for the solution.

Simple ANDS and ORS also are provided by diode circuits as is explained in the succeeding parts of this chapter.

Amplifiers

A relay can act as an amplifier because a small current applied to the relay coil can cause a much larger current to flow through the relay contacts (see Fig. 32*a*).

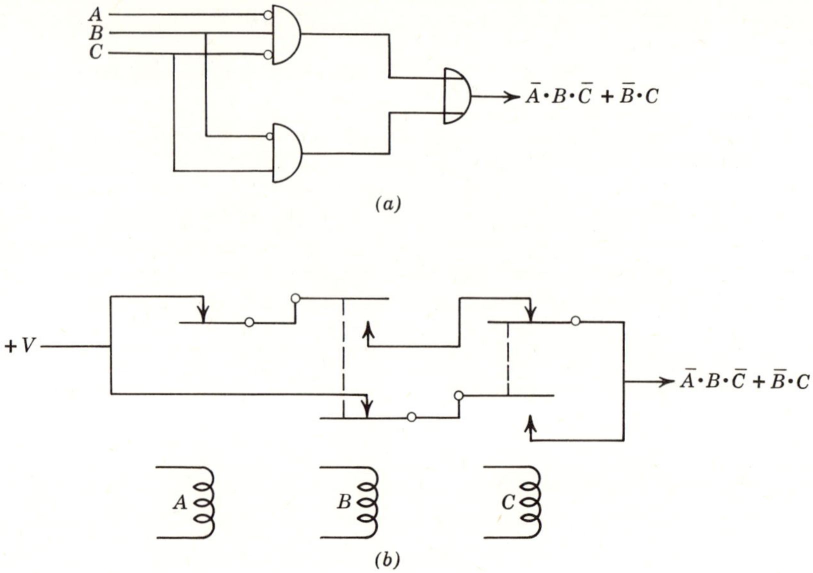

Figure 31 Graphical representation for $\bar{A}\cdot B\cdot\bar{C}+\bar{B}\cdot C$. (*a*) Logical block diagram. (*b*) Relay schematic.

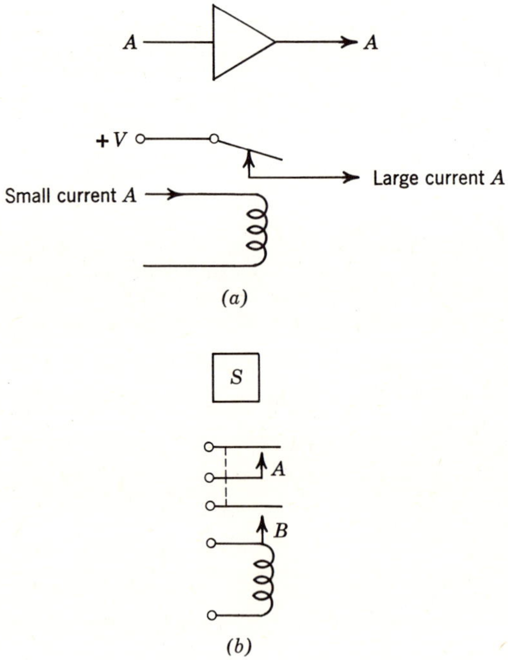

Figure 32 Amplifier and storage circuits. (*a*) Amplifier. (*b*) Storage cell.

Storage Circuits

An ordinary relay cannot be used for storage because the removal of current from the coil causes the associated contacts to open. A relay with holding contacts, however, may be used as a storage cell. An example of such a relay is shown in Fig. 32*b*. Contacts *A* are the normal contacts. Contacts *B* are the holding contacts. Once the coil is energized, current is applied to the coil through the *B* contacts to keep the coil energized even if the initial pulse is removed from the coil. A switch in series with the *B* contacts may be used to deenergize the relay coil. A pulse of current applied to the coil closes contacts *A* to store a ONE. If no pulse of current is applied to the coil contacts *A* remain open to store a ZERO.

Another form of storage circuit is the delay element. This is accomplished electronically by a one-shot multivibrator. This circuit is discussed in detail in the part on transistors.

Switching and Amplification

Diode circuits, unlike relays, may produce ANDS and ORS, but not NOTS. The NOT in this case may be produced by a transistor amplifier that inverts the signal at the same time that it amplifies it. The sequence of building blocks is

AND — OR — AND — ··· — NOT

Transistors may be combined into circuits that execute AND and OR functions at the same time that they act as inverting amplifiers. The net result is a sequence of building blocks such as

NAND — NOR — NAND —

Because transistors can be used for switching and amplification, they may be connected together into flip-flop circuits of all kinds which are used for storage.

Electromagnetic components also execute switching and amplification functions at the same time. It so happens, however, that the sequence of building blocks in a network in this case is

OR — INHIBIT — OR —

Example

Express $A+\bar{B}$

a. By means of NAND circuits.

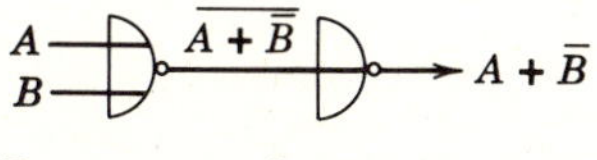

b. By means of NOR circuits.

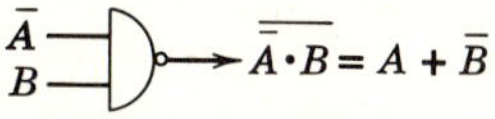

c. By means of INHIBIT circuits.

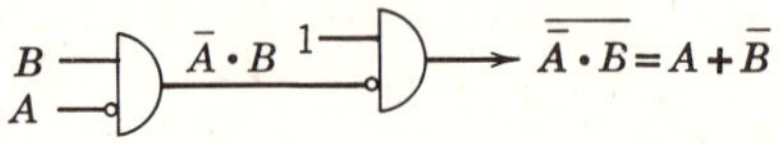

The succeeding paragraphs explain in detail how diode, transistor, and electromagnetic circuits operate.

* * * * * *

SEMICONDUCTOR DIODES

Basic Semiconductor Physics

From the standpoint of conductivity, there are three types of elements: conductors, nonconductors, and semiconductors. A conductor has free electrons which may be made to flow from point to point by the application of electric charge. A nonconductor has its electrons tightly bound, making electron flow very difficult. A semiconductor is not normally a conductor but may be made conductive under certain circumstances.

A typical semiconductor is silicon. As shown in Fig. 33, an atom of silicon consists of a nucleus with a +14 charge surrounded by 14 negatively charged electrons in three orbits. The electrons in the two inner orbits are tightly bound to the nucleus. The four electrons in the outer orbit are loosely bound. This picture therefore may be replaced by the equivalent simpler picture shown: a +4 core (representing the nucleus plus the tightly bound electrons) and four minus electrons.

In a crystal of silicon the atoms arrange themselves neatly in the structure shown in Fig. 33. Loose electrons from adjacent atoms pair off to form what are known as covalent bonds. Since practically all outer orbit electrons are paired off, there is a negligible number of free electrons available for conduction.

If a small impurity is embedded in the silicon, either an *n*-type or a *p*-type crystal may be formed. The *n*-type crystal allows the conduction of negative charges; the *p*-type crystal allows the conduction of positive charges.

The *n*-type crystal may be formed by adding a tiny amount of an element such as phosphorus which has five electrons in its outer orbit (Fig. 33). Four of the outer electrons in each atom of phosphorus form covalent bonds with electrons from atoms of silicon, thus leaving one electron free to wander about the crystal lattice. These negative free electrons can be made to flow through the crystal by application of a potential across the crystal. Because the phosphorus atoms donate electrons, they are called donors. Donor impurities introduce negative free electrons to produce *n*-type silicon; by donating negative electrons, the donor becomes positively charged.

The *p*-type crystals may be formed by introducing into the silicon tiny impurities of an element such as boron which has three electrons in its outer orbit (Fig. 33). The three outer electrons in each atom of boron form covalent bonds with three electrons from atoms of silicon. There remains one electron in a nearby atom of silicon that has no electron in the boron atom with which to pair off. We say the boron atom has a hole with a positive charge. If a potential is applied across the crystal, a negative electron is attracted to this positive hole. This electron leaves a hole in the atom from which it is taken. Then another electron fills the last hole formed, and so on. Even though electrons are actually moving, it is easier to explain semiconductor phenomena by saying that there is a flow of positive holes. Because the boron atoms accept electrons, they are called acceptors. Acceptor impurities introduce positive holes to produce *p*-type silicon. The acceptors by accepting electrons become negatively charged.

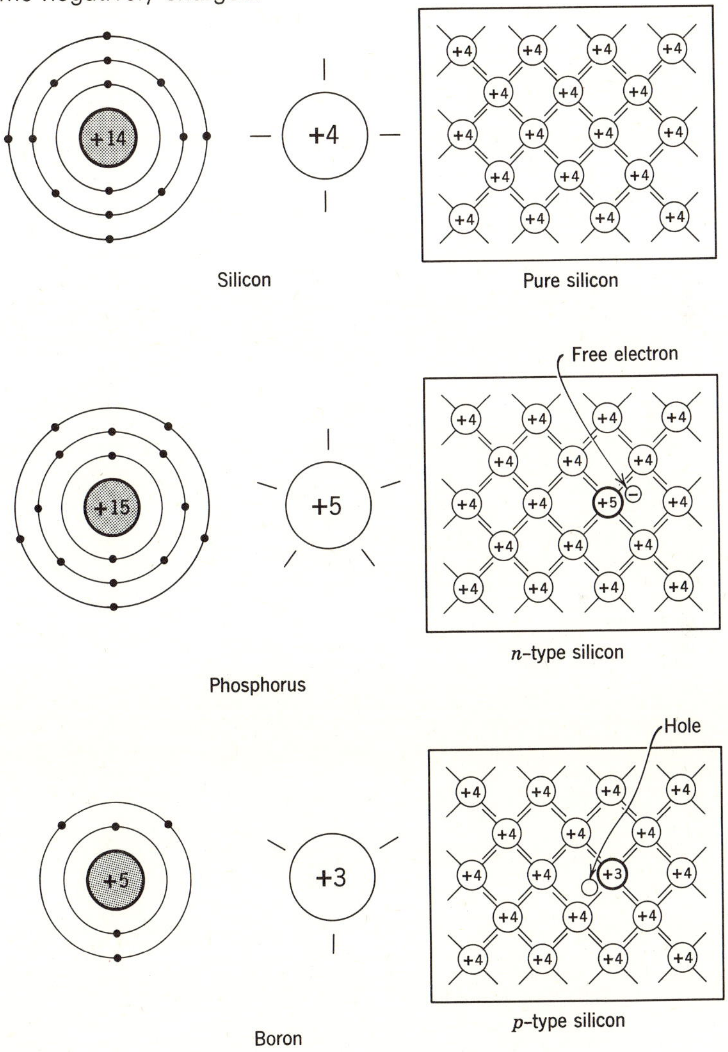

Figure 33 Pure, *n*-type, and *p*-type silicon.

Silicon Diodes

Silicon diodes are formed by alloying *n*- and *p*-type crystals to form an *n–p* junction, as shown in Fig. 34. At the junction, there is a crossover from the *n* side of free electrons which are attracted to the *p* side; as a result of this crossover, ionized positive charges are produced on the *n* side of the junction. Similarly, holes from the *p* side are attracted to the *n* side, leaving ionized negative charges on the *p* side of the junction. This diffusion process, as it is called, continues until a potential hill is set up that prevents further flow of electrons across the junction (Fig. 34*a*). Similarly, a potential hill to hole flow is also set up.

The junction is reverse biased if a battery is applied across the junction with the minus terminal connected to the *p*-crystal and the plus terminal to the *n*-crystal, as shown in Fig. 34*b*. Holes in the *p*-crystal are attracted to the

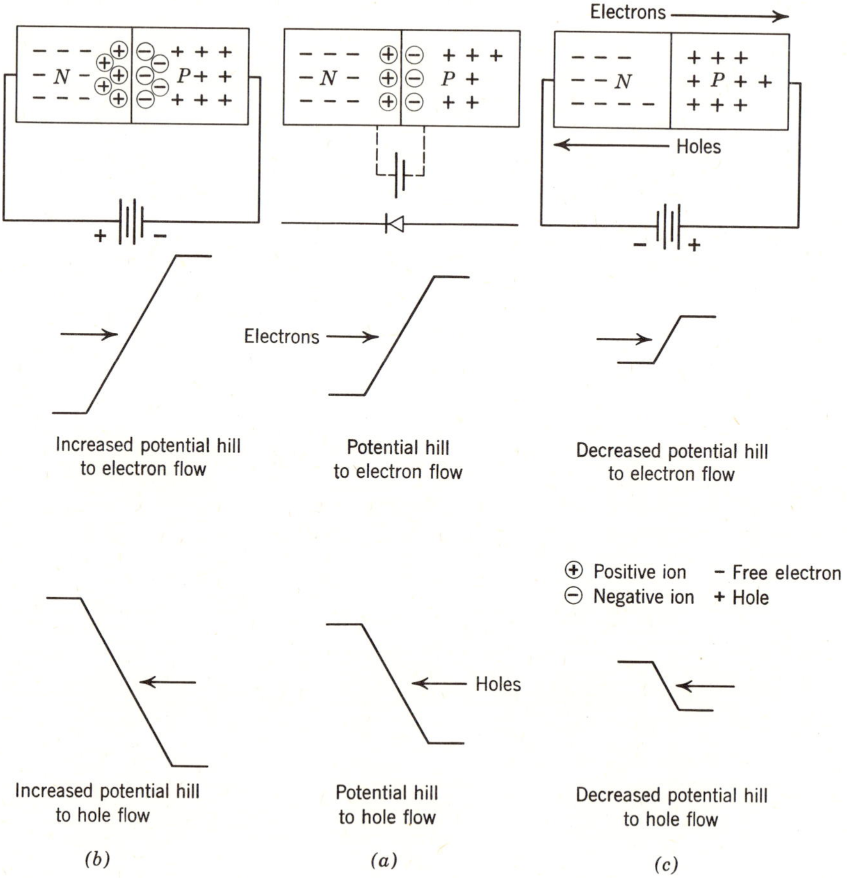

Figure 34 Diode. (*a*) No bias. (*b*) Reverse bias. (*c*) Forward bias.

minus terminal, leaving behind more negative ions. Similarly, free electrons in the *n*-crystal are attracted to the plus terminal, leaving behind more positive ions. As a result, the potential hill increases, and no electron or hole flow can occur across the junction.

On the other hand, the junction is forward biased if a battery is applied across the junction with the plus terminal connected to the *p*-crystal and the minus terminal to the *n*-crystal, as shown in Fig. 34*c*. Holes in the *p*-region are repelled by the positive terminal toward the junction where they decrease the number of negative ions. Similarly the free electrons in the *n*-region are repelled by the negative terminal toward the junction where they decrease the number of positive ions. The result is a reduction of the potential hill.

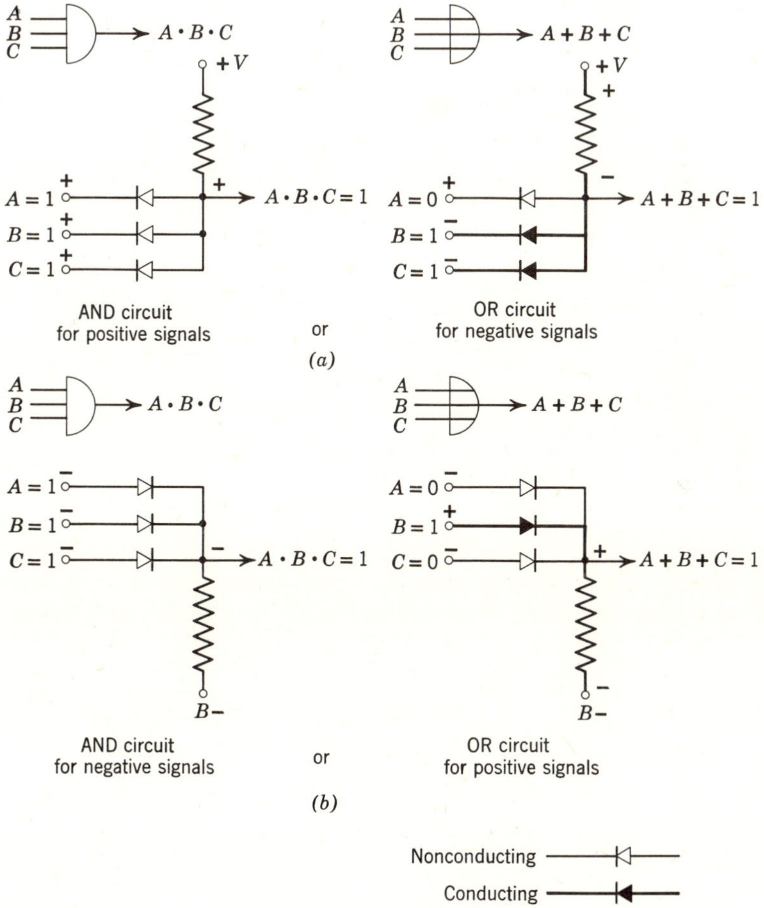

Figure 35 Diode switching circuits.

Electrons flow through the *p*-region, and holes flow through the *n*-region. This is current flow.

The *n–p* junction is therefore a diode. It conducts when the *p* is made positive relative to *n*, and it does not conduct when the *p* is made negative relative to *n*.

Diode Switching Circuits

A simple diode switching circuit which may be an AND or an OR is shown in Fig. 35*a*. The *p*-crystals of the three diodes are connected through a load resistor to a positive supply voltage, and the *n*-crystals are connected to either positive or negative potentials. If one of the *n*-crystals is negative, electrons flow through the diode and the load resistor; the voltage drop across the load resistor makes the output voltage negative. If all *n*-crystals are positive, none of the diodes conduct and no electrons flow through the load resistor; the output voltage is positive. If a positive potential is considered to be ONE and a negative potential ZERO, this is an AND circuit. If a negative potential is considered to be ONE and a positive potential ZERO, this same circuit is an OR circuit.

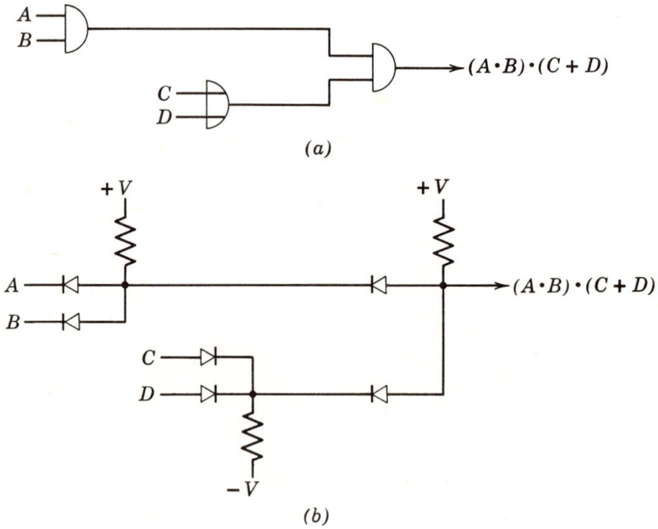

Figure 36 Graphical representation for $(A \cdot B) \cdot (C + D)$. (*a*) Logical block diagram. (*b*) Diode schematic.

Figure 35*b* shows an OR circuit for positive signals or an AND circuit for negative signals. When any input is positive, the associated diode conducts and the resultant voltage across the load resistor is positive. If all *p*-crystals are negative, none of the diodes conduct and the output is negative.

In almost all cases AND circuits for positive signals are equivalent to OR circuits for negative signals, and OR circuits for positive signals are equivalent to AND circuits for negative signals. For simplicity, all switching circuits are discussed under the assumption that positive signals are applied, unless otherwise stated.

Example

Draw a logical block diagram and the equivalent diode circuit to represent the following expression:

$$(A \cdot B) \cdot (C + D)$$

See Fig. 36 for the solution.

TRANSISTORS

N–P–N and *P–N–P* Junction Transistors

By forming two *p–n* junctions, as shown in Fig. 37*a*, an *n–p–n* junction transistor is produced. The *n*-crystal at the left is the emitter; the thin *p*-crystal in the middle is the base; the *n*-crystal at the right is the collector. The symbol for the *n–p–n* junction transistor is shown in Fig. 37*a*.

Figure 37*a* shows the potential hill across each of the two junctions of the *n–p–n* transistor when no potentials are applied to it. Under these conditions no electrons or holes may cross either junction.

If the emitter-base junction is reverse biased by making the base (*p*) negative with reference to the emitter (*n*) the potential hill at this junction is increased and no current may flow. If the collector-base junction is reverse biased by making the base (*p*) negative with reference to the collector (*n*), no current may flow across this junction. Under these conditions (Fig. 37*b*), the transistor is cut off.

If the emitter-base junction is forward biased and the collector-base junction remains reverse biased (Fig. 37*c*), the emitter-base junction potential hill is decreased. As a result, free electrons from the emitter are injected into the base. The extreme thinness of the base does not allow the electrons much time to combine with holes in the base. From the base, the electrons "slide down the potential hill" to the collector. Current flows. Notice that electrons flow opposite to the direction of the arrow on the emitter of the transistor symbol; in other words, the arrow indicates the direction of positive current flow.

Figure 38 shows the *p–n–p* junction transistor, its symbol, and the potential hills associated with the same combinations of bias as for the *n–p–n* previously discussed. Observe that all the battery potentials are opposite to the ones for *n–p–n* transistors in analogous circumstances. The potential hills,

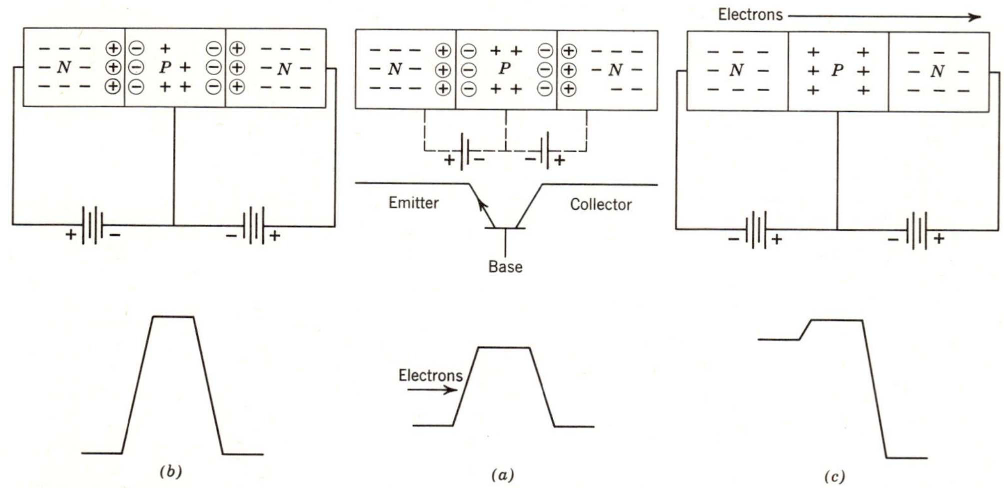

Figure 37 *N-P-N* transistor. (*a*) No bias. (*b*) Emitter-base reverse bias collector-base reverse bias. (*c*) Emitter-base forward bias collector-base reverse bias.

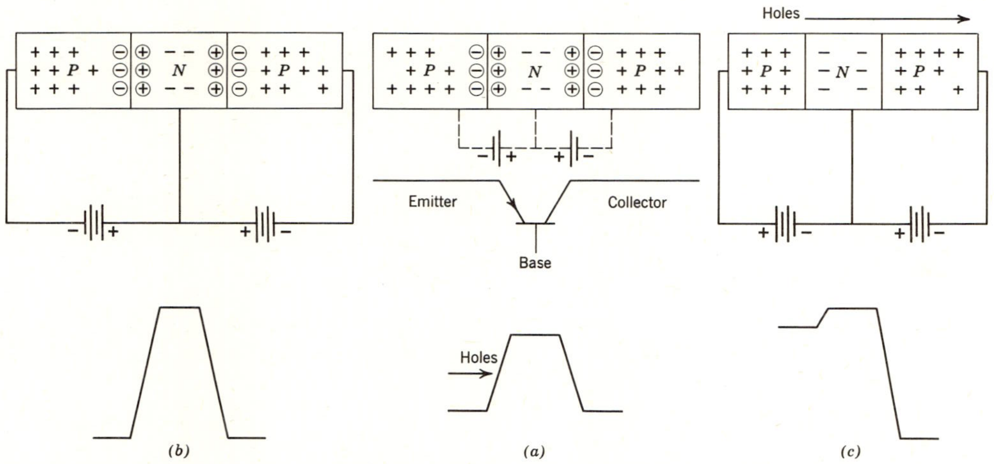

Figure 38 *P-N-P* transistor. (*a*) No bias. (*b*) Emitter-base reverse bias collector-base reverse bias. (*c*) Emitter-base forward bias collector-base reverse bias.

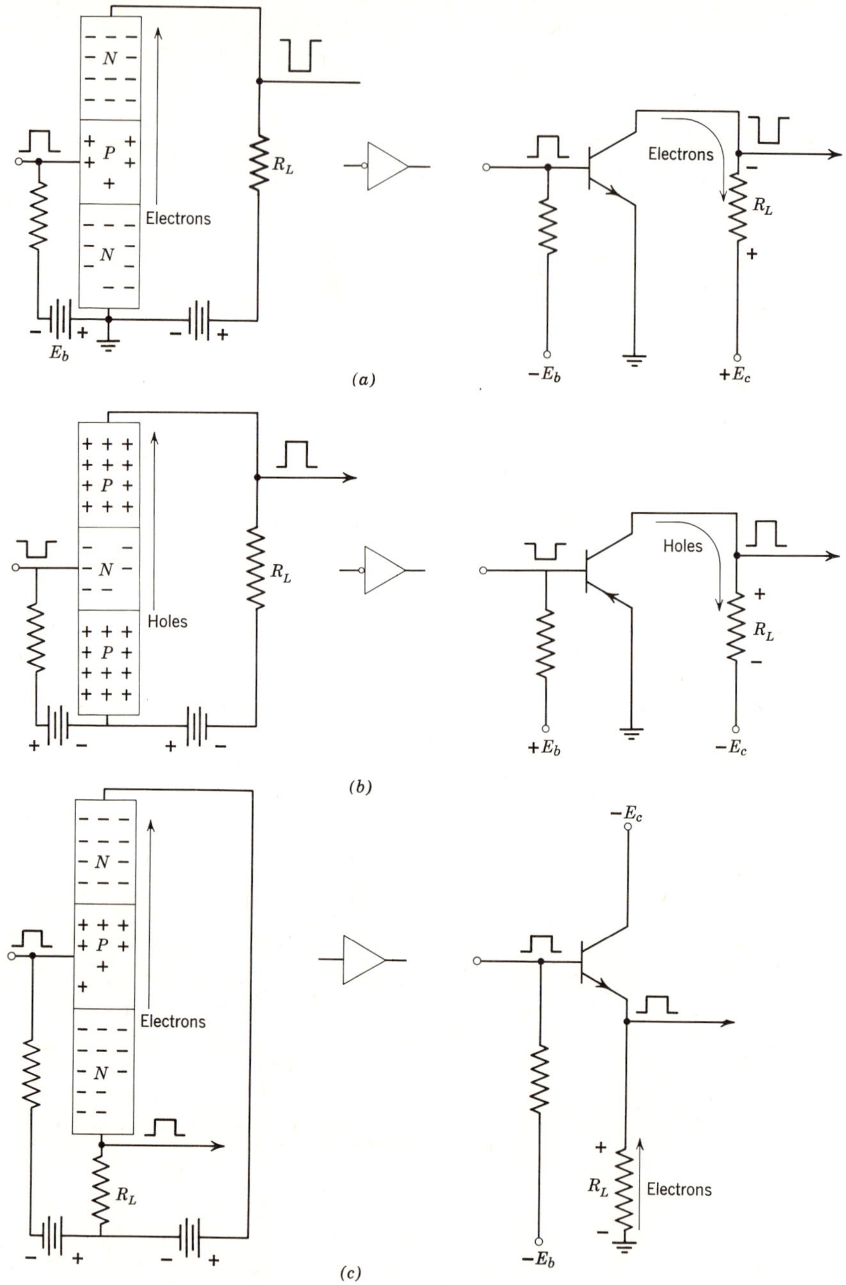

Figure 39 Transistor amplifiers. (*a*) *N-P-N* grounded emitter amplifier. (*b*) *P-N-P* grounded emitter amplifier. (*c*) *N-P-N* emitter follower.

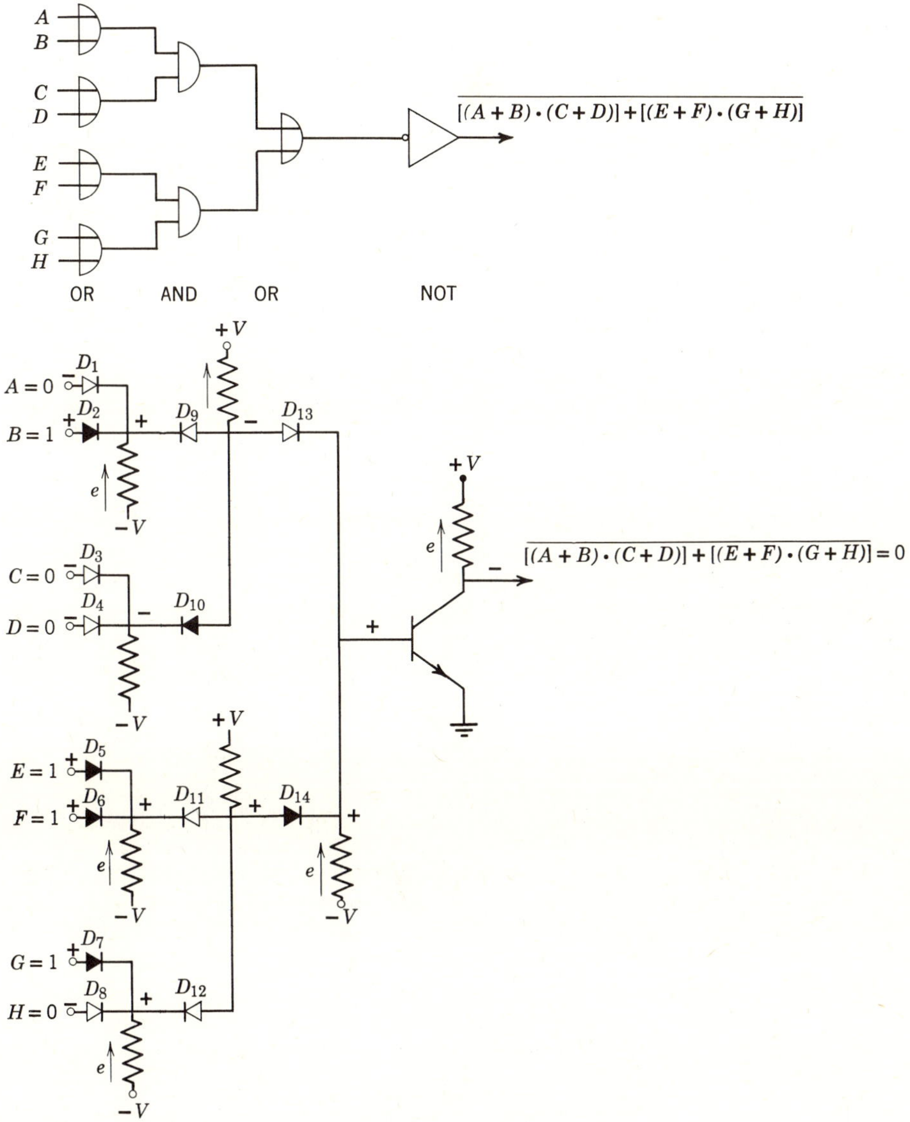

Figure 40 Diode-transistor logic.

in this case, are given with reference to hole flow. With the two junctions reverse biased, no holes may flow from the emitter. With the emitter-base junction forward biased and the collector-base junction reverse biased, the emitter-base potential hill is decreased allowing holes to be injected into the base. The holes then "slide down the potential hill" to the collector. Current flows. In this case the arrow of the emitter in the transistor symbol points in the same direction as hole flow.

Transistor Amplifiers

By connecting a transistor circuit like the one shown in Fig. 39*a*, amplification may be obtained. The emitter-base junction is reverse biased by E_b, and the collector-base junction is reverse biased by E_c. With no signal applied between the base and the emitter, this *n–p–n* transistor is cut off. When a positive signal is applied, the cut off bias is overcome and electrons flow as shown. Although the input signal may be small, the output signal developed across the load resistor R_L may be large: amplification occurs. Notice that with electrons flowing in the direction shown, the output polarity is opposite to the input polarity. This circuit, therefore, is an inverting amplifier.

Fig. 39*b* shows a similar circuit using a *p–n–p* transistor. Its operation is analogous to that of the *n–p–n* circuit, except that all polarities are in the opposite direction and current is achieved by hole flow instead of electron flow. This circuit, too, is an inverting amplifier.

An *n–p–n* emitter-follower circuit that amplifies without inversion is shown in Fig. 39*c*. The biasing arrangement is similar to the one used for the *n–p–n* grounded emitter amplifier. However, the load resistor R_L is connected between emitter and ground. As is shown in the illustration, electrons flowing through R_L produce an output that is of the same polarity as the input. The emitter-follower produces current amplification but not voltage amplification.

The diode logic previously described does not provide a complete system, since diodes do not amplify. By combining diode logic with a transistor inverting amplifier, as shown in Fig. 40, a practical system of logic may be obtained. The illustration shows a level of OR circuits (diodes D_1 to D_8), followed by a level of AND circuits (D_9 to D_{12}), followed by an OR circuit (D_{13}, D_{14}), followed by an amplifier that produces a NOT. The output of the entire network is, therefore, the complement of what is produced by the diode network itself.

Example

Draw a logical block diagram and the equivalent diode-transistor circuit to represent the following expression:

$$((\overline{A+B})+(\overline{C+D}))\cdot(\overline{E\cdot F})$$

To convert this to a group of terms under a complement bar, negate the two outside parenthetical expressions and change the dot between them to a plus:

$$((A+B)+(C+D))+(E \cdot F)$$

Simplification of the left larger parenthetical term produces

$$((A+B) \cdot (C+D))+(E \cdot F)$$

Figure 41 presents the logical and schematic representations for this expression.

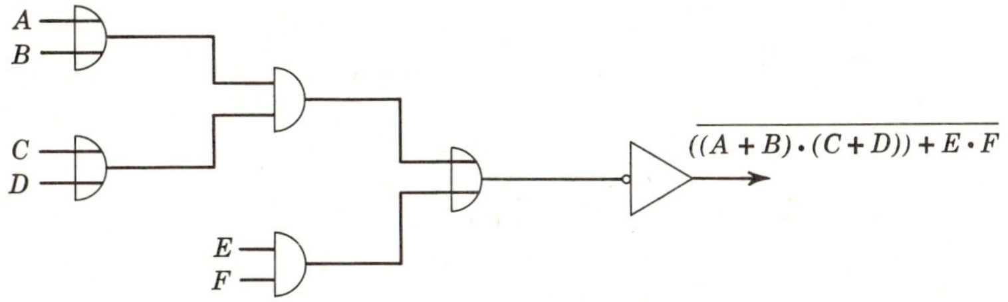

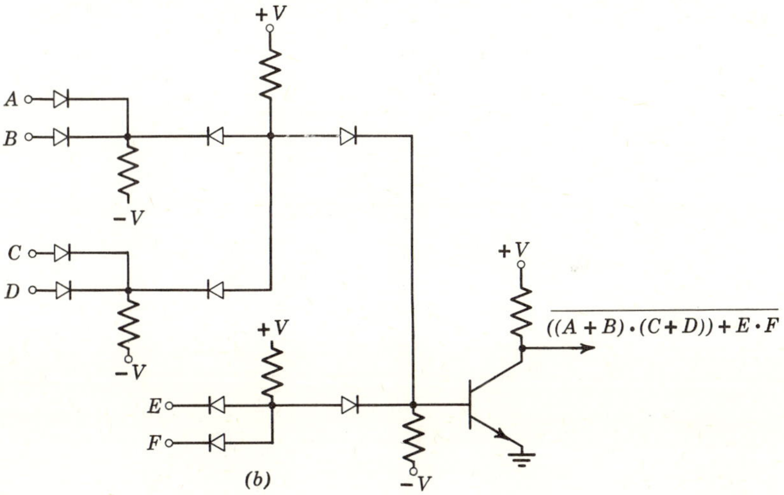

Figure 41 Graphical representation for $((A+B) \cdot (C+D))+E \cdot F$. (*a*) Logical block diagram. (*b*) Diode-transistor schematic.

Transistor Switching Circuits

Switching circuits may be produced by coupling transistors directly in series or in parallel. When *n–p–n* transistors are connected in series, as shown in Fig. 42*a*, the circuit is a NAND. Only when a positive signal is applied to both bases does electron current flow to produce a negative output across the load resistor. In this illustration, only $A=1$ and therefore no current flows, thus keeping the output positive — or $\overline{A \cdot B}=1$.

When n–p–n transistors are connected in parallel, the circuit is a NOR (Fig. 42*b*). If the base of either transistor is made positive, the transistor conducts, and the current flowing through the load resistor produces a negative output. This is the situation in the illustration, which produces an output of $\overline{A+B}=0$.

If serial and parallel circuits are made to share one load resistor, the output of the circuit is similar to that obtained with diode-transistor logic.

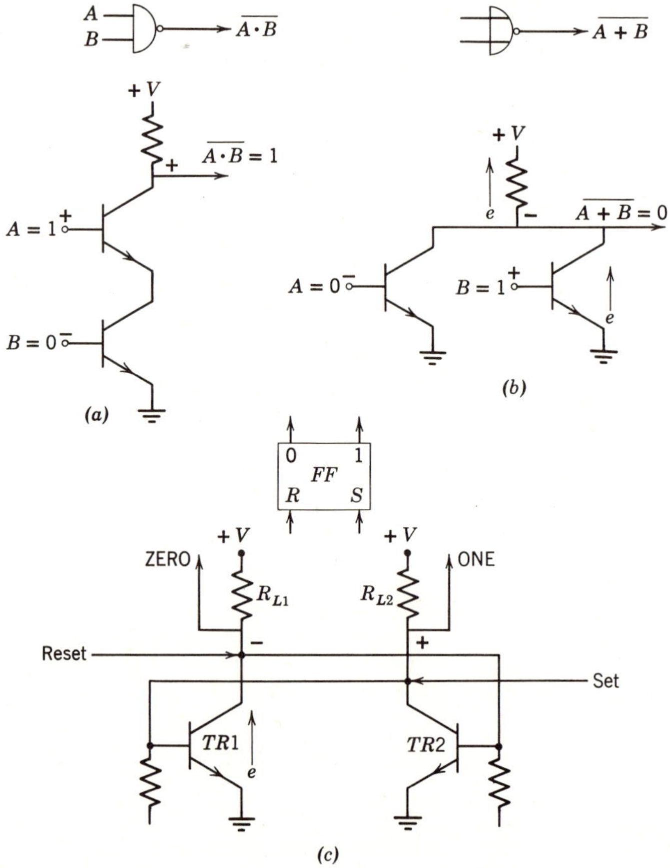

Figure 42 Directly coupled transistor logic. (*a*) NAND. (*b*) NOR. (*c*) Flip-flop (in set state).

Example

Draw a logical block diagram and the equivalent n–p–n directly coupled transistor circuit to represent the following expression:

$$((A+B)\cdot C+D)\cdot E+F$$

The solution is given in Fig. 43. If polarity inversions are disregarded, the parallel combination of *TR*1–*TR*2 produces $A+B$. By placing these transistors in series with *TR*3, the expression $(A+B)\cdot C$ is produced. Paralleling this with *TR*4 produces $(A+B)\cdot C+D$. Placing *TR*5 in series with this combination produces $((A+B)\cdot C+D)\cdot E$. Connecting *TR*6 in parallel with all this produces $(A+B)\cdot C+D)\cdot E+F$. This last expression shows how the currents in the various transistors combine. However, the load resistor produces the negative of this, or $((A+B)\cdot C+D)\cdot E+F$. Therefore, another inverting amplifier *TR*7 must be added to produce the result required.

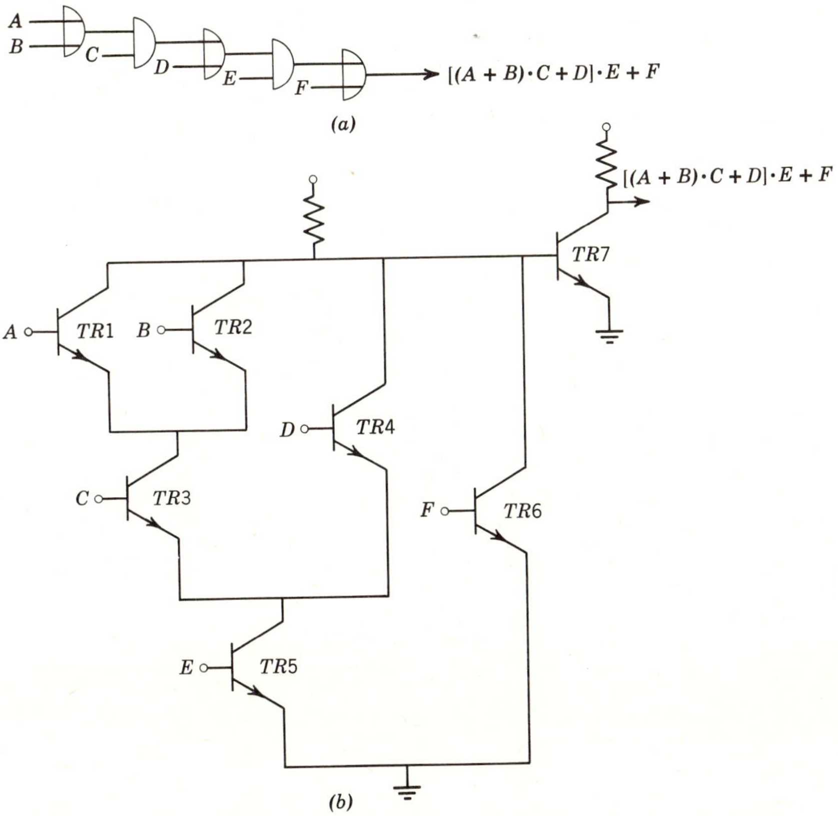

Figure 43 Graphical representation for $((A+B)\cdot C+D)\cdot E+F$. (*a*) Logical block diagram. (*b*) *n-p-n* transistor schematic.

Transistor Flip-Flop

A simple *n–p–n* transistor flip-flop is drawn in Fig. 42*c*. One transistor or the other is conducting at any one time. If *TR*1 is conducting, the negative potential produced at the *TR*1 collector by R_{L1} is fed to the base of *TR*2 to keep $TR2$ cut off. The nonconducting $TR2$ keeps its collector and, therefore, the base of $TR1$ positive. As a result, $TR1$ is maintained at high conduction and $TR2$ at cutoff. This is the set or ONE state. To flip the flip-flop to the ZERO state, a positive pulse may be applied to the collector of $TR1$ and to the base of $TR2$ to cause $TR2$ to conduct; $TR2$ conducting, in turn, cuts off $TR1$. The flip-flop may be flipped back to the ONE state by a positive set pulse applied to the collector of $TR2$ and to the base of $TR1$.

One-Shot Multivibrator

The one-shot multivibrator is a circuit that on application of an input trigger pulse produces an output pulse of measured width. The trailing edge of the output pulse may be used to activate a second circuit.

An example of a transistor one-shot multivibrator is shown in Fig. 44. Notice that it is obtained by a slight modification to the flip-flop circuit. A greater than cut off bias voltage keeps $TR1$ cut off. The resultant positive potential on the collector of $TR1$ is applied to the base of $TR2$, causing it to conduct. This is the stable state of this circuit.

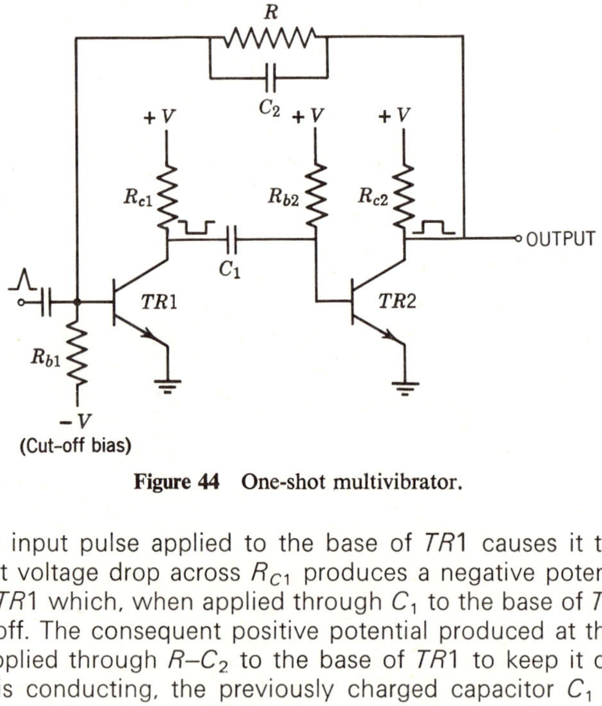

Figure 44 One-shot multivibrator.

A positive input pulse applied to the base of $TR1$ causes it to conduct. The resultant voltage drop across R_{C1} produces a negative potential on the collector of $TR1$ which, when applied through C_1 to the base of $TR2$, causes $TR2$ to cut off. The consequent positive potential produced at the collector of $TR2$ is applied through R–C_2 to the base of $TR1$ to keep it conducting. While $TR1$ is conducting, the previously charged capacitor C_1 discharges through $TR1$ and R_{b2}. As the discharge current decreases, the potential drop across R_{b2} decreases until the voltage at the base of $TR2$ rises above cut off. Once this happens, $TR2$ conducts and the resultant negative potential at the collector of $TR2$ is fed to the base of $TR1$ to keep $TR1$ cut off. The circuit is back to its stable state.

The amount of delay is determined by the length of time $TR2$ is kept non-conducting. This, in turn, is determined by the discharge time constant $C_1 R_{b2}$.

ELECTROMAGNETIC LOGICAL ELEMENTS

Electromagnetic Fundamentals

Logical circuits may be built of electromagnetic components as well as of transistor components. But there is one important difference between the two types of components: transistor components produce constant output signals; electromagnetic components cannot. Direct current flowing through a transistor produces a voltage drop across a load which can be detected by another circuit. Not so with magnetic energy flowing through a magnetic core. Only when magnetic energy is *changed*, is a voltage induced across a winding. This means that only dynamic techniques, pulse–no-pulse or

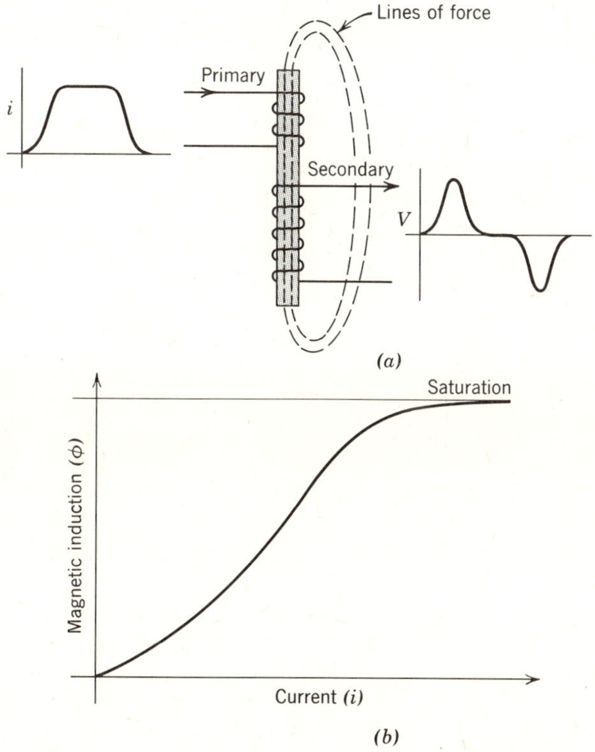

Figure 45 Transformer action. (*a*) Transformer. (*b*) Magnetic induction curve.

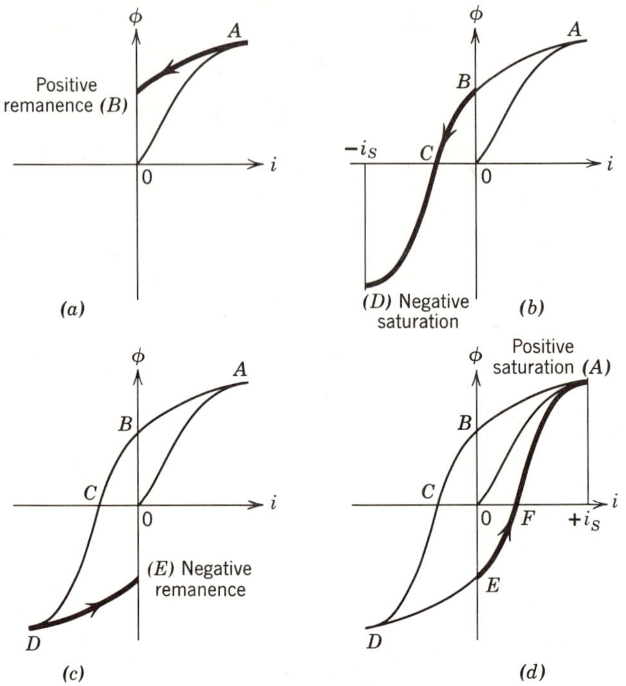

Figure 46 The hysteresis loop. (*a*) Positive current removed. (*b*) Negative current applied. (*c*) Negative current removed. (*d*) Positive current applied.

plus-pulse–minus-pulse combinations, may be used with electromagnetic components.

Two principles form the basis for almost everything that follows: transformer action and the hysteresis loop. The first shows the relationships among current, magnetic fields, and induced voltages. The second shows how magnetic energy is stored.

Figure 45*a* shows a transformer: an iron core around which are wound primary and secondary windings. If a pulse of current is applied to the primary, the magnetic field varies, thus inducing a voltage across the secondary. As the current increases, the lines of flux increase and a positive potential is produced across the secondary. During the flat portion of the applied current wave the current is not changing and neither is the magnetic flux. As a result, no voltage is induced across the secondary. When the current drops, the lines of flux collapse, and a negative potential is produced across the secondary.

This description of transformer action assumes that the magnetic core has a linear characteristic, that is, the magnetic induction of the core at all times varies with the applied magnetizing force which, in turn, varies with the applied current. But the magnetization curve is actually as shown in Fig. 45*b*.

The magnetic induction varies directly with the magnetizing force up to a point. After this point, any increase in applied magnetizing force has a very small effect on the magnetic induction. This point on the curve is called the point of magnetic saturation. At magnetic saturation very few lines are cut by the secondary and very little voltage is induced.

This nonlinear curve represents the behavior of a magnetic core when subjected to a magnetic field for the first time. After it has once become magnetized, changes in current flow through a winding cause the magnetic induction of the core to follow the hysteresis loop shown in Fig. 46. If after the core reaches magnetic saturation in the positive direction (point *A*, Fig. 46), the current through the winding is removed, then the magnetic induction does not drop to zero but to the positive remanence point (point *B*).

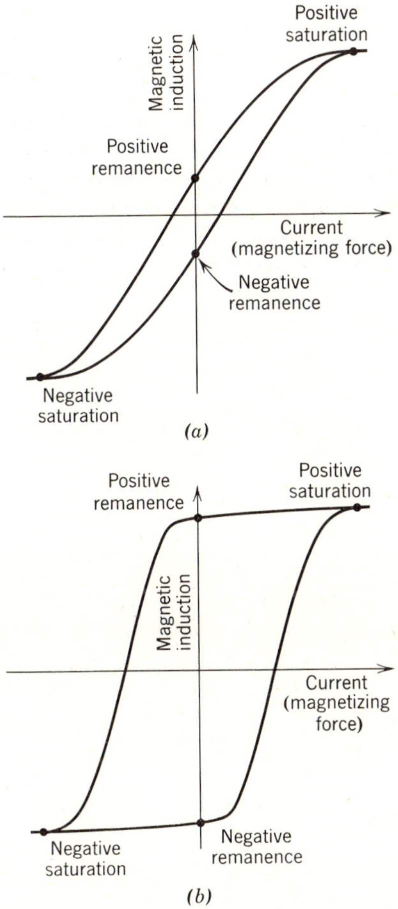

Figure 47 Difference between square-loop and nonsquare-loop cores. (*a*) Nonsquare-loop core. (*b*) Square-loop core.

If now current is allowed to flow through the winding in the opposite direction, the resultant magnetizing force makes the magnetic induction of the core follow loop *BCD* to the saturation point in the negative direction (point *D*). When the current is stopped, the magnetic induction falls to the negative remanence (point *E*). Reversing the current flow now causes the magnetic induction to vary along *EFA*. Thus, instead of following the same curve upward and downward, hysteresis makes the core follow one curve upward and another curve downward.

The shape of the hysteresis loop depends on the type of material used for a core. Iron cores such as those used for transformers have a nonsquare loop (Fig. 47*a*); ferrite and molypermalloy cores such as those used for many computer applications have a square loop (Fig. 47*b*). Note that the core with the nonsquare loop does not have a well-defined saturation line and the remanence points are fairly low.

Because it is needed for an understanding of practically all electromagnetic components, the hysteresis loop is explained by means of the domain theory. In brief, the domain theory states that a magnetic material is composed of many tiny magnets. With no magnetizing force applied, these tiny magnets are oriented in a random manner, causing no total field in any direction. With a magnetic force applied, the magnets are forced to line up. Once the magnets are fully aligned, further application of magnetic force has no effect on the magnetization of the core—saturation is reached.

The operation of a square-loop core is explained in Fig. 48. Assume the core is originally at negative remanence. At this point the tiny magnets are aligned, but not perfectly, with the south poles facing upward, let us say. If to the input winding is applied a pulse of current of such amplitude as to produce a magnetizing force smaller than the positive coercive force (point *F*), the magnets are rotated but not quite enough. When the pulse is removed, the magnets fall back to their original position. But if the pulse of current is of such magnitude as to produce a magnetizing force greater than the positive coercive force, then the magnets rotate past their horizontal orientations and fly toward positive saturation—with the north poles facing upward. This operation is analogous to that of a swinging door: if the door is pushed past the center point, it completes the swing even if the force is removed. The flipping pulse must be applied for a long enough time to supply the energy necessary to reorient each magnet. When the pulse is removed, the magnets become slightly disoriented—they fall to positive remanence. Flipping from the positive side to the negative side is similar except that it is accomplished with an opposite polarity pulse.

Cores for Storage

Magnetic cores used in computers are often doughnut-shaped. The advantage of the doughnut shape, or the toroid, is that very few lines of flux are lost; a complete circular path is provided for the lines of flux.

Doughnut-shaped magnetic cores with square hysteresis loops upon which are wound input and output windings make excellent storage cells. The positive remanence point may be called the ONE state and the negative remanence point the ZERO state. A ONE may be written into the core by applying a pulse of current in such a direction as to bring the core to positive saturation. When the pulse is removed, the core falls to positive remanence and remains there indefinitely. To write a ZERO into the core a pulse of current is applied to the input winding in the opposite direction, thus bringing the core to negative saturation. When the pulse is removed, the core falls to negative remanence and remains there indefinitely.

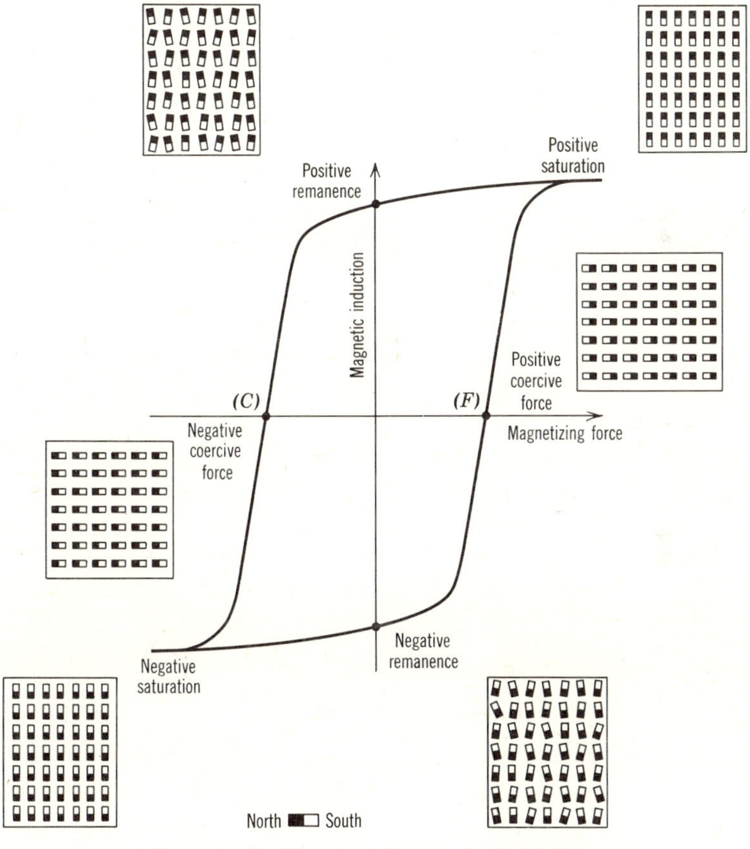

Figure 48 Explanation of square hysteresis loop.

To avoid ambiguity, a dot is placed near one end of the input winding to indicate whether a ONE or ZERO is written according to the following rule (see Fig. 49*a* and *b*).

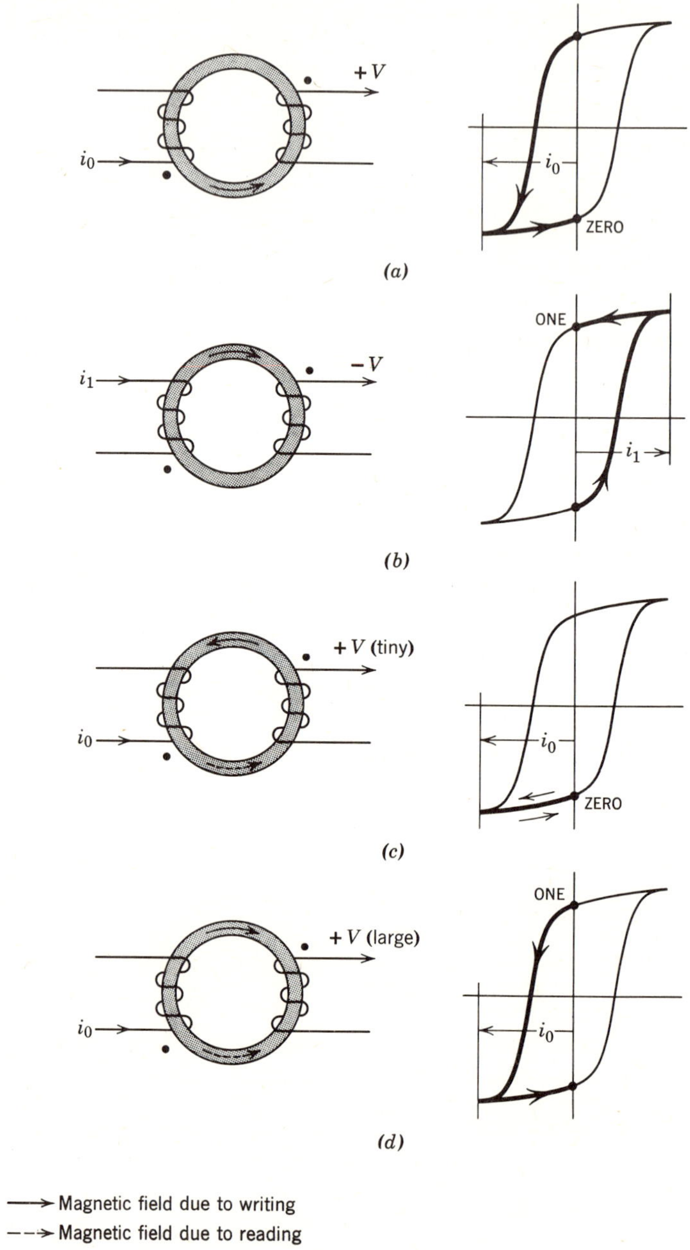

Figure 49 Doughnut-shaped magnetic core as storage element. (*a*) Writing ZERO. (*b*) Writing ONE. (*c*) Reading ZERO. (*d*) Reading ONE.

Current (i_0) fed to the dot side flips the core to the ZERO state; current (i_1) fed to the nondot side flips the core to the ONE state.

A dot is also placed near one end of the output winding to indicate whether a plus or minus output voltage is induced across it according to the following rule:

When flipping the core to the ZERO state the dot end of the output winding becomes positive; when flipping the core to the ONE state the nondot end of the output winding becomes positive.

Reading is accomplished as follows. A pulse which tends to flip the core to the ZERO state is applied to the input winding. If the core was storing a ZERO, the pulse causes the core to move along the negative saturation line. Since there is only a slight change in the lines of force, only a tiny voltage is induced across the secondary (Fig. 49*c*). If the core was storing a ONE, this pulse flips the core to the ZERO state. The change in lines of force induces a large voltage across the output winding (Fig. 49*d*). Therefore, no output voltage (or a tiny voltage) indicates the core was storing a ZERO, and an output voltage indicates the core was storing a ONE. Note that, after reading, the core is in the ZERO state in both cases.

Cores for Amplification

The doughnut-shaped square-loop core may also be used as an amplifier. A pulse applied to the input winding determines the state of the core. A pulse applied to the output winding causes current to flow in the load in accordance with what was stored in the core. The amount of energy flowing into the load is determined by the power applied by the pulse. This secondary pulse plays the same part in the magnetic amplifier that the collector voltage plays in the transistor amplifier.

OR and INHIBIT Circuits

The doughnut-shaped square-loop core with input and output windings may be used for switching if the two stable states of the core can be converted into discretely different signals across the output winding. This may be accomplished by adding a third winding to which a positive clock pulse is applied in order to switch the core to ZERO. If the core was storing ONE, the clock pulse causes it to reverse states and the changing field causes a positive pulse to be produced across the output winding. If the core was storing ZERO, the clock pulse does not reverse the state of the core and no voltage is induced across the output winding.

An OR circuit may be built of three cores connected as shown in Fig. 50*a*. A signal *A* is applied to the input winding of core 1, and signal *B* is applied to the input winding of core 2. The output winding of each of these cores is connected to one of the two input windings (*N*1 and *N*2) on core 3. The clock pulse *CP* is applied in series to one winding on each core.

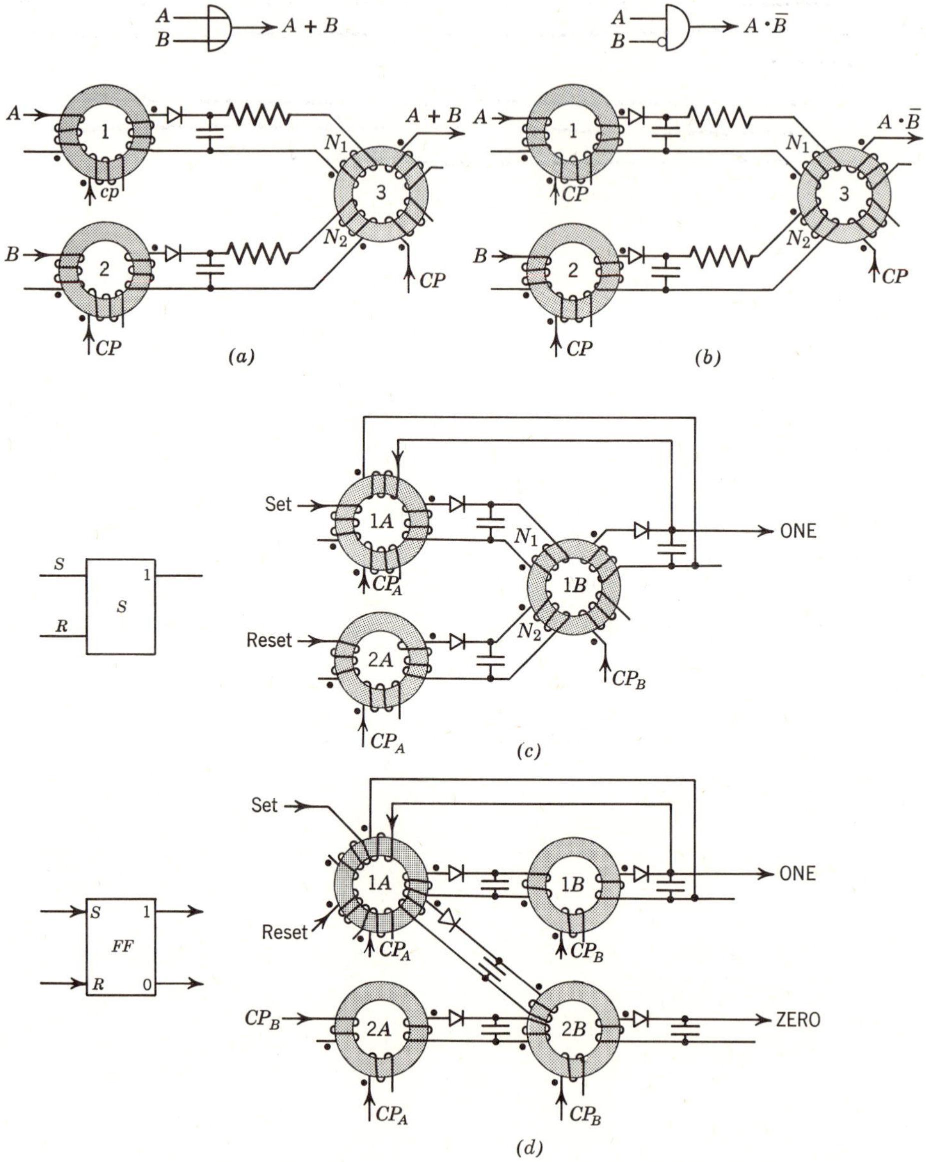

Figure 50 Magnetic-core logic. (*a*) OR. (*b*) INHIBIT. (*c*) Dynamic storage cell. (*d*) Dynamic flip-flop.

The circuit operates as follows. A pulse of current applied at A flips core 1 to the ONE state. The next CP flips core 1 back to the ZERO state, and induces a positive output voltage. This output voltage enters the nondot side of $N1$ to flip core 3 to the ONE state. The next CP flips core 3 to the ZERO state and produces an output voltage. If a current pulse is applied to B instead of to A, the first CP induces an output voltage which causes current to flow to the nondot side of $N2$ to flip core 3 to the ONE state; the following CP produces an output voltage as before. Since a pulse applied at either A or B (or both) produces a pulse at the output, this is an OR circuit.

To make sure that core 3 is completely flipped before the contents of core 1 are applied to core 3, a delay circuit is placed between cores, as shown in Fig. 50*a*. In this configuration when the CP is applied, if core 1 is storing ONE, it flips and an output pulse flows through the diode to charge the capacitor. After a delay determined by the charging of the capacitor, the capacitor discharges its current into the input winding of core 3.

The diode in the loop between cores prevents induced voltages from sending current backward from core 3 to core 1 or to core 2.

The INHIBIT function is produced by the circuit shown in Fig. 50*b*. On the surface, the OR and INHIBIT circuits look alike. But there is this important difference between them: in the OR circuit winding $N2$ is wound in the same relative direction as $N1$, whereas in the INHIBIT circuit $N2$ is wound in the opposite direction from $N1$. In the INHIBIT circuit a pulse at A sets 1 to the ONE state, and the following CP flips core 3 to the ONE state. The next CP flips core 3 to ZERO and produces an output pulse. If at the same time a pulse is applied at A a similar pulse is applied at B, core 2 is set to the ONE state. While the first CP is shifting the ONE from core 1 to $N1$, it is also shifting the ONE from core 2 to $N2$. Since $N1$ and $N2$ are wound in opposite directions, their magnetic fields cancel each other. The result is that core 3 does *not* flip to the ONE state and the following CP does *not* produce an output pulse. In other words, an output pulse is produced when A is present unless inhibited by a B pulse. The circuit produces $A \cdot \bar{B}$.

A very important fact to remember about these switching circuits is that the output occurs later in time than the inputs. In other words, there is a delay inherent to the magnetic-core switching circuit.

Example

Draw a logical block diagram to represent the implementation of the following expression by means of OR and INHIBIT circuits:

$$(((\bar{A} \cdot \bar{B}) + \bar{C}) \cdot \bar{D} + \bar{E}) \cdot \bar{F}$$

The solution is given in Fig. 51.

Dynamic Storage

A dynamic storage cell—one producing a train of pulses when storing ONE and no pulses when storing ZERO—may be built of three square-loop magnetic cores, as shown in Fig. 50*c*. The dynamic storage cell has an input core 1*A*, an output core 1*B*, and a reset core 2*A*. A positive pulse applied to the input core stores a ONE in it. CP_A shifts the ONE to the output core; CP_B shifts the ONE back to the input core. The ONE pulse is thus continuously shifted back and forth between cores 1*A* and 1*B* as long as clock pulses are applied. During each CP_B an output pulse is produced.

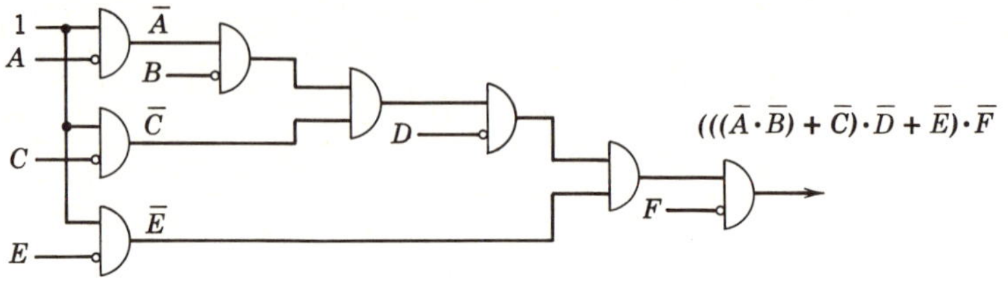

Figure 51 Logical block diagram using only OR and INHIBIT.

This situation continues as long as no signal is applied to reset core 2*A*. But if a pulse is applied to 2*A*, the next CP_A sends current through *N*2 to oppose the field produced by *N*1, thus preventing core 1*B* from flipping to the ONE state. As a result no output pulses are produced until a set pulse is once again fed to core 1*A*.

A dynamic flip-flop is shown in Fig. 50*d*. The dynamic flip-flop has four cores: an input core (1*A*), a ONE output core (1*B*), a ONES-generator core (2*A*), and a ZERO output core. The output of core 1*A* sets core 1*B* and resets core 2*B*. The output of core 1*B* sets core 1*A*. The output of core 2*A* sets core 2*B*.

The operation is as follows. A positive set pulse applied to 1*A* causes 1*A* to store a ONE. Clock pulse CP_A shifts this ONE to 1*B*; an alternate clock pulse CP_B shifts the ONE back to 1*A*. As long as these clock pulses are applied, the ONE bounces back and forth between 1*A* and 1*B*, and a ONE output pulse is produced during each CP_B.

Core 2*A* is made to store a ONE on each CP_B. CP_A attempts to shift this ONE to 2*B*, but the inhibit pulse from 1*A* prevents this. The result is that no output pulses are produced at the ZERO output line while the ONE output line produces a train of pulses.

If now a positive reset pulse is applied to 1*A*, it will store a ZERO. On CP_A there will now be no ONE transferred to 1*B* nor an inhibit pulse to 2*B*. The ONE from 2*A*, therefore, will be transferred to 2*B*. The result is that no output pulses are produced at the ONE output line while the ZERO output line produces a train of pulses.

Set and Reset pulses should not be applied at the same time, since they will cancel each other and the conditoin of the flip-flop will not change.

Notice that, if the output of the dynamic flip-flop is viewed only during CP_B, the output of the flip-flop is essentially the same as that of a static flip-flop.

SUMMARY

1. A device that acts like a switch may be used to form a switching circuit. A device that increases the energy in a signal may be used for amplification. An amplifier or any other device that can be made to possess two easily entered and easily distinguished stable states may be used for storage.
2. The basic switching building blocks are AND, OR, and NOT. However, all logical combinations may be obtained by using only *one* of the following blocks:

   NAND

   NOR

   INHIBIT
3. The relay may be used for switching, amplification, and storage. AND may be obtained by connecting relay contacts in series; OR may be obtained by connecting them in parallel; NOT may be obtained by using normally closed contacts. A storage cell is obtained by using a relay with holding contacts.
4. An AND circuit for positive signals is equivalent to an OR circuit for negative signals; an OR circuit for positive signals is equivalent to an AND circuit for negative signals.

* * * * * * *

5. The semiconductor diode may be used for switching only. A positive AND may be obtained by connecting to a common load the *p*-crystals of several diodes; a positive OR may be obtained by connecting the *n*-crystals.
6. In the grounded-emitter *n–p–n* transistor amplifier configuration, a NAND is obtained by connecting transistors in series; a NOR is obtained by connecting them in parallel. If transistors are connected in a series–parallel combination using a common load, the transistors in series produce ANDS; the ones in parallel produce ORS; and the common load causes the output to be complemented. Storage is obtained by connecting transistors in a flip-flop circuit.
7. The *p–n–p* transistor produces the same functions as the *n–p–n* in similar circuits, except that it handles negative pulses instead of positive pulses.
8. A magnetic-core switching circuit may be obtained by connecting the output windings of two cores to two separate input windings of another core. OR is produced if the two input windings are wound in the same direction; INHIBIT is produced if they are wound in opposite directions.
9. The square-loop magnetic-core switching circuit and flip-flop are dynamic—they respond to and produce pulses, not dc.
10. *Definitions to Remember*

    Switching Circuit. A circuit that produces an output for certain combinations of input.

    Flip-Flop. A 1-bit storage device with two input terminals and two output terminals. The device remains in either state until it is caused to change to the other state by the application of the corresponding signal. In either state, the signal on one output terminal is out of phase with the signal on the other output terminal.

* * * * * * *

Semiconductor. An element that possesses conductivity which is in between that of a conductor and of an insulator.
p-**Crystal.** A semiconductor to which acceptor impurities have been added.
n-**Crystal.** A semiconductor to which donor impurities have been added.
Acceptor. An element that, when used as an impurity in a semiconductor, introduces positive holes.
Donor. An element that, when used as an impurity in a semiconductor, introduces negative free electrons.
Hysteresis. The property of a magnetic material which prevents it from coming back to its original magnetic state after the magnetizing force is removed.
Magnetic Saturation. The point where any further increase in the magnetizing force applied to a magnetic material causes an almost negligible change in the magnetic state of the material. A material may be magnetically saturated in the positive or negative direction.
Square Hysteresis Loop. A loop whose upper and lower saturation lines are fairly flat.
Remanence. The magnetic state to which a magnetic material falls when the magnetizing force is removed. Materials have positive and negative remanence states.
Dynamic Storage Cell. A logical element which has two possible outputs; a continuous series of pulses (ONE) or of no pulses (ZERO). A set pulse flips the cell into the ONE state; a reset pulse flips the cell into the ZERO state.
Dynamic Flip-Flop. A circuit with two inputs and two outputs. The set input pulse produces a series of pulses on the 1-output line and no pulses on the 0-output line. The reset input pulse produces the reverse: no pulses on the 1-output line and a series of pulses on the 0-output line.

Exercises

1. Draw a logical block diagram of $A \cdot B$ with only the following circuits:
   a. NOR.
   b. NAND.
   c. INHIBIT.
2. Draw a logical block diagram of $A+B$ with only the following circuits:
   a. NOR.
   b. NAND.
   c. INHIBIT.
3. Draw a logical block diagram of $A \cdot B+A \cdot C+\bar{D}$, using only the following circuits:
   a. INHIBIT and OR.
   b. NAND.
   c. NOR.

4. Draw a logical block diagram of $(\bar{A}+B)\cdot(C+\bar{D})$, using only the following circuits:

   a. NOR.

   b. INHIBIT and OR.

   c. NAND.

5. Draw a logical block diagram of $A\cdot B+\bar{A}\cdot\bar{C}+\bar{B}\cdot\bar{C}$, using only the following circuits:

   a. NOR.

   b. INHIBIT and OR.

   c. NAND-NOR.

6. Draw a logical block diagram of $(A\cdot B\cdot\bar{C}+(\bar{D}+\bar{E})\cdot F)\cdot M+G\cdot\bar{H}$, using only the following circuits:

   a. AND-OR-NOT.

   b. OR-INHIBIT.

7. In the relay circuit of Fig. 31, if $A=0$, $B=C=1$, trace the path of current flow (if any) and determine if an output is produced.

8. Answer the following questions with reference to Fig. 52:

   a. Under what conditions is $FF1$ set? $FF2$ set?

   b. What does $CP1$ do? $CP2$?

   c. If $FF1$ is set and $FF2$ is reset, can output K be produced? Output L?

   d. What conditions are required to produce an output at L?

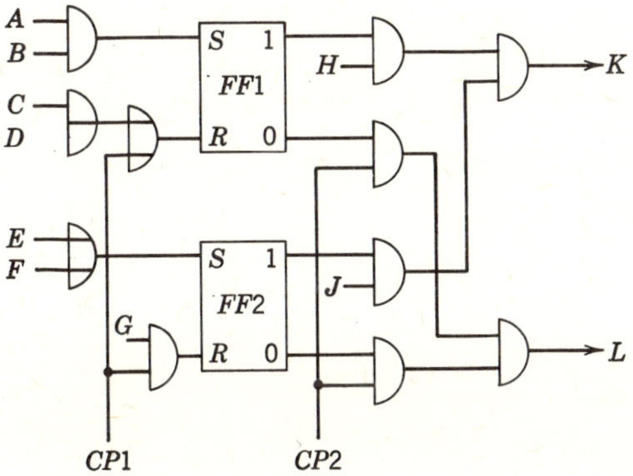

Figure 52 Logical block diagram for exercise 8.

* * * * *

9. In the diode–transistor circuit of Fig. 41, if $A=D=E=0$ and $B=C=F=1$, trace the path of current flow (if any) and determine if an output is produced.

10. In the transistor circuit of Fig. 43, if $E=F=0$ and $A=B=C=D=1$, trace the path of current flow (if any) and determine if an output is produced.

11. If in the transistor circuit of Fig. 43, transistor $TR2$ is defective and does not conduct, under the input conditions given, trace the current flow.

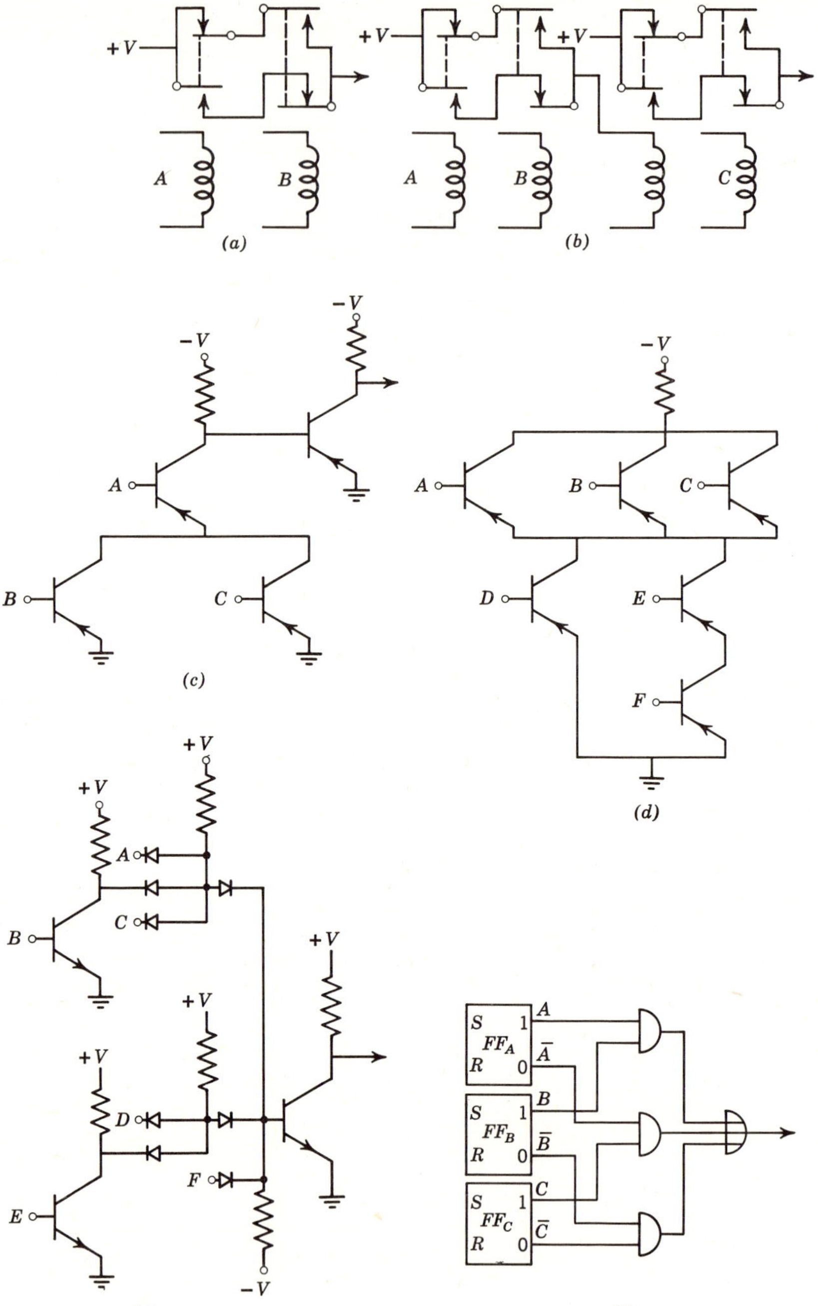

Figure 53 Logical circuits for exercises 19 and 20.

12. Trace the polarity changes across the coils in the magnetic-core circuit of Fig. 50*b* if $A=1$ and $B=0$, and determine if an output is produced.

13. In the transistor flip-flop of Fig. 42*c*, what happens if
   a. A positive pulse is applied to the base of *TR*2?
   b. A negative pulse is applied to the collector of *TR*2?
   c. A positive pulse is applied to the collector of *TR*1?
   d. A negative pulse is applied to the base of *TR*1?

14. If the core in this illustration is storing ZERO, that is, it is at its negative remanence point,

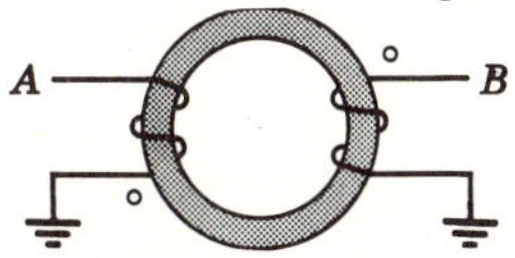

   a. Through what states does the core pass if a positive pulse and then a negative pulse are applied at *A*?
   b. At what point on the hysteresis loop does the state of the core stabilize?
   c. What are the answers to the above if the negative remanence point is considered to be a ONE?

15. Draw a magnetic-core switching circuit to represent
   a. $\bar{A} \cdot \bar{B}$
   b. $(A \cdot \bar{B}) \cdot (A+B)$

16. Draw a logical block diagram and an *n–p–n* transistor switching circuit for
   a. $A \cdot B$
   b. $(A \cdot \bar{B}) + (\bar{A} \cdot B)$
   c. $(A+B) \cdot (C+D) \cdot E$

17. Repeat exercise 16 for diode–*n–p–n* transistor circuit.

18. Draw a logical block diagram and a magnetic-core switching circuit for
   a. $(A+B+C)$
   b. $A+B+C$
   c. $(\bar{A}+\bar{B}) \cdot (A+B)$
   d. $A \cdot (B+C+D) + \bar{A} \cdot (E+F)$

19. Write the logical equation and draw the logical block diagram for each of the circuits in Fig. 52.

20. In Fig. 52*f*, if FF_A is set, FF_B and FF_C are reset, is an output produced?

CHAPTER 6

Translators

The basic switching circuits developed previously may be combined into larger units called functional building blocks. Among the simplest functional building blocks are the translators. A translator is a network that translates from one code to another. In the simplest case, the network may consist of a group of gates or of even only 1 gate. In the more complicated case, it may be a decoder or an encoder matrix.

GATES

In a sense, every gate is a translator: it translates a certain "message" at the input into a different "message" at the output.

Gates may be used to detect whether a certain combination of bits representing a special character is present. For instance, if a certain group of characters stored in a computer is delineated by < before the first and > after the last, a simple gate circuit may be used to detect these two conditions. The ASCII codes for the two special characters are

	A_8	A_7	A_6	A_5	A_4	A_3	A_2	A_1
<	0	0	1	1	1	1	0	0
>	0	0	1	1	1	1	1	0

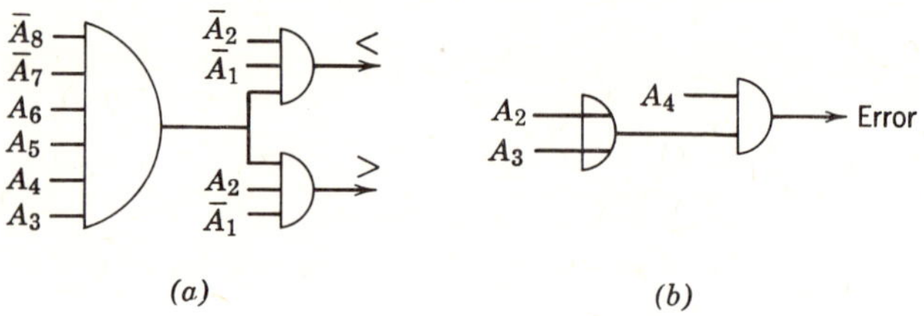

Figure 54 Combinatorial logic. (*a*) < and >. (*b*) Error.

where A_1 represents the least significant and A_8 the most significant positions. $<$ is, therefore, given by $\bar{A}_8\bar{A}_7A_6A_5A_4A_3\bar{A}_2\bar{A}_1$ and $>$ by $\bar{A}_8\bar{A}_7A_6A_5A_4A_3A_2\bar{A}_1$. The circuit to produce this is shown in Fig. 54*a*.

Example

Produce an "Error" pulse whenever any of the six forbidden combinations of *BCD* occurs.

All combinations of 4 bits in 8421 code are as follows:

BCD

	A_4	A_3	A_2	A_1
0	0	0	0	0
1	0	0	0	1
2	0	0	1	0
3	0	0	1	1
4	0	1	0	0
5	0	1	0	1
6	0	1	0	0
7	0	1	1	1
8	1	0	0	0
9	1	0	0	1

FORBIDDEN

	A_4	A_3	A_2	A_1
10	1	0	1	0
11	1	0	1	1
12	1	1	0	0
13	1	1	0	1
14	1	1	1	0
15	1	1	1	1

A study of the two groups shows that members of the forbidden group are different from the members of the *BCD* group in one of two ways: the simultaneous presence in the forbidden group of A_4 and A_2 or A_4 and A_3. The logical block diagram of Fig. 54*b*, therefore, may detect this condition.

DECODERS

A decoder is a device that translates a combination of signals into one of a group of signals. Some of the forms it may take are the tree and the rectangular matrix.

Relay Decoder

In Fig. 55 is shown an example of a relay tree decoder which chooses one out of 16 output lines when a 4-bit combination is applied to it. The input signals are applied to the relay coils; a ONE is represented by a current pulse, a ZERO is represented by the absence of a current pulse. The movable contact is forced downward for each of the relays to which a current pulse is applied; all other movable contacts remain in their upward positions. For each combination of ONE'S and ZERO'S applied, a different closed-circuit path is established. For instance, in the illustration 0101 is applied. As a result, the first and third (counting from the right) relays are activated. The $+V$ is therefore fed through the path indicated by the bold lines to choose line number 5.

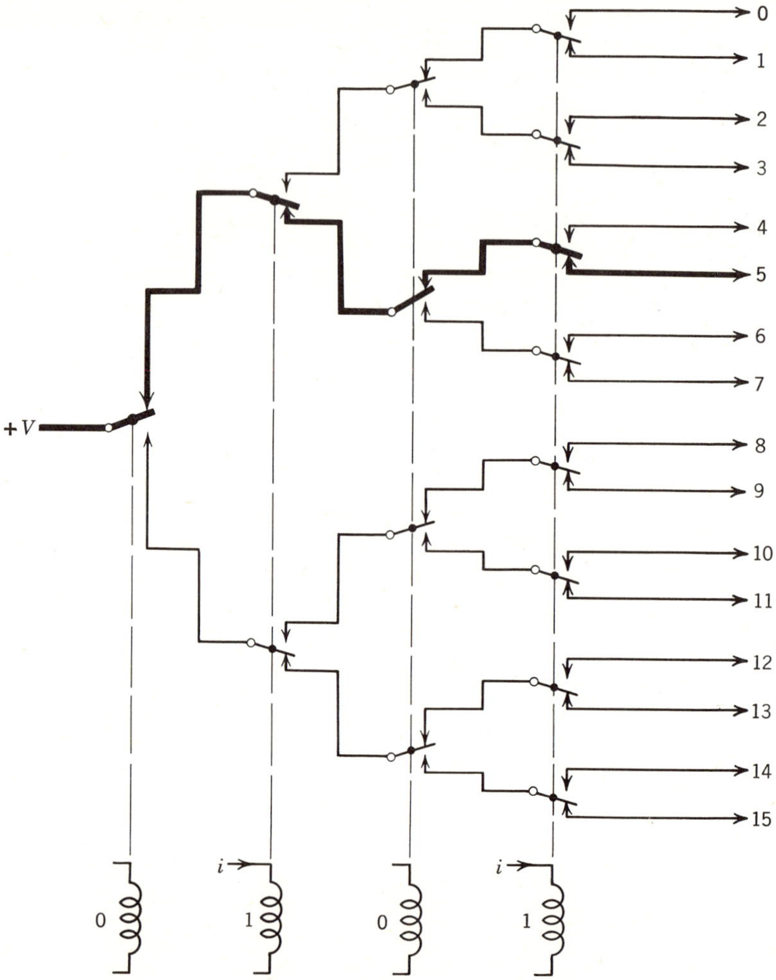

Figure 55 Relay tree decoder.

Diode Decoder

The decoder may be constructed of diodes in a rectangular matrix. Fig. 56*a* shows a diode decoder that decodes two bits into 2^2 or 4 possible combinations. Essentially this decoder consists of four AND circuits, each AND circuit being composed of two diodes attached to a horizontal line, and the resistor in the horizontal line. Two input bits are applied to each of the four AND circuits by sending a positive pulse to either the ONE or ZERO line of each of the two pairs of vertical lines. All other vertical lines are negative. Each horizontal line—AND circuits—which has a diode connected to a negative vertical line produces a negative output, since the diode conducts. The one horizontal line which is connected through diodes to the two positive vertical lines produces a positive output, since none of the diodes conducts. The illustration shows binary 10 decoded into 2. The bold, vertical lines are positive; all other vertical lines are negative. A positive potential applied to the two diodes attached to horizontal line 2 causes them to be open. No voltage drop is produced across *R* and a positive signal is developed at the output.

The diode matrix may be drawn more simply as shown in Fig. 56*b*. It is important to remember when using the shorthand dot matrix that the *n* sides of the diodes of a decoder are in the input lines.

**Example*

Draw a diode matrix to decode 3 bits into eight possible combinations. Figure 56*c* presents the dot matrix.

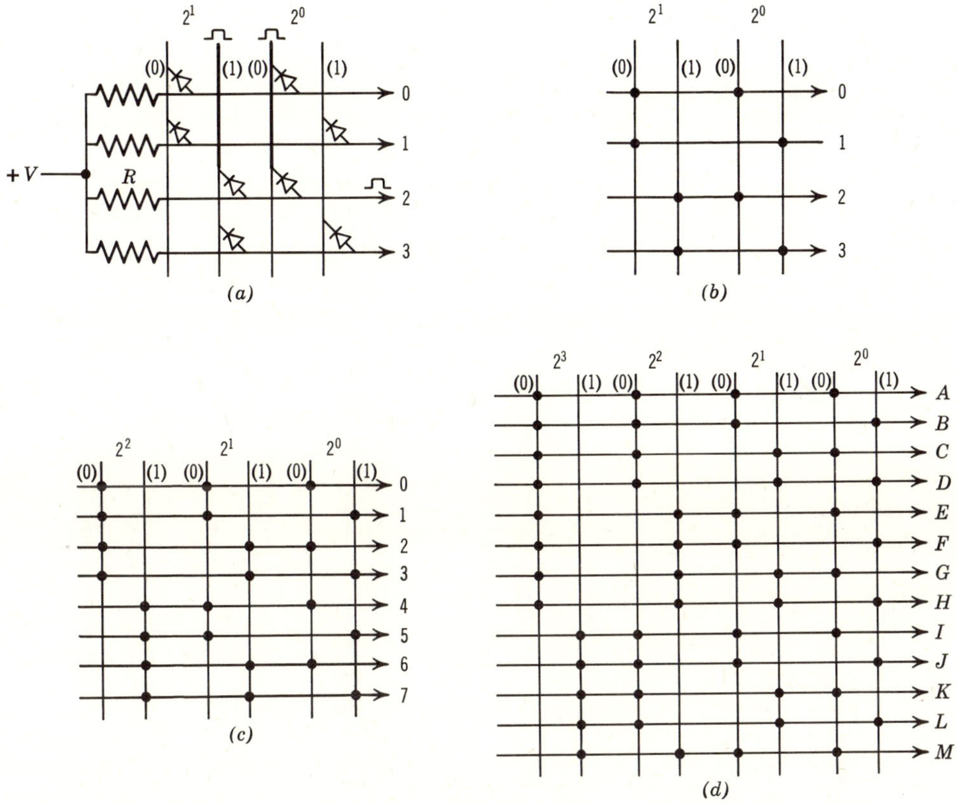

Figure 56 Rectangular matrix decoders. (*a*) Diode 2 × 2. (*b*) Dot 2 × 2. (*c*) 3 × 8 dot matrix. (*d*) 4 × 13 Dot matrix.

Example

Draw a diode matrix to decode the first 13 combinations of 4 bits in *BCD*. Figure 56*d* presents the dot matrix.

Example

Draw a decoder that produces three outputs as follows:

α when *BCD* is 0.
β when *BCD* is 1 to 10.
γ when *BCD* is 11.

The *BCD* and the decoded combinations may be listed as follows:

BCD				
A_4	A_3	A_2	A_1	
0	0	0	0	α
0	0	0	1	β
0	0	1	0	β
0	0	1	1	β
0	1	0	0	β
0	1	0	1	β
0	1	1	0	β
0	1	1	1	β
1	0	0	0	β
1	0	0	1	β
1	0	1	0	β
1	0	1	1	γ

From this list we notice that the conditions under which the three outputs are developed are as follows:

$$\alpha = \bar{A}_4 \cdot \bar{A}_3 \cdot \bar{A}_2 \cdot \bar{A}_1$$
$$\beta = \bar{A}_4 \cdot A_3 + \bar{A}_4 \cdot A_2 + \bar{A}_4 \cdot A_1 + \bar{A}_3 A_2 \bar{A}_1 + A_4 \bar{A}_3 \bar{A}_2$$
$$\gamma = A_4 \cdot \bar{A}_3 \cdot A_2 \cdot A_1$$

It is obvious, therefore, that the entire 4-bit matrix need not be drawn. Figure 57 shows the solution.

Coincident Current Selector

Another name for a decoder is selector. A coincident current selector is a device that activates one of several output lines when signals are applied to two input lines simultaneously. The selector consists of a group of square-loop cores arranged in an array of vertical columns and horizontal rows. A vertical input line threads all the cores in a column; and a horizontal input line threads all the cores in a row. A separate output winding is wound around each core in the array. Current pulses, each of which is only half the value needed to flip a core, are applied to one vertical line and one horizontal line. Only the one

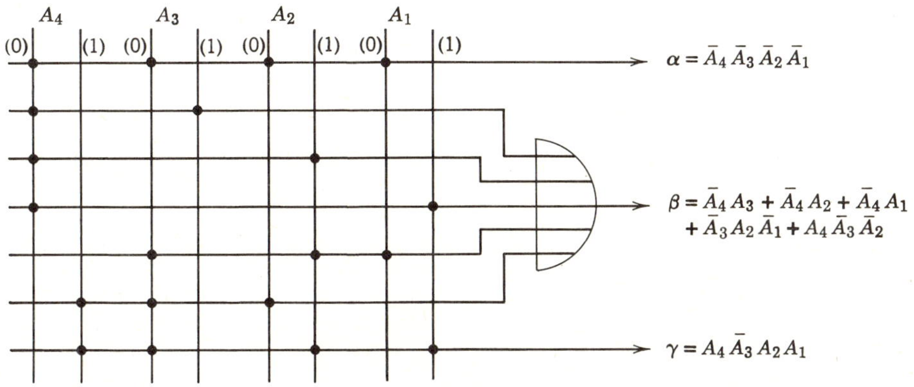

Figure 57 Reduced matrix decoder.

core in the array through which both activated lines pass receives enough magnetic energy to reverse states; a pulse is produced across its output winding.

Figure 58 shows a 3-column by 3-row coincident-current selector. The horizontal input lines are labeled X_0, X_1, and X_2. The vertical input lines are labeled Y_0, Y_1, and Y_2. Assume all cores in the array are originally at negative remanence. If now a half-current pulse—a pulse half the amplitude needed to bring a core to positive saturation—is applied to X_2, the cores in this row reach point A on the hysteresis loop (Fig. 58*b*). Likewise, a half-current pulse applied to Y_1 causes the cores in this column to reach the same point on the loop. Only the cross-hatched core receives enough magnetic energy to flip completely to positive saturation. When the half-current pulses are removed, the cross hatched core falls to the positive remanence point; all other cores fall to the negative remanence point.

Before being used again, the cores in the selector must be reset to negative remanence.

Note that, if the strength of the half-current pulse is increased slightly, the core's coercive force may be exceeded, and the core may flip completely with only one half-current pulse applied. For greater reliability of operation it is best to improve the distinction between the effects of single half-current pulses and double half-current pulses. This distinction may be improved by applying a d-c bias to all cores in the coincident-current selector. Core operation with d-c bias applied is indicated in Fig. 58*c*. The bias current places each core at negative saturation. One half-current pulse brings the core to the origin; two half-current pulses bring the core to positive saturation.

ENCODERS

An encoder is a device that translates one of a group of signals into a combination of signals. Mechanical, relay and diode matrix encoders are discussed below.

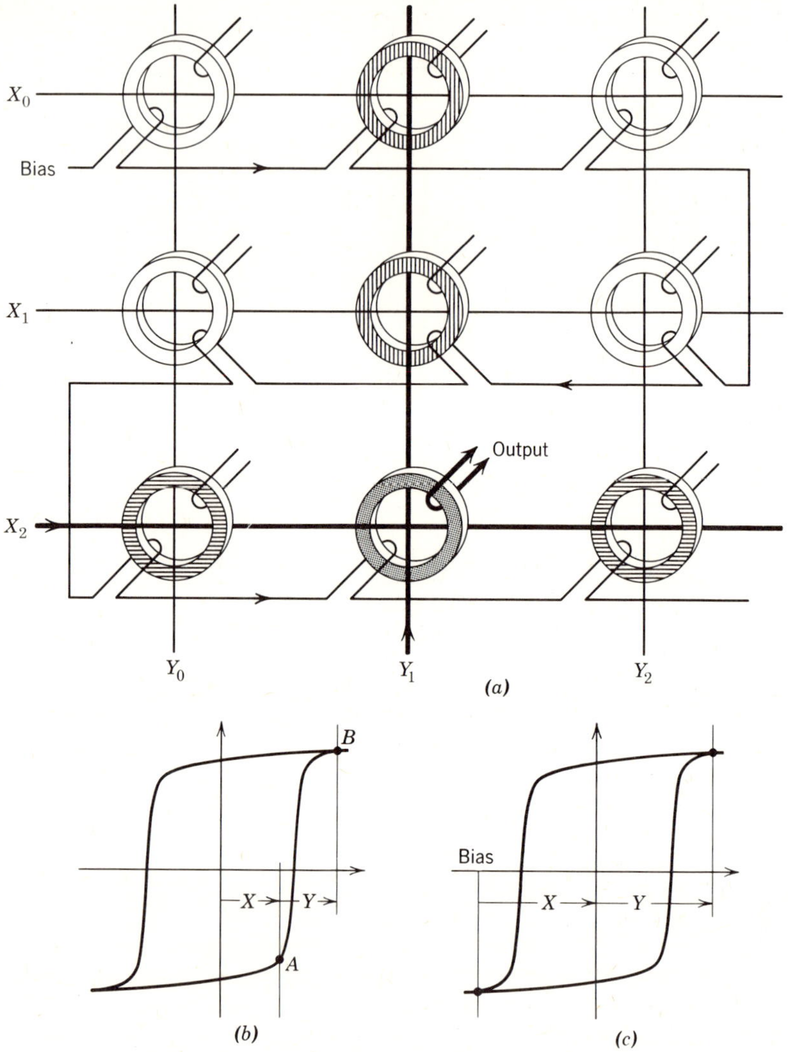

Figure 58 Magnetic coincident current selector. (*a*) Selector. (*b*) Loop without bias. (*c*) Loop with bias.

Mechanical and Relay Encoders

Figure 59 shows a mechanical encoder and a relay encoder. Both translate effectively from decimal (one of a group of ten signals) to binary-coded decimal (a combination of four signals). The mechanical encoder consists of ten vertical bars each having four evenly spaced ledges; and four horizontal bars possessing ledges in a pattern determined by the binary code for each

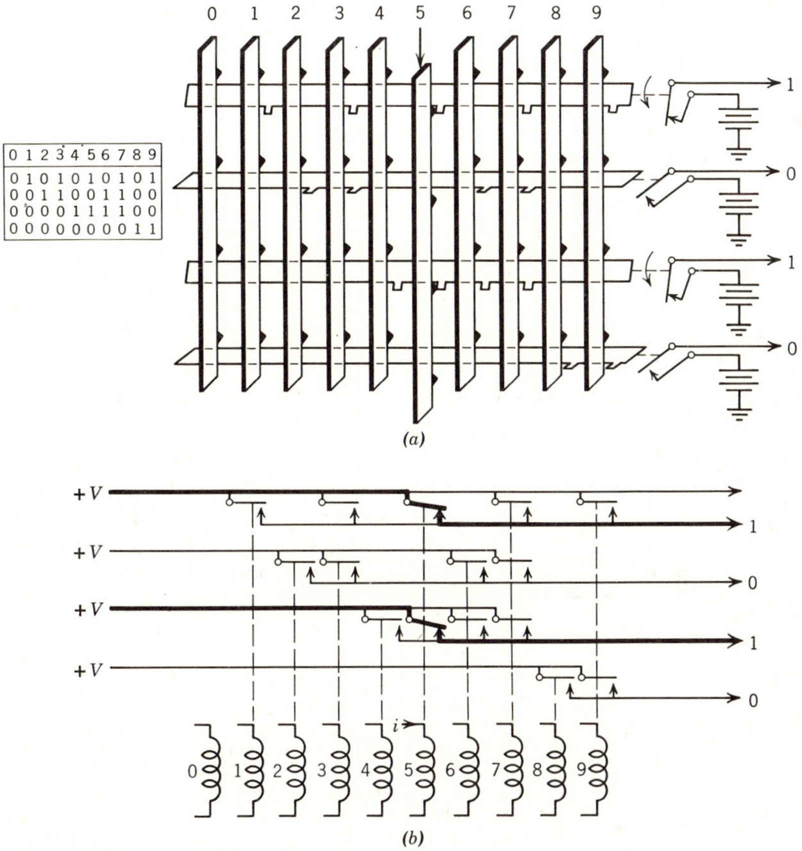

Figure 59 Encoders. (*a*) Mechanical encoder. (*b*) Relay encoder.

decimal number. The input signal consists of mechanical pressure applied in a downward direction to one of the vertical bars. Wherever the ledges on this bar strike the ledges on the horizontal bars, these horizontal bars are made to move in an arc. The horizontal bars are connected mechanically to a pair of electric contacts in such a way that, if the bar is moved, the contacts close, causing current to flow in the associated output line. In the illustration, bar 5 is depressed. The ledges on this bar hit the ledges on horizontal bars 1 and 3. Therefore, current flows through lines 1 and 3. If we consider the flow of current a ONE and the absence of current a ZERO, then the ouput is 0101, the binary-coded decimal equivalent of 5.

The relay encoder works in a similar manner. Instead of ten vertical bars it has ten relays. Instead of four horizontal bars it has four sets—or rather four possible sets—of contacts on each relay. These contacts are arranged analogously to the way the ledges are arranged on the horizontal bars. When

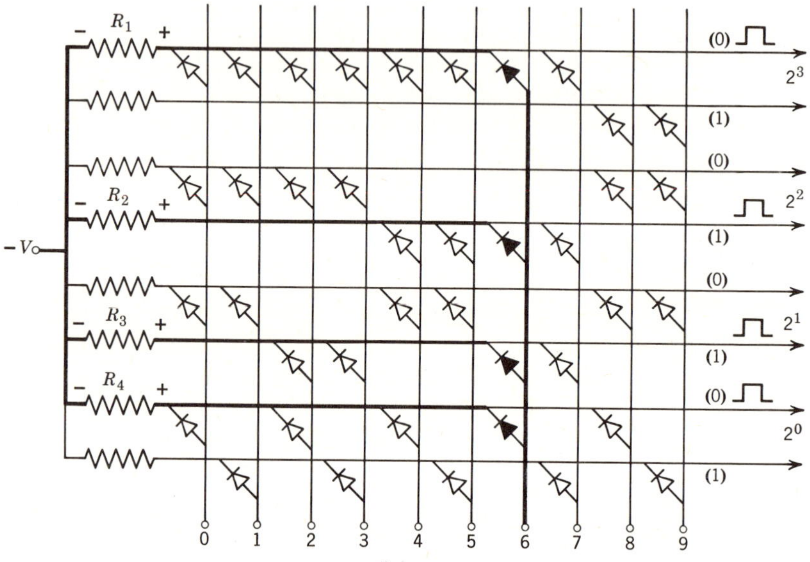

(*a*)

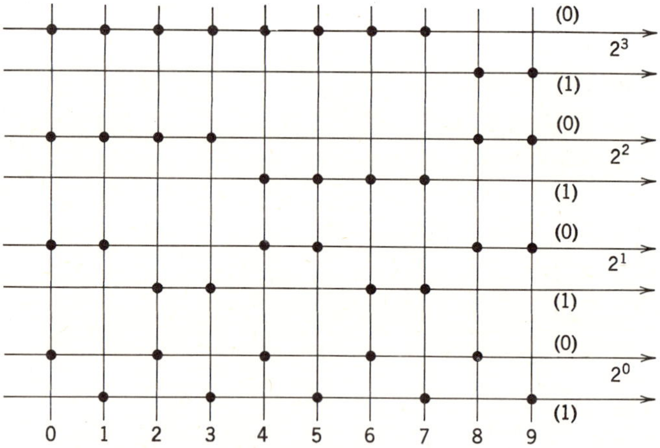

(*b*)

Figure 60 Diode encoding matrix-decimal to binary-coded decimal. (*a*) Diode matrix. (*b*) Dot matrix.

a signal is applied to relay 5, the first and third lines are activated as before to produce 0101.

Diode Encoders

Just as a decoder consists of a group of AND circuits, an encoder may be considered to consist of a group of OR circuits. A circuit which encodes decimal numbers to binary-coded decimal is given in Fig. 60*a*. The diodes along each horizontal line together with the resistor in each horizontal line compose an OR circuit. A signal applied to each of the ten vertical input lines feeds a positive potential to a different combination of four OR circuits. For instance, a positive potential applied to line 6 feeds current through the diodes shown to the four horizontal bold lines. As a result, positive signals are produced across *R*1, *R*2, *R*3, and *R*4. The output is therefore 0110 or binary 6.

Notice that for the encoder, the *p* sides of the crystal are in the input lines. Figure 60*b* shows the dot matrix equivalent of the diode encoder.

Example

Draw a dot matrix of an encoder to translate the alphabet into ASCII code. See Fig. 61 for the solution.

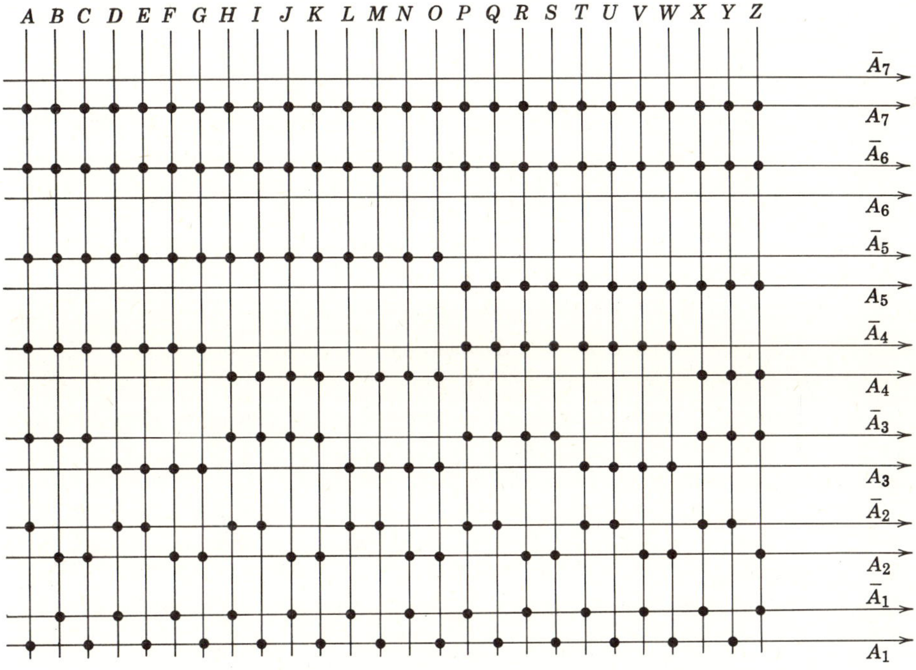

Figure 61 Alphanumeric characters to ASCII code encoder.

SUMMARY

1. Groups of gates may be used to produce combinations of output signals on the application of certain combinations of input signals.
2. When there is a pattern to the input signals, to the output signals, or to both, decoders and encoders may be used.
3. *Definitions to remember*
   Translator. A network to which are applied signals representing data in a certain code, and the output of which are signals representing the same data but in a different code.
   Encoder. A network (or mechanical device) of circuits in which only one input is excited at a time, and each input produces a combination of outputs.
   Decoder. A network of circuits which converts a combination of signals into an output on one of several output lines.
   Coincident-Current Selector. A circuit that activates one out of several output lines when current signals are applied coincidentally to two input lines.

Exercises

1. If a signal is applied to relay 7 in Fig. 59*b*, show the output current paths.
2. Draw a logical block diagram for detecting the presence of a Start of Header (SOH) character and of an End of Text (ETX) character. The ASCII codes are: SOH = 00000001 ; ETX = 00000011.
3. Draw a logical block diagram of a circuit to produce an "Error" signal when any of the 6 forbidden combinations of the 5421 code is applied.
4. Repeat exercise 3 for the Excess-3 code.
5. Draw a dot matrix to decode from 5211 code to decimal.
6. Repeat exercise 5 for Excess-3 code.
7. How many inputs (ONE and ZERO pairs) must be applied to a decoder to be able to produce 16 different possible outputs? 32?
8. In exercise 7, how many diodes are needed?
9. If 6 inputs (ONE and ZERO pairs) are applied to a decoder, how many different possible outputs can it have? Can the same number of different outputs be obtained by the use of two decoders, each with 3 inputs? If so, how?
10. The algebraic expression for a decoding network is

$$(\bar{A}\cdot\bar{B}+A\cdot\bar{B}+\bar{A}\cdot B+A\cdot B)\cdot(\bar{C}\cdot\bar{D}+C\cdot\bar{D}+\bar{C}\cdot D+C\cdot D).$$

Draw a diode circuit to represent this.

11. Draw a decoder dot matrix to translate 8421 code to the following:

A on numbers 0 to 3
B on numbers 4 to 9
C on numbers 10 to 15

12. Draw a dot matrix of a decimal to 5211 code encoder.

13. Draw a dot matrix of a decimal to Excess-3 code encoder.

14. How many bits are required to encode the 26 characters of the alphabet? 100 items? 56 items?

15. How many *X* and *Y* lines are needed by a coincident current selector to choose any 1 of a possible 1024 points? 4096?

16. In exercise 15, how many cores are required?

CHAPTER 7

Registers and counters

The functional building blocks of the previous chapter consist of combinational logic only—no timing considerations are involved. To obtain sequential logic—logic including the factor of time—clock pulse generators, temporary storage blocks called registers, and sequential counters are required.

The major part of this chapter is devoted to a discussion of various types of registers and counters and to the usefulness to which they may be put. Clock pulse generators, which are oscillators producing pulses of constant dimensions and constant frequency, are not discussed per se. The use of clock pulses in the operation of registers and counters, however, is an important part of this chapter.

REGISTERS

There are three types of registers: static, shifting, and recirculating. We describe each in turn.

Static Register

The static register consists of a group of flip-flops, or other storage devices, that is used to store a group of bits. The bits may be entered into and removed from the flip-flops in parallel or in series.

Figure 62*a* shows a static register with parallel bit flow. Inputs are represented as a_0 to a_3 for ONE'S and as $\bar{a}_0$ to $\bar{a}_3$ for ZERO'S. When a Read-In pulse is applied, the four flip-flops are set or reset according to the input signals applied—the register *stores* the input bits. When, at a future time, a Read-Out signal is applied, the contents of the flip-flops are output as shown, and they may be applied to another register or to some other functional building block. The contents of the flip-flops are undisturbed.

To reduce the number of lines needed, the register may be connected as shown in Fig. 62*b*. Here a ONE is input by applying a signal at a_0, a_1, a_2 or a_3; a

ZERO is input by the absence of a signal at one of these points. In this approach a Clear signal is applied after data is read out to bring all flip-flips back to ZERO before the read-in. If this were not done, a ZERO could not be written into a flip-flop that was previously storing a ONE.

The diagrams of Fig 62*a* and *b* may be simplified into the register diagram shown in Fig. 62*c*. In this illustration the 4 in the circles, indicates that 4 bits are input or output in parallel. To obtain serial flow, the same flip-flop arrangement is used, but timing pulses are needed to sequence the bits into and out of the appropriate flip-flops (see Fig. 63*a*). During read-in, a group of 4 bits is applied in sequence at the point labeled *a*, and a Read-In signal is applied for the length of 4 timing pulses. At time t_0 the first bit is applied to *FF*-0; during t_1 the second bit is applied to *FF*-1; during t_2 the third bit is applied to *FF*-2; and during t_3 the fourth bit is applied to *FF*-3. Similarly, on output, a long Read-Out pulse is applied, and successive *t* pulses read the bits out of successive flip-flops and place them at *A* in sequence.

A clear signal is needed after read-out to avoid confusion between a read-out and its succeeding read-in.

Figure 63*b* shows that the same effect may be achieved by means of delays. Again, a sequence of bits is applied at *a*. After a period of time equal to $D_1+D_2+D_3$, the Read-In pulse is applied to gate in in parallel, the first bit into *FF*-0, and the fourth bit into *FF*-3. Output is obtained by applying a short duration Read-Out pulse. The first bit is gated out of *FF*-0 immediately. After a delay of D_1, the second bit is gated out of *FF*-1, and so on. A sequence of 4 bits thus appears on the output line *A*.

The diagrams of Fig. 63*a* and *b* may be simplified into Fig. 63*c*

Shifting Register

A shifting register is one where data flow is obtained by shifting bits from cell to cell of the register. Shifting produces serial flow, although the rate of input shifting and output shifting may be different. Furthermore, either the input or the output may be executed in parallel.

Figure 64*a* shows a shifting register that operates serially upon read-in and upon read-out. Serial bits are applied at *a* or $\bar{a}$ while a long Read-In signal plus a group of clock pulses CP_1 are applied as shown. The first input bit sets or resets *FF*-3 when the first CP_1 is applied. The second CP_1 transfers the contents of *FF*-3 to *FF*-2 and at the same time transfers the second input bit to *FF*-3. Delay elements *D* are included to assure that a flip-flop does not flip before it has a chance to transfer its data to the following stage. After the fourth CP_1 is applied, the first bit is in *FF*-0 and the fourth bit is in *FF*-3. Read-out is produced by applying a long Read-Out signal plus a group of clock pulses CP_2 as shown. The first CP_2 shifts the bit in *FF*-3 to *FF*-2, the bit in *FF*-2 to *FF*-1, the bit in *FF*-1 to *FF*-0, and the bit in *FF*-0 out. Succeeding CP_2 transfer the respective bits another position to the right. After four CP_2, all the bits have been transferred out of the register.

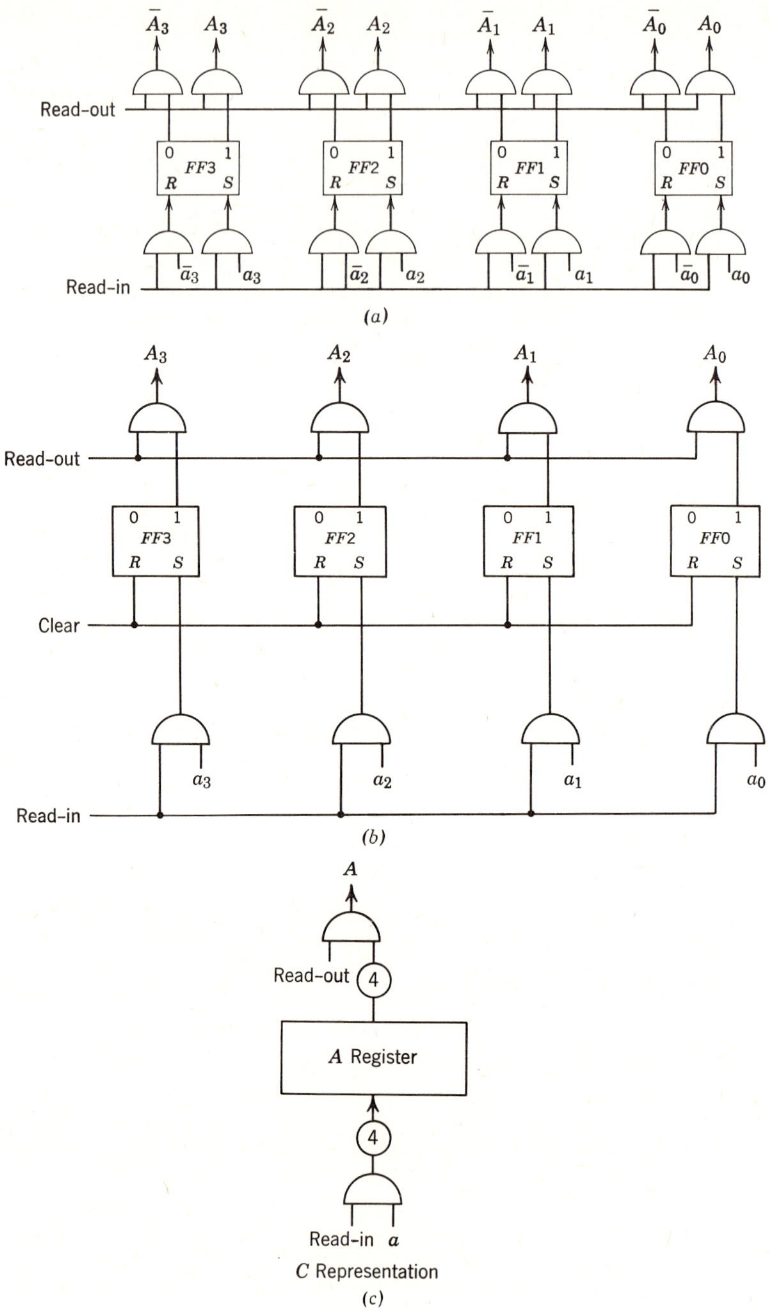

Figure 62 Register, Parallel flow. (*a*) One and zero outputs. (*b*) One output only. (*c*) Representation.

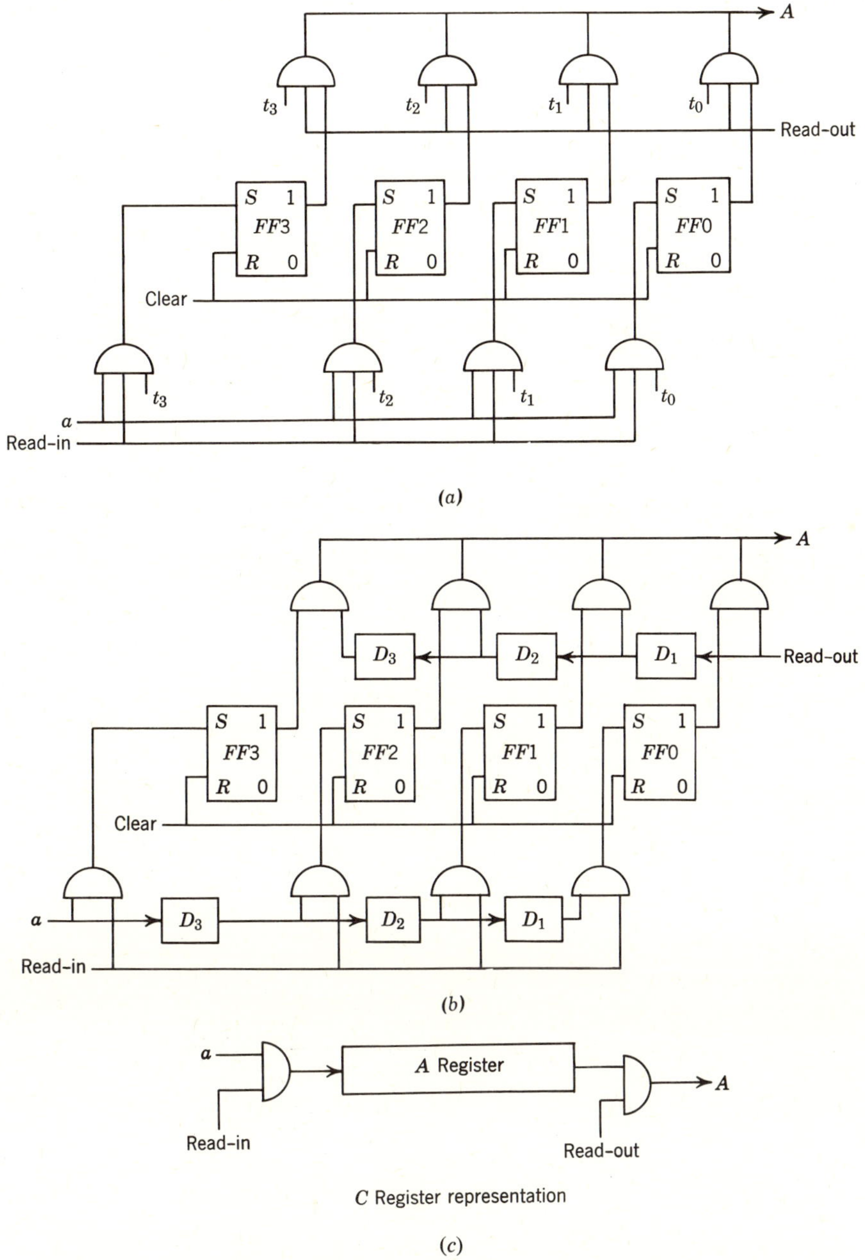

Figure 63 Register, Serial flow. (*a*) Use of timing pulses. (*b*) The use of delay elements. (*c*) Register representation.

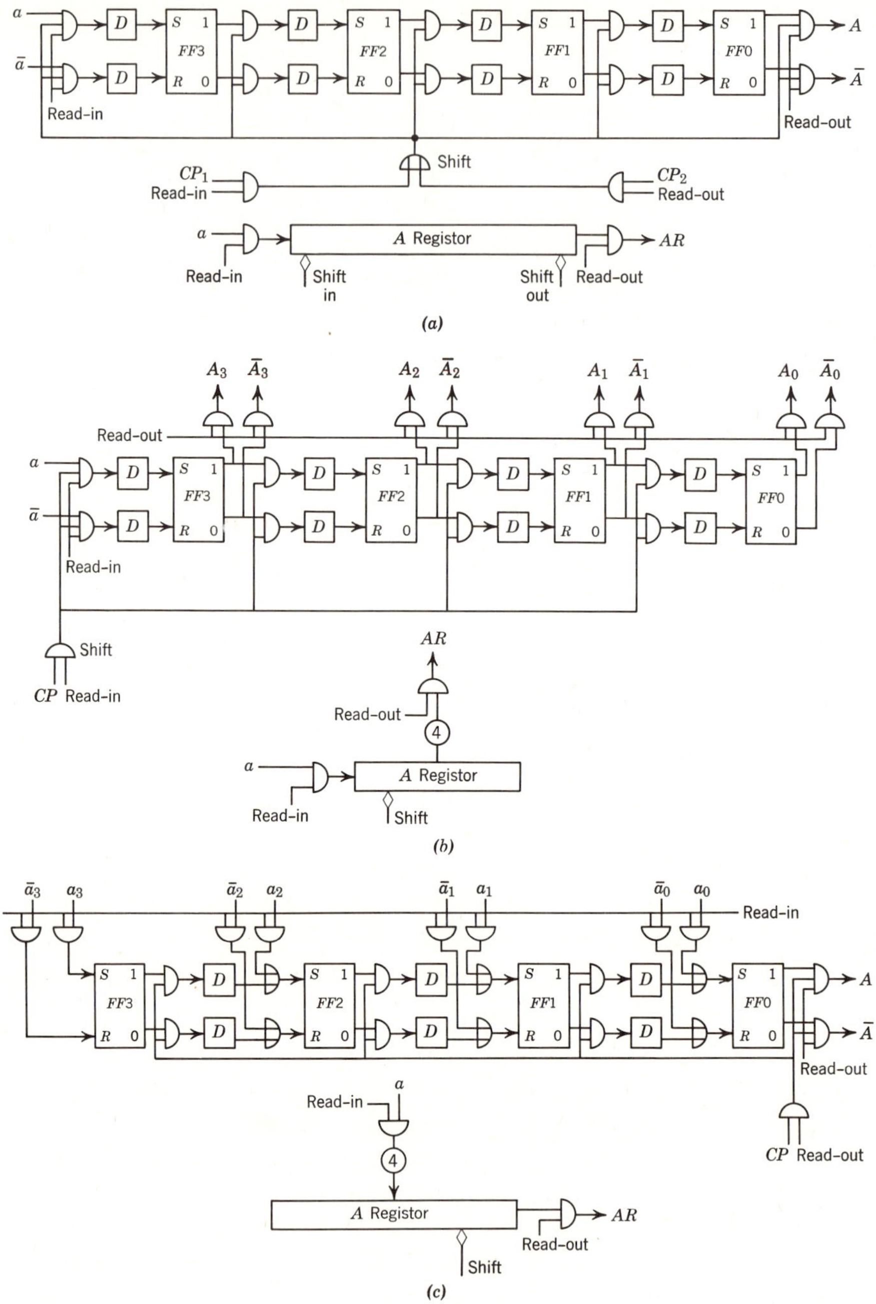

Figure 64 Shift registers. (*a*) Serial read-in, Serial read-out. (*b*) Serial read-in, Parallel read-out. (*c*) Parallel read-in, serial read-out.

By making CP_1 and CP_2 occur at different frequencies, input and output may be executed at different rates. When it is used for speed adjustment in this manner, the register is called a buffer.

A shifting register also may be used as another type of buffer, one that changes serial flow to parallel flow. Fig. 64*b* shows one such register. Here input bits are shifted in as before by the use of a long Read-In signal plus a series of four clock pulses *CP*. The four bits stored may be later read out by a Read-Out pulse that is applied simultaneously to all the output gates shown.

Another use of the shifting register is as a buffer that changes parallel flow to serial flow, as shown in Fig. 64*c*. A Read-In pulse applied to all the input gates transfers all four input bits to the four flip-flops as shown. Serial read-out is obtained by applying a long Read-Out signal plus 4 *CP*.

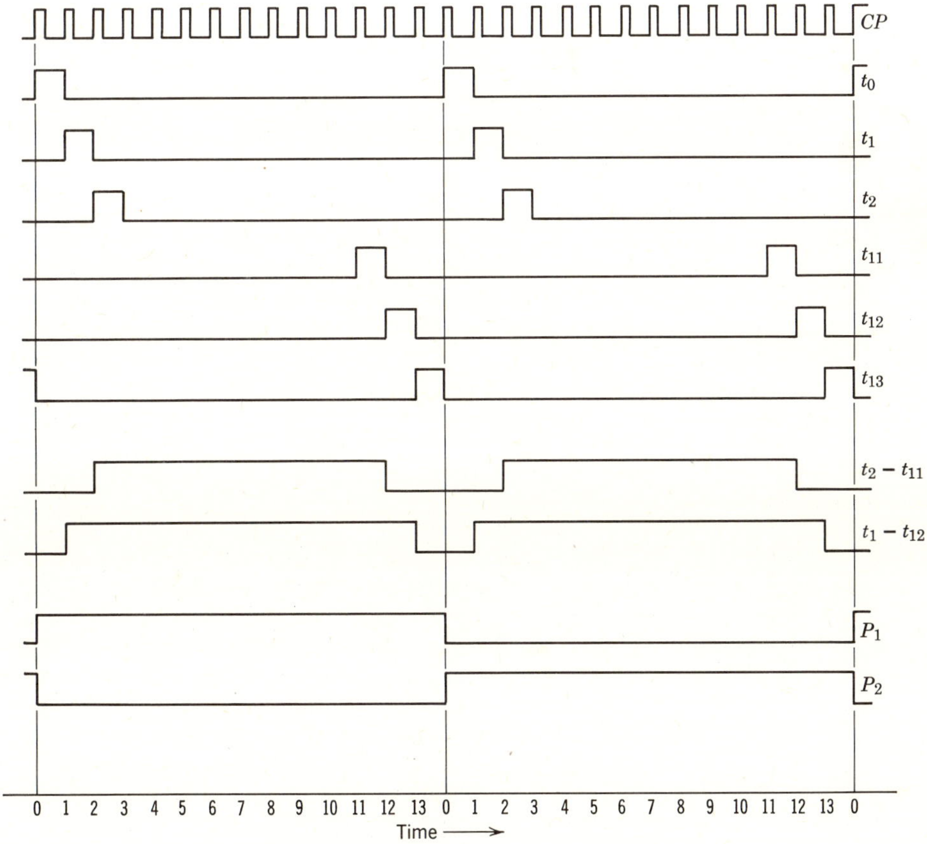

Figure 65 Clock, timing, and phasing signals.

Example

Assume two 10-bit serial sources—MR and AR. Assume a clock that produces clock pulses CP at a steady frequency. Assume the clock pulses are fed to a timing pulse generator (described later in this chapter) that divides the pulses into groups of 14 and that produces the subscripted t timing pulses and phases P_1 and P_2 (see Fig. 65).

Draw a diagram of an X Register to which the bits of MR are applied during t_2–t_{11} of phase P_1 whenever a control signal Y is present. During phase P_2 the contents of the X Register are shifted to the right one position during time t_1 if a control signal S is present. The rightmost bit is gated out, and at the same time a bit is gated in from AR to the leftmost position of the X Register.

A shift register diagram that accomplishes these tasks is shown in Fig. 66*a*.

Example

Assume that the same MR, AR, clock, timing, and phasing pulses are available as before.

Draw a diagram of an I Register to which 10 bits are applied in series during t_2–t_{11}; these bits come from MR during phase P_1, when control signal F is present, and from AR during phase P_2. Regardless of the phase, at time t_{13} all 10 bits are read out in parallel. If control signal Y is present, the 6 most significant bits are not read out.

A shift register diagram to solve this problem is shown in Fig. 66*b*.

Example

Assume the same clock, timing and phasing signals as before. Assume, too, the presence of a 12-bit serial source TR and of a 12-bit parallel source SR.

Draw a diagram of an M Register which during phase P_1 loads serially from TR at times t_1–t_{12} and unloads in parallel at time t_{13}; during phase P_2 it loads in parallel from SR during t_0 and unloads serially during t_1–t_{12}.

A shift-register diagram performing these tasks is shown in Fig. 66*c*.

Double Rank Shifting Registers

Transistor flip-flops may be used as storage cells in a shift register. As was shown previously, to reduce ambiguity of operation, a delay must be introduced between storage cells. Even more reliable operation can be obtained by means of a double-rank shift register. A double-rank shift register (Fig. 67*a*) has two storage cells for each bit. One storage cell ($FF0_A$, $FF1_A$, etc.,) stores the bit; the other cell ($FF0_B$, $FF1_B$, etc.,) acts as temporary storage during the transfer of the bit from one storage cell to the next. The block diagram shows the two storage levels connected by means of AND switches to produce right shifts. A right shift is accomplished by applying a CP_A pulse and then a CP_B pulse. The CP_A pulse primes the AND circuits to the temporary storage cells; bits stored in the data flip-flops $FF0_A$, $FF1_B$, etc., are fed to flip-flops $FF0_A$, $FF1_B$ and so on. The following CP_B pulse primes the AND circuits to the data storage cells;

data stored in the temporary storage cells are fed to the data flip-flops. Each succeeding pair of clock pulses shifts the data one bit position to the right.

Another set of AND circuits may be connected between flip-flops in such a manner as to shift bits from data cells to temporary storage cells, and then to data cells to the left to produce left shifts.

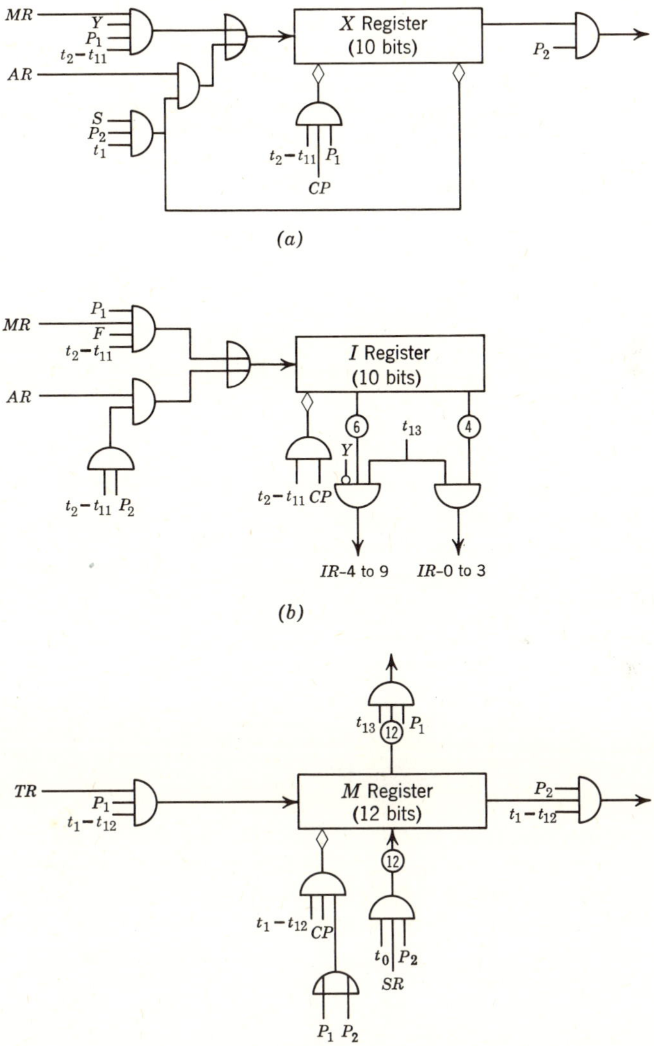

Figure 66 Examples of shifting registers. (*a*) Serial input, serial output. (*b*) Serial input, parallel output. (*c*) Serial in, parallel out; parallel in, serial out.

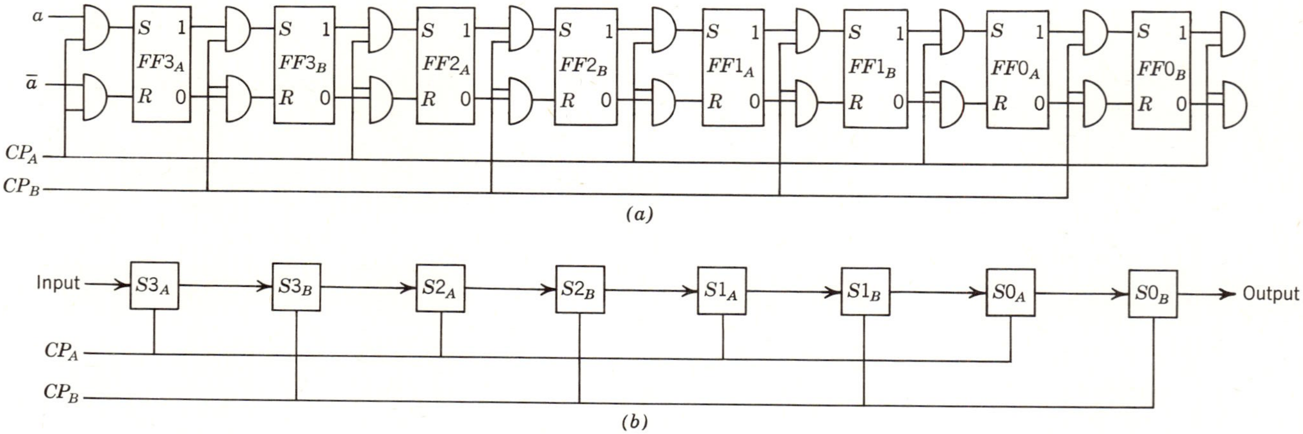

Figure 67 Double-rank shift register. (*a*) Logic diagram. (*b*) Abbreviated representation.

Recirculating Registers

A recirculating register is a register that stores data by recirculating it at a constant rate. An element, such as fused quartz, that possesses delay characteristics, may be connected in a circuit such as that shown in Fig. 68*a* to form a recirculating register. When a Read-In signal is applied, input signals consisting of an alternating wave for a ONE and no wave for a ZERO are applied to the piezoelectric quartz crystal on the left. The crystal converts the electrical waves into acoustic waves that travel along the fused quartz crystal. At a certain time later the acoustic waves impinge on the piezoelectric quartz crystal on the right, which converts the acoustic wave back into electrical energy. If a Recirculation signal is then applied, this electrical energy is amplified and is returned to the input. By keeping recirculation going in this way, the data may be stored indefinitely. To remove data from the register, a Read-Out signal is applied for the length of time necessary to remove all the pulses.

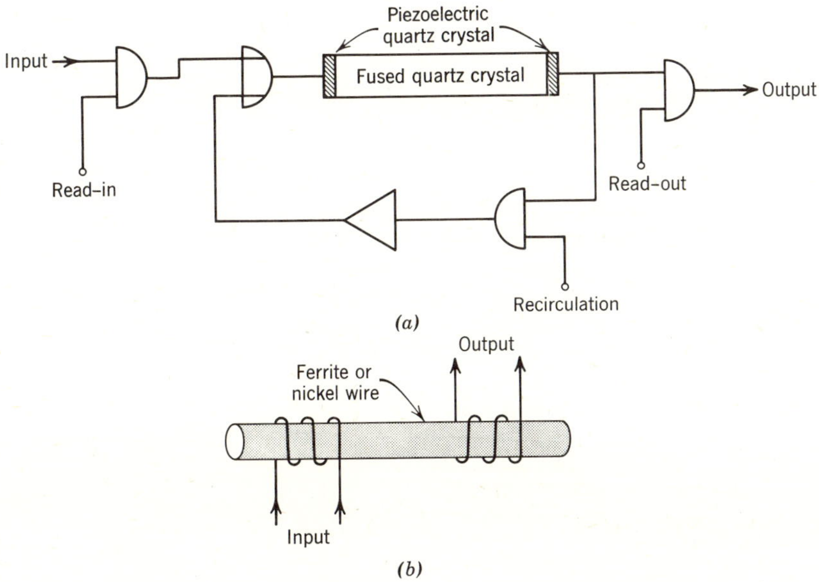

Figure 68 Recirculating registers. (*a*) Quartz crystal delay line. (*b*) Magnetostriction.

Notice that data may be read out and recirculated at the same time. In other words, the quartz delay line possesses nondestructive read-out.

Delay may be produced by using the magnetostrictive property of certain materials such as ferrite or nickel. A magnetostrictive material is one which converts magnetic energy into a mechanical movement, and vice versa. A magnetostrictive delay line composed of two coils wound on a piece of ferrite or nickel ribbon is shown in Fig. 68*b*. A pulse applied to the input coil produces a magnetic field which causes a mechanical deformation in the rod or ribbon. After a definite time, the mechanical deformation reaching the area within the output coil causes a change in magnetic field and thus induces a voltage in the output coil. This voltage may be amplified and fed back to the input coil to cause recirculation just as is done in the mercury delay line.

The shifting register also may be used as a recirculating register, as is shown in Fig. 69*a*. Four CP_A and four CP_B must be applied to shift four bits into the register. At the end of the fourth CP_B, the first bit is stored in $S0_B$ and the last bit in $S3_B$.

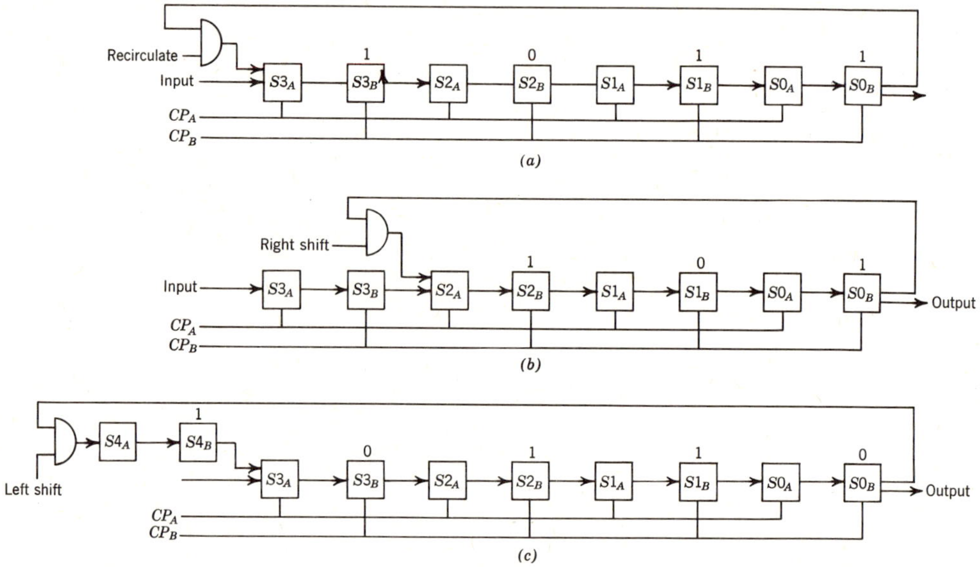

Figure 69 Recirculation and shifting. (*a*) Recirculating register. (*b*) Right shift—remove delay. (*c*) Left shift—add delay.

If now the Recirculation signal is applied, succeeding clock pulses cause bits from $S0_B$ to be shifted into $S3_A$. After four more CP_A and CP_B, all the bits are back to the same relative positions they were in upon completion of read-in.

If now the Right-Shift signal is applied (Fig. 69*b*), the total number of delay elements in the loop is ıeduced from eight to six. After the advent of three CP_A and CP_B, the first bit appears in $S0_B$. If now the Right-Shift signal is removed, the following CP_A and CP_B annihilate the first bit, and the rest of the number appears in the three rightmost positions of the register. The leftmost position contains ZERO.

Just as the removal of delay from the loop produces a right shift, the addition of delay produces a left shift. When the Left-Shift signal and four CP_A and CP_B are applied (Fig. 69*c*), the bits wind up in $S1_B$, $S2_B$, $S3_B$, and $S4_B$. If now $S4_A$ and $S4_B$ are cut off from the register, only the three leftmost bits are being stored in the register—$S3_B$, $S2_B$, and $S1_B$. The rightmost position, $S0_B$, is storing ZERO.

To feed information out of the register, a Read-Out signal (not shown) is applied for the time it takes four CP_A and CP_B to pass.

*Example

Assume the same clock, timing, and phasing pulses as before. Assume also a serial 10-bit source *AR*. Draw a diagram to show the serial load of a *D* Register during P_1 from *AR* at time t_2–t_{11}, when control signal *Y* is present, and recirculate and unload during P_2 at time t_2–t_{11}, when control signal *X* is present.

Figure 70*a* shows a recirculating shifting register diagram that accomplishes these tasks.

Shifting right or left also may be accomplished by controlling the number of clock pulses applied.

By connecting the output of the right side of the register to the input on the left side, a circular shift may be obtained. The difference between circular and noncircular shifts is that in the latter the bits shifted off the end are lost, whereas in the former they are placed in new positions at the opposite end of the register. Right and left circular shifts are explained with the aid of Fig. 71.

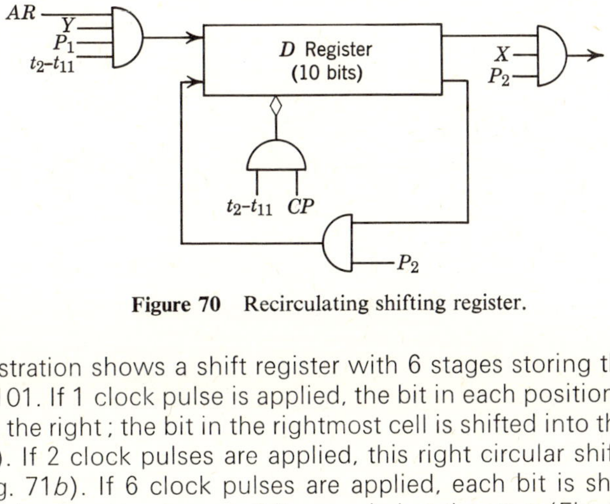

Figure 70 Recirculating shifting register.

The illustration shows a shift register with 6 stages storing the following 6 bits: 100101. If 1 clock pulse is applied, the bit in each position is shifted into the cell to the right; the bit in the rightmost cell is shifted into the leftmost cell (Fig. 71*a*). If 2 clock pulses are applied, this right circular shift is performed twice (Fig. 71*b*). If 6 clock pulses are applied, each bit is shifted 6 places, bringing it back to the same cell it occupied at the start (Fig. 71*c*). This is a normal circulation.

A circular left shift may be obtained by reversing the direction of flow shown. This implies the use of a new set of gates. However, if you realize that the circular right and circular left shift are related. no special gating is required. As is shown in Fig. 71*d*, if 5 clock pulses are applied, a circular right shift of 5 places is executed; but the result is equivalent to a circular left shift of 1 place. Similarly (see Fig. 71*e*), if 4 clock pulses are applied, a circular right shift of 4 places is executed, which is equivalent to a circular left shift of 2 places. Figure 71*f* shows that if 3 clock pulses are applied, this process may be called either a circular right shift or circular left shift of 3 places.

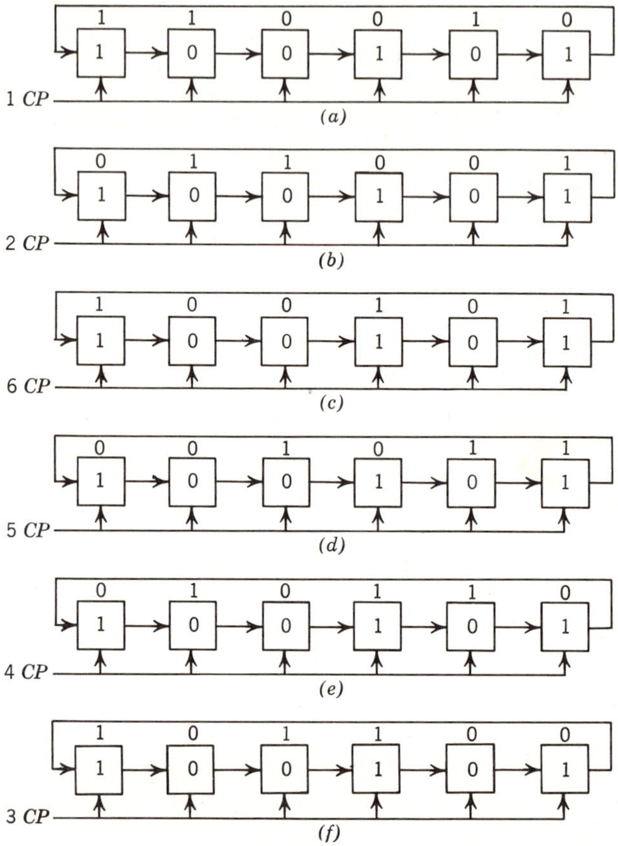

Figure 71 Circular shifting. (*a*) Right shift one place. (*b*) Right shift two places. (*c*) Recirculate. (*d*) Left shift one place. (*e*) Left shift two places. (*f*) Right shift *or* left shift three places.

COUNTERS

There are 4 types of digital counters in general use: modulus, ring, binary, and bit-coded. Each is described in turn.

Modulus Counter

A modulus counter is a device that produces an output pulse after a certain number of input pulses or multiple of this number are applied.

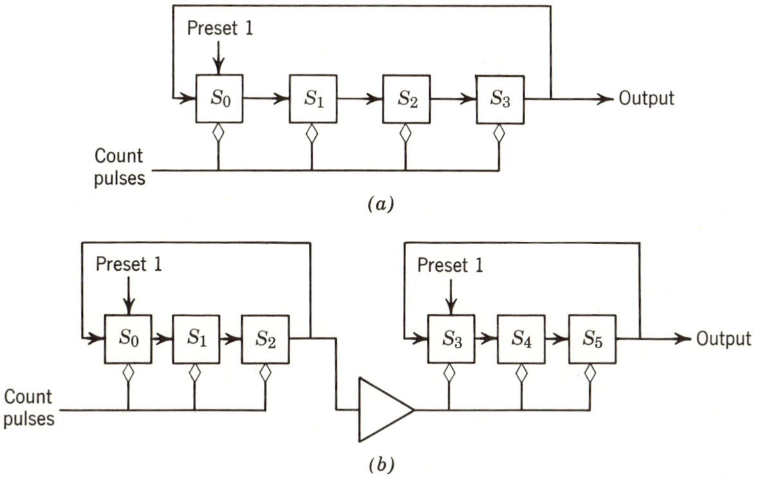

Figure 72 Modulus counters. (*a*) Modulo-4 counter. (*b*) Modulo-9 counter composed of two modulo-3 counters.

Figure 72*a* shows a shift register connected as a modulo-4 counter. A preset pulse sets S_0 before counting begins. Each count pulse applied acts as a shift pulse to produce a circular right shift of 1 place. After 4 count pulses, an output is produced. At the same time, the ONE is shifted into S_0 in order that counting may continue. After 4 more count pulses, another output is produced, and so on.

Figure 72*b* illustrates how a modulo-3 counter can feed another modulo-3 counter to produce a modulo-9 counter. The first counter produces a pulse after three counts. When this pulse is applied to the second counter, the ONE in the second counter moves to the next position. After two more counts of three, the ONE in the second counter is shifted to the output. Thus an output is produced after three times three or nine counts.

Example

Draw a diagram of a modulo-12 counter using only 7 storage cells.

The solution is given in Fig. 73. It consists of a modulo-3 counter feeding a modulo-4 counter. After each group of 3 count pulses, a pulse is applied to the modulo-4 counter. After 4 groups of 3 count pulses, the ONE in the modulo-4 counter appears at the output.

Ring Counters

A ring counter is a device consisting of a loop of interconnecting bistable elements, only one of which produces an output at any one time. Each successive count pulse causes a succeeding stage to produce an output. Two such counters are shown in Fig. 74.

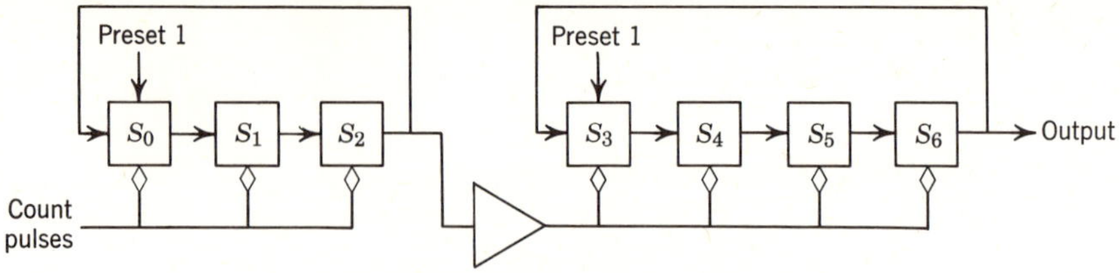

Figure 73 Modulo-12 counter.

The first (Fig. 74*a*) is obtained by modifying slightly the modulus counter. As successive count pulses are applied, outputs appear at 0, 1, 2, 3, and then at 0 again.

The second (Fig. 74*b*) is obtained by grouping flip-flops in such a way that when one stage is set, the previous stage is reset. Specifically, the counter works as follows: a start pulse sets *FF*0 at the beginning producing count 0. When a count pulse is applied, the ONE output of *FF*0 is gated into *FF*1 to set it; at the same time, the pulse is returned to the reset side of *FF*0 to reset it. An output now appears at 1. The next count pulse shifts this pulse to *FF*2 and at the same time resets *FF*1. This procedure continues as it counts 0, 1, 2, 3, and then back to 0, and so on.

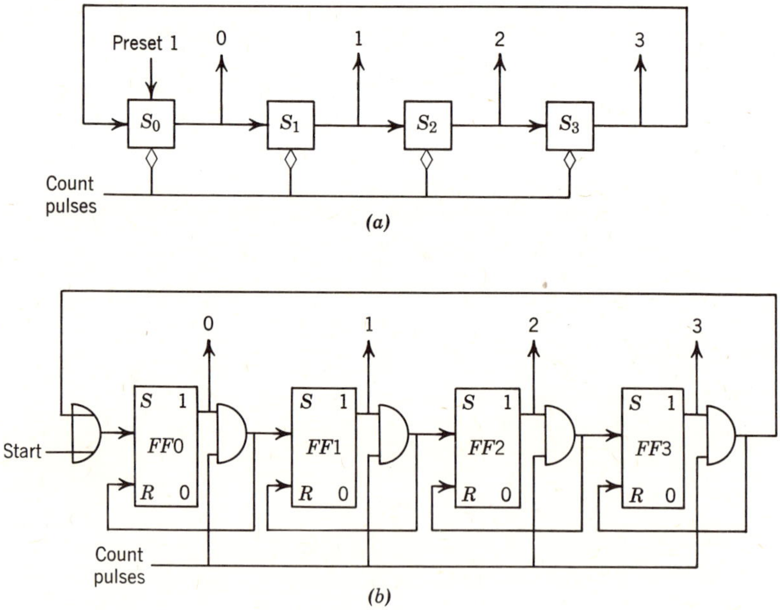

Figure 74 Ring counters. (*a*) Modification of modulus counter. (*b*) Set one stage; reset previous stage.

**Example*

Draw a diagram of a timing pulse generator producing the pulses given in Fig. 65.

Figure 75 presents the solution. This is a ring counter with 14 stages, and included are 3 additional flip-flops: two *R–S* flip-flops and one *T* flip-flop. One *R–S* flip-flop is set by a t_1 and reset by a t_{13}, thus producing a ONE output for the time beginning with the start of t_1 and ending with the start of t_{13}. Since the latter time coincides with the ending of t_{12}, this flip-flop produces t_1–t_{12}. Similarly, the second *R–S* flip-flop produces t_2–t_{11} by applying t_2 to the set side and t_{12} to the reset side. The *T* flip-flop produces the two phases. Assume that the first arriving t_0 places the flip-flop in the ONE state. Fourteen bit times later when t_0 arrives again, the flip-flop will be flipped to the reset state. Fourteen bit times after that a succeeding t_0 will flip the flip-flop back to the set state. Thus phases P_1 and P_2 are continuously produced.

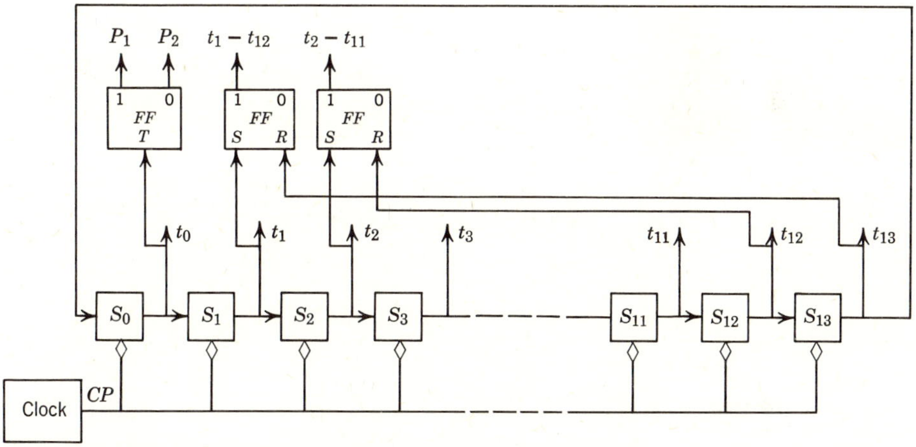

Figure 75 Timing pulse generator.

Binary Counter

A binary counter is a device that counts in the binary number system. The basic building block for a binary counter is the *T* flip-flop. This is true because it flips from 0 to 1 and then back to 0, and this is exactly the action required to count in the binary system.

As shown in Fig. 76*a*, the *T* flip-flop is logically equivalent to an *R–S* flip-flop with the feedback paths shown. An input pulse is applied to both input gates. If the flip-flop is storing ZERO, the upper gate opens to set the flip-flop. If the flip-flop is storing ONE, the lower gate opens to reset the flip-flop.

If each time the flip-flop is flipped to ZERO a positive pulse is fed to another

T flip-flop, this second flip-flop also flips back and forth but half as frequently.† If each time the second flip-flop is flipped to ZERO a positive pulse is applied to still another *T* flip-flop, this third flip-flop also flips back and forth but one-quarter as frequently. The result of placing in tandem such a group of *T* flip-flops is a binary counter (see Fig. 76*b*). The modulus of a 2-stage counter is 2^2; of a 3-stage counter 2^3; of a 4-stage counter 2^4. In other words, the modulus is 2 to an exponent given by the number of counting stages.

†*Note.* A capacitor is placed between stages in the binary counter diagram to show that the square wave produced when a flip-flop is flipped from the SET state to the RESET state is converted into a narrow positive trigger pulse for surer triggering of the succeeding stage.

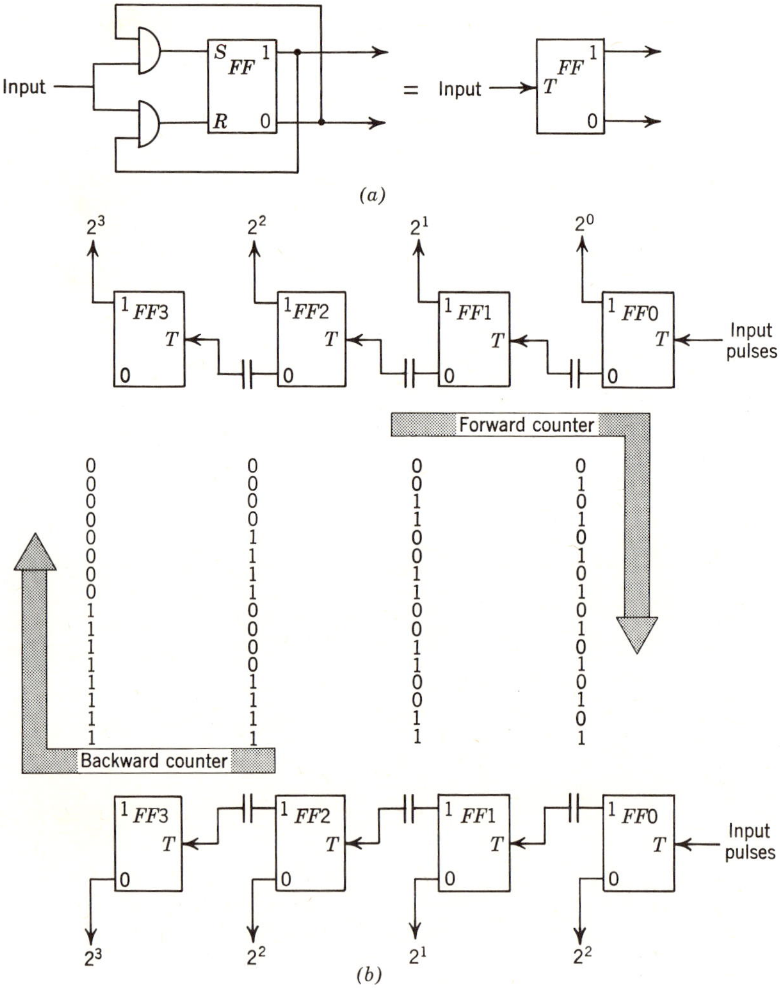

Figure 76 Binary Counter. (*a*) *T* flip-flop. (*b*) Binary counter.

The positive pulse produced when a flip-flop flips to ZERO is called a carry; the carry adds a ONE to the succeeding column. If the flip-flops are connected in such a way that a carry pulse is produced when flipping from ZERO to ONE, the result is a counter which counts backward (see bottom of Fig. 76*b*).

**Example*

Draw a diagram of a 2^6 forward-counting *P* counter which does the following.

1. During each P_1 phase it steps forward with the arrival of a t_0 pulse. However, if signal *S* is present but $\bar{A}$ is not, or *T* alone is present, then no stepping occurs.
2. If *A* and *N* signals are present, the counter is stepped again at t_{13}.
3. If either signal *T* or signals *A* and *S* are present, the 6 bits of *IR* are entered in parallel at t_0.
4. Read-out occurs in parallel during the P_2 phase at time t_0.

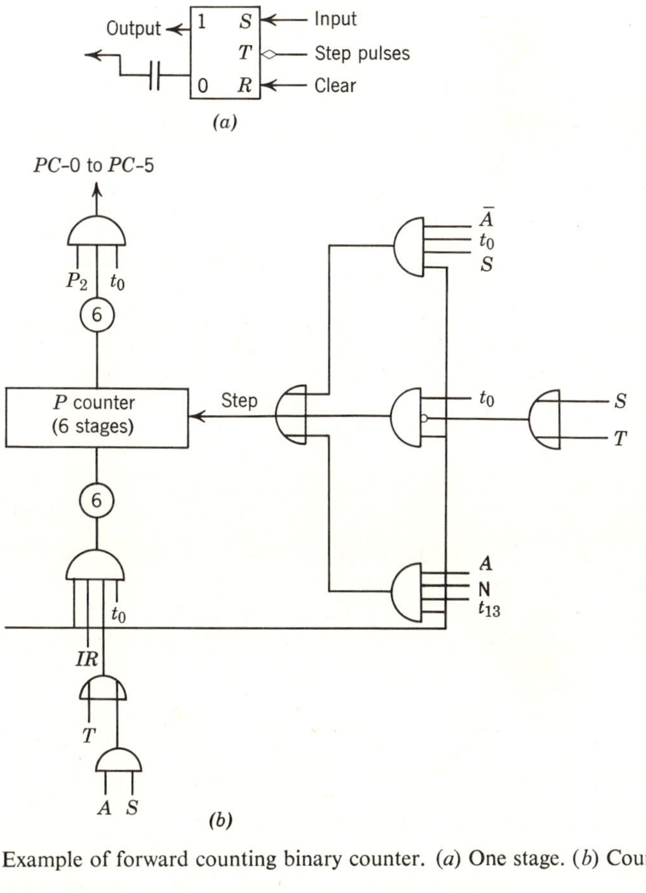

Figure 77 Example of forward counting binary counter. (*a*) One stage. (*b*) Counter.

Figure 77*b* shows the solution, and Fig. 77*a* shows one of the 6 stages of the counter. Notice that a Clear pulse applied simultaneously to all stages brings the counter back to zero.

**Example*

Draw a diagram of a backward counting *M* counter and an associated decoder, which starts counting with binary 11 (eleven), and with each timing cycle counts down until it reaches ZERO. Three signals issue from the decoder as follows:

$$\alpha — 1011$$
$$\beta — 1010 \text{ to } 0001$$
$$\gamma — 0000$$

A *D* signal is used to start the count. When in the α mode, the stepping occurs at t_{13}. When in the β mode the stepping occurs at t_1 but only if signal *S* is present.

Figure 78*b* shows the solution, and Fig. 78*a* presents one stage of the counter. The decoder is similar to the decoders discussed in the previous chapter.

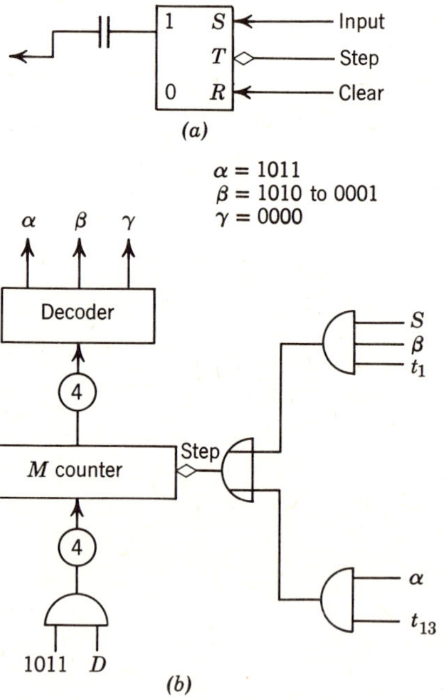

Figure 78 Example of backward counting binary counter. (*a*) One stage of counter. (*b*) Counter.

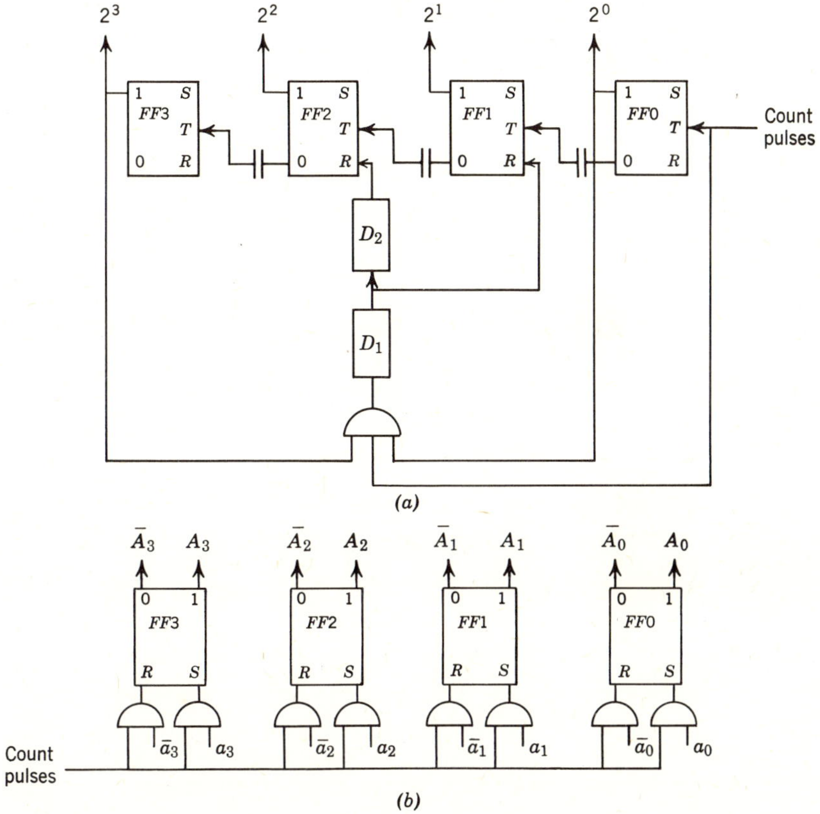

Figure 79 Bit-coded counters. (*a*) Binary-coded decimal counter. (*b*) General bit-coded counter. (*Note:* a_0 to a_3 and $\bar{a}_0$ to $\bar{a}_3$ are functions of A_0 to A_3 and $\bar{A}_1$ to $\bar{A}_3$.)

Bit-Coded Counter

A 4-stage counter counts to 16. By removing the last six binary combinations in the sequence, this counter can be made to count from 0 to 9. The last six binary combinations are removed by means of the AND circuit and delay elements shown in Fig. 79*a*. The counter operates normally until it reads 1001 or binary 9. When this occurs, *FF*0 and *FF*3 are storing a ONE—they prime the AND circuit. When the next count pulse arrives, *FF*0 is flipped to ZERO, and the AND circuit allows *FF*1 and *FF*2 to be reset to ZERO. Delay D_1 makes sure FF_1 is flipped to ZERO after the carry from *FF*0 had flipped *FF*1 to ONE. Delay D_2 makes sure *FF*2 is flipped to ZERO after the carry from *FF*1 had flipped *FF*2 to ONE. Flipping *FF*2 to ZERO produces a carry which flips *FF*3 to ZERO too. The tenth count pulse, therefore, makes the counter read 0000. Further counting is in normal binary until 1001 is again reached.

Instead of the above binary-coded decimal, the bit coding may follow many different rules or it may even be irregular. Regardless of the pattern, a 4 stage bit-coded counter may be depicted as the one shown in Fig. 79*b*. Here inputs a_0 to a_3 and $\bar{a}_0$ to $\bar{a}_3$ are functions of the A_0 to A_3 and $\bar{A}_0$ to $\bar{A}_3$ outputs. What these functions are is determined by the counting sequence desired.

Example

Determine the functions a_0 to a_3 and $\bar{a}_0$ to $\bar{a}_3$ to produce a counter that counts in the following order:

	A_3	A_2	A_1	A_0		A_3	A_2	A_1	A_0
0	0	0	0	0	5	0	1	1	1
1	0	0	0	1	6	0	1	0	1
2	0	0	1	1	7	0	1	0	0
3	0	0	1	0	8	1	1	0	0
4	0	1	1	0	9	1	1	0	1

Input a_0 should be activated whenever we want A_0 to switch from ZERO to ONE; this occurs when switching from count 0 to 1, count 4 to 5, and count 8 to 9. The output conditions at counts from which switching occurs are

Count 0	$\bar{A}_3$	$\bar{A}_2$	$\bar{A}_1$	$\bar{A}_0$	Count 8	A_3	A_2	$\bar{A}_1$	$\bar{A}_0$
Count 4	$\bar{A}_3$	A_2	A_1	$\bar{A}_0$					

Therefore

$$a_0 = \bar{A}_3\bar{A}_2\bar{A}_1\bar{A}_0 + \bar{A}_3A_2A_1\bar{A}_0 + A_3A_2\bar{A}_1\bar{A}_0$$

Similarly, input $\bar{a}_0$ should be activated whenever we want to switch from ONE to ZERO; this occurs from count 2 to 3, from count 6 to 7, and from count 9 to 0. Therefore

$$\bar{a}_0 = \bar{A}_3\bar{A}_2A_1A_0 + \bar{A}_3A_2\bar{A}_1A_0 + A_3A_2\bar{A}_1A_0$$

In a similar manner, a_1 should be activated when we want A_1 to switch from ZERO to ONE, and $\bar{a}_1$ should be activated when we want A_1 to switch from ONE to ZERO. Similarly for the other inputs. The remaining equations, therefore, are

$$a_1 = \bar{A}_3\bar{A}_2\bar{A}_1A_0$$
$$\bar{a}_1 = \bar{A}_3A_2A_1A_0$$

$$a_2 = \bar{A}_3\bar{A}_2A_1\bar{A}_0$$
$$\bar{a}_2 = A_3A_2\bar{A}_1A_0$$

$$a_3 = \bar{A}_3A_2\bar{A}_1\bar{A}_0$$
$$\bar{a}_3 = A_3A_2\bar{A}_1A_0$$

Simple 4-input gates may be used together with OR circuits to produce these functions, which then are applied as inputs to the general bit-coded counter given in Fig. 79*b*.

SUMMARY

1. Registers and counters are functional blocks that are needed to introduce the factor of time into logic structures.
2. A register introduces this time factor by acting as a temporary storage device. It may delay bits or a collection of bits to determine sequencing with reference to some operation; to adjust speed of bit flow; to vary type of bit flow; or to rearrange the combination of bits.
3. Registers normally include Read-In gates that determine when data are entered; and Read-Out gates that determine when data are taken out. Movement of bits between cells of a register is accomplished by means of clock and timing pulses, or by means of delay elements.
4. Shifting registers often consist of a group of flip-flops. A delay element may be connected between stages to assure that a flip-flop does not flip before it has a chance to transfer its contents to the succeeding flip-flop. A double-rank register produces the same results by applying different clock phases to alternate cells in the register.
5. A combination of bits in a register may be shifted right or left by controlling the number of clock pulses applied or by controlling the amount of delay.
6. A counter is a register that has been modified to produce a specific sequence of bit combinations.
7. Modulus and ring counters can count up to the number of stages in the counter. Two or more modulus counters may be combined to produce counts equal to the product of the individual counters. Binary and bit-coded counters can produce a total count equal to 2 taken to the power of the number of stages in the counter.
8. *Definitions to Remember*

   Clear. To restore a storage device to a prescribed state, usually Zero.

   Clock. A circuit or some physical arrangement that produces pulses at a steady rate.

   Clock Pulse. One of a stream of pulses occurring at a constant frequency.

   Register. A device or circuit used to store, temporarily, numbers consisting of several digits.

   Shifting Register. A register consisting of discrete storage cells, and in which bits may be advanced from one cell to the other by means of applied shift pulses.

   Double-Rank Register. A shifting register consisting of two rows of storage cells; one row for actual storage of the bits, the other row for temporary storage of bits while they are being shifted to another stage.

   Parallel Storage. Storage in which all bits, characters or words, are essentially equally available in space. Time is not one of the coordinates.

   Right Shift. An operation in which the bits in a register are moved a given number of positions to the right. Bits removed from the right-hand side are dropped.

Right Circular Shift. An operation in which the bits in a register are moved a given number of positions to the right. Bits removed from the right-hand side are reentered at the left.

Left Shift. An operation in which the bits in a register are moved a given number of positions to the left. Bits removed from the left-hand side are dropped.

Left Circular Shift. An operation in which bits in a register are moved a given number of positions to the left. Bits removed from the left-hand side are reentered at the right.

Modulus Counter. A device that produces an output pulse after a certain number of input pulses or multiples of this number are applied.

Ring Counter. A device consisting of a loop of interconnecting bistable elements, only one of which can be in a specified state at any time. Each successive applied pulse causes another element in the loop to switch to the specified state.

Binary Counter. A device or circuit that counts in the binary number system and produces numbers consisting of 1–0 combinations when pulses are applied to its input.

Bit-Coded Counter. A device or circuit that, when pulses are applied to its input, produces 1–0 combinations representing binary-coded numbers.

Buffer Storage. A storage device used to accommodate differences in the rate of flow or in the method of transmission between two devices when transmitting information from one to the other.

Exercises

1. In Fig. 63*a*, if the frequency of timing pulse input is 1 megacycle, how long should the READ-IN signal be? READ-OUT? What should the delays D_1 to D_3 be in fig. 63*b* to produce the same frequency of operation?
2. In exercise 1, how should the timing pulses be applied in order that output be in reverse order from input?
3. If input to the register in Fig. 64*a* is to be at a 100 kc rate and output at a 500 kc rate:
   a. What should the frequency of CP_1 be?
   b. Of CP_2?
   c. For a 10-stage register, what should be the length of READ-IN? READ-OUT?
4. If in Fig. 64*b*, the *CP* is 1 mc, how long would read-in take for a 10-stage register? If the READ-OUT signal is gated in by 1 clock pulse, how long does read-out take?
5. If in Fig. 64*c*, it takes 2 μs to read-in the data in parallel and 20 μs to read-out the data in serial from a 10-stage register, what is the clock frequency needed?

6. Draw a logical diagram of a double buffer such that when one buffer is loading, the other buffer is unloading and vice versa. All flow is parallel.
7. Repeat exercise 6 for serial flow.
8. Repeat exercise 6 for serial input and parallel output for both buffers.
9. Draw a logical diagram of a register that is loaded in parallel one-half register at a time and that then unloads the entire register in series.
10. What is the frequency of operation of a double rank shift register if the frequency of both CP_A and CP_B is 1 megacycle?
11. If 10011011 is stored in an 8-stage shift register, and 3 clock pulses are applied to cause a right shift of 3 places;
    a. What are the contents of the register after this operation?
    b. What are the contents after a shift left of 4 places?
    c. What would the contents be in each case if the shifts were circular?
12. Draw a logical diagram of a device that produces an output only for each alternate pulse applied.
13. What is the minimum number of total stages required to produce a modulus counter counting to 15? 10?
14. Draw a logical diagram of a 4-count binary counter plus a decoder which causes 1 out of 4 lines to be chosen for each of the 4 counts.
15. In Fig. 79*b*, determine a_0 to a_3 and $\bar{a}_0$ to $\bar{a}_3$ to produce a counter counting in Excess-3 code.
16. What is the highest number a 5-stage binary counter can count to? An 8-stage counter?
17. How many places must a binary number be shifted in order to;
    a. Multiply it by 4?
    b. Divide by 8?
    c. In what direction must the shift take place for each of the above?
18. How can shifting be used to extract the bit combination shown by means of a bar in each of the following cases?
    a. 1010111001
    b. 1010111001
    c. 1010111001

CHAPTER 8

Comparators and Adders

To perform arithmetic and other logical operations, several functional building blocks must be added to the arsenal developed up to this point. Among the most important of these functional building blocks are the binary comparator, parity generators and detectors, complementers, binary adders, binary subtractors, and accumulators.

BINARY COMPARATOR

Figure 80 presents a summary of facts given earlier on the binary comparator or exclusive OR circuit. Since this block compares two bits and produces a ONE when they are unequal and a ZERO when they are equal, it is an important functional block in the building of arithmetic units.

Example

Write the truth table, equation, and draw a logical block diagram for a device that compares two bits and produces a ONE when they are equal and a ZERO when unequal. Prove that this device produces the inverse of the binary comparator.

Figure 81 shows the truth table, equation, and logical block diagram. The equation is

$$K = A \cdot B + \bar{A} \cdot \bar{B}$$

The inverse of this is

$$\overline{A \cdot B + \bar{A} \cdot \bar{B}} = (\overline{A \cdot B}) \cdot (\overline{\bar{A} \cdot \bar{B}})$$
$$= (\overline{A \cdot B}) \cdot (A + B)$$

which is the equation for the binary comparator.

Notice that the equation for the inverse of the binary comparator is the equation representing the relation of "if and only if."

A	B	K
0	0	0
0	1	1
1	0	1
1	1	0

$$K = \bar{A} \cdot B + A \cdot \bar{B}$$

(a)

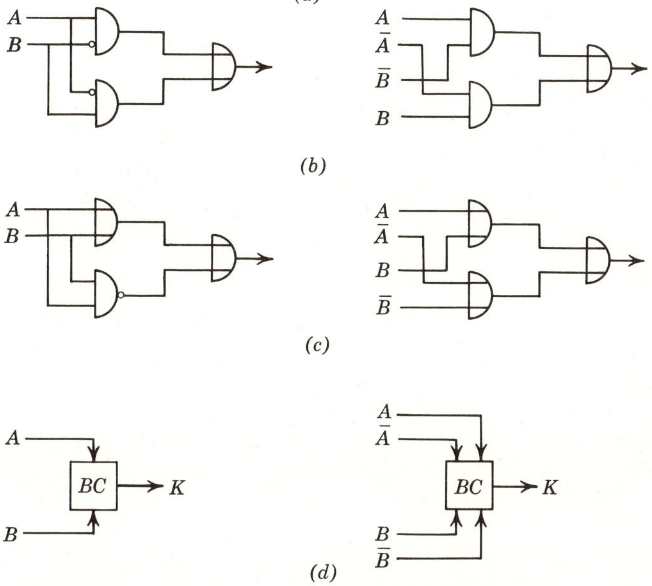

Figure 80 Binary comparator. (*a*) Truth table and equation. (*b*) $K = \bar{A} \cdot B + A \cdot \bar{B}$. (*c*) $K = (A + B)\,\overline{(A \cdot B)}$. (*d*) Representation.

**Example*

Draw a block diagram of a sign circuit (the reason for the name will become obvious in the chapter on arithmetic) using binary comparators, flip-flops, and gates, which performs according to the following truth table:

A	D	C	O	S
1	1	1	0	1
0	1	1	0	0
1	0	1	0	0
0	0	1	1	0
1	1	0	1	1
0	1	0	0	1
1	0	0	0	1
0	0	0	0	0

In this truth table, both *O* and *S* depend on the three variables *A*, *D*, and *C*.

A	B	K
0	0	1
0	1	0
1	0	0
1	1	1

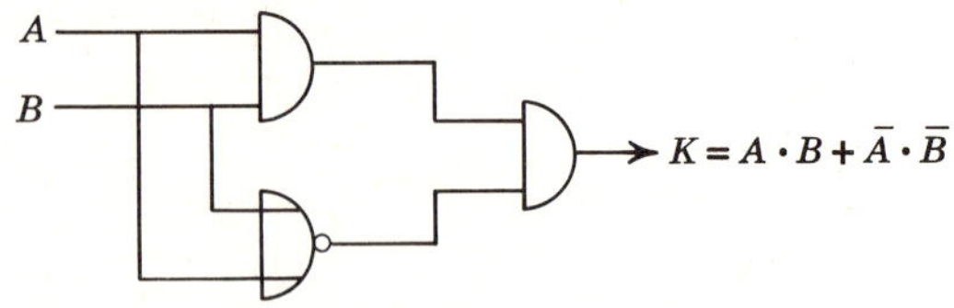

Figure 81 Inverse of binary comparator.

To obtain the block diagram shown in Fig. 82, which is the solution, one must observe that O is ONE or ZERO depending on whether the sum of the bits A, D, and C is odd or even, respectively. Following through a special case may help in understanding. Suppose $A=0$, $D=0$, and $C=1$. The output of $BC-O$ equals ZERO. This ZERO combined with $C=1$ causes $BC-1$ to produce a ONE. Since $\bar{A} \cdot \bar{D} \cdot C = 1$, the output of $BC-2$ is ZERO, which agrees with the table.

PARITY GENERATORS AND DETECTORS

As was indicated earlier, parity bits may be used for the checking of data. The extra bit that is placed next to the representation of a character is called a vertical parity bit. This is in contrast to horizontal parity, which is given by an extra character such that each bit position of this character is the parity sum of the bits of all the characters in that position. Table 18 shows the difference

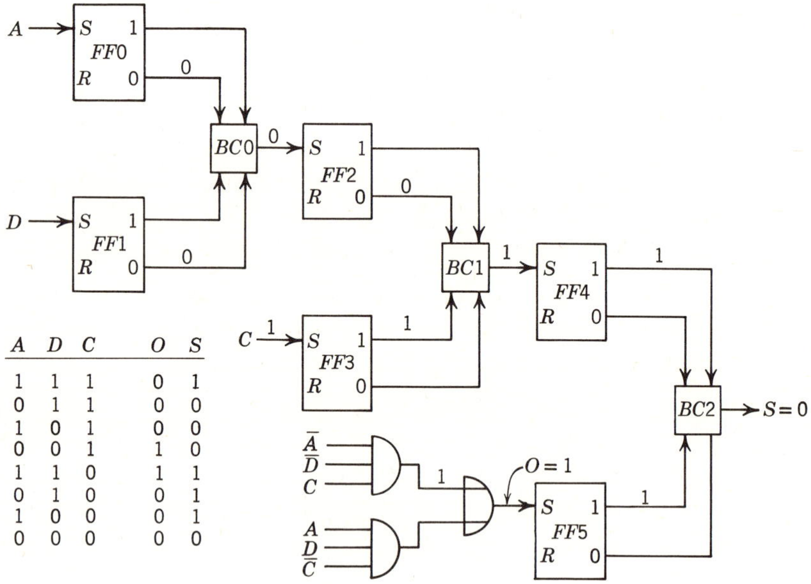

A	D	C	O	S
1	1	1	0	1
0	1	1	0	0
1	0	1	0	0
0	0	1	1	0
1	1	0	1	1
0	1	0	0	1
1	0	0	0	1
0	0	0	0	0

Figure 82 Sign circuit.

between vertical and horizontal even parity. Notice that the sum of all the bits across any row or along any column is even. The horizontal parity character is used for the checking of messages. The rules for generating the parity bits are similar for the two types of parity, except that different bit positions are summed in the two cases.

table 18 VERTICAL AND HORIZONTAL PARITY (EVEN)

Bit order \ Character order	1	2	3	4	5	6	7	8	9	10	Horizontal parity character
1	1	1	0	0	1	0	1	0	1	1	0
2	0	1	0	1	1	0	1	0	1	0	1
3	1	0	1	0	1	0	0	0	0	0	1
4	1	0	1	1	0	0	0	0	0	0	1
5	0	0	1	1	0	1	0	0	1	0	0
6	0	0	0	0	1	1	1	1	1	1	0
Vertical parity bit	1	0	1	1	0	0	1	1	0	0	1

Vertical Parity Generators and Detectors

Figure 83*a* shows a simple vertical parity generator for a character of 6 bits. At time t_0, the *T* flip-flop is reset. During each successive bit-time from t_1 to t_6, one of the succeeding bits is applied to the *T* flip-flop. A ZERO does not cause any change. But each successive 1 causes the flip-flop to change states. This means that if there are an odd number of 1's in the character, the state of the flip-flop will be ONE after t_6. At t_7 this ONE is gated out to become the parity bit.

If there are an even number of 1's in the character, the flip-flop will be in the ZERO state after t_6, and t_7 would gate 0 into the seventh or parity position.

Since in this system, there are always an even number of 1's to a complete character representation, the device is called an even parity generator.

A vertical parity detector works in a similar manner. As can be seen in Fig. 83*b*, during t_0, the *T* flip-flop is reset, and during t_1 to t_6 the 1's are summed. At t_7 the state of the *T* flip-flop is compared with the parity bit by means of a binary comparator. In the illustration the representation 0101100 is checked. After t_6, the flip-flop is in the ONE state. During t_7, this 1 is compared with. the 0 parity bit. The result is an output pulse signifying a parity error.

**Example*

Draw a block diagram of a vertical odd parity generator and detector for characters 11 bits long.

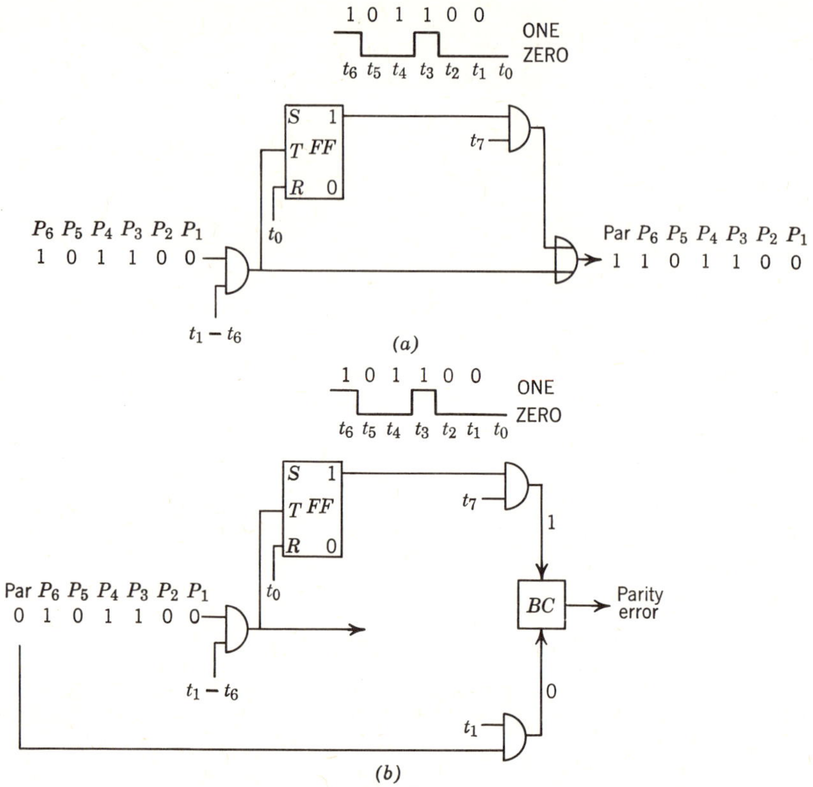

Figure 83 Vertical even parity generator and detector. (*a*) Parity generator. (*b*) Parity detector.

The solution is shown in Fig. 84. To achieve odd parity, the t_0 signal is used to set the flip-flop rather than to reset it, as was done for the even parity generator. The eleven bits of the character are gated in by t_1 to t_{11}. After an odd number of 1's have flipped the flip-flop, the flip-flop will be in state ZERO. After an even number of flips, the flip-flop will be in state ONE. At t_{12}, the state of the flip-flop is gated out to be the odd parity bit.

Similarly, for the odd parity detector, except that at t_{12} the state of the flip-flop is compared to the parity bit. If the two are the same—as is shown in the illustration—no output is produced. An odd parity error signal is produced if the two are not the same.

Horizontal Parity Generators and Detectors

Horizontal parity generators and detectors are constructed the same way as vertical parity generators and detectors, except that different bits are applied to the circuit. This is shown by example.

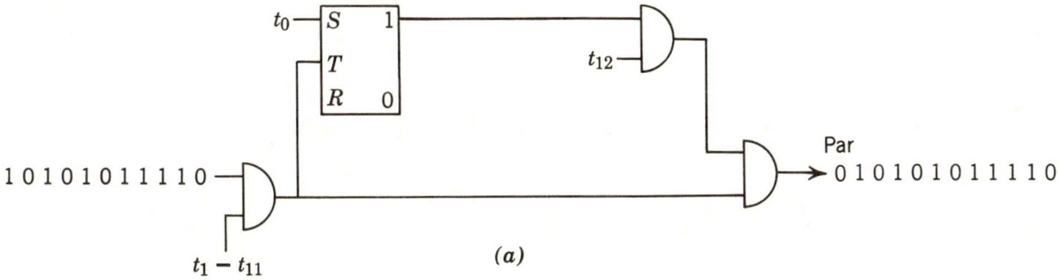

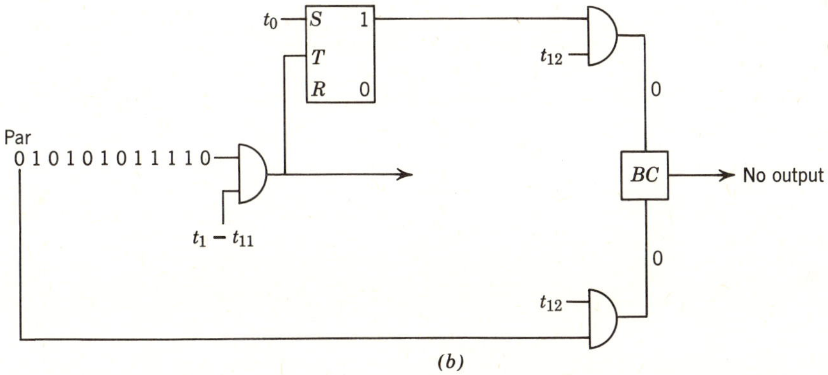

Figure 84 Vertical odd parity generator and detector. (*a*) Odd parity generator. (*b*) Odd parity detector.

Example

Given the following table of successive characters appearing at the times indicated:

	P_3	P_2	P_1	P_0
t_1	1	1	1	1
t_2	1	1	1	0
t_3	0	1	1	1
t_4	0	0	1	1
t_5	1	0	0	1
t_6	1	1	0	1
t_7	1	1	1	1
t_8	1	0	1	0
t_9	1	0	1	1
t_{10}	0	1	0	0
t_{11}	1	1	0	0

where the last character is the horizontal odd parity character for the 10 previous characters. Draw a block diagram of a detector that would check the horizontal parity character. For the case given, does a parity error exist?

	P_3	P_2	P_1	P_0
t_1	1	1	1	1
t_2	1	1	1	0
t_3	0	1	1	1
t_4	0	0	1	1
t_5	1	0	0	1
t_6	1	1	0	1
t_7	1	1	1	1
t_8	1	0	1	0
t_9	1	0	1	1
t_{10}	0	1	0	0
t_{11}	1	1	0	0

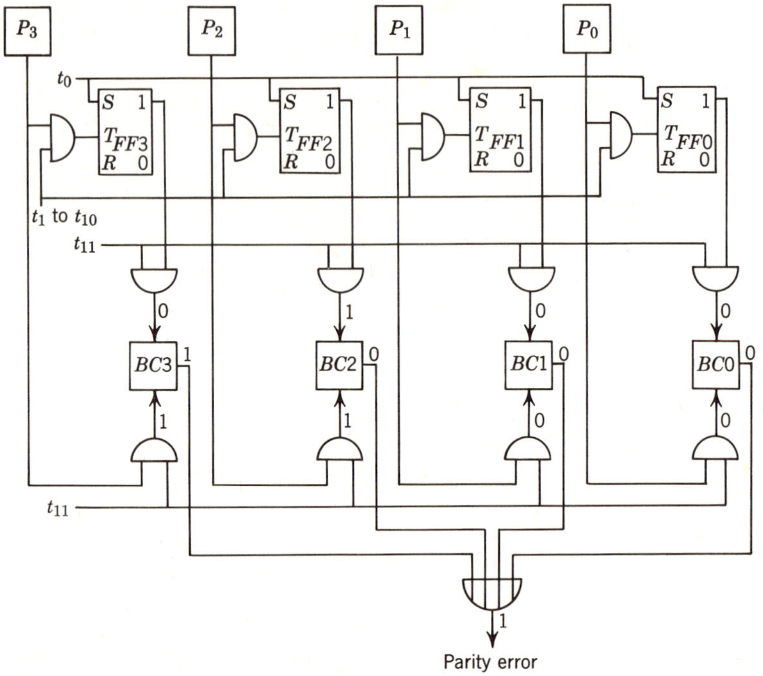

Figure 85 Horizontal parity detector.

The solution is given in Fig. 85. Essentially the circuit consists of four parity detectors similar to that given in Fig. 84. At t_0 the four T flip-flops are set. During t_1 to t_{10} the bits in each column are fed successively to the associated T flip-flop. With the bits given, the flip-flops are storing 0100 after t_{10}. At t_{11}, this is compared with 1100, and an error signal is produced.

COMPLEMENTERS

A complementer converts a binary number to its complement—1's complement or 2's complement.

A simple gate such as that shown in Fig. 86*a* is enough to produce the 1's complement of a binary number. Each bit of the character in the illustration is inverted as it passes through.

A 2's complementer is only slightly more complicated, as is shown in Fig. 86*b*. This circuit produces the 2's complement by following this procedure.

> Inspect each bit in turn, starting with the least significant bit. Do not change all zeros to the left of the first significant bit and the first significant bit. Change remaining ONE's to ZERO's and ZERO's to ONE's.

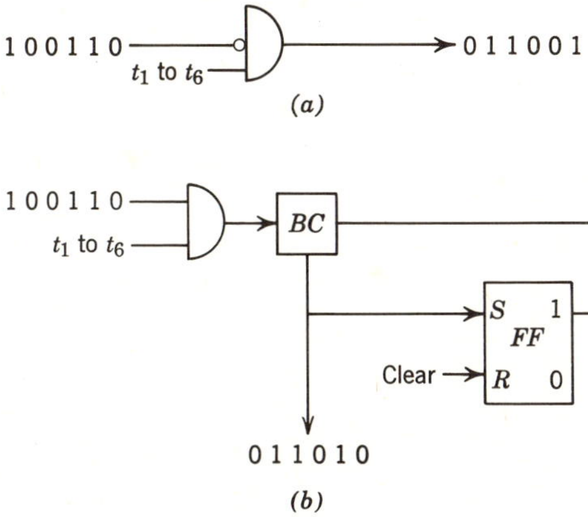

Figure 86 Complement generators. (*a*) 1's complement generator. (*b*) 2's complement generator.

The circuit works as follows. The flip-flop is first cleared to ZERO, thus making the lower input to the binary comparator ZERO. The bits of the number are applied to the other input to the binary comparator. If the bit is ZERO, a ZERO appears at the output. When the first ONE appears, a ONE appears at the output. It also sets the flip-flop to ONE and thus keeps a ONE at the lower input to the comparator. If the following input bit is a ONE, the two ONE's at the comparator produce a ZERO output. If a following bit is a ZERO, the ONE and ZERO combination produces a ONE output. The output is therefore the 2's complement of the input.

The illustration shows the character 100110 converted to its 2's complement, which is 011010.

Example

Draw a block diagram of a circuit that converts negative six-bit characters to their 1's complement but allows positive six-bit characters to pass through unchanged. A negative sign may be represented by a 1 in the least significant position; a positive sign may be represented by a zero in this position.

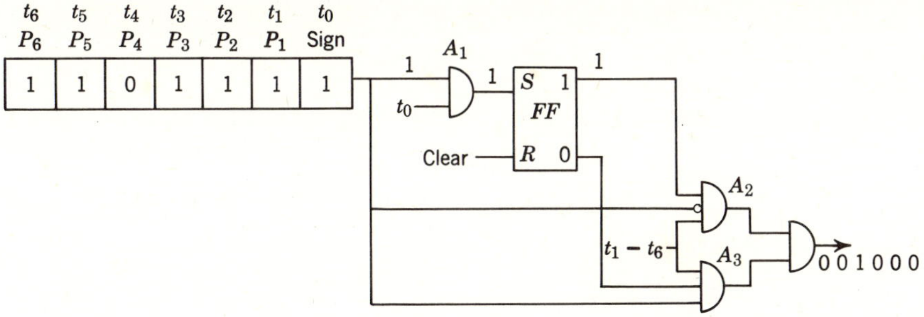

Figure 87 Complementer example.

The solution is shown in Fig. 87. At t_0, if the sign is minus, it sets the flip-flop; if it is plus, the flip-flop remains reset. If the flip-flop is set, the other bits are applied to A_2 and the 1's complement is output. If it is reset, the bits are applied to A_3 and the same bits appear at the output.

COINCIDENCE ADDERS AND SUBTRACTORS

Addition and subtraction are comparison-type processes: two numbers are compared to produce another number. The bits comprising the numbers may be compared one at a time—serially; or all at the same time—in parallel. The basic functional building blocks that may be used, in either serial or parallel arrangements, are the binary adder and binary subtractor.

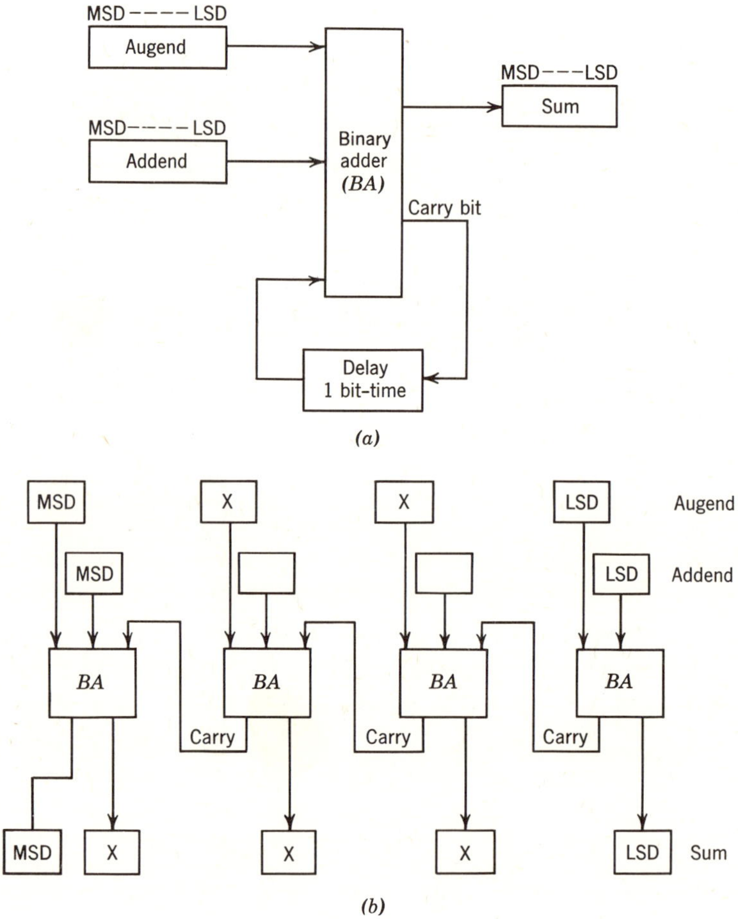

Figure 88 Serial and parallel addition. (*a*) Serial. (*b*) Parallel.

Serial and Parallel Addition

Figure 88 shows the difference in use of the binary adder (*BA*) in serial and parallel addition.

In serial addition only one binary adder is needed. During the first bit-time, the least significant augend and addend bits are applied to the binary adder to produce a sum bit and a carry bit. The carry bit is applied through a 1-bit-time delay circuit to the input side of the binary adder. During the second bit-time, the binary adder adds the second least significant augend and addend bits plus the carry bit from the least significant position. In each succeeding bit-time the following bits are added plus any carry from the previous position. After a word-time, a complete sum is produced.

A	*B*	*S*	*C*
0	0	0	0
0	1	1	0
1	0	1	0
1	1	0	1

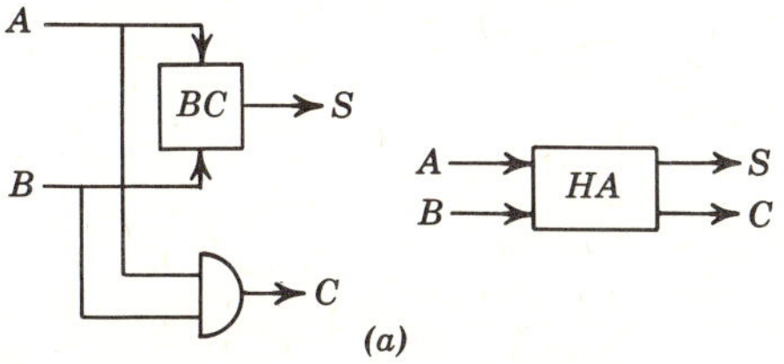

(*a*)

A	*B*	S_1	*C'*	*S*	*C*
0	0	0	0	0	0
0	0	0	1	1	0
0	1	1	0	1	0
0	1	1	1	0	1
1	0	1	0	1	0
1	0	1	1	0	1
1	1	0	0	0	1
1	1	0	1	1	1

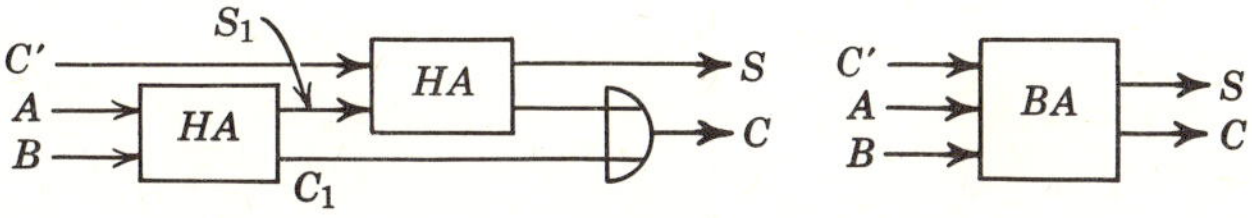

(*b*)

Figure 89 Half adder; binary adder. (*a*) Half adder. (*b*) Binary adder.

In parallel addition, as many binary adders are needed as there are bits to a word. The augend and addend bits in each position are added separately to produce all the bits of the sum and carries where appropriate. The carries are then applied to the following columns to modify the sum.

Binary Adder

The binary adder (*BA*) compares 2 bits (*A* and *B*) plus a carry bit (*C'*) to produce sum (*S*) and carry (*C*) bits. As has been shown previously, such a binary adder (*BA*) may be built of two half adders (*HA*), as is illustrated in Fig. 89*b*. This illustration is somewhat easier to understand if *HA* is drawn to consist of a *BC* and a gate. The first *HA* in Fig. 89*b* produces S_1 whenever *A* and *B* are unequal; the second *HA* produces *S* whenever S_1 and *C'* are unequal. The carry bit *C* is produced whenever *A* and *B* are equal to 1, or when S_1 and *C'* are equal to 1.

It also has been shown that the sum (S) and carry (C) equations may be expressed as follows:

$$S = \bar{A}\cdot\bar{B}\cdot C' + A\cdot B\cdot C' + \bar{A}\cdot B\cdot\bar{C}' + A\cdot\bar{B}\cdot\bar{C}'$$
$$C = A\cdot B\cdot C' + A\cdot B\cdot\bar{C}' + \bar{A}\cdot B\cdot C' + A\cdot\bar{B}\cdot C'$$

The logical block diagram representing these circuits is given in Fig. 90*a*.

Example

Show that the following expressions are equivalent to the above expressions for S and C:

$$S = C'(\overline{\bar{A}\cdot B + A\cdot\bar{B}}) + \bar{C}'(\bar{A}\cdot B + A\cdot\bar{B})$$
$$C = A\cdot B + C'(\bar{A}\cdot B + A\cdot\bar{B})$$

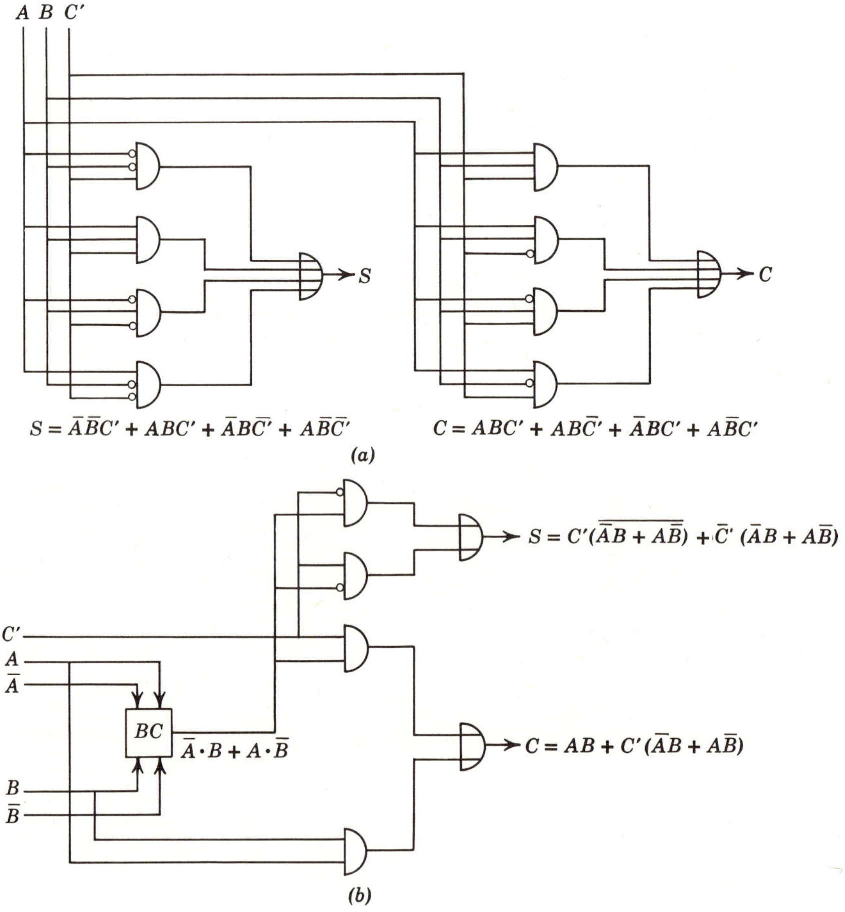

Figure 90 Two representations of a binary adder.

Draw a block diagram of this binary adder.

The C' and $\bar{C}'$ may be factored out of the sum equations as follows:

$$S = C'(\bar{A} \cdot \bar{B} + A \cdot B) + \bar{C}'(\bar{A} \cdot B + A \cdot \bar{B})$$

We know that

$$\bar{A} \cdot \bar{B} + A \cdot B = (\overline{\bar{A} \cdot B + A \cdot \bar{B}})$$

Therefore

$$S = C'(\overline{\bar{A} \cdot B + A \cdot \bar{B}}) + \bar{C}'(\bar{A} \cdot B + A \cdot \bar{B})$$

Similarly, the carry equation may be simplified by factoring as follows:

$$C = A \cdot B(C' + \bar{C}') + C'(\bar{A} \cdot B + A \cdot \bar{B})$$

This is equal to

$$C = A \cdot B + C'(\bar{A} \cdot B + A \cdot \bar{B})$$

The logical block diagram for the binary adder is shown in Fig. 90*b*. First a *BC* circuit is used to produce $\bar{A} \cdot B + A \cdot \bar{B}$. This expression is combined with C' in AND and INHIBIT gates to produce the following terms:

$$C'(\bar{A} \cdot B + A \cdot \bar{B})$$
$$\bar{C}'(\bar{A} \cdot B + A \cdot \bar{B})$$
$$C'(\overline{\bar{A} \cdot B + A \cdot \bar{B}})$$

$A \cdot B$ is produced by a simple AND circuit. The terms are then OR'd as shown.

**Example*

Draw a block diagram of an adder and complementer that operates as follows. When a Don't Complement signal is applied, it operates on the augend (A), addend (D) and carry (C') from the last position to produce the sum (S) and carry (C) bits. When a Complement signal is applied, the 1's complement of the addend is taken and added to the augend (D) and to the carry (C') from the last position. Do this by a coincidence circuit requiring binary comparators and gates.

Figure 91 illustrates the solution. The add table in the illustration is a truth table showing the conditions under which sum and carry bits are produced during simple addition. These conditions may be summarized by the following logical expressions:

$$S = A \cdot \bar{D} \cdot \bar{C}' + \bar{A} \cdot D \cdot \bar{C}' + \bar{A} \cdot \bar{D} \cdot C' + A \cdot D \cdot C'$$
$$C = A \cdot D \cdot \bar{C}' + A \cdot \bar{D} \cdot C' + \bar{A} \cdot D \cdot C' + A \cdot D \cdot C'$$

The complement and add table is a truth table showing the conditions under which sum and carry bits are produced if the addend bit is assumed to be complemented first. Note that the S and C bits are obtained by assuming a value of 1 for each D bit which is 0, and a value of 0 for each D bit which is 1. This truth table may be summarized by the following logical expressions:

$$S_C = \bar{A} \cdot \bar{D} \cdot \bar{C}' + A \cdot D \cdot \bar{C}' + A \cdot \bar{D} \cdot C' + \bar{A} \cdot D \cdot C'$$
$$C_C = A \cdot \bar{D} \cdot \bar{C}' + \bar{A} \cdot \bar{D} \cdot C' + A \cdot \bar{D} \cdot C' + A \cdot D \cdot C'$$

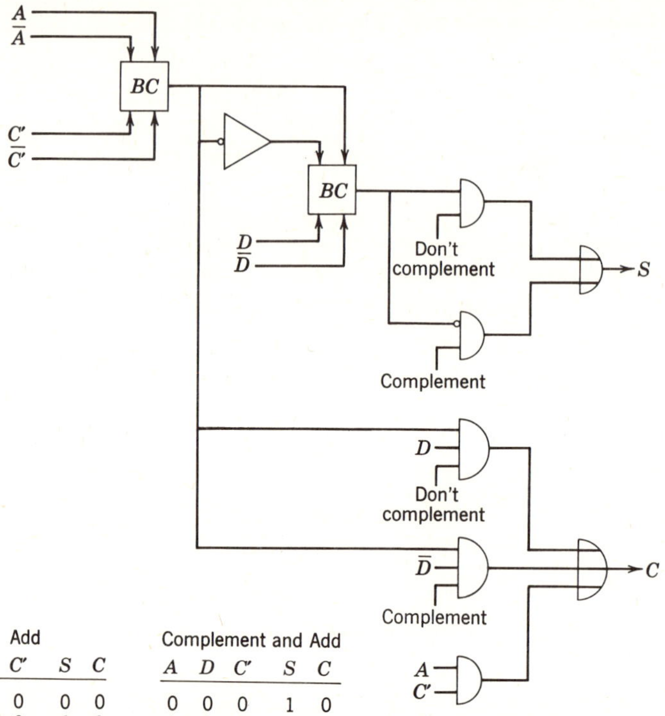

Add

A	D	C′	S	C
0	0	0	0	0
1	0	0	1	0
0	1	0	1	0
1	1	0	1	0
0	0	1	1	0
1	0	1	0	1
0	1	1	0	1
1	1	1	1	1

Complement and Add

A	D	C′	S	C
0	0	0	1	0
1	0	0	0	1
0	1	0	0	0
1	1	0	1	0
0	0	1	0	1
1	0	1	1	1
0	1	1	1	0
1	1	1	0	1

Figure 91 Adder and complementer.

M	S	B′	D	B
0	0	0	0	0
1	0	0	1	0
0	1	0	1	1
1	1	0	0	0
0	0	1	1	1
1	0	1	0	0
0	1	1	0	1
1	1	1	1	1

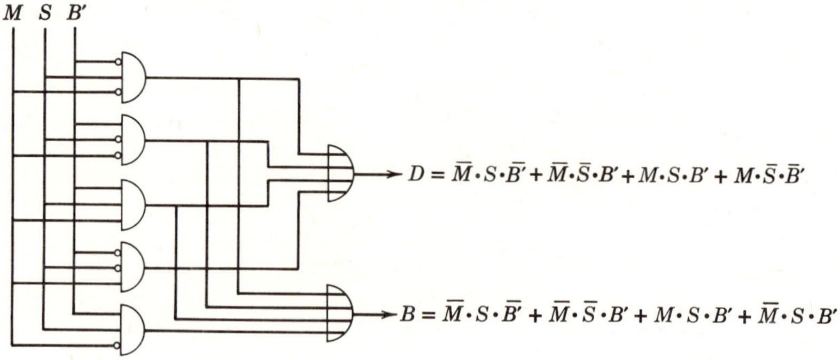

Figure 92 Subtractor.

If D and $\bar{D}$ are factored out, the expression for the simple sum may be rewritten:

$$S = \bar{D} \cdot (A \cdot \bar{C}' + \bar{A} \cdot C') + D \cdot (\bar{A} \cdot \bar{C}' + A \cdot C')$$

If D and $\bar{D}$ are similarly factored out of the expression for the sum assuming complementation of the addend bit, the sum expression may be rewritten:

$$S_C = \bar{D} \cdot (\bar{A} \cdot \bar{C}' + A \cdot C') + D \cdot (A \cdot \bar{C}' + \bar{A} \cdot C')$$

By a similar factoring procedure, the carry expressions may be rewritten:
No complementation

$$\begin{aligned} C_C &= D \cdot (\bar{A} \cdot C') + D \cdot (A \cdot \bar{C}' + \bar{A} \cdot C' + A \cdot C') \\ &= A \cdot C' + D \cdot (A \cdot \bar{C}' + \bar{A} \cdot C') \end{aligned}$$

Complementation

$$\begin{aligned} C_C &= \bar{D} \cdot (A \cdot \bar{C}' + \bar{A} \cdot C' + A \cdot C') + D \cdot (A \cdot C') \\ &= \bar{D} \cdot (A \cdot \bar{C}' + \bar{A} \cdot C') + A \cdot C' \end{aligned}$$

By studying the above expressions, several important facts come into view:

1. $(A \cdot \bar{C} + \bar{A} \cdot C')$ is common to several terms.
2. $(\bar{A} \cdot \bar{C}' + A \cdot C')$ is common to several terms.
3. $A \cdot C'$ produces a carry regardless of whether D or $\bar{D}$ is present, or whether the addend is complemented or not.

Because of these conditions, duplications may be avoided by using a *BC* to produce $\bar{A} \cdot C' + A \cdot \bar{C}'$. This is inverted to produce $A \cdot C' + \bar{A} \cdot \bar{C}'$. A second *BC* combines these terms with D and $\bar{D}$. The Don't Complement signal gates the output and the Complement signal gates the inverse out as the sum (S). To produce a carry (C) the output of the first *BC* is combined with D when a Don't Complement signal is applied; and it is combined with $\bar{D}$ when a Complement signal is applied. It also is produced when

$$A = C' = 1$$

Binary Subtractor

In a binary subtractor the minuend (M), subtrahend (S) and borrow (B') bits from the previous position may be combined to produce difference (D) and borrow (B) bits. The truth table and equations and block diagram derived from it are shown in Fig. 92.

ACCUMULATORS

An accumulator is a register that stores the augend before addition and the sum after addition. Two types of accumulators may be distinguished, as shown in Fig. 93. In the first (Fig. 93*a*), coincidence adders produce the sum of augend and addend, and then return it to the accumulator. In the second (Fig. 93*b*), logic is combined with the A register in a manner such that addition is performed by the accumulator itself.

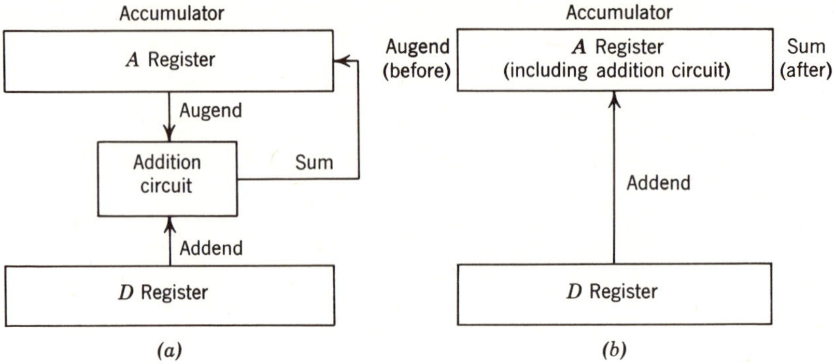

Figure 93 Accumulators. (*a*) Addition performed outside *AR*. (*b*) Addition performed within *AR*.

This last type of accumulator is especially useful for parallel addition. A superficial look would seem to indicate that parallel addition should take only 2 bit-times: one for producing the sum and one for modifying the sum with the carries. This would be true only if the carry bit produced in any one column affected only the sum bit in the following column. However, carries may propagate as can be seen from the following example:

```
 0 1 1 1 1 1 1   Augend
+0 0 0 0 0 0 1   Addend
 1 1 1 1 1 1     Carries
 -------------
 1 0 0 0 0 0 0
```

An accumulator that performs parallel addition with automatic propagation of carries is shown in Fig. 94. It consists of an upper row of flip-flops representing stages of the accumulator; a lower row of *R–S* flip-flops representing stages of the addend register; a series of addition gates A_1 controlled by an add pulse; a series of carry manufacturing gates A_3 controlled by a carry pulse; and a series of delays *D* and gates A_2 for controlling automatic carry propagation.

The circuit works as follows. After a number is applied to the addend register and another number to the accumulator, an add pulse is applied to all gates A_1. Those addition gates associated with addend flip-flops storing ONE produce output pulses which flip the associated accumulator flip-flop to produce a tentative sum.

As soon as this tentative sum is produced in the accumulator, a carry pulse is applied to all gates A_3. If the addend flip-flop is storing ONE and the associated accumulator flip-flop is storing ZERO, signifying that 1 was added to 1, a carry pulse is produced by A_3 and fed to the succeeding accumulator flip-flop through 0_2, delay *D* and 0_1.

If an accumulator flip-flop is storing a ONE and a carry is being applied to

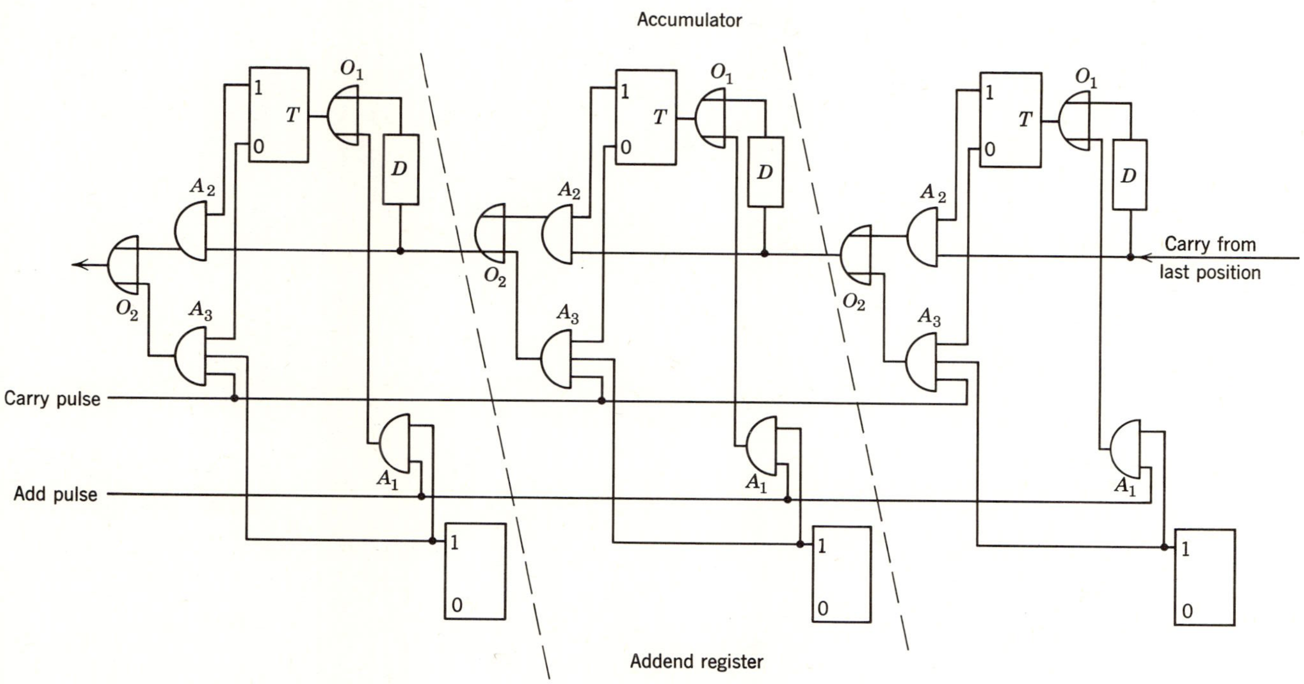

Figure 94 Parallel addition with automatic carry propagation.

it, obviously the flip-flop must be flipped to ZERO and a carry must be propagated to the following stage. These two actions are performed independently. The carry is applied to A_2 which propagates it to the following stage. After this occurs, the carry applied through D and 0_1 flips the accumulator stage. Delay D assures this independent action.

Example

Draw a block diagram of one stage of an accumulator that operates as the one described above, except when D is negative the 1's complement is taken and added to A.

Complement and add

A	D	S	C'	S	C
0	0	1	0	1	0
1	0	0	0	0	1
0	1	0	0	0	0
1	1	1	0	1	0
0	0	1	1	0	1
1	0	0	1	1	1
0	1	0	1	1	0
1	1	1	1	0	1

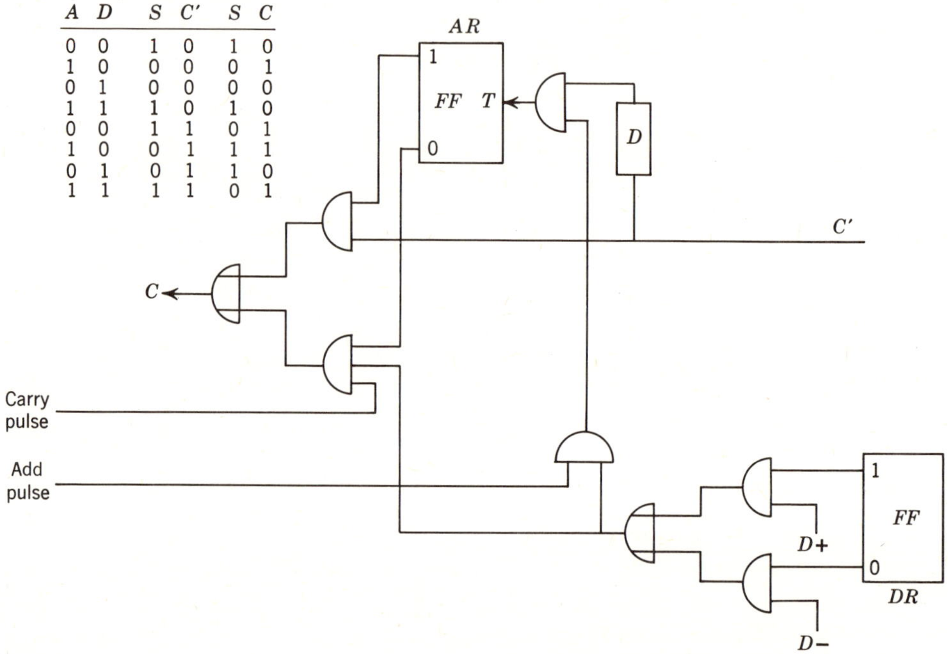

Figure 95 Accumulator stage.

The solution is shown in Fig. 95. Notice that when D equals minus, the main change is that $D=0$ is used to flip A and to combine with $A=0$ to produce a carry C, instead of $D=1$. [Compare the truth tables for the two cases to determine why.]

SUMMARY

1. A comparator device compares 2 or more bits or sets of bits according to a logical rule to produce a bit or set of bits.
2. A coincidence adder is a form of comparator: it compares augend and addend to produce an output sum.
3. Another type of adder uses the storage, counting, and carry propagation ability of an accumulator to perform addition.
4. Addition may be accomplished serially or in parallel. In the first case only one binary adder is required, and the bits are applied sequentially to it. In the second case, a separate binary adder is required for each bit.
5. Parallel addition is obviously faster than serial addition. However, it is not as fast as it may appear to be on the surface, since time is necessary for the propagation of carries.
6. A binary adder (*BA*) may take on many forms: it may be built of binary comparators (*BC*), half adders (*HA*) or of ordinary gates.
7. Among devices other than adders which may use comparators in their construction are parity generators and detectors and complement generators.
8. *Definitions to Remember*

   Half Adder (HA). A device that produces the binary sum and carry of two bits.

   Binary Adder (BA). A device that produces the binary sum and carry bits with each input combination of augend, addend, and previous carry bits.

   Vertical Parity Check. A comparison of the sum of 1 bits in a coded representation to determine if it is odd or even. It is used to check characters.

   Horizontal Parity Check. Comparison of the sum of 1 bits in each bit position of a group of characters to determine if it is odd or even. It is used to check messages.

   Parity Generator. A device that compares the bits of a character or the bits in each bit position of a group of characters, to produce an odd or even parity bit, or character, respectively.

   Parity Detector. A device that compares the bits of a character against its vertical parity bit, or the bits in each bit position of a group of characters against its horizontal parity character, to determine if an error has occurred during transmission.

   Complement Generator. A device that produces as output, the complement of its input.

   Binary Subtractor. A device that produces the binary difference and borrow bits, with each input combination of minuend, subtrahend, and previous borrow bits.

   Accumulator. A register that accumulates and stores results of arithmetic operations.

   Carry. The digit to be added to the next higher column when the sum of the digits in one column is greater than the radix.

Exercises

1. What would a device look like which compared 2 bits and produced an output only when both bits are 1? When both bits are 0?
2. How would you check the binary representation for a number to determine if it is odd or even?
3. Draw a block diagram of a device that would compare the four bits of a number to determine if it contains an odd or even number of 1's.
4. Given the following series of 8-bit characters:

		CHARACTERS C_0	C_1	C_2	C_3	C_4	C_5	C_6	C_7	C_8	C_9	C_{10}
	B_0	1	0	1	0	0	1	0	0	1	1	0
	B_1	0	0	1	1	0	0	0	0	1	1	0
	B_2	1	0	0	0	1	0	1	0	1	1	0
BITS	B_3	1	1	0	1	1	0	0	0	0	1	0
	B_4	0	1	0	0	1	0	0	0	0	1	0
	B_5	1	0	0	0	1	0	0	0	0	0	1
	B_6	1	0	1	0	0	0	0	1	1	0	1
	B_7	0	1	0	1	1	0	1	0	1	0	1

where B_7 is the odd vertical parity bit and C_{10} is the odd horizontal parity character.

   a. Which character is in error?
   b. In which bit position has this error most likely occurred?

5. Given the following series of 8-bit characters:

		CHARACTERS C_0	C_1	C_2	C_3	C_4	C_5	C_6	C_7	C_8	C_9	C_{10}
	B_0	1	0	1	1	0	0	1	0	0	0	1
	B_1	1	0	1	0	0	0	1	0	0	1	0
	B_2	1	1	1	0	0	0	1	0	1	0	0
BITS	B_3	1	1	0	1	0	1	1	0	0	1	0
	B_4	1	1	0	1	0	0	1	0	0	1	0
	B_5	1	0	0	1	1	0	0	0	1	1	0
	B_6	0	0	0	1	1	0	0	1	0	0	0
	B_7	1	0	0	0	1	0	0	0	1	1	1

   a. Are there any errors in the odd horizontal parity character?
   b. How many?
   c. Are there any odd vertical parity errors?
   d. Explain why.

6. If in Fig. 83*a* timing pulse t_6 were lost, what would be the output of the parity generator? If t_5 were lost?

7. Draw a logical block diagram of a parallel even bit vertical parity detector for seven-bit (excluding parity bit) coded characters.

8. If the device drawn in Fig. 85 showed a horizontal parity error, would you know in which bit position the error occurred? How would you modify the device in order to obtain this indication?

9. What would be the output of Fig. 86*a* if t_6 were lost? If t_3 were lost? What would be the output of Fig. 86*b* under similar circumstances?

10. Prove that the sum and carry output of a binary adder are equal to

$$S = (A + B + C')\,(A \cdot B \cdot C' + \bar{C})$$
$$C = B \cdot C' + A \cdot B + A \cdot C'$$

Use a Veitch diagram to aid you. Draw a block diagram of this adder.

11. If positive numbers are stored in absolute value binary form and negative numbers in 2's complement binary form, what would be the representation for the following numbers (use 4 bits plus sign bit):
   a. +1?
   b. −3?
   c. +8?
   d. −9?

12. If numbers are stored as given in the previous problem, what would the output of an adder be in terms of bit combinations after adding the following and before recomplementation of the result:
   a. +4 and +4?
   b. −2 and −2?
   c. +6 and −6?

13. If positive numbers are stored in absolute value binary form and negative numbers in 1's complement form, what would the output of the adder be after adding +6 and −6?

*14. Modify Fig. 91 to include timing required to add serially two numbers of 10 bits in length. The Complement and Don't Complement signals are produced during t_1 (by another circuit), and the addition takes place during t_2 to t_{12}.

15. If a parallel adder with self-carry propagation requires 1 μs to perform an addition and .1 μs for each carry propagation, how long would it take to add the following:
   a. 10101010 and 00101010?
   b. 01111111 and 00000001?
   c. 01111110 and 00000001?

16. Draw a logical block diagram of a device using *T* flip-flops that produces an output only when 1 of 7 bits is equal to 1.

CHAPTER 9

Bulk logic

A summary of computer building blocks is presented in Table 19. Small logical blocks are shown on the left, larger functional building blocks are shown in the center, and largest bulk logic on the right. Functional building blocks discussed up to this point are built of discrete components in a hierarchical system. Bulk logic, on the other hand, is produced by an array of components or by batch fabrication. Bulk logic may be a functional building block or even a group of functional building blocks.

table 19 COMPUTER BUILDING BLOCKS

Logical blocks			
AND	*Functional building blocks*		
OR	Binary comparator		
NOT	Half-adder	Encoder	*Bulk logic*
NAND	Binary adder	Decoder	Bulk storage
NOR	Parity generator	Register	Bulk switching
INHIBIT	Parity detector	Counter	Bulk storage and switching
Amplifier	Complement generator	Coincidence adder	
Delay	Complement detector	Accumulator	
Flip-flop			

In this chapter, bulk storage and bulk switching techniques are described in turn. This is followed by a discussion of bulk storage *and* switching, in which it becomes clear that storage and switching are often two sides of the same coin.

BULK STORAGE

Many characteristics are used for defining storage systems. But only two are used for most practical categorizations. They are (1) type of storage, and (2) method of address selection. After a brief discussion of a few of the more general characteristics, storage access and address selection are covered in more detail. This is followed by descriptions of bulk storage devices under each of the four major categories: sequential access storage, cyclic access storage, coordinate access storage, and content addressable storage.

General Characteristics of Storage Components

Storage components may be classified according to four different criteria:

1. Static or dynamic.
2. Volatile or nonvolatile.
3. Destructive read-out or nondestructive read-out.
4. Erasable or nonerasable.

A *static* storage component stores bits by staying in one of several stable states. A *dynamic* storage component stores data by continuous recirculation of a wave, pulse, or other physical quantity.

A *volatile* storage component loses the stored data with time or if the power is turned off. A *nonvolatile* storage component holds the data even after the power is removed.

A storage component with *destructive read-out* loses the data stored in it when the data is read out. A storage component with *nondestructive read-out* keeps the data stored in it intact even when read out.

In an *erasable* storage component the bits may be removed and other data may be written in the same place. In a *nonerasable* storage component the data cannot be erased.

Obviously a volatile component has limited application. The same is true for destructive read-out components, except that methods are available for countering the destructive read-out tendencies by appropriate storage system organization. Different timing arrangements must be made for static than for dynamic components. Nonerasable and erasable devices are extremely different from each other. Each is used in a different way. A synonym for nonerasable storage is read-only storage, and a synonym for erasable storage is read-write storage.

Storage Access

Types of access. Storage systems may be categorized according to the method of access to any one of the many storage addresses. There are three types of access as follows:

1. Sequential.
2. Cyclic.
3. Coordinate.

The three types of storage are described pictorially in Fig. 96.

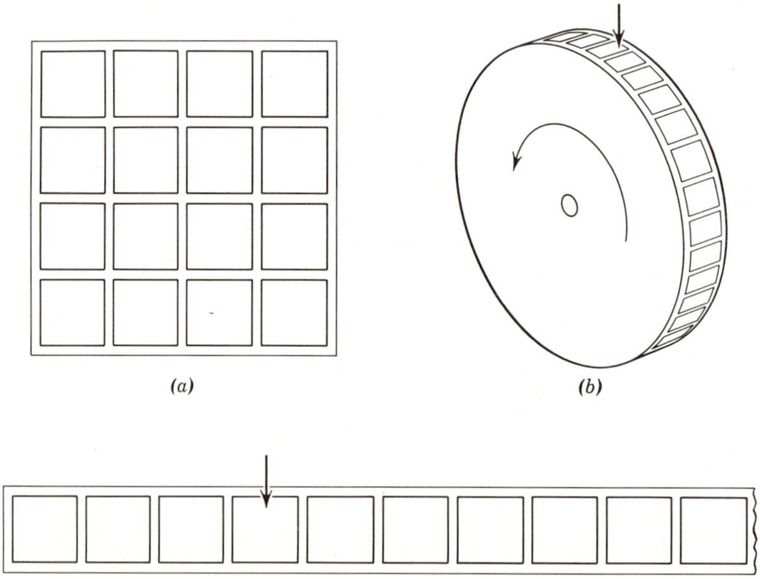

(a) (b) (c)

Figure 96 Types of storage access. (*a*) Coordinate access. (*b*) Cyclic access. (*c*) Sequential access.

In the sequential-access system a long group of storage cells moves in time with reference to an access device. Relative movement of storage cells with respect to the access device may be started and stopped at will, and each storage cell may appear only once at the access device during an operation.

In the cyclic access system a group of storage cells is arranged in time in such a manner that access may be gained to each cell once during each period of time called a cycle. Storage cells may be rotated past a stationary access device; or an access device may be rotated past a stationary group of storage cells; or the bits may be circulated through a closed-loop delay circuit. Several storage loops may be operated in parallel.

In the coordinate access system the storage cells are arranged in an array in space. To gain access to any one location, the address selector opens a path to one of the storage cells.

Latency, Access Time, and Cycle Time

The speed with which words may be written into or read from a storage device depends on the cycle time (Fig. 97). The cycle time is defined as the time between successive references to storage.

The cycle time consists of the access time plus a waiting time. The access time is the time between arrival of the signal activating the memory and the completion of write-in or read-out. The waiting time is the time the storage device needs to settle sufficiently so that the next reference to storage may be performed reliably.

The access time consists of the latency plus the transfer time. The latency represents the amount of time it takes to find the chosen address.

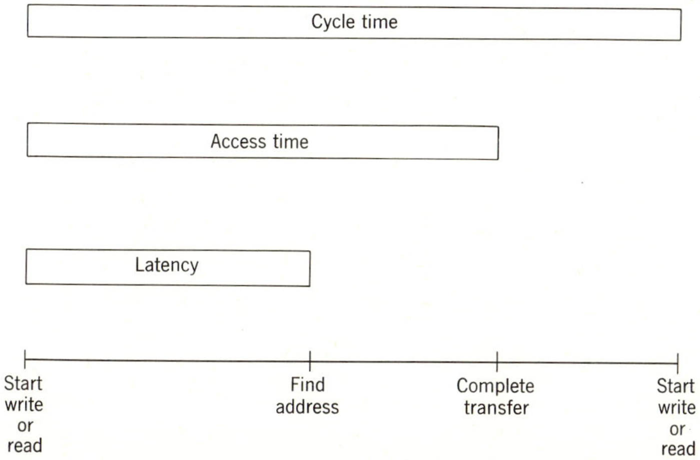

Figure 97 Latency, access time, and cycle time.

Latency is a factor in sequential and cyclic access storage devices (see Fig. 98). For sequential storage, the further away the addressed location is from the location where the read-write head is located, the greater the latency time. For cyclic storage, we speak of a maximum latency time and an average latency time. The maximum is given by the time of 1 revolution; this is the amount of time we must wait if the command for accessing arrives immediately after the addressed location passes under the head. If accessing commands arrive in a random manner, the average latency time will be one half of the maximum.

For coordinate access systems, the latency time may be considered to be zero.

Example

If a cyclic storage device possessing one head rotates at the rate of 600 revolutions per minute, what is the maximum latency time? The average latency time?

If it rotates at 600 revolutions per minute, it rotates at 600/60 = 10 revolutions per second. This means one revolution takes $\frac{1}{10}$ second or 100 ms, which is the maximum latency time. The average latency time 100/2 = 50 ms (see Fig. 98).

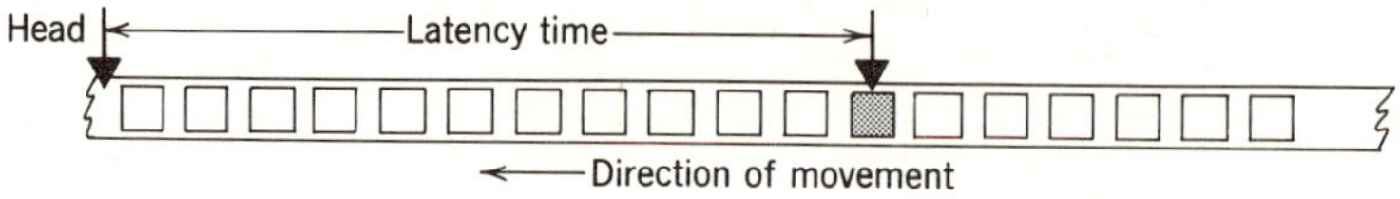

(a)

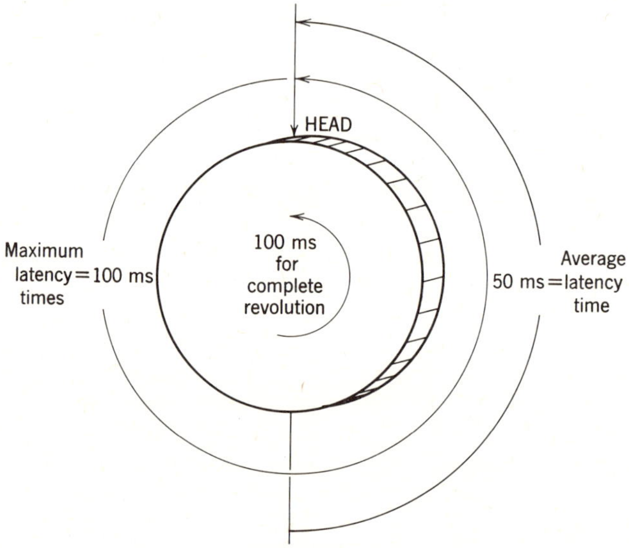

(b)

Figure 98 Latency time. (*a*) Sequential storage. (*b*) Cyclic storage.

Example

In the above example if 2 heads 180° apart are provided, what would the maximum and average latency time be?

Since we never need travel more than 180° to find an addressed location, the maximum latency time is one half of the previous maximum, or 50 ms. The average latency time is one half of the maximum or 25 ms.

Random access. An important class of storage devices possesses the property of random access. Random access storage refers to a device in which it takes just as long to obtain access to one address as it does to obtain access to another address. A coordinate access storage device possesses random access. A sequential access storage device, on the other hand, does not possess random access, since it takes a short time to gain access to a location at the start of the device and a much longer time to gain access to a location at the end of the device. The same is true of the cyclic access device: access time depends on what point in the cycle reference to an address is made.

The main advantage of a random access device is that it allows data to be stored and retrieved quickly. Since in any practical situation it is the relative speed that is important, the definition of random access has been distorted to refer to a device which allows access at a rate faster than the data is needed by the equipment served by the storage. For instance, a cyclic access device with a cycle time of 20 ms may be considered to be a random access device if it serves a device which cannot operate faster than once every 30 ms.

Address Selection

Two general ways exist for addressing data stored in a storage system. They are location addressing and content addressing. The first is a means of finding data when the physical location is known. The second is a means of finding data when something about its contents is known. A good everyday example of location addressing is the address we use for mail delivery. A good everyday example of content addressing is the word that appears on the top of each page of a dictionary. Location addressing has been used in computers since their advent. Content addressing is a newer more sophisticated scheme.

Location address selection. An addressing scheme is a means for labeling each storage cell. The simplest way to form an address is by giving a number to each storage cell or group of cells in the storage unit. Another way is by labeling each storage location by the number of the column and row in which it is found. In this case the address is effectively divided in two: a row address and a column address.

An address may be chosen by a simple decoder (Fig. 99*a*). A different output line is activated for a different combination of address bits.

When row and column addresses are used in a coordinate access storage unit, two address decoders are provided, one for the column address and one for the row address (Fig. 99*b*). The two chosen lines then produce coincidence at one storage location in the storage unit. In this scheme the storage device itself performs part of the selection.

The row address and column address schemes may be used for cyclic as well as for coordinate access devices. In the coordinate access device the row and column represent addresses in space. In the cyclic access device the column address is an address in space, whereas the row address is an address in time.

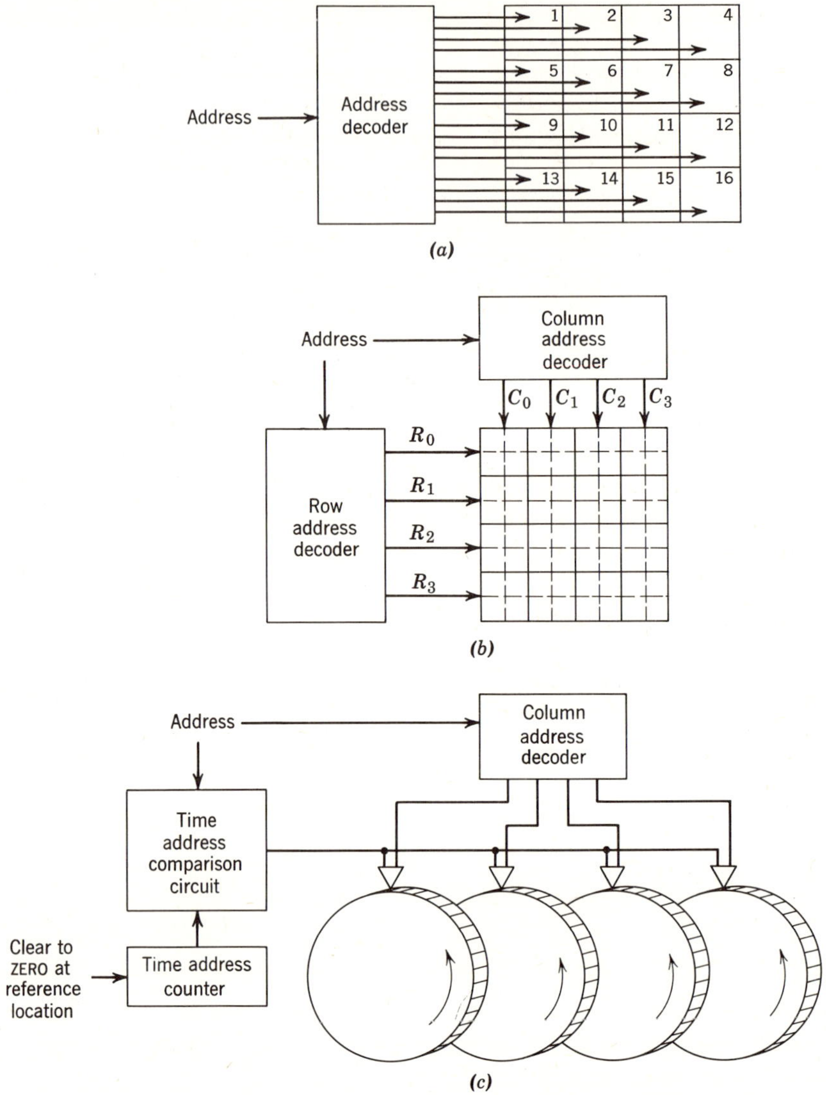

Figure 99 Location address selection. (*a*) Space-array address selection. (*b*) Coincident-storage address selection. (*c*) Space-time storage address selection.

Specifically, in a cyclic access device it takes a certain number of word-times for all the rows to pass through the access device. If one row is labeled as reference, all the other rows may be labeled in terms of the number of word-times needed to travel from the reference point to the designated row. This word-time number is the time address.

To find a time address, the row address is compared with the output of a clock ticking in synchronism with the storage device. When the two are alike, it signifies that the chosen row is passing through the access device. Figure 99*c* shows a cyclic access storage unit in which the columns are chosen by a column address decoder, and the rows are chosen by a time address selector. At the reference point on the storage device a pulse is applied to the word-time counter to clear it to 0. The word-time counter thus stores 0 during the period row 0 is passing through the access device. The word-time counter advances to 1 at the same time that row 1 passes through the access device. If the wanted row address is 1, the time-address comparison circuit produces an output pulse which allows writing or reading. If the wanted row address is not 1, the word-time counter is stepped again. This operation continues until comparison is achieved.

In contrast to the cyclic and coordinate access storage devices, it is normally impractical to address any location at random in a sequential access storage device. The usual approach is to store data groups according to a certain sequence, and then to read out a group at a time according to the same sequence. This may be called sequential addressing as opposed to the previously discussed random addressing.

Example

If a coordinate access storage device is to have 1024 locations, how many address bits would be required in order to be able to encode each location?

As was shown in Chapter 2 the number 1024 may be expressed as 2^{10}. Therefore, 10 bits are required.

Example

If the address decoder for the above storage device consisted of column and row decoders, how many bits would be handled by the column decoder? By the row decoder? How many columns and rows are there in this storage device?

There are 5 bits each for the row and column decoders. These 5 bits are each decoded into 32 outputs. A matrix of 32 rows and 32 columns produces a total of $32 \times 32 = 1024$ locations.

Example

Assume that there are 100 locations around each of several columns in a cyclic access storage device that has an average latency of 100 ms. If a read time-address 5 command is given for a certain column at the time that time-address 0 just comes under the read head, how long will it take to reach the data stored in time-address 5.

To answer this we must know how much time is consumed by a time-address. Since the average latency is 100 ms, it means that it takes 200 ms to complete a revolution. With 100 locations around the periphery, each time-address consumes 2 ms. Five time-addresses would thus take

$$2 \times 5 = 10 \text{ ms}$$

Example

Assume a storage system consisting of 4 separate cyclic access devices, each device having the following characteristics: 8 columns and 512 time-addresses. How many bits are needed to choose a device? A column within that device? A time address within this column? What are the total required address bits? How many storage locations are available in the whole storage system?

Two bits are required to choose 1 of 4 devices, 3 bits to choose 1 of 8 columns within this device, 9 bits to choose 1 of 512 time-addresses within this column. The total is $2+3+9=14$ bits. The total number of locations is

$$\text{(4 devices)} \times \text{(8 columns)} \times \text{(512 time-address)} = 16{,}384$$

This number is equivalent to 2^{14}, thus, checking that 14 bits are required for the address.

Content address selection. In the cyclic access device, the time address of each location in a column may be stored in that location instead of being counted externally. In that event, the time-address portion of the contents of a given location is compared with the required time-address to determine if they are the same; and when they are, read-out of that location can be performed.

If read-out occurs on comparison, why do the "time-addresses" have to be in order? They do not. If we wish, we may store "time-addresses" in haphazard manner; still the proper location will be accessed by the comparison circuit. If this is done, the "time-address" is called a key, and the process is labeled content addressing.

There is no special reason why the key need be a numeric character. It may be an alphanumeric character or a group of characters.

Content addressing may be done in serial or in parallel. Figure 100*a* shows a cyclic access storage device using serial content addressing. As the storage device rotates, the first character in each location, the key, is read out and compared with the desired key stored in the Key Register. When comparison is achieved the read circuits are activated, and they read out the contents of this chosen location. In the illustration, the key 2 is stored in the Key Register and the location storing 2*WYZ* is read out.

Figure 100*b* shows content addressing in parallel. The Key Register stores the key, and at one time the keys of all the locations are compared with this key. At the location where comparison occurs, read-out is performed. Nothing occurs at the other locations.

Obviously, the parallel method is much more powerful than the serial. Normally, when content addressing is discussed, the parallel type is assumed. All future references in this book to content addressing, therefore, will refer to the parallel type, unless we specifically state otherwise.

An extremely important variation to the basic content addressable storage device is the ability to access two or more locations storing the same key at the same time.

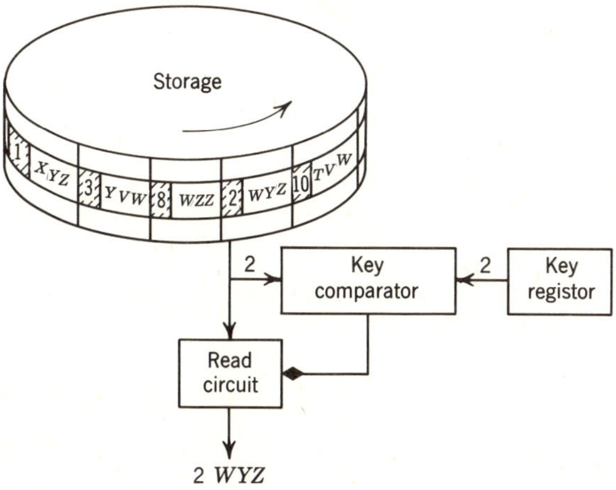

(a)

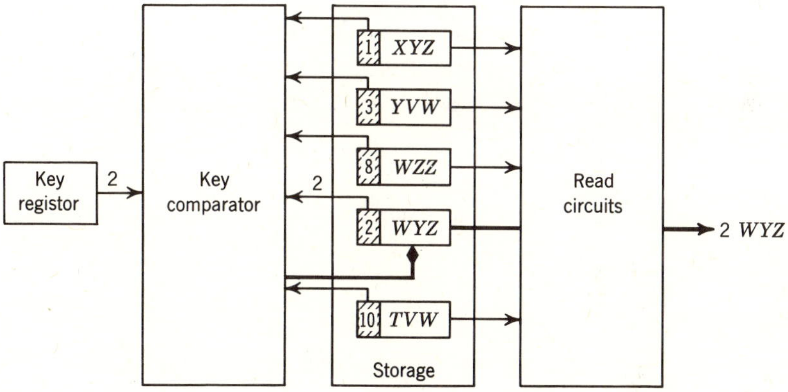

(b)

Figure 100 Content addressing. (*a*) Serial. (*b*) Parallel.

Example

With content addressing, how would you address an empty location for the purpose of entering data into it?

By convention, each empty location may be made to store a certain key—"*E*", for instance. When we want to write, we place *E* into the Key Register in order to fetch one of these empty locations. As part of the writing operation we enter the key which may be used later for retrieval of this data.

Sequential Storage

Three media commonly used for sequential storage are punched paper tape, punched card and magnetic tape. The first two store data mechanically, the last by a process of magnetization.

Punched paper tape. Data is stored on punched paper tape by means of patterns of holes as shown in Fig. 101. Each spot where a hole may appear is in effect a binary storage cell. It may store a hole (ONE) or a no-hole (ZERO). Writing is accomplished by means of a hole-punching machine. Reading may be performed by means of pins, brushes, or photocells. In the pin-sensing method, as the paper moves, a group of spring-loaded pins pushes against the paper. Where a hole is present, the pin falls through the hole; as the pin falls, it causes a switch to close and produce a pulse of current (ONE). The pin meeting a no-hole does not fall and does not cause a pulse of current (ZERO).

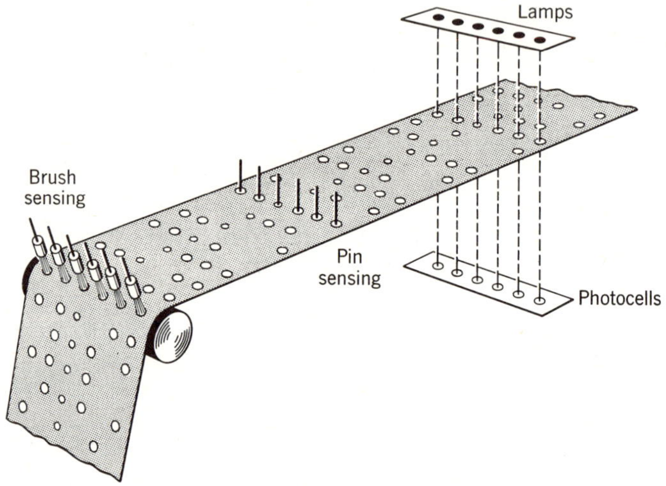

Figure 101 Methods of reading punched paper tape.

The holes and no-holes may be read by means of brushes. Wherever a hole is present, the brush closes the circuit with the contact on the opposite side to produce a ONE. Where a no-hole is present, no contact is made and a ZERO is produced.

In the photocell method a bank of six lamps shines at a row of code on the paper. On the opposite side of the paper is a bank of photocells. At a point where a hole is present light gets through and impinges on the associated photocell to produce current (ONE). At a point where a no-hole is present, no light passes and no current is produced by the associated photocell (ZERO).

The smaller holes are called sprocket holes. Their function is to allow the sprocket of a punched paper tape reader to move the paper at a constant rate.

Punched cards. A punched card is another storage device which stores data by means of punched holes. The main difference between punched paper tape and punched cards is that the former is a continuous record and the latter is a discrete record. This difference is significant in the selection of data-processing systems.

The most common punched card has 80 columns with 10 positions labeled 0 to 9 (Fig. 102). There are two unlabeled positions in the space above the 0-digit position: *X* (nearest the 0 position) and *Y*. Decimal digits may be written into each column by punching the appropriate spot. Letters may be written by punching two holes in each column; one hole is punched in either the 0, *X*, or *Y* row and the other hole is punched in a digit position. For some of the editing symbols three holes are necessary.

One method of writing is performed by means of machines which punch holes into appropriate positions when keys are depressed.

Reading may be accomplished by the brush-sensing or photocell methods. In the former method a roller moves the card along its breadth across a set of 80 brushes. At each hole a circuit closes; at each point where a no-hole exists the circuit stays open. How does the reader distinguish among pulses representing 9, 8, or 0? This is done by means of a clock which is activated when the card starts moving and counts 12 pulses. If the card is moved from its 9 position toward its *Y* position a pulse produced by a brush during count 1 represents a 9; a pulse produced by a brush at count 10 represents a 0.

To better organize the data, the punched card often is subdivided into fields, each field representing a given category of data and occupying a specific number of columns on the card. By looking at a sample of several items that may be stored under each category, the size of the fields may be decided on. This was done for a punched card system storing book titles and authors, and the field designations and sizes shown in Fig. 102 were arrived at. Notice that the size of an item such as "code" is determined mainly by the number of cards expected in the file.

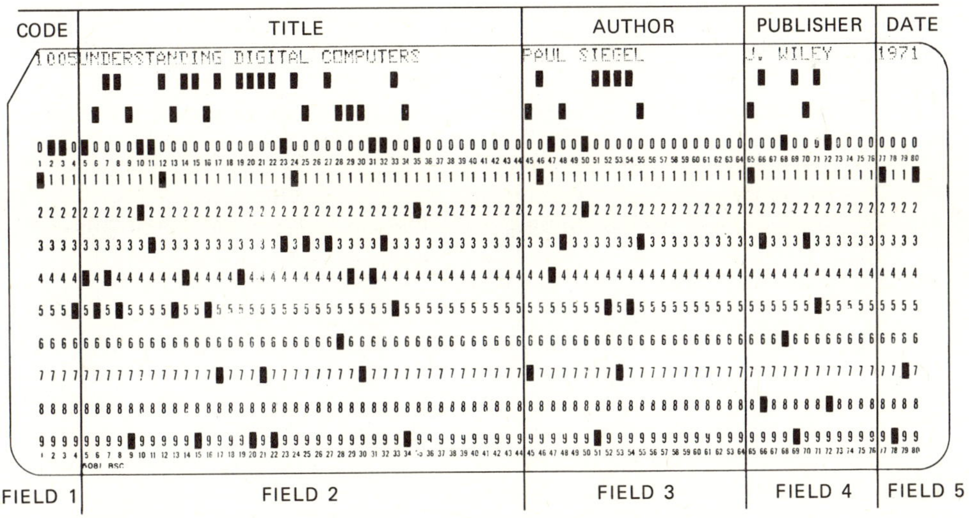

Figure 102 Punched card subdivided into fields.

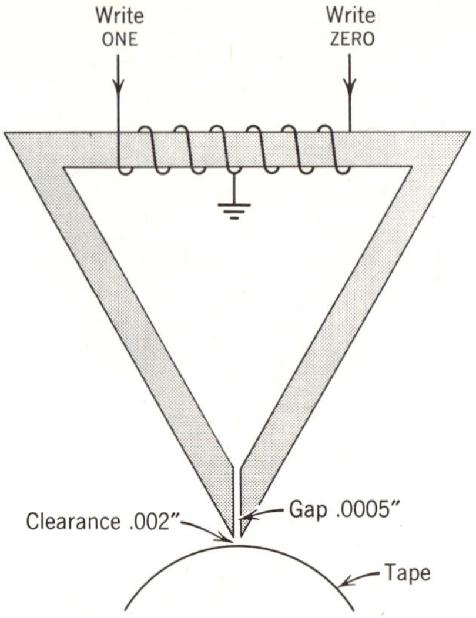

Figure 103 Magnetic write head.

Example

Assume the card shown in Fig. 102 is read by a card reader which has a clock that counts from 1 to 12 as the card is scanned from the 9 position to the *Y* position. In column 5, during which counts are pulses produced? In column 67?

In column 5, pulses are produced during count 1, representing position 9, and count 10, representing position 0. This reads *U*.

Magnetic tape. A square-loop magnetic mixture may be deposited on an acetate or Mylar tape to form magnetic tape. Thousands of bits of data may be stored on this magnetic tape, each bit being located in a small square on the tape. In effect, the tape is divided into many storage cells.

Writing is accomplished by means of a magnetic head constructed as shown in Fig. 103. The triangular material has an air gap of about .0005 in. When current is applied to the winding, a magnetic field flows through the head and across this tiny air gap. If the magnetic tape is close to the head—about .002 in. distant—the lines of flux affect the magnetic state of the tape near the point of the head. Sending current through the winding in one direction causes the simulated storage cell on the tape to saturate positively—store a ONE. Sending current through the winding in the opposite direction causes the simulated storage cell to saturate negatively—store a ZERO. By moving the tape and feeding successive data pulses to the winding, bits may be stored in successive locations on the tape. Figure 104 shows 4-19-2-7-25-2-8 recorded on the tape.

Reading is accomplished by means of a magnetic read head similar to the write head. As the magnetic tape with its stored bits is moved under the head, the magnetic field of each area induces a magnetic field in the head which induces a voltage across the output winding. The direction of the induced voltage depends on the direction of magnetization of the effective storage cell on the tape.

Like the punched paper tape, the magnetic tape provides a continuous record. Therefore, to distinguish groups of data bits, the contents of the magnetic tape are written into blocks, where each block consists of a series of characters with means for defining its beginning and/or end.

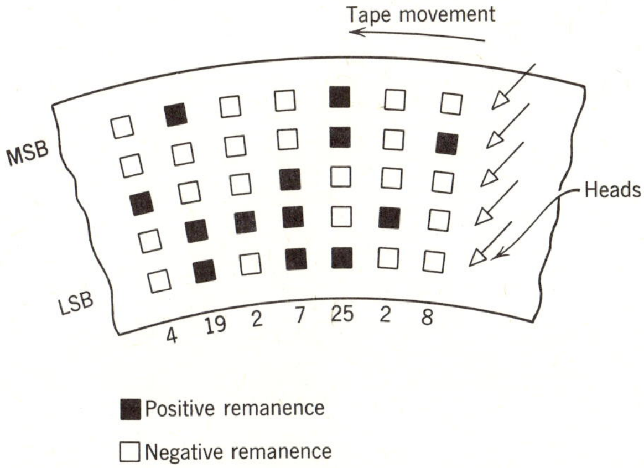

Figure 104 Tape recording.

Example

Assume a reel of magnetic tape is 2400 feet long and can store 500 characters per inch. If blocks are 2400 characters long, how many blocks may be stored on the tape (assuming space is not needed for anything else)? If the contents of the tape can be read at the rate of 120 inches per second, what is the access time to the center block, assuming tape reading starts from the beginning?

If the reel stores 500 characters per inch, it stores $500 \times 12 = 6000$ characters per foot. For a 2400-foot reel, it stores $6000 \times 2400 = 14{,}400{,}000$ characters. If there are 2400 characters to a block, there are $14{,}400{,}000/2400 = 6000$ blocks on the tape. If the tape is read at the rate of 120 inches per second, this is equivalent to $120/12 = 10$ feet per second. Since the center block is half way across the tape or 1200 feet, the access time to the center block is $1200/10 = 120$ seconds.

Cyclic Storage

Examples of cyclic access storage are the magnetic drum, magnetic disc, and magnetic card. The latter, in reality, is a hybrid between sequential and cyclic access storage.

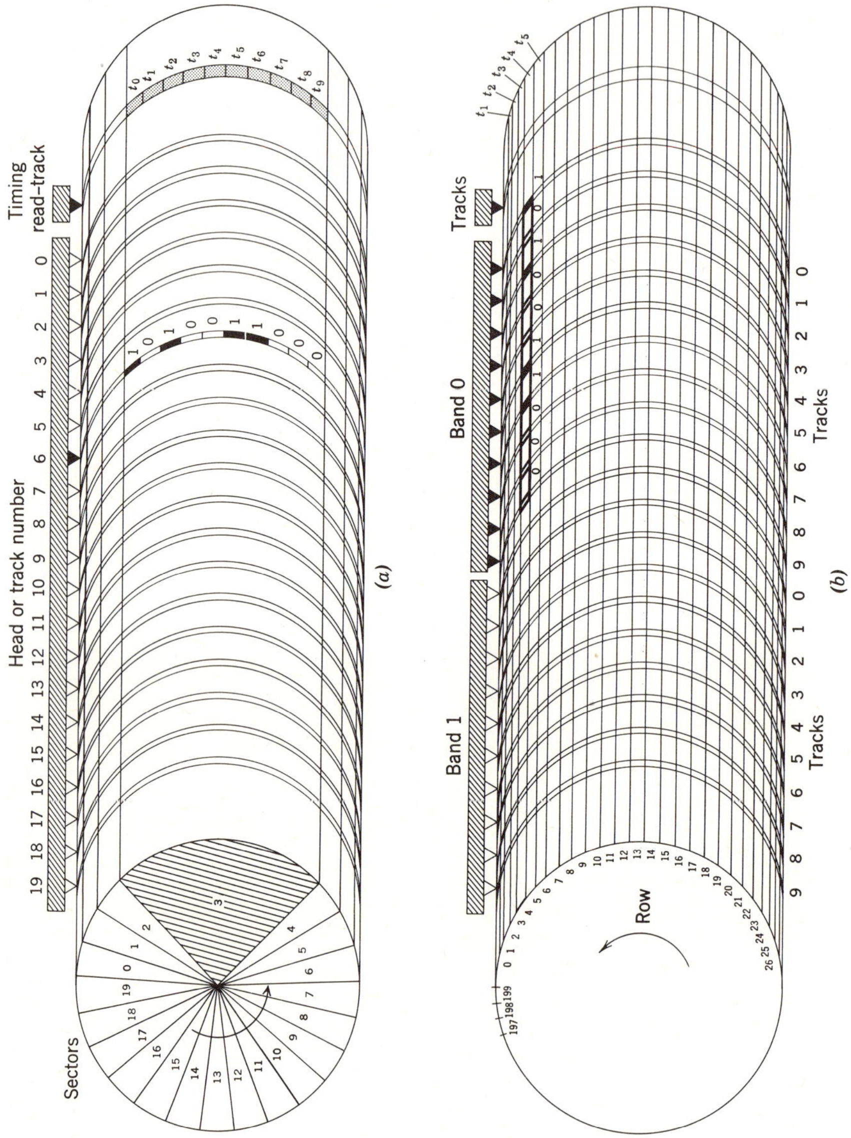

Figure 105 Magnetic drum. (*a*) Serial. (*b*) Parallel.

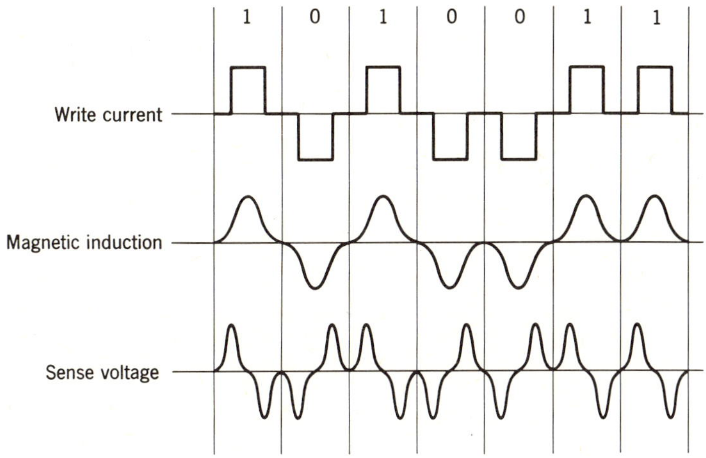

(a)

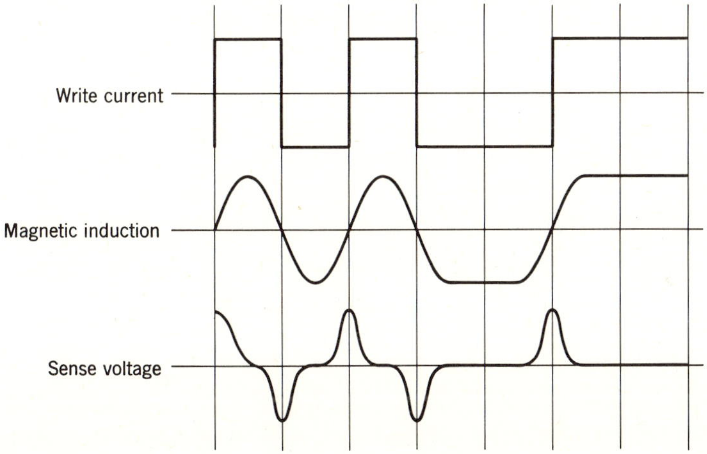

(b)

Figure 106 Types of magnetic recording. (*a*) Return-to-ZERO. (*b*) Nonreturn-to-ZERO.

Magnetic drum. Because tape is long, it takes time to write it or to read it. To speed writing and reading, several tapes may be wrapped around a rotating cylinder, and several more stationary heads may be added to take care of the extra tracks. This is essentially the description of a magnetic drum.

Figure 105*a* illustrates a magnetic drum with 20 data tracks and 20 sectors. Each data track has a magnetic head for reading and writing. Each sector consists of 10 rows. A specific location may be addressed by specifying the track number and sector number. In Fig. 105*a*, address 63 is illustrated as storing the following word:

0001100101

In this case a hatched area on the drum represents a positively saturated area, which in turn represents a ONE; and a clear area represents a negatively saturated area, which in turn represents a ZERO.

The drum is rotating constantly. To select a location on the drum for either writing or reading, the proper track is chosen by activating the appropriate read-write head. However, it must be activated only when the appropriate sector is underneath the heads. For instance, to read the data in the area shown in bold, the head servicing track 6 is activated as soon as the rows in sector 3 come under the heads.

Evidently the row must be chosen by some sort of timing arrangement. A timing track storing a succession of ONE's helps in this selection.

The above drum reads and writes in serial. Figure 105*b* shows a drum that reads and writes 10-bit words in parallel. The address of each location is given by a band number and a row number. Each band represents a group of 10 tracks, which store the 10 bits of a word. The illustration shows address 05 storing

0001100101

A timing track is needed in the parallel arrangement too. But notice that it takes only 1 pulse time to read out a 10-bit word, whereas it takes 10 pulse times in the serial arrangement.

Example

Assume that both the serial and parallel drums discussed above rotate at the rate of 3000 rpm. What is the maximum and average latency of each? What is the maximum and average access time of each?

In terms of revolutions per second, the rate of drum rotation is 3000/60 = 50. This means it performs a revolution in

$$\tfrac{1}{50} \text{ second} = .02 \text{ second} = 20 \text{ ms}$$

Therefore, the maximum latency for both drums is 20 ms, and the average latency for both is 20/2 = 10 ms.

In both drums there are 200 rows, and 200 timing pulses are needed, giving 20/200 = .1 ms per timing pulse. Thus, the transfer time for a word in the parallel case is .1 ms, and the transfer time for the serial case is .1 × 10 = 1 ms. Therefore, the maximum and average access times for the two cases in milliseconds are:

	Maximum Access Time	Average Access Time
Serial	20 + 1 = 21	10 + 1 = 11
Parallel	20 + .1 = 20.1	10 + .1 = 10.1

Several recording schemes are in use for magnetic drums. Two of these are the return-to-ZERO and the nonreturn-to-ZERO schemes. In the return-to-ZERO recording scheme, a ONE is recorded by feeding a positive current pulse through the write coil, and a ZERO is recorded by feeding a negative current pulse through the write coil. It is called return-to-ZERO because the current always passes through the ZERO point between pulses. Figure 106*a* shows the flux pattern on the drum as the combination 1010011 is recorded with the return-to-ZERO scheme. It also shows the voltage induced into the read coil as it passes under this track during reading. A ONE induces a positive pulse followed by a negative pulse; a ZERO induces a negative pulse followed by a positive pulse. To make sense of the pulses read, they are fed to a gate which opens only during the first half of each pulse period. All ONE's come through as positive pulses and all ZERO's as negative pulses.

The current, flux, and voltage waveforms in the nonreturn-to-ZERO recording scheme are depicted in Fig. 106*b*. Here a ONE is represented by a flow of positive current, and a ZERO by a flow of negative current. But the currents do not fall back to zero in every case. When reading a track storing 1010011 in this form, the induced voltage waveform is as shown. Pulses are not produced for each bit of information. Pulses are produced only when the data switches from ZERO to ONE or from ONE to ZERO. A positive pulse is produced when switching from ZERO to ONE, and a negative pulse is produced when switching from ONE to ZERO. To translate these pulses, a storage device—such as a flip-flop—is needed. A positive pulse is made to set the flip-flop to ONE. Each clock pulse gates the ONE output out. A negative pulse is made to reset the flip-flop. The ZERO output is then gated through by clock pulses.

Interestingly enough, a track on a magnetic drum may be used as a recirculating shift register. The arrangement which accomplishes this is shown in Fig. 107. It consists of a read head scanning a track and feeding the bits through an amplifier back to a write head which writes the data further

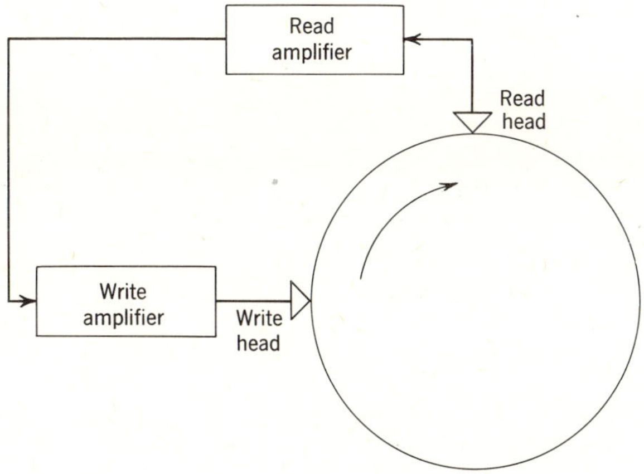

Figure 107 Drum recirculating register.

along on the same track. After a group of bits are read and rewritten, the read head appears at the point on the track where it can read the bits once more. This sequence may continue as long as the drum rotates. Several such recirculating registers may be built into one track.

Magnetic disc. Bits may be stored magnetically on a disc in a manner analogous to the way voice recordings are placed on discs. An example of the bit layout on a disc is shown in Fig. 108*a*. The disc is divided into four sectors and 100 tracks. The illustration shows address 101, representing sector 1 and track 01, storing word

0001100101

This magnetic disc can then store as much data as the previous magnetic drums. With discs, however, it is possible to group them and thus to build much larger storage units.

Figure 108*b* shows in schematic form how discs may be grouped. To locate any word, another number must be added to the address—the disc number. The illustration shows the location addressed by 2104, where 2 is the disc number, 1 is the sector number, and 04 is the track number.

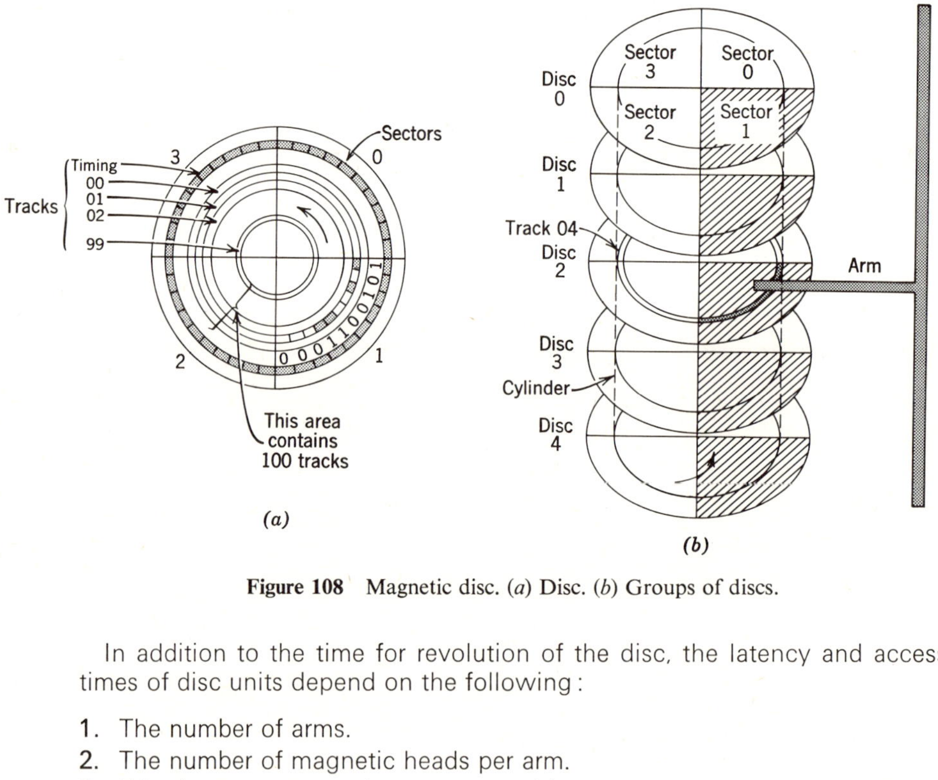

Figure 108 Magnetic disc. (*a*) Disc. (*b*) Groups of discs.

In addition to the time for revolution of the disc, the latency and access times of disc units depend on the following:

1. The number of arms.
2. The number of magnetic heads per arm.
3. Whether arms are stationary or movable.

If a 1-disc unit possesses a stationary arm with one magnetic head for each track, then the latency time depends on the disc revolution time, as it did for the drum. However, if only one magnetic head is provided in a movable arm, then latency time must be increased by the amount of time it takes to move the arm from one track to another.

For multiple disc units with an arm for each disc the same considerations apply. Notice that at any one time the head on each arm can access the same track number on each of the discs. Any track on a "cylinder" is thus accessible.

If only 1 arm is provided, then the latency time must be increased by the time it takes to move the arm from 1 disc position to another.

Example

Assume a disc storage device consisting of 10 discs each rotating at 3000 rpm. Each disc consists of 10 sectors with 10 bits per sector, and 100 tracks. One magnetic head is mounted on 1 arm that can be moved from disc to disc and also from track to track at any one disc. If it takes 40 ms for the arm to travel one half the total distance from the disc at one end to the disc at the other end, and it takes 25 ms for the arm to move the magnetic head across half the tracks (50) on a given disc, what is the average latency time? If a series of accesses apply to only 1 disc, what is the average latency time for this series?

The average latency time is equal to the time for the arm to move across one half the discs, plus the time for the arm to move across one half the tracks on a disc, plus one half the disc rotation time:

$$50 + 25 + \frac{3000}{60} \times \frac{1}{2} = 100 \text{ ms}$$

If accesses are all within a given disc, the time for movement of the arm from disc to disc does not apply. The average latency time then is only 50 ms.

Magnetic card. The cyclic magnetic drum and magnetic disc may be visualized to consist of several strips of magnetic tape mounted in parallel on a surface so that their ends meet. If you could visualize the mounting of these magnetic tapes on a surface without their ends meeting, you could obtain a good picture of the magnetic card.

By itself, the magnetic card is a sequential access device. However, if the magnetic card is placed on a revolving drum, it can be accessed in a cyclic manner. Figure 109 shows in outline a magnetic card storage unit. By a mechanical selection mechanism, one magnetic card is removed from a group of cards stored in a magazine and placed on a drum. The drum rotates continuously under a group of stationary read-write magnetic heads.

If it is assumed that there are 256 cards per magazine, that each card has 8 channels and that a different block is recorded starting at the top of each channel, then the address must specify the card and the channel on the card. For example, address 0366 would specify card 36 and the block written on channel 6 of that card.

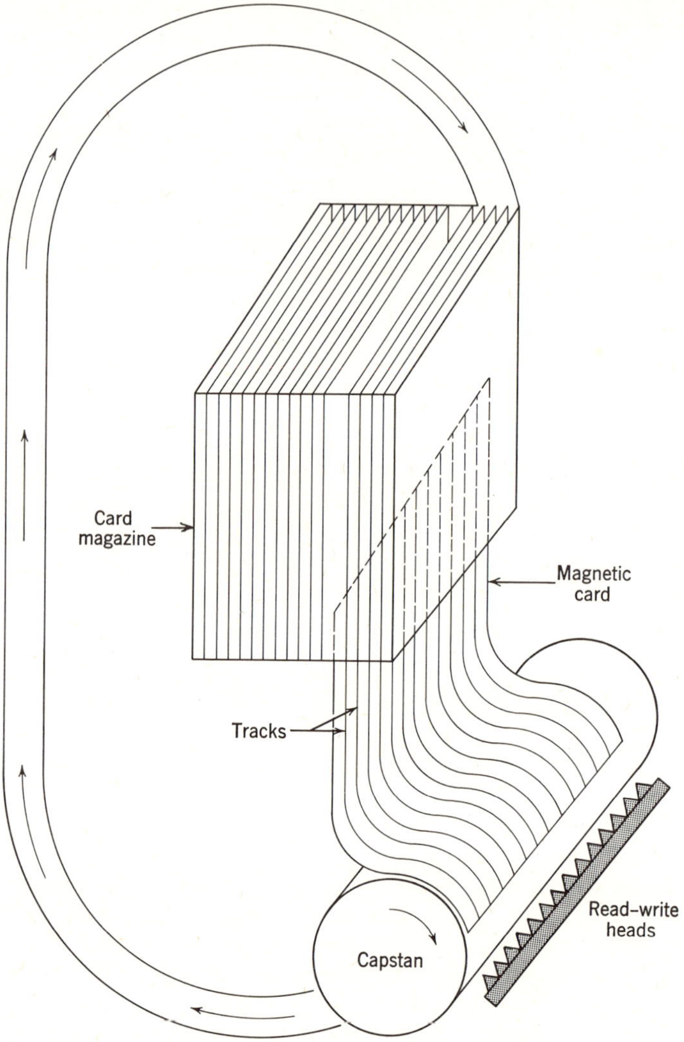

Figure 109 Magnetic card storage unit.

Example

If it takes on the average 125 ms from the time of addressing until the chosen magnetic card is placed on the drum, and the drum rotates at the rate of 1200 rpm what is the average latency time? If each band stores a block starting from the top, how long after the start of reading 1 block would it take before access can be obtained to another block?

The average latency time is

$$125 + \frac{1200}{60} \times \frac{1}{2} = 125 + 25 = 150 \text{ ms}$$

Since the drum rotates once in 50 ms, a block on the card may be accessed 50 ms after accessing another block on the same card.

Coordinate Storage

Coordinate access storage is commonly obtained by means of a matrix of storage elements. This matrix is stored on a plane which is similar to the coincident current magnetic core selection plane described in Chapter 6 (Fig. 58), except that two windings have been added. They are the data winding, *D*, which is used to write 0's or 1's: and the sense winding for reading out the 0's and 1's. Both thread all the cores in a serial manner, as shown in Fig. 109. The resultant array is called a coincident-current magnetic core storage plane.

Writing is illustrated in Fig. 110*a*. Core selection is accomplished by applying current pulses to a column (Y_2) and to a row (X_1). But these pulses are of smaller magnitude and even additively are not capable of flipping the chosen core. At the same time that these two pulses are applied, a pulse is applied to the data line (*D*), in one direction for a ONE, in the opposite direction for a ZERO. If a ONE pulse is applied, the *D*, *X*, and *Y* fields at the chosen core add to bring the core to the ONE state. If a ZERO pulse is applied, the *D* and *X* fields cancel each other and not enough flux is produced to flip the core to ONE; it stays in the ZERO state. All other cores definitely do not receive enough energy to flip.

Reading is illustrated in Fig. 110*b*. It is accomplished by applying half-current pulses to a column (Y_2) and a row (X_1) in such a direction as to cause the chosen core to flip to ZERO. If the chosen core was storing a ONE, the core flips to ZERO and during this reversal of flux produces an induced voltage across the sense winding. If the chosen core was storing a ZERO, there is no flux reversal and very little voltage is induced across the sense winding.

The above scheme is called coincident-current storage and the plane of nine magnetic cores is called a 3-by-3 (three rows by three columns) coincident-current storage plane. This scheme of storage may be expanded to include several planes, coincidence occurring simultaneously at similar points in each plane. In Fig. 111 is shown how three 3-by-3 coincident-current storage planes are connected to form a storage scheme capable of storing combinations of bits. Three current drivers X_0, X_1, and X_2 feed the rows of all three planes; and three column drivers Y_0, Y_1, and Y_2 feed the columns of all three planes. A separate data driver sends either a ONE or a ZERO pulse into the data winding of each plane; and a separate sense amplifier picks up the signal produced during reading across the sense winding of each plane.

The illustration shows what happens when the binary combination 101 is written into a group of cores. The cores are chosen by activating drivers X_1

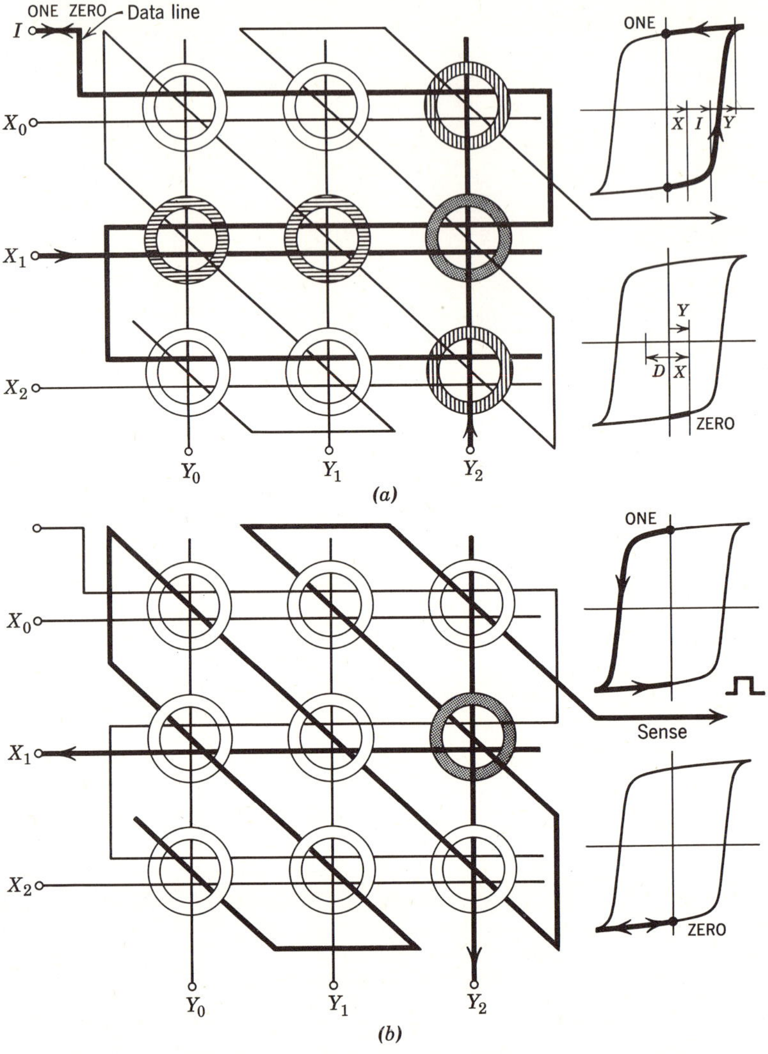

Figure 110 Coincident-current storage plane. (*a*) Writing. (*b*) Reading.

and Y_2. The drivers send current flowing through the row and column lines shown in bold in each plane, selecting core *A* in plane 0, core *B* in plane 1, and core *C* in plane 2. At the same time, data drivers 0 and 2 are caused to send ONE- producing current through the cores in plane 0 and 2 respectively. The X_1, Y_2, and data pulses add to flip the cores *A* and *C* to the ONE state. Data driver 1, on the other hand, sends ZERO-producing current through the cores of plane 1. This current cancels the effect of the X_1 current in core *B*, thus leaving only Y_2 to produce flux. This flux is not enough to flip core *B*. Upon

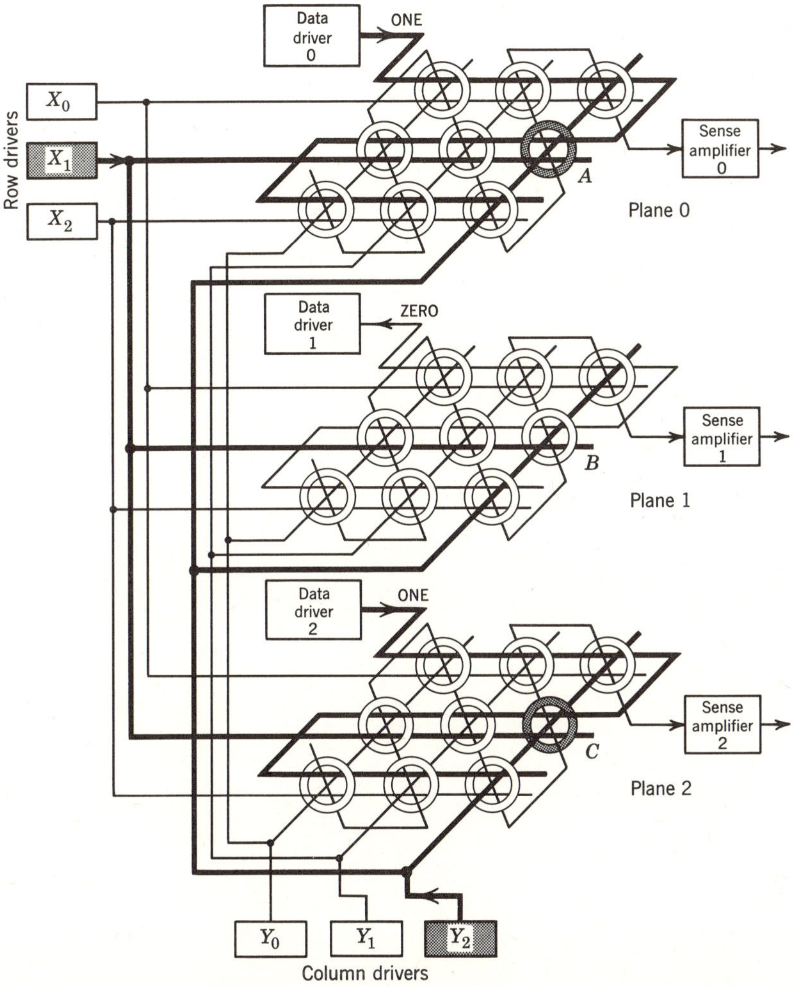

Figure 111 Three planes of coincident-current storage.

completion of writing, therefore, cores A, B, and C are storing the combination 101.

To read this combination, half-current pulses are produced by X_1 and Y_2, but in the opposite direction. The two pulses in coincidence are strong enough to flip a core to the ZERO state. Cores A and C flip from the ONE state to the ZERO state; the reversals in flux produce output voltages in the sense windings of planes 0 and 2. The respective sense amplifiers amplify these output pulses. Core B does not flip since it is already in the ZERO state; no voltage is produced across the sense winding of plane 1, and nothing is amplified by sense amplifier 1.

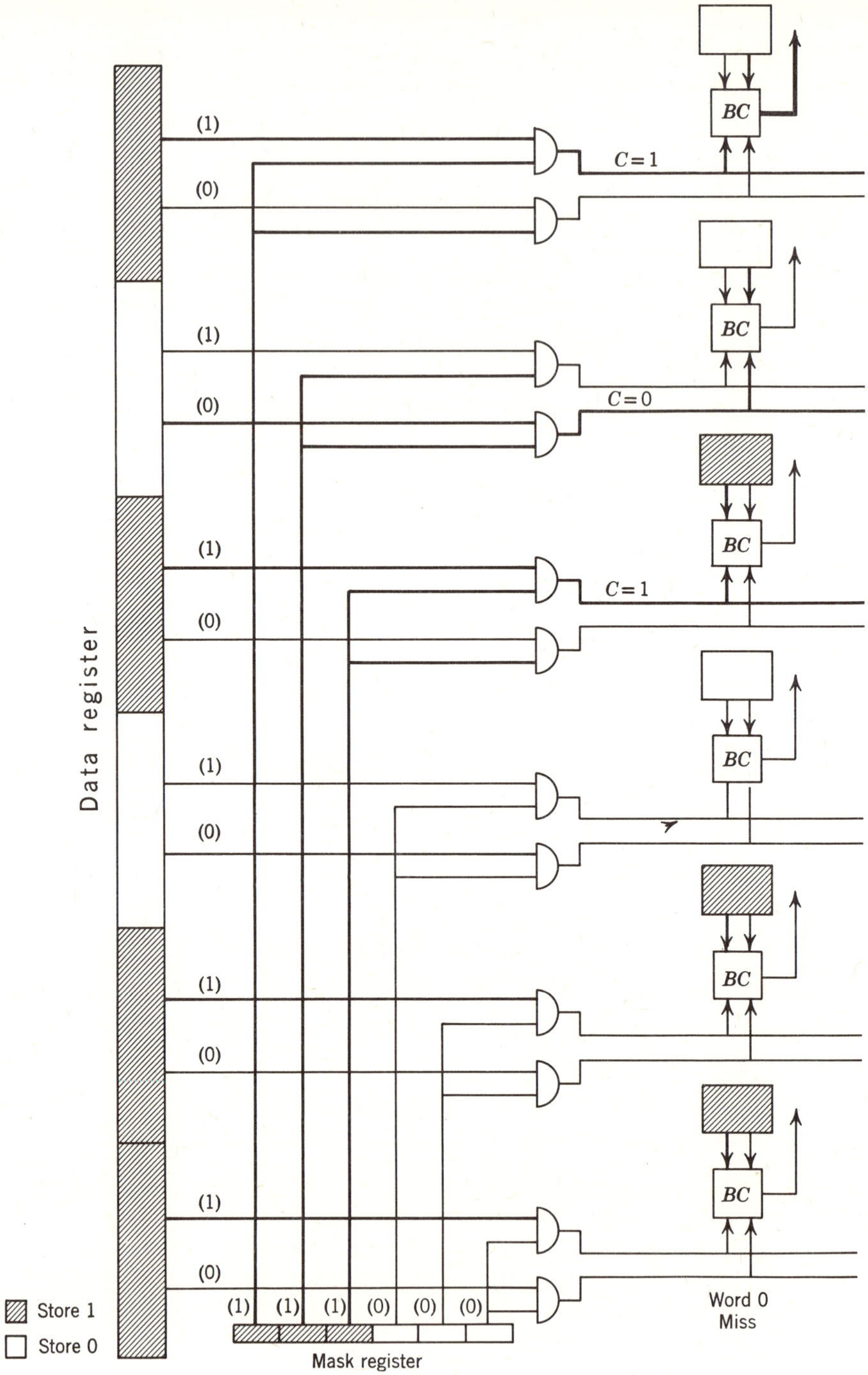

Figure 112 Content addressable storage.

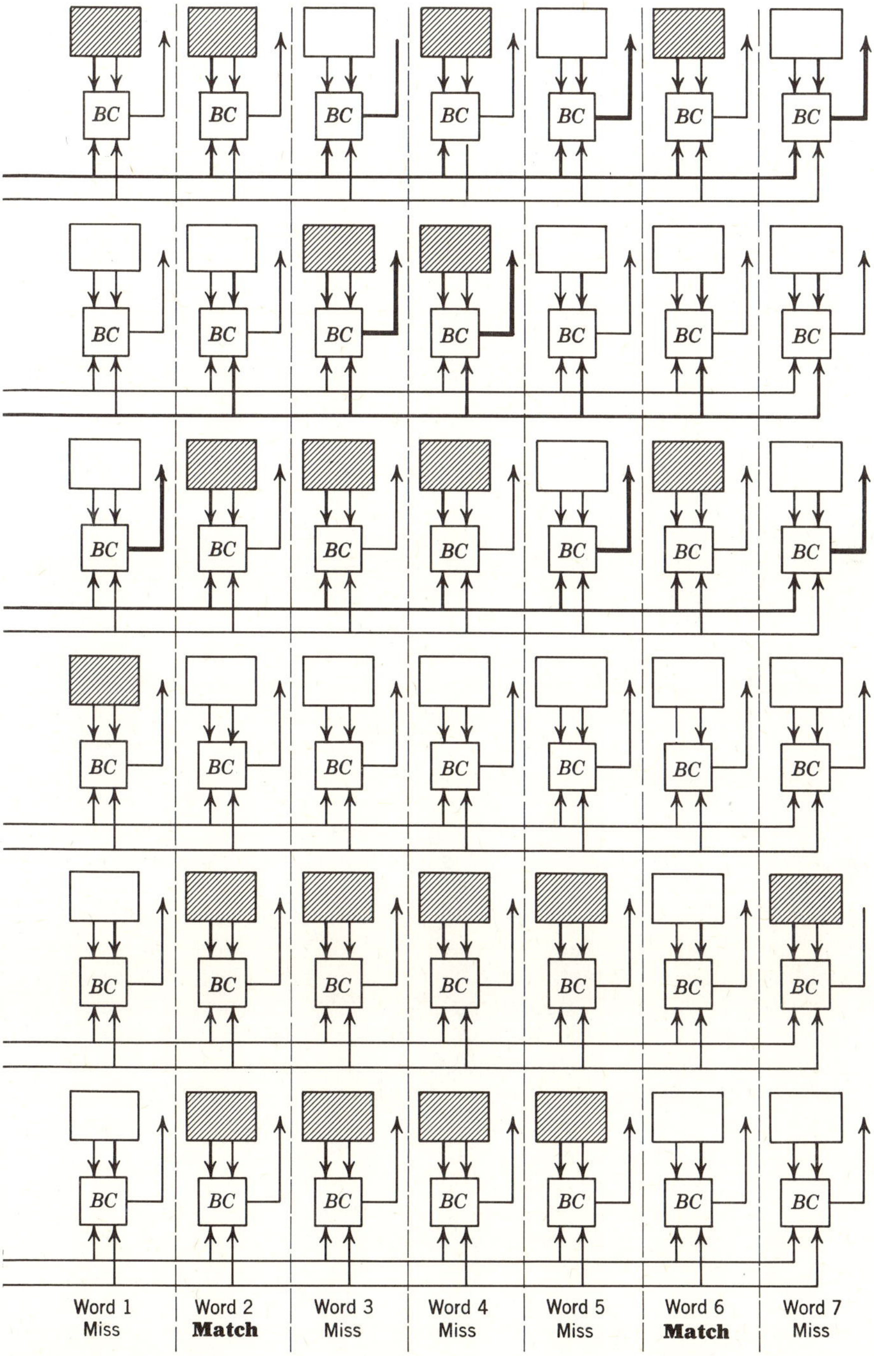
BC
Word 1
Miss
Word 2
Match
Word 3
Miss
Word 4
Miss
Word 5
Miss
Word 6
Match
Word 7
Miss

Example

Can you build a coincident-current magnetic core storage unit with X and Y pulses of half-current amplitude? How?

If half-current pulses are applied to the chosen core it will flip. This is alright for storing a ONE. To store a ZERO, we would have to apply an inhibit current to the data line.

Example

How many planes and how many cores per plane would be needed for a unit storing 100 words, each word 10 bits long? How many X and Y coordinates do we need?

Since 100 words are needed, 100 cores are required per plane. To be able to store a different bit in each of the 10 positions, 10 planes are required. To choose 1 out of 100 words would require a 10×10 matrix.

Example

What is the latency time of a coincident-current magnetic-core storage unit? What is the access time?

The latency time is zero: no time is needed to find an address. The access time is the time it takes to write data into the cores or to read out the data.

Content Addressable Storage

Figure 112 shows in schematic form a content addressable storage unit consisting of a 6-bit data register (*DR*), a 6-bit mask register (*MR*) and 48 storage cells each with an associated binary comparator (*BC*). These cells are grouped into 8 words of 6 bits each. *DR* holds the word that will be compared with each of the 8 words in storage. The *MR* holds a word that indicates which of the data bits are to be masked and which not: a 1 in *MR* means the associated data bit is not to be masked, a 0 indicates the bit is to be masked. The combined output of *DR* and *MR* is the associative criterion C, and it is this value against which all storage cells are compared.

Before continuing with the discussion of this comprehensive illustration, it may be best to consider what happens at the 1-bit level. Figure 113*a* shows this by block diagram and by truth table. The outputs of *MR* and *DR* are combined so that if $MR=1$, the associated value of *DR* becomes C, whereas if $MR=0$, *DR* is not gated out and a "don't care" condition occurs. The criterion C is compared with the contents of the storage cell S in the binary comparator *BC*. If the two are equal, no pulse is produced and the detector D remains in the matched state that it is placed in at the beginning. If C and S are unequal, then *BC* produces a pulse that places D in the miss state.

Returning to Fig. 112, it can be seen that for the example given, $DR=101011$ and $MR=111000$, only the three criteria lines shown are activated. Each of these lines is compared at the same time with the associated bits of each of the eight words in storage. At each *BC* where S and C are unequal, an output is produced which flips the detector associated with that word to the miss state. In the example given, there are only two words that do not have any output

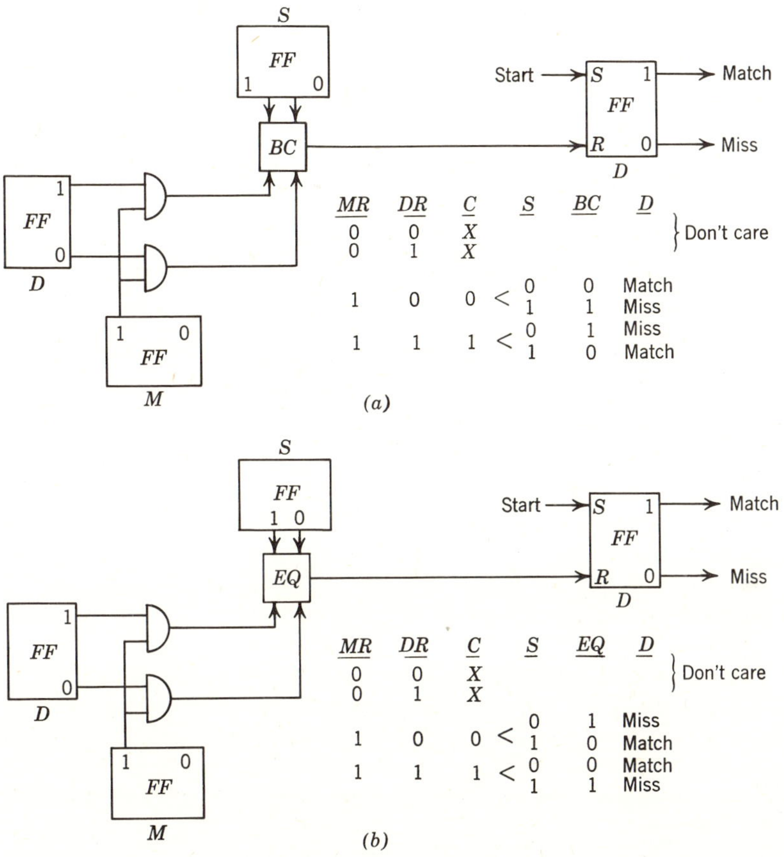

Figure 113 Searching against an associative criterion. (*a*) Match against criterion. (*b*) Match against inverse of criterion.

pulses produced and, thus, that remain in the match state. These are words 2 and 6, the chosen words.

Now that the search has located the word or words storing the same bits as the associative criterion, all that remains to do is to read out each of the two words in turn.

To write into the storage unit, a search must be made of empty locations. Empty locations may be identified by a special tag such as 000. Thus to write in an empty location, 000xxx is stored in *DR* and 111000 in *MR*, where *X* may be either 1 or 0. A search of the storage unit with the contents as given in the illustration would produce a match for words 5 and 7. Writing can then take place first into word 5 and then into word 7.

A comparison may be obtained between *C* and *S* for any Boolean expression, not only for the exclusive OR represented by the *BC*. Table 20 shows the results obtainable with several Boolean expressions.

table 20 LOGICAL COMPARISON OF 2 VARIABLES

C	*S*	Exclusive OR	Equivalence	AND	OR	NOR	NAND	INHIBIT
0	0	0	1	0	0	1	1	0
0	1	1	0	0	1	0	1	0
1	0	1	0	0	1	0	1	1
1	1	0	1	1	1	0	0	0

Example

What logical block must be substituted for *BC* in Fig. 112 in order to produce a match only when the inverse of the criterion is stored?

An equivalence block will do the job, as shown in Fig. 113*b*. In this case an output is produced whenever *C* and *S* are equal, and this output flips the detector to the miss state. When *C* and *S* are unequal, the detector remains in the match state.

Figure 114a Integrated circuit chip near grains of rice. (courtesy Texas Instruments Co).

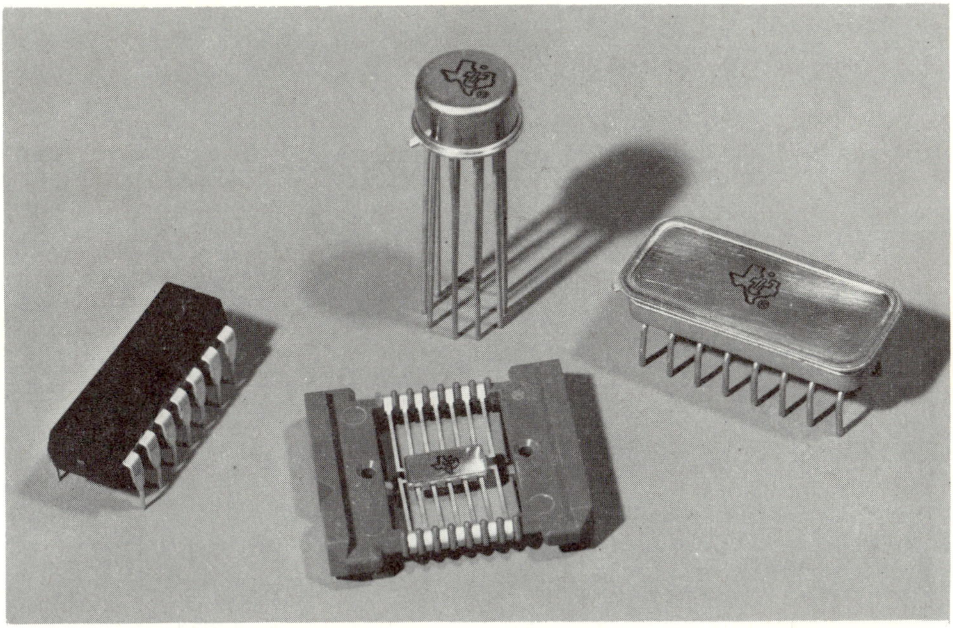

Figure 114b Integrated circuit packages. (courtesey of Texas Instruments Co).

BULK SWITCHING

Instead of building discrete logical building blocks out of individual transistors, we may build a large array of logical building blocks by forming a group of junctions in one chip of silicon. This can be done by a batch fabrication technique. The resultant device may be a complete functional building block or even a group of functional building blocks occupying a tiny space (see Fig. 114).

After describing the basic method of manufacturing these transistor-like arrays, we discuss several of these logical arrays. After that, the Metal Oxide Silicon (MOS) technique for accomplishing the same ends is considered briefly.

Batch Fabrication of Integrated Transistor Circuits

As has been shown previously, a diode consists of a *p–n* junction, as illustrated in Fig. 115. The *p*-type crystal consists of a crystal of silicon with boron impurities; and the *n*-type crystal consists of a crystal of silicon with phosphorus impurities. In addition, conductors are attached to both sides of the *p–n* junction.

This diode may be manufactured by the following technique (see Fig. 116). Start with a wafer of *n*-type silicon (Fig. 116*a*). Place it in an oven and heat it in the presence of oxygen to about 1000°C until an extremely thin layer of

Figure 115 *P-N* junction diode.

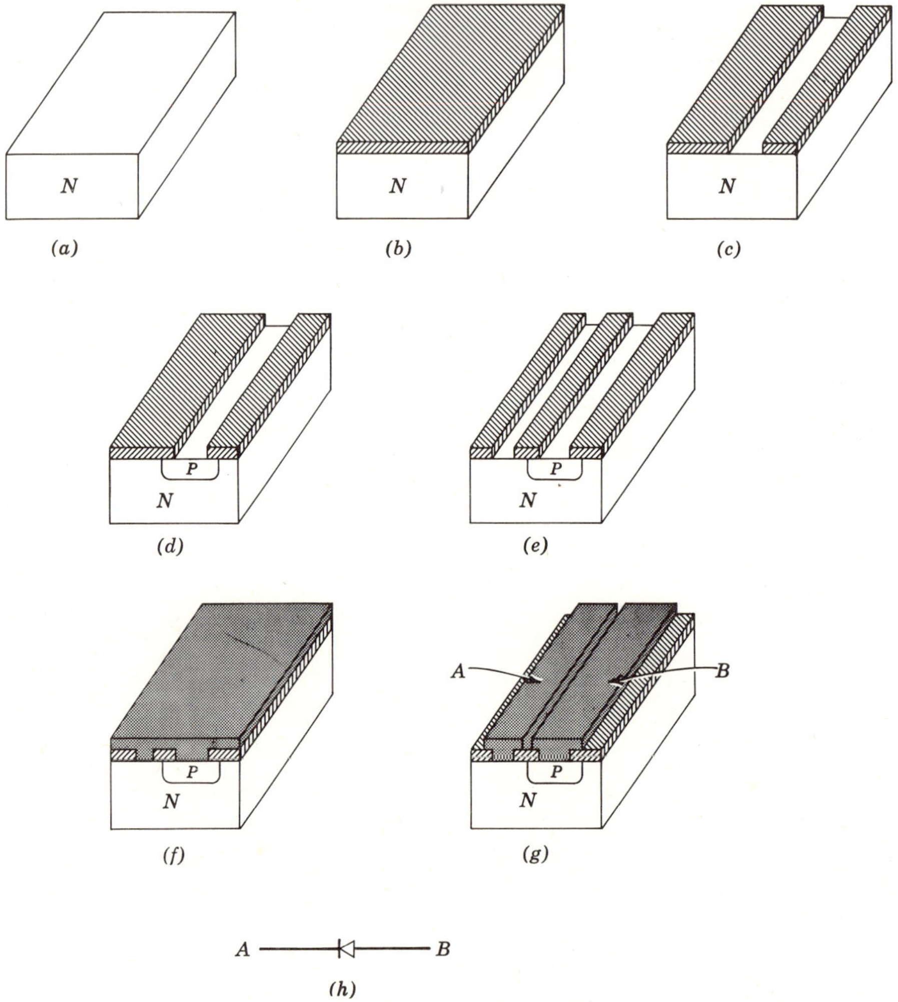

Figure 116 Manufacturing diode with integrated circuit techniques. (*a*) *N*-type wafer. (*b*) Silicon dioxide growth. (*c*) Etching. (*d*) Boron diffusion. (*e*) Etching. (*f*) Metalization. (*g*) Etching interconnection pattern.

silicon dioxide is grown on the surface (Fig. 116*b*). Then etch a pattern in this silicon dioxide layer (Fig. 116*c*) in the following manner:

1. Cover the crystal with a photosensitive material.
2. Place a light mask over area desired.
3. Expose the crystal to ultraviolet light.
4. Remove the mask and apply hydrofluoric acid. Areas that were unexposed to the light are etched; the acid has no effect on the previously exposed areas.

The next step is to diffuse boron into the *n*-type material to form a *p*-type area (Fig. 116*d*). This is the basic *p–n* junction. By an etching technique similar to the one done in Fig. 116*c*, the pattern of Fig. 116*e* is made. After this, aluminum is evaporated over the surface (Fig. 116*f*) and again etching is used, this time to form the interconnection pattern (Fig. 116*g*).

Merely by modifying the masks an array of junctions can be formed. Since a given *p*-type material has a certain amount of resistivity per given length, the technique lends itself toward fabrication of resistors as well as diodes. Figure 117 shows a three-dimensional view of a simple diode-resistor combination. It is made from a basic *n*-crystal into which the pattern of *p*-type areas is infused. The large snake pattern *p*-type area representing the resistor is infused at the same time. The aluminum is deposited in the areas shown in black to provide the terminals. If a minus voltage is applied to *A*, the device is an OR circuit: if a plus signal is applied to *B*, *C*, or *D*, a plus output is produced at *E*.

Integrated Circuit Arrays

Figure 118 shows a complete *BCD* to decimal decoder on one chip of silicon. After a silicon dioxide layer is grown over an *n*-type silicon crystal, a pattern of 10 horizontal bars is etched in this layer. Boron is then infused into these areas to make them *p*-type. After another layer of silicon dioxide is grown, a pattern of all the boxes labeled *N* in the illustration is etched out, and phosphorus is infused to make these areas *n*-type. Each horizontal bar now represents a group of 8 diodes with common *p*-areas, and with all the *p*-areas connected to a resistor (the long *N* area). Again, a layer of silicon dioxide is grown, this time the pattern shown in black is etched, and aluminum is evaporated to form the interconnection pattern.

Notice that an entirely different decoder may be obtained by merely modifying the mask used before the metalization step in order to connect different diodes to the various vertical lines.

Example

What happens when 0101 is applied to the above decoder?

The first, fourth, fifth, and eighth vertical bars have signals applied to them. Under these circumstances, the only horizontal bar that has a signal applied to every connected diode is line 5. A signal is produced across the resistor in this line.

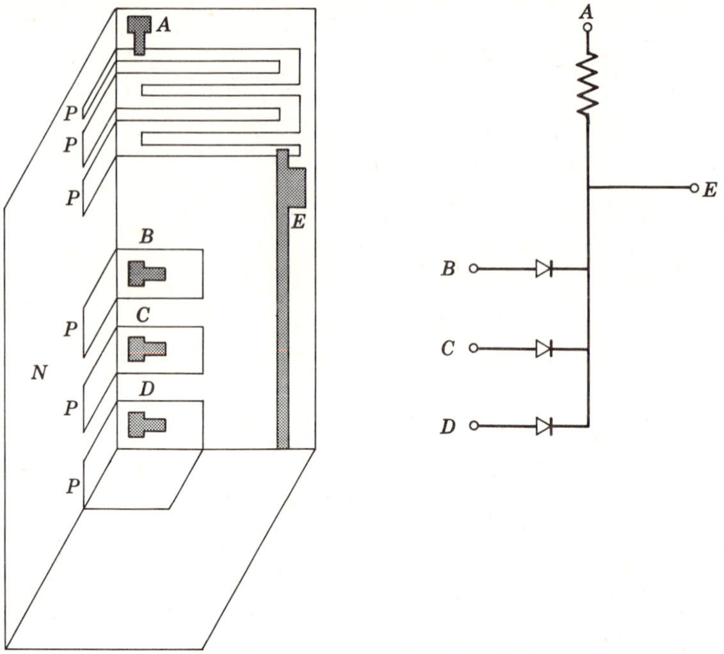

Figure 117 Integrated OR circuit.

If we can form diodes, we can form transistors by the same process. Figure 119*a* shows a NAND circuit comprised of diodes and a transistor. Figure 119*b* shows the same circuit as it would appear in an integrated circuit layout. In this case, we start with a *p*-type silicon crystal. First, the *n*-type layers are diffused. This is followed by the *p*-type layer diffusion and, then, *n*-type layers near the top. After this, the interconnection patten is applied to the surface, as shown in black.

The *N, P, N* layers on the right represent the *n–p–n* transistor. The four *N* areas embedded within the central *p*-area represent four diodes with their *p*-areas common. The large *p*-area at the left represents a resistor.

By the same technique, adders and any other functional building block used for switching may be manufactured. When a decoder such as that shown in Fig. 118 is produced, it is called medium-scale integration (MSI). When about 100 or more circuits are placed on a chip it is called large-scale integration (LSI).

Metal Oxide Silicon (MOS)

Batch fabrication of switching circuits also may be accomplished via the Metal Oxide Silicon (MOS) approach. The basic construction of an MOS element is shown in Fig. 120*a*. It consists of three terminals called the

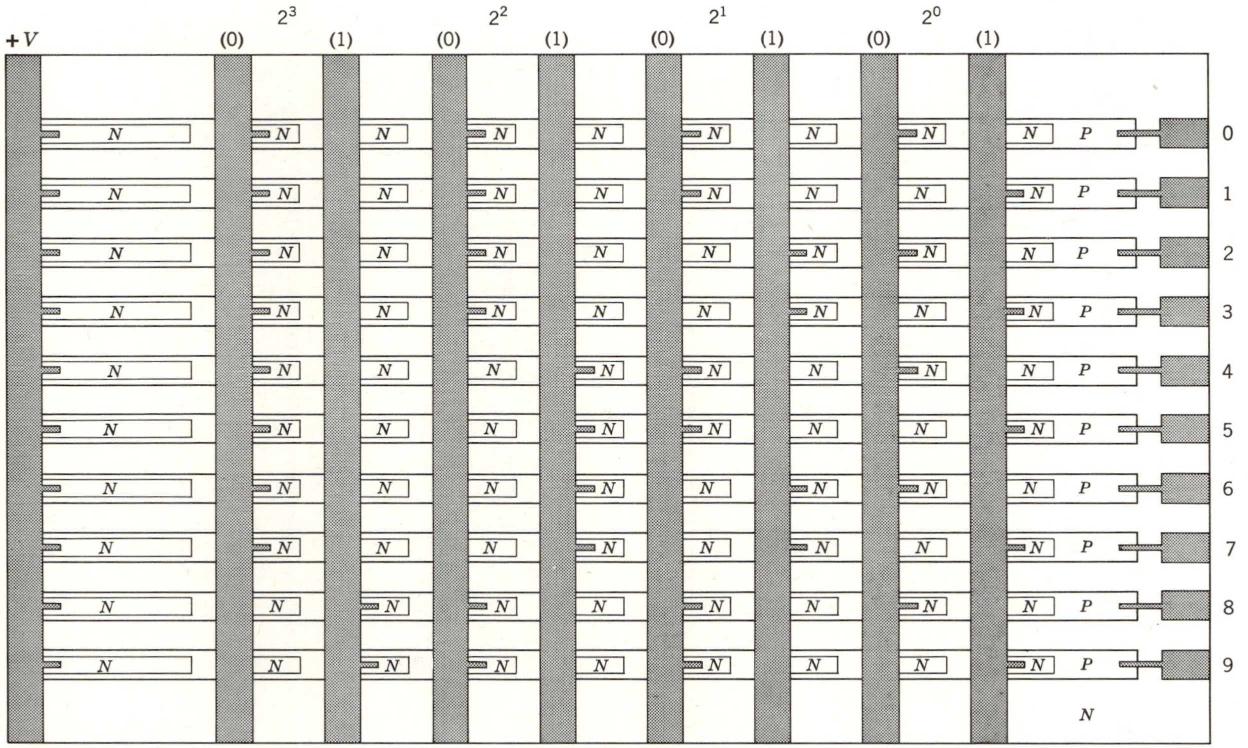

Figure 118 Decoder—*BCD* to decimal.

source, gate, and drain, which correspond to the emitter, base, and collector of an ordinary *p–n–p* transistor. The gate is made of metal over a silicon dioxide insulator area. The source and drain are *p*-areas diffused into an *n*-type silicon crystal. Holes can be made to flow between source and drain only by making the gate sufficiently negative with respect to the source. This negative potential produces a field that controls the hole flow. Figure 120*b* shows the symbol for the MOS device.

By placing two MOS devices in parallel as shown in Fig. 120*c*, a NOR is produced. If a negative signal is applied to either *A* or *B*, current flows through the MOS device and a positive signal is produced.

By placing two MOS devices in series as shown in Fig. 120*d*, a NAND circuit is formed. Only if negative pulses are applied to both *A* and *B* does current flow and produce a positive output across the resistor.

By batch fabrication techniques similar to the ones described above, many MOS devices can be placed on one chip of silicon to achieve MSI and LSI.

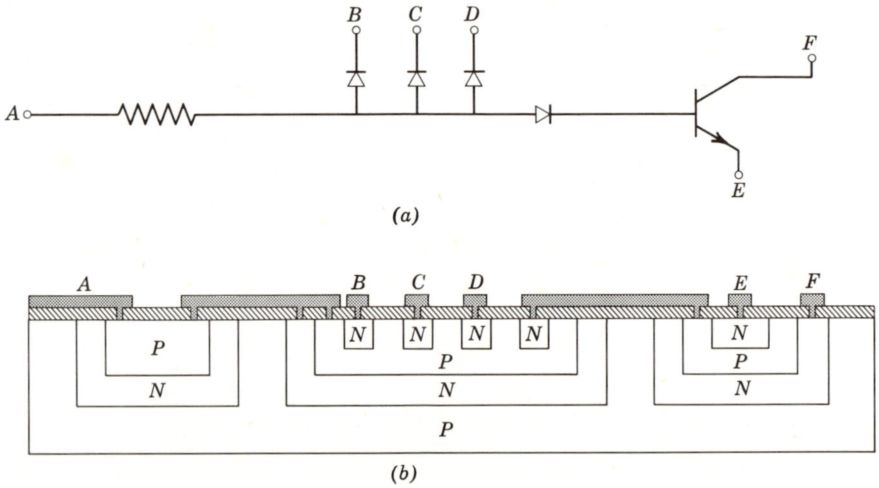

Figure 119 NAND circuit. (*a*) Diode-transistor. (*b*) Integrated circuit.

BULK STORAGE AND SWITCHING

By an extension of the above batch fabrication techniques as well as by other electronic and mechanical techniques, combinations of bulk storage and switching devices may be obtained.

The NOR Flip-Flop

We have seen how the NOR circuit may easily be fabricated by integrated circuit techniques. If this can be done, so can a flip-flop be fabricated, since a flip-flop may be considered to consist of two NORs the output of each forming an input to the other as shown in Fig. 121*a*.

Specifically, this flip-flop works as follows. If a negative Set pulse is applied to N_1 at the same time as a negative CP (Fig. 121*c*), then its output is made positive. NOR circuit N_2 inverts this to a negative pulse representing a ONE output. This negative output is fed to N_4, which together with the negative pulse from N_3 causes a positive output. This positive output, in turn, is applied as input to N_2 to keep the flip-flop in the ONE state, even after the Set pulse is removed.

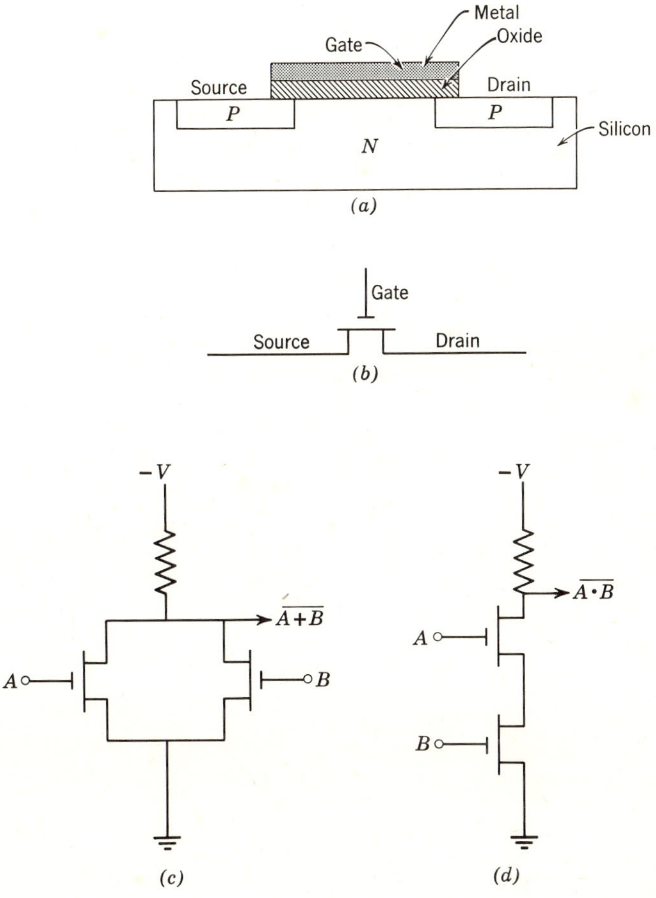

Figure 120 MOS logic. (*a*) MOS construction. (*b*) MOS symbol. (*c*) NOR. (*d*) NAND.

To reset this flip-flop, a negative Reset pulse is applied to N_3 at the same time as a negative CP (Fig. 121*d*). The resultant positive output is inverted by N_4 to produce a negative ZERO output. Again the feedback keeps the flip-flop in this state: the minus output of N_4 is applied to N_2; the two minus inputs at N_2 produce a positive output that is returned to N_4 to keep its output negative.

The NOR gates may be built of transistors embedded within a silicon crystal, and the connections among the transistors may be accomplished by means of a metalization pattern.

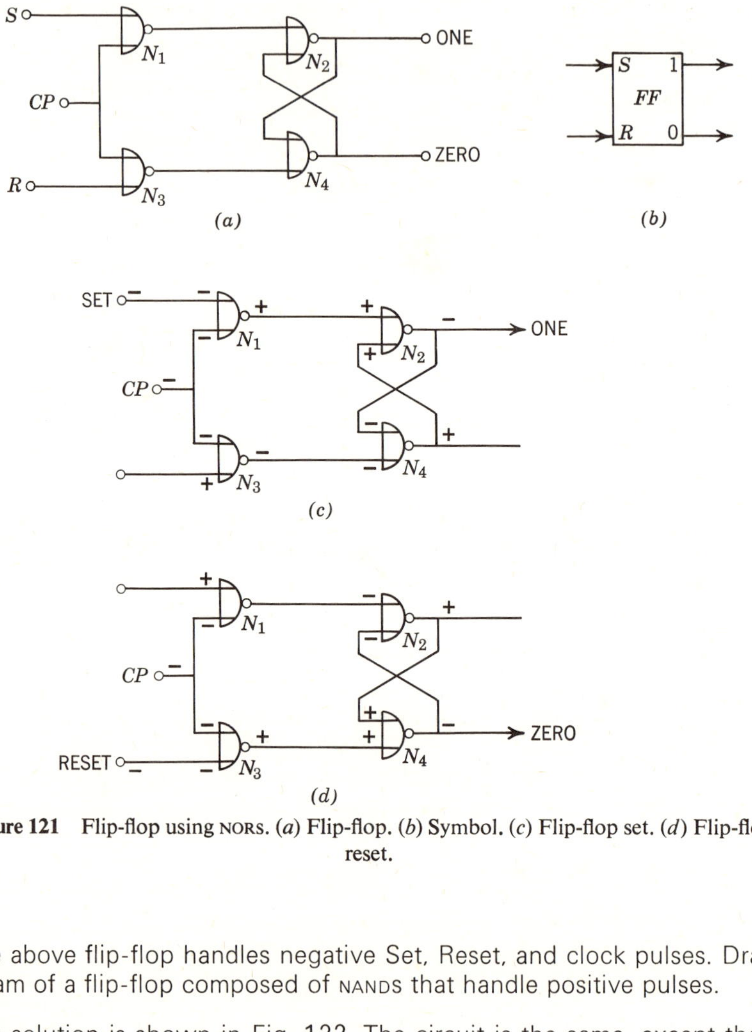

Figure 121 Flip-flop using NORS. (*a*) Flip-flop. (*b*) Symbol. (*c*) Flip-flop set. (*d*) Flip-flop reset.

Example

The above flip-flop handles negative Set, Reset, and clock pulses. Draw a diagram of a flip-flop composed of NANDS that handle positive pulses.

The solution is shown in Fig. 122. The circuit is the same, except that all NORS are replaced by NANDS. The illustration shows the circuit placed into the Set state. Positive Set and *CP* pulses applied to N_1 produce a minus pulse that is inverted to a positive ONE output by N_2. The feedback from N_2 to N_4 causes the latter to produce a minus which, when returned to N_2, maintains the ONE output state even after the Set pulse is removed.

Registers and Counters

By placing many such flip-flops in a crystal of silicon, we can fabricate a complete register or a complete counter on one crystal. And this has been done.

Read-Only Storage

We have learned how a switching circuit—a NOR—can be converted to a storage circuit—a flip-flop. Now we shall see that what is nominally a storage circuit—a read-only store—is in actuality a switching circuit—an encoder.

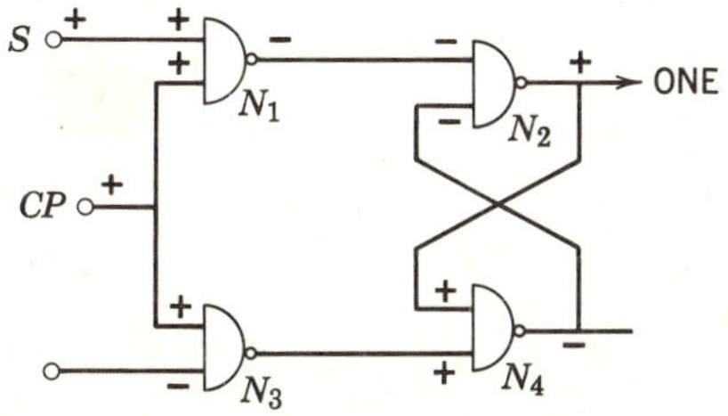

Figure 122 Flip-flop using NANDS.

In fact, we shall explain the operation of a transformer read-only store by comparing it to a transformer encoder. This is done in Fig. 123, where the upper illustration presents a transformer encoder, and the lower illustration presents an equivalent read-only store.

The transformer encoder consists of 4 *U*-cores made of low remanence ferrite that are linked by drive lines or not, as shown. Across each *U*-core is a magnetic *I*-core with a secondary winding surrounding it. When current is sent through drive line *A*, pulses appear at the sense 0 and 2 outputs, since they are the only two places where transformer action occurs; no pulses appear at the sense 1 and 3 outputs. The encoded output word is 0101. When current is sent through drive line *B*, pulses appear at the sense 1 and 3 outputs, since they are the only places where transformer action occurs; no pulses appear at the sense 0 and 2 outputs. The encoded output word in this case is 1010.

In the read-only store the drive lines are replaced by copper ladders etched onto a piece of plastic tape. *U*-cores are placed through holes in the tape between rungs of the ladders and mate with *I*-cores on the other side. To obtain an output equivalent to the one obtained by the encoder, holes must be punched in sides of the ladders as shown. If a hole is punched in an inner side of a ladder, the circuit on this side is broken, forcing current to travel down the outer side; the result is no transformer action and a ZERO is produced at the secondary winding. If, however, a hole is punched in an outer side of a ladder, current is forced to travel through the inner side, causing transformer action to occur and to produce a ONE at the secondary.

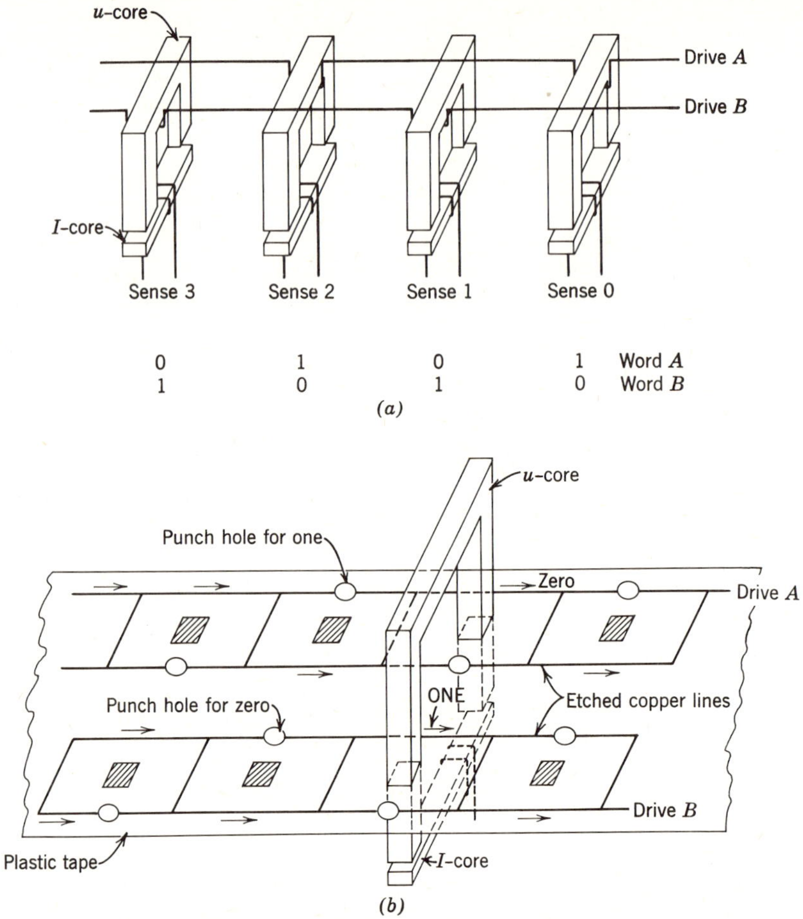

Figure 123 Transformer read-only storage.

Many tapes of this kind, each with a different combination of holes, may be placed in a stack.

Data storage is on the tape. Although it is not done frequently, the tape can be removed and replaced with a new tape punched with a different set of holes representing new data. Perhaps this device should have been called delayed write—quick read instead of read-only.

Mechanical Switching and Storage

The printer is one form of mechanical switching and storage. The printer translates from one code to another and stores the data on paper. Many types of mechanical printing mechanisms are available. Four generic types are discussed briefly.

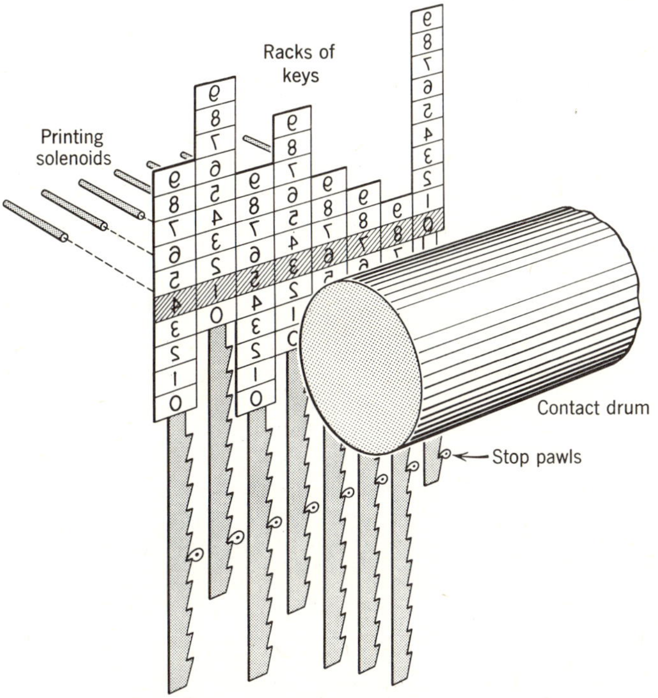

Figure 124 Rack-type printing mechanism.

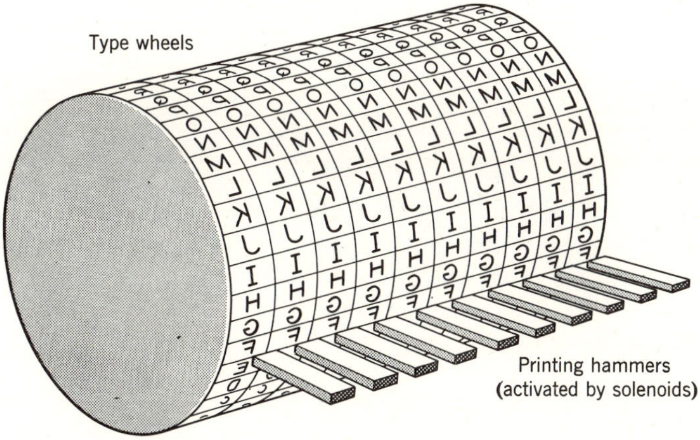

Figure 125 Type-wheel printing mechanism.

Figure 124 shows a simple system in which all the characters are aligned in a vertical rack. Characters are chosen for printing by pushing the racks upward against springs and stopping each rack in its movement at the appropriate time by a stop pawl. After all the racks are in position, printing plungers force the keys against carbon and paper. The racks are then brought back to their neutral position. The paper and carbon are moved a little, the racks are adjusted again, and the plungers cause the next line to be printed. Several adding and calculating machines print in this manner.

Figure 125 illustrates the type-wheel printer. In this type of printing mechanism, several wheels, one for each print position on a line, are mounted on a steadily rotating axle. Each type-wheel has embossed around its periphery all the characters which may be printed. At any one time during the rotation of the type-wheels, the same character appears in printing position at each wheel. Printing is accomplished by striking a hammer onto carbon and paper at each printing position along the line at the appropriate time. This means that all the a's in a line are printed first, then all the b's, all the c's, etc. One revolution of the type-wheels is needed to print one line of data. As soon as a line is printed, the paper and carbon are moved and the characters of the next line are printed during the next revolution of the type-wheels.

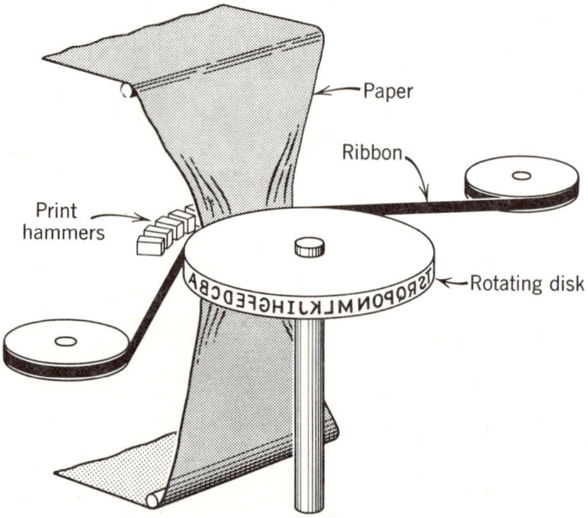

Figure 126 Spinning-disk printing mechanism.

The spinning-disk type of printing mechanism is shown in Fig. 126. In this case, all the characters are embossed around the periphery of one horizontal disk. The paper is fed vertically and follows the curvature of the disk. Arranged in an arc on the opposite side of the paper are the solenoids, one for each printing position along a line. As the disk rotates, different characters appear at different points along the line. As the appropriate character appears in a desired printing position, the associated print hammer is activated by a solenoid. One revolution of the disk is needed to print a line. If a series of a's is desired across the line, the solenoids are activated in sequence. If all the characters are desired in sequence across the line, all the hammers are activated at once.

Another type of printing mechanism uses a matrix composed of pins. Different characters are printed by producing impressions on paper with different configurations of pins. Figure 127 shows character impressions produced when a matrix of 35 pins, 5 columns of 7 pins each is used.

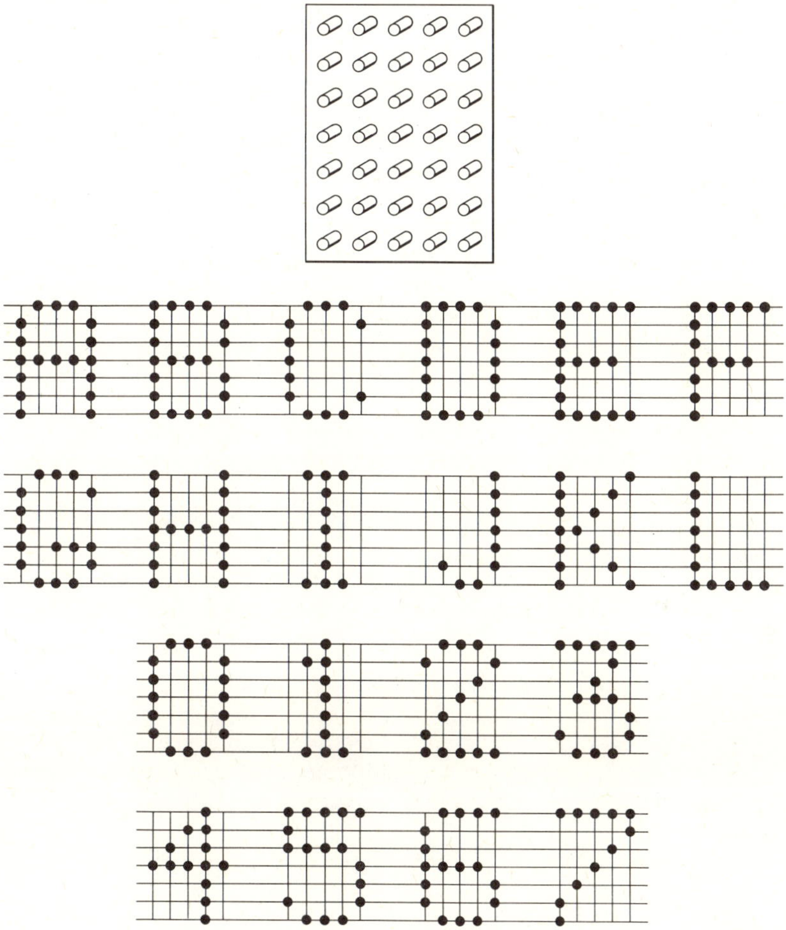

Figure 127 Matrix-type printing.

SUMMARY

1. Bulk logic is logic produced by batch fabrication techniques, and it may consist of a complete functional building block or of several functional building blocks.
2. Two major methods of categorization of storage devices are by means-of-access and type-of-address selection. Access may be sequential, cyclic, or coordinate. Address selection may be by location or by content.
3. Among sequential storage devices are the ones that deal with unit records—punched cards; and the ones that deal with continuous records—punched paper tape and magnetic tape.
4. Among cyclic access devices are the magnetic drum and the magnetic disc. These devices have time-addresses as well as space addresses.
5. The magnetic card has some of the characteristics of a sequential access device as well as some of the characteristics of a cyclic access device.
6. The coordinate access device has only space addresses. The coincident current magnetic-core storage device is an example.
7. In content addressable storage no location address is given. The storage may be searched to find stored data matching a given tag, a criterion determined by a Boolean expression, or functions such as "more than" and "less than."
8. Batch fabrication may be used to manufacture switching circuit arrays of integrated circuits on small chips of silicon. The process consists of masking, etching, impurity diffusion, and metalization steps. Changing patterns accomplished by changing masks produces changed circuits and thus changed logic.
9. The close relationship between storage and switching is indicated by the following:

   A flip-flop may be built of 2 NORS
   A read-only storage device acts as an encoder

10. *Definitions to Remember*

    Static Storage. A storage device that stores bits by staying in one of several stable states.
    Dynamic Storage. A storage device that stores bits by continuous recirculation of a wave or other physical phenomena.
    Volatile Storage. Storage that loses its data with time or when the power is turned off.
    Nonvolatile Storage. Storage that does not lose its data even when the power is turned off.
    Destructive Read-Out. Storage in which the data is changed when it is read out.
    Nondestructive Read-Out. Storage in which bits remain stored even after they are read out.
    Erasable Storage. Storage in which bits may be replaced by other bits.
    Nonerasable Storage. Storage that does not allow bits to be erased.
    Sequential Access Storage. A storage device whose individual locations are

arranged in time in such a manner that access to any one location may be normally obtained only once during an operation.

Cyclic Access Storage. A storage device whose individual locations are arranged in time (as well as in space) in such a manner that access to any one location may be obtained repeatedly at a certain rate.

Track. That portion of a moving type storage medium (tape, drum, etc.) which is accessible to a given writing or reading station.

Band. A group of tracks that often are written onto or read from at one time.

Coordinate Access Storage. A storage device whose word locations are arranged in space.

Random Access Device. A device in which it takes as long to obtain access to one address as it does to any other address.

Coincident-Current Storage. A bulk storage device composed of storage cells in a rectangular array. Data is written into and read from a location by sending current coincidentally to the column and row lines in which the location occurs.

Continuous Record. A record where a long stream of data is stored on one unit. A good example is magnetic tape.

Unit Record. A record where a small group of characters is stored as one item. Unit records are easy to file. Punched cards are an example.

Content Addressable Storage. A storage device that searches for data by comparing the contents of all of its storage cells with a given word or part of a word.

Associative Criterion. The word or part of a word against which the contents of the cells of a content addressable storage device are compared.

Latency Time. The time required to find an address in a storage device.

Access Time. The time required to complete a transfer to or from a storage device.

Cycle Time. The time between references to a storage device.

Medium Scale Integration (MSI). A batch fabrication technique which produces up to 100 integrated circuits on a semiconductor chip.

Large Scale Integration (LSI). A batch fabrication technique which produces more than 100 integrated circuits on a semiconductor chip.

Exercises

1. Given a magnetic tape which is 2400 feet long and is able to record 500 characters per inch.
   a. How many blocks consisting of 2000 characters each can be stored on this tape if we assume that a gap of .8 inch is inserted between blocks?
   b. How many such blocks can be recorded if the recording density is 250 characters per inch?

2. Assume in exercise 1 above that the tape can be read at the rate of 100 inches per second and that 10 ms is required to get the tape unit started.
   a. How long will it take to reach the eleventh block?
   b. How long will it take to read the data in this block off the tape after this point has been reached?
3. For exercise 2 above, give the following:
   a. The latency time.
   b. The access time.
   c. The maximum latency time (in the general case).
   d. The average latency time (in the general case).
4. Given a drum (as per Fig. 105) with 8 data tracks, each track consisting of 128 sectors, each sector being 32 bits long:
   a. What are the total number of sector locations which may be addressed?
   b. How many bits are required to address these locations?
   c. How many timing pulses must there be on the timing track?
5. Assume that the drum in exercise 4 above has stationary read-write heads and rotates at 3000 rpm.
   a. What is the maximum latency time?
   b. What is the average latency time?
   c. What is the average access time?
   d. What is the time from start of one timing pulse to the start of the following timing pulse?
6. Given a drum with 16 stationary heads serving 16 data tracks addressed as 0 to 15. Each track consists of 256 sectors addressed as 0 to 255. Each sector is 64 bits long, and the drum rotates at 3600 rpm. How long will it take to get to address 3–100 where 3 is the track address and 100 is the sector address, if the drum has just finished reading 2–000? Assume that the time for switching from one head to another is negligible.
7. Given a drum for parallel writing and reading, which consists of 16 bands each band consisting of 32 tracks, and each track divided into 2048 rows:
   a. How many addressable locations are there?
   b. How many bits are needed to encode an address?
8. Assume the drum in exercise 7 above has stationary heads and is rotating at 2400 rpm.
   a. What is the maximum latency time?
   b. What is the average latency time?
   c. What is the average access time?
   d. How many timing pulses are needed in the timing track?
9. Given a drum with 8 tracks, each consisting of 4096 sectors and rotating at 3600 rpm. The drum has one stationary head provided per track.
   a. What is the maximum latency time?
   b. What is the average latency time?
   c. What are **(a)** and **(b)** if 2 heads 180° apart are provided for each track?
   d. What are **(a)** and **(b)** if 4 heads 90° apart are provided for each track?
10. Given a disc system consisting of 16 discs each consisting of 512 tracks, each track storing 32 sectors, each 1024 bits long. All discs rotate at 1200 rpm. A

positioning arm associated with each disc possesses 8 heads and may be moved to any one of 64 positions along the disc. The arm positioning time varies from 100 ms, when moved 1 position; to 200 ms, when moved across the whole range; with 150 ms considered to be the approximate average.

a. What is the maximum and average latency time (which includes arm positioning time)?

b. What is the maximum and average access time?

11. A coincident-current magnetic storage device stores 4096 words, each 32 bits long.

a. How many planes are required?

b. How many cells per plane are required?

c. How many *x* address bits are required?

d. How many data drivers are required?

12. A coordinate storage unit is designed so that each cycle consists of a read followed by a write; after a settling time during which the circuits are brought back to normal, another cycle starts. The latency time is 4 μs, read time 10 μs, write time 10 μs, and settling time 5 μs. What is the cycle time?

13. Given a content addressable storage unit using 16-bit words, the least significant 8 bits of which are used for comparison.

a. What should the contents of the mask register be?

b. What should the contents be if the most significant 8 bits are used for comparison?

section III

FUNCTIONAL UNITS OF A DIGITAL COMPUTER

In this section the logical and functional building blocks developed in the last section are combined into the five functional units of a typical computer: memory, input, output, arithmetic, and control. Each of these functional units is discussed in detail in a separate chapter, except for input and output. The last two are discussed in one chapter because of their fundamental similarities.

By way of introduction into the functional description of computers and their components, the first chapter of this section describes the languages of computation. This is done from the point of view of the machine, the programmer and the ultimate user.

After all the functional units are described, all the pieces are combined into a specimen computer in the last chapter. This specimen machine is described in enough detail to provide an integrated picture of a digital computer.

CHAPTER 10

Machine language and programming

A digital computer is comprised of five functional units each performing its own function. In order that these units operate in unison, there must be communication among them. This internal communication is facilitated by defining basic data units and data and instruction words based on these units.

This internal language, or machine language, may be used by a person to define a task for the machine to execute. Unfortunately, this is not the language of human problem solving. For this reason, higher level languages have been developed that allow the programmer to define his problem in terms closer to those understood by humans.

BASIC DATA STRUCTURE

There are two viewpoints of the basic data structure: logical and physical. The first is determined by the intrinsic nature of data; the second by the physical devices used to store the data. For this reason this physical aspect is best referred to as storage structure instead of data structure.

Logical Data Units

Figure 128 shows possible relationships among logical data units. The atomic unit is the bit. Bits may be encoded into digits or into characters. Four bits are sufficient to encode the 10 digits. Six bits are sufficient to encode the digits, the letters of the alphabet plus a few punctuation marks. However, in many cases, 8 bits are used in order to make 2 digits fit into a space of 1 character.

A word consists of a group of bits, digits, or characters. The illustration, for instance, shows a word consisting of 32 bits, or 8 digits or 4 characters.

There are two kinds of words: the instruction word and the data word. The instruction word is active. It operates on the passive data word.

A group of instruction words designed to perform a specific task is called a program.

Several words may be grouped into records; several records may be grouped into blocks; and several blocks may be grouped into files.

Digits and characters are almost always fixed in size. Words and records may be fixed or variable in size. Although they can be fixed, as a rule, blocks and files are variable in size.

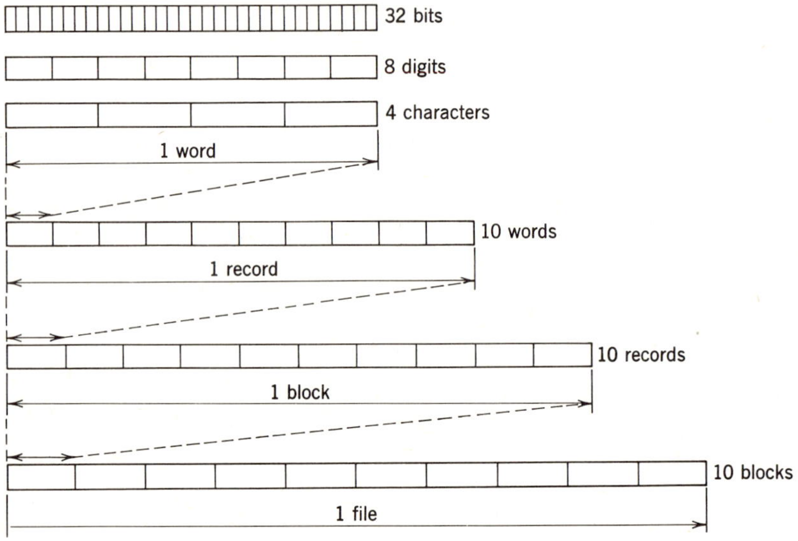

Figure 128 Logical data units.

Physical Storage Units

Physical storage units vary with the type of storage device used (see Fig. 129). In the coordinate access unit bytes are used. The byte is a unit into which a digit or a character may fit. In the previous example, the byte is 8 bits long and could accommodate 2 digits or 1 character. If the byte were 6 bits long, it could accommodate either 1 digit or 1 character. If it were 12 bits long, it could accommodate 3 digits or two 6-bit characters.

In the sequential access device that uses unit records, such as punched cards, the physical record is determined by the size of the card. The logical record may be equal to this or may consist of several physical records, or several records may be placed on a card, and so forth. On the card itself, there are fields consisting of groups of characters. Several of these fields which are of varying sizes comprise a physical record.

In the sequential access device using continuous records, such as magnetic tape, the file consists of the complete length of tape. This physical file may store several logical files, or several physical files may be needed to store one logical file.

In the cyclic access device, such as a magnetic disc, sectors are used. They may or may not be the same size of a word or of a record.

In general, transmission among storage devices is by bit, by byte, or by word.

INSTRUCTION WORD

In general, the instruction word consists of two parts: the command portion and the address portion. The command specifies the operation to be executed by the machine. The address portion specifies the location where the operand or operands are stored.

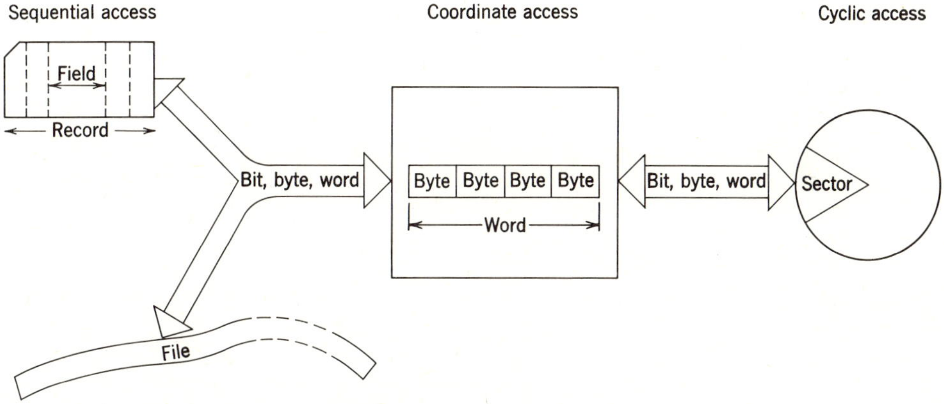

Figure 129 Physical storage units.

Types of Commands

One way of classifying computer commands is as follows:

1. Arithmetic and Logic.
2. Transfer.
3. Branch.
4. Input and Output.
5. Miscellaneous.

Arithmetic commands include add, subtract, multiply, divide, and so on; logic commands are the ones that perform various types of Boolean comparisons such as OR, AND, and exclusive OR.

Since arithmetic and logical commands normally are executed in the arithmetic unit, transfer commands are required to bring operands to and remove results from this unit. Data also must be transferred into and out of other registers in the computer.

The forte of the computer is that it can follow one sequence of instructions under one set of conditions and another sequence of instructions under another set of conditions. A command that enables the computer to make this basic type of decision is called a branch command. A branch command may cause a change in instruction sequencing if the result of a previous operation is negative, or when two operands are equal, or under many other criteria.

The input commands enable data to be entered into the computer from external input devices; output commands enable data to be sent from the computer to output devices. Also included in the input-output category are commands such as rewind the tape that control input and output device operation.

Miscellaneous commands include many that are discussed in future chapters.

Levels of Addresses

There are 3 levels of addressing: 0, 1, and 2. In level 0, the address refers to the operand; no reference is made to the storage unit. In level 1, the address refers to the location in the storage unit where the operand is stored. In level 2, the address refers to another address where the operand is stored.

Level 0 is called immediate addressing, since the address itself is the operand. Level 1 is called direct addressing: the address refers to the data wanted directly. Level 2 is called indirect addressing: the address refers to the data wanted indirectly, via another address.

Example

Given the following words stored at the following locations in storage:

Address	*Word Stored*
500	864
864	325

If the address associated with a given instruction is 500, what is the operand under the following conditions:

a. Immediate addressing.
b. Direct addressing.
c. Indirect addressing.

The answer is shown in Fig. 130. Under immediate addressing, the address itself—500—is the operand. Under direct addressing, the word stored at address 500, which is 864, is the operand. Under indirect addressing, the 864 found at location 500 represents the address of the operand; the operand then is 325.

Types of Instruction Words

Instruction words are distinguished mainly by the number of addresses specified. For the most part, computers have been designed to work with direct addresses and with indirect addressing made possible for special

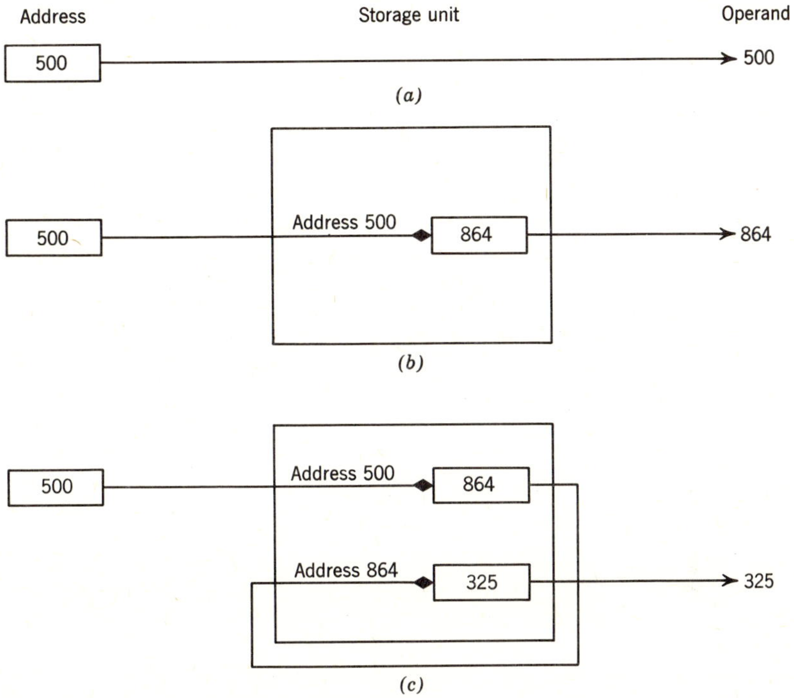

Figure 130 Levels of addressing. (*a*) Level 0: immediate. (*b*) Level 1: direct. (*c*) Level 2: indirect.

instructions. One-, two-, three-, and four-address instructions have been used. Some machines have been designed primarily around indirect addressing. The major types of instruction words are described below.

One-address instruction. When only one direct address is specified, the machine executes the given command upon the operand found in the location specified by the address. Since most arithmetic operations require at least two operands—augend and addend, multiplicand and multiplier—the computer must be built so that one operand is brought into the arithmetic unit during one instruction, and the other operand is brought into the arithmetic unit during the following instruction; during the second instruction the arithmetic operation is performed. The sequencing of the instruction words in the program is performed by an instruction counter. As soon as one instruction is completed, the instruction counter is advanced by one. The new reading of the instruction counter specifies the address of the next instruction to be executed. The machine thus automatically chooses instructions stored in successive memory locations.

Two-address instruction. The two-address instruction consists of a command, an address specifying the operand, and an address specifying the location of the next instruction word to be executed. The two-address machine does not need an instruction counter. The two-address instruction is often referred to as a 1-plus-1-address instruction.

Three-address instruction. The three-address instruction consists of a command and three addresses. The first two addresses specify two operands; the third address specifies the location in memory where the result should be stored. Machines using the three-address instruction need an instruction counter to sequence instructions in the program.

Four-address instruction. The four-address instruction has a command and four addresses. The first two addresses specify two operands. The third address specifies the location of the result. The fourth address indicates the location of the next instruction to be executed. Machines using the four-address instruction need no instruction counter.

Indirect address instruction. The address portion of an instruction may be an indirect address. One form such an indirect address may take is that of a content address. In content addressing a tag is given, and after the tag is found the associated word is read out. The content address instruction leads to a computer organization much different from the one the direct address instruction leads to.

DATA WORD

The data word is the operand. It may be given in binary or coded decimal form, in integral or in fractional form, in absolute value-plus-sign or in complement form, in fixed point or in floating point, and in fixed size or in variable size.

Binary versus Coded Decimal Words

In binary, the numerical operand is given in terms of binary equivalents. Characters are not usually used; if they are, special binary combinations are needed. In coded-decimal, the digits of the operand may be represented by 4-bit combinations; characters may be represented by bit combination of 6 or more.

Example

Express 542 by means of a binary data word of 12 bits.

DIVIDE BY 2	QUOTIENT	REMAINDER	
542/2	271	0	—LSD
271/2	135	1	
135/2	67	1	
67/2	33	1	
33/2	16	1	
16/2	8	0	
8/2	4	0	
4/2	2	0	
2/2	1	0	
1/2	0	1	—MSD → 1000011110

In terms of 12 bits, it is 001000011110.

Example

Express 542 by means of a binary-coded decimal word of 3 digits.

The binary coded decimal combinations for these digits are

5	0101
4	0100
2	0010

Therefore, the data word is expressed as

0101 0100 0010

Integral versus Fractional Words

When integral data words are used, the binary or decimal point is assumed to be to the right of the LSD. When fractional data words are used, the binary or decimal point is assumed to be to the left of the MSD.

The range of absolute values of numbers in a fractional computer is between 0 and 1 regardless of the number of bits, or whether it is given in binary or decimal form. In an integral computer, the range varies with the number of bits or digits.

Example

In a binary fractional computer, give the range of numerical values handled under the following circumstances:

a. Binary 6 bits
b. Binary 12 bits
c. Decimal 2 digits
d. Decimal 3 digits

The ranges are as follows:

a. .000000 to .111111, which is equal to decimal 0 to 63/64
b. .000000000000 to .111111111111, which is equal to decimal 0 to 4095/4096
c. .00 to .99
d. .000 to .999

Example

What is the range of numbers in a machine that handles integral numbers 3 digits long? 6 digits long?

In the first case the range is 000 to 999.
In the second case the range is 000000 to 999999.

Absolute Value-Plus-Sign versus Complement Form

The sign of a data word may be specified by an extra bit, a 1 representing a minus sign, and a 0 a plus sign. This is absolute value-plus-sign form. Data words also may be expressed in 1's complement form for binary and 9's complement form for decimal.

Example

What is the total range of numbers in an integral computer that uses 8-digit words?

Answer: −99999999 to +99999999

Example

Express the range of numbers using fractional numbers 8 digits long with negative numbers given in complement form.

Answer:

ABSOLUTE VALUE FORM	COMPLEMENT FORM
−.99999999	1.00000000
00000000	0.00000000
+.99999999	0.99999999

Here a 0 to the left of the MSD indicates a positive number and a 1 to the left of the MSD indicates a negative number in complement form.

Fixed Point versus Floating Point

Computers handling digits with the decimal or binary point assumed to be on the left end or at the right end are called fixed-point computers. Computers using the significant digits multiplied by a base to an exponent are called floating-point computers. A data word in a floating point computer is composed of two parts: the mantissa and the characteristic. The mantissa consists of a group of significant digits with the decimal point to the left of the MSD. The characteristic specifies the exponent. The base is not recorded; it is understood that the base is 10 in a decimal machine, and 2 in a binary machine.

To distinguish between minus and positive exponents, the following characteristic encoding system may be used in decimal machines. An exponent of 0 is encoded as 50. Positive exponents are encoded as numbers above 50; negative exponents are encoded as numbers below 50.

In a 10-digit data word the eight most significant digits may be used for the mantissa and the two least significant digits for the characteristic.

Example

Express the following fixed point numbers in floating point form:

54000000
.0000000843
360743000000

The floating point representations are as follows:

Fixed Point	Exponent Form	Floating Point Mantissa	Floating Point Characteristic
54000000	$.54 \times 10^8$	54000000	58
.0000000843	$.843 \times 10^{-7}$	84300000	43
360743000000	$.360743 \times 10^{12}$	36074300	62

Fixed Size versus Variable Size

The examples given above all show fixed-size data words. Computers may be built with variable-size words, that is, words consisting of a variable number of digits or characters. To make this technique feasible, a special character may be used to indicate the end of the word. In some computers part of the instruction word may be used to specify the size of the data word referred to.

INTERNAL COMMUNICATION

In general, the digital computer is composed of five functional units; memory, input, output, arithmetic, and control. The memory stores instruction and data words, and makes them available when needed. Instruction and data words are fed into the machine through the input unit, and out of the machine through the output unit. Most arithmetic and logic operations are executed in the arithmetic unit. The control unit sees to it that instructions are properly sequenced and executed.

Each area in the machine does its job and then communicates with another area.

Computer Data Paths

The five functional units of a digital computer and the data paths connecting these units are shown in Fig. 131. Each of the functional units has a register which receives and transmits data and thus acts as the link between the rest of the machine and the functional unit of which it is a part. This register acts as a buffer. The arithmetic unit contains several registers for storing operands.

Both data and instruction words are loaded into the machine via input controllers. Inputs are of 2 kinds: direct and batched. Direct is represented by a keyboard being used to enter data into the machine as it is prepared. Batch is represented by a punched card reader which is entering a quantity of data that have been previously punched into the cards. Words are entered into the input register. Input control circuits operate on these words before they are sent elsewhere.

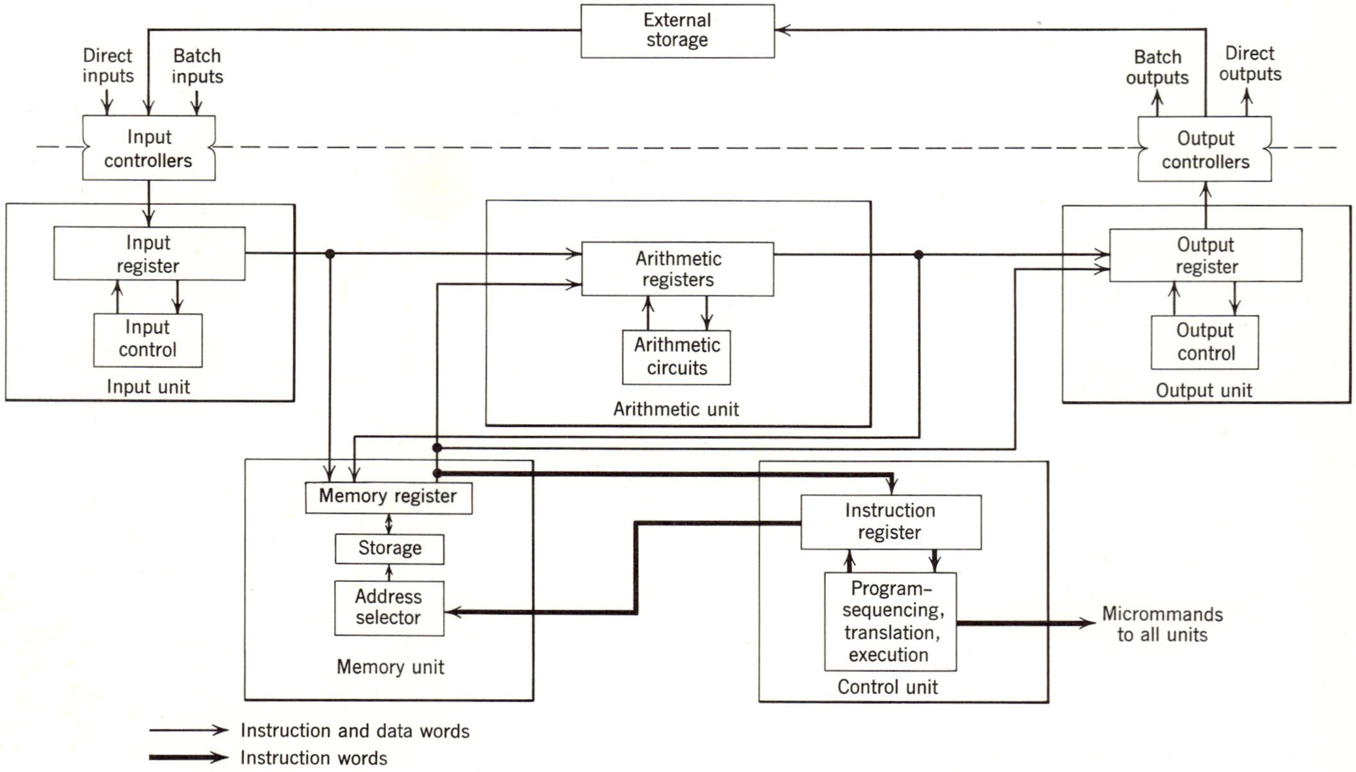

Figure 131 The functional units of a digital computer.

From the input register data words usually go to memory. When each word is needed, it is fed to the arithmetic unit for computation. Results of computations may be returned to memory. If these results are to be communicated to the outside world, they are forwarded to the output register and, from there, to an output unit via an output controller.

The output may be direct or batched. A direct output is represented by a line printout. A batched output is represented by a file that has been updated and is being written onto a reel of magnetic tape.

The input and output registers may be combined into one register called the input-output register. In fact, in most cases the functions of the input and output units are so similar that they may be performed by one unit, called the input-output unit.

Another purpose for input-output is to connect external mass storage devices, such as magnetic drums and discs, in order to enlarge the effective storage capacity of the computer.

The instruction word is fed as part of a program, from the input register to the memory. In some machines it is stored in the same section of the memory as the data words. In other machines the two types of words are stored separately.

A portion of the control unit causes a group of instructions in a program to be taken out of the memory in a definite sequence. Each instruction word is fed to the instruction register and then interpreted by the associated control circuits. The command is converted into a group of microcommands—signals which are fed to various gates and circuits throughout the machine to cause the indicated command to be executed. The address portion of the instruction is interpreted, and signals are fed to the memory unit to allow the appropriate operands to leave the memory or to enter it.

Because in many machines, instruction words look like data words, instruction words may be fed to the arithmetic unit and modified arithmetically.

Instruction words may be output directly or in a batched manner, or they may be stored in external storage, in the same manner as data words.

Methods of Data Transmission

Words may be transmitted from point to point within the machine serially, in parallel, or in serial-parallel. The method of data transmission depends for the most part on the number system used and the speed of machine operation required.

As we have learned, in a binary number system, the bits composing the word may flow through the machine in a serial or in a parallel manner. In serial flow, bit follows bit. A basic register consists of a string of binary storage cells equivalent to the number of bits to a word (Fig. 132*a*). Bits enter the most significant end of the register. The least significant bit is applied first, followed by other bits in order, until the most significant bit is entered. As each bit is entered, the previous bits are shifted within the register.

In parallel flow, all bits of a word are applied simultaneously to all the storage cells in the register (Fig. 132*b*). If a word consists of ten bits P_0 to P_9 ten bit-times t_0 to t_9 are required to shift all the bits into the register when data is transmitted serially. Similarly, ten bit-times are required to shift all the bits out of the register to some other register or to another circuit. In parallel flow, one bit-time is required to bring all ten bits into the register or out of it.

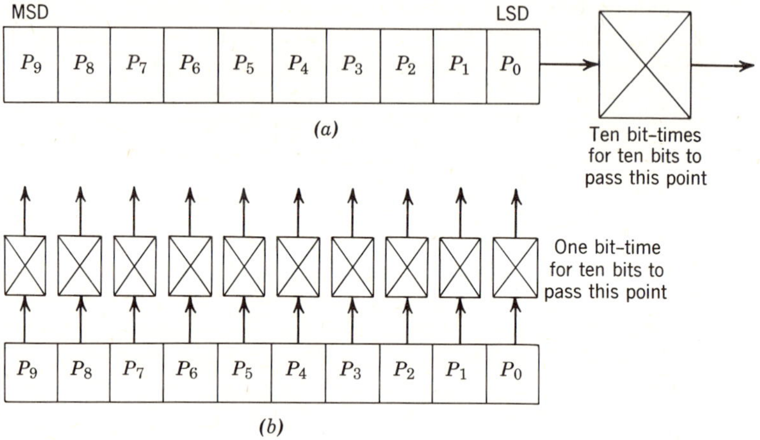

Figure 132 Methods of transmission of binary words. *(a)* Serial. *(b)* Parallel.

Example

If a word consists of 10 bits, how many bit-times are required to shift it into or out of a register if serial transmission is used? Parallel?

In serial transmission 10 bit-times are needed to shift the word into or out of a register. In parallel transmission only one bit time is needed.

Obviously, parallel data transmission is speedier than serial data transmission. Notice, however, that in parallel transmission a separate channel is required for each bit, whereas only one channel is required for serial flow regardless of the number of bits per word.

Example

If a coded-decimal number system with 4 bits to a digit is used, how many bits are needed to encode 10 digits? If serial transmission is used, how many bit-times are needed to bring a word into or out of a register? How many bit-times are needed for parallel transmission?

For 10 digits, 40 bits are needed. Since it takes a bit-time to shift each bit, it would take 40 bit-times to transfer a word in serial. In parallel, it would take only 1 bit-time.

Although it takes only 1 bit-time to execute the transfer in the parallel case, 40 channels are required. Thus the serial transmission is too slow and the parallel transmission is too expensive in required equipment. A good compromise between transmission time and the number of channels may be obtained by using serial-parallel data transmission.

In serial-parallel flow (Fig. 133) the digits of a word are transported in serial; and the bits comprising each digit are transported in parallel. Effectively there is a separate channel for each order of bits. To handle the 4-bit, 10-digit word, we may use a serial-parallel register consisting of four subregisters, each subregister handling in serial one bit of each digit. The subregister may be labeled according to the order of bit flowing through it. In the illustration, the top subregister is the first-order subregister and the bottom one is the fourth-order subregister. The data transmission path consists of four channels, and ten bit-times are required to transmit a word.

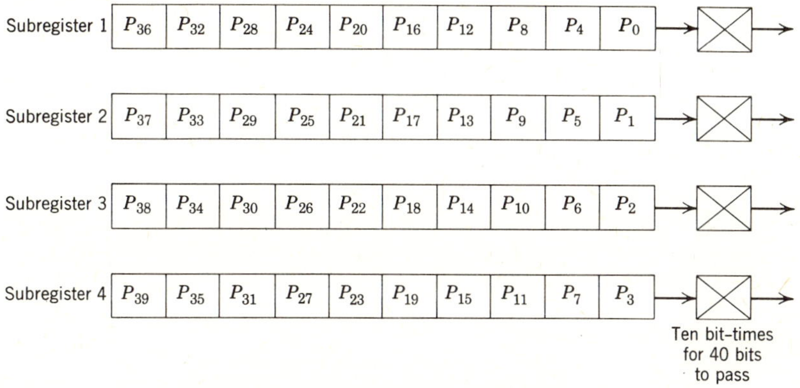

Figure 133 Serial-parallel data transmission.

Example

If serial-parallel transmission is used how many bit-times would it take to transfer a 10-digit word consisting of 4-bit digits?

Since effectively there are 4 parallel paths for the 40 bits, it means that 10 bit-times are required for the transfer.

Example

If in the previous example the number of bits to a digit is increased to 6, what effect would it have on the speed of word transfer? On the number of subchannels?

The speed of word transfer will not change, but the number of subchannels would increase to 6, one for each bit comprising a digit.

Checking

Every computer has definite language rules and definite rules for transmission of data. To increase the reliability of the computer, words are periodically fed through checking circuits.

In a binary computer, a parity-check bit may be attached to one of the words and transmitted as part of the word. The parity-check bit is chosen so that the sum of all the ONE'S in the word is odd. At strategic locations in the machine, parity-check circuits look at the word to determine whether the sum of the ONE'S is odd or even. If the sum is even, the machine knows a mistake has occurred. It can then stop the machine or merely warn the operator by lighting a light on the control panel.

In a coded-decimal machine, parity bits may be added to each digit combination. In effect, each digit in a word is tested.

Other redundancy checks such as the forbidden-combination check may be used to test the correctness of data flow throughout the machine.

MACHINE LANGUAGE

Machine language is the language of internal communication. By writing a program in machine language, a user may communicate to the computer the task to be executed. A simple program consists of a group of instruction words operating on a group of data words.

Since the advent of high-level languages machine language programming is rarely used. However, because it more clearly defines the nature of the computer, some basic programming techniques are described below in terms of machine language.

Preparation of Programs

The program of instructions tells the computer what to do. To make sure the computer does exactly what we want, we must detail every step in the process, and we must detail each step by instruction words following the format understood by the machine.

To make each instruction explicit, we must be sure of the address of each required data word, and the address of each instruction word. Therefore, before computation begins, the data words are loaded into one group of addresses in memory, and the instruction words are loaded into another group of addresses.

The basic method of preparation of programs can best be understood by following a simple example. For the following examples assume we have a machine with a one-address instruction code of six digits, two digits for the command and four digits for the address as follows:

COMMAND	ADDRESS
XX	XXXX

Part of the command code is as follows:

01 *Store* the contents of the arithmetic register into the memory location specified by the address.

02 *Transfer* the contents of the location specified by the address from the memory to the arithmetic register (after first clearing it of its previous contents).

03 *Add* the data word stored in the location specified by the address to the word stored in the arithmetic register.
04 *Subtract* the data word stored in the location specified by the address from the word stored in the arithmetic register.
05 *Input* a block of four data words from external storage to the four consecutive locations in memory beginning with the one specified by the address.
06 *Output* to external storage a block of 4 data words stored at the four consecutive locations in memory beginning with the location specified by the address.
07 *Test:* Compare contents of location specified by the address to the contents of the arithmetic register. If they are unequal, execute next instruction. If they are equal, execute the 2nd following instruction.
08 *Jump* to the location specified by the address.
09 *Halt* the computer.

Example

How many commands are possible to encode in the above computer? How many locations are available in memory?

Two decimal digits for the command allow for the encoding of 99 commands. Four decimal digits for the address allow for the encoding of 9999 addresses.

Example

Prepare a program which will execute the following:

$$450{,}000 + 380{,}000 - 240{,}000 - 650{,}000$$

First we enter these operands on punched paper tape or whatever external storage means is used. Then the following program is prepared:

Instruction		
Command	Address	Explanation
05	1000	*Input* the four data words into the locations specified by the following addresses: DATA WORDS — ADDRESSES 450000 — 1000 380000 — 1001 240000 — 1002 650000 — 1003
02	1000	*Transfer* the contents of the location specified by address 1000 (which is 450,000) into the arithmetic register.
03	1001	*Add* the contents of the location specified by address 1001 to the contents of the arithmetic register; store sum in the arithmetic register.

		450000 (In arithmetic register at start) 380000 (In address 1001) 830000 (In arithmetic register at end)
04	1002	*Subtract* the contents of the location specified by address 1002 from contents of the arithmetic register; store difference in arithmetic register.
		830000 (In arithmetic register at start) −240000 (In address 1002) 590000 (In arithmetic register at end)
04	1003	*Subtract* the contents of the location specified by address 1003 from the contents of the arithmetic register; store difference in arithmetic register.
		590000 (In arithmetic register at start) −650000 (In address 1003) −060000 (In arithmetic register at end)
01	1004	*Store* the result of the calculation into the location specified by address 1004
		−060000 (In address 1004)
06	1004	*Output* the contents of address 1004 (plus that of 1005, 1006, and 1007 which contain nothing) to external storage.
09	0000	*Halt* the computer.

After this program is prepared, it is loaded into the machine so that the instructions in the sequence are in consecutive memory locations starting with the location given by address 0001, as follows:

	Instruction	
Location of Instruction	Command	Address
0001	05	1000
0002	02	1000
0003	03	1001
0004	04	1002
0005	04	1003
0006	01	1004
0007	06	1004
0008	09	0000

If now the start button is pushed, each instruction is performed in the sequence given by the program.

Looping

Looping is one means for economizing in the use of instructions. To understand the need for this economy, study the following example.

Example

Write a program to add the operands stored in locations 0401 to 0416 and to store the sum in 0425.

The solution is given in Table 21.

table 21 SIMPLE SUMMATION PROGRAM

Location of Instruction	Instruction: Command	Instruction: Address	Comments
0001	02	0401	*Transfer* (0401) into Arithmetic Register
0002	03	0402	*Add* (0402)
0003	03	0403	*Add* (0403)
0004	03	0404	*Add* (0404)
0005	03	0405	*Add* (0405)
0006	03	0406	*Add* (0406)
0007	03	0407	*Add* (0407)
0008	03	0408	*Add* (0408)
0009	03	0409	*Add* (0409)
0010	03	0410	*Add* (0410)
0011	03	0411	*Add* (0411)
0012	03	0412	*Add* (0412)
0013	03	0413	*Add* (0413)
0014	03	0414	*Add* (0414)
0015	03	0415	*Add* (0415)
0016	03	0416	*Add* (0416)
0017	01	0425	*Store* sum in 0425
0018	09	0000	*Halt*

Note: (0401) means the contents of the location addressed as 0401.

You will notice from this example that the same command—*Add*—is used 15 times. The only difference between one instruction and another is the address. You can visualize the waste of instructions even better if the list contained 100 or 1000 operands, a not unusual situation.

Looping corrects for this situation as follows (see Fig. 134). The instructions necessary to execute the basic repetitive task are written only once. Before these instructions are placed initializing instructions that take care of the first case to be executed. After the basic task is executed, a test is performed to determine whether the last case has been executed. If not, we make a modification and return to execute the operation on another operand. This sequence forms a loop. If the test indicates that the last case has been executed, an exit jump out of the loop is executed.

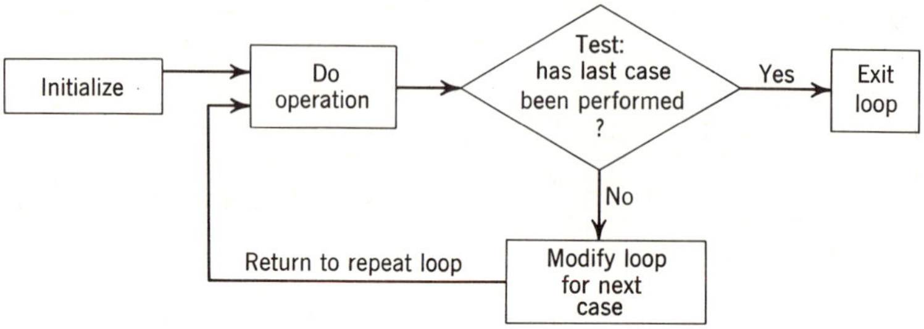

Figure 134 Basic program loop.

Example

Execute the same problem as in the previous example with the aid of a loop

The solution is shown in Table 22. Notice how the instructions are grouped to show the 5 main functions of a loop.

Initialization, the function of the first 4 instructions, is needed to assure that 2 memory locations whose contents keep changing during the course of the program are storing the proper value at the start. These locations are:

1. 0428 which is used for storing the count of the number of times the loop has been executed. It is initialized to 000401, the address of the first operand.
2. 0429 which is reserved for the sum. It is initialized to 000000.

Instructions at locations 0005, 0006, and 0007 execute the addition. After the "sum" (000000 at the start) is brought into AR, the first operand—the contents of 0401—are added to it and the result is returned to the "sum" location.

Next comes the *Test*. Instruction 0008 is used to transfer into AR the count of the number of times addition was performed. The instruction at 0009 then tests to determine whether this count is equal to 0416, meaning that 16 operands have been summed. Of course, during the first iteration, it is not, and a jump is made to location 0012—the start of the modify instructions.

The purpose of the modify instructions is to condition the loop so that the next operand is summed during the next iteration. Instructions at 0012, 0013, and 0014 add 000001 to the count of 000401 to produce a new count of 000402, which value is returned to the "count" location, 0428. Instruction 0015 adds 030000 to this new value producing 030402; 0016 then stores it in location 0006.

Once this is accomplished, instruction 0017 executes a jump to repeat the loop starting with the instruction at 0005.

The do instructions now add the second operand to the "sum," and again a test is made.

After 16 additions the count is 0416, and the result of the test is that the instruction at 0011 is executed, causing an exit from the loop.

table 22 SUMMATION SUBROUTINE

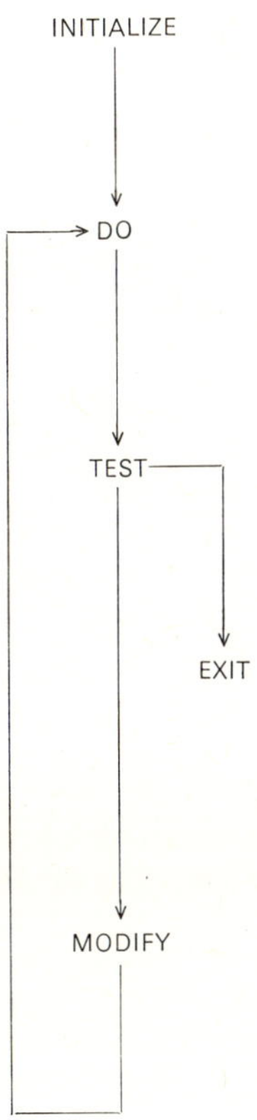

Location of Instruction	Instruction: Command	Instruction: Address	Remarks
0001	02	0420	*Transfer* 000401 to AR
0002	01	0428	*Store* in "count" location
0003	02	1000	*Transfer* 000000 to AR
0004	01	0429	*Store* in "sum" location
0005	02	0429	*Transfer* "sum" to AR
0006	03	0401	*Add* 1st (2nd, etc., during succeeding iterations) operand to (AR)
0007	01	0429	*Store* in "sum" location
0008	02	0428	*Transfer* count of 000401 (000402, etc., during succeeding iterations) to AR
0009	07	0419	*Test* if 16th operand was added
0010	08	0012	If not, *Jump* to 0012
0011	09	0000	If yes, exit loop by halting
0012	02	0428	*Transfer* count of 000401 (000402, etc., during succeeding iterations) to AR
0013	03	1001	*Add* 000001
0014	01	0428	*Store* in "count" location
0015	03	1002	*Add* 030000 to (AR)
0016	01	0006	*Store* 030402 (030403, etc., during succeeding iterations) in 0006
0017	08	0005	*Jump* to 0005 to repeat loop

Storage Assignments

0401	1st operand	0420	000401	1000	000000
0416	16th operand	0428	"count"	1001	000001
0419	000416	0429	"sum"	1002	030000

Subroutines

Suppose that a program is needed which requires the same group of instructions to be executed several times at various locations in the program. One method of accomplishing this task would be to repeat this set of instructions at each point where it is needed. A more efficient way would be to write this group of instructions once, and to call for its execution at each point in the program that it is needed. A group of instructions used in this way to carry out a well-defined mathematical or logical operation is called a subroutine.

The process of using subroutines is not as simple as we have implied. The main program that calls for the subroutine must notify the subroutine what operand or operands to use, where to store the sum, and where to return to in the main program upon completion.

The following example explains the use of subroutines.

Example

Write a main program that calls a subroutine to solve the following problem:

$$C = \text{Sum of } A + \text{Sum of } B$$

where A consists of 16 operands stored in 0401 to 0416 and B consists of 18 operands stored in 0501 to 0518.

Since a summation is required twice, let us make it a subroutine. Obviously, this summation subroutine should be similar to the summation program presented earlier. It is with the exception of two changes (see Table 23):

1. Initialization instructions are missing. Initialization is accomplished by the main program, and initialization may be different for each call of the subroutine.
2. The *Halt* instruction in location 0011 has been replaced with a *Jump* instruction. Upon completion of the subroutine, the *Jump* instruction transfers control back to the main program.

The instructions stored in 0005, 0006, 0007, 0008, 0009, 0011, 0012, and 0014 are different during the second call of the subroutine from what they are during the first call. To understand this, it is necessary to follow the sequence of instructions in the main program (Table 24).

Part 1 of the main program consists of 2 types of initialization and then a jump to the subroutine. The first type of initialization (instructions at 5001, 5002, 5003, and 5004) is the same as the one that was accomplished by the first 4 instructions of Table 22. The other type of initialization is one in which we find the following:

MAIN PROGRAM INSTRUCTIONS	INITIALIZE	SUBROUTINE LOCATIONS	WITH	INSTRUCTIONS
5005 5006		0005		020429

5007 5008	0006	030401
5009 5010	0007	010429
5011 5012 5013	0008 & 0012	020428
5014 5015	0009	070419
5016 5017	0011	085021
5018 5019	0014	010428

The last instruction in part 1 of the main program causes control to transfer to the first instruction of the subroutine. The subroutine is executed, using the initialized instructions, thus causing the sum of *A* to be obtained.

The exit instruction of the subroutine returns machine control back to part 2 of the main program, according to the previously planted 085021 instruction.

Part 2 does essentially the same operation as part 1, but initializes the subroutine to handle *B* operands. When the last instruction of part 2 causes a jump to the subroutine, this time different instructions are executed, as follows:

SUBROUTINE LOCATIONS	INSTRUCTIONS
0005	020529
0006	030501
0007	010529
0008	020528
0009	070519
0011	085041
0012	020528
0014	010528

The net result is that the sum of *B* rather than the sum of *A* is obtained, and a return is made to part 3, rather than to part 2.

Part 3 of the main program merely subtracts the sum of *B* from the sum of *A* and stores the remainder in the "result" location.

table 23 SUMMATION SUBROUTINE

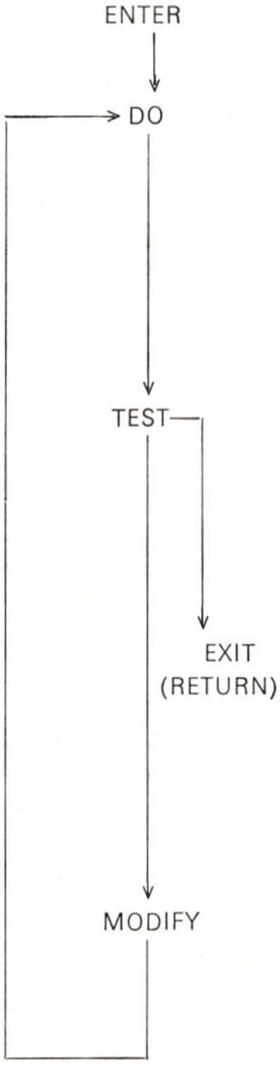

Location of Instruction	Number of Sub-routine Call	Instruction: Command	Instruction: Address	Remarks
0005	1	02	0429	*Transfer* "sum A" to AR
	2	02	0529	" "sum B" " "
0006	1	03	0401	*Add* A operand
	2	03	0501	" B "
0007	1	01	0429	*Store* in "sum A" loc.
	2	01	0529	" " "sum B" "
0008	1	02	0428	*Transfer* "count A" to AR
	2	02	0528	*Transfer* "count B" to AR
0009	1	07	0419	*Test* if 16th A added
	2	07	0519	" " " B "
0010		08	0012	If not, *Jump* to 0012
0011	1	08	5021	If yes, *Jump* to part 2 of main program
	2	08	5041	If yes, *Jump* to part 3 of main program
0012	1	02	0428	*Transfer* "count A" to AR
	2	02	0528	" "count B" " "
0013		03	1001	*Add* 000001
0014	1	01	0428	*Store* in "count A"
	2	01	0528	" " "count B"
0015		03	1002	*Add* 030000 to (AR)
0016		01	0006	*Store* in 0006
0017		08	0005	*Jump* to 0005 to repeat loop

Storage Assignments

0401	1st A operand	0501	1st B operand	1000	000000
0416	16th A operand	0518	18th B operand	1001	000001
0419	000416	0519	000518	1002	030000
0420	000401	0520	000501		
0421	020429	0521	020529		
0422	030401	0522	030501		
0423	010429	0523	010529		
0424	020428	0524	020528		
0425	070419	0525	070519		
0426	085021	0526	085041		
0427	010428	0527	010528		
0428	"count A"	0528	"count B"		
0429	"sum A"	0529	"sum B"		
		0530	"result"		

table 24 PROGRAM FOR FINDING SUM A MINUS SUM B

	Location of Instruction	Instruction: Command	Instruction: Address	Remarks
Part 1	5001	02	0420	Initialize "count A" with 000401
	5002	01	0428	
	5003	02	1000	Initialize "sum A" with 000000
	5004	01	0429	
				Preset Subroutine:
	5005	02	0421	Loc. 0005 with 020429
	5006	01	0005	
	5007	02	0422	,, 0006 ,, 030401
	5008	01	0006	
	5009	02	0423	,, 0007 ,, 010429
	5010	01	0007	
	5011	02	0424	,, 0008 ,, 020428 & 0012
	5012	01	0008	
	5013	01	0012	
	5014	02	0425	,, 0009 ,, 070419
	5015	01	0009	
	5016	02	0426	,, 0011 ,, 085021
	5017	01	0011	
	5018	02	0427	,, 0014 ,, 010428
	5019	01	0014	
	5020	08	0005	*Jump* to start of subroutine
SUBROUTINE (Table 23)				
Part 2	5021	02	0520	Initialize "count B" with 000501
	5022	01	0528	
	5023	02	1000	Initialize "sum B" with 000000
	5024	01	0529	
				Preset Subroutine:
	5025	02	0521	Loc. 0005 with 020529
	5026	01	0005	
	5027	02	0522	,, 0006 ,, 030501
	5028	01	0006	
	5029	02	0523	,, 0007 ,, 010529
	5030	01	0007	
	5031	02	0524	,, 0008 ,, 020528 & 0012
	5032	01	0008	
	5033	01	0012	
	5034	02	0525	,, 0009 ,, 070519
	5035	01	0009	
	5036	02	0526	,, 0011 ,, 085041
	5037	01	0011	
	5038	02	0527	,, 0014 ,, 010528
	5039	01	0014	
	5040	08	0005	*Jump* to start of subroutine
SUBROUTINE (Table 23)				
Part 3	5041	02	0429	*Transfer* "sum A" to AR
	5042	04	0529	*Subtract* "sum B"
	5043	01	0530	*Store in* "result"

HIGH LEVEL LANGUAGE

Machine language is tedious and inflexible. Command writing is tedious because of the numerical code which must be remembered. Address writing is tedious because of the great amount of bookkeeping that must be done. The inflexibility of machine language becomes obvious if we try to move a program of instructions from one area of memory to another. All the instructions are now stored in different locations and, if any of the instructions refer to another instruction word in the group, the address is obviously wrong. In addition to these objections, machine language follows a format that is too stilted with reference to problems that a programmer is interested in solving.

For these reasons and additional ones, high-level languages have been developed. Among the many in existence, two representative types are discussed: assembly language and FORTRAN. The first removes much of the tediousness and adds a little flexibility. The second goes further by allowing the programmer to write programs in terms closer to the way in which he thinks of his problems.

Assembly Language

Two ideas are important for understanding assembly languages. The first is symbolic instructions. The second is relative addressing.

A symbolic instruction is one in which the command and address are not given numerically, but by name. For the command a simple mnemonic code called a symbolic command may be used. For the simple machine discussed in this chapter the symbolic code may be like this:

Numeric Code	Operation	Symbolic Code
01	*Store*	STR
02	*Transfer*	TFR
03	*Add*	ADD
04	*Subtract*	SUB
05	*Input* a block to Memory	INP
06	*Output* a block to Ext. Storage	OUT
07	*Test*	TST
08	*Jump*	JMP
09	*Halt*	HLT

Addresses also may be referred to symbolically. Instead of calling an address by its number, it may be called by a name that is representative of its function or of some other characteristic. The use of this simple expedient saves the programmer much housekeeping. He writes the address by name at the time that he writes each instruction. He does not need to determine exact addresses.

But, it may be pointed out, he must determine the exact addresses sooner or later. The answer is that this task must indeed be done, but not by the programmer. As long as the program is completely defined, an assembler program built for this special purpose, translates each of the assembly language instructions into machine language instructions. This program does the tedious bookkeeping job.

The mere use of symbolic addresses is not enough guidance for the assembler, especially if we want to have the capability of moving a program or subroutine from one area in memory to another. Relative addressing is needed. By relative addressing is meant that we count locations from a given base address. For instance, if an address is labeled symbolically as A, then the succeeding addresses may be called $A+1$, $A+2$, and so on. Hence, if the assembler program knows the location in which it places A, it can determine the exact addresses of $A+1$, $A+2$, and so on.

table 25 SUMMATION SUBROUTINE IN ASSEMBLY LANGUAGE

Location of Instruction		Symbolic Instruction		
Direct	Symbolic and Relative	Command	Address	Remarks
0005	*D*0	TFR	SUM	*A* or *B* depending on which call
0006	*D*+1	ADD	OPERAND	
0007	*D*+2	STR	SUM	
0008	TEST	TFR	COUNT	
0009	*T*+1	TST	TEST	
0010	*T*+2	JMP	MODIFY	
0011	EXIT	JMP	RETURN	To part 2 or part 3 depending on which call
0012	MODIFY	TFR	COUNT	
0013	*M*+1	ADD	1	
0014	*M*+2	STR	COUNT	
0015	*M*+3	ADD	ADD	ADD constant = 030000
0016	*M*+4	STR	*D*+1	
0017	*M*+5	JMP	*D*0	

Example

Write the main program of Table 24 and the subroutine of Table 23 in assembly language.

The subroutine is given in Table 25 and the main program is given in Table 26. Notice that the address of each instruction is given by a symbolic and relative address that represents the part of the subroutine that it is in. Thus address 0008 is labled the TEST address: this is where the group of instructions dealing with the test starts. Address 0009 is labeled *T*+1, meaning that it follows directly after the TEST address. Notice how the whole program is much easier to understand, although nothing has been fundamentally changed.

Notice also that constants may be given a name too. In the table, named constants are underlined for clarity.

table 26 PROGRAM FOR FINDING SUM A MINUS SUM B IN ASSEMBLY LANGUAGE

Location of Instruction		Symbolic Instruction		
Direct	Symbolic and Relative	Command	Address	Remarks
5001	*P*1	TFR	FIRST *A*	Intialize "count *A*"
5002	*P*1+1	STR	COUNT *A*	
5003	*P*1+2	TFR	ZERO	Initialize "sum *A*"
5004	*P*1+3	STR	SUM *A*	
5005	*P*1+4	TFR	TFR SUM *A*	Preset subroutine
5006	*P*1+5	STR	*D*0	
5007	*P*1+6	TFR	ADD *A*	
5008	*P*1+7	STR	*D*+1	
5009	*P*1+8	TFR	STR SUM *A*	
5010	*P*1+9	STR	*D*+2	
5011	*P*1+10	TFR	TFR COUNT *A*	
5012	*P*1+11	STR	TEST	
5013	*P*1+12	STR	MODIFY	
5014	*P*1+13	TFR	TEST *A*	
5015	*P*1+14	STR	*T*+1	
5016	*P*1+15	TFR	JUMP RETURN	
5017	*P*1+16	STR	EXIT	
5018	*P*1+17	TFR	STR COUNT *A*	
5019	*P*1+18	STR	*M*+2	

table 26 (cont.)

Location of Instruction		Symbolic Instruction		
Direct	Symbolic and Relative	Command	Address	Remarks
5020	*P*1+19	JMP	*D*0	*Jump* to subroutine entrance
5021	*P*2	TFR	FIRST *B*	Initialize "count *B*"
5022	*P*2+1	STR	COUNT *B*	
5923	*P*2+2	TFR	ZERO	Initialize "sum *B*"
5024	*P*2+3	STR	SUM *B*	
5025	*P*2+4	TFR	TFR SUM *B*	Present subroutine
5026	*P*2+5	STR	*D*0	
5027	*P*2+6	TFR	ADD *B*	
5028	*P*2+7	STR	*D*+1	
5029	*P*2+8	TFR	STR SUM *B*	
5030	*P*2+9	STR	*D*+2	
5031	*P*2+10	TFR	TFR COUNT *B*	
5032	*P*2+11	STR	TEST	
5033	*P*2+12	STR	MODIFY	
5034	*P*2+13	TFR	TEST *B*	
5035	*P*2+14	STR	*T*+1	
5036	*P*2+15	TFR	JMP RETURN	
5037	*P*2+16	STR	EXIT	
5038	*P*2+17	TFR	STR COUNT *B*	
5039	*P*2+18	STR	*M*+2	
5040	*P*2+19	JMP	*D*0	*Jump* to subroutine entrance
5041	*P*3	TFR	SUM *A*	
5042	*P*3+1	SUB	SUM *B*	
5043	*P*3+2	STR	RESULT	

Fortran

There is generally a one-to-one relationship between assembly language instructions and machine language instructions. No such simple relationship exists between FORTRAN (FORmula TRANslation) instructions and machine language instructions. One FORTRAN instruction, which is better known as a statement, may be translated into a group of machine instructions. This is done by a program called a compiler.

Statements written in FORTRAN follow rigid rules so that they would be translatable into machine language instructions. The statements used in this language are modifications of formulas and expressions.

Notice in the following example the vast reduction in work required to program in FORTRAN instead of in assembly language.

Example

Write the previous summation subroutine (Table 25) and the program for finding the sum of *A* minus the sum of *B* (Table 26) in FORTRAN.

The solution is shown in Table 27 and Table 28. The summation subroutine is extremely simple. The first statement names the subroutine and specifies the variable to be handled by it, *X*. The variable *X* stands for the operand, and statement 3 says that the succeeding operand should be added to a given operand and the result then should be labeled the operand. Statement 2 says that the operation specified by statement 3 should be repeated 15 times, for $I = 1$ up to $I = 15$. After this, the subroutine comes to an end.

table 27 SUMMATION SUBROUTINE IN FORTRAN

Statement Number	Compiler Statement
1	SUBROUTINE SUM (*X*)
2	*D*O 3 *I* = 1, 15
3	*X*(*I*) = *X*(*I*)+*X*(*I*+1)
4	END

Table 28 shows the main program. Statement 10 merely names the program. Statement 11 defines two groups of operands, *A* and *B*, each consisting of 16 words. Statement 12 calls in the SUM subroutine and asks it to operate on operands *A*. Statement 13 also does this except that it asks the subroutine to operate on operands *B*. Statement 14 states that the sum of *B* should be subtracted from the sum of *A* and stored in a location labeled as *C*.

table 28 PROGRAM FOR FINDING SUM *A* MINUS SUM *B* IN FORTRAN

Statement Number	Compiler Statement
10	DIFFERENCE OF SUMS
11	DIMENSION *A* (16), *B* (16)
12	Call SUM (*A*)
13	Call SUM (*B*)
14	*C* = SUM (*A*)−SUM (*B*)

Other High-Level Languages

The above example, although a simplified case, shows the power of a high-level language. FORTRAN is used for scientific and other problems that require extensive manipulation of mathematical expressions. Many other high-level languages are available. Among the most common are ALGOL (ALGOrythmic Language), which also is used for scientific work; COBOL (COmmon Business Oriented Language), which is used extensively for business operations; and PL/I (Programming Language I), which combines features from FORTRAN, COBOL, and other languages.

There also are languages at a higher level than the ones mentioned above. These languages enable the businessman, social scientist, economist, psychologist, historian, or any man with a problem to use a computer for its solution with a minimal knowledge of the computer. Among them are BASIC, which allows practically anyone to sit at a terminal remotely connected to a computer and do numerical calculations, and AESOP, which enables an individual to enter in and retrieve data from a data base stored in a computer via a remote terminal possessing a display screen.

SUMMARY

1. There are two ways of viewing the data structure: logically and physically. logically the sequence from small to large units is as follows: bit-digit-character-word-record-block-file. Physical units depend on the structure of the storage device.
2. There are two types of words: instruction words and data words. The instruction word consists of a command and an address. it operates on a data word that may be in fractional, integral, or floating point form.
3. The type of instruction word is determined mainly by the type of address used—direct or indirect—and the number of addresses per instruction word: 1, 2, 3, or 4.
4. There are five general categories of commands:
   Arithmetic and Logic, which execute basic operations.
   Transfer, which move data from 1 point to another within the machine.
   Input-Output, which move data into and out of the machine.
   Branch, which modify the sequence of instruction flow.
   Miscellaneous.
5. Words flow from register to register in series, in parallel, or in series-parallel. At various locations, the words may be checked by a parity or a forbidden combination check.
6. Programming may be accomplished by listing a group of instruction words in either direct or symbolic form; or by writing statements in a more advanced language, providing a compiler exists for their conversion into machine instruction words.

7. *Definitions to Remember*

Word. A set of bits or digits treated by the computer as a unit.

Data Word. A data word consists of numbers or characters to be processed. It may consist of digits and sign.

Instruction Word. A word used to inform the machine what operation to perform. It consists of a command and one or several addresses.

Fixed-Point Computer. A computer in which the decimal or binary point is assumed to be in a fixed location.

Floating-Point Computer. A computer which carries data words in exponential form. It can deal directly with fractional as well as integral numbers.

Fixed Word. A word possessing a fixed number of digits or characters.

Variable Word. A word composed of a variable number of digits or characters.

Command. The portion of the instruction which tells the machine what to do.

Address. An expression which designates the location of a character or word in a storage device.

Characteristic. That part of a floating point representation which indicates the size of the exponent.

Mantissa. That part of a floating point representation which specifies the significant digits of the number.

Immediate Address. An address in the instruction word which is the operand itself. It is also called a O-level address.

Direct Address. An address in the instruction word which indicates the location where the referenced operand is to be found. It is also called the first level address.

Indirect Address. An address in the instruction word which indicates a location where the *address* of the referenced operand is to be found. Also called second-level address.

Symbolic Address. An address in the instruction word which is given by a name or a mnemonic code to specify a storage location within the context of a particular program.

Relative Address. An address that specifies location only with reference to a base address.

One-Address Instruction. An instruction with only one address. The address indicates the operand on which the operation is to be performed.

Two-Address Instruction. An instruction with two addresses. One address specifies an operand and the other specifies the address of the next instruction.

Three-Address Instruction. An instruction with three addresses. These addresses specify the two operands and the address of the result.

Four-Address Instruction. An instruction with four addresses. These addresses specify the two operands, the result, and the address of the instruction to be executed next.

Indirect Address Instruction. An instruction word in which the address part is given in indirect form.

Serial Transmission. All bits of a word are transmitted sequentially.

Parallel Transmission. All bits of a word are transmitted simultaneously.
Serial-Parallel Transmission. All bytes are transmitted serially; but the bits that make up the digits are transmitted in parallel.
Subregister. A portion of a register handling a group of bits flowing serially in serial-parallel transmission.
Program. The complete sequence of instruction words or statements needed for a computer to accomplish a given task.
Loop. A self-contained series of instructions in which the last instruction can cause a modification and make the series repeat itself, until a terminal condition is reached.
Subroutine. A well-defined portion of a program that is called on by the main program or routine for execution, after which control is returned to the main routine.
Assembly Language. A language in which instructions are written with symbolic commands and symbolic and relative addresses.
Assembler. A program that translates instructions given in assembly-language form into machine-instruction words.
Compiler Language. A language in which are used problem-oriented statements that do not bear a 1-to-1 relationship with machine instructions.
Compiler. A program that translates compiler language statements and compiles them into machine-instruction words.

Exercises

1. A word has 48 bits.
   a. How many 4-bit digits can this represent?
   b. How many 6-bit characters can this represent?
   c. How many 8-bit characters can this represent?
2. Given a machine that has a 42-bit word consisting of seven 6-bit bytes. Transmission occurs only by word or by byte. How many 4-bit digits may be stored in a word?
3. Given a computer with a 24-bit word divided into 4 bytes. How would you arrange its communication with another computer that has a 48-bit word divided into 8 bytes?
4. Given a computer that stores words 10 bytes long, each byte consisting of 6 bits. A punched card reader reads a card record of 80 characters into the computer.
   a. If a logical record consists of 160 characters, how many punched cards must be read to enter one logical record?
   b. If cards are read at the rate of 480 per minute, how many logical records are entered per second?
   c. How many characters are entered per second?

5. In exercise 4 above, if the speed of internal transfers are 6 μs per character, how can we match the card reader speed to the internal machine speed?

6. It takes 1 μs to transfer a bit in serial transmission.
   a. How long will it take to transfer a 6-bit byte?
   b. A 10-byte word?
   c. A physical record of 80 characters?
   d. A logical record of 160 characters?

7. In exercise 6, how much time would be required to execute transfer of a physical record if parallel transmission were assumed by byte? By word?

8. Assume that to the computer in exercise 4 above there is connected a disc with 19,200 bits per track and that all words are stored serially by bit.
   a. How many logical records could be stored in 1 track?
   b. If the disc could transfer in or out at 2 μs per bit, how long would it take to transfer a logical record?

9. Given the Instruction:

   ADD 0501

   At address 0501 is stored 0520, and at 0520 is stored 4673. Determine the operand under each of the following addressing schemes:
   a. Immediate
   b. Direct
   c. Indirect

10. If in a binary computer using 1-address instructions we want to be able to have 32 commands and 4096 storage locations, how many bits would we need per command? Per address? Per instruction word?

11. If the computer in exercise 10 above used 2-address instructions, how large would the instruction word need to be?

12. Assume that the 32 commands and 4096 storage locations are needed for a computer using decimal numbers,
    a. How many digits would be needed for a 1-address instruction word? A 2-address instruction word?
    b. With this size instruction word, what is the total possible number of commands? What is the total possible number of address locations?

13. The number of bits required for an instruction word is 20, but 40 bits are needed for the data word.
    a. How can we resolve the conflict for a fixed word computer?
    b. How can we resolve the conflict if 40 bits were needed for the instruction word and 20 for the data word?

14. What is the 12-bit binary equivalent of
    a. 647?
    b. 580?
    c. 346?

15. What is the binary-coded decimal equivalent of
    a. 100010?
    b. 111001?
    c. 101011?

16. What is the equivalent mathematical operation of the following:
   a. A right shift executed on a binary number?
   b. A right shift executed on a decimal number?
   c. A left shift on a binary number?
   d. A left shift on a decimal number?
17. What is the range of numbers in a computer that uses fractional numbers?
18. What is the range of numbers in a computer using integral numbers when a word consists of
   a. 10 bits?
   b. 10 digits?
   c. 5 digits?
19. Express the following absolute value-plus-sign decimal numbers in 9's complement form:
   a. −.5463
   b. 9743
   c. −2589
20. Express the following fixed point numbers in floating point form:
   a. 346000000
   b. .000000000093
   c. 5434.673
21. Given a word of 8 bytes, each byte being 6 bits long. Transmission from 1 register to another can occur at the rate of 1 μs per bit.
   a. How long would it take to transfer a word, if transmission were in serial? Parallel? Serial-parallel?
   b. How many channels are needed for each of the above?

   Note: use assembly-type instructions given in this chapter in the following two exercises.
22. Write a program to input 96 words into successive memory locations starting with address 6000. Use a loop.
23. Write a program to add 5 to each of a group of numbers stored in addresses 7000 to 7050. Store the results in the same addresses.

CHAPTER 11

Memory unit

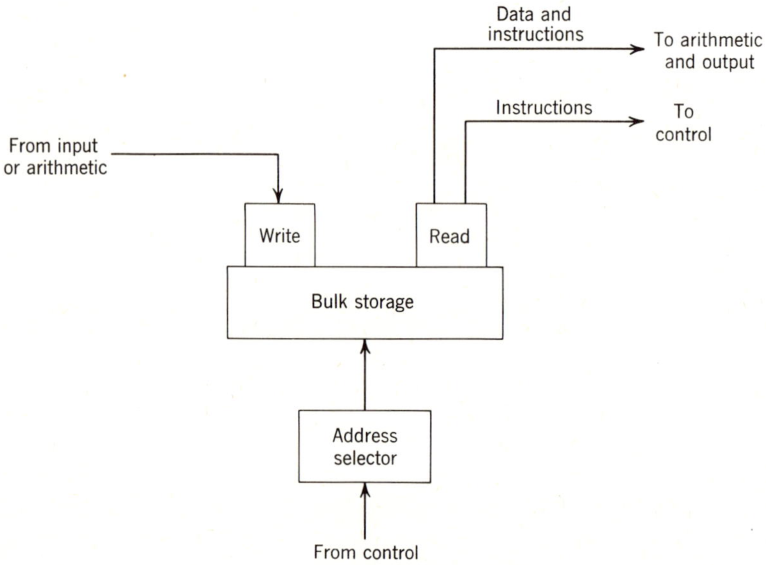

The memory unit consists of: a bulk storage which stores data and instruction words; an address selector which chooses the location in memory to be written into or read out of; and write and read circuits which perform the actual writing and reading.

The memory serves two functions. It stores the program of instructions, and it stores the data words upon which the instructions operate. The instructions are read out of memory into the control unit by the part of the control unit concerned with instruction sequencing; the sequencer chooses the appropriate address and activates the read circuits at the correct times.

Aside from the sequencing, words are written into or read out of memory as determined by the instruction words. There are two kinds of instruction words which refer to memory: the write and the read. In the write-type instruction, the address selector is activated to choose the address, and signals are applied to the write circuits to allow the data to be stored. In the read-type instruction, the address selector is activated, and signals are applied to the read circuits to allow data to be read.

WHAT IS MEMORY?

What is the difference between storage and memory? Storage is a generic term. Storage is used throughout the computer: flip-flops provide bit storage; registers provide word storage; magnetic disc units provide bulk external storage; read-only storage devices are used as encoders.

None of them is memory. Memory is bulk storage that can be written into as well as read from. It is internal storage: there is ready and quick communication between memory and the other functional units of the computer.

The primary component of memory is usually a coordinate access storage unit or a cyclic access storage unit. Sequential access storage units are inappropriate for this use. Some modern computers may have content addressable memories.

COORDINATE ACCESS MEMORY

The coordinate access memory is well established. It provides high-speed access, and is especially appropriate for computers that use 1- and 3-address instruction words. Its common representation is as some form of coincident current magnetic core storage unit.

Coincident-Current Magnetic-Core Memory

Coincident-current magnetic-core memories have been built to store up to millions of bytes or words, and they are capable of being accessed in nanoseconds (thousandths of a microsecond). For purposes of exposition, however, a memory capable of storing sixty-four 6-bit bytes is shown in Fig. 135. It consists of six storage planes, each plane consisting of eight columns and eight rows of cores. Each core has column, row, data, and sense windings threading through it according to the pattern shown previously in Fig. 111. Column address and row address decoders select the core in each plane to be written into or to be read from. Each decoder converts three address bits into 1 of eight lines. The drivers supply the necessary power and the proper polarity of current required in the address selection process. Data drivers (*D*) convert the individual ONE's and ZERO's into pulses which either add to or subtract from the flux in the chosen core of each storage plane. Sense amplifiers (*S*) pick up voltages during read-out and convert them to ONE's and ZERO's. Flip-flops are used to feed ONE's back to the data drivers to rewrite them into the cores from which they have just been read out.

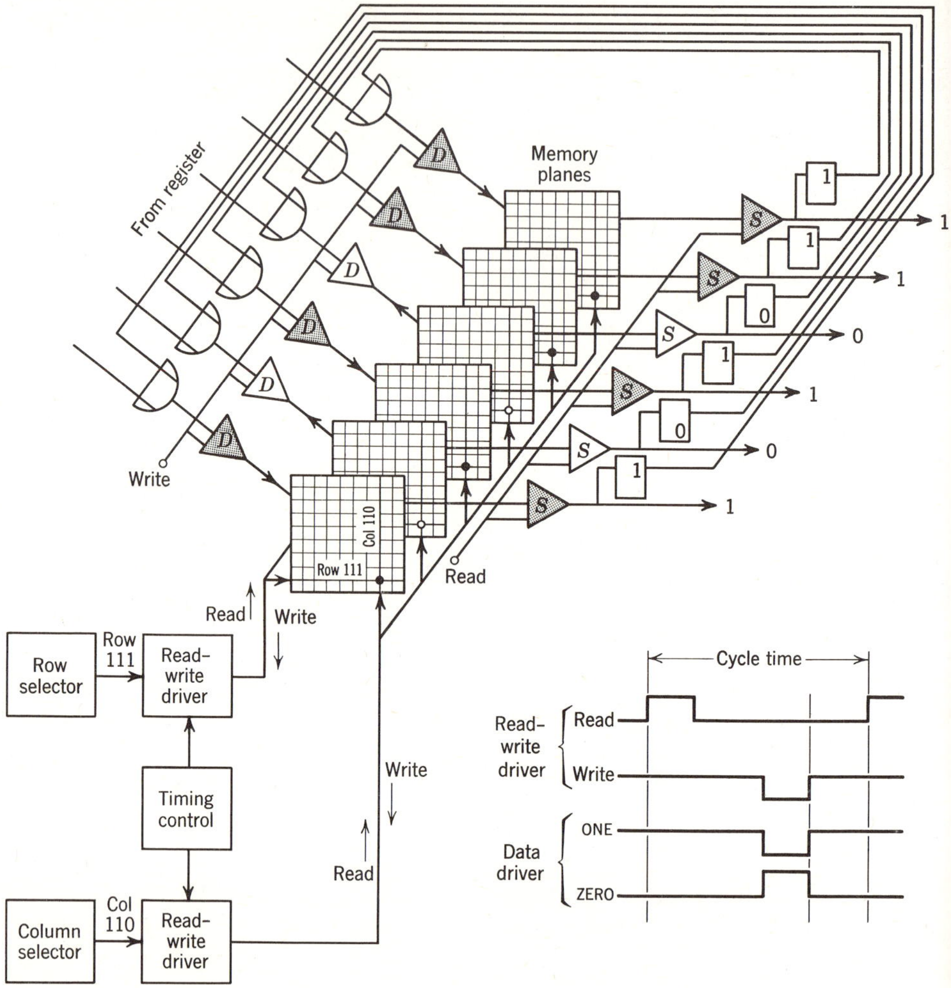

Figure 135 Coincident-current memory.

The basic timing cycle of the memory is determined by the timing control. The timing control produces read-phase pulses followed by write-phase pulses at a definite frequency. The time between the advent of one read-phase pulse and the next is the cycle time.

During the read phase, half-current pulses are applied to the chosen column and row in a direction which would cause the core to flip to the ZERO state. If a Read control signal is present at the sense amplifiers, the voltages induced across the sense windings in each plane are fed through the sense amplifiers to the output. At the same time the ONE's set the associated flip-flops.

During the write phase, half-current pulses are applied to the chosen column and row in a direction which would cause the core to flip to the ONE state. If this is the rewrite portion of a read operation, a Write signal appears at all the data drivers and all 1-bits are rewritten into memory. A Write signal also appears at all the data drivers during an ordinary Write instruction. In this case, the entering bits are written into the chosen cores in each storage plane.

The illustration shows a "read 110111," where 110 is the column address and 111 is the row address being accessed. The Read command is converted to a Read signal followed by a Write signal. The column address 110 is decoded to choose column 6; the row address 111 is decoded to choose row 7. The timing control sends a read-phase pulse through the decoders to cause reading. The word 101011 is stored in the chosen cores. During reading the cores storing ONE's produce output pulses whereas the others do not. The sense amplifiers convert these pulses to standard pulses representing ONE's. Thus at the output is found 101011. The ONE's also set the flip-flops shown. When the timing control switches to the write phase, these ONE's are rewritten into the cores from which they were read out.

Example

Given a computer with a 1-address instruction in binary form. We want to execute 64 commands and we want a memory that can store 4096 words. How many bits are needed for an instruction word? To be able to enlarge the memory capacity of the machine at a future date to 16,384 words, how large should the instruction word be made? What would be needed to make the modification, assuming 4096 word memory modules are available?

To encode 64 commands, 6 bits are needed. To encode 4096 addresses, 12 bits are needed. Therefore, $12+6=18$ bits are needed if only 4096 words are to be accessed. To enlarge the memory capacity to 4 times its original size ($4 \times 4096 = 16{,}384$), 2 extra address bits are needed, making the required instruction word 20 bits long. The modification would consist of adding 3 additional 4096-word memory modules, each with its own address selector. In addition, a simple decoder will be added that would take the additional 2 bits of the address and would decode them to choose 1 of the 4 modules.

Timing

As has been stated, the cycle time of the coincident current magnetic-core memory is from the start of a read-phase pulse to the start of the next read-phase pulse. Because the cores possess destructive read-out, data must be rewritten immediately after reading to avoid loss. Therefore, a constant read-write cycle is assumed, and the access for either reading or writing can be made only once per cycle. The frequency of memory access is 1 over the cycle time.

Bits may be written into or read from a coordinate access memory in parallel. This means that reference may be made in only 1 bit-time. Obviously, the efficient use of this type of memory would require the remainder of the computer to use parallel transmission. If for some reason, transmission within the computer is in serial or serial-parallel, a buffer register is required within the memory unit. During writing, the bits of a word are transferred in serial from another register to this buffer register; as soon as the complete word is in the buffer, the address selector and write circuits are activated to write the word in parallel into the memory. During reading, the address selector and read circuits are activated to read a word out of memory in parallel into the buffer register; then the word is transferred serially to another register.

Example

If the time from the start of the read-phase pulse to the start of the next read-phase pulse is .2 μs, how frequently can writing take place? What must we do to double the frequency of writing?

If the cycle time is .2 μs, the frequency of writing or reading, is

$$\frac{1}{.2} \times 10^{-6} \text{ second} = 5 \times 10^{6} \text{ cycles} = 5 \text{ megacycles}$$

To double this frequency to 10 megacycles, the cycle time must be cut in half to .1 μs.

Example

Assume a computer using 10-bit words in serial transmission, which possesses a coordinate access memory with a cycle time of .2 μs. The bit-time of the computer is .1 μs. How frequently can reading from memory take place?

Since the bit-time is .1 μs, it takes $10 \times .1 = 1$ μs to transfer 10 bits in serial to the buffer. After this, .2 μs are required for the actual access. Therefore, the effective cycle time is stretched from .2 μs to 1.2 μs. The frequency of reading may be

$$\frac{1}{1.2} \times 10^{-6} \text{ second} = .83 \times 10^{6} \text{ cycles} = .83 \text{ megacycles}$$

Write and Read Instructions

Figure 136 shows the relationships between the memory and the registers to and from which words are transferred. All words may be fed to a bus, and from the bus to all other storage points, or vice versa. Words on the bus enter only registers whose input gates are opened; on the other hand, output gates allow words from registers to be returned to the bus. The address selector acts as a group of input gates for the memory.

If instruction sequencing is disregarded for the moment, instructions may be divided into memory and nonmemory instructions. The nonmemory instruction makes no reference to memory. The memory instruction, on the other hand, does make reference to memory. It may be pure transfer of data or an arithmetic-type instruction in which the transfer is part of a larger operation.

In the one-address machine, memory instructions may be divided into two classes: write and read. In the write instruction, a word stored in one of the registers and fed to the bus is allowed to be written into the memory by activating the write circuits and by applying the proper signals to the address selector. In the read instruction, one of the words stored in memory, as determined by signals applied to the address selector, is fed to the bus; from the bus the word enters the register whose gates are open. The write or read circuits are activated by microcommands. The address selector is activated by the address.

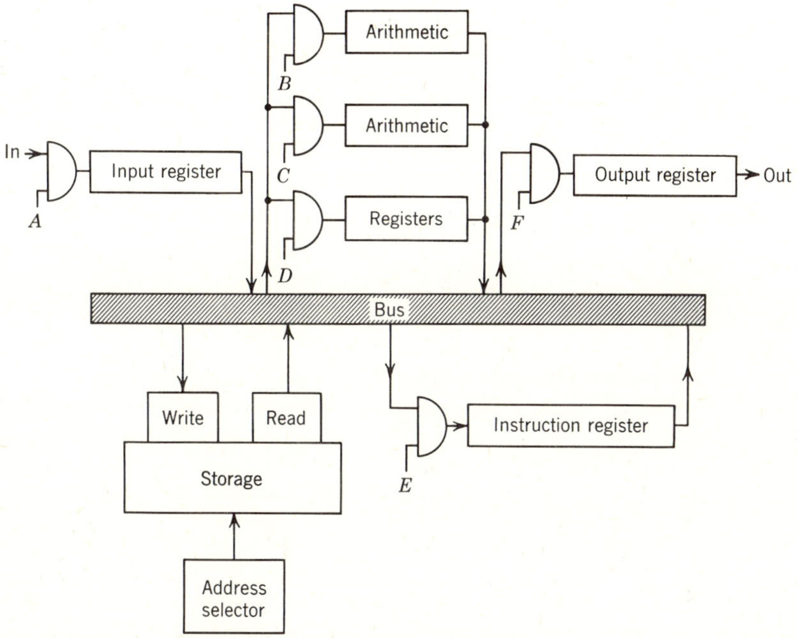

Figure 136 Data transfer by means of bus.

In the 3-address machine, very few instructions are of the nonmemory type. Practically all instructions are simultaneously of the write and read types. The three addresses normally represent two operands and a location for the result. Three memory cycles are needed for each command: two cycles for reading the two operands out of two memory locations, and a third cycle for writing the result of the arithmetic or other operation back into a memory location.

Example

Assume that two parallel computers possess memory units with the same cycle times. One computer uses a 1-address instruction, and the other uses a 3-address instruction. To add *A*, *B*, and *C*, to subtract *D*, and to store the result in location Z, the two machines need instructions that contrast as follows:

1-Address	*3-Address*
Read in A	Read A, Add B, Store in X
Add B	Read (X), Add C, Store in Y
Add C	Read (Y), Subtract D, Store in Z
Subtract D	
Store in Z	

Assume that arithmetic operations can be performed in a cycle time or less and that one cycle time is needed for reading the instruction word from memory to the control unit. Which computer will take longer to execute the given instructions?

In the 1-address computer, 5 instruction words are needed. Therefore, 10 cycle times are consumed: 5 for reading out the instruction words, 5 for the accesses indicated by the instructions. In the 3-address computer, only 3

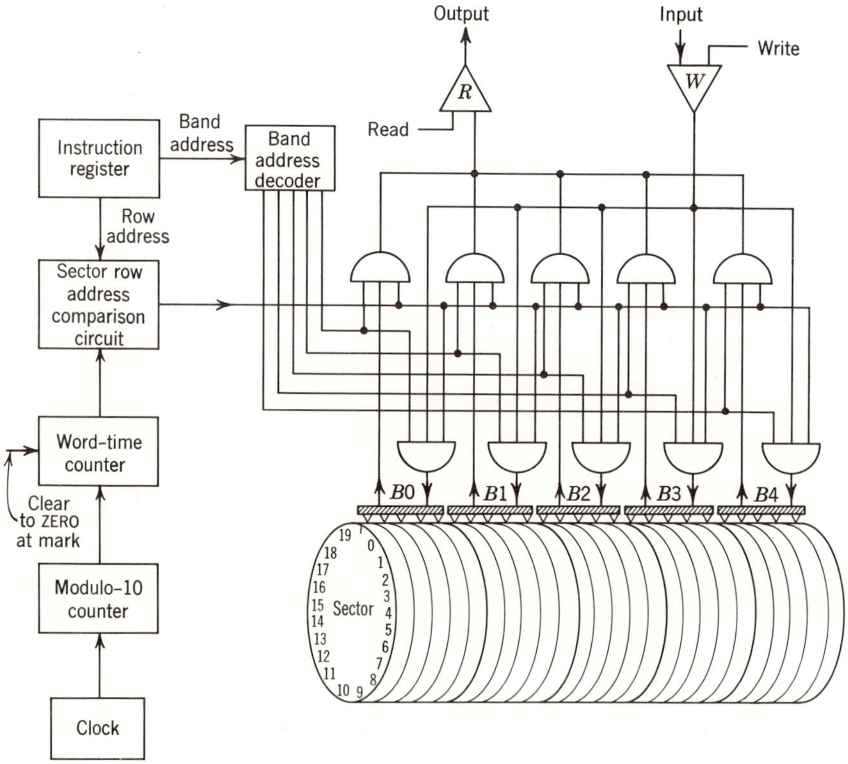

Figure 137 Magnetic-drum memory.

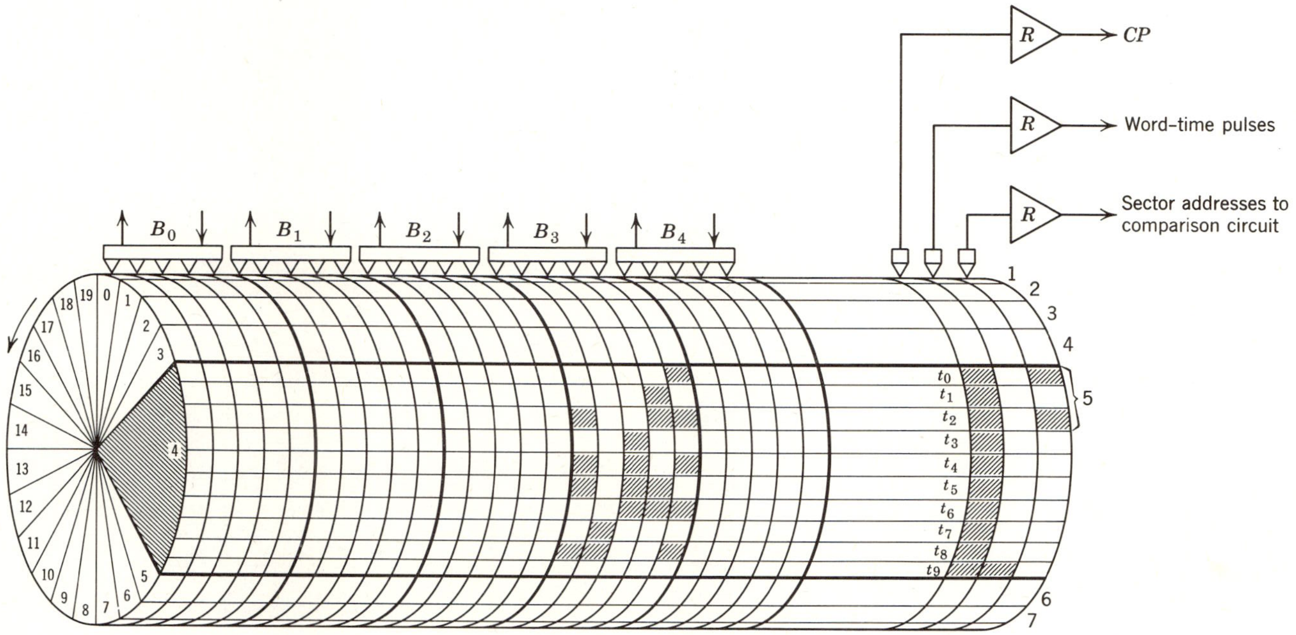

Figure 138 Magnetic-drum with timing tracks.

cycle times are needed to read the 3 instruction words out of memory. But for each instruction, 3 accesses are required, giving a total of 9 cycle times for the execution portion. The total time for executing these 3 instructions is 3+9 = 12 cycle times. The 3-address machine takes a longer time.

Notice that this is not always true. See if you can find a situation in which the 3-address computer is faster?

CYCLIC ACCESS MEMORY

The cyclic access memory is more appropriate for use in computers with 2- and 4-address instruction words with data transmission in serial or serial-parallel. Its most common representation is as a magnetic-drum storage unit.

Magnetic Drum Memory

A simplified magnetic drum memory capable of storing 100 words is shown in Fig. 137. The drum is divided into five bands, each band consisting of five tracks and storing 20 words. The words are nine 5-bit digits long; but ten digit spaces are provided in each row of the sectors in a band to allow space between words (Fig. 138). It takes 20 word-times to complete one revolution of the drum. In other words, every 200 bit-times the same sector appears at the heads of any one band.

The band address decoder chooses one of the five bands as determined by the band address digits in the instruction. The sector address comparison circuit together with the modulo-10 counter and the word-time counter determines the point in time when the chosen band is opened for writing or reading.

Each symbol for read-write head, gate, and amplifier represents five such components, one for each track in a band. The read lines are connected to gates (in practice these gates also amplify) and the outputs of all the gates are fed to a group of five read amplifiers. Similarly one group of five write amplifiers feeds the gates to each of the bands.

The memory operates as follows. When the command portion of the instruction calls for a write operation, a Write signal opens the five write amplifiers for a period of a word-time. At the same time, the band address decoder decodes the band address and places an alerting signal to both the read and write gates of the chosen band.

The sector address is fed to the sector address comparison circuit where it is compared with the output of a word-time counter. The word-time counter is fed from a modulo-10 counter which, in turn, is fed by a clock. Starting with the reference point on the drum, the clock produces one pulse per bit-time in synchronism with the appearance at a head of each successive bit on a drum track. After each group of 10 bits, the modulo-10 counter produces a pulse indicating that a word-time has passed. This pulse steps the word-time counter which thus always stores the word-time representing the sector presently under the heads. When the contents of the word-time counter are the same as the contents of the sector address portion of the instruction register, the sector address comparison circuit produces a signal which opens the chosen band write gate to allow the nine digits of the word to be written into the memory.

Reading is performed in a similar manner except that the read amplifiers are activated by a Read microcommand.

It is possible to simplify the sector address circuits considerably by properly utilizing extra tracks on the drum. By permanently storing 1-bits in each bit-row space of a timing track, these pulses can be read as clock pulses. No separate clock circuit is needed. By storing a ONE pulse in each sector of another track, these may be read as word-time pulses. No separate modulo-10 counter is needed. It is even possible to do away with the word-time counter by storing the word-time on each sector of a separate track. The clock pulses and word-time pulses may be used for control functions too.

A drum constructed in this manner is shown in Fig. 138. Please note that the number actually stored in each sector space of the word-time track does not represent the address for the sector in which it appears but for the following sector. The reason for this is that it takes a word-time for the comparison to take place. Since the drum rotates during this word-time, at coincidence the drum is ready for writing into or reading from the following sector.

The illustration shows the drum storing 987654321 in band 3, sector 4. This word is read by placing into the machine an instruction reading "read 304" where the first digit represents the band and the next two digits the sector. The band address decoder alerts the gates feeding the band-3 heads. Now if row 0 is under the head when band selection occurs, sector address number 1 is fed to the comparison circuit. Since no coincidence occurs, no reading takes place. No coincidence occurs until sector 3 passes under the heads. Then when the word-time pulse occurs, the gates of band 3 open to allow the reading of sector 4. The gates are open for nine bit-times.

Example

Assume a decimal computer using the above drum memory and capable of executing 30 different commands. If a 2-address instruction word is used, how many digits are needed to encode an instruction? With this size instruction word, what is the maximum size drum that can be accessed?

To encode 30 commands, 2 digits are required. To encode an address, 1 digit is required to choose 1 of 5 bands, and 2 digits are required to choose 1 of 20 sectors. Since 2 addresses are needed, the necessary digits per instruction word are

$$2 + 3 + 3 = 8$$

Since 3 digits are used to encode an address, a drum with a maximum capacity of 1000 locations may be accessed. They may divide as 10 bands each with 100 sectors or as 100 bands each with 10 sectors.

Example

If the computer in the above example used a 4-address instruction, how could it be stored? Could this instruction refer to a larger memory?

For a 4-address machine, the digits required are

$$2 + 3 + 3 + 3 + 3 = 14$$

One way of storing this instruction would be to use two words as follows:

Word 1:

Command (first half)	*Address 1*	*Address 2*
1	3	3

Word 2:

Command (second half)	*Address 3*	*Address 4*
1	3	3

With this arrangement, only 7 digits are stored per word. Since we have room for 9, each address may be increased by 1, to make it 4 digits long. With 4 digits 10,000 locations may be accessed.

Timing

The frequency of access depends not only on the drum rotation speed but also on the sequence of address selection. If the sectors are accessed at random, then the frequency of access is twice the number of revolutions per second. (Why?) But if addresses are chosen in order, several accesses can be made during a revolution, and the frequency of access is increased.

Example

If a magnetic drum with 10 sectors per band is rotating at the rate of 4800 rpm, what is the frequency of access if addresses are chosen at random? If they are chosen in sector sequence?

The drum rotates at

$$\frac{4800}{60} = 80 \text{ rps}$$

Since the latency time is the time for one half a revolution, the frequency of access is

$$80 \times 2 = 160$$

If addresses are chosen in sequence, however, 10 accesses are made per revolution, making the frequency of access

$$80 \times 10 = 800$$

Obviously a cyclic access memory slows down the operation of a computer using parallel data transmission. However, if a cyclic access memory is wanted a buffer register is required in the memory unit. During writing, a complete word is transferred at one time from another register to the buffer register; then the address selector and the write circuits are activated to allow serial writing into the cyclic access memory. During reading, the address selector and read circuits are activated to allow a word to be read in serial into the buffer register; as soon as the complete word is in the buffer register, the word is transferred in parallel to another register.

Write and Read Instructions

Selecting instructions stored in succeeding memory locations is not the best way to choose successive instructions in a routine when cyclic access storage is used. The reason is that in this type of storage, address locations are constantly changing and the next available address location after the completion of an instruction depends on the time that is necessary to complete the instruction. This means that on an average it would take one half the time of one revolution to access an instruction.

However, if the address of the next instruction in the sequence is stored in the instruction word, this address can be chosen in a manner that would cut down the time to access the succeeding instruction. This is the reason for preferring 2- and 4-address instructions for cyclic access memories.

Since the second address of a 2-address instruction refers to a location storing an instruction word, it prepares the memory for a read. The first address may prepare the memory for reading or writing, depending on the command part of the instruction. The 2-address instruction, thus, requires a minimum of two references to storage: one for the second address which chooses the instruction word, another for the operand given as the first address of the chosen instruction.

A 4-address instruction is similar to a 3-address instruction, except that the address of the next instruction to be executed is added to the instruction word. Normally, the first 2 addresses go with successive readings of the 2 operands; the third address goes with the writing of the result; the fourth address goes with the reading of the next instruction word.

Example

Assume a computer that uses a cyclic access memory with fixed heads and that has 2-address instruction words. The memory has 10 bands each band storing 100 sectors. One revolution of the storage device takes 10 ms. The access time for a word is equivalent to the time it takes one sector to pass under the head, or a sector-time. If an instruction stored in band 1 sector 03 consists of a command that takes .4 ms to execute after the first address is read out of memory, what should be the second address of this instruction for the greatest efficiency?

It takes 1 sector-time to read out the operand. Since it takes an additional .4 ms or 4 sector-times to execute the command, the total elapsed time is 5 sector times. This means that the second address may be at band 5 sector 8, or in sector 8 of any other band.

Example

Assume a computer with a storage device as in the above example except that the sectors store 4-address instruction words. If an instruction is stored in band 2, sector 08, and the various parts of the instruction consume the following amounts of time:

Reading of first operand	1 sector-time
Reading of second operand	1 sector-time
Remainder of command execution	3 sector-times
Writing of result	1 sector-time
Reading of next instruction	1 sector-time

what should the first operand, second operand, result, and next instruction addresses be?

If the instruction is in band 2, sector 08, the first operand should be in sector 09 of any band, and the second operand should be in sector 10 of any band. Since it requires three additional sector-times to execute the command, the result location should be in sector 14 of any band, and the address of the next instruction should be in sector 15 of any band.

CONTENT ADDRESSABLE MEMORY

Memories that use the principle of content addressing recently have become the object of interest. For computers possessing this type of storage unit, instruction words may be written in symbolic form. The programmer does not have to keep track of the exact locations where data is stored; and neither does an assembler or compiler.

Names may be given to individual instruction words, to operand locations, and to files of data. In the former case, the name is a tag that is stored with the instruction or operand; a request to retrieve this name causes the given instruction or operand to be read out. In the latter case, the name is a tag that is stored with each item in the file; a request to retrieve this name, causes each of the items in the file to be read out in sequence.

Similarly, to load a file into memory, a search is made to find all locations storing a tag representing an empty location. Each of the group of words in the file is written into a different empty location. Also the empty tag is replaced with the tag representing the file name, thus readying the file for future retrieval.

Notice that the basic cycle of the content addressable memory is a search followed by either a read, a write, or a sequence of reads or writes.

An extremely important advantage of content addressable memories is that logic operations may be performed in the memory unit. For instance, instead of retrieving data when the tags match, we may retrieve them under the condition when the stored tag is larger than or smaller than the given tag. Other criteria may be that the wanted tag is between given limits or has a maximum or minimum value.

It is possible to combine the content addressable memory with a directly accessed memory. The content addressable memory may store the names of blocks of storage; the blocks themselves may be in the directly accessed memory. A normal counter may be used to choose the words of the block in sequence.

SUMMARY

1. The main component of memory is a multiword storage unit which is internal to the computer and which is erasable.
2. For direct addressing the coordinate or cyclic access storage unit is used; for indirect addressing the content addressable storage unit may be used.
3. The coordinate access memory fits in well in a parallel computer using 1- or 3-address instruction words.
4. The cyclic access memory fits in well in a serial or serial-parallel computer using 2- or 4-address instruction words.
5. Content addressable memory may be used in computers in which file searches and semantic manipulations are more important than numerical calculation.

Exercises

1. Given a binary computer using 1-address instruction words and having 128 commands and four 16K (where $K = 1024$) memory modules. How many bits are needed for the command? The address? The instruction word?
2. Given a binary computer using 3-address instruction words and having 64 commands and sixteen 4096-memory modules. How many bits are needed for the command? The address? The instruction word?
3. Given a decimal 3-address computer using binary instruction words. If 64 commands are encoded and 261,824 memory words are stored, how many bits are needed for the command? The address? The instruction word?
4. In exercise 3 above how many 6-bit characters may be stored in a data word that is the same size as the instruction word?
5. Why must each cycle in a coincident current magnetic core memory consist of a read and a write, regardless of the command executed?
6. In a coincident current magnetic core memory having a cycle time of .4 μs, what is the maximum possible frequency of reading? Writing?
7. A coordinate access memory has a .2 μs cycle time and is used in a serial machine that possesses 60-bit words.
   a. How can the memory be matched to the remainder of the computer?
   b. If a bit-time is .2 μs, how long would it take to transfer the 60 bits of a word from a register to the memory?

8. If in exercise 7 above, data transmission is in serial-parallel form with a 6-bit character transferred at a time, how long would it take to accomplish the transfer?

9. Given a coordinate access memory with a .5 μs cycle time. If it is assumed that a given arithmetic command can be executed in the same cycle that a transfer is made, how long would it take to fetch an instruction from memory and execute it if the following occurs:
   a. 1-address instruction words are used?
   b. 3-address instruction words are used?

10. If in exercise 9 above, the arithmetic part takes 5 cycles in addition to the transfer cycle, how long would the instruction fetching and execution take?

11. Given, a 2-address instruction computer with a cyclic acce~s memory that can execute 100 different commands and that transmits data in serial-parallel. A word is 10 digits long, 4 bits to a digit.
   a. How many locations can the memory consist of?
   b. If 1000 words are stored in a band, how many bands are there? How many tracks are there?

12. If in exercise 11 above a 4-address computer is assumed, how many bands are there?

13. A serial computer possesses a drum memory that rotates at 3600 rpm. There are 50 sectors to a track, each sector storing a word of ten 4-bit digits.
   a. What is the average latency time?
   b. What is the transfer time?
   c. What is the maximum possible frequency of sector access?

14. Assume in exercise 13 above that data transmission in the remainder of the computer was in parallel.
   a. How could the drum be matched to the remainder of the machine?
   b. If it took 1 bit-time to execute a parallel transfer, where bit-times are obtained from clock pulses on the drum, then how long would it take to transfer a word from the drum to another register?

15. A drum rotates at 4800 rpm and has 100 sectors on a track, and it is used in a 2-address instruction computer.
   a. If address locations are chosen at random, how much time would be required on an average to fetch an instruction word and to execute it?
   b. How long would it take if addresses are chosen to minimize access time?

16. In exercise 15 above, what would the values be for a 4-address instruction computer?

*17. Draw a logical block diagram of a coincident current magnetic core memory consisting of twelve 64-bit planes to and from which data are read from or to a memory register. Read occurs during time t_0; serial flow through a parity detector to other registers occurs during t_1-t_{12}. Writing occurs by a serial transfer to MR via a parity bit generator during t_1-t_{12}; parallel write from MR to core occurs during t_{13}. Show the row and address selectors and the signals required to activate them.

CHAPTER 12

Input-output system

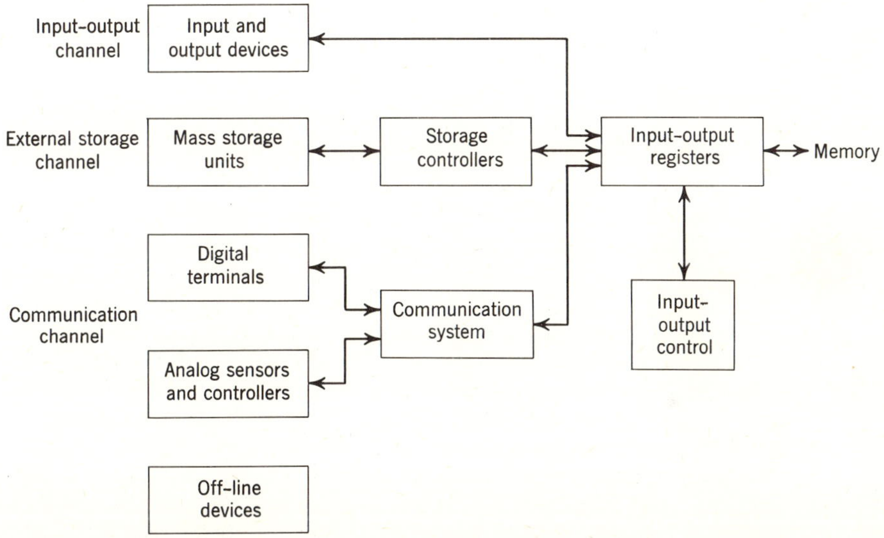

The input-output system is the link between the computer and the outside world. As a link, it consists of parts that are integral with the computer, parts that are external to the computer but that are connected directly to it, and parts that are not connected to the computer in any way. In the first category are the input-output register(s) with the associated I/O control. Their major function is to send data to and to receive data from memory whenever they are called on to do so. In the second category are three types of channels to which are connected a variety of external devices as follows:

1. *Input-output channel.* Input and output devices that send and receive data.
2. *External storage channel.* Mass storage units that enhance the storage capability of the computer.

3. *Communication channel.* External devices are of two types:
   a. Terminals that allow people to interact directly with the computer, either locally or remotely via a communication system.
   b. Analog sensors that pick up and transmit data about physical process; and controllers that accept computer commands and cause changes to the physical processes.

The above devices may be connected to the input-output register either directly or via a controller, a multiplexer or other device.

The above 3 channels are on-line, that is, they are connected to the computer and are under control of a program in the computer. The third category, however, consists of devices that are not connected to the computer at all and are considered to be off-line.

After a discussion of the 3 on-line channels, means for transmission of data to and from the various devices together with the problems of matching these devices to the computer are detailed. A brief description of input-output instructions follows. A review of some off-line devices completes the chapter.

INPUT-OUTPUT CHANNEL

This is the simplest type of channel. Input devices transfer data to the I/O register and from there to memory. Data to be output are transferred from memory to the I/O register, and from there to the output device.

Input Devices

Among input devices commonly in use are input typewriters, punched card and paper tape readers, and printed document readers.

Input typewriter. A typewriter or keyboard is normally supplied to allow maintenance and operating personnel to input special data for control, diagnosis, and maintenance.

Card and paper tape readers. After a programmer writes a program, he may store the instructions in a batch of punched cards. This deck of cards is loaded at one time into a punched card reader and, when the load button is pressed, the entire program is entered into the computer's memory.

In addition to instructions, the punched card also may be used to input data.

Batch input of data also may be executed by paper tape readers.

Printed document readers. Sophisticated devices are on the market for input directly from printed documents, thus, removing the necessity for keypunching of the data onto punched cards or other media. Two major types of such devices are the magnetic ink character readers (MICR) and the optical character recognition (OCR) equipment. MICR equipment reads a stylized MICR font adopted by the American Bankers Association. The characters are written in magnetic ink; as each character is moved under the MICR head, a unique electrical waveform is induced that depends on the type of character. MICR font can be found on the bottom of most American bank checks. An OCR device reads a stylized OCR font (Fig. 139) and converts each character into a unique binary coded output; it is in general use for reading cash register tapes, credit cards, and ZIP codes. More advanced OCR equipment is available that can read many other fonts.

Figure 139 Stylized OCR font.

Output devices

Among the output devices commonly in use are the typewriter, card punch, paper tape perforator, the high speed printer, and the graphical plotter.

Output typewriter. This is usually the same as the input typewriter. It prints out messages to maintenance and operating personnel that notify them of status and other information they require to properly execute their tasks.

Card punch and paper tape perforator. After a program written in a high-level language is entered by means of a card reader, a compiler in the computer translates the instructions into machine instructions, and they are punched out on cards. They now are available for future input.

Data also may be punched out on cards.

Paper tape perforators are used for data primarily.

High speed printer. The high-speed printer is one of the most important output devices. The high-speed printer prints a line of up to 160 characters at a time at a rate of up to several thousand lines per minute. Notice that to print a line at a time, a buffer holding the contents of a line is needed. These printers also respond to formatting control characters, which are useful for printing on preprinted forms.

Graphical plotter. There are two major types of graphical plotter in general use. There are the drum type and the flatbed type. In the drum type, the pen moves along one axis and the paper along the other. In the flatbed type (see Fig. 140), the pen is moved in both the *X* and *Y* axes, although the paper remains fixed.

EXTERNAL STORAGE CHANNEL

In this channel, several mass storage units are connected to the I/O register via a storage controller, another component in the control path between computer and external device.

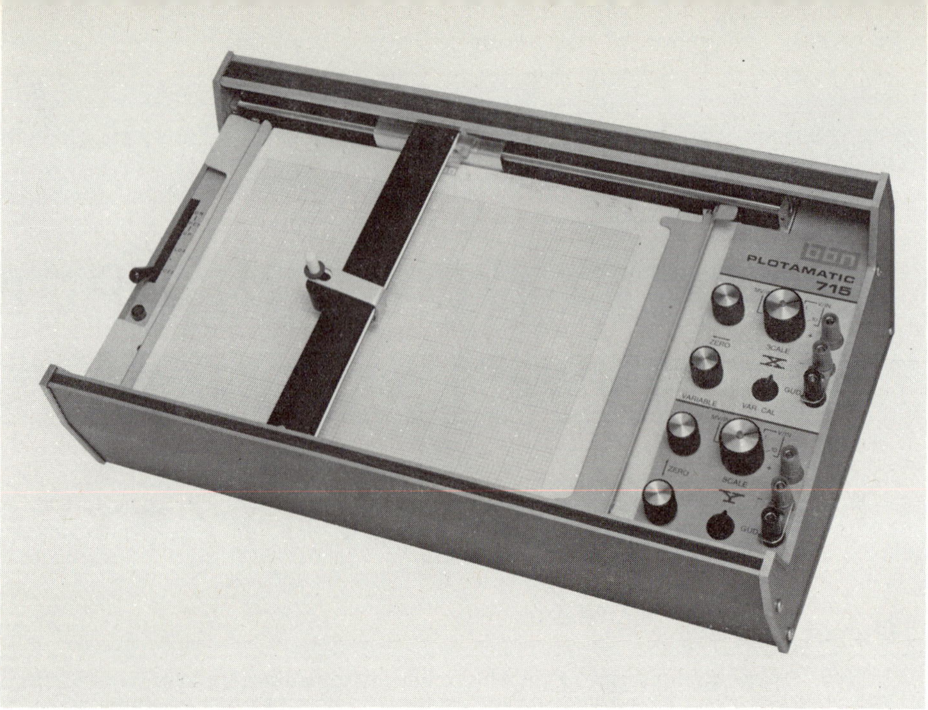

Figure 140 X/Y Recorder (courtesy of Bolt Beranek and Newman, Inc.).

Mass Storage Units

Mass storage units store large volumes of data. They may be programs or operating data. Whenever needed, these data are transferred to memory and operated on. If changes are made to the data, the new values are returned to the mass storage unit. Mass storage units may be viewed as extensions to the memory of the computer.

Two types of mass storage units are in general use: the sequential access magnetic tape unit, and the cyclic access magnetic drum, disc and card units.

Magnetic tape unit. Because of its sequential nature, the magnetic tape unit inputs and outputs a block at a time, consisting of a record or of a group of records. The channel must be designed to transfer blocks.

Magnetic drum, disc, and card units. These devices are cyclic and allow random access, that is, they allow the access time to one location to be the same (within certain limits) as to another location. Still, because of the delays involved in the process, when a location is accessed, usually a complete sector—which may or may not be equivalent to a block—is transferred.

Storage Controllers

The storage controller enables several mass storage devices to be connected onto one channel. There are magnetic tape, disc, and card controllers. Although many of their basic functions are the same, different controllers are needed in each case because of the different methods of implementation used in the mass storage devices they control. Only the magnetic tape controller is discussed here.

Magnetic tape controller. The magnetic tape controller operates as follows. First the central processor forwards the address of the chosen tape unit to the controller. Here an address decoder causes the appropriate tape unit to be queried. If the tape unit is not busy doing something, nor inoperative, a Ready signal is returned. Next the function code is forwarded to a function decoder in the controller. The output signal is applied to the chosen tape unit to cause it to execute one of several functions. Some general functions are:

1. *Read*—To cause magnetic tape to move forward and activate read heads. Data read out is forwarded to I/O register via controller. This continues until End of Block symbol is detected. The tape unit then is caused to stop within the gap between blocks.
2. *Write*—To cause magnetic tape to move forward and activate write heads. Data from I/O register is written onto tape via controller. After it is written, it is immediately read and returned to the controller which then compares the data read with the data written to see if they are the same. The tape unit is made to stop within the gap between blocks.
3. *Erase.* To cause magnetic tape to move forward and erase its contents.
4. *Backspace.* To cause magnetic tape to move backward and activate read heads. The data is sent to controller which ignores them. When the controller recognizes the gap between blocks it stops.
5. *Rewind.* To cause magnetic tape to move backward until the start of the tape reel.
6. *Write EOB.* To write a special coded combination representing the EOB symbol.

Most magnetic tape controllers enable one or several tape units to be rewound at the same time that another tape unit is writing or reading. By the judicious use of buffers, it is possible to have an arrangement where one tape unit is reading, another is writing, and still another is rewinding, all at the same time.

COMMUNICATION CHANNEL

Figure 141 shows the basic configuration of a communication channel for digital data. At the remote end, it consists of a group of terminals connected to a line concentrator and a data set. The line concentrator acts as a rotary switch that connects each of the remote terminals in turn to the data set. The data set sends and transmits to and from the data set at the other end via a transmission line. At the other end, several such data sets are connected to the I/O register via a communications multiplexer, which acts as a rotary switch for the data sets in a manner similar to the way the line concentrator acted for the remote terminals.

Methods of channel sharing other than multiplexing may be used. The concentrator is not always necessary.

Analog devices, sensors and controllers, may be connected into the system in place of the remote terminals.

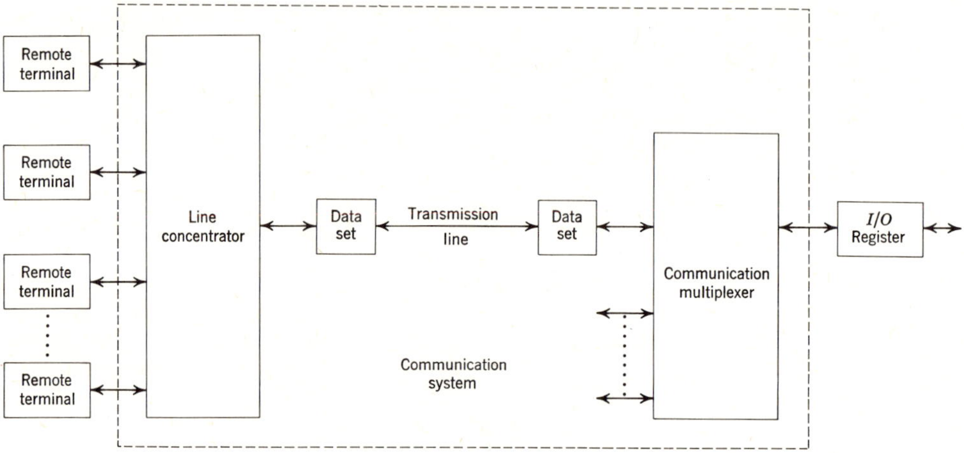

Figure 141 Digital communication channel.

Remote Terminals

A tremendous variety of remote terminals exist. Only teletype, telephone, keyboard, and display devices are discussed here.

Teletype. The teletype terminal is good for input and for output. As a key on the typewriter-type keyboard is depressed, a coded bit combination representing the chosen character (see Table 10 in Chapter 2) is produced and transmitted. Similarly for output: as each coded bit combination is received, it is decoded and the chosen character is printed.

Telephone. The ordinary telephone set with touch tone keyboard also may be used for remote input and output. Codes may be introduced via the keys; output may be by audio voice recording.

Keyboard. A keyboard may be arranged to transmit a character at a time, or a group of characters may be stored in a buffer and then transmitted at one time as a complete message. Similarly, output may arrive and be printed a character at a time, or it may arrive as a complete message and may be stored in the buffer before being printed.

Display. Television-type displays can be used to output graphical information. Devices called light pens have been developed which allow this display device to be used for input as well. The light pen may be pointed toward a drawn object and an associated keyboard may be used to give the computer instructions with reference to this object. In addition, the light pen may be used to "draw" graphs on the display screen, and these graphs may be entered into the computer's memory. An example of such a device is shown in Fig. 142.

Line concentrator

This is a device which scans each of the remote terminals to determine if it wants to transmit. If it does, it connects this terminal to the communication line. Similarly, when data arrives, the line concentrator connects the appropriate remote terminal and forwards the data to the terminal for output. Other functions such as checking, message formatting, and communication control, also may be included in the line concentrator.

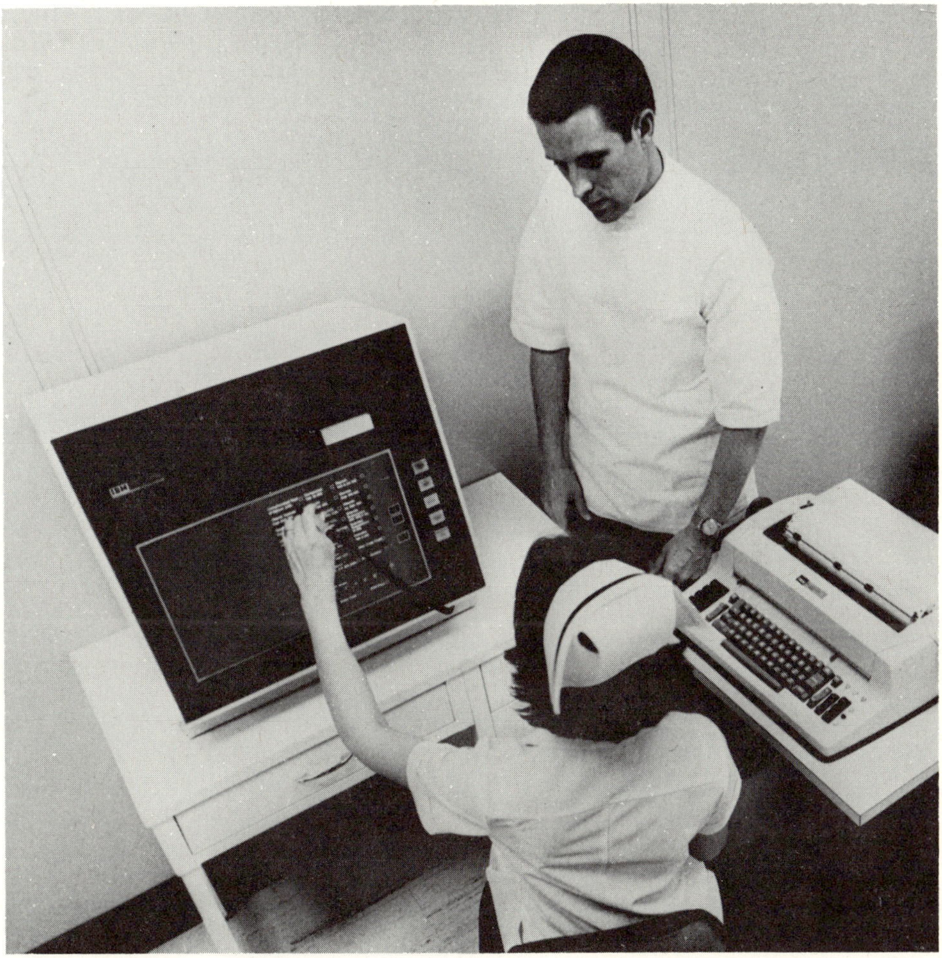

Figure 142 Optical Image Unit (courtesy of IBM).

Data Sets and Data Transmission

There are three aspects of data sets and data transmission that are important to know. They are the type of modulation, the mode of connection of data sets, and the method of data transmission.

Modulation. The data set modulates the data bits, that is, converts them into a form in which they can be transmitted through the medium. At the other end, the data set demodulates the data bits, that is, converts them into the original form.

Among the many forms of modulation for data sets, two are in general use. They are phase shift and multiple frequency. The former is used in teletype where a mark (ONE) produces one audio tone and a space (ZERO) produces another audio tone; each of these tones is represented by a phase shift in the frequency of transmission. For teletype this transmission frequency is between 45 and 75 bits per second. At the other end the data set demodulates the wave into the original mark (ONE) and space (ZERO), respectively.

Figure 143 Acoustic coupler (courtesy of OMNITEC).

Multiple frequencies are used in touch tone telephones. Here, depressing a key causes a coincidence of two audio frequencies, a different combination for each key. In this form, the data is transmitted over 2000 to 2400 bits-per-second telephone lines. At the other end filters in the data set separate the wave into its original components.

A brilliant technique for using the ordinary telephone handset as a data set is by means of an acoustic coupler (see Fig. 143). The acoustic coupler accepts a stream of bits and produces modulation as an audio tone. The telephone handset, which rests in a cradle of the acoustic coupler, picks up the tone and transmits it. During reception, the audio tone from the handset is picked up by the acoustic coupler which demodulates it into a bit stream.

Connection mode. The mode of connection between data sets may be simplex, duplex, or half-duplex. They are as defined in Fig. 144. Simplex transmission means only 1-way transmission. Duplex means simultaneous 2-way transmission. Half-duplex means 2-way transmission but not simultaneously (first 1 then 2 in the illustration).

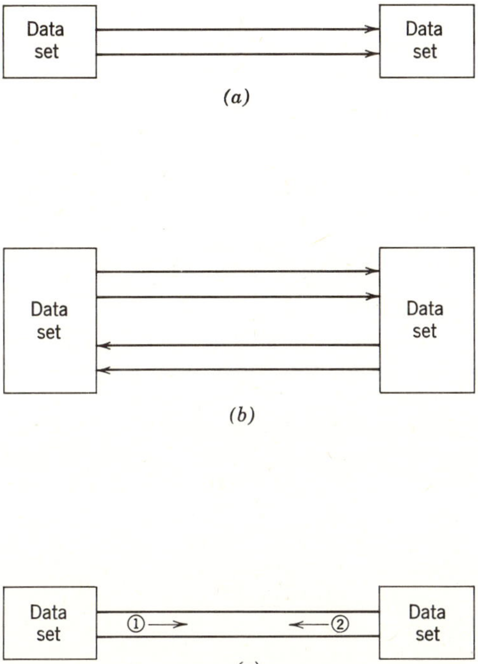

(c)

Figure 144 Mode of data set connection. (*a*) Simplex. (*b*) Duplex. (*c*) Half duplex—2 wire.

Example

Assume in Fig. 144 that data sets can transmit at 2000 bits per second and that characters are 7 bits long. Assume further that a 100-character message is to be transmitted from the left data set to the right data set and that a similar message must be sent in the opposite direction. Compare the time it would take to accomplish this task in the duplex mode with the time to accomplish it in the half-duplex mode.

A 100-character message consists of $100 \times 7 = 700$ bits. Since it takes 1 second to transmit 2000 bits, it should take

$$\frac{700}{2000} = .35 \text{ sec.} = 350 \text{ ms}$$

to complete transmission of a message. In the duplex mode both transmissions occur at the same time. Therefore, it will take 350 ms to complete the task. In the half-duplex mode, one transmission must be completed before the other can start. This means that the time for the task is

$$350 \times 2 = 700 \text{ ms}$$

(Actually, it is a little longer because it takes time for a data set to switch from the receive mode to the transmit mode.)

Methods of data transmission. Transmission may be in serial or in parallel. It is serial when the data set is built to handle bits; it is parallel when it is built to handle characters.

Data sets may be characterized as synchronous or asynchronous. A synchronous data set is one that must be furnished the bits at a regular rate. An asynchronous data set need not have its bits supplied at a regular rate.

In synchronous transmission, clocks are used to relate the arriving bit stream to time so that the bits of the message may be identified. In asynchronous transmission, some other means, for instance, detectors which determine the location of bits, must be used.

In teletype, transmission may be considered to be asynchronous by character, synchronous by bit. Each character arrives at an irregular rate. However, each character is framed with Start and Stop bits. When the group of bits arrives at the data set at the other end, the Start bit turns on a clock that produces clock pulses to sample the arriving bits. This process is stopped by the Stop bit.

The telephone company also provides broad band TELPAK and PCM (pulse code modulation) communication. Transmission via TELPAK may occur at frequencies of 40,800 to 500,000 bits per second. PCM carrier transmission is available in a hierarchy of three levels: T_1, which operates at 1.544 megabits per second and accommodates 24 voice-grade channels simultaneously; T_2, which operates at 6.3 megabits per second and accommodates 96 voice-grade channels simultaneously; and T_4, which operates at 181 megabits per second and accommodates 4032 voice grade-lines simultaneously.

Communication Multiplexer

Multiplexing is the technique whereby several data sets communicate with one computer channel simultaneously. The multiplexer generates successive time slots, each of which is assigned to a different data set.

Normally messages sent via data sets consist of a group of characters. In the general case the number of characters to a message is variable, and the message is framed with an SOH (Start of Heading) symbol at the start and an ETX (End of Text) symbol at the end.

When used with parallel data sets which transmit and receive a character at a time, the multiplexer interleaves the transmission of a character via one data set on one time slot with the transmission of another character—via another data set—on another time slot. In this way, it is possible to transmit a character via each data set connected to the multiplexer and then to come back to the first data set and start another series of character transmissions.

Of course, the multiplexer must choose the character for each data set from a different message. And when the sequence is repeated, the communications multiplexer must choose the second character in each of the same messages.

For any one data set, the above process starts when an SOH is detected and ends when an ETX is detected by the multiplexer.

Similar considerations apply for reception. On receipt of individual characters, they must be assembled into different messages.

When used with serial data sets, the multiplexer may convert each character into a serial stream of bits before the transmission by the data set. After reception, the serial bit stream is converted into characters. Interleaving may be character by character or bit by bit.

Other functions that the multiplexer may perform are the checking of messages and the control of data transmission. Common checking techniques are vertical and horizontal parity checking. When a complete message has been received, an acknowledgment is normally returned to the originator. If checking indicates the message was received in error, some multiplexers return a Request Repeat message. When this control message is received at the originating end, the message is sent out again.

Many of the above transmission control, checking, and message assembly and disassembly functions may be executed by the processor internally.

Example

Refer to Fig. 145. Assume a situation in which the memory is storing 100 messages each 10 characters long where a character consists of 8 bits. By means of programming, the first character of each message is removed in turn, after which the second character of each is removed in turn, and so on. As each character is removed, it is forwarded via the I/O register and multiplexer to the associated data set for transmission. If each of the 100 data sets transmits at the rate of 2000 bits per second, how fast must the characters be transmitted to the multiplexer? How long is the scan time of the multiplexer? What part of this time is available for each of the data sets?

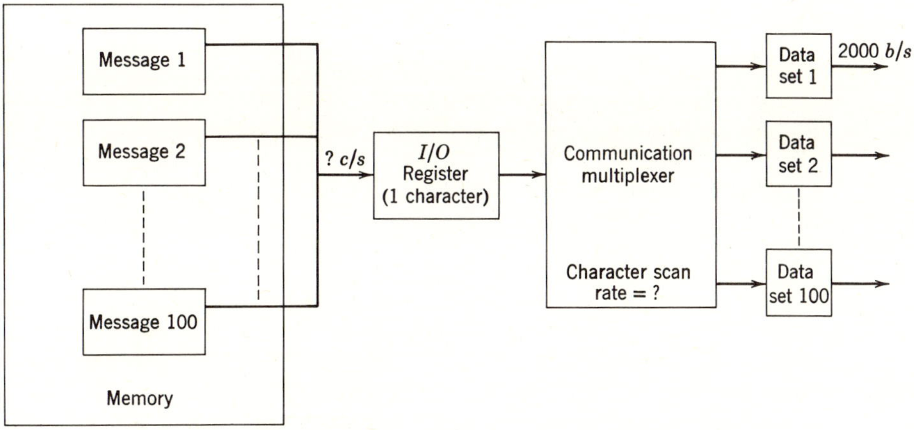

Figure 145 Output transmission via communication multiplexer.

See Fig. 145. Each data set transmits at 2000 bits per second, which is equal to $2000/8 = 250$ characters per second. Since we want to take care of 100 data sets, it means that the rate of character arrival at the multiplexer must be 100 times greater, or $250 \times 100 = 25{,}000$ characters per second.

To accommodate 100 data sets, the multiplexer must scan fast enough to take care of a character on each of them and come back in time to handle the succeeding character on the data set. The time between the arrival of a character and the arrival of the succeeding character on a data set is the reciprocal of the transmission rate, or $1/250 = 4$ ms. This is the scan time of the multiplexer. Since it must take care of 100 data sets during that time, it means that only one-hundredth of the scan time, or .04 ms is available for each data set.

Other Methods of Channel Sharing

The communication multiplexer allows several devices on slow communication lines to be matched to a fast computer. Another way of doing this is to connect several external devices to the same channel and use scanning, polling, or addressing to choose the desired external device.

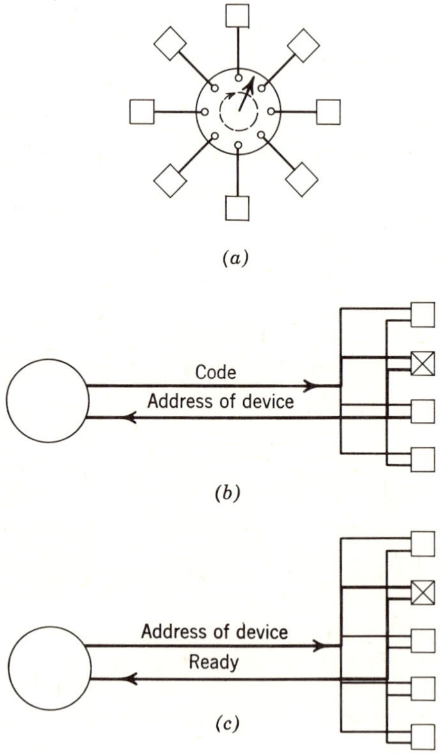

Figure 146 Scanning, polling, and addressing. (*a*) Scanning. (*b*) Polling. (*c*) Addressing.

Scanning (Fig. 146*a*). In this approach for selecting an external device each device is connected in turn. If it is ready and wishes to be connected, a connection is made and transmission occurs. Immediately thereafter the next device is connected. This occurs until all devices have been queried, after which the scan is repeated.

Polling (Fig. 146*b*). A code asking for a device that is ready to transmit or to receive is sent out. The one device that is ready is connected to the channel, and the device sends its address. If two devices are ready at the same time, some type of priority mechanism must be designed. More will be given about priority later.

Addressing (Fig. 146*c*). The address of the external device is sent out, and the chosen device sends back a signal indicating it is ready. If it is not, it sends back a Not Ready signal.

Direct Analog Input-Output

Some inputs to the computer may arrive in analog form. This analog data is picked up by sensors of natural phenomena being studied by scientists, or of physical processes occurring in industry. Some analog quantities which we may want sensors to pick up are pressure, temperature, humidity, flow of a liquid, stress, speed of movement or of rotation. To feed such data from a sensor directly into a computer we need an analog-to-digital converter.

At the output end of the computer, a digital-to-analog converter may be needed to convert digital results of calculations into a form which may enable a controller to control an output mechanism.

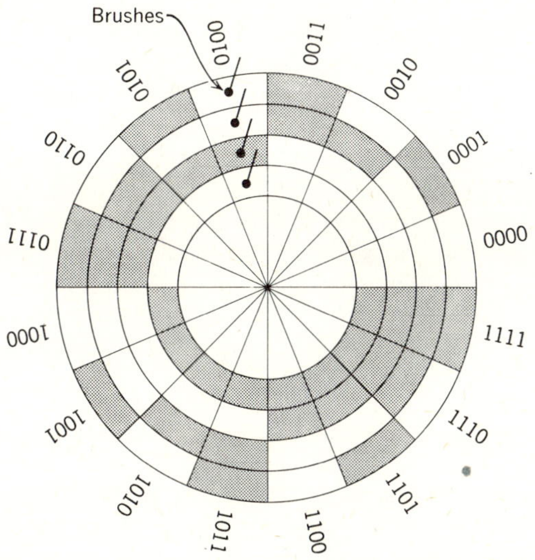

Figure 147 Analog-to-digital converter, mechanically operated.

Analog-to-digital converters. A simple mechanically operated converter may be built by encoding a physical representation of a code onto a disk rotated by a shaft. Figure 147 shows a disk with such a binary pattern. The dark areas represent conducting surfaces and the light areas insulating surfaces. An electric brush connected to a source of power is in contact with each channel. As the shaft rotates, current flows through some channels and not through others, depending on the configuration of conducting and insulating areas.

The illustration shows the disk stopped in a position to cause the brushes to read 0100: only the brush in the second inner channel is on a conducting surface and thus conducts current.

Example

If the brushes in Fig. 147 are on the border between 0100 and 0011, what are the possible bit combinations that can be read? What should we do to avoid this ambiguity?

Eight different combinations, as follows:

0000
0001
0010
0011
0100
0101
0110
0111

To avoid this ambiguity the binary coded decimal should be replaced with reflected binary (See Appendix).

Digital-to-analog converters. A digital-to-analog converter may be built by a process of weighting. This process is outlined in Fig. 148 for a 3-bit number. Switches are used in each bit position to connect a battery or not, depending on whether there is a ONE or a ZERO in that position. The battery voltages are proportional to the weights of the associated bit positions. The illustration shows that, for the binary combination 101, the 4-V battery and the 1-V battery are in series to produce an analog output of 5 V.

Of course, practical circuits are not built this way. The bits may be stored in flip-flops. The switches may be transistor switches activated by the outputs of the flip-flops. The actual summing of voltages may be obtained by the proper use of resistor networks.

DATA TRANSFER

Data transfer between various external devices and the computer may be under computer control or under joint computer and external device control.

Since external devices are in general slower than the computer, means must be provided for matching the two more carefully. The use of the I/0 register as a buffer helps in this process. So does multiplexing, as has been shown. Another important method is by concurrency: the execution of I/O operations simultaneously with internal processing operations.

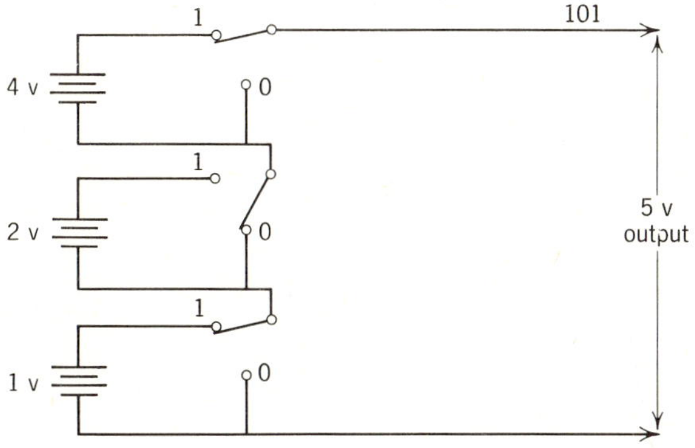

Figure 148 Digital-to-analog converter.

Computer Control

Because input-output devices are as a rule slower than internal memory and because they are of the sequential or cyclic access form, more efficient input-output transfers are obtained by executing transfers a block at a time rather than a word at a time. If internal transmission is word oriented, it means that a means of counting words must be provided. The technique is fixed or flexible depending on whether blocks consist of a fixed number of words or are variable in size.

Fixed length block transfer. Transfer of a fixed number of words at a time, whether the group be called a block or a sector, occurs often between memory and external storage devices such as the magnetic disc unit or the magnetic drum. Figure 149 shows the execution of the transfer of a sector consisting of a fixed number of words from a magnetic disc unit to memory. In addition to the I/O register, instruction register and address selector which perform the expected functions, we need a word counter, an adder, and a sector size decoder.

The general sequence of events in the execution of an input instruction is as follows. First, the word counter is cleared to zero. A word is transferred from the disc unit to the I/O register. The contents of the word counter are added to the initial address from the instruction register, and the result—the initial address—is applied to the address selector. The address selector thus chooses the location for the first word, and the word transfer is executed. After the word transfer, the word counter is stepped to one and the sequence is repeated. This time the address selector chooses the next succeeding address location to store the second word. This sequence is repeated until the sector size decoder finds that the word counter is storing the sector size, and then a signal is produced to cause the operation to end.

How does the computer know where on the disc to obtain each word? The answer is that the disc input instruction stores *two* addresses: the initial memory address and, also, the initial disc address. In one-address instruction machines, the sector address may be included with the command part of the instruction. If this is not possible, two instruction words may be used.

Normally, the disc can be made to choose succeeding addresses in time for succeeding transfers to memory. If this cannot be done, a counting mechanism similar to the one described above may be used to choose external storage addresses in sequence.

The disc output instruction works in a similar way. The initial address in memory is read out into the I/O register and from there into the initial address of the disc unit. After one is added to both counters, the sequence is repeated. This continues until the sector size decoder finds the last word of the sector is being transferred. On its completion, the disc output operation ends.

If internal transmission is executed in terms of characters instead of words, the same technique may be used except that the word counter is replaced by a character counter.

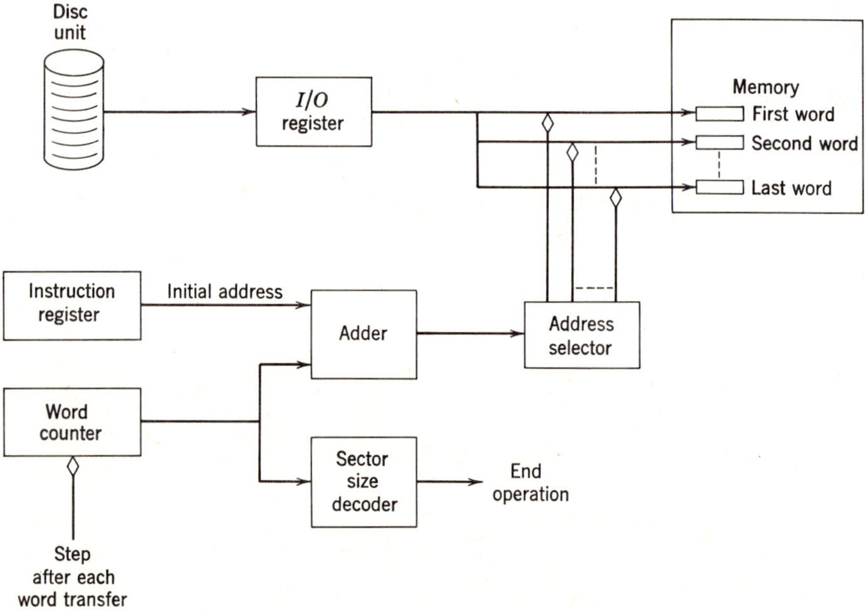

Figure 149 Transfer of fixed length sector.

Example

Given a computer with character-oriented data transmission and with a disc unit consisting of sectors 50 characters in size. An instruction reads:

> "*Input* disc sector 35 to succeeding memory locations starting with address 543"

What does the character counter read when the transfer executed by this instruction is completed? To which memory locations will the characters of the sector be transferred?

Since there are 50 characters to a sector, the character counter must read 50 when the transfer is completed. If the first character is forwarded to memory address 543, the last character is forwarded to the fiftieth location after that which is 592.

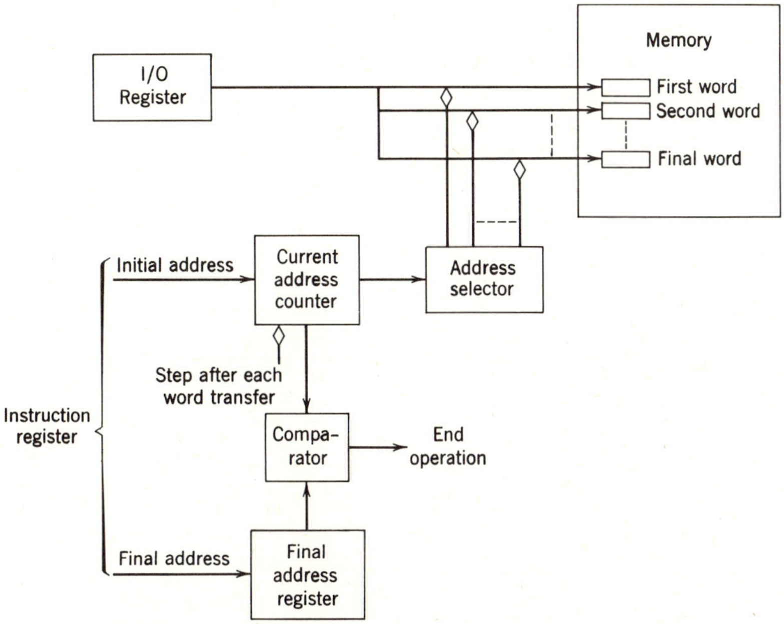

Figure 150 Transferring variable length block to memory.

Variable length block transfer. If a block is of variable length, the transfer to memory may be accomplished by making the instruction specify the final address as well as the initial address. The outline of this technique is given in Fig. 150. At the start of the execution of an input instruction, the initial and final addresses are read into the current address counter and the final address register, respectively. A word is transferred from the I/O device to the I/O register. The contents of the current address register are applied to the address selector, and the word is transferred from the I/O register to the initial address location in memory. After the word transfer, the current address counter is stepped by 1 and the process is repeated. The second word, thus, is stored in the succeeding memory location. This process continues until the contents of the current address counter are the same as the contents of the final address register. At this time the comparator produces a pulse that brings the operation to an end.

Another way of executing such an operation is by storing in the instruction word the initial address and a count of the number of words. Instead of the final address register, another counter would be included. At the start it would accept the count from the instruction word. After each word transfer this counter would be made to step down 1. When the counter reached zero, the operation would be brought to an end.

Still another method, which is commonly used in batch I/O devices, for instance magnetic tape units, is to store an End of Block (EOB) character at the end of each block. During read-in, a detector is needed to check for the appearance of this symbol. When it occurs, the operation is ended.

Output instructions are executed in a similar manner.

Example

When transferring a block of 100 characters from addresses 700 to 799 in memory to magnetic tape in a system that is using EOB characters, what must the last step be after counting 100 word transfers?

To make certain that this block could be read out at some future time, an EOB symbol must be manufactured and written onto the tape as the last step.

Control words, With the counting technique described above, a current address counter and a final address register are needed for each channel. If, in addition (as we shall discuss later in this chapter), we want to have several devices connected to each channel, the hardware proliferation mounts. A simpler hardware situation results from the use of control words.

A control word is a word in memory that stores the current and final addresses, plus other data, related to I/O control of a specific external device. A different control word is stored for each of the external devices used. Since the control word is manufactured by programming means, it may be modifed to suit various situations. If a new external device is added to the system, a new control word may be stored to take care of it. For these reasons and more, the control word introduces a great deal of flexibility in input-output operations.

Figure 151 is a diagram of an input transfer that is using the control word technique. Ten external devices are used for input at different times. Corresponding to these 10 devices are 10 control words that are stored in memory at address locations corresponding to the associated devices. For instance, CW2, which is the control word for device number 2, is stored at address 502.

An input instruction referring to device number two is executed in the following sequence. The input instruction sends out a signal to determine if device number two is ready. If it is, it is activated for reading, and address 502 in memory is accessed to read out CW2 into the current address counter and the final address register (step ①). After this, the sequence is similar to the one given above: the address selector chooses successive locations in memory② to store succeeding words entering the I/O register③. At the end of the block, the comparator is activated⑤ to bring the operation to an end.

A similar sequence of events occurs for an output instruction, except that words are removed from succeeding locations in memory and are transferred via the I/O register to the chosen external device.

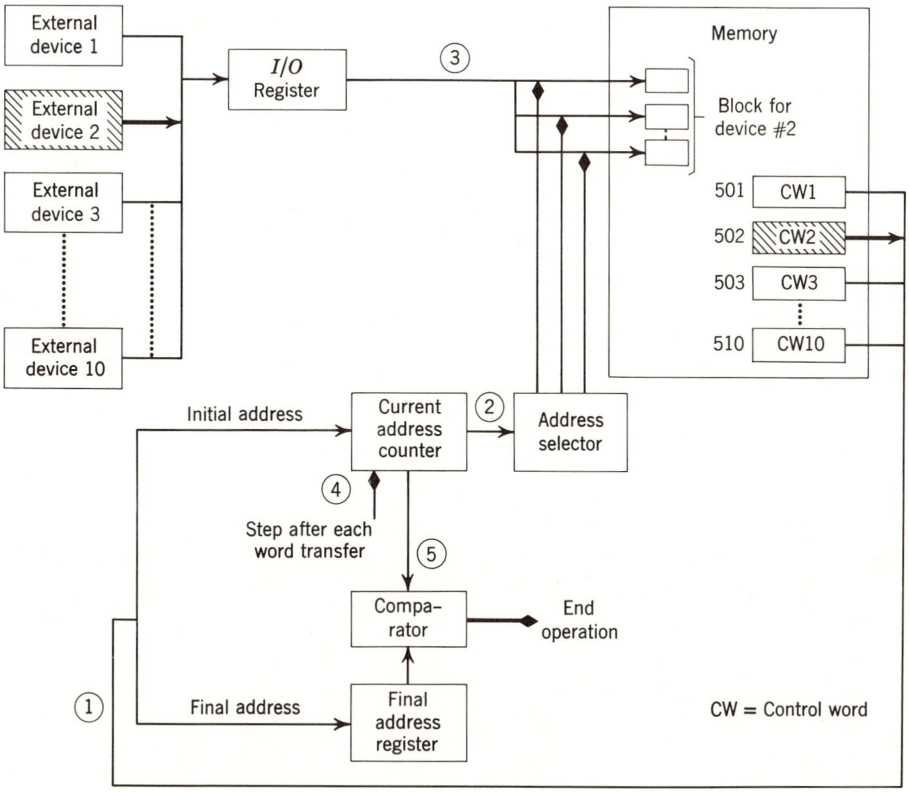

Figure 151 Control words for input transfers.

Example

Assume that the external devices in Fig. 151 are all output devices and that the arrows between memory and I/O register and between I/O register and external devices all point in the opposite direction. We want to transfer a 100-word block stored in successive addresses in memory starting at address 801 to external device number 10, which may be a printer. What should the control word be? Where should it be stored?

The control word consists of the initial address and the final address. The initial address where the first word is to be found is 801 ; the final address is 100 locations further, or 900. The control word thus is

801–900

Since it refers to device number 10, it should be stored at address 510.

Mutual Control by Computer and External Device

Assume that we have a situation where data arrive at random from some external device, an analog-to-digital converter, for example. Whenever it arrives, it must enter the computer. It can do this by shifting into a register. But how can we make certain that it is transferred to memory without causing havoc with operations currently being executed in the computer? Two techniques for doing this are discussed. They are sampling and program interrupt.

Sampling. In this approach, bits are shifted into an I/O register until the register is full. When this occurs, a flip-flop is set. The program in the computer periodically causes a signal to sample the state of this flip-flop. Whenever it finds that the I/O register is full, it institutes a transfer from the I/O register to memory.

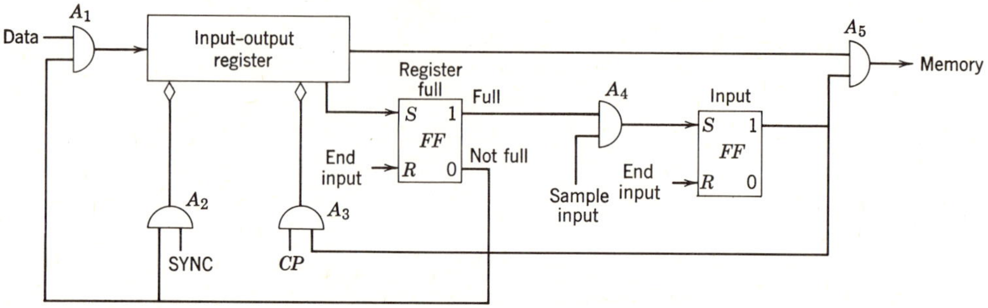

Figure 152 Random input with sampling.

Figure 152 shows an example of this system. It consists of an input-output register, two flip-flops and several gates. As each bit is applied to gate A_1, a sync pulse is applied to A_2 to allow this bit to be shifted into the register. When the register is full, the Register Full flip-flop is set. If now the Sample Input signal arrives, the input flip-flop is set. Once this happens, A_3 allows computer clock pulses *CP* to shift the bits out of the register via gate A_5 to memory. When the register is emptied, the End Input signal resets both flip-flops. With the input flip-flop reset, no data can be shifted out of the register. With the Register Full flip-flop in the Not-Full position, A_1 and A_2 are made ready for more data entry.

Program interrupt. For a computer that is always working on the same program, the sampling approach may be all that is needed. Whenever the I/O register is full, the program can be set up to transfer the data and to operate on them. But for a computer that is busy on many types of programs and expects inputs from and produces outputs to a variety of external devices, the sampling approach is inadequate. What is needed is a means for interrupting the program currently being executed to execute the input or output transfer; and to achieve this interruption in a manner that allows the computer to return to the point of interruption in the original program on completion of the transfer.

A simplified diagram of the program interrupt cycle is shown in Fig. 153. A given program is in progress when an input arrives and causes an interrupt signal①. At a convenient point, such as after the completion of the instruction currently being executed, the program in progress is halted and the address of the next instruction in the sequence is stored in a special register or a given location in memory②. This is followed by transferring control③ of the computer to the address where the first instruction of the new program is stored. This "called in program" causes input and executes other necessary instructions. On its completion, another interrupt is produced④. The address that had been stored on the initial interruption is returned⑤ and, thus, the instruction sequencing continues from where it left off in the "program in progress."

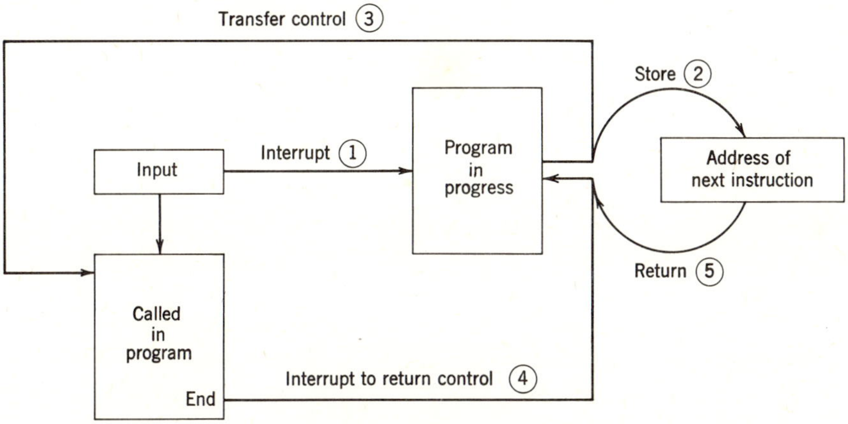

Figure 153 Program interrupt cycle.

In a practical situation, interrupts may be produced by any of several input or output lines. Figure 154 shows in simplified form a typical interrupt mechanism for handling four input lines. Separate registers and request flip-flops are provided for each input. An interrupt caused by a given input calls a program that is different from the one caused by a different input. The interrupt subroutine makes the proper choice. In addition to the instruction counter and address selector, which are always needed, the diagram shows an interrupt subroutine address register and an instruction counter store register, plus other logic.

Specifically the sequence of events is as follows. Input B arrives and fills the register. When full, the Request B flip-flop is set①. At an appropriate time during instruction execution, a Check Interrupt Request signal determines if any of the Request flip-flops is set②. Since Request B flip-flop is set, a signal is produced that causes the contents of the instruction counter to be transferred to the instruction counter store register③. After this, the contents of the interrupt subroutine address register are transferred to the instruction counter④ and instruction sequencing resumes with the instructions in the interrupt

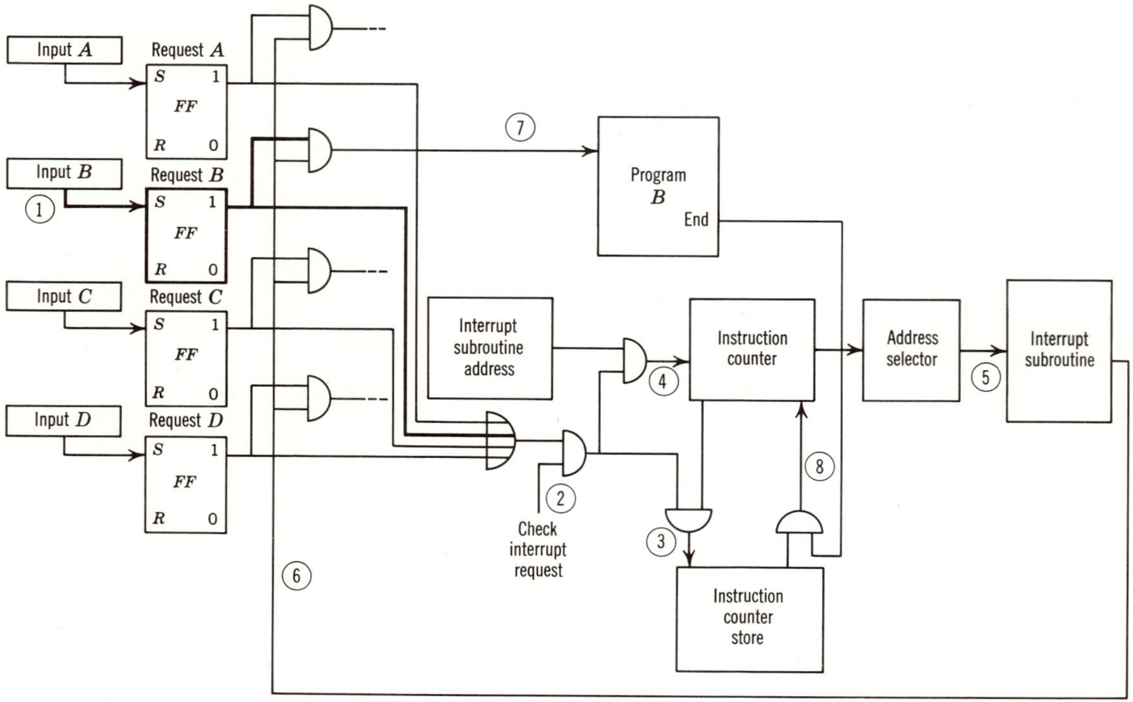

Figure 154 Interrupt mechanism.

subroutine⑤. One of the first things the interrupt subroutine does is to check the state of each of the Request flip-flops⑥ to determine at which register data has arrived. In the present case it finds that Request B flip-flop is set and, therefore, causes a jump to program B⑦. After program B reaches its end, a signal is produced that gates what was previously stored in the instruction counter store register back to the instruction counter⑧. Since the instruction counter is now storing the address of the instruction, following the one completed previous to the interrupt of the original program, instruction sequencing continues from where it had left off.

What do we do if two Request flip-flops go on at the same time? Obviously a system of priorities must be worked out. The interrupt subroutine checks the Request flip-flops according to their order of priority.

In some computers a hardware scanner may accomplish the same task as is performed by the interrupt subroutine.

Concurrency

The third and probably the most important present method for matching the slow speed of external devices to the fast speed of the computer is by executing input-output operations concurrently with internal processing. Two techniques for achieving concurrency are cycle stealing and multiple memories. The first is a means for interleaving I/O operations within the internal instruction stream. The second is a means for executing I/O operations in parallel with the internal instruction stream.

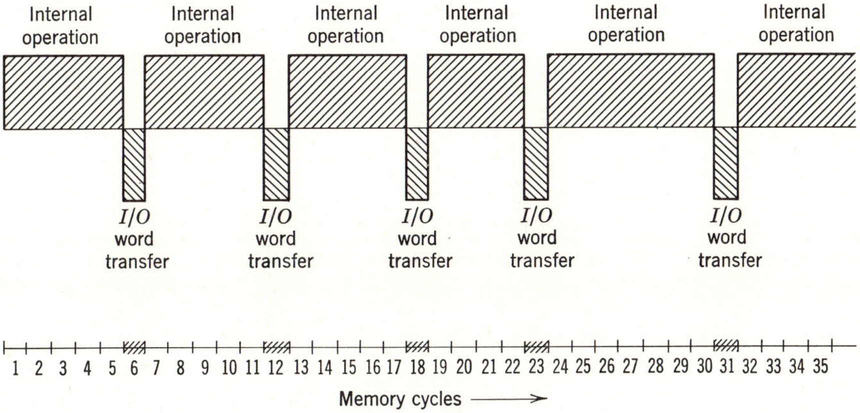

Figure 155 Cycle stealing.

Cycle stealing. Figure 155 shows what is meant by cycle stealing. The timing of operations executed by computers may be given in terms of memory cycles. Thus a *Read* instruction may take two cycles: one for fetching the instruction from the memory, the other for executing the transfer. As will be shown in the following chapter, some instructions, for instance, *multiply*, may take many more cycles, the actual number being variable. Cycle stealing is the process of removing one or more memory cycles in between instructions in the instruction stream and of using them for I/O operations. The illustration shows memory cycles 6, 12, 18, 23, and 31 being stolen for the transfer of I/O words.

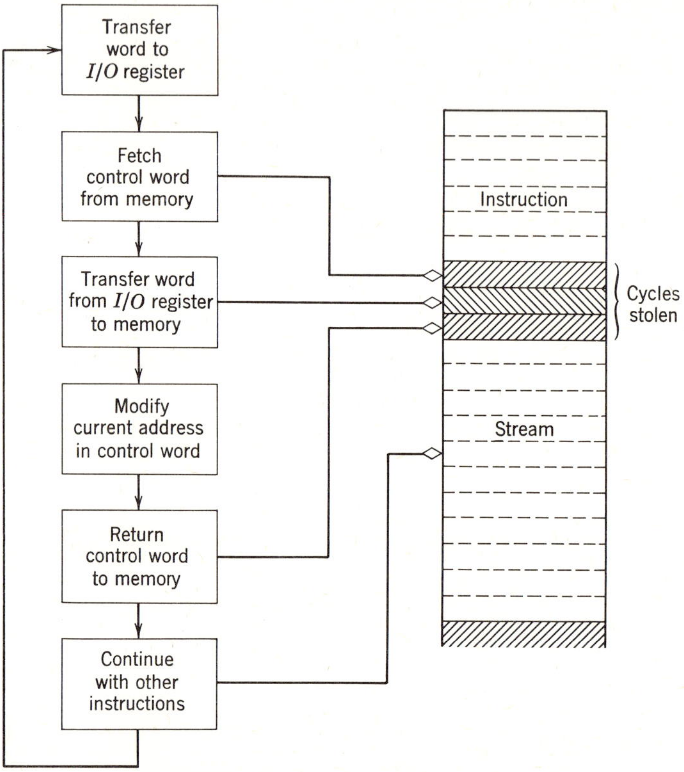

Figure 156 Cycle stealing with control words.

Figure 156 shows how data may be input by means of cycle stealing in conjunction with control words. While the computer is executing instructions, the I/O register is accepting input data. As soon as the I/O register is full, and the instruction presently being executed comes to an end, 3 memory cycles are stolen. The first cycle is for the purpose of fetching the control word from memory. The current address of the control word is then forwarded to the address selector, and the word in the I/O register is transferred to the location in memory represented by this address; this occurs during the second cycle. After this is done, 1 is added to the current address and the control word is returned to its location in memory during the third cycle. The computer now continues with its normal instruction sequencing. Meanwhile another word is loaded into the I/O register. When the register is again full, the above sequence is repeated. This continues until all the words in the block have been transferred. At this time, the current address is equal to the final address, a condition that causes the operation to come to an end, probably by introducing an interrupt.

Example

Assume a computer with a memory that has a cycle time of 1 μs and in which the average instruction takes 4 cycle times to execute. A magnetic tape unit can transfer characters to an I/O register at a 100 kc rate. Each word consists of 4 characters. To transfer the word from the I/O register to the memory, 4 cycles must be stolen. How many instructions are executed on an average between successive input word transfers?

Since the magnetic tape unit executes character transfers at the rate of 100 kc and there are 4 characters to a word, the I/O register fills up at the rate of 100 kc/4 = 25 kc. The time between successive accesses to memory is, therefore, 1/25,000 = 40 μs. This is equivalent to 40 cycles. Subtracting the 4 cycles that must be stolen for the transfer leaves 36 cycles for execution of instructions. At an average of 4 cycles to an instruction, 36/4 = 9 instructions are executed between successive word transfers.

To reduce the number of cycles that must be stolen during each transfer, a live control word register may be used for each channel. This one register can serve the needs of all devices connected to this channel. At the start of the data transmission, the appropriate control word is read into the control word register. Here it remains until completion of the I/O operation. Only 1 cycle must be stolen for each word transfer instead of the 3 cycles previously used.

Multiple memory modules. Another method of achieving concurrency is by the use of multiple memory modules, each separately addressable. With this approach, while instructions with associated data are being obtained from one memory module and executed, the external device may be transferring data to or receiving data from another memory module. Instruction sequencing is under control of the instruction counter. Input-output transfers are under control of a separate counter.

There is no reason why a memory module that has been loaded via the I/O register then cannot be switched for use in instruction sequencing.

INPUT-OUTPUT INSTRUCTIONS

Input-output instructions may be subdivided into the following three categories: control, transfer, and editing and formatting.

I/O Control

Control instructions depend a great deal on specific characteristics of external devices and I/O organizational approaches such as the use of control words, cycle stealing, interrupts, and priorities.

Among instructions that depend on the device characteristics are the ones that turn them on, the ones that check their status, and special instructions. Most devices have a manual switch to turn them on. However, devices such as magnetic tape units, which must be made to rotate before writing or reading can take place, sometimes require special instructions that start them rotating; a transfer instruction follows after a delay. If the computer uses a cycle stealing approach, this type instruction is not necessary, as it is made part of the transfer instruction. (Student: Why?) Any device may be inoperable or, in a concurrency approach, busy doing something else. For this purpose, instructions are provided that check the status of the external devices. For systems using program interrupt, the occurrence of an error or fault during execution of a transfer sets a status flip-flop and introduces an interrupt. One of the instructions in this interrupt routine is a device status checking instruction. Under special instructions may be listed the following:

1. *Rewind Tape.* After a reel of magnetic tape has completely unwound itself onto the take-up reel, this instruction causes the tape to be rewound back onto the original reel.
2. *Backspace.* On magnetic tape, reverse the tape and bring it back to before the beginning of a block.
3. *Skip Block.* Do not read block and go to succeeding block.

Among instructions that depend on the organizational approach are the following?

1. *Set Interrupt Permit On.* Set a flip-flop that allows the interrupt mechanism to operate.
2. *Reset Interrupt Permit Off.* Reset a flip-flop to prevent the interrupt mechanism from operating.

Transfer

Although transfer instructions may be written in many different ways depending on the nature of the external device, essentially there are only two types of transfers: input and output.

In addition to specifying the direction of transfer, the instruction also must specify the size of the transfer and the locations in both the external device and the memory. Some computers specify all this in the instruction itself. Others use indirect means such as control words. These control words are developed by the program.

Editing and Formatting

When executing an output instruction such as Print or Display, the message developed by a program may need to be modified to make it easy for a human being to comprehend. For instance, a number such as 543 may be stored in a 10-digit word computer as 0000000543. Before this is output, it is edited by removing the seven zeroes in the most significant positions. This is called zero suppression. In addition, data may be added to certain places, and symbols used for internal control may be removed from other places.

The output message also needs formatting. Some operations included in this area are paragraphing, line spacing, and tabulation. Because it is so intimately tied to the output operation itself, formatting often is accomplished by inserting control characters into the output message that is being sent to the printer or display unit.

OFF-LINE DEVICES

Many devices are used off-line. Among them are related processing equipment, for instance, check sorters and punched card and tabulating equipment; data entry devices for the preparation of data to be entered into the computer; and converters for converting data stored on a given medium to data stored on another medium. Only data entry devices and converters are discussed below.

Data Entry Devices

The keypunch has been a standard data entry device for a long time. It is a mechanical device that accepts 80-column cards and that punches appropriate holes in them when the operator depresses the keys. Because punched card input is so slow, the data on the punched cards often were transferred to magnetic tape or a magnetic disc either via an off-line converter or via the computer.

To make data preparation more efficient, direct key-to-tape and key-to-disc units have been developed. Some of them are single operator units; some accommodate several operators at a time.

Key-to-tape units. When we realize that the contents of a stack of 10,000 punched cards may be placed onto a 1200-foot reel of magnetic tape which is only $8\frac{1}{2}$ in. in diameter, we begin to perceive some of the advantages for entering data directly by keyboard to magnetic tape. If we include a buffer and a display in the unit, we discover many more advantages.

A key-to-magnetic tape unit has a buffer in order that it can store record formats and other control data which are entered via the keyboard. When data is to be entered, one of the stored formats may be displayed on the screen. This format display plus a guiding cursor allow the operator to follow the displayed format in his data preparation. As he keys his characters, they appear on the screen in the appropriate locations. The message at the same time is stored in the buffer and can be corrected at any time during the entry process. On completion of record entry, a special key is depressed which causes the stored record to be written onto the magnetic tape.

This data entry device allows data already stored on the magnetic tape to be verified. It also allows the searching for a record previously prepared to which corrections need to be made. The use of the buffer allows many other functions to be included.

Similar devices have been designed to transfer data directly to magnetic disc and to magnetic tape cassette. In the latter case, provision often is made to transfer the data from casette to magnetic tape. Many other combinations are possible.

Multi-station units. Since operators are slow, several operators may be accommodated by one data-entry device. All the keyboard stations are connected to the buffer. More control must be associated with the buffer to assure that no operator interferes with the keying of another operator. In fact, minicomputers may be used in the place of the simple buffer and control. Of course, this allows the use of programs to achieve a greater degree of flexibility in data preparation.

Although these units are off-line devices, many of them have provision for connection to a communication line. In the latter cases, they are essentially sophisticated remote terminals.

Converters

Many different converters have been in use. Among the more common ones are the card-to-magnetic tape converter and the high-speed line printer whose input is magnetic tape. The latter has been replaced in many cases by a computer output microfilmer (COM).

Punched-card-to-magnetic-tape converter. In broad outline, the punched-card-to-magnetic-tape converter works as follows. A punched-card reader transfers the data stored on the punched card to buffer storage. A tape-handling device then transfers the data stored in the buffer to magnetic tape.

Computer output microfilmer (COM). The COM takes the computer output that has been written onto magnetic tape and converts it into an alphanumeric printout on microfilm. The magnetic tape is read and its contents is applied to a CRT character generator which produces character symbols to be displayed on the CRT screen. A microfilm camera then records the characters onto microfilm.

The COM can operate at speeds of 20,000 lines per minute. The microfilm occupies considerably less room than does paper. Readers are available for viewing the microfilm and printers are available for producing hard copies.

COM's also may work directly off the computer.

SUMMARY

1. The input-output system consists of a functional input-output unit that is integral with the computer, plus external equipment some of which are on-line and others off-line.
2. There may be 3 types of on-line channels. Examples of external devices in each of the 3 channels are as follows:

   External Storage. Magnetic tape, magnetic drum, magnetic disc, and magnetic card.

   Input-Output. I/O typewriter, card punch and reader, paper tape punch and reader, MICR and OCR, and high-speed printer.

Communication. Remote terminals, line concentrators, data sets, multiplexers; analog sensors, analog-to-digital converters, digital-to-analog converters, and controllers may replace remote terminals.

3. For efficiency, transfer of data along the on-line channels normally occurs in larger units than a word. The transfer may be under computer control only, or it may be controlled jointly by the computer and the external device. The block transferred may be fixed in length or variable.
4. To transfer the proper number of words (or characters) in a block, a counting mechanism is needed. If the block size is fixed the process is automatically completed when the last count is reached. If the block size is variable, the final address or the number of words to be transferred is included in the instruction or in a control word stored in memory to which the instruction refers. In other situations an EOB designates the end of a block.
5. For closer interaction between external devices and the computer a sampling technique or a program interrupt technique is used. In the former, scanning occurs at a certain rate and transfers are executed whenever data appears at a given register. In the latter, entry of data causes an interrupt that stops execution of the present program long enough to execute an I/O program; on completion of the I/O program, the interrupted program returns to the point of interruption and resumes sequencing. Priorities are used to choose between different inputs that are producing interrupts at the same time.
6. As a rule, external devices are slower than the computer. Three techniques are used to produce a better match: buffering, multiplexing, concurrency. The first is a transfer-rate adjusting device. The second allows several devices to transfer data through the same channel. The third allows I/O transfers to occur concurrently with instruction execution.
7. Concurrency may be achieved by stealing cycles from the main instruction stream to execute successive word transfers, or by using multiple memory modules to allow I/O transfers to be executed simultaneously with internal instructions.
8. Input-output instructions are of three varieties: control, transfer, and editing and formatting.
9. Off-line devices are used to enter data into external storage and batch I/O devices, and to convert data stored in one storage medium to data on another storage medium. Among off-line devices are the key punch, card-to-tape converter, the tape driven high-speed printer and the computer output microfilmer.
10. *Definitions to Remember*

    External Storage. Data stored on a medium that is not a permanent part of the computer.

    On-Line. An operation that is tied directly to the computer and is under control of the program in the computer.

    Off-Line. An operation that proceeds completely independent of computer operation.

    Line Concentrator. A device that allows several remote terminals to be connected to one communication line.

Simplex. A line providing data transmission in one direction.
Duplex. A line allowing simultaneous data transmission in both directions.
Half-Duplex. A line allowing transmissions in both directions but not simultaneously.
Synchronous Data Set. A data set that must be furnished the data bits at a clocked rate.
Asynchronous Data Set. A data set that does not have to have the data bits supplied to it at a clocked rate.
Converter. A device for coverting data stored in one form into data in another form.
Control Word. A word storing data that may be of aid in the execution of an instruction.
Program Interrupt. A term meaning to temporarily disrupt the normal sequencing of a program when a certain event occurs. Usually, normal sequencing can be resumed from that point at a later time.
Multiplexer. A device that allows several external devices to be connected to one I/O channel.
Scanning. The examination of each of a group of items, channels, or devices in turn.
Polling. Interrogating a group of devices in a channel by a code. The device that is ready returns an appropriate reply.
Cycle Stealing. A term meaning to remove one or more memory cycles in the instruction stream for use in other operations, usually I/O transfers.
Editing. This term signifies the adding, deleting, and modifying of data before outputing a message.
Formatting. This signifies placing a message into a form to make it more understandable to a human being. It includes paragraphing, tabulation, and line spacing.

Exercises

1. A communication multiplexer is capable of transmitting to and receiving from the computer at the rate of 40,000 characters per second. The remote terminals connected to it via transmission lines transmit and receive at the rate of 2400 bits per second. If there are 6 bits per character, what is the maximum number of remote terminals that may be transmitting or receiving at one time?
2. Suppose that in exercise 1 above, the communication lines can transmit at 2400 bits per second, but each remote terminal averages only 48 bits per second. If a line concentrator were connected in each of the lines, what is the maximum number of remote terminals that may be accommodated?

3. Two terminals, A and B, are connected together via transmission lines transmitting 225 character messages, where each character is 8 bits long, at a rate of 1800 bits per second. One message is to be transmitted from terminal A to terminal B, and another message is to be transmitted from terminal B to terminal A.
   a. What is the transmission time if the terminals are connected in a duplex arrangement?
   b. What is the transmission time in a half-duplex arrangement where 20 ms are needed for a terminal to switch from receiving to transmitting.
4. A punched card reader can read six hundred 80-column cards per minute.
   a. What is the average rate of character entry into the associated computer?
   b. How much faster is a magnetic tape unit with a character transfer rate of 80 kc?
5. A magnetic tape unit has a character transfer rate of 50 kc. The average time to start the tape moving is 25 ms, and the average time needed to stop tape movement is 50 ms.
   a. How long will it take to complete the transfer of a 500-character message if the tape is not moving at the start? If it is moving?
   b. How long will it take to complete the transfer of a 5000-character message under similar circumstances as in exercise **a** above?
   c. If the tape in exercise **b** is halted between successive transfers, what's the minimum time that the tape unit can not be used per transfer?
6. Assume a computer that uses control words to control the transfer of 100-character blocks. Control words for external devices 1 through 10 are stored in memory addresses 0400 to 0409, respectively. In the character-oriented memory, 10 message areas are reserved starting with address 1000 for the first character of the block from device 1 and ending with address 1999 for the storage of the last character of the block from device 10.
   a. When external device number 2 is activated, which address must be accessed to retrieve the appropriate control word?
   b. What is stored in this control word, if it consists of a current and a final address?
   c. What is stored in this control word, if it consists of a current address and a character count?
   d. Which memory address receives the tenth character of the block?
   e. What does the current address counter read when the last character of the block is transferred?
7. A communications multiplexer scans inputs from 100 lines, each line transmitting at 1200 bits per second.
   a. What is the maximum time the scanner may use for a complete scan, if inputs are accepted a bit at a time?
   b. What is the maximum time the scanner may use for a complete scan, if inputs are first combined into 8-bit characters?
   c. What is the maximum possible transfer rate between the communications multiplexer and the computer?
8. A computer memory possesses a cycle time of 1 μs. An external device feeds data into the computer by stealing 1 cycle for the transfer of each character. If

the character transfer rate of the external device is 50 kc, what proportion of the total computer time is stolen for the transfer?

9. In exercise 9 above, what would the proportion of stolen time be if the I/O register gathered 4 characters together before executing the 4-character word transfer during a cycle time?

10. A magnetic tape unit stores 1000-character blocks in 8 parallel bit tracks at a density of 500 bits per inch. A $\frac{3}{4}$ in. gap is placed between blocks. It takes 25 ms to start the tape moving, and it moves at the rate of 100 inches per second.
  a. How long would it take from a standstill to the start of the fifth block?
  b. How long would the actual data transfer of the fifth block take?

11. A punched card reader reads 600 cards per minute. On each card is encoded a separate instruction. How much time is available in the computer to read and to execute each instruction before the next one arrives?

12. Given a magnetic disc unit possessing several discs rotating at 2400 rpm. On each disc surface are 256 tracks, 16 sectors to a track, a sector consisting of sixty-four 8-bit characters, making a total of 8192 bits total per track. An arm containing a group of 16 heads, one for each of 16 different tracks is provided for each disc surface. By making the arm capable of moving to any of 16 different positions, each of the tracks on a surface may be covered. Moving the head to an adjacent position takes 20 ms; to the furthest position, takes 60 ms. Although the I/O register used with the disc is a character in size, computer words stored in memory are 4 characters in length.
  a. If the chosen track is one of 16 already in position, how long will it take on an average to complete a transfer of the contents of a sector to memory?
  b. How long will it take on an average if the chosen track is in the next adjacent position? If it is in the furthest possible position?
  c. If the sector contents are to be transferred to successive locations in memory starting with address 0512, which memory location will receive the last word?

13. A high-speed line-at-a-time printer can print 600 lines per minute, 120 characters per line. The time required to execute a line spacing is 10 ms. The block transferred to the printer unit consists of 120 message characters plus 10 characters for control of the printer.
  a. If all 120 characters are printed on one line, how long does it take to execute the print operation?
  b. How long does it take if 20 characters are printed on each of 6 lines?
  c. What must the character transmission rate from the computer to the printer be?

*14. Draw a block diagram of an input-output unit that accepts 10 bits plus sign (least significant) from a punched-paper tape reader in octal form during a Read-In instruction. When the I/O register is full, the bits are shifted out in serial during $t_1 - t_{11}$. During a Punch instruction, the 11 bits are shifted from MR into the I/O register in serial during $t_1 - t_{11}$. When the register is full, paper tape is punched with the equivalent octal digits, serially by digit.

CHAPTER 13
Arithmetic and logic unit

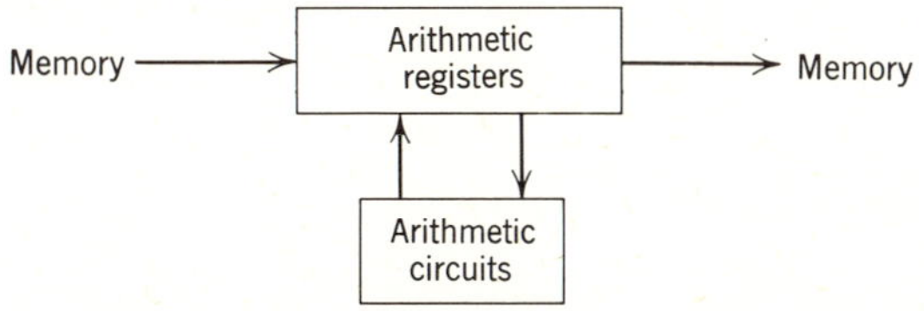

The majority of the basic computer operations are executed by the Arithmetic and Logic unit. Among the common instructions executed by this unit are:

Add
Subtract
Quantitative comparisons
Multiply
Divide
Shifting
Boolean comparisons

This unit consists of several arithmetic registers plus arithmetic circuits. The registers receive operands from memory. The arithmetic circuits process the contents of the registers in accordance with the instruction requirements. The result that is stored in one of the registers then is transferred from this register back to memory.

ADDITION

The primary component of the Arithmetic and Logic unit is the adder. As we have learned previously, for binary computers, addition may be in serial or in parallel. In the first case, only 1 bit-adder is required with the carry resulting from addition of a bit pair being returned to it during addition of the succeeding bit pair. In the second case a bit-adder is needed for each bit pair to be added, and carries are handled afterward.

Here, the emphasis is placed on addition in coded-decimal machines that execute addition in a serial-parallel manner.

Serial-Parallel Addition

The outline of the method for adding two numbers consisting of binary-coded decimal digits is shown in Fig. 157. The addend register (*XR*) and the accumulator (*AR*) each consist of four subregisters, one for each of the four bit orders of a digit. The adder consists of four bit adders, one for each bit in a digit, and a corrector. The carry is applied through a bit-time delay to the lowest order bit adder.

The four bits of the least significant digit of the augend and addend are applied simultaneously to the four bit adders. After carries have propagated through the bit adders, a 4-bit sum digit plus a possible carry bit from the fourth-order adder are produced. These bits are modified by the corrector; the resultant 4-bit sum is sent to the accumulator, and any carry is transmitted through the delay element to arrive at the first-order bit adder at the same time that the four bits of the following digit are being applied to the bit adders. Succeeding digits are added in a similar manner. After a word-time the addition is complete.

Example

Assume the number 35764 is stored in *XR* and the number 18983 is stored in *AR*, both in binary-coded decimal form. What are the bit combinations in each of the *X* subregisters and *A* subregisters? What are the bit combinations stored in *AR* after the addition is executed?

The bit combinations are:

In *XR*

Bit Order	3	5	7	6	4
4	0	0	0	0	0
3	0	1	1	1	1
2	1	0	1	1	0
1	1	1	1	0	0

In *AR*

Bit Order	1	8	9	8	3
4	0	1	1	1	0
3	0	0	0	0	0
2	0	0	0	0	1
1	1	0	1	0	1

After the addition, *AR* should store the result, 35764+18983 = 54747, as follows:

Bit Order	5	4	7	4	7
4	0	0	0	0	0
3	1	1	1	1	1
2	0	0	1	0	1
1	1	0	1	0	1

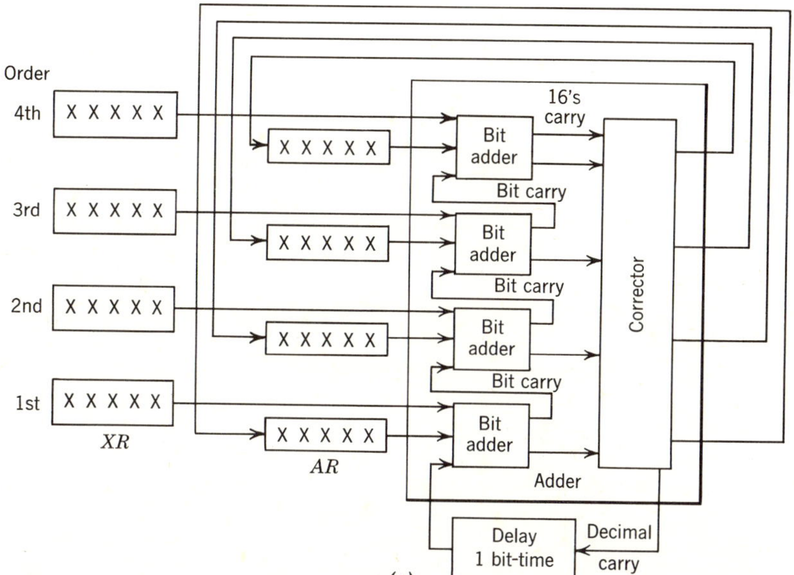

(a)

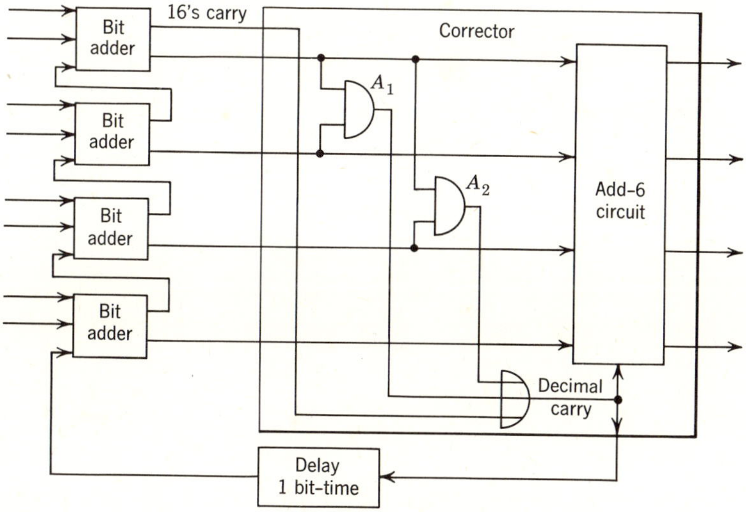

(b)

Figure 157 Serial-parallel addition of binary-coded decimal numbers. *(a)* Serial-parallel addition. *(b)* Corrector.

The corrector is required because the rules of binary addition are not completely obeyed when adding binary-coded decimal numbers. In the addition of binary-coded decimal numbers, the following three general situations may occur:

1. The sum is less than 10: no carry occurs, no carry is needed.
2. The sum is between 10 and 15: no carry occurs, but a carry is needed.
3. The sum is 16 or more: a 16's carry occurs, but a 10's carry is needed.

In the first case, no correction is needed. However, a corrector is needed to take care of cases 2 and 3. An example of such a corrector is shown in Fig. 157*b*.

In case 2, no decimal carry is produced but one is needed. To correct for this situation, means must be present to detect when the tentative sum is between 10 and 15. This can be done if we note that for each of these digits a ONE is present simultaneously in the fourth- and second-order bits or in the fourth- and third-order bits; and this situation is not true for any other digit. Gate A_1 in the corrector detects the first situation, and A_2 detects the second situation. If either of these situations occurs, a decimal carry pulse is produced and applied through the delay circuit to the first-order bit adder. Since a decimal carry is thus added to the following digit, 10 must be subtracted from the present digit. The subtraction of 10 may be performed by adding 6 and ignoring the carry which occurs from the fourth-order bit. Ignoring this carry is equivalent to subtracting 16. This correction is accomplished by the add-6 circuit as soon as the developed decimal carry is applied to it.

In case 3, a 16's carry is produced but a 10's carry is needed. We correct the sum by adding binary 6. The 16's carry is applied to the decimal carry line to be returned to the first-order bit adder through the delay, and also to activate the add-6 circuit.

Example

Add 4 and 3. Is a corrector needed?

$$\begin{array}{r} 0100 = 4 \\ \underline{0011} = \underline{3} \\ 0111 = 7 \end{array}$$

No corrector is needed.

Example

Add 6 and 8. Show correction needed.

$$\begin{array}{rrl} 0110 = & 6 & \\ \underline{+1000} = & \underline{8} & \\ 1110 = & 14 & \text{Binary} \\ \underline{+0110} = & \underline{+6} & \text{Correction} \\ 1\ 0100 = & 14 & \text{Binary-coded decimal} \end{array}$$

Example

Add 7 and 9. Show correction needed.

$$
\begin{array}{rcll}
0111 & = & 7 & \\
+1001 & = & \underline{9} & \\
1\ 0000 & = & 16 & \text{Binary} \\
+0110 & = & \underline{6} & \text{Correction} \\
1\ 0110 & = & 16 & \text{Binary-coded decimal}
\end{array}
$$

Overflow

Addition of the two 5-digit numbers 35764 and 18983 given above produces another 5-digit number: 54747.

Occasionally a carry occurs from the most significant position. Since the sum now possesses more digits than can be contained in a register, this carry is called an overflow.

The occurrence of overflow indicates that the machine has manufactured a number which is greater than the maximum allowable number. If the machine handles fractional numbers, the occurrence of overflow indicates that a number 1 or greater has been manufactured (Fig. 158).

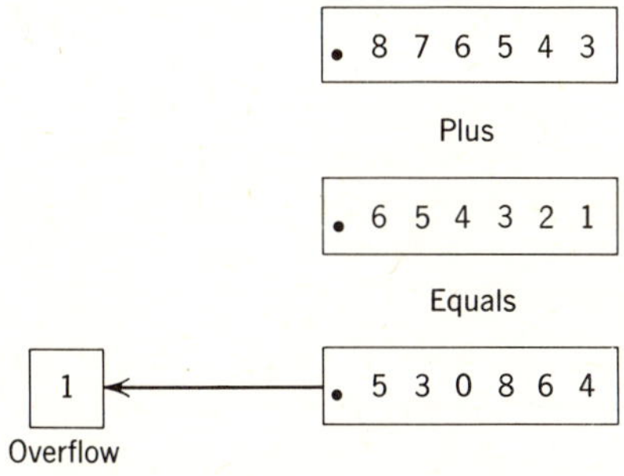

Figure 158 Production of overflow.

The overflow is usually fed to a flip-flop. This overflow is used to control arithmetic operations, especially those involving the use of complements as discussed in the following.

ALGEBRAIC ADDITION

The adder produces the absolute-value sum of the augend and addend. This is all right if addition of magnitudes is required. To perform algebraic addition, the signs of the operands must be taken into account. As we have learned in Chapter 3, when the signs of the operands are alike, the operands are added. When the signs are unlike, the smaller operand is subtracted from the larger, and the result is given the sign of the larger. The same result may be obtained by adding the complement of the negative number to the true value of the positive number. Simple methods for performing these two types of addition are given below.

Algebraic Addition of Numbers in Absolute-Value-Plus-Sign Form

Algebraic addition may be performed by means of a circuit similar to that shown in Fig. 159. The circuit consists of a binary comparator, an adder, and two subtractors. At the start of algebraic addition, the sign bits of the two operands *A* and *B* are fed to the binary comparator, while the digits themselves are applied to a group of gates. If the two signs are alike, the operand digits are allowed to flow to the adder. If the signs are unlike, the switches allow digits *A* and *B* to be fed to the two subtractors. Subtractor 1 subtracts the addend *B* from the augend *A*, and subtractor 2 subtracts augend *A* from addend *B*. The subtractor that subtracts the larger number from the smaller number produces a carry; this carry inhibits the result of this subtractor.

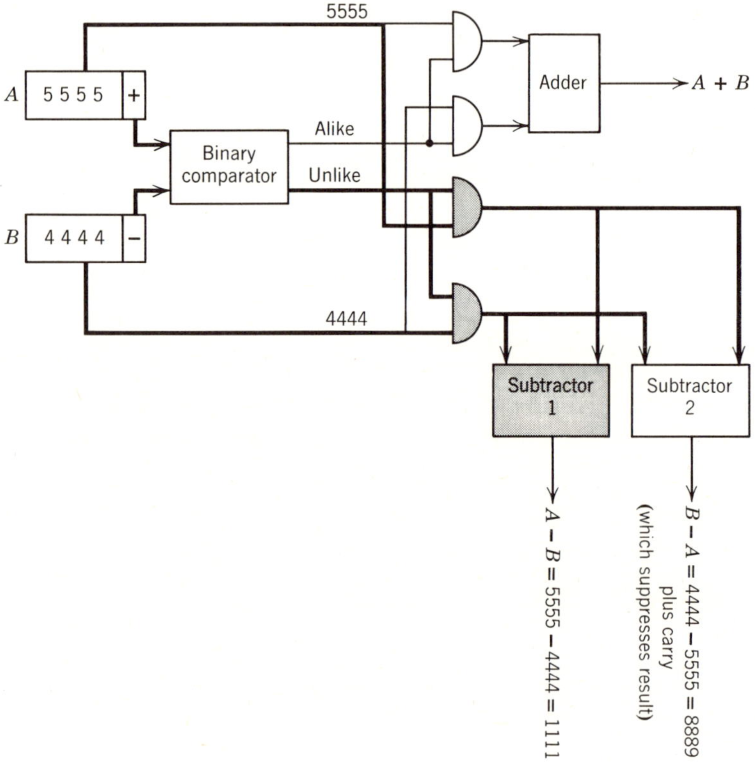

Figure 159 Algebraic addition, absolute value plus sign form.

Example

Add +5555 to −4444. Indicate what happens in Fig. 159 during this addition.

The comparator activates the unlike control line, and the two numbers are fed to the subtractors. Subtractor 1 produces 5555−4444=1111 and subtractor 2 produces 4444−5555 which gives 8889 and a carry. The carry inhibits this last result. The sign of the result must be determined by separate circuitry.

Algebraic Addition by the Use of Complements

A better way of accomplishing algebraic addition on numbers given in absolute-value-plus-sign form is to complement negative numbers and then add. Positive results are produced in absolute-value form. Negative results, on the other hand, are given in complement form and should be recomplemented when removed from the arithmetic unit.

A circuit which performs this operation is shown in Fig. 160. Figure 160*a* shows the input and adder circuits, and Fig. 160*b* the output circuits. Complementer 2 takes the 2's complement of the augend arriving to the *A* register if the sign is negative. Complementer 1 complements the addend arriving to the adder if the sign is negative. The output is transmitted through complementer 3 which is under control of the sign circuits consisting of four flip-flops and two binary comparators. The presence of a signal to complement the output depends on the relative signs of augend and addend, and the presence or absence of overflow.

This algebraic adder operates as follows. First the augend is transmitted to *AR* through complementer 2 by means of a transfer instruction. The first bit arriving at the complementer is the sign bit which acts as a control signal for the remaining bits. If the sign bit is plus, the complementer allows the bits of the number to pass through it unchanged; if the sign is negative, the number is complemented as it passes through.

Next, an add instruction pulls the addend from the location in memory specified by the address and sends it through complementer 1 to the adder. Again, complementation occurs only if the sign is negative. The addend and augend hit the adder at the same time. The adder produces the sum which is returned to *AR*; in some cases it also produces an overflow which is applied to the sign circuits.

The result of addition is transmitted from *AR* through complementer 3 to the memory or to the output register by means of another transfer instruction. Complementation or no complementation of the output is determined by the sign circuits, which operate as follows. When the augend is originally applied to *AR*, the sign bit sets or resets the *A* sign flip-flop depending upon whether it is minus or plus. Similarly, when the addend enters the adder, the sign bit sets or resets the *X* sign flip-flop, depending upon whether it is minus or plus. If the outputs of the two sign flip-flops are alike, the set sign flip-flop is reset;

if unlike, it is set. If no overflow occurs upon completion of the addition, the modify sign flip-flop is reset; if overflow occurs, it is set. The outputs of the set sign and modify sign flip-flops are compared. If they are alike, the *A* sign flip-flop is reset; if they are unlike, it is set.

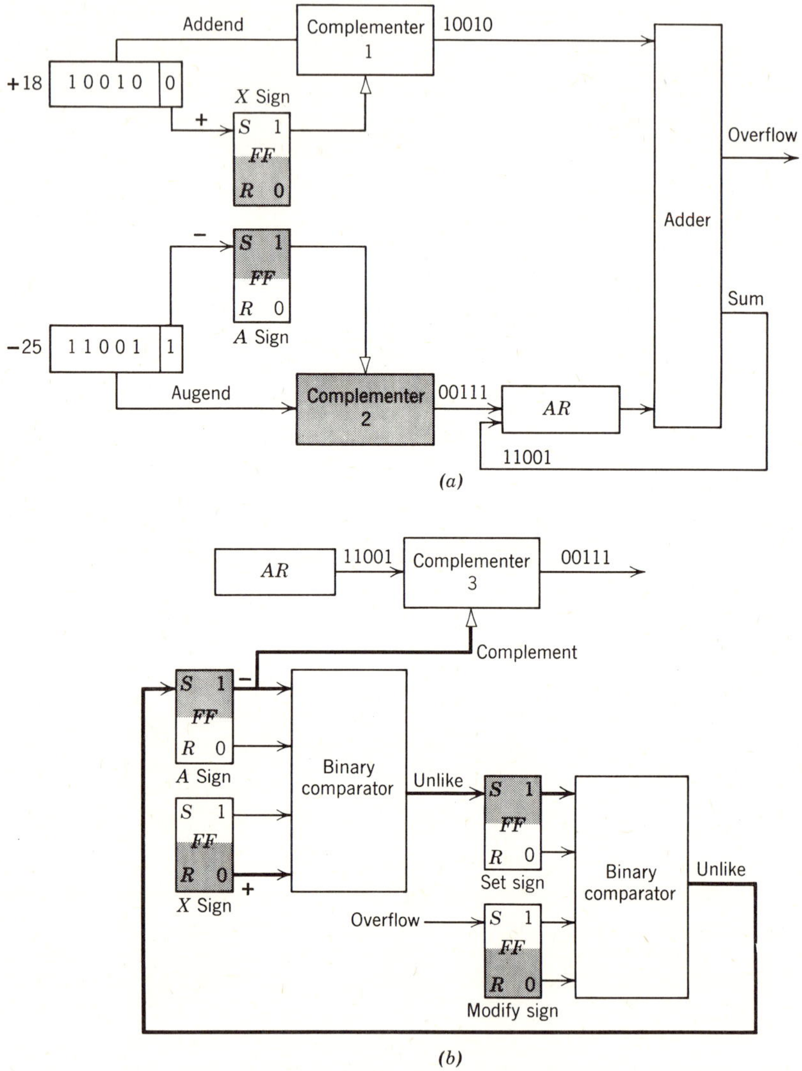

Figure 160 Algebraic addition by adding complements of negative numbers. (*a*) Complementation on input and addition. (*b*) Complementation on output.

Example

Show diagramatically what happens when +18 and −25 are added algebraically.

The events are shown in Fig. 160. The sign bits appear first. Because there is a ONE (signifying minus) in the least significant place of the augend, the number 11001 is complemented to 00111 which is applied to *AR*. Next, the addend, 10010 is fed directly through because a ZERO signifying plus, is present in the least significant position. These two numbers are added in the adder to produce

$$\begin{array}{r} 10010 \\ \underline{00111} \\ 11001 \end{array}$$

which is fed to *AR*.

When the augend and addend were applied, the *A* sign flip-flop was set and the *X* sign flip-flop was reset. As a result, the unlike output of the comparator was activated to set the set sign flip-flop. Since no overflow was produced by the adder, the modify sign flip-flop is reset. The unlike output of the comparator causes complementer 3 to complement the output as it is transferred, and it also sets the *A* sign flip-flop to feed a minus signal out.

Not all three complementers are needed. By proper gating it is possible to use one complementer for several operands. It is also possible to combine the summing and complementing functions in one circuit. Many other arrangements are possible.

If negative numbers are stored in the machine in complement form and positive numbers in absolute-value form, no sign circuits such as those described above are needed. For instance, numbers may be stored according to the following rules.

DECIMAL	ABSOLUTE VALUE PLUS SIGN	2'S COMPLEMENT	MACHINE FORM
+4	+0100		0 0100
+2	+0010		0 0010
−2	−0010	1110	1 1110
−4	−0100	1100	1 1100

A ZERO in the most significant position represents a positive number and a ONE in the most significant position represents a negative number in complement form.

The use of this extra bit simplifies addition as can be seen from the following examples.

Examples

	DECIMAL	ABSOLUTE VALUE PLUS SIGN	MACHINE FORM
I	+3	+0011	0 0011
	+7	+0111	0 0111
	+10	+1010	0 1010 = +1010

II	+3	+0011	0 0011
	−7	−0111	1 1001
	−4	−0100	1 1100 = −0100
III	−3	−0011	1 1101
	+7	+0111	0 0111
	+4	+0100	(1) 0 0100 = +0100 (Disregard carry)
IV	−3	−0011	1 1101
	−7	−0111	1 1001
	−10	−1010	(1) 1 1010 = −0110 (Disregard carry)

QUANTITATIVE COMPARISONS

If we can perform algebraic addition and subtraction, we can make quantitative comparisons such as determining if a given number is greater than or smaller than another number. Alternatively we can determine if a number is between a lower and an upper limit.

Greater Than and Less Than

To determine if a given number A is greater than or smaller than B, B is subtracted from A and the sign is checked. If the sign is minus, A is smaller; if the sign is plus, A is larger.

Example

Determine if A is larger or smaller than B if $A = 2$ and $B = 5$

$$\begin{array}{r} A = 2 \\ B = \underline{5} \quad \text{subtract} \\ -3 \end{array}$$

The sign of the difference is minus; therefore, A is smaller than B.

Example

Determine if A is larger or smaller than B if $A = 10$ and $B = 3$

$$\begin{array}{r} A = 10 \\ B = \underline{\ 3} \quad \text{subtract} \\ +7 \end{array}$$

The sign of the difference is plus; therefore, A is larger than B.

Example

Determine if the ASCII code for L is larger or smaller than the ASCII code for Z (see Appendix).

$$\begin{array}{rl} L = 100\ 1100 & \\ Z = \underline{101\ 1010} & \text{subtract} \\ -000\ 1110 & \end{array}$$

The sign of the difference is minus; therefore, L is smaller than Z.

Between Limits

If a given number B is between two limits A and C, then the following condition holds true:

$$A < B < C$$

In other words, B is greater than A and less than C. This means that two algebraic subtractions must be performed and the signs of the differences must be as follows:

$$\begin{array}{rlrl} B & & B & \\ \underline{A} & \text{subtract} & \underline{C} & \text{subtract} \\ + & & - & \end{array}$$

Example

Is a given number 5 between the two limits of 1 and 8?

$$\begin{array}{rlrl} 5 & & 5 & \\ \underline{1} & \text{subtract} & \underline{8} & \text{subtract} \\ +4 & & -3 & \end{array}$$

Since the first difference is + and the second − this number is between the two limits.

Example

Is a given number 20 between the two limits of 21 and 28?

$$\begin{array}{rlrl} 20 & & 20 & \\ \underline{21} & \text{subtract} & \underline{28} & \text{subtract} \\ -1 & & -8 & \end{array}$$

Since both signs are minus, this number is not between the two limits.

MULTIPLICATION

Multiplication may be accomplished by shifting or by a process of repeated addition.

Multiplication by Shifting

Placing a binary number in a register and shifting the contents to the left causes an extra zero to appear in the least significant position. Effectively the original number is multiplied by 2.

We must be certain of one condition, however, and that is that the most significant digit is never shifted out of the register.

Example

Given the binary number 11011 stored in a 7-bit register. How would you multiply it by 4? Could you multiply it by 8 by shifting?

The number 11011 which is equivalent to decimal 27 is originally in the register as follows

		1	1	0	1	1

To multiply by, 4, we shift left 2 places, which gives

1	1	0	1	1	0	0

This is equivalent to 108.

We could not multiply the original number by 8 by shifting. Multiplying by 8 would require 3 left shifts. If this were done, the most significant digit would be shifted out of the register.

Placing a decimal number in a register and shifting to the left multiplies the number by 10. As with the binary case, we must be careful that the most significant digit is not shifted out of the register.

Example

Given the decimal number 55 stored in a 5-digit register. How would you multiply it by 1000.

Store the number in the register as follows:

			5	5

Shift the contents 3 places to the left. The result is

5	5	0	0	0

Binary Multiplication

The following is a simple example of binary multiplication.

```
    1101      Multiplicand
    1011      Multiplier
    ----
    1101      First partial product
   1101       Second partial product
  0000        Third partial product
 1101         Fourth partial product
 -------
10001111      Product
```

Each partial product is determined by the corresponding multiplier bit: if the multiplier bit is ONE, the multiplicand is set down as a partial product; if the multiplier bit is ZERO, zeros are set down for the partial product. Each successive partial product is shifted one position to the left before it is added.

To mechanize this multiplication, each successive multiplier bit is detected in turn, and the bit is used to open a gate to allow the multiplicand to be added to the contents of the accumulator. After each multiplication the accumulator contents are shifted right before the following partial product is added; this is equivalent to shifting the following partial product to the left and then adding. The accumulator builds up accumulated partial products until finally it is storing the product.

Example

Show each step in the process of binary multiplication by repeated addition for the following:

```
 1101
x1011
-----
```

The process is summarized as follows:

```
  :1101:
  :1011:        Add (to cleared AR)
  ------
  :1101:
  : 110:1       Shift right
  :1101:        Add
  --------
 1:0011:1
  :1001:11      Shift right
  :0000:        Add
  ---------
  :1001:11
  :0100:111     Shift right
  :1101:        Add
  ----------
 1:0001:111
  :1000:1111    Shift right
```

A 4-bit binary multiplication circuit which operates in this manner is shown in Fig. 161. It consists of four registers, one for storing the multiplier, one for the multiplicand, and two for the product (one for the most significant half and another for the least significant half) plus an overflow flip-flop for storing the fifth bit obtained while developing partial products; an adder; two control flip-flops, one to store the multiplier bit being considered at a certain time, the other to control shift and add operations; and a counter to count the number of times shift and add operations are being performed.

Details of operation are as follows. At the start the multiplicand is stored in *DR* and the multiplier in *XR*. The contents of *XR* are shifted right, and the least significant bit of the multiplier is fed to multiplier bit flip-flop. If the bit is ONE, the flip-flop is set; if it is ZERO, the flip-flop is reset.

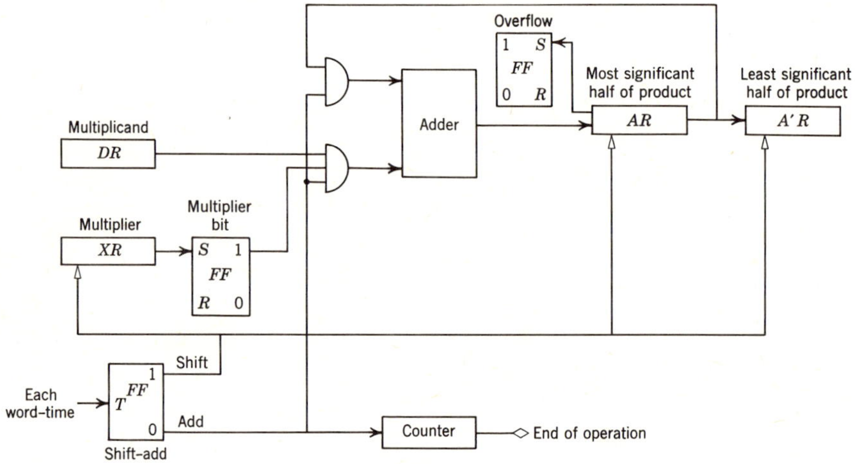

Figure 161 Mechanization of binary multiplication.

During the next step, if the multiplier bit flip-flop is reset, the multiplicand is not allowed to enter the adder. If the flip-flop is set, the multiplicand is allowed to be applied to the adder. Simultaneously, the contents of *AR* (0000 at the start) are also applied to the adder. The first partial product is developed in *AR*; if an overflow bit is developed it is stored in the overflow flip-flop.

The next step is to shift the partial product in the accumulator to the right. At the same time, the next multiplier bit is shifted into the multiplier bit flip-flop. During the following step, the multiplicand is added to the first shifted partial product if the multiplier bit flip-flop is set; nothing is added if the flip-flop is reset.

This sequence of shift and add steps is under control of the shift-add flip-flop. During each step a signal is applied to flip its output state. At the start it is set and produces a shift signal which is applied to *XR* and *AR*. The following signal resets the flip-flop to produce an add signal. The add-signal is applied to the adder input gates as shown.

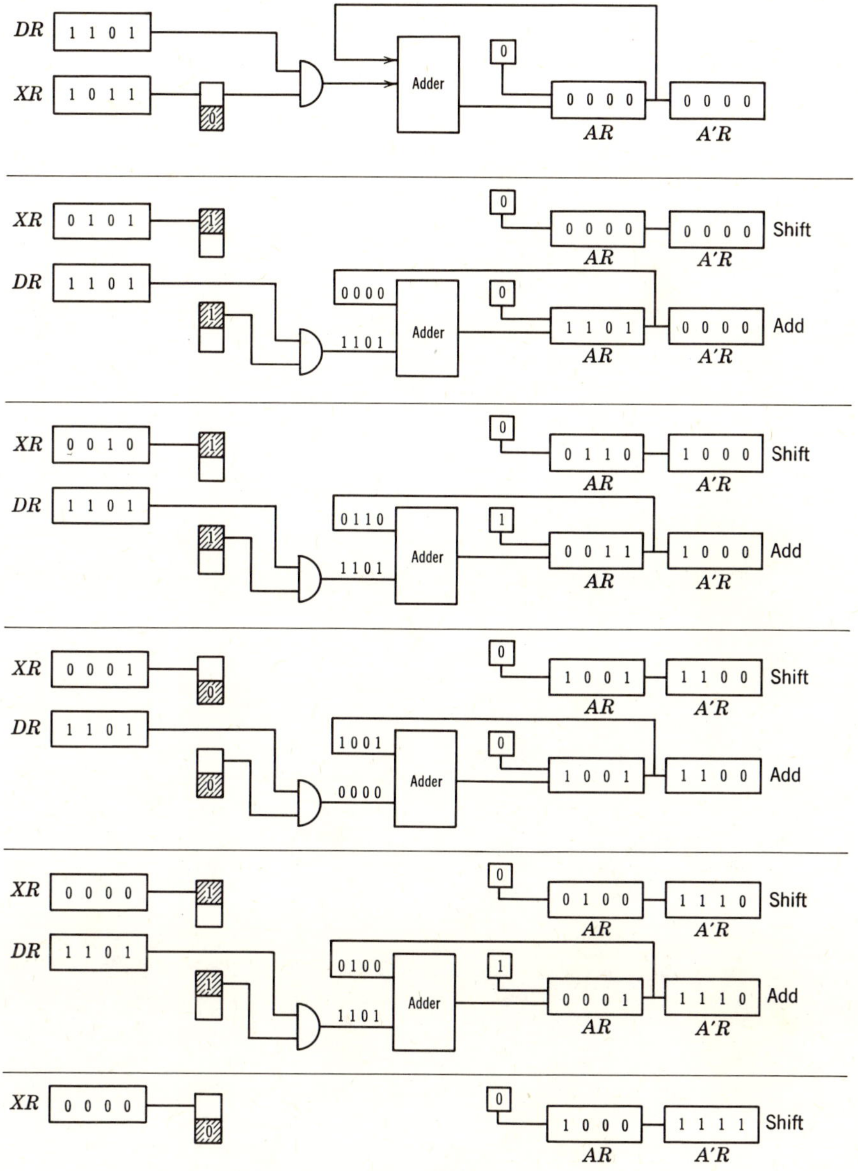

Figure 162 Steps in binary multiplication.

Every time the shift-add flip-flop produces an add signal the signal steps a counter. After a count of 4 signifying that all multiplier bits have been taken care of, the counter produces an end-of-operation signal.

Example

Show the contents of *XR*, *DR*, *AR* and *A'R* during each step of the multiplication of 1101 by 1011.

The answer is given in Fig. 162.

Note that, during the step where a bit at the least significant end leaves *XR*, a bit enters the most significant end of the *A'* register. When all the bits in *XR* have been shifted out, the *A'* register is filled with bits. Because of this relative timing, *XR* may double as the *A'* register. When this is done, only three registers are needed: *AR*, *XR*, and *DR*. Upon completion of the multiplication operation, the most significant half of the product is stored in *AR* and the least significant half in *XR*. The simplified multiplication circuit thus looks as shown in Fig. 163.

Decimal Multiplication

One of the most common machine methods for performing decimal multiplication is by a process of repeated addition.

Example

$$728 \times 451 = 328328$$

MULTIPLIER DIGIT	REPEATED ADDITION		PARTIAL PRODUCTS
1	728	=	728
	728		
	728		
5	728	=	3640
	728		
	728		
	728		
4	728	=	2912
	728		
	728		
	328328		328328

When mechanized, the machine performs essentially the same process except that the partial products are accumulated as we go along, and that right shifts of accumulated partial products rather than left shifts of multiplicands are performed. As in binary multiplication, each multiplier digit, in turn, starting with the LSD, determines whether the multiplicand should be added or not. But there is this difference. In binary multiplication only one addition is involved for each multiplier bit. In decimal multiplication the multiplicand

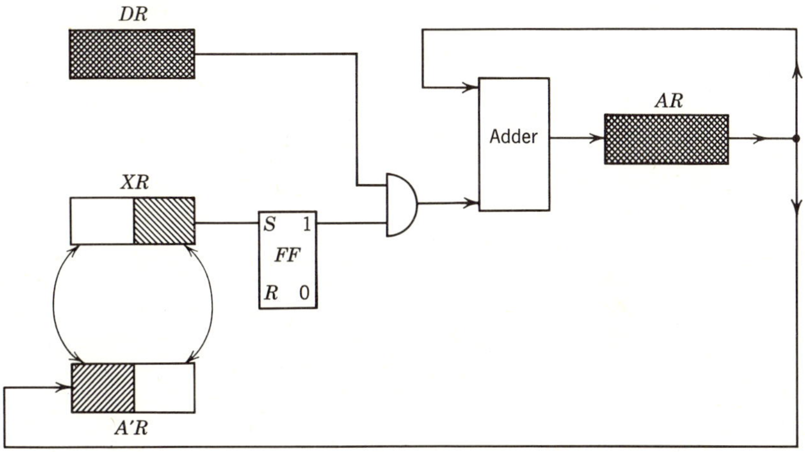

Figure 163 Storing least significant half of product in *XR*.

must be added to the accumulated partial product a number of times as given by the value of the multiplier digit. In decimal multiplication a counter is needed to keep track of the number of additions performed.

Figure 164 is a block diagram of a decimal multiplication circuit. Note that, except for the backward-counting counter, this circuit is practically the same as the binary multiplication circuit.

This circuit operates as follows. First the multiplicand is stored in *DR*, and the multiplier in *XR*. Secondly, the contents of *AR* (0 at the start) are shifted right, and the rightmost digit is shifted into the most significant end of *XR*. At the same time the contents of *XR* are shifted right, and the LSD is fed to the backward-counting counter.

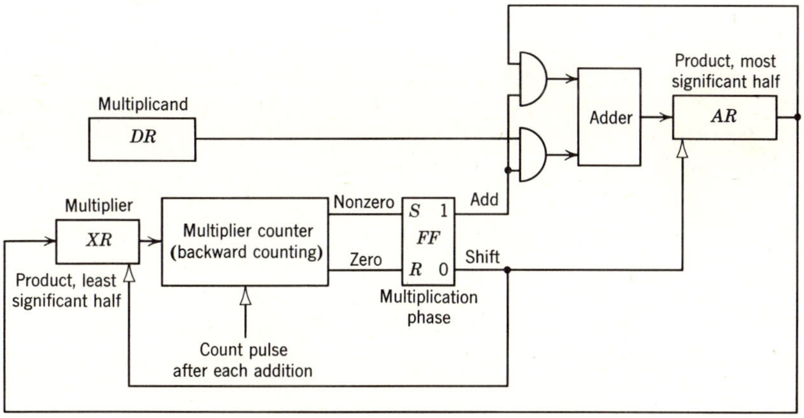

Figure 164 Mechanization of decimal multiplication.

If this counter is storing any digit but 0 during the next step, it allows the multiplicand (in *DR*) to be added to the accumulated partial product (in *AR*). During this addition the counter is stepped down 1. If the counter still does not read 0, the multiplicand is added again to the accumulated partial product; again a pulse applied to the counter causes it to step down 1. In this way the multiplicand is added the number of times given by the multiplier digit.

As soon as the counter reads 0, it resets the multiplication phase flip-flop which then produces a shift signal. The shift signal causes *AR* and *XR* to shift right, and the next multiplier digit to be transferred to the counter.

Now that there is a number other than 0 in the counter, an add phase is introduced. Add and shift phases alternate in this way until a counter (not shown) which is counting shift phases produces an end-of-operation signal.

Example

What are the contents of *DR*, *XR*, *AR*, and the counter at the start of the multiplication of 728 by 451? What are the contents of these registers at the end? After multiplier digit 5 has caused 728 to be added 5 times?

At the start:

$$DR = 728$$
$$XR = 451$$
$$AR = 0$$
$$\text{Counter} = 0.$$

At the end:

$$DR = 728$$
$$XR = 328$$
$$AR = 328$$
$$\text{Counter} = 0.$$

On completion of the series of additions caused by multiplier digit 5:

$$DR = 728$$
$$XR = 284$$
$$AR = 371$$
$$\text{Counter} = 0.$$

DIVISION

Division may be accomplished by shifting or by a process of repeated subtraction.

Division by Shifting

Placing a binary number in a register and shifting the contents to the right causes the least significant bit to be lost and a zero to appear in the most significant position. Effectively the original number is divided by 2.

If the least significant bit that is lost happens to be a 1, the result is approximately one half.

Example

Given the binary number 1011100 stored in a 7-bit register. How would you divide by 4? How inexact would division by 8 be using the shifting process?

The number 1011100, which is equivalent to decimal 92 is originally in the register as follows:

1	0	1	1	1	0	0

To divide by 4, we shift to the right two places, which gives

0	0	1	0	1	1	1

This is equivalent to 23.

To divide by 8, we should shift one more place to the right giving

0	0	0	1	0	1	1

which is equivalent to decimal 11. Since one half of 23 is 11.5, the result is incorrect by .5.

Placing a decimal number in a register and shifting to the right divides the number by 10. As with the binary case, we must be careful of digits at the least significant end being lost.

Example

Given the decimal number 43470. How would you divide by 10? How inexact would division by 100 be if the process of shifting is used.

The number is stored as

4	3	4	7	0

To divide by 10, shift one place to the right, giving

0	4	3	4	7

To divide by 100, shift one more place to the right, giving

0	0	4	3	4

Since the true answer is 434.7, it is inexact by .7.

Division by Repeated Subtraction

Division may be accomplished by means of a series of right shifts and subtractions. Since the more general case is that of decimal division, it is described here. (The binary case is given as an exercise for the student to do after he masters the decimal case)

The restoring method of division was explained in Chapter 3. Briefly, the method consists of successively subtracting the divisor from the most significant digits of the dividend until a negative remainder (indicating an overdraft) occurs. The divisor is then added to the negative remainder to restore the balance. The number of subtractions, not including the restored one, is the most significant quotient digit. Then the divisor is shifted right and successively subtracted again until a negative balance is produced, after which it is restored. The number of subtractions not including the restored one determines the next most significant quotient digit, etc.

For ease in mechanization, the subtractions are replaced by the addition of complements. The example of restoring division shown on page 345 is the same as the one presented in Chapter 3 except that the addition of complements is shown at each step where a subtraction is called for.

Note that a carry is produced from the most significant position when the remainder is positive, and no carry is produced from the most significant position when the remainder is negative. During the addition of a 10's complement each time a carry is produced from the most significant position, a 1 is added to the value of the quotient digit. Each time no carry is produced, a restoring addition followed by a shift operation is introduced. The presence or absence of a carry from the most significant position may thus be used to control the division operation.

A simplified block diagram of a circuit operating on these principles is shown in Fig. 165. It consists of three registers, *AR*, *DR*, and *XR* for storing the dividend, divisor, and quotient; a complementer flip-flop and complementer for complementing the divisor when required; a shift-add flip-flop for flipping between the shift and add phases; and a counter for accumulating each quotient digit. The steps in the division process are as follows:

1. The dividend is fed to *AR*, and the divisor to *DR*.
2. Division is started by resetting the shift-add flip-flop and setting the complementer flip-flop. The first allows addition to take place; the second causes 10's complementation of the divisor before it is added to the dividend. The resultant sum is stored in *AR* as a partial accumulated remainder.
3. If an overflow is produced, it steps the counter and allows another addition of the 10's complement to take place.
4. The counter continues counting until no overflow is produced. The no-overflow condition resets the complementer flip-flop. During the next step, therefore, the divisor is not complemented; it is simply added. This restoring addition produces a carry. However, A_3 is inhibited by the reset output of the complementer flip-flop and, therefore, does not step the counter.
5. The reset output of the complementer flip-flop is delayed a word-time by D_1 after which it sets the shift-add flip-flop. The set output causes the quotient in the counter to be shifted into *XR*, and the accumulated partial remainder in *AR* to shift left. Shifting the accumulated partial remainder left produces the same relative results as shifting the divisor to the right.

Example of restoring division

$$365\overline{)452980}^{\;1241}$$

			OPERATION	QUOTIENT DIGITS	
		452980			
		635	Add complement	(1)	
	(1)	087980			
		635	Add complement		
No carry		722980			
		365	Add to restore		
	(1)	087980			
		9635	Shift and add complement	1	
	(1)	051480			
		9635	Add complement	(2)	
	(1)	014980			
		9635	Add complement		
No carry		978480			
		0365	Add to restore		
	(1)	014980			
		99635	Shift and add complement	1	
	(1)	011330			1241
		99635	Add complement	2	
	(1)	007680			
		99635	Add complement	3	
	(1)	004030			
		99635	Add complement	(4)	
	(1)	000380			
		99635	Add complement		
No carry		006730			
		00365	Add to restore		
	(1)	000380			
		999635	Shift and add complement	(1)	
	(1)	000015			
		999635	Add complement		
No carry		000650			
		000365	Add to restore		
	(1)	000015			

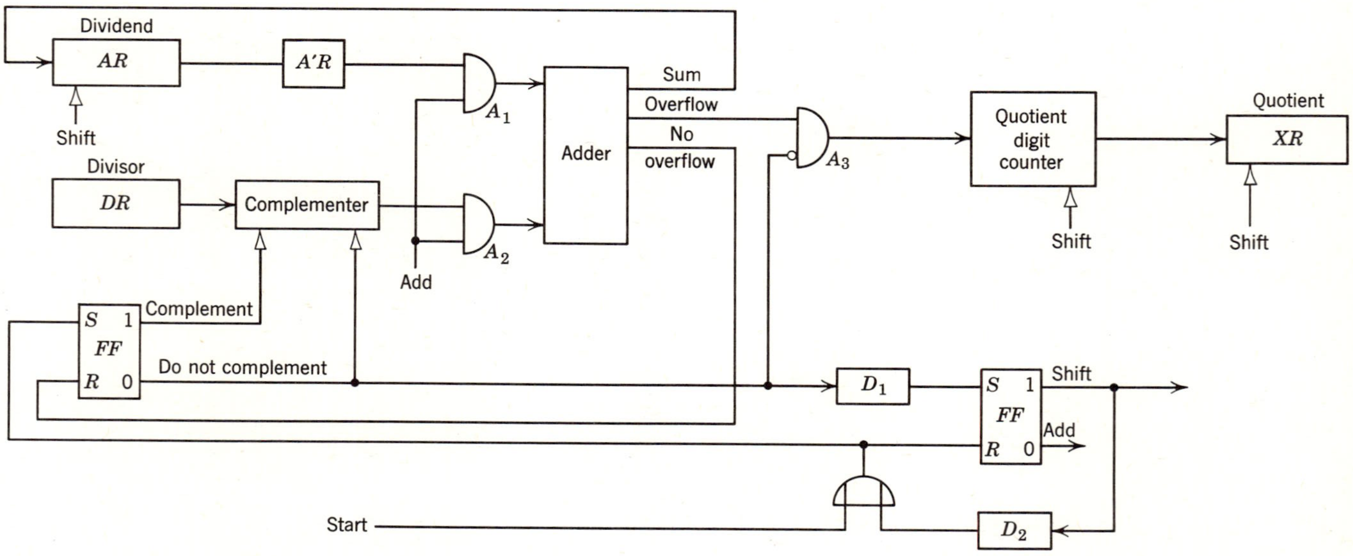

Figure 165 Mechanization of restoring division.

6. One word-time after the shift pulse is produced, the output of D_2 resets the shift-add flip-flop to cause the adder to add again, and it sets the complementing flip-flop to cause the divisor to be complemented before addition. The sequence for developing the next most significant quotient digit is thus introduced.
7. A separate counter (not shown) may be used to count the number of quotient digits developed. When a complete word is produced, the operation stops. At the end, the remainder is stored in *AR* and the quotient in *XR*. The last step in some machines is the interchanging of the contents of *AR* and *XR*. This is done in order to be consistent with the usual requirement of having useful results available in the accumulator.

Example

In the division example given, what are the contents of *AR*, *A'R*, *DR*, and *XR* at the start? What are the contents after the first "shift and add complement" step?

At the start the dividend is stored in *AR'* and *A'R*

4	5	2	—	9	8	0
	AR				*A'R*	

the divisor in *DR*:

3	6	5

Nothing is in *XR*:

0	0	0

After the first "shift and add complement" step the contents of *AR*, *A'R* are as shown in the example except shifted one place to the left:

5	1	4	—	8	0	0
	AR				*A'R*	

Register *DR* is still storing the divisor:

3	6	5

Register *XR* has just received the first quotient digit:

1	0	0

NONARITHMETIC MANIPULATION

Bits, digits, characters, or words may be manipulated by means of Boolean comparisons and by circular shifts.

Boolean Comparisons

Table 29 shows some of the Boolean comparisons that may be executed by a computer on a pair of bits.

table 29 LOGICAL COMPARISON OF TWO VARIABLES

VARIABLES X	Y	EXCLUSIVE OR	EQUIVALENCE	AND	OR	NOR	NAND	AND NOT	OR NOT
0	0	0	1	0	0	1	1	0	1
0	1	1	0	0	1	0	1	0	0
1	0	1	0	0	1	0	1	1	1
1	1	0	1	1	1	0	0	0	1

How data may be rearranged can be seen from the following example

Example

Given the following binary number

10011100

stored in an 8-bit register. Extract the four most significant bits.

This can be done by executing an AND comparison between this number and the following number:

11110000

Performing the AND comparison produces the following:

$$\begin{array}{r} 10011100 \\ \underline{11110000} \\ 10010000 \end{array}$$

Example

Given a number 10011001. Insert a bit into each odd position whether there is a bit there or not.

This may be accomplished by the use of an OR comparison with a word containing in each odd position 1 and in each even position 0:

$$\begin{array}{r} 10011001 \\ \underline{10101010} \\ 10111011 \end{array}$$

Circular Shift

A circular shift may be used to rearrange bits or digits in a word. A circular right shift is demonstrated by the first example following and a circular left shift by the example after that.

Example

Perform a circular right shift 2 times on the following:

10100011

The result is

11101000

Example

Perform a circular left shift 3 times on the following:

92176543

The result is

43921765

SUMMARY

1. The arithmetic unit usually consists of a group of registers (*AR*, *DR*, and *XR*) for storing operands, and arithmetic circuits such as adders, complementers, sign-determining circuits, and counters to perform the arithmetic operations.
2. Binary numbers may be added in serial or in parallel. Coded-decimal numbers are usually added in serial-parallel. Because a carry from the last-order bit of a digit is not necessarily a decimal carry, a corrector is made part of the adder.
3. By an extension of the arithmetic operation, quantitative comparisons, such as less than, greater than, and within limits may be performed.
4. Binary multiplication may be accomplished by shifting left or by a succession of add-shift operations. Decimal multiplication may be accomplished in similar ways. However, a group of adds instead of only one add must be performed before a shift is executed; the number of adds is determined by the magnitude of the multiplier digit.
5. Binary division may be accomplished by shifting right or by a succession of subtract-shift operations. Decimal division may be accomplished in similar ways. However, a successive series of subtractions must be followed by a restoring division and a shift.
6. Nonarithmetic manipulations of data may be performed by means of circular right and left shifts and by means of Boolean comparisons.
7. *Definitions to Remember*
   Overflow. The occurrence of a carry from the most significant position.
   Exceed-Capacity Overflow. An overflow that implies that the result of an operation is a number greater than the capacity of a register.

Exercises

1. Assume 463 is stored in *AR* and 275 is stored in *XR*, both in binary-coded decimal and in serial-parallel fashion.
   a. What are the bit combinations in the subregisters of *AR*?
   b. What are the bit combination in the subregisters of *XR*?
   c. What are the bit combinations stored in the subregisters of *AR* after addition?
2. What type of correction is needed when adding the following numbers given in binary-coded decimal form:
   a. 5 and 4?
   b. 7 and 8?
   c. 9 and 8?
3. A serial-parallel adder such as the one shown in Fig. 157 can sum 2 digits in 10 μs. How long should a complete addition take when adding:
   a. 2463 and 1521?
   b. 4999 and 5999?
   c. In which of the above does overflow occur?
4. Follow binary addition rules to add the following numbers in excess-3 code and determine what corrections must be made in each case to restore the resultant sum to excess-3 code:
   a. 2+3.
   b. 5+5.
   c. 8+9.
5. Draw a logical block diagram of a corrector which would convert a binary adder into an excess-3 adder (use results from exercise 4 as a guide.)
6. A binary multiplier like the one shown in Fig. 161 multiplies 110111 by 111000.
   a. How many shift steps are executed?
   b. How many add steps?
   c. Indicate the contents of *AR* after each shift.
   d. If a transfer, a shift, and an add each requires 1 μs to execute, how long would it take to execute this multiplication?
7. A decimal multiplier such as that shown in Fig. 164 multiplies 654 by 347. If a transfer, a shift, and an add each requires 1 μs to execute, how long would it take to execute the complete multiplication?
8. For each of the following, what are the equivalent binary-coded decimal values, assuming the 2's complement is used for negative numbers. Express the algebraic sum in the same form.
   a. $\begin{array}{r} +2 \\ \underline{+6} \end{array}$

b. $\begin{array}{r} +3 \\ -5 \\ \hline \end{array}$

c. $\begin{array}{r} -4 \\ -8 \\ \hline \end{array}$

9. What is the value of *A* relative to *B* under each of the following circumstances:
   a. *B* is subtracted from *A* and the difference is positive.
   b. *B* is subtracted from *A* and the difference is negative.
   c. *A* is subtracted from *B* and the difference is positive.
   d. *A* is subtracted from *B* and the difference is negative.
10. In which of the following is *B* between a lower limit of *A* and an upper limit of *C*? In which is *B* below *A*? In which is *B* above *C*?
    a. *B* subtract *A* = plus; *B* subtract *C* = minus
    b. *B* subtract *A* = minus; *B* subtract *C* = minus
    c. *B* subtract *A* = minus; *B* subtract *C* = plus
    d. *B* subtract *A* = plus; *B* subtract *C* = plus
11. Assume the uppercase characters of the alphabet are in USASCII code (as shown in the Appendix).
    a. Which has a larger numerical value: *Q* or *S*?
    b. How would you sort all the uppercase characters into alphabetical order?
    c. If the digits 0 to 9 were included, where would they appear? Where would they be with EBCDIC?
12. If 621 is multiplied by 298, what are the contents of *DR*, *XR*, and *AR* at the following times:
    a. The start of multiplication?
    b. After the completion of the series of additions caused by the first multiplier digit?
    c. At the end?
13. If 974215 is divided by 113 using the restoring method, what are the contents of *AR*, *DR*, and *XR* at the following times:
    a. The start of division?
    b. After first shift-and-add-complement step?
14. How would you extract all even column bits of an 8-bit number?

*15. Draw a block diagram of an arithmetic unit that consists of an adder and complementer and 3 registers similar to *AR*, *DR*, and *XR*. This unit executes in serial the following operations on 10-bit + sign (least significant bit) numbers:

Clear Add
Add
Subtract
Shift Right
Multiply

All negative numbers are converted to their 2's complement form before being operated on.

CHAPTER 14

Control unit

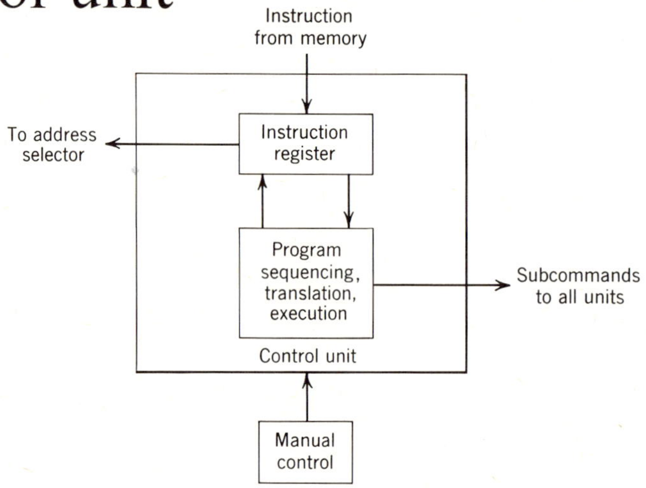

The control unit consists of an instruction register that accepts instruction words from memory; and control circuits that sequence, translate, and execute these instructions.

These events usually are accomplished by a partnership of the memory and control units in a basic machine cycle. Special instructions allow instruction sequencing to be modified depending on specified conditions. The control unit also is capable of modifying an instruction before it is executed.

The prime purpose of the control unit, therefore, is to sequence operations so that all parts of the computer can work together in the most efficient way. As was mentioned previously, concurrency of operation is one important way of achieving this.

All these topics are discussed in this chapter. In addition, the last part discusses advanced topics in computer organization.

BASIC MACHINE CYCLE

Automatic control of a digital computer may be divided into four functions as follows:

1. Sequencing of instructions.
2. Translation of commands.
3. Translation of addresses.
4. Execution of microcommands.

These functions are performed as part of a basic machine cycle which depends for the most part on the instruction code. In addition, there may be instructions that refer only implicitly to addresses.

Sequencing of Instructions

One- and three-address instruction machine. In a computer using a one-address or a three-address instruction code, sequencing is accomplished by means of an instruction counter which provides the address of the next instruction word to be executed and a flip-flop which divides the sequence into a FETCH phase and an EXECUTE phase. The other major parts of the control unit are the instruction register which stores the command and address of the instruction word, and the address selector (actually part of memory) and command decoder which translate the two parts of the instruction into signals which cause execution of the instruction.

A block diagram of such a sequencing unit is shown in Fig. 166. The following is the sequence it follows. Upon completion of an instruction, the instruction mode flip-flop is set to the FETCH state. In this state, it allows the address stored in the instruction counter to choose the next instruction word from memory① to be transferred to the instruction register. As soon as the word is completely in the instruction register, the instruction mode flip-flop is reset to the EXECUTE state. In this state, gates A_2 and A_3 allow the address part of the instruction to be transmitted to the address selector and the command to the command translator. The address selector chooses the location to be read from or written into②. The command translator translates the command into microcommands which execute the instruction on the operand specified by the address. One of the microcommands is a count pulse which steps the instruction counter to the next address. After execution of the instruction, the instruction mode flip-flop is set to the FETCH state to start a new cycle.

Example

Assume the following three instructions are stored at addresses designated:

	Instruction	
Address of Instruction	Command	Address
0800	TFR	0525
0801	ADD	0526
0802	STR	0527

At the start, 0800 is placed in the instruction counter and a series of 3 FETCH–EXECUTE cycles occurs during execution of these 3 instructions. What are the contents of the IC and IR during each of the 6 steps?

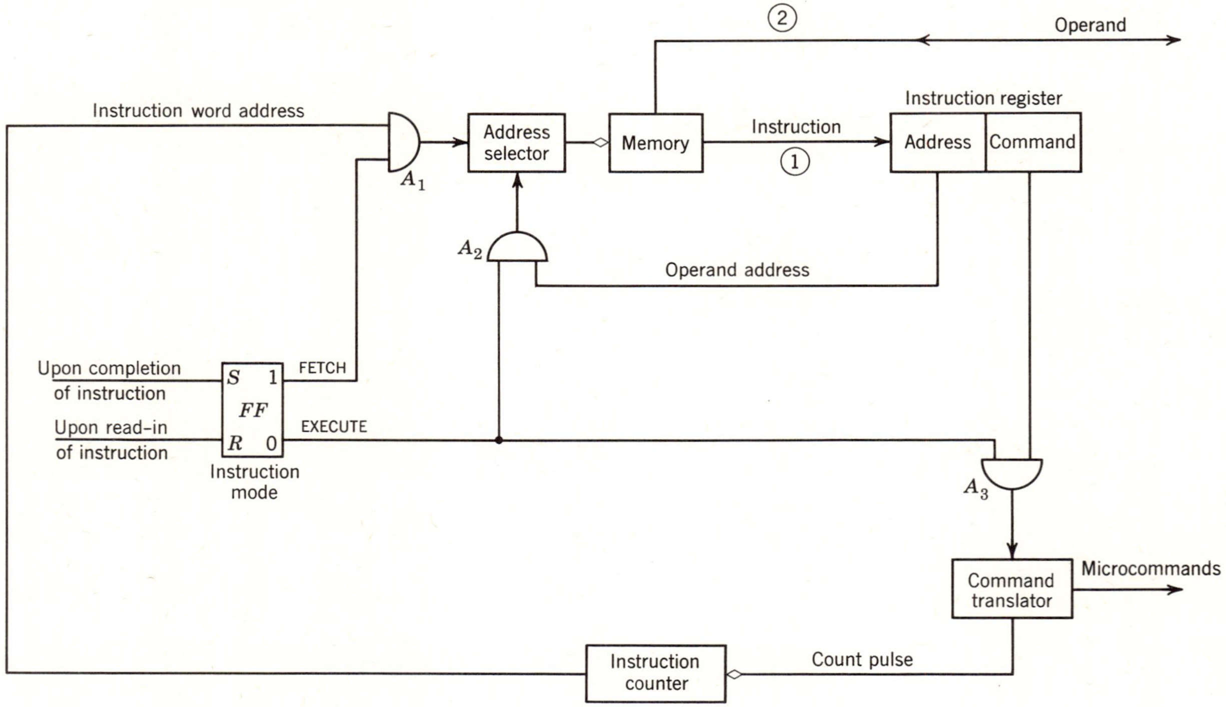

Figure 166 Sequencing the one-address computer.

The contents of *IC* and *IR* for the 6 steps are as follows:

Step	*IC* Contents	*IR* Contents
FETCH 1	0800	02 0525
EXECUTE 1	0801	02 0525
FETCH 2	0801	03 0526
EXECUTE 2	0802	03 0526
FETCH 3	0802	01 0527
EXECUTE 3	0803	01 0527

During the first FETCH the contents of address 0800 are fetched from memory and stored in *IR*. Code 02 represents the Transfer command. During the first EXECUTE, a 1 is added to the contents of *IC* changing them to 0801. During the succeeding FETCH the contents of this new address will be stored in *IR*. And so on.

Two- or four-address instruction machine. In a machine using a two-address instruction code, no instruction counter is needed; the address of the next instruction to be executed is given in the instruction word. The two-address instruction code may be specified with a cyclic access memory. Since in this type of memory time is required for finding an address, the basic machine cycle consists of four steps instead of two. These four steps are:

1. Search for operand.
2. Translate and execute microcommands on operand.
3. Search for next instruction.
4. Read next instruction into instruction register.

A modulo-4 cycle counter may be used to sequence through these four steps.

A sequencing unit to be used with a drum memory and a two-address instruction is shown in Fig. 167. Everything above the horizontal dashed line is part of the memory. Everything below the dashed line is in the control unit. Sequencing is performed by the two units working closely together.

The sequence is as follows. When the cycle counter reads ①, the data address is fed to the memory control circuits. The column address is applied to the column address selector which primes the appropriate drum heads. The row address is transmitted to the row address register where it is applied to one side of a comparator.

Upon completion of read-in of row address into the row address register, the cycle counter is stepped to ②. Every word-time the row address of the row currently under the heads is applied to the other side of the comparator. When the two addresses are alike, the comparator sends an activating signal to A_5 and A_6. Gate A_5 allows the operand to be read off the chosen head and to be applied to the arithmetic circuit (data may also go from the arithmetic unit to the memory). At the same time A_6 allows the microcommands to be transmitted to the arithmetic unit where they perform the operation called for.

As soon as the memory's part of the job is complete, the cycle counter is stepped to ③. After the entire operation is completed, an operation-complete

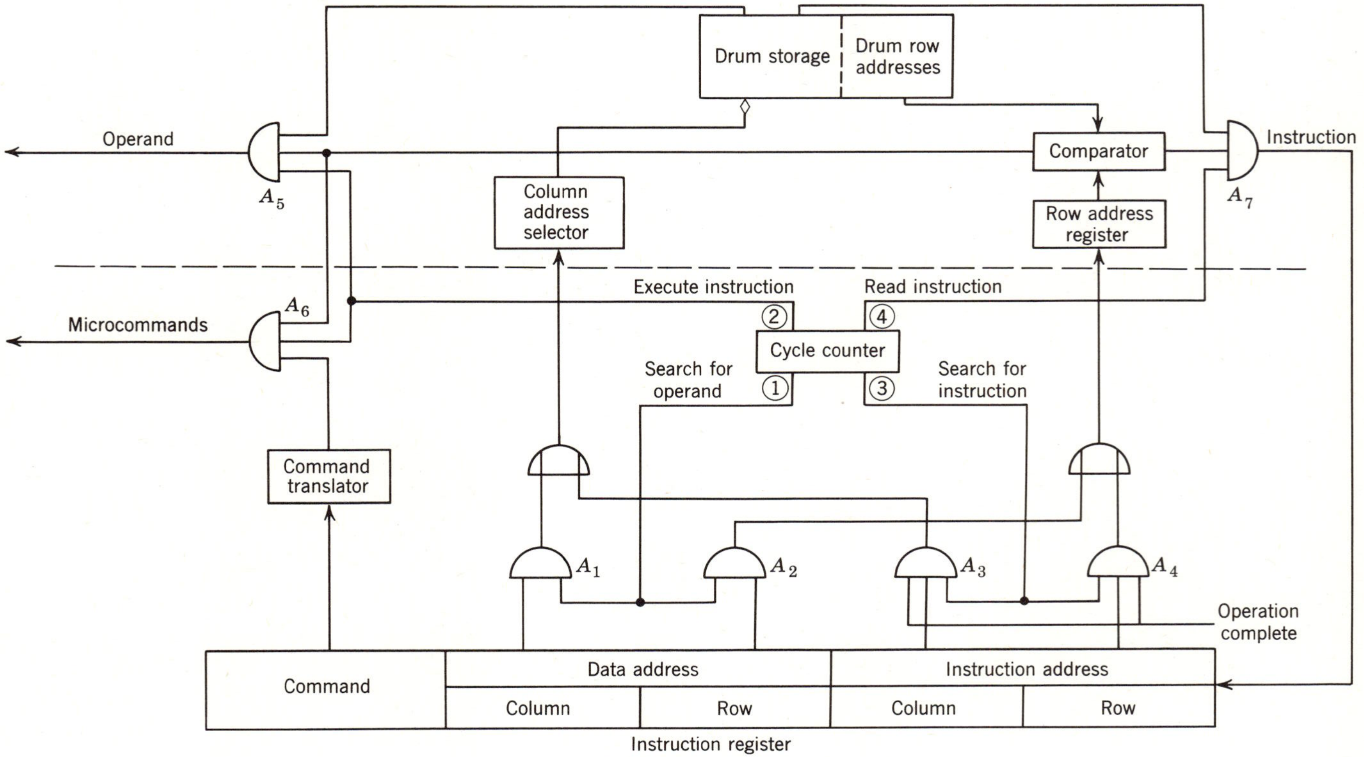

Figure 167 Sequencing the two-address computer. (Above dashed line—memory; below dashed line—control.)

signal is applied to gates A_3 and A_4, and the instruction column address is fed to the column address selector and the instruction row address to the row address register to begin the search for the next instruction.

Upon completion of read-in of the instruction row address into the row address register, the cycle counter is stepped to ④. After the comparator produces a coincidence pulse, the instruction word is fed through A_7 to the instruction register. The cycle counter is then stepped back to ①, and the sequence is repeated for the new instruction.

The first two steps in the cycle are concerned with the operand; the second two steps are concerned with the instruction.

Example

Given a computer with a 10-column 100-row drum memory and with the following two instructions stored at the locations given:

Instruction Location			Data		Instruction	
Column	Row	Command	Column	Row	Column	Row
7	00	TFR	3	10	7	60
7	60	ADD	5	70	7	100

If a revolution of the drum takes 100 ms, a Transfer instruction 1 ms and an add instruction 2 ms, prepare a table showing the steps in the two instruction cycles and the time to complete each step.

The steps and timings are as follows:

Cycle	Step	Operation	Row Movement	Time (in ms)
1	1	Transfer data address	1	1
	2	Compare until match	2–9	9
		Transfer operand and execute	10	
	3	Transfer instruction address	11	1
	4	Compare until match	12–59	49
		Transfer instruction	60	
2	1	Transfer data address	61	1
	2	Compare until match	62–69	10
		Transfer operand and execute	70–71	
	3	Transfer instruction address	72	1
	4	Compare until match	73–99	28
		Transfer instruction	100	
			Total	100

Machines using three-address instruction codes are sequenced by means of an instruction counter. Machines using four-address instruction codes are sequenced by a cycle counter. In both the three- and four-address machines, more steps must be included to take care of the two operands and the result.

Example

Draw block diagrams and describe the sequencing cycles for the three-address computer and the four-address computer. [This example is left as an exercise for the student.]

The machine cycles given above apply for simple transfer, arithmetic, and input-output instructions. If the command calls for a lengthy operation such as multiplication, the execution step may be extended by transferring control to arithmetic control. If the command calls for a lengthy input-output instruction such as the writing of a whole block of words into memory, the execution step may be extended by transferring control to the input-output control. In both cases, upon completion of the execution sequence control is transferred back to the control unit which continues in a normal manner (see Fig. 168).

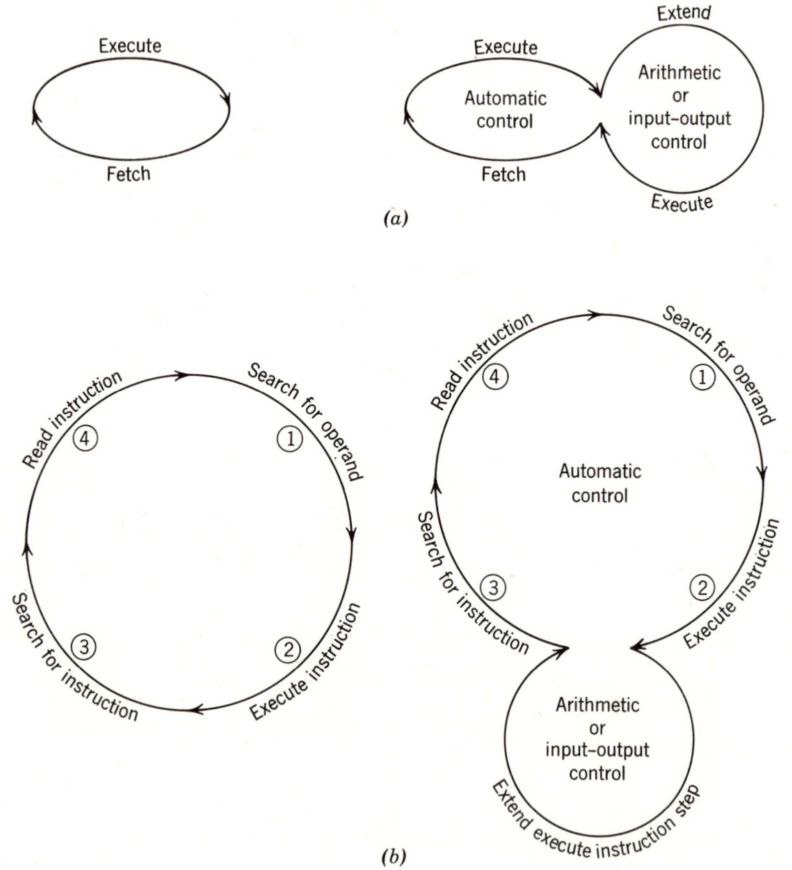

Figure 168 Extending the machine cycle. (*a*) One-address instruction. (*b*) Two-address instruction.

Where concurrency is used, the control unit may be sequencing at the same time as the I/0 control is in operation. This subject is discussed later in this chapter.

Translation of Commands

As soon as the instruction word appears in the instruction register, the command signals are applied to a command decoder which produces one output line for each code combination. This output line is then fed to an encoder which produces the microcommands needed to perform the instruction.

Different microcommands are encoded for different instructions. For instance in a "*Read* from memory to *AR* "instruction, the following microcommands may be needed:

1. Open read amplifiers.
2. Reset *A* register sign flip-flop (to read ZERO unless a minus pulse flips it to ONE).
3. Open input gate to *AR*.
4. Shift word into *AR*.
5. Operation-complete signal.
6. Block recirculation gate of *AR*.

Any one microcommand may be used by several commands. For instance, a right-shift microcommand may be part of a right-shift instruction, and it may also be part of a multiplication instruction.

To summarize, the list of microcommands represents the available micromachine operations, and each command is translated into the group of microcommands needed to perform the indicated operation.

Translation of Addresses

At the same time that the command translator is producing microcommands, the address selector is translating the address part of the instruction into a signal which activates the appropriate location in memory. In a variable address machine, a sequence of memory locations is activated.

Example

If the instruction word for a variable length word machine is given by specifying the address of the first character plus the number of characters to the word, how may addressing be mechanized?

The address of the first character is fed to an address counter and the number of characters is fed to a count-down counter. The first character in the word is read out. After this a pulse is applied to the address counter and to the count down counter. The address counter next chooses the succeeding character, after which a count pulse is again applied to both counters. This process continues until the count-down counter reads 0. At this point a zero output detector attached to the count-down counter causes the addressing operation to come to an end.

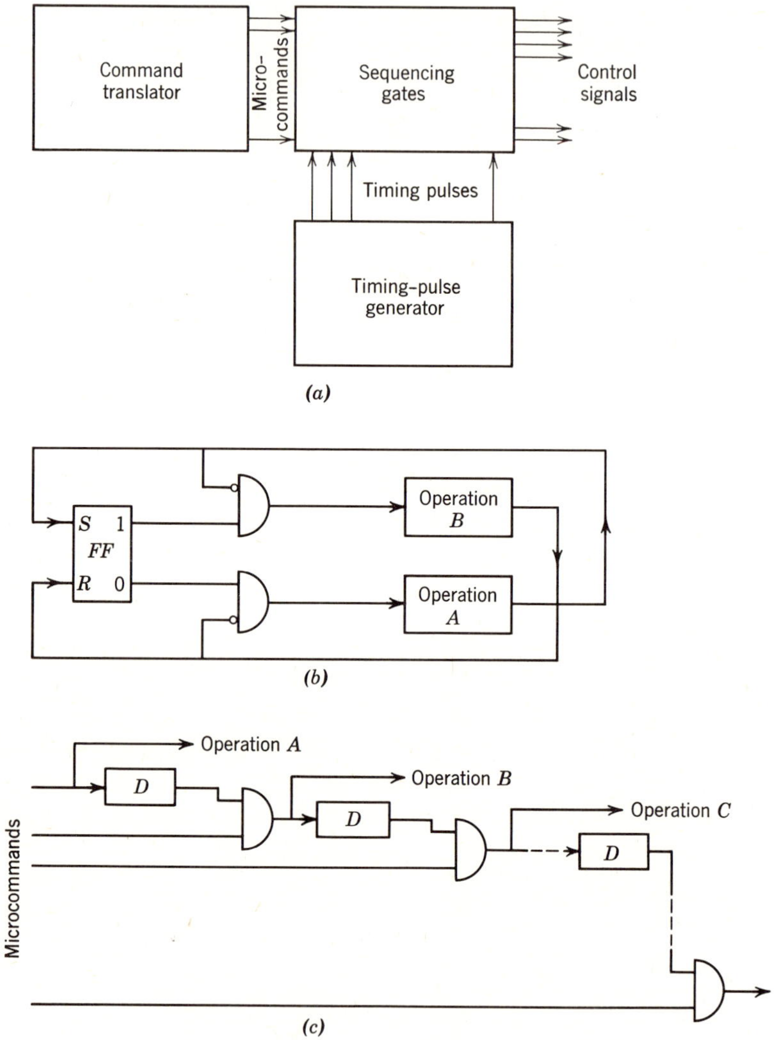

Figure 169 Synchronous and asynchronous operation. (*a*) Synchronous. (*b*) Asynchronous with flip-flops. (*c*) Asynchronous with delays.

Execution of Microcommands

To be effective, microcommands must be executed at the proper times. For instance, in the above example, if the sign bit is the first one transferred, the sign bit would be allowed to enter the sign flip-flop at time t_0. But the gate to *AR* would not be opened until time t_1, allowing all the other bits to enter *AR*. Similarly, the operation-complete signal is usually not allowed to operate until the end of the word-time.

Execution of microcommands may be performed in one of two ways: synchronously or asynchronously. In the synchronous machine (Fig. 169*a*) a timing-pulse generator produces a set of timing pulses for each cycle. A microcommand is gated with a timing pulse in a sequencing gate to produce a control signal effective at the appropriate time. These sequencing gates may be scattered throughout the machine. In the asynchronous machine a central timing-pulse generator is not used. As soon as one operation is completed, the next is allowed to take place. Asynchronous operation is easily accomplished by means of flip-flops in circuits such as that shown in Fig. 169*b*. With the flip-flop reset, operation *A* is performed. Upon completion of operation *A*, a signal sets the flip-flop to allow operation *B* to be performed. Asynchronous operation may also be accomplished by means of delay elements in a circuit such as that shown in Fig. 169*c*.

Very few machines are entirely synchronous or entirely asynchronous. Most of them use a combination of both techniques. In many machines it is difficult to separate the microcommands from the control signals.

In many computers, there are several instructions which may be performed in one word-time or in some other standard length of time. The timing is usually set up to take care of these situations easily. When a more complicated instruction such as a multiplication requiring repeated addition is called for, one of the microcommands may transfer machine control to the arithmetic control unit. Basic microcommands are fed to the arithmetic control, where counter, flip-flops, complementing and other circuits are in control of sequencing the steps of the operation. Upon completion of the operation, the operation-complete signal transfers control back to the control unit. A similar operation occurs when executing a block transfer into or out of the computer.

Implied Address Instructions

An implied address instruction does not call for an operand to be applied to or removed from memory, but to an operand addressed by a previous instruction. For such an instruction, the address part may be used to hold bits to modify the command part of the instruction. The basic machine cycle is not altered; some signals are merely interpreted in a different way.

An example of an implied address instruction that modifies the contents of an arithmetic register is a shift instruction. For instance, in a right-shift instruction, the address part of the instruction may be used to specify the number of shifts to be performed. During translation of "right shift," the machine produces a microcommand which prevents the contents of the address part of the instruction from entering the address selector and causes it to be applied to a counter instead. This counter controls the number of places to be shifted.

MODIFICATION OF INSTRUCTION SEQUENCE

The sequence of instructions to be executed may be modified by a branch or halt instruction. The branch instruction may cause the following instruction not to be in the normal sequence. The halt instruction may stop the instruction sequencing entirely.

Branch Instructions

Unconditional jump. The simplest type of branch instruction is the unconditional jump. The unconditional jump instructs the computer to choose the next instruction from the address specified in the instruction word. The mechanization is fairly easy. When an unconditional jump command is translated by the machine, a microcommand is fed to the address selector to prevent the address portion of the instruction word from affecting the memory. Instead, a different microcommand gates the address into the instruction counter. After the operation-complete signal is received, the computer sequences to the instruction stored at the address present in the instruction counter. Instructions sequence normally from this new address until another branch instruction is executed.

An unconditional jump is used in one- and three-address machines. It is not needed in two- and four-address machines since, in effect, an unconditional jump is part of every instruction word. [Explain.]

Conditional jump. A more sophisticated branch instruction is the conditional jump which allows the computer either to sequence normally or to jump to an instruction out of sequence based upon conditions present within the machine. In other words, the conditional jump chooses among alternatives, and it makes its decision on the basis of some important fact.

Some conditions commonly used by digital computers as criteria for deciding whether to perform a jump or not are as follows:

1. Occurrence of a minus accumulator as a result of a previous arithmetic operation.
2. Occurrence of overflow as a result of a previous arithmetic operation.
3. The presence of a special symbol such as an *EB* (end of block).
4. The presence of a signal indicating a faulty input-output device.

As a matter of fact, any yes-no condition which may be stored in a flip-flop may form the basis for a decision to perform or not to perform a jump.

In a one- or three-address computer, the conditional jump instruction may read as follows:

> Look at the accumulator sign flip-flop. If it is storing plus (flip-flop reset), sequence normally. If it is storing minus (flip-flop set), sequence to instruction located at address given by instruction word.

Example

How can the above conditional jump instruction be mechanized?

The mechanization may be accomplished as shown by the simplified block diagram in Fig. 170*a*. The command is translated into several microcommands one of which is the sense sign. This microcommand senses the state of the A sign flip-flop. If it is plus, A_2 sends a signal to A_3 to allow a count pulse to step the instruction counter to the next address. If it is minus A_1 sends a signal to A_4 to allow the address part of the instruction to be fed to the instruction counter.

In a two- or four-address computer, the conditional jump may read as follows:

> Test the contents of the A sign flip-flop. If it is storing plus (reset), choose the next instruction from location specified by instruction address. If it is minus (set), jump to instruction location specified by data address.

Example

How can the above conditional jump instruction be mechanized?

A simplified block diagram of a possible mechanization of this instruction is shown in Fig. 170*b*. Again, a sense sign microcommand looks at the state of the A sign flip-flop. If it is reset, A_2 sends a signal to the group of gates A_3 to allow the instruction address to be fed to the address selector. If the flip-flop is set, a signal from A_1 opens the group of gates A_4 to allow the data address to be fed to the address selector.

Compare. The conditional jump instruction may be used together with a subtraction instruction to compare numbers. One number B is subtracted from the other number A. If the difference $A-B$ is negative, it implies that B is the larger. The subtraction instruction is followed by a conditional jump—a jump if minus—instruction. Thus a jump occurs if B is larger than A.

The subtraction and jump on minus instructions may be combined into one comparison instruction. For a one-address machine, the comparison instruction may read as follows:

> Compare the word in the accumulator with the word stored in the location given by the address. If the operand in the address is less than or equal in magnitude to the word present in the accumulator, perform the next instruction in sequence. If the operand is greater in magnitude than the value present in the accumulator, jump to the second following instruction.

The skip of one instruction is easily accomplished by feeding two count pulses to the instruction counter instead of one.

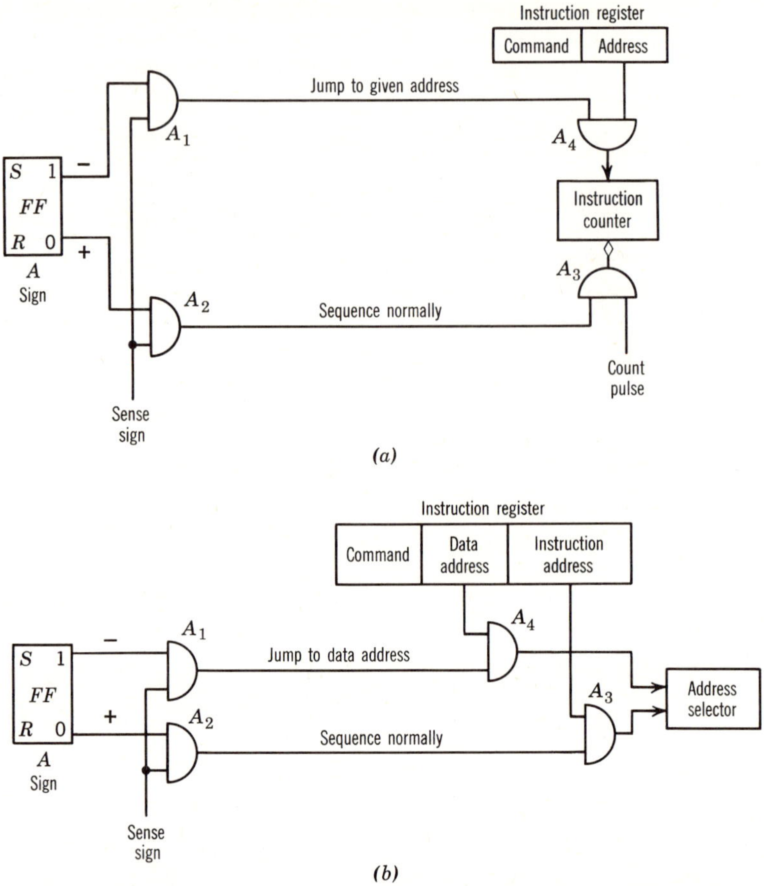

Figure 170 The jump instruction. (*a*) One-address instruction. (*b*) Two-address instruction.

In a two-address comparison instruction, the data address specifies the operand, and the instruction address specifies the location of the next instruction if the operand is smaller or equal in magnitude to the accumulator contents. If the operand is larger than the contents of the accumulator, the machine jumps to a specified address.

Halt Instructions

The basic machine cycle may be modified by a simple halt instruction. A halt instruction is needed because, if left to its own devices, the computer would sequence indefinitely. Usually when a halt instruction stops computer operation, a lamp on the panel lights up to indicate this fact.

A more sophisticated type of halt instruction may be built similar in operation to the conditional jump. The instruction senses the state of a flip-flop. If it is reset, sequencing occurs normally. If it is set, the computer halts.

INSTRUCTION MODIFICATION

The instruction word itself may be modified within the computer. The major method of doing this is by modifying the address, and the easiest way to accomplish this is by indexing. Another method is by the use of indirect addressing.

Indexing

By the use of a special register, called an index register, together with associated logic, the counting and testing needed for executing a program loop are greatly simplified. Also, the index register enables the programmer to write subroutines using relative addresses, that is, addresses relative to a base address stored in the index register. More than 1 index register may be used, and changes must be made to the instruction word to accommodate indexing. In addition means must be provided to simplify the storage of returns from the subroutine to the main routine.

Program loops and subroutines. Table 30 compares the summation subroutine covered earlier in Table 25 of Chapter 10 with a much more simple program obtained by using an index register.

Notice that without an index register a count of the number of operands summed takes place in M to $M+2$. Also $M+3$ and $M+4$ modify $D+1$ so that the *next* operand—not the present one—is summed in the next iteration. Notice also that, since the same AR must be used both for summing and for counting, the sum and the count are continually transferred to and from AR.

An index register (NR) enables the counting and modification to be accomplished more or less automatically, thus, cutting down the number of instructions required dramatically. In this illustration, the *ADD instruction is not the same as the ADD instruction (without *) : before the addition is executed, the count, which is stored in NR, is added to the address part of the instruction (000000 in this case). Thus if NR is preset to 0401, it means that the first operand, the one stored at 0401, is summed.

The *ADD instruction is followed by a TST, which in this case has the following meaning:

> Compare the contents of NR with the contents of the memory location specified by the address part of the instruction. If the contents of NR are less than the contents of the memory location, add 1 to the count in NR and execute the following instruction. If the contents of NR are equal to the contents of the memory location, jump to the 2nd following instruction.

table 30 SUMMATION SUBROUTINE USING INDEX REGISTER

Without Index Register		With Index Register		
Location	Instruction	Location	Instruction	Remarks
*D*0	TFR SUM	*D*0	TFR ZERO	Clear *AR* to zero to start
D+1	ADD OPERAND	*D*+1	*ADD ZERO	Address is 0000
D+2	STR SUM			
TEST	TFR COUNT			
T+1	TST TEST	TEST	TST TEST	Includes *M* to *M*+5
T+2	JMP MODIFY	*T*+1	JMP *D*+1	Previously *M*+6
EXIT	JMP RETURN	EXIT	STR SUM	Extra instruction for storing sum
		E+1	JMP RETURN	
MODIFY	TFR COUNT			
M+1	ADD 1			
M+2	STR COUNT			
M+3	ADD ADD			
M+4	STR *D*+1			
M+5	JMP *D*0			

Since the TST includes the counting, no MODIFY instructions are necessary; the next instruction, *T*+1, is a jump to *D*+1 for the next iteration of the loop.

The second time the *ADD instruction is executed, the new contents of *NR*, or 0402, are added to the address part of the instruction, thus causing the second operand to be added.

The iterations continue until *NR* stores 0416. At this point the TST causes a jump to EXIT. Here the sum is stored, and then a return is made to the main program.

Example

Assume that the above program loop is to be executed on 50 operands stored in locations 0400 to 0449. What should be stored in *NR* before the loop is started? What should the operand of the TST instruction be?

Since the first operand is in 0400, this is the value with which *NR* is preloaded. During each TST, 1 is added to the contents of *NR*. Hence, after 50 operands have been added, *NR* is storing 0449. Therefore, the operand of the TST instruction should be the address where 000449 is stored.

Table 31 compares the "Sum *A* minus Sum *B*" program covered earlier in Table 26 of Chapter 10 with a much more simple program obtained when using an index register.

Without an index register, two memory locations ("Count *A*" and "Sum *A*") must be initialized, and 8 subroutine instructions must be preset before the subroutine may be called.

With an index register, the procedure is simplified. A new instruction, Set *NR* (SNR), is used to initialize *NR*. Thus, *SNR* FIRST *A* transfers the contents of the "First *A*" location to *NR*. In addition, the subroutine must be preset to tell it where to store the sum, what test value should be used, and to what instruction in the main program to return to. This is done for *A* operands in part 1 and for *B* operands in part 2. Part 3 is unchanged.

table 31 SUM *A* MINUS SUM *B* PROGRAM, USING INDEX REGISTER

Without Index Register		With Index Register	
Location	Instruction	Location	Instruction
*P*1	TFR FIRST *A*	*P*1	SNR FIRST *A*
*P*1+1	STR COUNT *A*		
*P*1+2	TFR ZERO		
*P*1+3	STR SUM *A*		
*P*1+4	TFR TFR SUM *A*		
*P*1+5	STR *D*0		
*P*1+6	TFR ADD *A*		
*P*1+7	STR *D*+1		
*P*1+8	TFR STR SUM *A*	*P*1+1	TFR STR SUM *A*
*P*1+9	STR *D*+2	*P*1+2	STR EXIT
*P*1+10	TFR TFR COUNT *A*		
*P*1+11	STR TEST		
*P*1+12	STR MODIFY		
*P*1+13	TFR TEST *A*	*P*1+3	TFR TEST *A*
*P*1+14	STR *T*+1	*P*1+4	STR TEST
*P*1+15	TFR JMP RETURN	*P*1+5	TFR RETURN
*P*1+16	STR EXIT	*P*1+6	STR *E*+1
*P*1+17	TFR STR COUNT *A*		
*P*1+18	STR *M*+2		
*P*1+19	JMP *D*0		

table 31 (cont.)

*P*2	TFR FIRST *B*	*P*2	SNR FIRST *B*
*P*2+1	STR COUNT *B*		
*P*2+2	TFR ZERO		
*P*2+3	STR SUM *B*		
*P*2+4	TFR TFR SUM *B*		
*P*2+5	STR *D*0		
*P*2+6	TFR ADD *B*		
*P*2+7	STR *D*+1		
*P*2+8	TFR STR SUM *B*	*P*2+1	TFR STR SUM *B*
*P*2+9	STR *D*+2	*P*2+2	STR EXIT
*P*2+10	TFR TFR COUNT *B*		
*P*2+11	STR TEST		
*P*2+12	STR MODIFY		
*P*2+13	TFR TEST *B*	*P*2+3	TFR TEST *B*
*P*2+14	STR *T*+1	*P*2+4	STR TEST
*P*2+15	TFR JMP RETURN	*P*2+5	TFR RETURN
*P*2+16	STR EXIT	*P*2+6	STR *E*+1
*P*2+17	TFR STR COUNT *B*		
*P*2+18	STR *M*+2		
*P*2+19	JMP *D*0		
*P*3	TFR SUM *A*	*P*3	TFR SUM *A*
*P*3+1	SUB SUM *B*	*P*3+1	SUB SUM *B*
*P*3+2	STR RESULT	*P*3+2	STR RESULT

Example

Write a subroutine that would read each of 50 operands in turn, multiply it by .10, and store the product. The operands are stored in 0700 to 0749, the .10 factor in 0800, and the products are to be stored in 0750 to 0799. To what should *NR* be preset? (000050 is stored in location 0801.)

The subroutine is:

*D*0	RED	0800
D+1	MPY	0000
D+2	STR	0050
TEST	TST	0801
T+1	JMP	*D*0
EXIT	JMP	RETURN

If *NR* is preset to 0700, the first operand to be multiplied by .10 is the one stored in the location given by 0700+0000 = 0700. Succeeding operands are taken from 0701, 0702, and so on. The first product is stored in 0700+0050 = 0750. Succeeding products are stored in 0751, 0752, and so on.

To simplify programming further, some computers have special registers or storage locations for storing return addresses. In this manner, the return can be made part of the "Jump to subroutine" instruction.

Instruction variations. Indexing may take on a variety of forms. Some of the more common arrangements and general approaches to their implementation are shown in Fig. 171. Part (a) of the illustration shows the implementation of a simple 1-address instruction with no indexing. The address is applied to an address selector, which locates the proper location in memory from which the operand is read (or into which an operand is written). The command is applied to a decoder which converts it to microcommands that are applied to the operand.

Part (b) of the illustration shows indexing with one index register. The address part of the instruction is not applied directly to the address selector. First, it, as well as the index register contents, is applied to an adder. The sum, which is called the effective address, is applied to the address selector. The instruction word stores an index code that indicates whether or not indexing should be applied to this instruction. If the code indicates yes, the index register is activated and its contents forwarded to the adder. If not, nothing is forwarded from the index register to the adder, thus allowing the effective address to be the same as the address given in the instruction.

Since an index register is such a useful device, why settle for one? Why not have several? One register may be used to count one thing while another register is counting something else. One index register may be utilized by one subroutine, and another index register may be utilized by another subroutine. To accomplish this, the instruction word must include a code for specifying the appropriate index register, and another logical unit, called an index selector, must be added to choose the wanted index register from all those available (see Fig. 171*c*).

Example

If a 24-bit 1-address instruction word is used to choose one of 2048 memory locations and 1 of 128 commands, how many index registers can it handle?

$$\begin{array}{rl} 11 & \text{bits are needed to encode 2048 addresses} \\ \underline{7} & \text{bits are needed to encode 128 commands} \\ 18 & \end{array}$$

Thus, 6 bits remain to encode index registers. With 6 bits 64 combinations may be encoded. However, since one of the combinations must be used to specify no indexing, 63 index registers can be handled.

As long as we have a simple counting arrangement, why limit ourselves to counting by 1? We can just as easily count by 2's, 3's, 7's, or by any other increment that we specify. As Fig. 171*d* shows, we may make the increment part of the instruction word. This increment code is decoded to determine by how much the index register contents are increased each time a count pulse is applied. The remainder of the indexing operation is the same as previously.

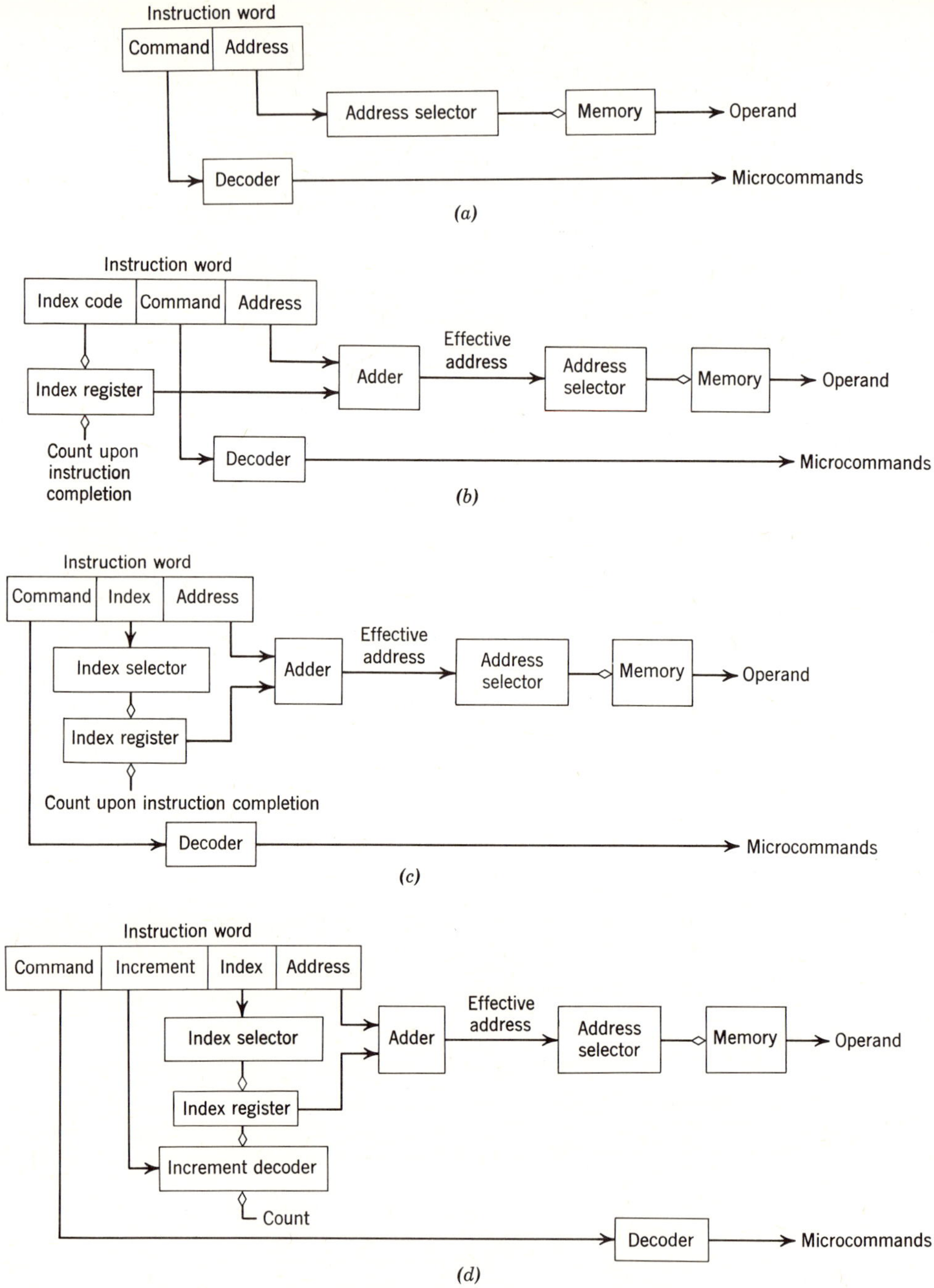

Figure 171 Forms of indexing (*a*) No indexing. (*b*) One index register. (*c*) Several index registers. (*d*) Changing the increment.

Example

Assume that we have a computer in which each character has a separate address. What should we set the increment to if we want to transfer data from an external peripheral unit—for instance, disc—to memory, in words that are 4 characters long?

We set the increment to 4. This will cause each successive word to be accessed in turn.

Of course it should be realized that if we have a 2-address instruction, separate indexing may be applied to each address.

Indirect Addressing

Another method for achieving flexibility in addressing is by indirect addressing. The basic technique consists of finding an address, reading out its contents, and using this as the actual address to access an operand. More sophisticated approaches to indirect addressing may be obtained by the use of control words.

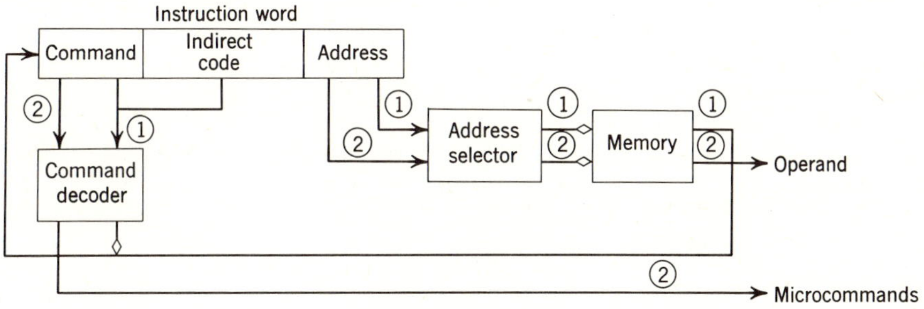

Figure 172 Indexing.

Basic technique. The basic technique for indirect addressing in a 1-address computer is shown in Fig. 172. In addition to the command and address, the instruction word stores an indirect addressing code which is applied to the command decoder. The command decoder, in turn, causes the word read out of memory to be applied to the instruction register. The new address selects the operand to which the microcommands of the command decoder are applied.

One purpose for indirect addressing is shown in Fig. 173. Here the main routine may store an indirect address for return from a subroutine, before it makes a choice among three different subroutines to enter each via a separate indirect address. Regardless of which subroutine is chosen, control is always returned to the same point in the main routine.

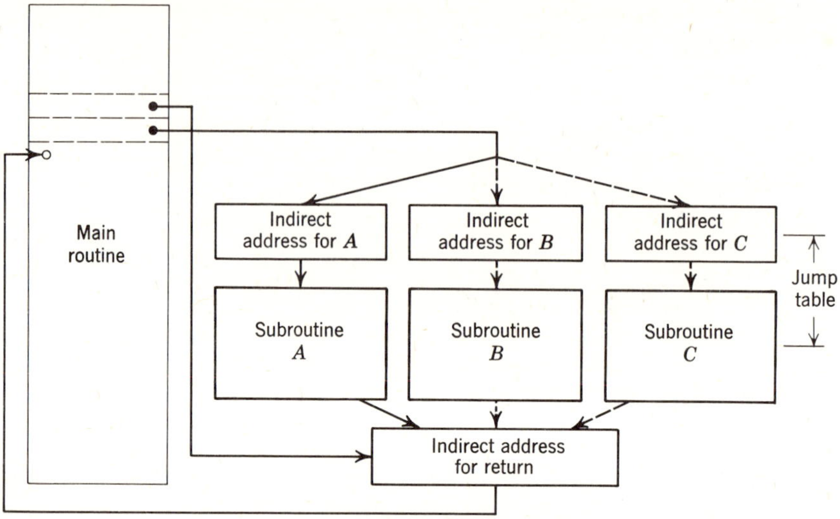

Figure 173 Indirect addressing.

Example

Given a situation where three different products are sold. These products have code numbers 0, 1, and 2, respectively. For each product there is a different method of calculating commissions as given by subroutine *A*, *B* and *C*, respectively. Each of these subroutines is of different size. Explain how you would use indirect addressing to jump to the appropriate one of the 3 subroutines.

Prepare a table as follows:

			Jump Table	
Product Code	Subroutine	Location of Start of Subroutine	Location	Instruction
0	*A*	0500	0400	Jump to 0500
1	*B*	0508	0401	Jump to 0508
2	*C*	0525	0402	Jump to 0525

The last instruction in the main routine is a

"Jump to (0400 + product code)"

If the product code is 0, the jump is executed to 0400, where "Jump to 0500" is stored. At this location the first instruction of subroutine *A* is stored. If the product code is 1, the jump is executed to 0401. Here "Jump to 0508" is stored, which takes us to the first instruction of subroutine *B*. Similarly, with product code 2, indirect address 0402 leads us to address 0525.

I/O control words. An input-output device may transfer and receive a block of words at a time. Indirect addressing enables us to address a whole block by means of one word—a control word. As was stated previously, a control word is a word stored in a given location in memory, and which specifies the beginning and ending address to or from where in memory the block is being transferred. An alternate form specifies the beginning address and the number of words to the block.

Figure 174 shows several levels of indirect addressing using control words. Figure 174*a* indicates address selection with no indirection. Figure 174*b* indicates how a block of words may be transferred using one level of indirection. The input-output instruction refers to the proper I/O device, which is obtained via the I/O selector. Based on which I/O device has been chosen, the I/O control forwards the address of the appropriate control word to the address selector ①. The control word is read out of memory and stored in I/O control ②. At the start, the beginning address in the control word, chooses the first location in memory to be accessed. After a word is transferred, a 1 is added to this beginning address thus causing the next location to be accessed for the second transfer, and so on. When the beginning address in the control word equals the terminating address, the block transfer is completed.

A separate control word is stored in a different location for each of the many I/O devices in a computer system. By means of programming, the contents of any of these control words may be changed.

Example

Assume a character addressed computer system with several I/O devices, each numbered, and each having an associated control word stored in memory starting with address 0201. The following three I/O commands are given:

1. Input a block from magnetic tape (unit 1) to addresses 0530 through 0575 in memory.
2. Output a block from memory addresses 0630 to 0651 to magnetic card (unit 2).
3. Transfer a sector 25 characters long from magnetic disc (unit 3) to memory addresses 0872 to 0896.

What are the control words and where are they stored?

Since the units are labled 1, 2, and 3, the control words are stored in addresses 0201, 0202, and 0203.

Control word 1 stores

0530	0575

Control word 2 stores

0630	0651

Control word 3 stores

0872	0896

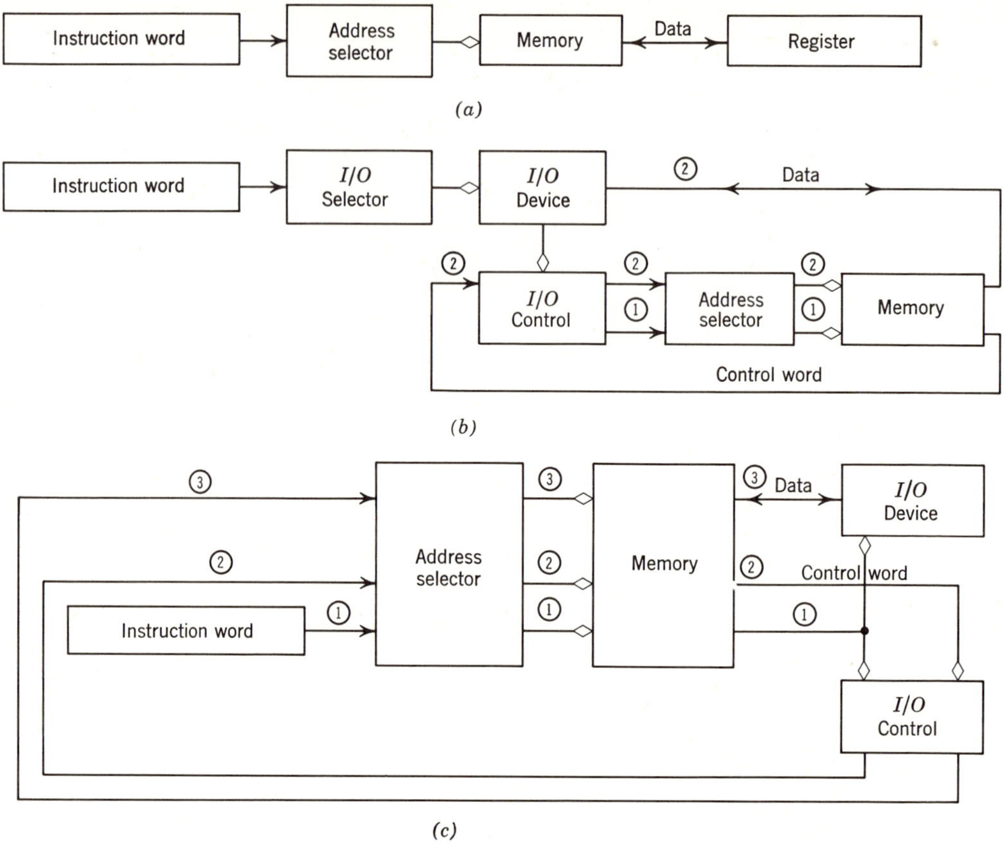

Figure 174 Indirect addressing with *I/O* control words. (*a*) No indirection. (*b*) One level of indirection. (*c*) Two levels of indirection.

Control words may be used in 2 levels of indirect addressing as shown in Fig. 174*c*. The input-output instruction refers to a memory address that stores a code which activates the appropriate I/O device①. It is also an address which the I/O control uses to locate the associated control word in memory②. The control word is used by the I/O control as before to control the data transfer.③

Example

Assume a character addressed computer that requires 4 characters to define an address with a communication multiplexer connected to 100 channels. Assume further that a control word consists of 8 characters. If the lowest-order address locations starting with address 0001 are reserved for channel codes and control words, how many address locations must be reserved? Where is the code for channel 5 stored? Where is the control word for channel 5 stored?

The 100 channels are numbered 1 to 100. Since the codes are 4 characters each, they are stored in 4-location groups starting with the following addresses:

Channel	Address
1	0001
2	0005
3	0009
4	0013
.	.
.	.
.	.
100	0397

Since control words are 8 characters long, their starting addresses are as follows:

Channel	Control Word Address
1	0401
2	0409
3	0417
4	0425
.	.
.	.
.	.
100	1193

The code for channel 5 is stored at 0017. The code reads 0433 which is the address of the associated control word. As previously, the control word stores the beginning and ending locations to be accessed.

The two levels of indirect addressing provide greater flexibility, since the contents of every memory location may be modified by program.

CONCURRENCY

The modern sophisticated computer possesses a great deal of concurrency in order to make the overall system more efficient. Some of this concurrency is machine-oriented. Some of it is program-oriented.

Machine-Oriented Concurrency

Machine-oriented concurrency may take the form of cycle stealing, interleaving, or multiprocessing. The main difference among them is the way arithmetic and I/O execution cycles relate to memory cycles (see Fig. 175).

Cycle stealing. In cycle stealing (Fig. 175*a*), arithmetic execution cycles coincide with memory cycles, until a word is to be transferred between memory and I/O. At this time, one of the memory cycles is stolen from the arithmetic unit and used by the I/O. On completion of the word transfer, the succeeding memory cycles again are provided to the arithmetic unit.

Interleaving. In interleaving, certain defined memory cycles are used by different units. In Fig. 175*b*, for instance, the arithmetic unit uses every other memory cycle, and the I/O uses the memory cycles in between. One simple way of implementing this is by means of 2 instruction counters, one sequencing for the arithmetic unit, the other sequencing for the I/O unit.

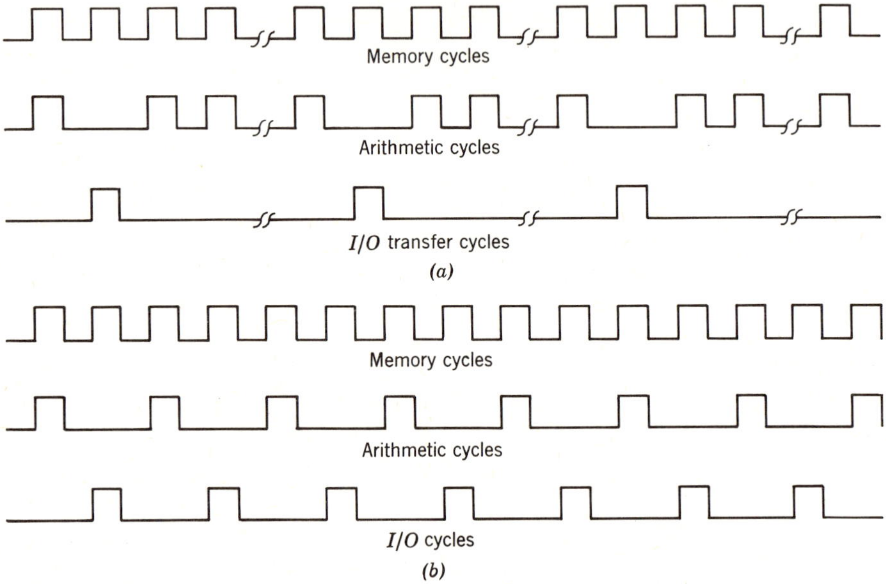

Figure 175 Machine-oriented concurrency. (*a*) Cycle stealing. (*b*) Interleaving.

Program-Oriented Concurrency

Concurrency may be obtained by the way programs are handled in a computer system. A computer may execute one program at a time. The program is executed until the point is reached where data must be entered. At this point, I/O is executed. On its completion, the program may continue. Figure 176*a* gives an idea of the inefficiency of this type of operation: when arithmetic is performed, I/O is idle; when I/O is performed, arithmetic is idle. Multiprogramming and time-sharing are techniques for improving this situation.

Multiprogramming. Multiprogramming is a technique for handling 2 or more programs simultaneously. Figure 176*b* gives an indication of the basics of the process for 2 programs. Program *A* is executed. As soon as a point is reached where I/O is needed, it is introduced. As this I/O is executed for program *A*, program *B* may be started. As soon as program *B* requires I/O, it is introduced providing the I/O for program *A* has been completed. On completion of I/O, the original programs may be continued. A system of interrupts enables the computer to jump from one task to another in this manner.

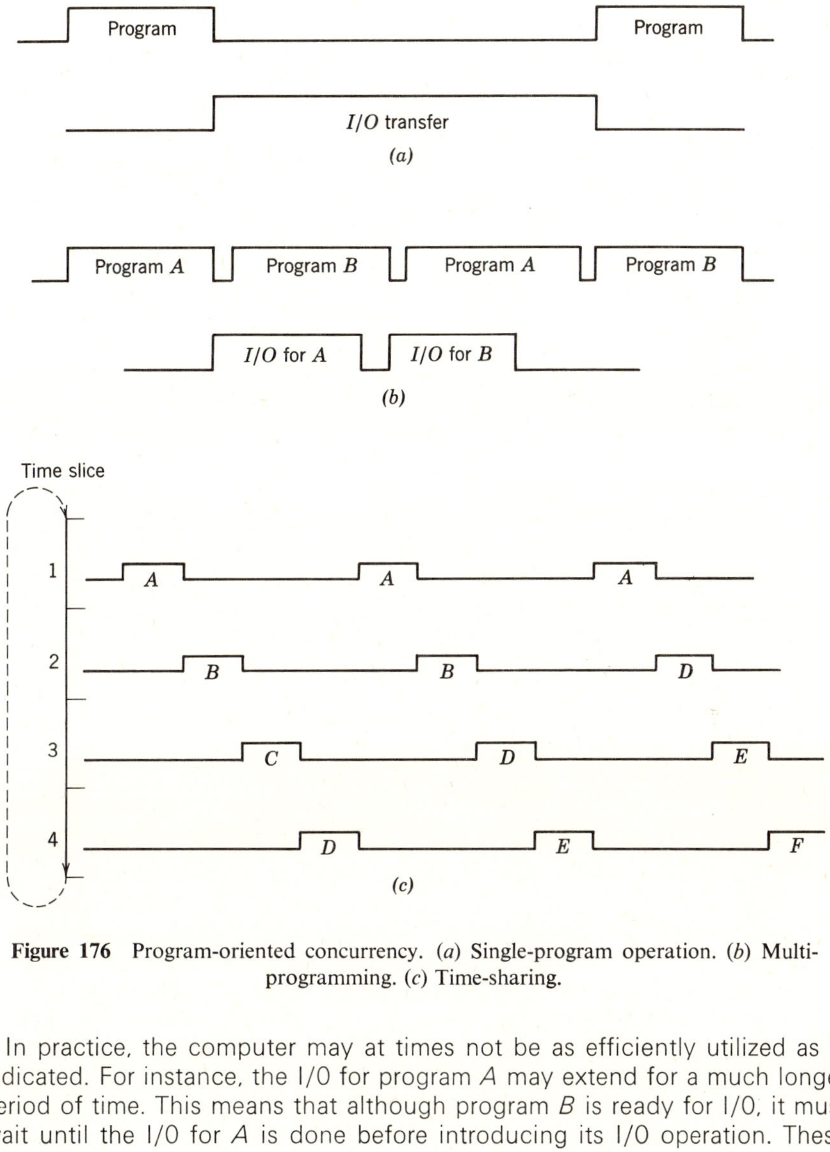

Figure 176 Program-oriented concurrency. (*a*) Single-program operation. (*b*) Multiprogramming. (*c*) Time-sharing.

In practice, the computer may at times not be as efficiently utilized as is indicated. For instance, the I/O for program *A* may extend for a much longer period of time. This means that although program *B* is ready for I/O, it must wait until the I/O for *A* is done before introducing its I/O operation. These types of problems are compounded if more than 2 programs sre executed simultaneously. Each job has different characteristics, and it is normally the task of a separate scheduling program to arrange execution of the programs in a manner that will use the computer system in the most efficient way.

Time-sharing. Multiprogramming is fine for batch processing tasks. A more sophisticated approach is needed for an on-line system in which people interact with individual programs stored in the central computer. Although efficiency of program execution is always important, it is not as important in this case as being able to answer each individual within seconds. Time-sharing gives the system this capability.

In time-sharing, time is divided into slices. During each time-slice, a different program is executed. If a program is not completed during a time-slice, it is set aside and after other programs have received their time-slices, this program receives another slice of time. In this manner, all users interacting with long programs must wait.

Figure 176*c* shows a very simple time-sharing system using 4 time-slices. A clock in the system counts 1, 2, 3, 4 and then repeats the count. During time-slice 1, part of program *A* is executed; the status of the program is saved for later execution. During time-slice 2, part of *B* is executed and its status is saved. During time-slice 3, *C* is executed and a response is returned to the user. During time slice 4, part of program *D* is executed. At the start of the new count, another portion of *A* is executed in slice 1, and *B* is completed in slice 2. Since *C* is out of the system, *D* may be completed in time-slice 3. A new program *E* now may be handled in time-slice 4. And so on.

What size time-slices to use, whether the size should vary according to the situation, what to do when requests arrive when all time-slices are occupied, how to assign priorities to programs when conflicts occur, and how to protect one program from another are only a few of the tasks performed by a supervisor program that must be part of a time-sharing system.

* * * * *

Advanced concepts

Control depends on the philosophy of machine organization. Basically, control must sequence instructions in the most efficient manner. We have learned that indirect addressing aids control considerably. Here, several other methods for achieving indirection and concurrency are discussed. Here, concurrency achieved via multiprocessors, multiple processors, and array processors is discussed. This part ends with a discussion of firmware, a technique encouraged by LSI technology that promises to have a profound impact on all the computer organization of the future.

Indirection

Indirection can take on many forms. Different techniques produce different objectives. The techniques discussed here are content addressing, list processing, paging, cache memory, and the push-down stack.

Content addressing. Content addressing is an indirect method for getting to the specific location where the data is stored. Figure 177 presents 2 simple cases of content addressing. In Fig. 177*a* the name of an item wanted, or a tag, is given. A search is executed to find where in memory a word with this tag is stored. When this match location is found, an access to this location is executed. In Fig. 177*b*, the same procedure is followed except that a match is found at several locations. Each of these locations then is accessed in turn.

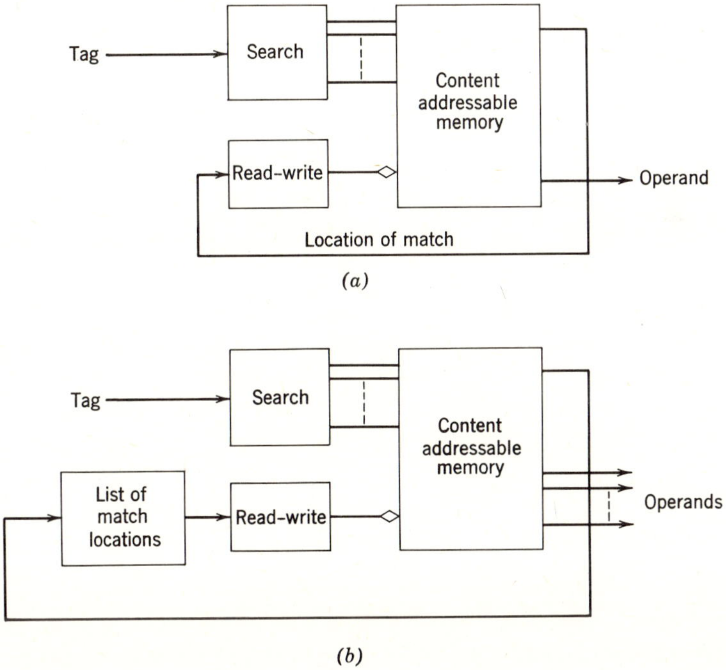

Figure 177 Content addressing. (*a*) Single match. (*b*) Multiple matches.

With content addressing, many other criteria of search may be applied in addition to matching against a tag. We may match against two or more tags related according to any Boolean expression. We may find all words possessing tags either greater than or less than the given tag. We may find words that are between limits set by 2 tags. There are many other possibilities.

List processing. List processing is similar to content addressing in that storage and retrieval is achieved by virtue of membership in a class. Membership is signified by placing all the items of a class in the same list.

To understand what is meant by a list, refer to Fig. 178. As shown in Fig. 178*a* and *b*, each data word and each instruction word has stored with it a link address. This link refers to the location of the next data or instruction word in the list, as shown in Fig. 178*c*. Any word in a list may refer to a sublist as can be seen in Fig. 178*d*. To signify the end of a list or sublist, a null is placed in the link area of the last word.

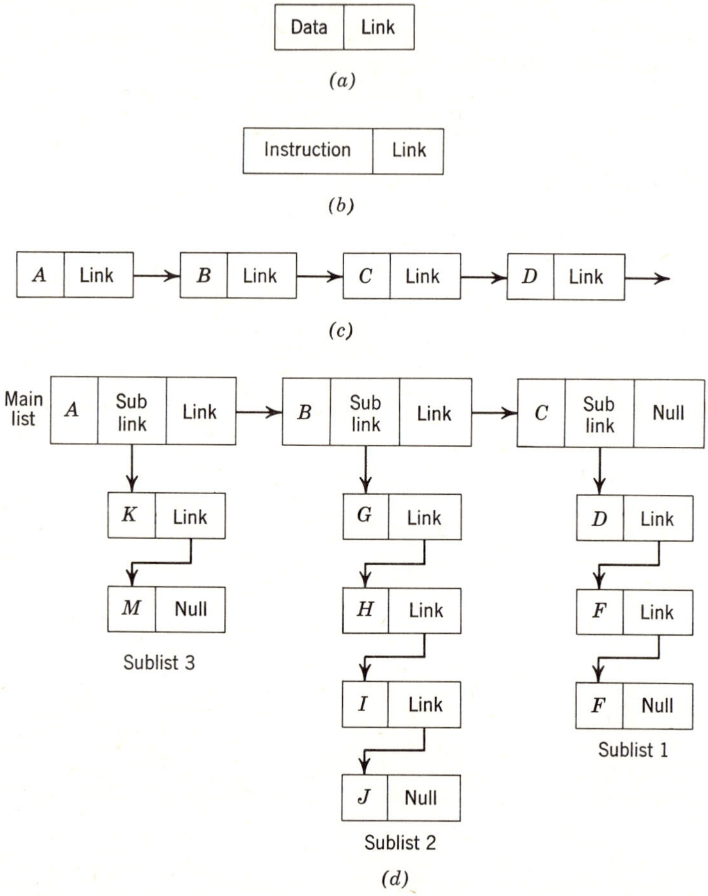

Figure 178 List structures. (*a*) Data word. (*b*) Instruction word. (*c*) List. (*d*) Multiple lists.

To locate a given word, a key is given and the appropriate lists and sublists are searched. For instance, if the key of *BH* is given, a search of the main list locates *B*, and a search of the associated sublist locates *H*. A list search, therefore, is similar to a table look-up operation.

Notice that one important advantage of list processing is that each succeeding word need not be contiguous to the previous word, which provides extreme flexibility in allocating and deallocating storage space in memory. Even for this allocation process a list is used: all empty space is linked together and labeled the list of available storage.

Hence, we perceive that addressing in the usual sense does not exist. The sequencing of instructions is determined by the links in the instruction words, and subroutines are determined by means of sublists.

Although list processing may be performed on conventional computers, special computers have been designed specifically for handling lists. Basically these machines perform in the following ways.

1. They fetch the next instruction via the link field of the current instruction directly or through several levels of indirection.
2. They find the operand directly or through several levels of indirection.
3. They cause appropriate data transfers to take place while assuring that all links have been appropriately set. For instance, to insert a data word with key *AL* requires that the link of the first word in sublist 3 (Fig. 178*d*) be changed to refer to the new word; and that this replaced link be inserted into the new word.
4. They execute instructions such as insert, delete, search, and compare.

Paging. This is another technique of indirection. The address is given in symbolic or logical form and the hardware translates it into a physical address. In addition, reference can be made to a bundle of locations by giving a page number; or reference can be made to a bundle of pages by giving a segment number. This technique is extremely useful in time-sharing systems, where it allows each user in effect to have his own personal storage—or as it is called, "virtual memory." It also allows programs associated with different users to be swapped in and out of memory from and to external storage in accordance with the changing activity pattern.

First, refer to Fig. 179*a* to determine how simple paging works. The logical address consists of a page number and a word number. In effect, the page number is the base address and the word number is the address relative to this base. To translate the logical address to a physical address, a page table is searched for an entry storing the given page number. When this page number is found, the block number that is stored within the same entry is transferred to the most significant end of the physical address register while the word number is transferred to the least significant end of the same register. This register now is storing a normal physical address and can be used for finding the desired location.

Thus far, we have one level of indirection. With segmentation, we may achieve another level of indirection. With each user of a time-sharing system may be associated a group of segment numbers, each of which may represent a different program. Each segment number consists of a group of page numbers. It is possible for a given page number to be part of several segment numbers.

Figure 179*b* shows the system in operation. The logical address consists of a segment number, a page number, and a word number. Each user has a segment table and a page table associated with him. When a user gets on the system, the segment table register is loaded with the base address of his segment table. When the segment number is added to this base address, the appropriate entry is found. The associated page-table base address locates the origin of the appropriate page table. The page number is added to this origin to locate the appropriate entry, and the associated block number is transferred to the most significant end of the physical address register while the word number is transferred to the least significant end.

Because each level of indirection requires another memory access, the above technique is slow. However, by using associative storage, as shown in Fig. 180, the access time is greatly improved. Here the segment number-page number is applied as a group to an associative or content addressable storage device, which looks at all entries to determine which one has this number. The associated block number and the word number make up the physical address as before.

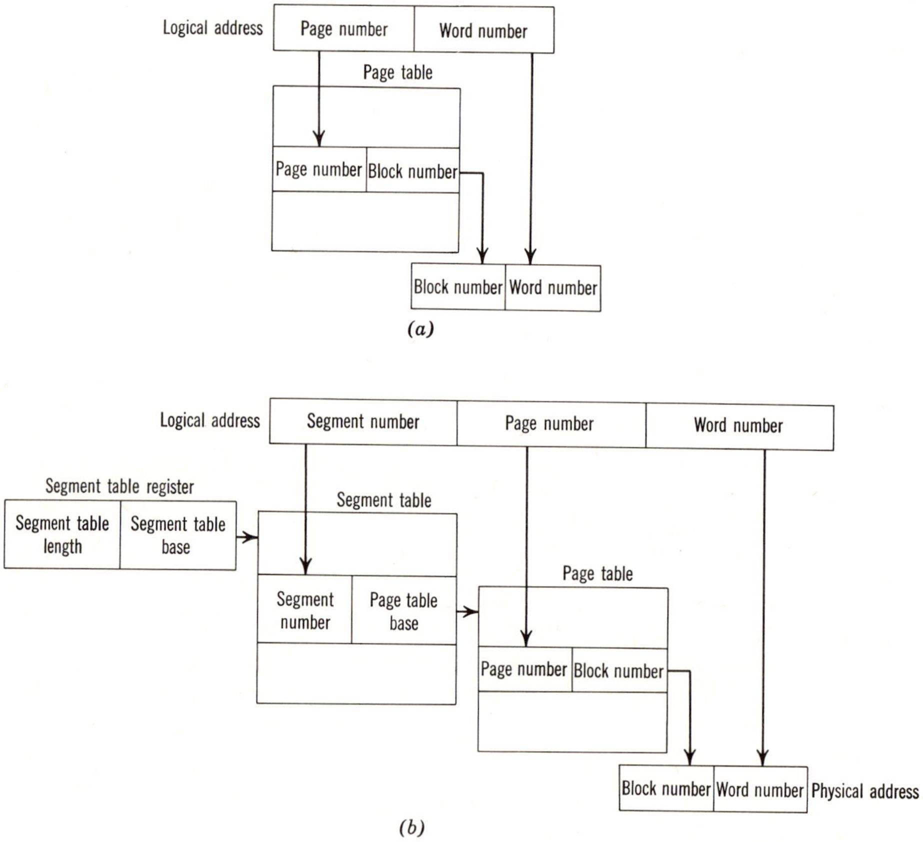

Figure 179 Paging. (*a*) Without segments. (*b*) With segments.

Cache memory. Still another type of indirection may be achieved by placing a buffer memory between the address request and the memory. The buffer, otherwise known as a cache memory, is smaller but much faster than the main memory. The main advantage to this system is fast data access.

Figure 181 shows an example of a cache and main memory working together. The main memory is divided into 32 sectors each sector consisting of 1000 locations. The cache stores 8 of these sectors that are in current use. In the present example, they are sectors 1, 9, 10, 17, 14, 12, 23, and 31, as can be seen from the contents of the associative storage that works with the cache. When a main memory address, such as 14–500 is applied (Fig. 181*a*), the associative storage is searched to locate sector 14 within the cache. When it is found, location 500 within it is read out of the cache. Since no reference is made to the memory, the access is achieved at the faster rate available from the cache.

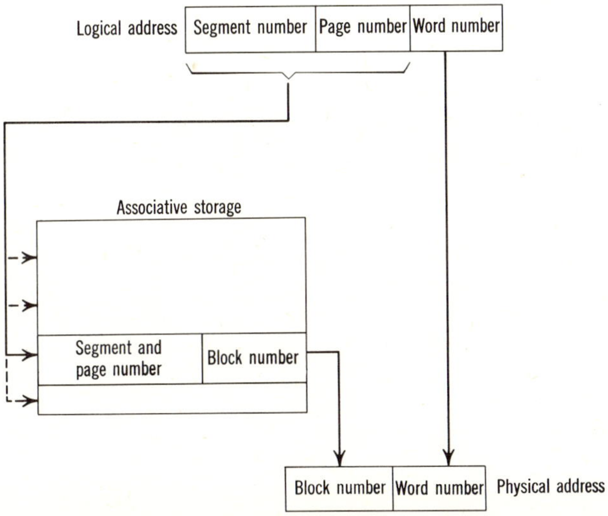

Figure 180 Paging with associative storage.

If a main memory address, such as 16–700 is applied (Fig. 181*b*), a search of the associative storage indicates that sector 16 is not in the cache. Under these circumstances, the entire sector is transferred from main memory to the cache so that succeeding references to sector 16 can be executed at a faster rate. In the example, sector 31, which has been the least active of the 8 in the cache, is removed from the cache to make room for sector 16.

Although most accesses are made via the cache, the programmer is entirely unaware of its presence. He asks for main memory addresses. The hardware takes care of the accesses. It has been found that in most cases the speed of this system is equal to about 80% of what it would be if the main memory had the speed of the cache. This is because of the fact that in most programs the probability is very high that succeeding data accesses ask for data words close to data words previously accessed.

Push-down stack. The less a computer must concern itself with addresses, the higher the level of indirection it operates at, and the closer it gets to being compatible with the problem-solving needs of people. The push-down stack enables this kind of operation. Computers built around the principle of the push-down stack handle high-level languages directly.

The push-down stack consists of a group of registers connected in such a way that each successive input is entered into the top register. As this input occurs, whatever has been stored in the top register is transferred to the one below it, and so on down the stack. Outputs are always taken from the top register, and whenever this occurs the contents of all the registers below it are

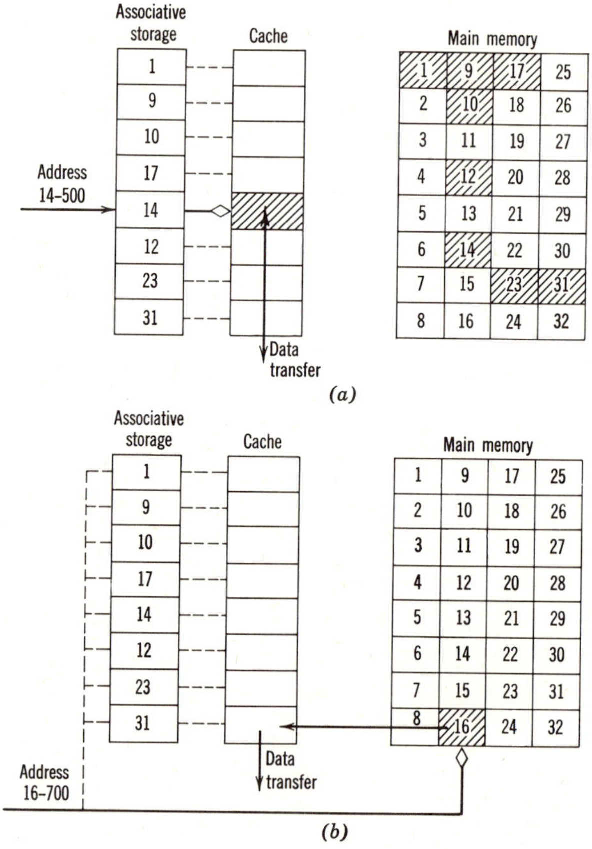

Figure 181 Operation of cache memory. (*a*) Requested address in cache. (*b*) Requested address not in cache.

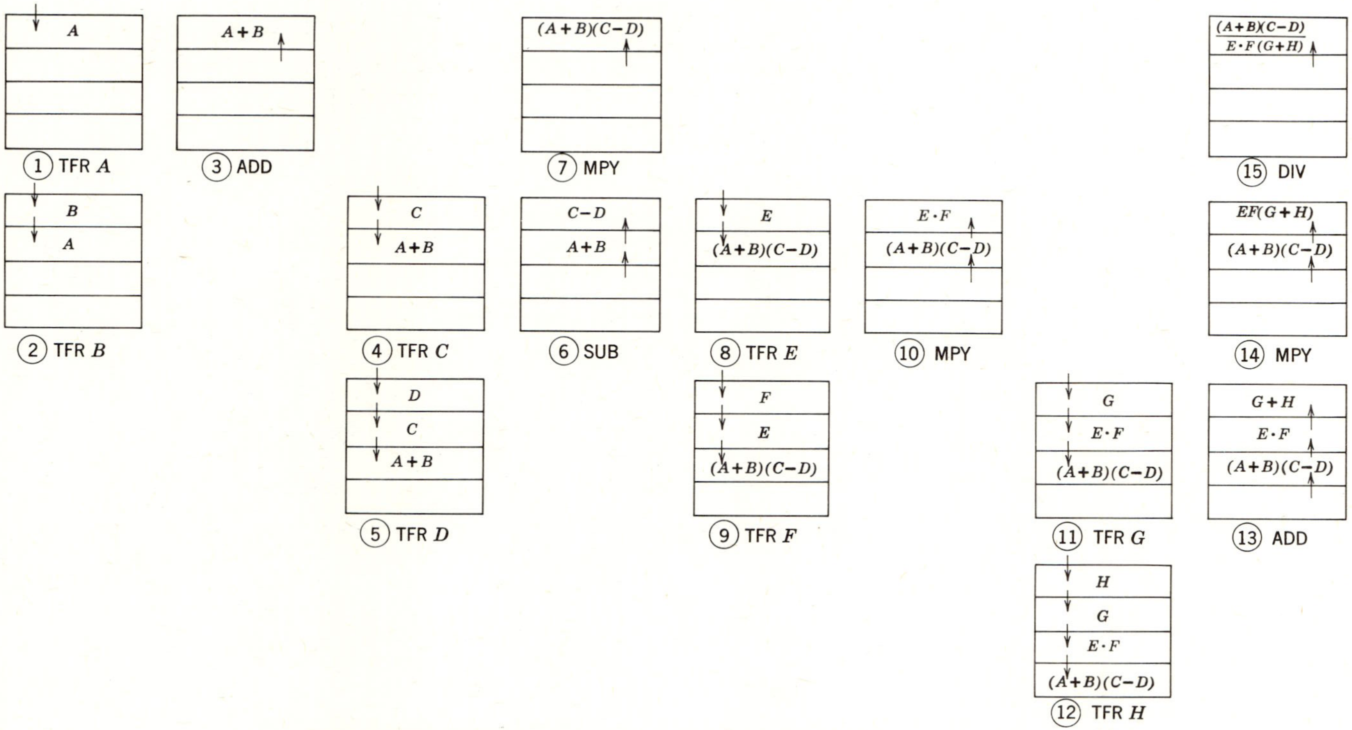

Figure 182 Calculation of $(A+B)\,(C-D)/EF(G+H)$ using a push-down stack.

transferred to the registers above. The operation of the push-down stack is analogous to the operation of the spring-loaded plate holder found in restaurants: the plate placed on top is the first one to be removed.

To understand the use of a push-down stack, assume a calculation must be performed to obtain

$$\frac{(A+B)(C-D)}{E\cdot F(G+H)}$$

Normally, to solve this problem, each instruction must refer to an address. Figure 182 shows that addresses need not be included in the instructions if a push-down stack is used. The illustration shows the sequence of states of a 4-register stack as the instructions required to solve this problem are executed. The instructions are numbered in sequence. The small arrows between registers of the stack show the direction of data flow. Thus data is pushed down in the first column, popped up in the second column, pushed down in the third, popped up in the fourth, and so on.

Specifically, the sequence of events is as follows. The *A* operand is read into the top of the stack①. This is an instruction with an address. This is followed

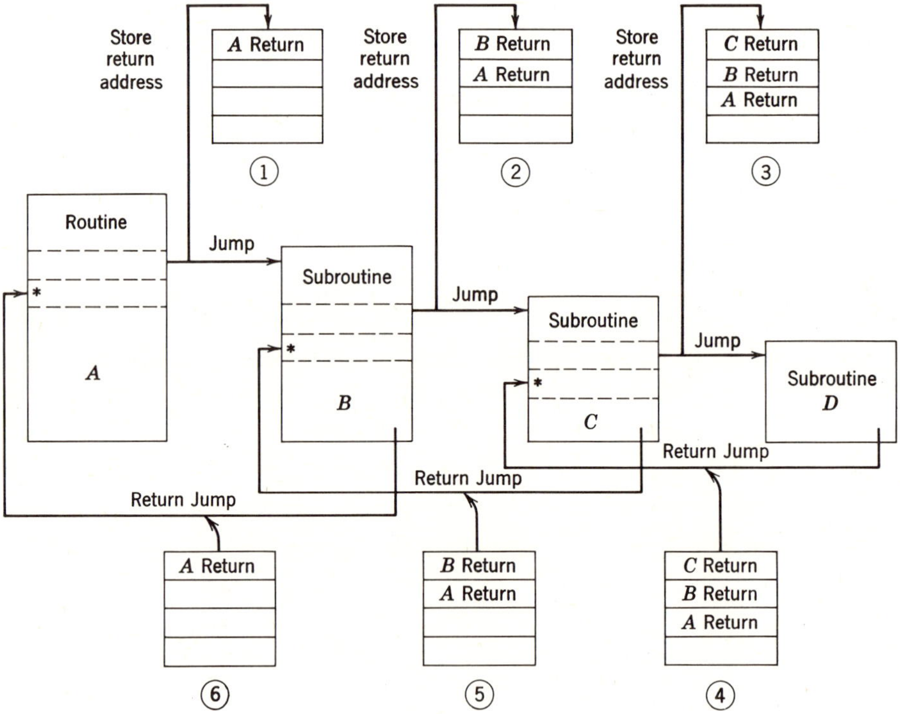

Figure 183 Subroutine nesting with aid of push-down stack.

by a similar instruction that reads in the *B* operand②. As the *B* operand enters the top of the stack, the *A* operand is pushed to the second level. An implied address ADD instruction now causes the *A* and *B* operands to be taken from their respective locations and added; the result is returned to the top of the stack③. The fourth and fifth instructions read in *C* and *D* while they push down $(A+B)$. An implied address SUB instruction produces $(C-D)$ and stores it at the top of the stack, while $(A+B)$ is pushed up to be immediately below the top⑥. Another implied address instruction, MPY, produces $(A+B) \cdot (C-D)$ and stores it on top of the stack⑦. The operation is similar for the remaining steps 8 to 15.

Notice that access to memory is needed only to obtain the operands. If the result obtained in the fifteenth step is the final answer, it is then stored. If not, the above process may be continued.

The power of the push-down stack can be further displayed by describing its use in nesting of subroutines. Nesting is the situation occurring when one subroutine calls another subroutine, and this latter subroutine calls still another subroutine. This nesting of subroutines may occur at many levels. Where do we store successive return addresses and how do we go back up the subroutine "staircase"?

Figure 183 describes how nesting is accomplished with the aid of the push-down stack. In this illustration during execution of routine *A* a jump into subroutine *B* is executed; during execution of subroutine *B* a jump into subroutine *C* is executed; and during execution of subroutine *C* a jump to subroutine *D* is executed. As each successive jump is made, the return address is stored in a push-down stack ①, ② and ③. When the last subroutine is being executed the push-down stack is storing the *C* return at the top④. On completion of subroutine *D* a return is executed to this location, thus allowing subroutine *C* to be completed. At this point, the *B* return is removed from the top of the push-down stack,⑤ and a return to this location in *B* is executed. On completion of *B*, the *A* return is made⑥.

Multiprocessors, Multiple Processors, and Array Processors

We have described 2 types of concurrency: independent I/O operation while arithmetic operations are taking place, and multiprogramming. Here we discuss concurrency that results from increasing the number of processors working together. A very simple type uses the principle of "look-ahead." Other systems of this kind are the multiprocessor, multiple processor, and array processor. In addition to improving the efficiency, these systems may increase availability (time the system is operating successfully). Some of them can perform tasks that cannot be done any other way.

Look-Ahead Processor. In a 1-address computer, instructions are sequenced through two phases: FETCH and EXECUTE. To speed up the machine, two arithmetic units are provided—one for each phase. While an instruction is being executed, the system looks ahead and fetches the next instruction.

On completion of the execution of the first instruction, the second instruction is ready for immediate execution.

This is true in all cases except where a choice is made, such as in conditional branch instructions. In such cases the look-ahead assumes the result of the branch instruction and fetches accordingly. In the few instances where it guesses wrong, the system must repeat the fetch. Even with this consideration, the system is faster than without the look-ahead.

Multi-Processor. The multiprocessor (Fig. 184) is a modular system consisting of several memory, processor, and I/O control modules. The processor module may be considered to be a combination arithmetic and logic unit plus a sequence control unit. Processor and I/O control modules share the same memory.

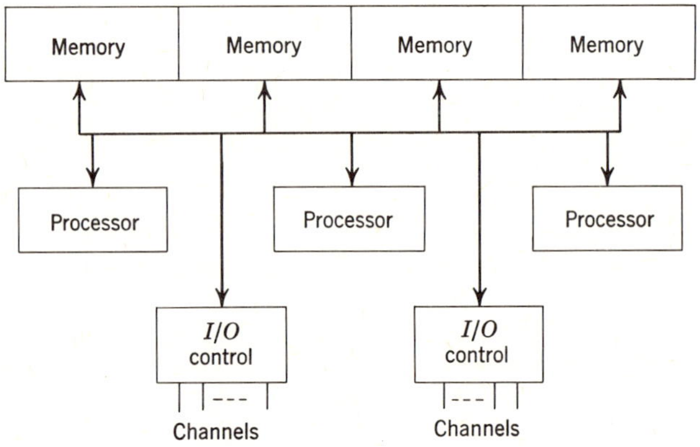

Figure 184 Multiprocessor.

Each processor may sequence and operate on a different program stored in memory. Each processor may ask for data to be retrieved from external storage; one of the I/O control modules will find the data for it. Meanwhile the processor may execute other operations. In other words, multiprogramming takes place.

What keeps one module from interfering with another? Often one processor module is designated the master and the others the slaves. This means that the master has access to the system software that controls the system and maintains the integrity of operations within the system. In other systems, a different processor module may become a master at a different time.

One big reason for building multiprocessors is to achieve availability. In many time-sharing or other on-line systems, the time that the system is not functioning properly must be kept to an infinitesimal amount. For instance, could we tolerate a breakdown in an on-line military information system during a military operation?

High availability can be achieved because of the redundant modules in the system. As soon as it is known that a processor module is faulty, it may be

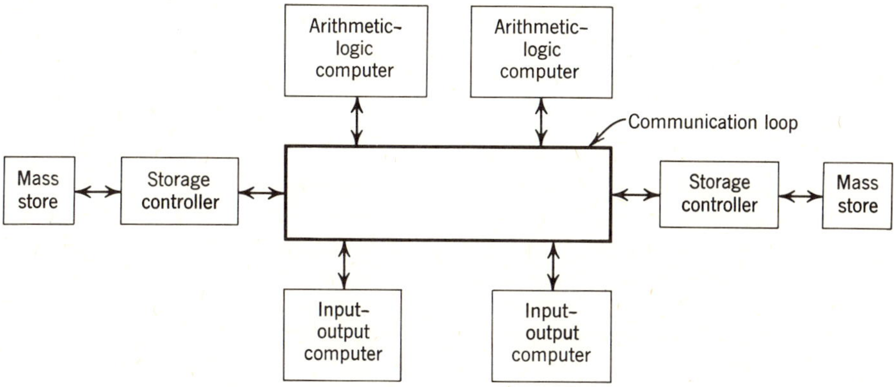

(a)

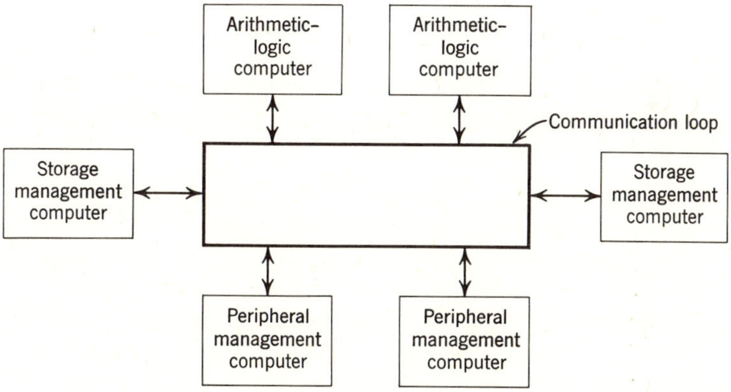

(b)

Figure 185 Multiple processors. (*a*) Common among all devices. (*b*) Common among processors only.

switched out of the system and the other processor modules are given its tasks to execute. Similarly, this is true for I/O control modules. When a memory module is faulty, the other memory modules are made to store its programs and data. Should one of the peripherals or its controller fail, other peripherals are switched in.

The switching capability required, plus the software to support module switching as well as the recovery procedures needed to put the system back on the air, make the multiprocessor complicated.

Multiple Processors. When processors share memory, we call the system a multiprocessor. If they do not share memory, that is, each processor has its own memory, then the system consists of multiple processors and is called a multi-computer. In a multi-computer each computer is independent of the others.

This implies that some type of communication system must exist among the computers.

Figure 185*a* shows one possible configuration. Here 4 independent computers (2 Arithmetic Logic Computers and 2 Input/Output Computers) and 2 storage controllers, with associated mass storage units, are connected to a common communication loop. When one ALC wants to transfer data to another ALC, it merely forwards a message to it, indicating where in the mass storage unit the data may be found. The ALC receiving the message then fetches the data.

Figure 185*b* shows another possible configuration. Here, there are only computers communicating with each other, each computer executing a specific class of tasks : 2 computers do arithmetic, 2 take care of terminals and peripherals, and 2 control storage.

Since multi-computer systems possess modularity and redundancy, they can be used to build highly available systems. Manufacturers of mini-computers like this approach, since it allows a user to build a large system out of many small computers.

If the system modularity is carefully designed, the multi-computer system may allow for adaptability to change. When system redesign is called for, modules, not complete systems, are replaced.

Array Processors. Multiprocessors and multi-computers allow for parallel processing. Instead of having to do the parts of a long task in sequential order, it is possible to divide the task in such a way that several sections of it are executed at the same time. By following this type of thinking to its logical conclusion, we arrive at an array processor.

Figure 186 is a very simplified diagram of an array processor. It consists of an array of 16×16 identical processors, making a total of 256. There is a central control to the system as well as individualized sequence controls within each of the processors. Each processor can communicate with memory as well as with the 4 processors adjacent to it.

This type of computer organization enables a single instruction stream to process several data streams simultaneously. It is useful for the solution of partial differential equations and pattern recognition problems. As may be imagined, programming this type of computer is complex.

The development of the array processor has been encouraged by the drastic miniaturization of components as well as the advent of LSI. Bulk fabrication techniques with which LSI chips are manufactured can most economically be accomplished if there is a great deal of repetitiveness. And this is provided by the array processor.

Firmware

Many different types of computer organization have been developed and proposed. Also the nature of LSI is such that it is forcing manufacturers to produce processors in volume. How can the two opposing forces—variety and mass production—be reconciled? The answer is, by building generalized

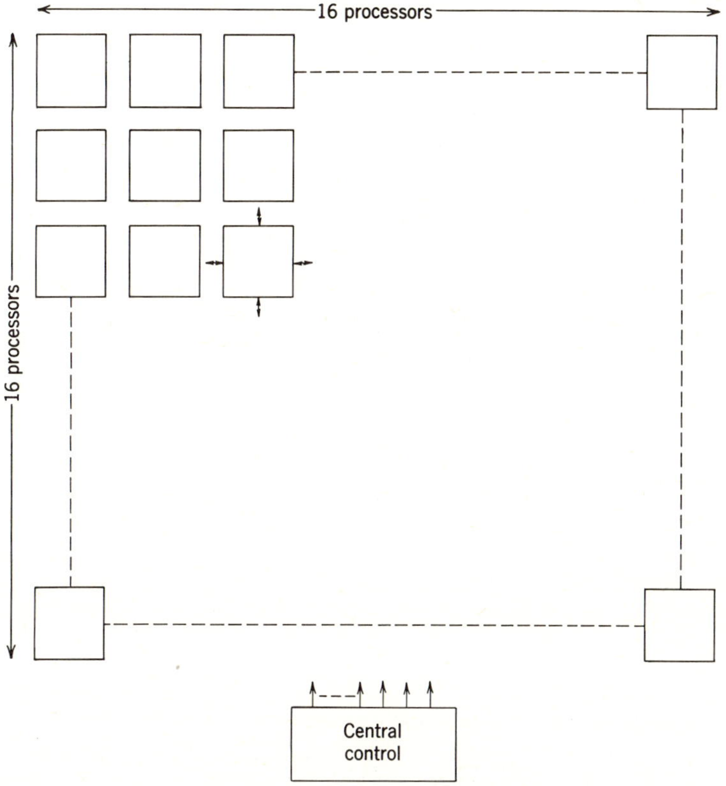

Figure 186 Array processor.

computers that can be specialized to specific tasks by means of firmware—something between hardware and software.

To understand what we mean by firmware, let us return to Chapter 9 where we discussed a read-only memory. The point was made that a read-only memory is similar to an encoder. This means that the sequence of micro-commands that is required to execute a given command could be stored in a read-only storage device just as readily as it can be wired into the logic. This has been done. These microcommands are stored in hardware.

On a higher level, if a computer does not have a command as part of its repertoire, a subroutine called a macro may be preprogrammed and stored in memory so that when a program calls for this function the macro is executed. For instance, if square roots are very commonly used by a program, but the computer possesses no such machine command, a square-root macro may be written; when the high-level program is executed, any reference to square root causes the macro to be executed. From the point of view of the program, the macro is just another command. The macro is software.

The macro is written by using the normal commands of the computer. But let us suppose that the computer had no commands—only microcommands. For every command that is wanted, a subroutine is written with these microcommands and stored in a ready-only memory that is a fundamental part of the control unit. This is not hardware and is not software, but it is firmware.

With firmware, the same basic processor may be used for many different specialized applications by changing the firmware. Furthermore, one computer can be made to operate like another. Programs written for one computer can be made to run on another. When new commands are required, they easily can be added to the repertoire.

Read-only memories for storing microprograms can be made of LSI and, thus, have much faster access times than do conventional core or other magnetic main memories. Firmware is faster than software.

* * * * *

SUMMARY

1. The control unit consists of an instruction register and of automatic control circuits.
2. The automatic control determines the basic machine cycle which consists of sequencing the instructions, translation of commands and addresses, and execution of microcommands. Sequencing is accomplished in cooperation with the memory unit. For complicated instructions the execution stage may be extended by the arithmetic or input-output controls.
3. A one-address computer is sequenced by an instruction counter. A flip-flop may be used to step from the FETCH phase, in which the instruction word is read from the memory to the instruction register, to the EXECUTE phase, in which the address and command are translated and the microcommands are executed on the operands. Sequencing of the three-address computer is similar.
4. A two-address computer is sequenced by means of a four-stage cycle counter. The four stages are as follows:
   a. Search for operand.
   b. Execute instruction.
   c. Search for next instruction.
   d. Read next instruction into instruction register.

   Sequencing the four-address computer is similar.
5. The instruction word consists of a command and an address or a group of addresses. In the translation stage the address portion(s) of the instruction is fed to an address selector which allows the path to the chosen location in memory to be opened; and the command is fed to a command translator which produces a microcommand for each of the small operations required to execute a complete instruction.

6. During the execution phase the microcommands are converted to control signals occurring at the appropriate times for the execution of the required instruction.

7. The basic machine cycle assumes an instruction requiring reference to memory. If the instruction does not require such reference, the address part of the instruction may be vacant or its contents may be sent to a special encoder which produces additional microcommands.

8. The basic machine cycle may be modified by a branch instruction. In the one- or three-address computer, a jump to an instruction out of sequence occurs by sending the address part of the instruction to the instruction counter. In the two- or four-address computer, a jump occurs by feeding the data address, instead of the instruction address, to the address selector.

9. An instruction may be modified by means of indexing and indirect addressing. Indexing simplifies the writing of program loops and enables relative addresses to be used for subroutine instructions. Indirect addressing enables an individual to use one instruction to effectively modify many and to address a whole block by means of 1 word.

10. Computers use concurrency of operation to achieve efficiency. This concurrency may take the form of trying to operate different parts of the computer simultaneously or of trying to execute several programs simultaneously.

11. *Definitions to Remember*

Microcommand. One of the many operations that must be performed in order to complete a command. *Example:* opening a gate, or resetting a flip-flop, or causing a register to shift its contents to the right.

Synchronous Computer. A computer whose microcommands are executed at times controlled by a master clock.

Asynchronous Computer. A computer whose microcommands are not executed according to times from a master clock; one operation begins after the previous operation is completed.

Branch Instruction. An instruction which may cause the machine to choose the next instruction out of the usual sequence. *Example:* the unconditional and conditional jumps and comparison instructions.

Unconditional Jump. An instruction which always causes the machine to execute a specified instruction out of the normal sequence.

Conditional Jump. An instruction which causes the machine to execute a specified instruction out of the normal sequence, only if certain conditions are met.

Comparison Instruction. An instruction which compares two numbers to see which is larger or smaller and then performs a jump on the basis of the results.

Conditional Halt Instruction. An instruction which causes the machine to come to a halt only if a halt switch on the control panel is thrown.

Index Register. A counter used to modify address portions of instructions before the instructions are executed.

Push-Down Stack. A register stack in which the last item entered is the first item available, and the relative position of the other items is pushed back one.

Nesting. The process of embedding a subroutine within another subroutine. This may be done to many levels.
Concurrency. The process of performing several different operations simultaneously within the computer.
Multiprocessing. The division of a computer system into functional units that execute their tasks simultaneously.
Multiprogramming. A technique for executing several programs simultaneously.
Time-Sharing. An extended form of multiprogramming in which slices of time are allotted to the various programs in order to achieve fast computer response for users interacting with the system.

Exercises

1. Assume the following 1-address instructions are stored at the addresses indicated:

	Instruction	
Address of Instruction	Command	Address
0205	TFR	0963
0206	SUB	0964
0207	JUMP on MINUS	0965

At 0963 and 0964 are stored the operands 65.74 and 66.58, respectively. At the start 0205 is in *IC* and a series of FETCH–EXECUTE cycles is performed. What are the contents of *IC* and *IR* during each of these steps?

2. Given a 2-address computer using a drum for memory. The drum has 16 columns and 120 rows. It takes 60 ms to complete a revolution, and a Transfer, Add, or a Store may be executed in the time it takes a row to pass under the head. How long should it take to execute the following:

Instruction Location		Instruction				
			Data		Instruction	
Column	Row	Command	Column	Row	Column	Row
2	25	TFR	8	35	2	63
2	63	ADD	8	05	2	84
2	84	SUB	8	45	2	90

Assume that *IC* is at 2–25 at the start and at 2–90 at the end.

3. How many memory accesses must be made to completely handle
   a. a 3-address instruction?
   b. a 4-address instruction?
4. In Fig. 167, what would happen if the topmost input line to gate A_6 were disconnected?
5. Assume a character-oriented computer in which each character has an address, and variable length words are added one character at a time, the carry produced being delayed for combining with the addition of the succeeding 2 characters. The addressing scheme should be oriented to read out from memory to arithmetic register the LSD first or the MSD first?
6. Draw a block diagram to show how, during a shift instruction, the contents of the address part of a 1-address instruction are not sent to the address register but to a shift counter.
7. In a 4-address computer, the compare instruction may have more choices built into it than a compare for a 1-address computer. How may a compare for a 4-address instruction read?
8. How may the test instruction read in:
   a. a 2-adress computer?
   b. a 3-address computer?
   c. a 4-address computer?
9. We want to write a routine to obtain the square root of each of a group of 150 numbers stored consecutively in memory starting with address 0640.
   a. What should the index register be preset to?
   b. What should the test compare against?
   c. If each of these numbers were 4 characters long, each character being addressable, what should the increment part of the instruction be set to? How does this change (**b**) above?
10. In a character-addressed computer, where each instruction word is 8 characters long, how should the instruction counter count?
11. How can we use nesting to solve:

$$\text{sine}(\sqrt{X} \log X)$$

12. Assume that 2-level indirect addressing is used in connection with a communication multiplexer serving 256 channels. The lower end of memory starting with location 0001 is used for the codes, each of which is 4 characters long, and the control words, each of which is 6 characters long.
   a. Where is the fifth code stored?
   b. Where is the tenth control word stored?
   c. How much of memory is reserved for codes and control words?
13. Assume a multiprogramming system in which 10 programs are being executed simultaneously. On an interrupt, one of these programs is halted, and the new program initiated. On completion of the new program, the one that was halted is reinitiated, and it continues from the point where it had stopped. How can the availability of many index registers aid in the execution of the above procedure?

14. How many times must the content address memory be accessed to read one operand?

*15. Draw a block diagram of a control unit for a 1-address synchronous serial by bit computer, which can execute the following commands:

Store
Clear Add
Add
Subtract
Multiply
Shift Right
Input
Punch
Jump
Set NR
Test NR
Jump on Minus
Halt

on operands consisting of 10 bits and sign bit (least significant) plus parity bit (most significant). The instruction word stores 6 bits to locate 1 of 64 words in memory. It also includes a sign that is minus when indexing is called for, and plus when it is not.

CHAPTER 15

A specimen computer

We now know of what building blocks computers are built. We know now how building blocks may be combined to perform an array of computer functions. We know how to combine functional building blocks into the major functional units that any digital computer must possess. Now let us see how the functional units work together by describing an integrated specimen computer.

The specimen computer presented is not a complete machine; it is a skeleton. However, the skeleton is good enough so that if enough flesh is added to the bones the computer can be made operable.

The specimen computer is not typical of the way present-day machines are designed. It is not intended to be. Instead it is presented for the purpose of reviewing the major fundamental points developed in this book.

After a general description, the 4 major functional units of the computer are described. This is followed by a brief discussion of the part of the computer that makes the whole device practical: the console. The chapter is completed with a discussion of programming, operation, and maintenance of the specimen computer.

GENERAL DESCRIPTION

Computer Characteristics

The specimen computer is a binary fractional fixed-point machine possessing 13 commands and a memory with a capacity of 64 words. The one-address instruction word is 12 bits long: 4 bits to encode the 13 commands; 6 bits to encode the 64 memory addresses; 1 sign bit to specify whether the instruction should be modified by *NR*; and 1 parity bit for checking. To simplify the logic of the machine, the data word is also 12 bits long: 10 magnitude bits, 1 sign bit, and 1 parity bit.

A coincident-current magnetic-core type of storage is utilized for the memory. This type of storage requires parallel read-in and read-out. The arithmetic unit, on the other hand, operates serially. As is shown later, a buffer register is utilized to make the memory and arithmetic units compatible.

The external storage medium is punched paper tape encoded in binary-coded octal.

In the paper tape the bits are stored as holes for ONE's and no-holes for ZERO's. In the inside of the computer, ONE's are stored as 0-v levels, and ZERO's as −6-v levels. Machine timing signals are pulses of 6-v amplitude.

The ONE's and ZERO's are operated upon by means of diode AND and OR circuits. Since after four levels of logic the data signal is deteriorated, a transistor amplifier is used to restore its energy. Two types of amplifiers are provided, one to reverse the polarity in order to produce the NOT function, and one merely to amplify and not change the polarity. For delay and control functions, direct-coupled transistor flip-flops are used.

These basic building blocks are combined into gates, registers, counters, selectors, generators, detectors, and adders which are needed to breathe life into the machine.

The essential characteristics of the computer are given in Table 32.

table 32 CHARACTERISTICS OF SPECIMEN COMPUTER

Language	
Number system	Binary
Number range	Magnitude less than one
Number designation	Fixed point
Bit representation	ONE = 0-v level ; ZERO = −6 v level
Type of transmission	Serial ; writing and reading are in parallel
Word size	12 bits ; 10 magnitude bits, 1 sign bit, 1 parity bit ; parity bit not present in arithmetic and input-output units
Instruction code	One-address
Composition of instruction word	Parity / Address: Column, Row / Command / Sign X / XXX XXX / XXXX / X
Composition of data word	Parity / Magnitude / Sign X / XXXXXXXXXX / X
Machine timing	Synchronous Word-time = 14 bit-times
Instruction repertoire	1 * Store 0001 2 * Transfer 0010 3 * Add 0011 4 * Subtract 0100 5 Input 0101 6 Punch (output) 0110 7 Test *NR* 0111

table 32 (cont.)

	8	Jump	1000
	9	Halt	1001
	10	* Multiply	1010
	11	* Shift Right	1011
	12	Set *NR*	1100
	13	Jump on Minus	1101
	* *NR* modifiable instructions if sign of instruction word is negative		
Checking scheme	Parity-bit detector in memory unit		
Memory			
Type	Coincident-current magnetic core		
Capacity	64 words		
Construction	12 8×8 core planes		
Input-output			
Type	Punched paper tape reader and punch		
Number system	Binary-coded octal		
Arithmetic			
Type of algebraic addition	Negative numbers converted to 2's complement and added		
Type of multiplication	Sequence of alternate additions and shifts		
Speed	Addition: 1 word-time Multiplication: 22 word-times *NR* modification: 1 extra word-time		

Computer Organization

A system block diagram showing the major functional blocks within each of the functional units of the specimen computer is drawn in Fig. 187.

The memory consists of 12 magnetic-core coincident-current planes driven by column and row address selectors. Data arrives at the memory unit serially and leaves it serially. Access to the coincident-current planes, however, is in parallel. The *MR* acts as a buffer to convert parallel read-out data to serial form, and serially arriving data into parallel form for writing into the cores. A parity-bit detector checks the data as it is removed from memory.

A parity-bit generator generates an extra bit according to the rules of parity just before a word is written into memory.

Machine words are in binary. However, instruction and data words are written in binary-coded octal form onto punched paper tape. These are then fed to memory via the input-output register. The three bits of each octal digit are applied directly to the appropriate storage cells of the input-output register.

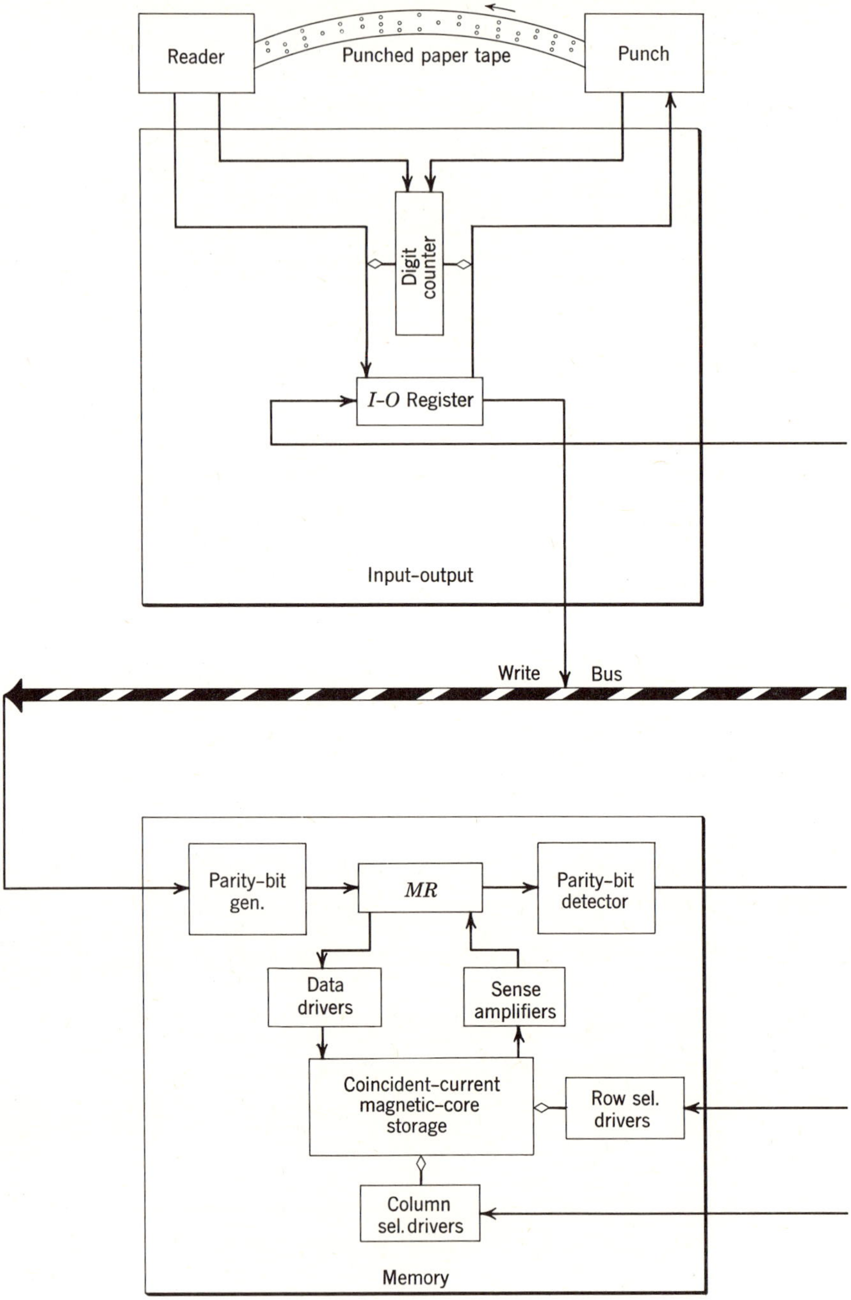

Figure 187 Block diagram of specimen computer.

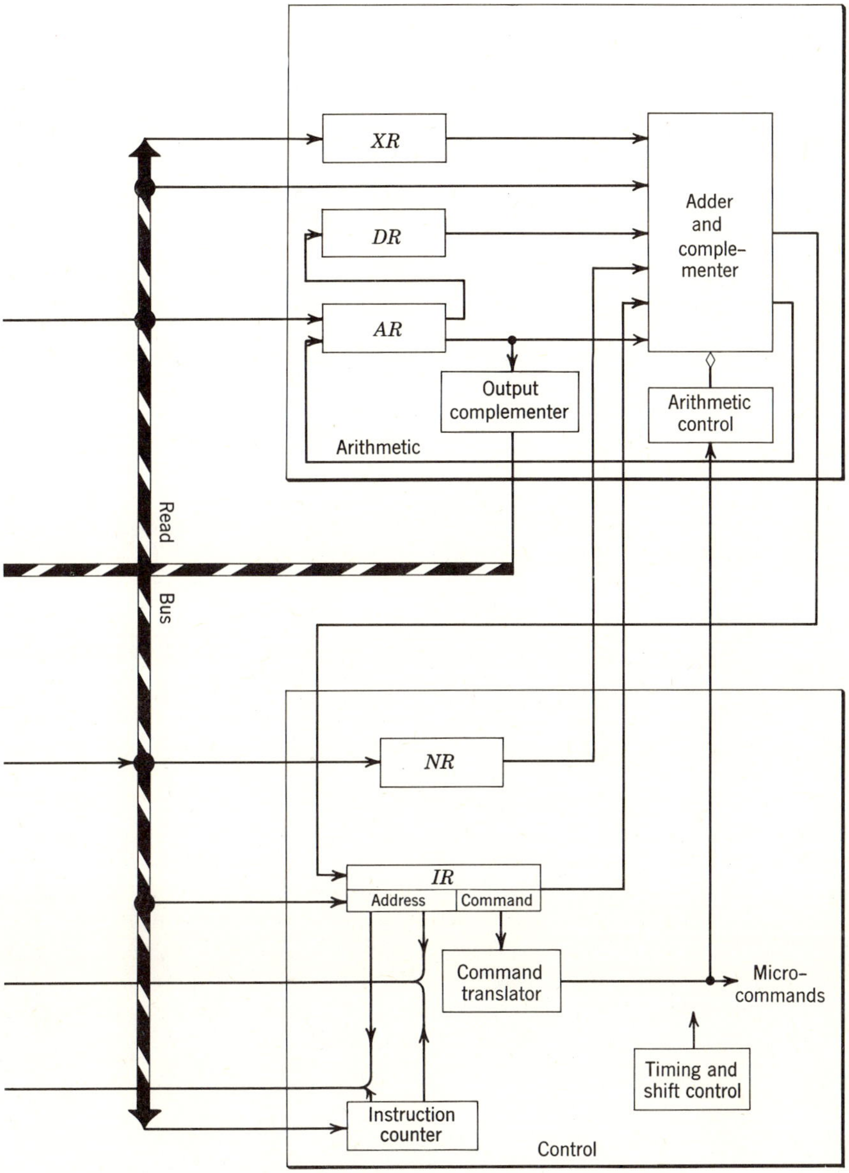

Figure 188 Memory of specimen computer.

The read-in is under control of a digit counter. Output from the input-output register to memory is in serial. Words are sent serially into the input-output register and then fed from the separate storage cells to the punch under control of a digit counter.

The arithmetic unit executes arithmetic operations. Words are applied from memory to the adder and complementer. The adder and complementer converts negative numbers to their complement form; it leaves positive numbers unchanged. It also algebraically adds to or subtracts from the number previously stored in *AR*. Multiplication is performed by a series of additions and shifts under control of the multiplier, which is read directly into *XR*. All results are stored in *AR*, from which point they are returned to memory via an output complementer that brings the numbers back to absolute-value-plus-sign form.

The control unit determines the sequencing, translation, and execution of the instructions. From memory the instructions are transmitted to *IR*, where the instruction bits remain while being translated by the command translator and the column and row address selectors. The command translator produces microcommands which activate the appropriate gates to perform the necessary steps in the operation. The timing and shift control determines in what sequence the microcommands are performed. At the end of an operation the instruction counter is stepped; its contents are fed to the column and row selectors to choose the next instruction to be executed. *NR* is used to modify instructions: before execution of an instruction having a negative sign, the contents of *NR* are added to the contents of *IR* in the adder; the new instruction is returned to *IR*, translated and executed.

MEMORY (Fig. 188)

The memory consists of twelve 64-bit magnetic-core planes, one plane for each of the 12 bits to a word. Column and row selectors and read-write drivers (*RW*) choose the appropriate address by a coincidence of column and row currents. Data write amplifiers (*D*) cause ONE's and ZERO's to be written into the chosen core in each plane. Sense amplifiers (*S*) amplify output signals leaving each plane during read-out. Reading and writing are accomplished in parallel. The *MR* acts as a buffer to convert parallel data into serial form for outward transmission, and serially arriving data into parallel form for writing into the core planes. A parity detector is in the serial read-out path. A parity-bit generator is in the serial read-in path.

Read-Write Cycle

The memory operates in a read-write cycle which takes one word-time, as shown in Fig. 189. Parallel reading occurs during the first bit-time, serial transmission to and from *MR* occurs during the next 12 bit-times, and parallel writing occurs during the last bit-time.

During a read-type instruction—Transfer, Add, Subtract, Multiply, Punch—read and rewrite microcommands are produced by the control unit. The read microcommand operates at t_0 to transmit the 12 bits of the word in parallel to *MR*. At t_1 to t_{12}, the bits are transmitted serially through the parity detector to the arithmetic or output units. Because of the destructive read-out of magnetic cores, at t_{13} the bits of the word are removed from *MR* and rewritten into memory.

During a write-type instruction—Store, Input, *SNR*—no read microcommand occurs; nothing happens during t_0. During t_1 to t_{11}, the bits of the word are transmitted serially from the arithmetic or output units to *MR* through the parity generator. At time t_{12} a parity bit is generated. At time t_{13} the 12 bits of the word including the recently produced parity bit are written in parallel into memory.

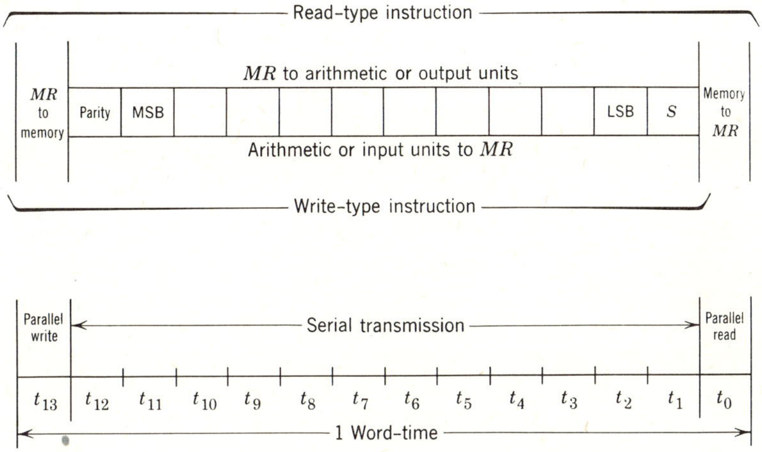

Figure 189 Read-write cycle.

Address Selection

The address is chosen by a 6-bit combination arriving from the instruction counter or from the address part of the word in the instruction register. In the first case, an instruction is read out of memory into the instruction register. In the second case an instruction word or data word is read from or written into memory.

The address is divided into a 3-bit column address and a 3-bit row address, each of which is fed to a diode selector. The selector decodes the bits into a signal on one of 3 output lines. The activated line opens the associated driver. During a write operation, current is made to flow in one direction; during a read operation, current is made to flow in the opposite direction through this driver.

Writing and Reading

One bit of each word is stored in one core in each plane. The lowest plane stores the sign, the next plane the least significant bit, followed by the other bits in order, and the topmost plane stores the parity bit.

Writing of a bit in the chosen core of each plane is accomplished by a coincidence of three currents: the column current, the row current, and the data current. One column driver feeds current through the chosen column of each plane, and one row driver feeds current through the chosen row in each plane. Separate data drivers feed each plane. In planes where we want to write a ONE, the data current is in a direction aiding the row and column currents. In planes where we want to write a ZERO, the data current is in a direction opposing the row and column currents. In the first case the chosen core flips; in the second case it does not.

Reading is performed by reversing the row and column drive currents. The outputs are introduced into the sense amplifiers, one for each plane. The sense amplifiers convert the signals into pulses of standard amplitude before they are transmitted to *MR*.

M Register

The *MR* is a shift register capable of accepting data in serial or in parallel, and transmitting it in serial or in parallel. During reading (t_0), the 12 bits from the 12 sense amplifiers are fed through 12 gates to each of the 12 storage cells of *MR*. Once in the register, timing pulses t_1 to t_{12} shift the bits from one storage cell to the next, and from the LSD through a parity bit-detector to the bus. During this same time a recirculation gate is opened to allow the bits to feed back to the other end of the register; this is done to maintain the bits in storage. At t_{13} the bits are applied through the data drivers to the same cores in memory from which the bits were removed.

If writing is taking place, bits are transmitted serially at times t_1 to t_{11} to the parity-bit generator. Out of the generator the eleven bits plus a parity bit are transmitted during t_1 to t_{12} to *MR*. This time the recirculation gate is inhibited, so that the new bits replace the old. Again, at t_{13}, the 12 bits are applied in parallel through the data drivers to the chosen cores.

Parity-Bit Detection and Generation

The 10 magnitude bits of the word may contain an odd or an even number of 1-bits. If the number of ONE's is odd, a ZERO is recorded for the parity bit; if the number of ONE's is even, a ONE is recorded for the parity bit. Thus the sum of all the ONE's in the word (excluding the sign bit) should always be odd.

The parity-bit detector tests for this condition. In essence it is nothing more than a trigger flip-flop which reverses states with each ONE. After all the bits pass through, a timing pulse t_{12} samples the state of the flip-flop. If it reads ONE, everything is alright. If it reads ZERO, indicating an even count of ONE's, the stop flip-flop is set. This flip-flop, in turn, stops the computer.

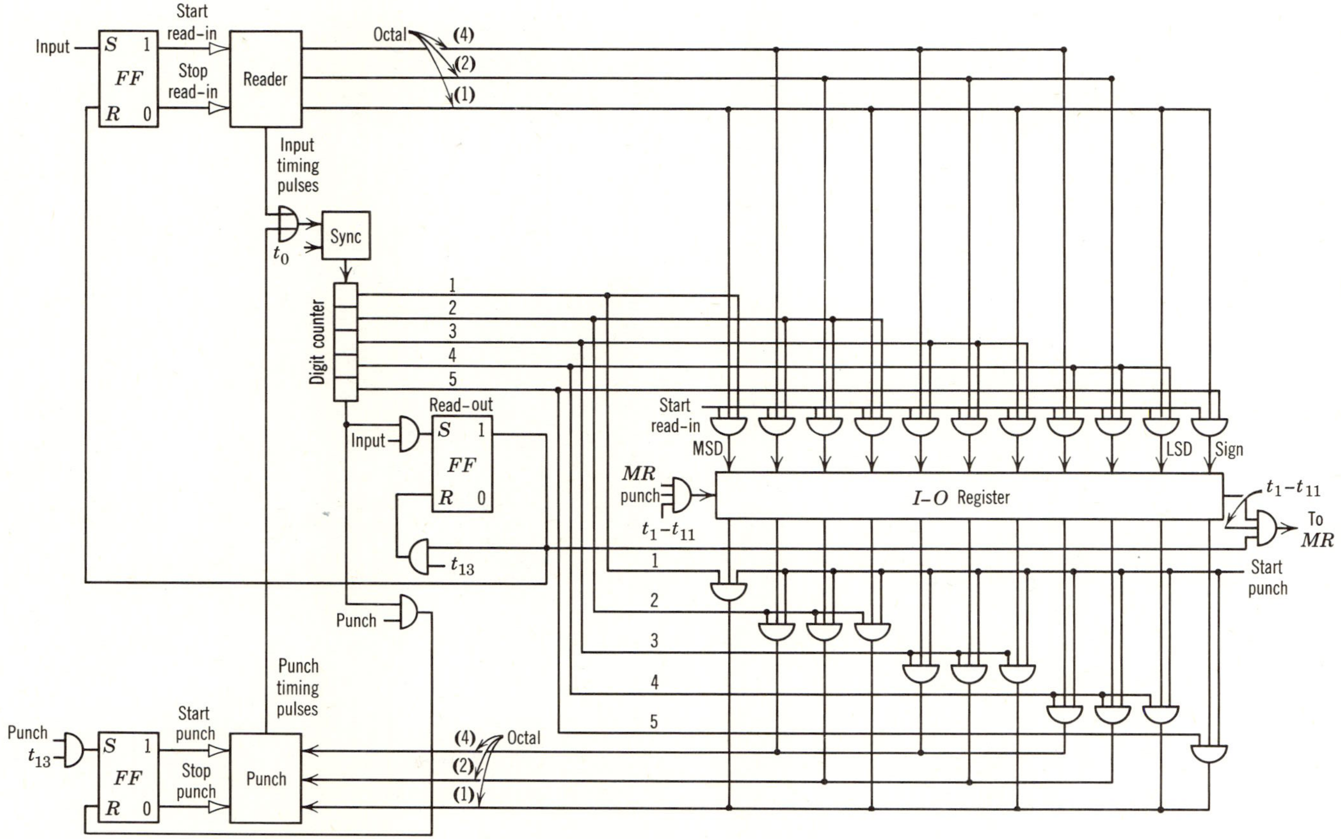

Figure 190 Input-output of specimen computer.

INPUT-OUTPUT (Fig. 190)

The external storage medium for the specimen computer is punched paper tape. Instruction and data words are entered onto punched paper in octal form: the 10 bits plus sign bit are represented by 3 octal and by 2 binary digits, as shown in Fig. 191. An input instruction causes the bits of each octal digit to be entered into the appropriate storage cells in the input-output (*I-O*) register under control of the digit counter; when the register is full, the bits are shifted out serially into *MR*. During a punch instruction, the bits are shifted serially from *MR* to the *I-O* register; when the register is full, the bits of each octal digit are removed under control of the digit counter and are punched on paper tape.

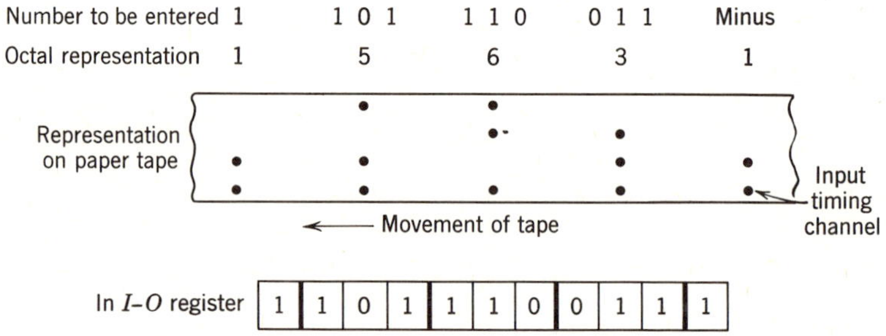

Figure 191 Punched paper tape format.

Input Instruction

An Input instruction produces the input command signal which sets the read-in flip-flop and turns on the paper tape reader. At the same time that the reader reads the three bits of each octal digit, it also reads an input timing pulse. The input timing pulse is applied to the synchronizer which produces a sync pulse occurring at t_0. The sync pulse steps the digit counter to 1. The 1-output of the digit counter plus the "start read-in" signal from the read-in flip-flop allow the most significant bit to enter the most significant storage cell of the *I-O* register. As the three bits of the next octal digit are read, the associated input timing pulse becomes a sync pulse which steps the counter to number 2. The 2-output of the digit counter plus the "start read-in" signal allow the next most significant three bits to enter into the three next most significant storage cells of the *I-O* register.

As each octal digit is read, the associated sync pulse steps the counter to cause the bits to be entered into progressively less significant storage cells until, at count 5, the sign is entered in the least significant position. Also at the count of 5, the read-out flip-flop is set. The set output resets the read-in flip-flop whose output in turn shuts off the reader.

The read-out flip-flop is turned on at time t_0. During t_1 to t_{11} the bits in the *I-O* register are shifted through the output gate to *MR*. During t_{12} a parity bit is generated, and during t_{13} the whole word is written into the address in memory specified by the instruction word.

At t_{13}, too, the read-out flip-flop is reset. The *I-O* register is clear and ready for another input or punch instruction. Figure 191 shows the relationships among the number to be entered, its octal representation, and its representation on paper tape, and in the *I-O* register.

Punch Instruction

During t_0 of a Punch (output) instruction, a read microcommand causes read-out of the word from memory into *MR*. During t_1 to t_{11}, the bits are shifted out of *MR* into the *I-O* register. At t_{12} the parity detector generates a pulse to stop the computer if the number does not meet the parity rule. The word transferred from memory remains in the *I-O* register. At t_{13} the "start punch" flip-flop is set to turn on the punch, and to halt computer sequencing until the punch finishes its job.

The punch produces punch timing pulses which are converted to sync pulses at time t_0. These sync pulses step the digit counter in the same way they do during the input operation. In the 1-output position the most significant bit is applied to the punch. In the succeeding positions of the counter, lower significant bits are transferred in groups of three to the punch. During step 5, the sign bit is transferred and the start punch flip-flop is reset to stop the punch. The Stop Punch signal also allows the End-of-operation signal to be produced to enable instruction sequencing to continue.

ARITHMETIC (Fig. 192)

The arithmetic unit executes the Add, Subtract, Shift-right and Multiply instructions. Before these instructions may be executed, a Transfer instruction brings an operand into *AR*. The second operand is entered by the arithmetic instruction. After the arithmetic operation is performed, the result may be returned to memory by means of a Store instruction. For all operations except multiply, negative operands are stored in arithmetic registers and are operated upon in 2's complement form. This means that complementation may occur during the input or output of a negative word.

General Description

The arithmetic unit consists of three arithmetic registers—*AR*, *DR*, and *XR*—an adder and complementer, an output complementer, sign circuits, multiply counter, and several flip-flops.

AR and *DR* are 10-bit shifting recirculating registers. *AR* is the accumulator, and *DR* stores the multiplicand. Shift pulses are under control of the timing and shift control. (Shift pulses are not shown at the registers.) Both *AR* and *DR* have separate flip-flops for storing the *A* and *D* signs.

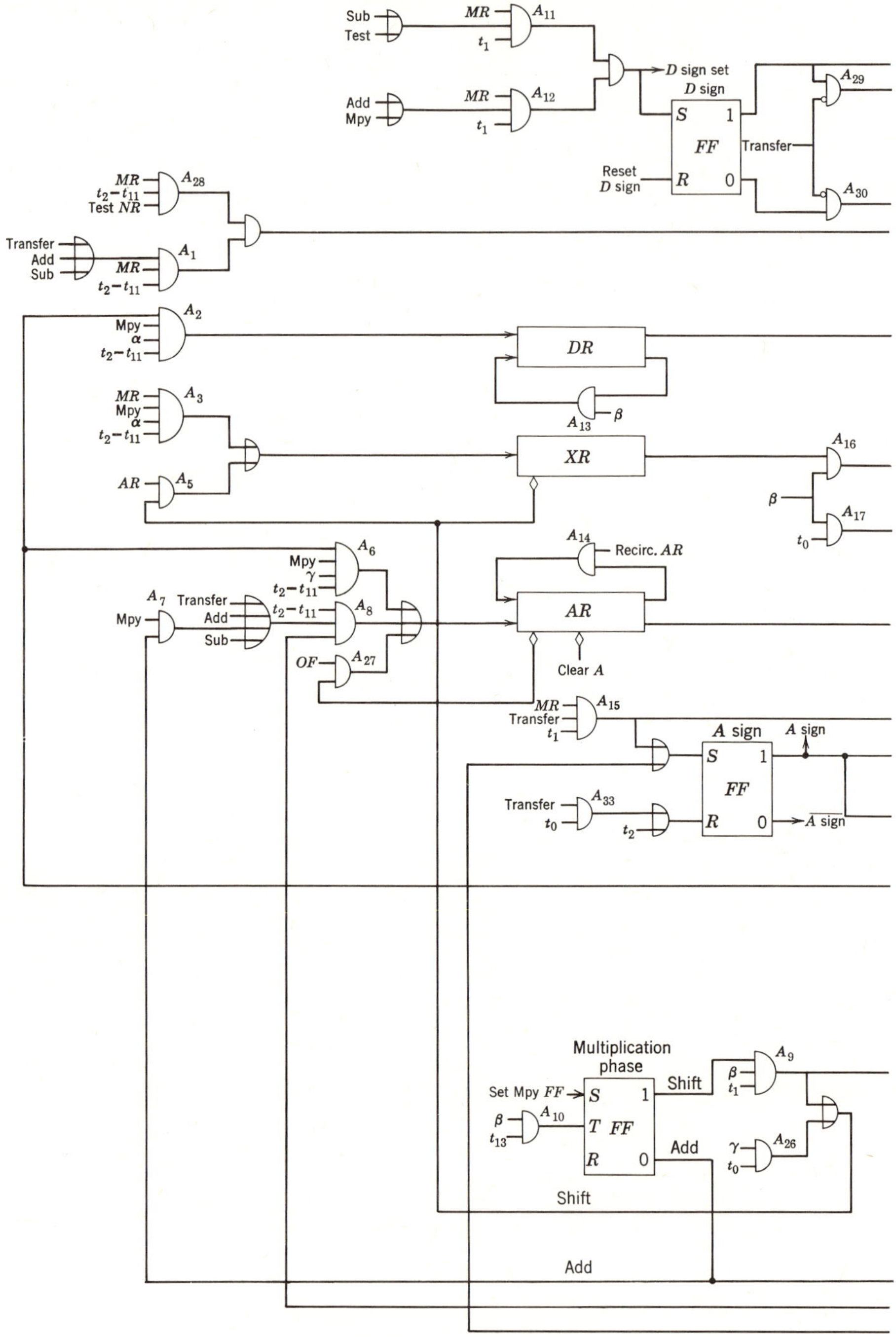

Figure 192 Arithmetic unit.

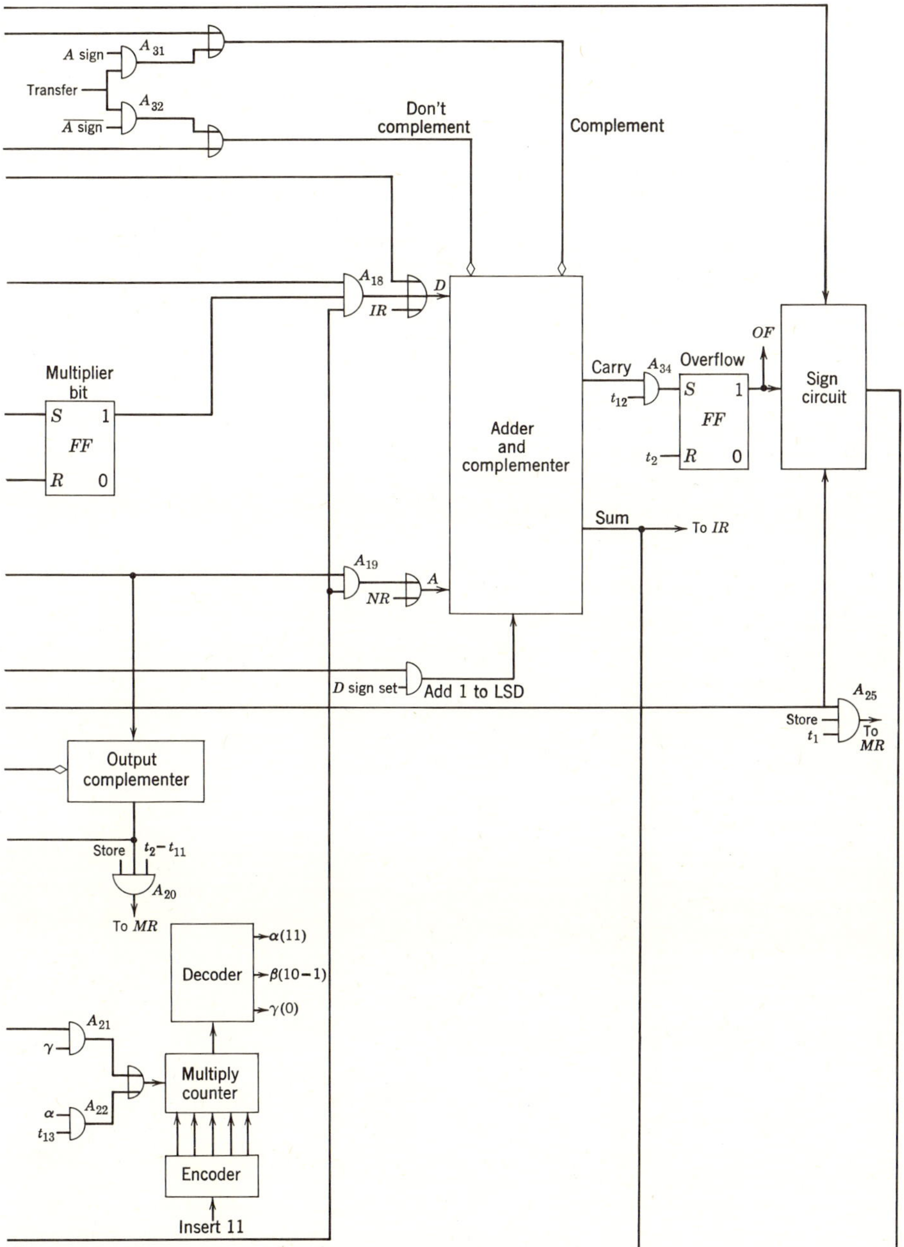
A sign
A_{31}
Transfer
A_{32}
$\overline{A\ \text{sign}}$
Don't complement
Complement
A_{18}
D
IR
Multiplier bit
S 1
FF
R 0
Adder and complementer
Carry
A_{34}
t_{12}
Overflow
S 1
FF
t_2
R 0
OF
Sign circuit
Sum
To IR
A_{19}
A
NR
D sign set
Add 1 to LSD
A_{25}
Store
t_1
To MR
Output complementer
Store
t_2-t_{11}
A_{20}
To MR
Decoder
α(11)
β(10−1)
γ(0)
A_{21}
γ
A_{22}
α
t_{13}
Multiply counter
Encoder
Insert 11

XR is a 10-bit shifting register for storing the multiplier. Associated with *XR* is a multiplier-bit flip-flop which controls the addition of the multiplicand to the accumulated partial product during the repeated addition and right-shift process used in multiplication.

The adder and complementer produce the sum or difference of the two terms applied to it and returns the result to *AR*. Whenever necessary, the adder complements and adds at the same time.

The output complementer converts results that are in 2's complement form back to absolute-value form while they are being transferred to memory.

The sign circuits determine whether the sign of the result, as stored in the *A* Sign flip-flop, should be positive or negative. This it does under control of the *A* and *D* Sign flip-flops and the presence or absence of overflow, from the adder and complementer.

The multiply counter together with its associated encoder and decoder, and the multiplication-phase flip-flop control the more extensive sequencing required to execute a Multiply instruction.

The Adder and Complementer

The adder and complementer is of the serial type. The augend and addend bits plus the carry bit from the previous position are combined in this circuit, and the sum bit is fed to the accumulator. The carry bit is delayed one bit-time and returned to the input of the adder in time to be combined with the next most significant augend and addend bits.

The augend is applied to the adder from *AR* which is storing negative words in complement form. The addend, on the other hand, is applied directly to the adder in absolute-value form. If the addend is positive, the adder behaves as any normal adder. If the addend is negative, the adder complements the addend and then adds. To convert the sum from 1's complement to 2's complement, a 1 is added to the *LSD*.

The adder and complementer is shown in Fig. 193. Notice that this circuit is the same as for the 1's complementer and adder given in Fig. 91 of Chapter 8, plus a small change that is needed to convert the 1's complement to the 2's complement. This change consists of inserting into the carry output a pulse obtained during t_1. After a delay, which in the specimen computer is achieved by timing pulses, this 1 is added into the *LSD* position—the t_2 position.

Add, Transfer, and Subtract Instructions

Before an Add instruction is given, the augend is present in absolute-value or complement form in *AR*, and the *A* Sign flip-flop is storing its sign.

When the Add command is translated, it produces read and rewrite micro-commands; at the same time, the address part of the instruction chooses the appropriate location in memory to be read. The word is read out of memory in parallel into *MR* during t_0. During t_1, if the sign bit is 1, it is applied via A_{12} to produce a *D* Sign Set signal. This signal then is sent to the carry circuit of the adder. It also sets the D sign flip-flop. If the sign is plus, the D Sign Set signal is not produced and the D sign flip-flop remains reset (this is the state in which the Reset D Sign signal placed it during t_0). During t_2 to t_{11} the 10 magnitude bits are transferred from MR to the adder and complementer via A_1. These are the bits labeled D in the adder and complementer diagram. At the same time that the magnitude bits of the addend (D bits) are being applied to the adder, the 10 augend bits stored in the A register (A bits) also are applied.

If the D sign flip-flop is set, the adder and complementer complements and adds; a 1 is added to the t_2 or LSD position. If the D sign flip-flop is reset, the adder produces simply a sum. As each sum bit is produced, it is fed back to AR. Thus after time t_{11}, the complete sum is stored in AR.

The sign of the sum is determined by the sign circuits. The sign of the sum depends upon the following factors:

1. The sign of D.
2. The sign of A.
3. The presence or absence of a carry from the most significant position (overflow OF).

The signs of D and of A are compared at t_1 immediately after the D sign flip-flop has received the addend sign bit, and the result of the comparison is stored in a flip-flop. If overflow occurs, at t_{12} it enters the sign circuits to modify its output. At t_{13}, the sign circuits set the A sign flip-flop under the conditions given in Table 33. Under all other conditions occurring during an Add instruction, the A sign flip-flop remains reset because of the Reset A Sign signal applied to it during t_0.

table 33 DETERMINATION OF SIGN OF SUM

Input			Output
A Sign	D Sign	Overflow	A Sign
−	−	Yes	−
+	−	Yes	+
−	+	Yes	+
+	+	Yes	+
−	−	No	−
+	−	No	−
−	+	No	−
+	+	No	+

A Transfer instruction is executed in a manner similar to the Add instruction except that AR and the A sign flip-flop are cleared to 0 during t_0, and the sign is transferred during t_1 to the A sign flip-flop instead of to the D sign flip-flop.

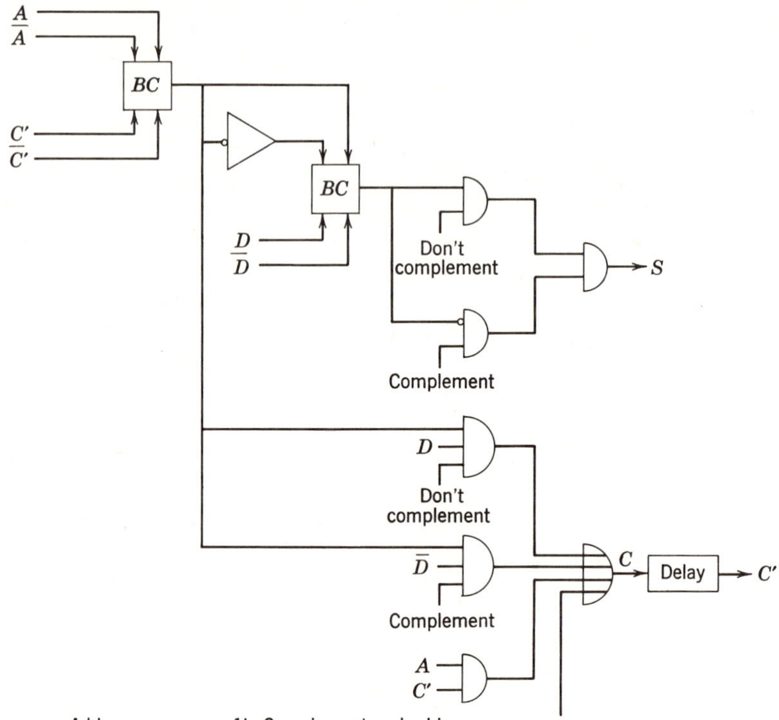

Add					1's Complement and add				
A	*D*	*C'*	*S*	*C*	*A*	*D'*	*C'*	*S*	*C*
0	0	0	0	0	0	0	0	1	0
1	0	0	1	0	1	0	0	0	1
0	1	0	1	0	0	1	0	0	0
1	1	0	0	1	1	1	0	1	0
0	0	1	1	0	0	0	1	0	1
1	0	1	0	1	1	0	1	1	1
0	1	1	0	1	0	1	1	1	0
1	1	1	1	1	1	1	1	0	1

Figure 193 Adder and complementer, 2's complement.

During t_2 to t_{11}, the magnitude bits applied to the adder through A_1 are added to zero coming from *AR*. The sum which is the same as the input word is sent to *AR*. Thus a simple transfer occurs from memory to *AR*, and it occurs this way if the *A* sign flip-flop is reset. If the *A* sign flip-flop is set, the complement of the word is sent to *AR*.

During algebraic subtraction, the adder operates the same way as during algebraic addition. The only difference is that the *D* sign flip-flop is set when the sign is *plus*, and *reset* when the sign is *minus*. Thus complementation during algebraic subtraction occurs at opposite times to its occurrence during algebraic addition.

Right Shift and Multiply Instructions

AR, *DR*, and *XR* are of the shifting type; they shift only when shift pulses are applied to them from the timing and shift control. When ten shift pulses are applied, all ten bits in the register are shifted out. If at the same time the recirculating gates in *AR* and *DR* are activated, the ten bits return to their original positions in the register after shifting.

To obtain a one-place right shift of a word stored in *AR*, only one shift pulse is applied. To obtain a right shift of two places, two shift pulses are applied, and so on. A right-shift instruction has a number in the address part specifying the number of shifts. This number is decoded to produce a signal which is applied to the timing and shift control; this circuit, in turn, produces the appropriate number of shift pulses to be applied to *AR*.

The ability to recirculate the contents of *AR* and *DR* and to perform a right shift in *AR* and *XR* makes these registers adaptable to the addition and right-shift process of multiplication. Also important for the multiplication process are: the multiplier-bit flip-flop which determines whether the least significant bit of the multiplier is 1 or 0; the multiplication-phase flip-flop which causes alternate add and shift stages; and the multiply counter with its encoder and decoder for controlling the sequencing of the multiplication instruction.

A multiplication is translated into several microcommands, one of which is "insert 11." At t_0 the insert-11 signal is applied to the encoder which inserts the binary equivalent of 11 into the multiply counter. With the aid of the decoder, the counter controls the 22 steps of the multiplication process, as follows.

During the first word-time, the number 11 is decoded into an α signal which controls rearrangement and transfer of words to take part in the multiplication operation. During the following 20 word-times, the counter is stepped *down* once every alternate word-time, and the decoder produces a β signal to allow the multiplication-phase flip-flop to control the shift and add stages. During the 22nd word-time, the counter is stepped down to 0, which is decoded as γ. The γ signal rearranges the words so that the product appears in *AR*.

The actual steps in the multiplication process are as follows. At t_0, α is produced. At t_0, also, the multiplier stored in memory is read into *MR*. During t_1, the sign is transferred from *MR* to the *D* sign flip-flop. During t_2–t_{11}, the word is transferred to *XR* via A_3. Note that the word enters *XR* in absolute-value form. At the same time that the multiplier magnitude bits are entering *XR*, the previously stored multiplicand bits in *AR* are transferred to *DR* via the output complementer and A_2. The output complementer converts the word into absolute-value form. Thus at the end of the first word-time of the multiplication, *DR* is storing the multiplicand, and *XR* is storing the multiplier.

During α, the sign circuits compare the two signs. If they are unequal, they set the *A* sign flip-flop. If they are equal, the *A* sign flip-flop stays reset.

At t_{13} the multiply counter is stepped down and the decoder produces β. At t_1 the coincidence of β and the shift signal produced by the multiplication-phase flip-flop produce a pulse at A_9 which causes *AR* and *XR* to shift one place to the right with the least significant bit of *AR* entering *XR* through A_5, the overflow bit entering the most significant position of *AR*, and the least significant bit in *XR* entering the multiplier-bit flip-flop through *AR*. If the least significant bit of *XR* is ONE, it sets the multiplier bit flip-flop. If it is ZERO, the flip-flop remains reset because of the pulse applied to it at t_0. At t_{13}, A_{10} produces a pulse which reverses the state of the multiplication-phase flip-flop and brings it to the add state. During the next word-time, A_{18} is open if the multiplier-bit flip-flop is set, and closed if the flip-flop is reset. If gate A_{18} is open, the multiplicand is shifted into the adder at the same time that the contents of *AR* (0 to start) are also shifted into the adder via A_{19}. The sum—the first partial product—is returned to *AR* via A_8. The multiplicand remains in *DR* since the recirculation gate is open. At the end of this word-time (at t_{13}), the multiplication-phase flip-flop is flipped to the shift state. As soon as this happens, the multiply counter steps down to 9.

Since the output of the decoder is still β, the shift and add stages are repeated as before. This shifting and adding under control of the least significant multiplier bit are performed for each of the ten multiplier bits. After 20 word-times the most significant 10 bits of the product appear in *AR*. The least significant 10 bits are in *XR*. The product is in absolute-value form.

To simplify mechanization as far as other instructions are concerned, during γ the absolute-value form of the product in *AR* is converted into complement form if the *A* sign flip-flop is set—storing a minus. This is easily accomplished by feeding the product from *AR* through the output complementer back to *AR* via A_6. The final shift signal to position the product properly is caused by the combination of γ and t_0 in gate A_{26}. The least significant 10 bits of the product remain in *XR* in absolute value form.

Store Instruction

The Store is a write-type instruction. At t_1, the sign is transferred from the *A* sign flip-flop via A_{25} to *MR*. During t_2–t_{11}, the contents of the register are transferred via the output complementer, which converts the word to absolute-value form, through A_{20} to *MR*. During t_{12}, the parity generator generates the appropriate parity bit, and during t_{13} the entire word is written into the location in memory specified by the address.

CONTROL (Fig. 194)

The control unit accepts instruction words from memory, modifies the address if the instruction is *NR* modifiable, and produces the microcommands and other control signals needed to execute the instructions. After the instruction is executed, an instruction counter (*IC*) is stepped to choose the location in memory from which the next instruction is read. The sequencing may be modified by a jump instruction.

Instruction Sequencing

Instruction sequencing of non-*NR* modifiable instructions is under control of the instruction-phase flip-flop. Upon completion of an instruction, the flip-flop is reset to the FETCH state. When the instruction-phase flip-flop is in this state, the contents of the instruction counter are applied to the column and row selectors to read the next instruction into *IR*.

At the end of the word-time, at t_{13}, the instruction-phase flip-flop is flipped to the EXECUTE state. In this position, the address part of the instruction is applied to the column and row selectors to choose the operand, and the command decoder and microcommand encoder translate the command into microcommands. The microcommands plus the timing and shift pulses control the execution of the instruction.

The execution takes one word-time for all Instructions except multiply. In the latter instruction an insert-11 microcommand is applied to the multiply counter which then takes over sequencing.

A microcommand produced for every instruction is the operation-complete pulse. This signal steps *IC* by one. At the end of the word-time, or for multiply at the end of the last word-time, the operation-complete pulse resets the instruction-phase flip-flop to the FETCH state, and the sequence repeats.

If the sign of the instruction is minus, the *N* sign flip-flop introduces an extra operation into the sequence. At time t_0, the *N* sign flip-flop is reset. At time t_1, the minus sign sets the flip-flop. As a result, the instruction bits entering from *MR* during t_2 to t_{11} are applied to the adder. During t_6 to t_{11}, the *NR* bits are also applied to the adder. The sum is immediately fed to *IR*.

While the addition is taking place, the instruction-phase flip-flop remains in the FETCH state since the *N*-minus signal inhibits the set input. As soon as the addition is completed at t_{12}, the *N* sign flip-flop is reset, and at t_{13} the instruction-phase flip-flop is set to EXECUTE. The remainder of the sequence is as before.

Addressed and Implicitly Addressed Instructions

Implicitly addressed nonmemory instructions are executed slightly differently from instructions possessing addresses. During the EXECUTE phase of an instruction with an address, the address bits are applied to the column and row selectors while the shift control feeds pulses to the appropriate register or registers to accomplish the transfer of data.

During an implicitly addressed instruction such as a right shift, the "open RS decoder" microcommand inhibits the inputs and the selectors, and sends the six most significant bits of *IR* to the right-shift decoder. The right-shift decoder decodes the bits representing the number of places to be shifted into a signal which causes the shift control to produce the number of shift pulses required to accomplish this shift.

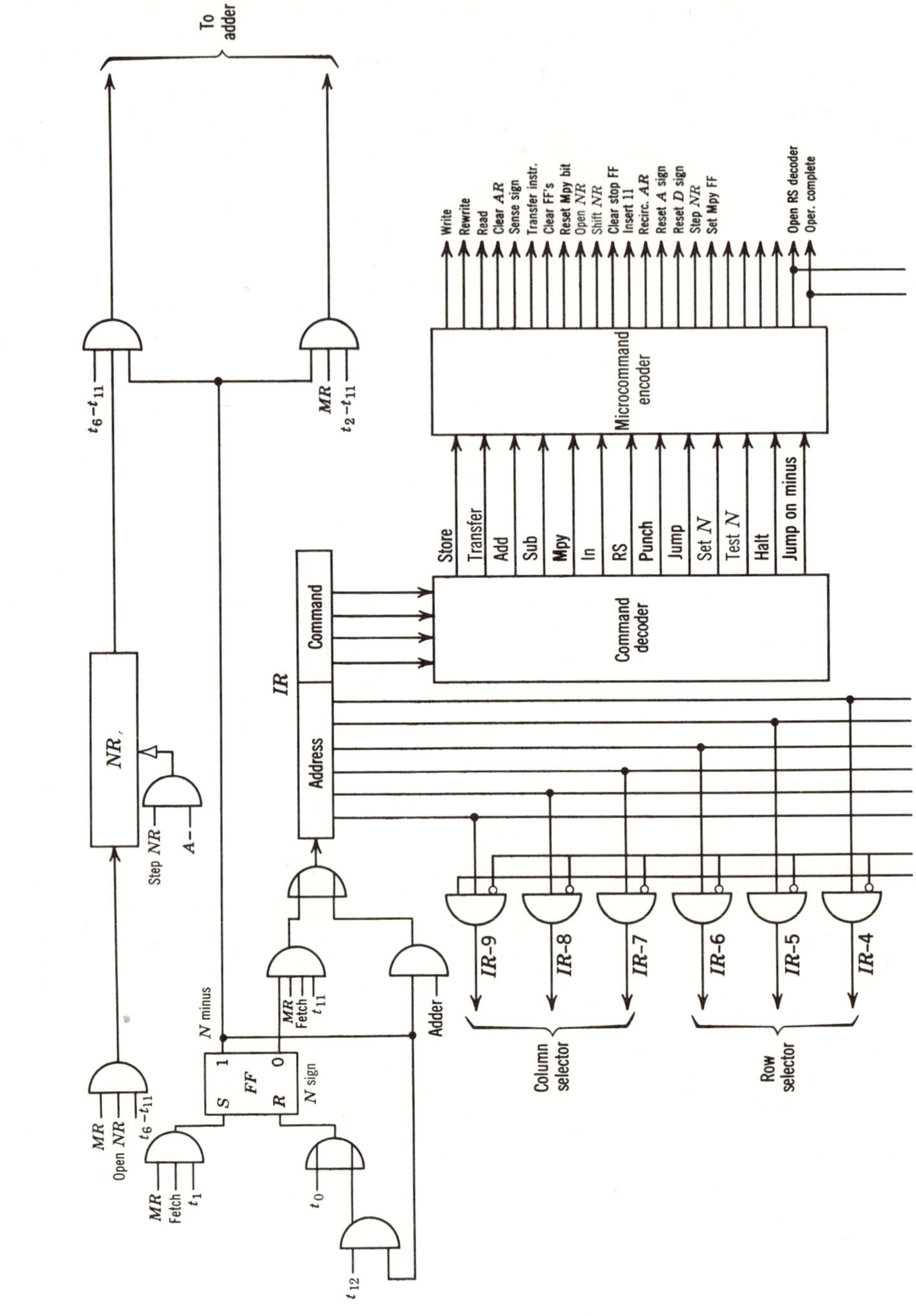
To adder
t_6–t_{11}
MR
t_2–t_{11}
NR
Step NR
A –
MR
Open NR
t_6–t_{11}
MR
Fetch
t_1
N minus
FF
S 1
R 0
N sign
t_0
t_{12}
MR
Fetch
t_{11}
Adder
IR
Command
Address
Command decoder
Store
Transfer
Add
Sub
Mpy
In
RS
Punch
Jump
Set N
Test N
Halt
Jump on minus
Microcommand encoder
Write
Rewrite
Read
Clear AR
Sense sign
Transfer instr.
Clear FF's
Reset Mpy bit
Open NR
Shift NR
Clear stop FF
Insert 11
Recirc. AR
Reset A sign
Reset D sign
Step NR
Set Mpy FF
Open RS decoder
Oper. complete
IR-9
IR-8
IR-7
IR-6
IR-5
IR-4
Column selector
Row selector

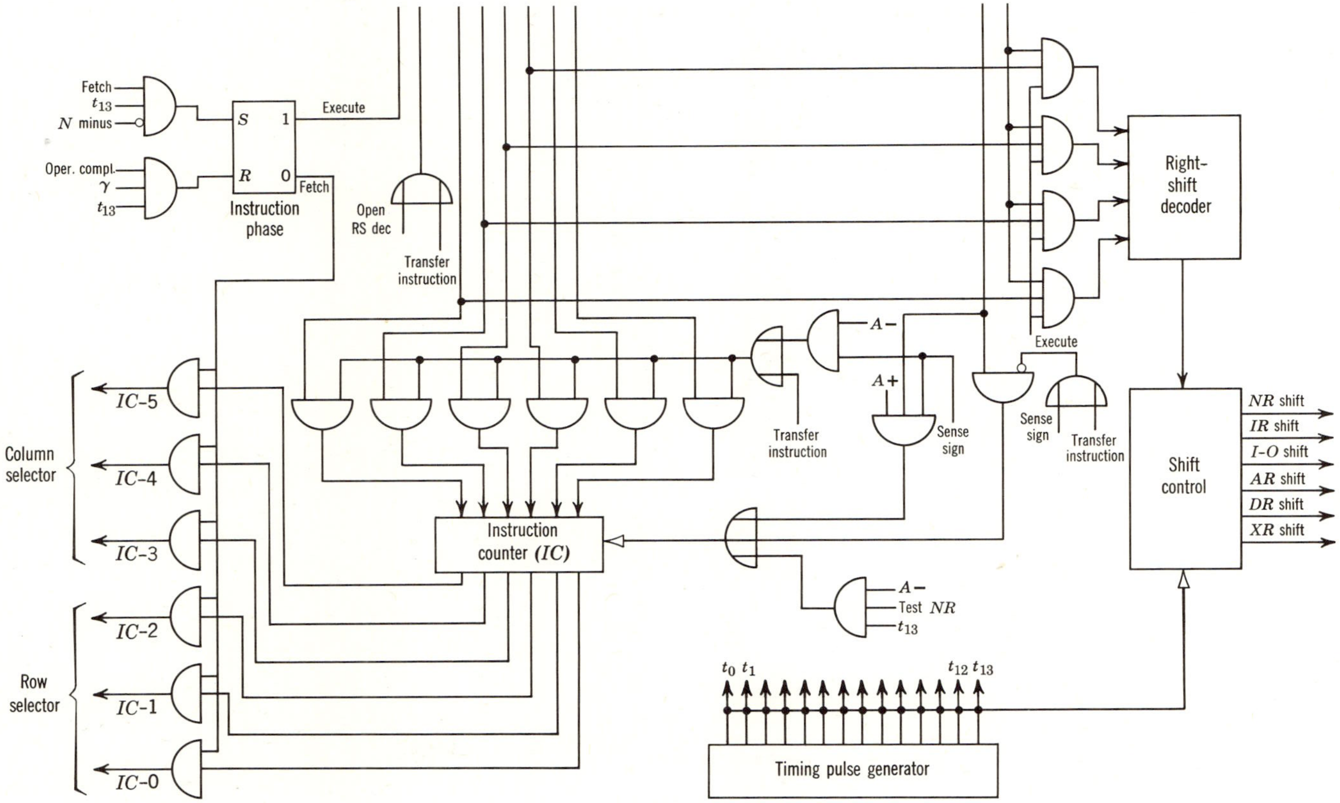

Figure 194 Control unit of specimen computer.

Modifying the Sequence

The basic machine sequence may be modified by a jump or a jump-on-minus instruction. One of the microcommands produced during the translation of the jump command is "transfer instruction." This signal inhibits the selectors, and causes the address to be transmitted to the instruction counter. The operation-complete pulse is prevented from stepping the instruction counter so that during the next FETCH phase the next instruction to be executed is obtained from the address in the instruction counter.

The Jump-on-Minus instruction transfers the address to *IC* only if the sign of *AR* is minus. The sense sign microcommand and the *A* Minus signal open the gates to *IC*. At the same time the sense sign micro-command inhibits the operation-complete pulse from stepping the *IC*. During the presence of *A*+ and Sense Sign signals, the operation-complete pulse steps the instruction counter normally.

Use of *NR*

To use *NR* in a program loop requires two instructions: Set *NR* and Test *NR*. The first stores a number in *NR* before the start of a loop. The second tests the loop each time the series of operations is performed to see if the loop should be broken. If no jump should occur out of the loop, a count pulse is applied to *NR* and the loop is repeated.

The Set *NR* command is translated into several microcommands, among which are read, rewrite, and open *NR*. The read microcommand causes the word given by the address part of the instruction to be read out into *MR* during t_0. During t_1 to t_{11}, the bits of the word are transmitted out of *MR*. However, the open *NR* and t_6–t_{11} signals allow only the six most significant bits to be shifted into *NR*.

The Test *NR* instruction acts as a combination comparison and count *NR* instruction. The comparison is performed by means of the following subtraction:

Contents of *NR* – contents of test location

where the test location is given by the address part of the instruction. The difference is stored in *AR*. The relative value of the two terms is determined by the *A* sign flip-flop. Since both terms are positive, a negative sign for the difference indicates the *NR* count has not reached the test number. Under these conditions *NR* is stepped once (by the step *NR* microcommand) and the instruction counter is stepped twice. The instruction counter is stepped once normally by the operation-complete pulse, the second time at t_{13}. If the *A* sign flip-flop is positive, the instruction counter is stepped only once.

The Console

The console (Fig. 195) stores controls and indicators for the performance of the following five functions:

1. Power control.
2. Operation control.
3. Program test.
4. Manual input.
5. Register display.

The logic associated with each of these groups is discussed briefly below. (This logic is not included in the logical block diagrams in order to keep these diagrams simple.)

Power Control

In this group are included the a-c power and d-c power switches and the fuses. The switches are merely for turning on the power and activating the machine's power supplies, and the fuses are for the protection of the several power supplies required for a digital computer.

Operation Control

In this group are included the start, stop, and mode switches; and the operate, paper-punch-on, and tape-reader-on indicators.

The start and stop switches control machine sequencing. The start push button clears the instruction counter to 0, and then allows the operation-complete pulse to step the instruction counter to maintain instruction sequencing. As long as the operation-complete pulse is allowed to step *IC*, the operate lamp is lit. When the stop push button is depressed, the operation-complete pulse is inhibited from stepping *IC* and sequencing stops.

The mode switch has three positions: automatic, test, and load. In the automatic position, normal sequencing occurs. In the test position the program test switches are made operative. In the load position, the number 40 is introduced into the instruction counter, and then automatic sequencing begins. If the location 40 in memory is storing the first instruction of the loading routine, a program stored on paper tape may be entered into memory.

The paper-punch-on and tape-reader-on indicators are in series with the on-off switches of the respective devices. They therefore light when these equipments are operating.

Program Test

In this group are included the one-instruction, break-point, and jump–no-jump switches; and the halt, parity error, and overflow indicators.

The one-instruction switch executes one instruction of the program at one time. Activation of the switch produces a simulated operation-complete pulse which steps the instruction counter. The instruction stored in this new location given by the instruction counter is then executed. The normally produced operation-complete pulse is inhibited, and sequencing stops until the one-instruction switch is depressed again.

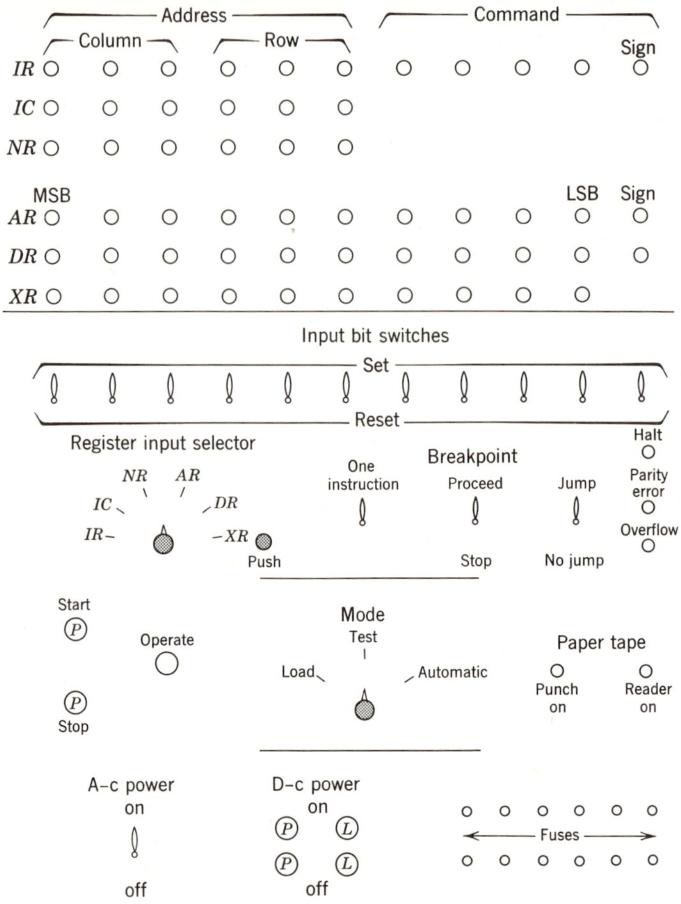

Figure 195 Control panel of specimen computer.

The breakpoint and jump–no-jump switches are used together. The breakpoint switch causes the computer to stop at key points in the program being tested. The jump–no-jump switch may then be used to continue normal machine sequencing or to modify sequencing. In the stop position the breakpoint switch causes the computer to stop at the occurrence of a conditional jump instruction: the combination of the breakpoint stop signal plus the jump signal inhibits the operation-complete pulse from stepping the instruction counter, and inhibits gates between the address part of the instruction register and the instruction counter. When the breakpoint switch is placed in the proceed position, one of the above paths is opened: the gates between *IR* and *IC* if the jump–no-jump switch is in the jump position; the gate allowing the operation-complete pulse to step the counter if the jump–no-jump switch is in the no-jump position.

The halt, parity error, and overflow indicators light whenever the indicated conditions occur. The overflow lights only when the overflow represents an exceed-capacity.

Manual Input

Manual input is controlled by the input-bit switches and the register input selector. Bits are entered by placing the input bit switches in the ONE or ZERO positions. The setting of the register input selector determines to which register this number is transferred. The actual shifting of the bits into the chosen register starts when the push button is depressed.

Register Display

The register indicator lamps are connected to the outputs of each of the flip-flops comprising the registers. An indicator is lit when a ONE is stored; unlit when a ZERO is stored.

PROGRAMMING

Most programming is not done in machine code but in a programming language, such as FORTRAN. However, the specimen computer has such a small memory that it could not store the compiler necessary to translate from FORTRAN to machine code. In addition, the specimen computer cannot handle alphanumeric characters. Nevertheless the programming sequence is given here, starting with the FORTRAN statements, in order to review the major steps. After the FORTRAN statements are converted to machine code, the code is loaded and debugged before actual execution.

Fortran Program

The program to be developed is one for finding the smallest number in a group of 60 numbers. Basically the program is as follows. The 60 numbers are stored on the punched paper tape, and the routine asks the tape reader to read-in one word at a time and store it in a location in memory called the "latest number location." This latest number is compared with the smallest number obtained from the previous comparison. If the latest number is the smaller of the two, the latest number is transferred to the smallest number location. If the previous smallest number is still the smallest, the next word is read-in from the tape for another comparison. This loop is repeated until 60 numbers have been compared. After this the smallest number is punched onto paper tape.

table 35 SPECIMEN COMPUTER COMMAND CODE

Decimal	Command Code: Octal	Command Code: Binary	Command Code: Name	Description
1	01	0001	Store	* STORE *AR* contents in location given by address.
2	02	0010	Transfer	* TRANSFER TO *AR*, contents of location given by address.
3	03	0011	Add	* ADD algebraically contents of location given by address to *AR* contents; leave sum in *AR*.
4	04	0100	Subtract	* SUBTRACT algebraically contents of location given by address from *AR* contents; leave difference in *AR*.
5	05	0101	Input	INPUT a word from punched paper tape to location given by address.
6	06	0110	Punch	PUNCH onto paper tape word stored in location given by address.
7	07	0111	Test *NR*	TEST *NR* by subtracting contents of location given by address from *NR* contents. If difference is plus, sequence normally; if minus, step *NR* and jump to instruction stored in location following next location.
8	10	1000	Jump	JUMP to instruction stored in location given by address.
9	11	1001	Halt	HALT computation.
10	12	1010	Multiply	* MULTIPLY *AR* contents by contents of location given by address; leave product in *AR*.
11	13	1011	Shift right	SHIFT RIGHT *AR* contents a number of places given in address part of instruction.
12	14	1100	Set *NR*	SET *NR* by transferring to it address bits of word stored in location given by address.
13	15	1101	Jump on minus	TEST sign of *AR* and JUMP ON MINUS to instruction at location given by address; if it is plus, sequence normally.

* These commands are modified by *NR* when the sign of the instruction word is minus.

table 36 NUMBER COMPARISON

Location of Instruction	Instruction Code: Command	Instruction Code: Address	Explanation	FORTRAN Statement Number
01	14	16	SET *NR* to 1.	
02	05	21	INPUT first word from paper tape to *smallest number* location.	1
03	05	20	INPUT (second) word from paper tape to *latest number* location.	3
04	02	21	TRANSFER *smallest number* to *AR*.	
05	04	20	SUBTRACT *latest number* from *smallest number*.	4
06	15	11	JUMP ON MINUS to instruction stored in 11. If *AR* is plus, sequence normally.	
07	02	20	TRANSFER *latest number* to *AR*.	5
10	01	21	STORE *latest number* as *smallest number*.	
11	07	17	TEST *NR* to see if 59 comparisons have been made. If so, sequence normally. If not, add one to *NR* contents and jump to instruction in 13.	2
12	10	14	JUMP to 14.	
13	10	03	JUMP to 03 to repeat loop.	
14	06	21	PUNCH *smallest number*.	6
15	11	00	HALT.	
16	00	01	Constant.	
17	00	73	Octal for 59 (for testing count).	
20			*Latest number* location.	
21			*Smallest number* location.	

If

$$\text{smallest number} = X$$

$$\text{latest number} = Y$$

the FORTRAN statements of this number comparison program are given in Table 34. The first statement asks for an input of a word into the "smallest number" location. Statement 2 states that the following 3 statements (through statement 5) should be repeated 59 times: first the next word is taken off the tape and placed in the "latest number" location; if the difference $X-Y$ is less than or equal to 0, return to statement 2 to repeat the loop; if the difference is greater than 0 go to the next statement (5) where the "latest number" is substituted for the "smallest number." After the loop is executed 59 times, taking care of the 60 words, statement 6 causes the "smallest number" to be punched.

table 34 NUMBER COMPARISON PROGRAM

Statement Number	Statement
1	INPUT *X*
2	*DO* 5 *I* = 1, 59
3	INPUT *Y*(*I*)
4	*IF* (*X*−*Y*(*I*)) 2, 2, 5
5	*X* = *Y*(*I*)
6	PUNCH *X*
7	END

Machine Code

The above FORTRAN statements, if they are inserted into a computer that also stores a FORTRAN compiler, are translated into machine code. These statements usually are entered via punched cards. Assume that this is accomplished by a specimen computer similar to the one presented here but that it is of greater capacity and capability. The result of this translation is shown in Table 36. The command code of the specimen computer is presented in Table 35 for reference.

Notice that some statements such as numbers 1, 3, and 6 have a 1-to-1 correspondence with instructions in machine code. Other statements are converted into a group of instructions:

Statement 4 is translated into Transfer, Subtract, and Jump-on-Minus instructions.

Statement 5 is translated to a Transfer and Store.

Statement 2 is translated into a Test *NR* and two Jump instructions.

To be able to do the looping, however, the first instruction in the table, Set *NR*, is needed to initiate the count operation.

Also notice that the order of the instructions is not exactly the same as for the FORTRAN statements.

Loading

The FORTRAN compiler usually punches out punched cards with the above machine code in them. They then are loaded into the computer. Assume that in the "sophisticated" specimen computer the code is produced in octal form on the tape, and this tape then must be reinserted. When this is done the words of the program should be stored in locations 01 to 21. How do we go about entering these words into their proper locations?

Loading is accomplished by means of a punched paper tape reader and a loading routine stored in memory; this routine is called into operation when the mode switch is placed in the load position. The location in which the first instruction of the program is to be stored is entered manually by means of the input-bit switches and the register input selector.

The sequence of operations required to load a program is as follows. First the program is punched onto paper tape; in addition to the actual program, the number of words in the program—17 or octal 21 in the previous illustration—is punched as the *first* word. This tape is mounted on the reader which is then placed into operation. By means of the input-bit switches, the location of the first word of the program—01 in our examlpe—is entered. The register input selector is placed in the *AR* position and the push button is depressed. This causes the number stored on the panel to be transferred to *AR*. After this is accomplished, the mode switch is placed in the load position, causing the computer to start sequencing with the instruction in location 40, the first instruction of the loading routine.

The loading program stores an input-instruction constant which is continuously modified to cause entry of succeeding words on tape to successive memory locations. At the start of the routine, the address of the first word of the program is added to the input-instruction constant and, when it is executed, the first instruction word is transferred to the first address reserved in memory for the program. *NR* keeps count of the number of words entered, and also modifies the input-instruction constant each time the loop is repeated.

The entire loading program is shown in Table 37. In step 40, the address of the first program word is stored. In step 41, the first word on the tape, specifying the number of program words, is stored. In steps 42 and 43, the input-instruction constant is subtracted from the "location of the first word,"

−07 00000	Input instruction constant
−00 00001	"Location of first program word"
−07 00001	Input instruction

and the resultant input instruction is stored for later use. In step 46, *NR* is set to 0 in preparation for the program loop occupying steps 47 to 50. Step 47

table 37 LOADING ROUTINE FOR SPECIMEN COMPUTER

Location of Instruction	Instruction Code: Command	Instruction Code: Address	Explanation
40	01	55	STORE "location of first program word" (previously transferred from panel to *AR*).
41	05	56	INPUT first word from tape into "number of program words" location.
42	02	54	TRANSFER input-instruction constant to *AR*.
43	04	55	SUBTRACT "location of first program word" from input-instruction constant. *Result:* – INPUT 01.
44	01	57	STORE in input-instruction word location and
45	01	47	STORE in 47.
46	14	53	SET *NR* to 0.
47	–05	(01)	INPUT (first) instruction word of program into the (first) location of the program.
50	07	56	TEST *NR* to see whether the specified number of program words have been transferred to memory.
51	11	00	HALT computer if all program words have been entered.
52	10	47	JUMP to 47 to repeat loop if all program words have not yet been entered.
53	00	00000	Constant.
54	–05	00000	Input-instruction constant.
55			Address of first instruction word stored here.
56			Number of program words location.
57			Input-instruction word location.

stores the manufactured input instruction. The first time it is executed, the first program word is transferred from the tape to the first location in the program. This is immediately followed by a test to see whether the specified number of program words has been entered. During the first time through the loop, the computer jumps to location 52, at which point a jump to the instruction in 47 causes the loop to repeat.

During the second time through the loop, *NR* stores a 1, thus sending the second program word to the following location in memory. Each successive program word is entered into a successive memory location until all words have been entered. At this point the Test-*NR* instruction causes the computer to sequence to 51, and the machine halts.

Program Debugging

Programming is the art of describing a task so completely that a machine can perform it by following blindly the step-by-step procedures given. Because of this requirement for meticulous detail, the first results of a programmer's efforts are rarely correct. To test out or debug the program, the programmer has program test controls available to him. In the specimen computer, he has the one-instruction, breakpoint, and jump–no-jump switches. These program test switches are used together with the register display lights to find mistakes in the program.

The machine-coded number-comparison program may be debugged with the aid of the one-instruction switch and the register indicators. After the program is loaded, and a group of 60 punched numbers is mounted on the paper tape reader, the one-instruction switch is depressed. The first instruction of the program is executed after which the contents of *IC*, *IR*, *AR*, and *NR* are viewed on the panel. The one-instruction switch is depressed again, the second instruction in the program is executed, and the contents of the same registers are viewed once more. In this way, the results of each instruction are apparent, and the programmer can tell if there is a mistake in the program. A group of numbers to be compared and the contents of the registers during such a step-by-step operation are shown in Table 38.

The above procedure may become tedious, especially in long, complicated programs. Faster debugging may be obtained by placing the break-point switch on stop. The computer sequences until it reaches a branch instruction, and then stops to allow the programmer to view the contents of the registers. After he is satisfied, he flips the breakpoint switch to the proceed position, and the computer sequences until the next breakpoint is reached. Table 38 shows the contents of the registers at each break-point in the above program.

When the computer stops at a breakpoint, a negative number in *AR* signifies that a jump will be executed next. If the programmer feels that the result of the previous operation is in error—the contents of *AR* should be +, for instance—he may test his belief by throwing the jump–no-jump switch to the no-jump position before throwing the breakpoint switch to proceed. If the machine now produces expected results, his hunch was correct.

table 38 DEBUGGING NUMBER-COMPARISON ROUTINE

Numbers to be Compared		Contents of Registers During Each Step of Routine				
		IC	*IR*	*AR*	*NR*	
1st	1200	01	14 16		1	
2nd	1300	02	03 21		1	
3rd	0500	03	05 20		1	
4th	0700	04	02 21	1200	1	
5th	1400	05	04 20	−0100	1	
.	.	06	15 11	−0100	1	Breakpoint
.	.	11	07 17	−0072	2	Breakpoint
.	.	13	10 03	−0072	2	
.	0200	03	05 20	−0072	2	
60th	0600	04	02 21	1200	2	
		05	04 20	0700	2	
		06	15 11	0700	2	Breakpoint
		07	02 20	0500	2	
		10	01 21	0500	2	
		11	07 17	−0071	3	Breakpoint
		13	10 03	−0071	3	
		03	05 20	−0071	3	
		04	02 21	0500	3	
		05	04 20	−0200	3	
		06	15 11	−0200	3	Breakpoint
		11	07 17	−0070	4	Breakpoint
		13	10 03	−0070	4	
		03	05 20	−0070	4	
		04	02 21	0500	4	
		05	04 20	−0900	4	
		.		.	.	Breakpoint
		.		.	.	
		.		.	.	
		.		.	.	Breakpoint
		03	05 20	−0002	72	
		04	02 21	0500	72	
		05	04 20	+0300	72	
		06	15 11	+0300	72	Breakpoint
		07	02 20	+0200	72	
		10	01 21	0200	72	
		11	07 17	−0001	73	Breakpoint
		13	10 03	−0001	73	
		03	05 20	−0001	73	
		04	02 21	0200	73	
		05	04 20	−0400	73	
		06	15 11	−0400	73	Breakpoint
		11	07 17	0000	73	Breakpoint
		12	10 14	0000	73	
		14	06 21	0000	73	
		15	11 00	0000	73	

Compilers have features that allow the programmer to debug the program while it is being compiled.

OPERATION AND MAINTENANCE

Normal Operation

Once a program is loaded and debugged, the mode switch is placed in the automatic position, and the computer executes the program. During operation, the register display lights flash on and off to indicate the changing contents of the registers. All is well, provided the following lights are on:

1. Operate.
2. Paper punch on.
3. Tape reader on.

The halt, parity, and overflow indicators are normally not on. Upon completion of a routine, the halt indicator goes on. If it goes on before the routine is completed, it indicates that a machine malfunction has occurred:

1. In the memory or arithmetic units if the parity indicator goes on at the same time.
2. In the arithmetic unit if the overflow indicator goes on at the same time.

Test Routine

To forestall the occurrence of machine breakdown during operation, the specimen computer may be tested beforehand by means of a test routine. A test routine simply makes the machine go through its paces. It consists of a group of instructions utilizing all the variations of machine commands and transferring words to and from every address in memory. At the end of the routine, the final result is compared with what the result should be if all the operations have been properly performed. If the two are alike, the machine is in operating order. If the two are unlike, something is wrong with the machine and it should be debugged before a program is run on it.

Diagnostic Routine

A more sophisticated form of trouble-finding routine is the diagnostic routine. This routine not only tests the machine to see if it is operating but also determines in what area the trouble is! The operation of this routine is based on the fact that every instruction utilizes only certain functional blocks, some functional blocks being shared by several types of instruction. The routine may therefore determine the cause of trouble by a process of elimination.

In outline, the diagnostic routine may operate as follows. First, since a comparison of numbers is required for practically every test, the adder is tested first. This is done by performing a series of additions on a set of standard numbers and then comparing the final result obtained with the correct sum. If the two are unlike, something is wrong with the adder. If the two are alike, the adder is tested further by means of a series of subtractions.

DR and *XR*, the multiplier-bit flip-flop, and the multiply counter are tested by performing several multiplication instructions on standard numbers and then comparing the results obtained with the correct results. If the results are unlike, the actual location of arithmetic malfunction may be pinned down further by performing right-shift instructions.

If the arithmetic unit has been tested and found to be in operating order, a series of store and transfer instructions transmitting a definite number between *AR* and every address in memory is performed. At the end of this series, the word finally found in *AR* is compared with the original word. If they are alike, the memory is in operating order; if not, the memory is not functioning properly.

If both the arithmetic and memory units are functioning properly, the control unit may be tested by performing jumps and *NR* modifiable instructions. Again, a comparison may be used to determine if the control is functioning properly.

Next the reader and input unit are tested by entering a word from the reader into memory, and then comparing this word with the same word stored in another location in memory. If the two are unlike, a malfunction is present in either the reader or the input unit. If the two are alike, the input system is in operating order.

Naturally, the routine is more devious than described. By a judicious choice of instructions and factors to be transferred and operated upon, it is possible to develop a diagnostic routine which would narrow the malfunction to a very small area in the machine. The routine may be written so that, when a malfunction is discovered, a code number specifying the functional area at fault is punched out on the paper tape.

Exercises

1. Assume that the specimen computer is to be modified to handle data words consisting of 4-bit decimal digits.
   a. If each digit has its own parity bit, how many bits are needed per data word? What is the maximum possible size of the number that can be stored in a data word?
   b. How many planes are required for the coincident-current memory?
   c. If 64 storage locations are needed, how many commands may be encoded, assuming that the instruction word is of the same size as the data word?
   d. How would you modify the parity detection circuit in the memory unit to handle the 2 digits of the word?
   e. How would you modify the arithmetic unit to handle the 2 digits of the word?

2. Assume the specimen computer is to be modified to handle 8-bit USASCII characters instead of words.

a. How large should *AR* be?

b. If two 8-bit characters are used per instruction word, one for the command, the other for the address, how many storage locations may be accessed? If 16 commands are required, how many index registers may be accessed?

c. Assume that the computer has a 2-address instruction word, where each address gives the location of an operand and each address is modifiable by 1 of 15 index registers. Assume that the memory is to be enlarged to 4096 locations and the commands increased to 256. What would the instruction word format be? What affect would this change have on instruction sequencing?

d. If a data word in the above consists of a variable number of characters, and each address in the instruction refers to the most significant character of the word, how must the format be modified to indicate data word size? How must the control unit be modified to handle this variable size word?

3. Assume that data transmission throughout the specimen computer were parallel by the 8 bits of a USASCII character.

a. Would a read-write cycle be needed?

b. How would it be different from the one used in the specimen computer?

c. Would MR be needed?

d. How would you modify the parity detector?

4. Would the timing pulse generator be needed if we replaced the memory unit by one possessing nondestructive readout? If not, how could sequencing be achieved?

5. Assume the memory unit uses a magnetic drum.

a. How would you store words, if data transmission throughout the computer were serial by bit? Would you need a timing pulse generator?

b. How would you store words if data transmission were in parallel:

6. Assume a computer in which it takes a memory cycle to read or write a character. Assume, too, that simple arithmetic manipulations, for example, those required for addition, can be accomplished during such a read or write cycle. Determine how many memory cycles are needed to execute the following:

a. A 1-address instruction word consists of 3 characters: 1 for the command, two for the address. A data word consisting of 3 characters is to be stored.

b. A 2-address instruction word consists of 5 characters: 1 for the command, 2 for each operand address both of which refer to operands. Two data words consisting of 6 characters each are to be added and the sum left in *AR*.

c. A 1-address instruction word consists of 2 characters: 1 for the command, 1 for the address. Assume that 56 is previously stored in *AR*. Multiply it by 23, using a process similar to the one used by the specimen computer, except modified for decimal operation.

7. Assume a computer similar to the specimen computer, except that it has an expandable memory. This expansion is achieved by adding memory modules similar to the 64-word memory the specimen possesses.

a. To be able to access 16 such memory modules, how many additional address bits are needed?
b. How can these extra address bits be added without modifying too much the organization of the specimen computer?
c. How would you modify the address selection circuits to accommodate this memory modularity?

8. In the input-output system of the specimen computer, replace the paper tape reader with one reading 8-hole tape. This would allow input and output of 8-bit characters.
a. How would you modify the I/O unit to receive these 8-bit characters, and to transmit 2-character words in parallel to other areas of the computer. For output, it would receive in parallel 2-character words and would transmit 1 character at a time to be punched.
b. Assume data is stored in the above punched paper tape reader as a block consisting of 10 characters. How would the I/O unit need to be modified to allow 1 instruction to cause a transfer of a complete block from reader through I/O register to memory?
c. If (**b**) above were handled by means of a 4-character control word stored in memory, what should the control word read if we want the first word of the block to be entered into address 20?
d. How many memory cycles would (**c**) above take, assuming a cycle-stealing approach in which the control word must be read out of memory and the modified control word returned to memory for each data word transferred?

9. How would you modify the I/O unit if paper tape is replaced with punched cards?

10. How would you change the adder and complementer if the binary words in the specimen computer are to be added in parallel?

11. How would you modify the arithmetic unit of the specimen computer to execute the following:
a. Add Magnitude—addition without reference to the signs of the operands?
b. Floating-point Addition?
c. Logical Multiply—compare each bit in *AR* with the corresponding bit of the operand. Store its original value in *AR* if the corresponding bit of the operand is the same; store 0 in *AR* if the two compared bits are different?

12. The overflow listed in Table 33 is not an overflow alarm which may occur on completion of an arithmetic operation.
a. What is the difference between the two types of overflow?
b. Under which of the conditions given in Table 33 should an overflow alarm occur?

13. Assume that the control unit of the specimen computer is to be modified to sequence asynchronously. However, instead of using delay elements (as per Fig. 169*c*) a counter (as per Fig. 79) is used. How would this affect the control?

14. How would you modify the control unit of the specimen computer:
a. To sequence 3-address instructions?
b. To sequence 4-address instructions?

APPENDIX
Codes

Numbers and alphabetical and other control characters may be represented by many types of codes, some of which have become standard. Numeric codes (both ordinary and reflected) and 2 of the standards are described below.

NUMERIC CODES

Only 4 bits are needed to encode a number. However, 5, 6, or even 7 bits may be needed to make the code error detecting and error correcting.

Four-Bit Codes

Codes may be weighted or nonweighted. A weighted code is obtained by placing a weight on each order bit. For instance, binary coded decimal is obtained by weighting the bits 8421. Table A1 shows several possible weighted codes.

table A1 WEIGHTED 4-BIT CODES

Order of Bit	Order of Bit	Order of Bit
4 3 2 1	4 3 2 1	4 3 2 1
5 2 1 1	6 2 2 1	7 3 2 1
4 3 1 1	3 3 2 1	4 4 2 1
5 3 1 1	4 3 2 1	5 4 2 1
6 3 1 1	5 3 2 1	6 4 2 1
4 2 2 1	6 3 2 1	7 4 2 1
5 2 2 1	2 4 2 1	8 4 2 1

Among the nonweighted codes are the excess-3 and the excess-6 codes. The excess-3 code has a value equal to 3 more than the bit value it would have using 8421 weights; the excess-6 code has a value equal to 6 more than the 8421 value.

Table A2 presents values for two weighted and two nonweighted codes.

table A2 EXAMPLES OF WEIGHTED AND NONWEIGHTED CODES

	Weighted		Non-Weighted	
Decimal	8421	5421	Excess-3	Excess-6
0	0000	0000	0011	0110
1	0001	0001	0100	0111
2	0010	0010	0101	1000
3	0011	0011	0110	1001
4	0100	0100	0111	1010
5	0101	1000	1000	1011
6	0110	1001	1001	1100
7	0111	1010	1010	1101
8	1000	1011	1011	1110
9	1001	1100	1100	1111

In several coded-decimal systems, replacing 0's with 1's and 1's with 0's produces the 9's complement. Codes that have this happy facility are called self-complementing codes. Several examples of self-complementing codes are given in Table A3.

table A3 SELF-COMPLEMENTING CODES

Decimal	2421	5211	4311	4221	3321	Excess-3
0	0000	0000	0000	0000	0000	0011
1	0001	0001	0001	0001	0001	0100
2	0010	0011	0011	0010	0010	0101
3	0011	0110	0100	0011	0011	0110
4	0100	0111	0110	1000	0101	0111
5	1011	1000	1001	0111	1010	1000
6	1100	1001	1011	1100	1100	1001
7	1101	1100	1100	1101	1101	1010
8	1110	1110	1110	1110	1110	1011
9	1111	1111	1111	1111	1111	1100

Error Detecting Codes

An error detecting code is one in which at least 2 bits must change when going from the representation of one digit to the representation of another. This may be accomplished by a parity bit added to the 8421 code, as shown in Table A4. In this code to switch from 1 to 3, not only must order bit 2 be switched from 0 to 1, the parity check bit also must be switched from 0 to 1.

Three other error detecting codes are given in Table A4. In each of these—2 out of 5, modified bi-quinary and modified qui-binary—each digit must have two and only two ONE'S. Obviously, then, 2 bits must be changed to accomplish a change in digit representation.

table A4 ERROR DETECTING CODES

	8421 with Parity Check	2 out of 5	Modified Bi-Quinary	Modified Qui-Binary
Order of Bit	5 4 3 2 1	5 4 3 2 1	7 6 5 4 3 2 1	7 6 5 4 3 2 1
Weight	Check 8 4 2 1	7 4 2 1 0	5 0 4 3 2 1 0	8 6 4 2 0 1 0
Decimal				
0	1 0 0 0 0	1 1 0 0 0	0 1 0 0 0 0 1	0 0 0 0 1 0 1
1	0 0 0 0 1	0 0 0 1 1	0 1 0 0 0 1 0	0 0 0 0 1 1 0
2	0 0 0 1 0	0 0 1 0 1	0 1 0 0 1 0 0	0 0 0 1 0 0 1
3	1 0 0 1 1	0 0 1 1 0	0 1 0 1 0 0 0	0 0 0 1 0 1 0
4	0 0 1 0 0	0 1 0 0 1	0 1 1 0 0 0 0	0 0 1 0 0 0 1
5	1 0 1 0 1	0 1 0 1 0	1 0 0 0 0 0 1	0 0 1 0 0 1 0
6	1 0 1 1 0	0 1 1 0 0	1 0 0 0 0 1 0	0 1 0 0 0 0 1
7	0 0 1 1 1	1 0 0 0 1	1 0 0 0 1 0 0	0 1 0 0 1 0 0
8	0 1 0 0 0	1 0 0 1 0	1 0 0 1 0 0 0	1 0 0 0 0 0 1
9	1 1 0 0 1	1 0 1 0 0	1 0 1 0 0 0 0	1 0 0 0 0 1 0

Error Correcting Codes

An error correcting code is one which cannot only detect that an error exists but can specify in which bit position it occurs; by flipping this bit value it corrects the error. To be error correcting, *three* bits must change when going from one digit representation to another: two to detect the error, and the third to locate the bit position at fault.

Notice that the use of horizontal together with vertical parity can produce error correcting capability if the message is short.

table A5 8421 CODE WITH ERROR CORRECTING BITS

	Check Bits			Bit Order			
Digit	C_3	C_2	C_1	4	3	2	1
0	1	1	1	0	0	0	0
1	0	0	0	0	0	0	1
2	1	0	0	0	0	1	0
3	0	1	1	0	0	1	1
4	0	1	0	0	1	0	0
5	1	0	1	0	1	0	1
6	0	0	1	0	1	1	0
7	1	1	0	0	1	1	1
8	0	0	1	1	0	0	0
9	1	1	0	1	0	0	1

By introducing three types of vertical parity check bits with the 8421 code, an error correcting code may be obtained, as shown in Table A5. The three check bits check different bit combinations as follows:

Parity Check Bit	Order Positions			
	4	*3*	*2*	*1*
C_1		X	X	X
C_2	X		X	X
C_3	X	X		X

This means that with the following

Check Bit Failures an error has occurred in *Bit Order*	
C_1, C_2 & C_3	1
C_1 & C_2	2
C_1 & C_3	3
C_2 & C_4	4

REFLECTED NUMBERS

When counting in a positional number system, occasionally all the digits of a number must be changed in order to obtain the following number in sequence. For instance, the number after 199999 is 200000. If the indicator of a mechanized counter should fall somewhere between these two numbers, the actual number read out may vary anywhere from 100000 and 299999.

table A6 REFLECTED NUMBERS

Decimal	Reflected Decimal	Reflected Octal	Reflected Quarternary	Reflected Binary
0	0	0	0	0
1	1	1	1	1
2	2	2	2	11
3	3	3	3	10
4	4	4	13	110
5	5	5	12	111
6	6	6	11	101
7	7	7	10	100
8	8	17	20	1100
9	9	16	21	1101
10	19	15	22	1111
11	18	14	23	1110
12	17	13	33	1010
13	16	12	32	1011
14	15	11	31	1001
15	14	10	30	1000
16	13	20	130	11000
17	12	21	131	11001
18	11	22	132	11011
19	10	23	133	11010
20	20	24	123	11110
21	21	25	122	11111
22	22	26	121	11101
23	23	27	120	11100
24	24	37	110	10100
25	25	36	111	10101
26	26	35	112	10111
27	27	34	113	10110
28	28	33	103	10010

When we are interested in reducing the error which can be produced by a counter—as we are when converting an analog signal to digital form—a reflected form of the number system may be used. The reflected form possesses the quality that two adjacent numbers differ from each other in the value of only one of the digits. This means that regardless of how many digits a number possesses, only one of two possible digit combinations may be read at any one point.

Examples of reflected number systems are given in Table A6. Figure A1 is a pictorial illustration of the reflected binary system with a 2^4 modulus. Because

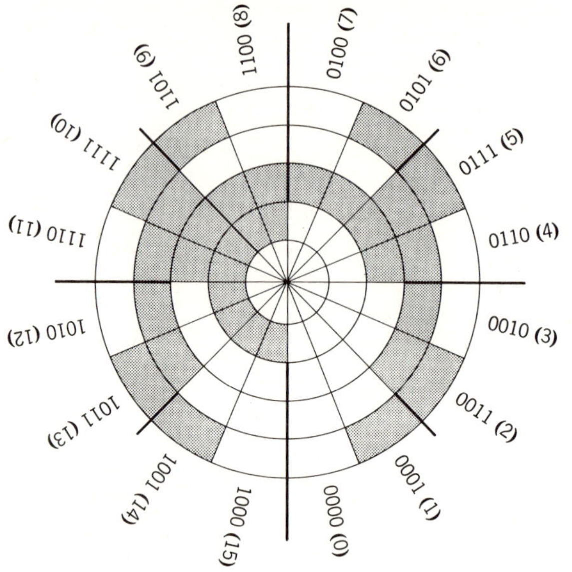

Figure A1 Reflected binary in modulus 2^4.

the number after 15 is 0, the number system may be represented by a circle with 16 subdivisions as shown. A black area represents a bit of ONE and a blank area represents a bit of ZERO. Note that the pattern of the three outside bands on the left half of the circle is the mirror image of the pattern on the three outside bands on the right side of the circle. If the two outside bands are considered, the pattern in each quarter circle is the mirror image of the pattern in the adjacent quarter circle. If only the outside band is considered, the pattern in each eighth-circle is a mirror image of the pattern in the adjacent eighth-circle. Similar mirror images or reflected patterns exist in all reflected number systems.

STANDARD CODES

To accommodate the characters of the alphabet as well as the digits and a few other control characters requires 6 bits. One such 6-bit standard called the Transcode is shown in Table A7. The table shows that it is a subset of the 8-bit EBCDIC (Extended Binary Coded Decimal Interchange Code) obtained by dropping bits in order positions 7 and 8. The 8-bit code is needed to accommodate upper- and lowercase letters as well as a host of control characters required for communication purposes.

table A7 EXTENDED BINARY CODED DECIMAL INTERCHANGE CODE (EBCDIC)

Order of Bit Character	8-Bit EBCDIC 87654321	6-Bit Transcode 654321	Bit Order Character	8-Bit EBCDIC 87654321
0	11110000	110000		
1	11110001	110001		
2	11110010	110010		
3	11110011	110011		
4	11110100	110100		
5	11110101	110101		
6	11110110	110110		
7	11110111	110111		
8	11111000	111000		
9	11111001	111001		
A	11000001	000001	*a*	10000001
B	11000010	000010	*b*	10000010
C	11000011	000011	*c*	10000011
D	11000100	000100	*d*	10000100
E	11000101	000101	*e*	10000101
F	11000110	000110	*f*	10000110
G	11000111	000111	*g*	10000111
H	11001000	001000	*h*	10001000
I	11001001	001001	*i*	10001001
J	11010001	010001	*j*	10010001
K	11010010	010010	*k*	10010010
L	11010011	010011	*l*	10010011
M	11010100	010100	*m*	10010100
N	11010101	010101	*n*	10010101
O	11010110	010110	*o*	10010110
P	11010111	010111	*p*	10010111
Q	11011000	011000	*q*	10011000
R	11011001	011001	*r*	10011001
S	11100010	100010	*s*	10100010
T	11100011	100011	*t*	10100011
U	11100100	100100	*u*	10100100
V	11100101	100101	*v*	10100101
W	11100110	100110	*w*	10100110
X	11100111	100111	*x*	10100111
Y	11101000	101000	*y*	10101000
Z	11101001	101001	*z*	10101001

Another standard is USASCII (United States of America Standard Code for Information Interchange). The coded representations for alphabetic and numeric characters in this standard are given in Table A8. A 7-bit subset obtained by dropping the bit in order position 8 also is shown.

table A8 UNITED STATES OF AMERICA STANDARD CODE FOR INFORMATION INTERCHANGE

Bit Order	8-Bit 87654321	7-Bit 7654321	Bit Order	8-Bit 87654321	7-Bit 7654321
Character			Character		
0	00110000	0110000			
1	00110001	0110001			
2	00110010	0110010			
3	00110011	0110011			
4	00110100	0110100			
5	00110101	0110101			
6	00110110	0110110			
7	00110111	0110111			
8	00111000	0111000			
9	00111001	0111001			
A	01000001	1000001	*a*	01100001	1100001
B	01000010	1000010	*b*	01100010	1100010
C	01000011	1000011	*c*	01100011	1100011
D	01000100	1000100	*d*	01100100	1100100
E	01000101	1000101	*e*	01100101	1100101
F	01000110	1000110	*f*	01100110	1100110
G	01000111	1000111	*g*	01100111	1100111
H	01001000	1001000	*h*	01101000	1101000
I	01001001	1001001	*i*	01101001	1101001
J	01001010	1001010	*j*	01101010	1101010
K	01001011	1001011	*k*	01101011	1101011
L	01001100	1001100	*l*	01101100	1101100
M	01001101	1001101	*m*	01101101	1101101
N	01001110	1001110	*n*	01101110	1101110
O	01001111	1001111	*o*	01101111	1101111
P	01010000	1010000	*p*	01110000	1110000
Q	01010001	1010001	*q*	01110001	1110001
R	01010010	1010010	*r*	01110010	1110010
S	01010011	1010011	*s*	01110011	1110011
T	01010100	1010100	*t*	01110100	1110100
U	01010101	1010101	*u*	01110101	1110101
V	01010110	1010110	*v*	01110110	1110110
W	01010111	1010111	*w*	01110111	1110111
X	01011000	1011000	*x*	01111000	1111000
Y	01011001	1011001	*y*	01111001	1111001
Z	01011010	1011010	*z*	01111010	1111010

Copies of the complete EBCDIC and USASCII as well as of other standards may be obtained from the American Standards Association, Inc., 10 East 40th Street, New York, New York, 10016.

Glossary

Acceptor. An element which when used as an impurity in a semiconductor, introduces positive holes.

Access time. The time it takes to complete a transfer to or from a storage device.

Accumulator. A register which accumulates totals and stores the results of most arithmetic operations.

Address. An expression which designates the location of a character or word in a storage device.

Amplifying element. A device which increases or maintains the energy of signals representing bits or digits.

AND element. A device which produces an output only when all input signals are present.

Assembler. A program that translates instructions given in assembly language form into machine instruction words.

Assembly language. A language in which instructions are written with symbolic commands and symbolic and relative addresses.

Associative criterion. The word or part of a word against which the contents of the cells of a content addressable storage device are compared.

Asynchronous computer. A computer whose microcommands are not executed according to times from a master clock ; one operation begins after the previous operation is completed.

Asynchronous data set. A data set that does not have to have the data supplied to it at a clocked rate.

Band. A group of tracks which are often written onto or read from at one time.

Base. Number of digits (or bits) to a number system.

Binary. Involving the integer two.

Binary adder (BA). A device which produces the correct binary sum and carry bits with each combination of augend, addend, and previous carry bits.

Binary coded-decimal notation. A decimal number system in which each digit is represented by a group of bits (for instance, 8421, excess-3 systems).

Binary comparator (BC). A device that produces a ONE when its two input bits are unequal and a ZERO when equal. A quarter adder.

Binary counter. A device or circuit that counts in the binary number system: produces numbers consisting of 1–0 combinations when pulses are applied to its input.

Binary point. The point that marks the separation between integral powers of 2 and fractional powers of 2.

Binary subtractor. A device that produces the binary difference and borrow bits, with each input combination of minuend, subtrahend, and previous borrow bits.

Bit. One of the two elements used in the binary number system. Also one of the two elements used in coded-decimal systems.

Bit-coded counter. A device or circuit that, when pulses are applied to its input, produces 1–0 combinations representing binary-coded numbers.

Bit-time. The time for the passage of a bit in a serial system, for the passage of a word in a parallel system, and for the passage of a digit in a serial-parallel system.

Block. A group of words considered or transported as a unit, particularly with reference to input and output.

Branch instruction. An instruction which may cause the machine to choose the next instruction out of the usual sequence. *Examples:* Unconditional and conditional jumps and comparison.

Breakpoint. A point in a routine where the computer may be stopped by the operator for a check of the routine.

Breakpoint switch. A switch which causes the computer to stop at certain instructions in the program; for instance, at conditional jumps or at conditional halts.

Buffer storage. A storage device used to accommodate differences in the rate of flow or in method of transmission between two devices when transmitting data from one to the other.

Carry. The digit to be added to the next higher column when the sum of the digits in one column is greater than the radix.

Channel. A path along which data may flow.

Character. A digit, letter, or punctuation symbol, or their coded representations.

Characteristic. That part of a floating-point representation which indicates the size of the exponent.

Clear. To restore a storage device to a prescribed state, usually ZERO.

Clock. A circuit or some physical arrangement which produces pulses at a steady rate.

Clock pulse (CP). One of a stream of pulses occurring at a constant frequency.

Coincident-current selector. A circuit that activates one out of several output lines when current signals are applied coincidentally to two input lines.

Coincident-current storage. A bulk storage device composed of storage cells in a rectangular array. Data is written into and read from a location by sending current coincidentally to the column and row lines in which the location occurs.

Command. The portion of the instruction that tells the computer what to do (add, transfer, etc.).

Comparator. A functional building block which determines whether two input pulse combinations are the same or different.

Comparison instruction. An instruction that compares two numbers to see which is larger or smaller and then performs a jump on the basis of the result.

Compiler. A program that translates compiler language statements and compiles them into machine instruction words.

Compiler language. A language in which are used problem-oriented statements that do not bear a 1-to-1 relationship with machine instructions.

Complement. 10's—The number that must be added to the given number to obtain the modulus in the decimal system.

9's—One less than the 10's complement.

2's—The number which must be added to the given number to obtain the modulus in the binary system.

1's—One less than the 2's complement.

Complement generator. A device that produces as output, the complement of its input.

Concurrency. The process of performing several different operations simultaneously within the computer.

Conditional halt. An instruction which causes the machine to come to a halt only if a halt switch on the control panel is thrown.

Conditional jump. An instruction which causes the machine to execute a specified instruction out of the normal sequence, only if certain conditions are met.

Content addressable storage. A storage device that searches for data by comparing the contents of all of its storage cells with a given word or part of a word.

Continuous record. A record where a long string of data is stored on one unit. A good example is magnetic tape.

Control word. A word storing data that may be of aid in the execution of an instruction.

Converter. A device for converting data stored in one form into data in another form. This device usually operates externally to the computer itself.

Coordinate access storage. A storage device whose word locations are arranged in space.

Cycle stealing. The removing of one or more memory cycles in the instruction stream for use in other operations, usually I/O transfers.

Cycle time. The time between references to the storage device.

Cyclic access storage. A storage device whose word locations are arranged in time (as well as space) in such a manner that access to any one location may be obtained repeatedly according to a definite rate.

Data word. A data word consists of numbers or characters which are to be processed. A number word may consist of digits and sign.

Decimal counter. A counter which counts in the decimal number system—produces numbers consisting of combinations of digits 0 to 9—when pulses are applied to its input.

Decoder. A network of AND circuits which is used to convert a combination of signals into an output on one of several output lines.

Destructive read-out. Storage in which the data is changed when it is read out.

Detector. A functional building block which produces a pulse when certain combinations of pulses are applied to it.

Diagnostic routine. A routine placed in the computer which is used to determine the cause of a malfunction in the computer or a mistake in coding.

Digit. A symbol representing one of the elements in a positional number system.

Direct address. An address in the instruction word that indicates the location where the referenced operand is to be found. Also called the 1st level address.

Donor. An element that, when used as an impurity in a semiconductor, introduces negative free electrons.

Double-rank register. A shift register consisting of two rows of storage cells: one row for actual storage of the bits, the other row for temporary storage of bits while they are being shifted to another stage.

Duplex. A line allowing simultaneous data transmission in both directions.

Dynamic flip-flop. A circuit with two inputs and two outputs. The set input pulse produces a series of pulses on the 1-output side and no pulses on the ZERO output line. The reset input pulse produces the reverse.

Dynamic storage. A storage device that stores bits by continuous recirculation of a wave or other physical phenomenon.

Dynamic storage cell. A cell which has two possible outputs: a continuous series of pulses (ONE) or of no pulses (ZERO). A set pulse flips the cell into the ONE state; a reset pulse flips the cell into the ZERO state.

Editing. The adding, deleting, and modification of data before outputing a message.

Encoder. A network of OR circuits in which only one input is excited at a time and each input produces a combination of outputs.

Erasable storage. Storage in which bits may be replaced by other bits.

Excess-3 code. A number code in which the decimal digit is represented by the binary equivalent of the number plus 3.

Exceed-capacity overflow. An overflow that implies that the result of an operation is a number greater than the capacity of a register.

Exclusive OR circuit. A circuit which produces an output only when either one or the other of two inputs but *not both* are present.

External storage. Data stored on a medium that is not a permanent part of the computer.

Fixed-point computer. A computer in which the decimal or binary point is assumed to be in a fixed location.

Fixed word. A word possessing a fixed number of digits.

Flip-flop (R–S). A 1-bit storage device with two input terminals and two output terminals. The device remains in either state until caused to change to the other state by the application of the corresponding signal. In either state, the signal on one output terminal is out of phase with the signal on the other output terminal.

Flip-flop (J–K). This is the same as an R–S flip-flop except that, when set and reset pulses are applied simultaneously, the state of the device flips.

Floating-point computer. A computer which carries data words in exponential form. It can deal directly with fractional as well as integral numbers.

Forbidden-combination check. A check which tests for occurrence of a nonpermissible code combination.

Formatting. Placing a message into a form to make it more understandable to a human. It includes paragraphing, tabulation, and line spacing.

Four-address instruction. An instruction with 4 addresses. These addresses specify the two operands, the result, and the address of the next instruction to be executed.

Fractional computer. A computer dealing with fractional numbers, that is, numbers smaller in magnitude than one.

Gate. Another name for a switching circuit.

Read-in—switching circuit which allows data to be written into a register.

Read-out—switching circuit which allows data to be read from a register.

Generator circuit. A circuit which generates a certain combination of pulses under certain circumstances.

Half-adder (HA). A device which produces the binary sum and carry of two bits.

Half-duplex. A line allowing transmission in both directions but not simultaneously.

Horizontal parity check. The comparison of the sum of 1 bits in each bit position of a group of characters to determine if it is odd or even. It is used to check messages.

Hysteresis. The property of magnetic materials which prevents them from coming back to their original magnetic state after the magnetizing force is removed.

Hysteresis loop. A graphical representation of the variation in the state of a magnetic material as the magnetic force applied to it is varied in the plus and minus directions.

Immediate address. An address in the instruction word that is the operand itself. It also is called a 0-level address.

Index register. A counter that is used to modify address portions of instructions before the instructions are executed.

Indirect address. An address in the instruction word that indicates a location where the *address* of the referenced operand is to be found. Also called 2nd level address.

Indirect address instruction. An instruction word in which the address part is given in indirect form.

Inhibit element. A device which allows a signal to pass through only when another signal is not present.

Instruction word. A word used to inform the machine what operation to perform. It consists of a command and one or several addresses.

Integral computer. A computer dealing with whole numbers, that is numbers above 1 in magnitude.

Jump. An instruction which conditionally or unconditionally directs the computer to the next instruction. It usually alters the normal instruction sequencing.

Large Scale Integration (LSI). A batch fabrication technique which produces more than 100 integrated circuits on a semiconductor chip.

Latency time. The time it takes to find an address in a storage device.

Least significant digit (LSD). The rightmost digit of a number.

Left circular shift. An operation in which bits in a register are moved a given number of positions to the left. Bits removed from the left-hand side are reentered at the right.

Left shift. An operation in which the bits in a register are moved a given number of positions to the left. Bits removed from the left-hand side are dropped.

Line concentrator. A device that allows several remote terminals to be connected to one communication line.

Loop. A self-contained series of instructions in which the last instruction can cause a modification and can make the series repeat itself, until a terminal condition is reached.

Magnetic saturation. The point where any further increase in the magnetizing force applied to a magnetic material causes an almost negligible change in the magnetic state of the material. A material may be magnetically saturated in one of 2 possible directions.

Malfunction. A failure in operation of the computer hardware.

Mantissa. That part of a floating point representation which specifies the significant digits of the number.

Medium Scale Integration (MSI). A batch fabrication technique which produces up to 100 integrated circuits on a semiconductor chip.

Memory. Internal storage forming an integral part of the computer and directly controlled by the computer.

Microcommand. One of the many operations that must be performed in order to complete a command. *Examples:* opening a gate, resetting a flip-flop, causing a register to shift its contents to the right.

Modulus. One more than the maximum number attainable in any practical counting device.

Modulus counter. A device which produces an output pulse after a certain number of input pulses or multiples of this number are applied.

Most significant digit (MSD). The leftmost digit of a number.

Multiplexer. A device that allows several external devices to be connected to one I/O channel.

Multiprocessing. The division of a computer system into functional units that execute their tasks simultaneously.

Multiprogramming. A technique for executing several programs simultaneously.

***n*-crystal.** A semiconductor to which donor impurities have been added.

Nesting. The process of embedding a subroutine within another subroutine. This may be done to many levels.

Nondestructive read-out. Storage in which bits remain stored even after they are read out.

Nonerasable storage. Storage which does not allow the bits to be erased.

Nonvolatile. Storage which does not lose its data even when the power is turned off.

Nonreturn-to-zero magnetic recording. Magnetic recording in which a ONE is written when current flows in one direction, and a ZERO is written when current flows in the opposite direction. Current passes through the zero point only when a ONE is followed by a ZERO, or a ZERO is followed by a ONE.

Octal notation. A system for representing numbers in the radix of 8.

Off-line. An operation that proceeds completely independent of computer operation.

On-line. An operation that is tied directly to the computer and is under control of the program in the computer.

OR element. A device which produces an output if one or all of its input lines are energized. This circuit performs the inclusive OR function.

Order. Rank of bit position in a coded decimal system.

One-address instruction. An instruction word with only 1 address. The address indicates one of the operands upon which the operation is to be performed.

Overflow. The occurrence of a carry from the most significant position of a word.

***p*-crystal.** A semiconductor to which acceptor impurities have been added.

Parallel storage. Storage in which all bits, characters or words are essentially equally available in space. Time is not one of the coordinates.

Parallel transmission. All bits of a word are transmitted simultaneously.

Parity check. Comparison of sum of 1 bits in a coded representation to see if it is odd or even.

Parity detector. A device that compares the bits of a character against its vertical parity bit, or the bits in each bit position of a group of characters against its horizontal parity character, to determine if an error has occurred during transmission.

Parity generator. A device that compares the bits of a character or the bits in each bit position of a group of characters, to produce an odd or even parity bit, or character, respectively.

Polling. Interrogating a group of devices in a channel by a code. The device that is ready returns an appropriate reply.

Program. The complete sequence of instruction words or statements needed for a computer to accomplish a given task.

Program interrupt. To temporarily disrupt the normal sequencing of a program when a certain event occurs. Usually normal sequencing can be resume from that point at a later time.

Push down stack. A register stack in which the last item entered is the first item available, and the relative position of the other items is pushed back one.

Pyramid or tree. A decoding network which looks like a pyramid.

Quarter-adder. A device which produces a ONE when its two input bits are unequal and a ZERO when equal. A binary comparator.

Radix. See base.

Random access device. A device in which it takes as long to obtain access to one address as it does to any other address.

Reading. The process of determining what bits or digits are stored in a storage device. The data may or may not be erased during reading.

Recorder. A device which is used to manually write onto a document or storage medium.

Rectangle. A modified matrix.

Redundancy check. A check which uses extra digits to help detect malfunctions and mistakes.

Register. A device or circuit used to store temporarily numbers consisting of several digits.

Relative address. An address which is easily converted to an absolute address by adding or subtracting a factor.

Remanence. The magnetic state in which a magnetic material falls when the magnetizing force is removed. Materials have positive and negative remanence states.

Return-to-zero Magnetic recording. Magnetic recording in which a ONE is written by a pulse of current rising to a level and then returning to zero; and a ZERO is written by a pulse of current rising to a level in the opposite direction and then returning to zero.

Right circular shift. An operation in which the bits in a register are moved a given number of positions to the right. Bits removed from the right-hand side are reentered at the left.

Right shift. An operation in which the bits in a register are moved a given number of positions to the right. Bits removed from the right-hand side are dropped.

Ring counter. A device consisting of a loop of interconnecting bistable elements, only one of which can be in a specified state at any time. Each successive applied pulse causes another element in the loop to switch to the specified state.

Routine. A set of instructions arranged in sequence which directs a computer to perform a certain operation or series of operations.

Sampling instruction. An instruction which looks at the state of the input register. If it is not full, the next instruction in sequence is executed. If it is full, the contents are transferred to the memory and an instruction out of sequence is executed next.

Scanning. The examination of each of a group of items, channels, or devices in turn.

Selector. A circuit which chooses instructions to be executed.

Self-checking code. A coded-decimal system in which it is easy to check each character because of a redundancy in each character.

Self-complementing code. A code in which all numbers may be converted to their 9's or 1's complements by inverting 1's and 0's.

Semiconductor. An element which possesses conductivity that is in between that of a conductor and of an insulator.

Sense amplifier. An amplifier plus the associated circuitry required to convert storage output signals into a form which makes them understood by the rest of the computer.

Sequential access storage. A storage device whose word locations are arranged in time in such a manner that access to any one location may normally be obtained only once during an operation.

Serial-parallel transmission. All digits are transmitted serially; but the bits which make up the digits are transmitted in parallel.

Serial storage. Storage in which time is one of the coordinates used to locate any given bit, character or word.

Serial transmission. All bits of a word are transmitted sequentially.

Shifting register. A register that consists of discrete storage cells, and in which bits may be advanced from one cell to the other by means of applied shift pulses.

Significance. Rank of digit position in a number.

Simplex. A line providing data transmission in one direction.

Square hysteresis loop. A hysteresis loop where the upper and lower saturation lines are fairly flat.

Static storage. A storage device which stores bits by staying in one of several stable states.

Storage element. A device which is used to store bits or digits either temporarily or permanently.

Stored program computer. A computer whose program is stored in the memory of the machine. The program is usually prepared on an external storage medium and then fed to the memory.

Subregister. A portion of a register that handles a group of bits flowing serially in serial –parallel transmission.

Subroutine. A well-defined portion of a program that is called on by the main program or routine for execution, after which control is returned to the main routine.

Switching circuit. A circuit that produces an output for certain combinations of input.

Symbolic address. An address in the instruction word that is given by a name or a mnemonic code to specify a storage location within the context of a particular program.

Sync pulse. A pulse produced on coincidence of input timing pulse from external storage and timing pulse from computer. This pulse is used to gate the associated digit into the input register.

Synchronizer. A storage device used to compensate for a difference in a rate of flow of data or the time of occurrence of events when transmitting data from one device to another.

Synchronous computer. A computer whose microcommands are executed at times controlled by a master clock.

Synchronous data set. A data set that must be furnished the data bits at a clocked rate.

Temporary storage component. A component which stores bits for a short time; a delay element.

Test routine. A routine which tests for proper functioning of the computer.

Three-address instruction. An instruction with 3 addresses. These addresses specify the two operands and the address of the result.

Time-sharing. An extended form of multiprogramming in which slices of time are allotted to the various programs in order to achieve fast computer response for users interacting with the system.

Timing pulse. A pulse always occurring at a definite point in a repeated cycle.

Track. That portion of a moving type storage medium (tape, drum, etc.) which is accessible to a given writing or reading station.

Translator. A network to which are applied signals representing data in a certain code and the outputs of which are signals representing the same data but in a different code.

Truth table. A statement of all conditions of a problem in tabular form.

Two-address instruction. An instruction word with 2 addresses. One address indicates one of the operands upon which the operation is to be performed; the other address indicates where in memory can be found the next instruction.

Unconditional jump. An instruction which always causes the machine to execute a specified instruction out of the normal sequence.

Unit record. A record where a small group of characters is stored as one item. Unit records are easy to file. Punched cards are an example.

Variable word. A word composed of a variable number of characters.

Vertical parity check. A comparison of the sum of 1 bits in a coded representation to determine if it is odd or even. It is used to check characters.

Volatile storage. Storage which loses its data with time, or if the power is turned off.

Writing. The process of placing bits or digits into a storage device.

Word. A set of bits or digits which is treated by the computer as a unit.

Word space. The space (usually in storage) occupied by a word, plus the space between words if present.

Word-time. The time it takes for a word space to pass by a certain point. Used especially in reference to serial storage devices.

Word-time address. Numerical value given to the word space in storage with reference to a certain zero point in time. Used especially in reference to serial storage devices.

Write amplifier. An amplifier plus the associated circuitry required to convert computer data signals into the form needed for driving a storage device.

BIBLIOGRAPHY

1. *Computer Oriented Mathematics*, National Council of Teachers of Mathematics, 1201 16th St. NW, Washington, D.C. See the chapter entitled "Repetitite Processes and Approximations."
2. N. Ya Vilenkin, *Successive Approximation*, Pergamon Press, Oxford/Macmillan Company, New York, 1964. This book presents several methods of successive approximation using geometric concepts.
3. James R. Newman, *The World of Mathematics*, Simon & Schuster, New York, 1956, see especially Vol I, Part III, "Arithmetic, Numbers, and the Art of Counting;" and Vol III, Part XIII, "Mathematics and Logic." Very interesting exposition of the basics of these subjects.
4. *Language and Symbology of Digital Computer Systems*, RCA Service Company, 1959. Logic symbols.
5. Ivan Flores, *Computer Design*, Prentice Hall, Englewood Cliffs, New Jersey, 1967. Logic and numbers.
6. *Boolean Algebra—A Self-Instructional Programmed Manual*, Prentice Hall, Englewood Cliffs, New Jersey, 1966. This book discusses number systems, truth tables, Venn diagrams, and minimization techniques. It is simple, easy to use, and covers all the basic ideas.
7. Morton Nadler, *Topics in Engineering Logic*, Pergamon Press, New York, 1962. Logic, Veitch diagrams.
8. H. Graham Flagg, *Boolean Algebra and Its Application*, John Wiley & Sons, New York, 1964. A good description of algebra of classes, switching algebra and simplification methods, plus more advanced subjects.
9. R. K. Richards, *Digital Computer Components and Circuits*, Van Nostrand, Princeton, New Jersey, 1957. An extensive discussion of diode, transistor, vacuum tube, and electromagnetic logic circuits.
10. A. J. Meyerhoff (ed.), *Digital Applications of Magnetic Devices*, John Wiley & Sons, New York, 1960. A thorough discussion of the use of magnetic devices for computer switching, amplification, and storage.

11. S. L. Oppenheimer, *Semiconductor Logic and Switching Circuits*, Charles E. Merrill Books, Columbus, Ohio, 1966. Solid state digital circuits and switches for the technician.

12. W. S. Bennett, *Binary Logic*, McGraw Hill Book Company, New York, 1963. Switching logic, including hydraulic, pneumatic, mechanical, optical, and so on.

13. Robert G. Middleton, *Elements of Transistor Technology*, Howard W. Sams, New York, 1963. A simplified discussion of transistor circuits.

14. Seymour Schwartz, *Selected Semiconductor Circuits Handbook*, John Wiley & Sons, New York, 1960. Specific switching circuits, amplifiers, and power-supply building blocks.

15. Samuel H. Caldwell, *Switching Circuits and Logical Design*, John Wiley & Sons, New York, 1967. More than 600 pages of information about switching circuits and switching algebra, as well as more advanced topics in logic design. It describes relay, electronic, and solid state switching circuits.

16. ITT Federal Electric Corporation, *Transistors, A Self-Instructional Programmed Manual*, Prentice Hall, Englewood Cliffs, New Jersey, 1962. A simplified description of the basics of transistors, including their use in logic circuits. A self-learning text.

17. A. S. Hoagland, *Digital Magnetic Recording*, John Wiley & Sons, New York. A discussion of magnetic recording used in storage devices. Calculus is used.

18. Raymond E. Miller, *Switching Theory*, Vol I, "Combinational Circuits" John Wiley & Sons, New York, 19—. A discussion of many combinational circuits.

19. David C. Evans, "Computer Logic and Memory", *Scientific American* September 1966. A discussion of computer logic, flip-flops, registers, and memory.

20. R. K. Richards, *Arithmetic Operations in Digital Computers*, Van Nostrand, Princeton, New Jersey, 1955. Configurations of a variety of serial and parallel logic diagrams for accomplishing arithmetic and related operations.

21. Van Ness, *Principles of Punched Card Data Processing*, Business Press, Elmhurst, Illinois, 1967. It includes coverage of all punched card equipment, operations, and practices.

22. McGill, *Punched Cards: Data Processing for Profit Improvement*, McGraw Hill Book Company, New York, 1962.

23. Raymond M. Warner Jr. (ed.), *Integrated Circuits, Design Principles and Fabrication*, McGraw Hill Book Company, New York, 1965. A thorough discussion of the theory, design, and techniques of fabrication of integrated circuits.

24. E. M. Award et al., *Automatic Data Processing*, Prentice Hall, Englewood Cliff, New Jersey, 1966. A quarter of the book is on punched cards and their use.

25. Edward Keonjian, *Microelectronics: Theory, Design, and Fabrication*, McGraw Hill Book Company, New York, 1963. A comprehensive description of semiconductor integrated circuits of various types.

26. James A. Taunt, *Digital Tape Drives*, Business Press, Elmhurst, Illinois, 1965. A good coverage of the mechanical and electronic features of the magnetic tape drive. It discusses many design problems common to other storage devices.

27. Adi J. Khambata, *Introduction to Integrated Semiconductor Circuits*, John Wiley & Sons, New York, 1963. A descriptive discussion on fundamentals, design, logic, and fabrication of integrated circuits.

28. Fred J. Gruenberger, Daniel D. McCracker, *Introduction to Electronic Computers*, John Wiley and Sons, New York, 1963. A simple introduction to computers and programming. It discusses assemblers and FORTRAN.

26. P. A. Stark, *Digital Computer Programming*, Macmillan and Company, New York, 1967. It is easy to follow and includes FORTRAN IV.

30. D. D. McCracken, *Guide to FORTRAN IV Programming*, John Wiley and Sons, New York, 1965. A paperback that is a simple and straightforward exposition of the use of FORTRAN in solution of problems by computer. It includes a great many examples.

31. Eric A. Weiss, *Programming the IBM* 1620, McGraw Hill Book Company, New York, 1965. A simple exposition of how to program a specific computer in FORTRAN.

32. James H. Howard, *Electronic Information Display System* Spartan Books, 1965. This book covers many types of displays and their applications.

33. Ivan E. Sutherland, "Computer Inputs and Outputs," *Scientific American*, September 1966. An extremely interesting survey of the methods of inputting and outputting information, especially via graphic displays.

34. John R. Pierce, "Transmission of Computer Data," *Scientific American*, September 1966. A general discussion of various data transmission techniques.

35. J. R. Ziegler, *Time Sharing Data Processing Systems*, Prentice Hall, Englewood Cliffs, New Jersey 1967. A good general description of time-sharing applications.

36. D. F. Parkhill, *Challenge of the Computer Utility*, Addison-Wesley Publishing Company, Reading, Massachusetts, 1966. A discussion of the use of time-sharing to develop utilities that dispense computer power, as an electrical utility dispenses electrical power.

37. W. Buchholz, *Planning a Computer System*, McGraw Hill Book Company, New York, 1962. Advanced concepts of control and organization. It should be read only after the student has obtained a thorough mastery of this text book.

38. Walter J. Karplus, *On-Line Computing*, McGraw Hill Book Company, New York, 1967. A description of on-line systems from several points of view, plus the descriptions of many applications.

39. R. M. Fano, and F. J. Corbato, "Time Sharing on Computers," *Scientific American*, September, 1966. A general discussion of time-sharing.

Literature about specific computer systems can be obtained from the following manufacturers.

1. *Burroughs Corporation.* 6071 Second Ave, Detroit, Michigan.
2. *Control Data Corporation.* 8100 34th Ave S., Minneapolis, Minnesota.
3. *Digital Equipment Corporation.* 141 Main St., Maynard, Massachusetts.
4. *Honeywell, Inc.,* EDP Division. 60 Walnut Street, Wellesley Hills, Massachusetts.
5. *IBM Corporation,* Data Processing Division, 112 East Post Road, White Plains, New York.
6. *National Cash Register Company,* Main and K Sts, Dayton, Ohio.
7. *Radio Corporation of America,* EDP Division, Cherry Hill, New Jersey.
8. *Xerox Data Systems,* 701 South Aviation Boulevard, El Segundo, California.
9. *UNIVAC Division, Sperry Rand Corporation,* P.O. Box 8100, Philadelphia, Pennsylvania.

Index

Abacus, 3
Access, coordinate, 198
cyclic, 198, 209
random, 201
sequential, 198
time, 199
Accumulator, 189, 325, 407
Accuracy of computer, 7
Acoustic coupler, 300
Add 6 circuit, 328
Addend, 51
Adder, abacus, 3
binary, *see* Binary adder
coincidence, 184
half, 83, 95, 185
parallel, 185
quarter, 83, 95
serial, 185
serial-parallel, 326
specimen computer, 410
Addition, absolute value, 51
algebraic, 51, 185, 329
binary, 32
serial and parallel, 185
serial-parallel, 326
using complements, 52, 331
Address, 201
column, 201
content, 204
direct, 248
immediate, 248
indirect, 248
levels, 248
row, 201
time, 202
Addressing, for channel sharing, 305
Address selection, 201, 403
Address translation, 359
Algebra of classes, 74
Alphanumeric code, 45, 438
Amplification, 96
Amplifying circuits, electromagnetic, 131
relay, 107
transistor, 120
Analog computer, 6
Analog-to-digital converter, 305
AND element, graphical, 77
expression, 79
inverted, 81
logical block, 93
mechanical, 105
relay, 105
silicon diode, 112
AND–OR relationship, 81
Approximation formula for square root, 61
Arithmetic, of specimen computer, 407
and logic unit, 325
Array processor, 390
Associative addressing, 204
Associative criterion, 222
Associative law, 79
Asynchronous operation, 361
Asynchronous transmission, 302
Augend, 51

Band, 212
Base, 27
Batch fabrication of integrated circuits, 225

Binary adder, block diagram, 97, 185
expression, 84, 95
truth table, 84
Binary arithmetic, 32, 62
Binary comparator, definition, 83, 93
expression, 83, 176
inverse of, 176
logical block diagram, 95, 176
truth table, 83, 176
Binary number system, 29
Binary-octal equivalents, 39
Binary point, location of, 64
Binary subtractor, 189
Bit, 30
order, 44
Block, 307
Block diagrams, logical, 93
Block transfer, 307
Boolean comparison, 348
Branch instruction, 362
Breakpoint, 420
Building blocks, functional, 243
logical, 105
summary, 196
Bulk, logic, 196
storage, 197
switching, 225
Bus, memory, 283

Cache memory, 383
Calculating machines, 4
Card reader, 294
Carry, end-around, 52, 63
propagation of, 190
Casting out 7's, 69
Casting out 9's, 69
Channel, 293
sharing, 304
Characteristic, of a number, 253
Checking, casting out 7's, 69
casting out 9's, 68
circuits, 257
duplication, 67
forbidden combination, 44
inverse arithmetic, 67
parity, 45
specimen computer, 397
Clock pulse, 153, 167
Code, alphanumeric, 45, 438
command, for specimen computer, 398
EBCDIC, 45, 438
error correcting, 435
excess 3, 434
excess 6, 434
modified bi-quinary, 435
modified qui-binary, 435
nonweighted 4-bit, 434
reflected, 436
self-checking, 44
self-complementing, 434
7-bit, 438
standard, 438
teletype, 46
Transcode, 47, 438
two out of five, 435
USASCII, 45, 438
weighted bit, 434
Coded-deciman notation, 39
Coincidence Adder, 184
Coincident-current selector, 144
Coincident-current storage, 217, 279
Column address, 201
Command, 247
Command code, *see* Instructions
Command translator, 359
Communication channel, 294
Communication devices, 297
Commutative law, 79
Comparison instruction, 363
Complementer, 5421 code, expression, 86
truth table, 86
Complement form for numbers, 251
Complement generator, 182
Complements, principle of, 40
1's and 2's, 44
9's and 10's, 43
Computer, analog, 6
digital, 6
fractional, 251
functional organization of, 12
integral, 251
output microfilmer, (COM), 320
specimen, characteristics of, 398
Concentrator, line, 299
Concurrency, 315, 375
Conditional halt, 365
jump, 418
Console, of specimen computer, 418
Content addressable storage, 222
Content address selection, 204, 379
Continuous record, 209
Control, arithmetic, 358, 415

asynchronous, 361
input-output, 307, 317
of specimen computer, 414
synchronous, 361
unit, 352
word, 310, 373
Converter, analog-to-digital, 305
digital-to-analog, 305
magnetic tape to high-speed printer, 320
punched card to magnetic tape, 320
Coordinate access storage, 198, 217
Core, magnetic, 125
storage array, 217
Corrector, for binary-coded decimal adder, 326
Counter, backward counting, 169
binary, 168
cycle, 355
decimal, 171
forward counting, 167
instruction, 353
modulus, 164
ring, 165
Counting, 26
Counting board, 3
Crystal, silicon, 110
Cycle, machine, 352
of memory, 280
stealing, 315, 375
time, 273, 199
Cycle counter, 355
Cyclic access storage, 198, 209

Data entry devices, 319
Data paths, 253
Data set, 300
Data structure, 245
Data transmission, 255, 300
Data units, 245
Data word, 250
Decimal counting, 27, 29
Decimal point, location of, 64
Decoder, coincident current, 144
definition, 141
diode matrix, 142
integrated circuit, 227
relay tree, 141
Detector, definition of, 140
end-of-block, 310
forbidden combination, 8421 code, 141
Diagnostic routine, 429
Digit, 1
Digital-to-analog converter, 306
Diode, silicon, 112
translator, 142
Disc, magnetic, 214
Display, 298
Distributive law, 79
Division, mechanization of, 342
pencil and paper method, 55
repeated subtraction method, 56
restoring method, 56
Domain theory, 128
Dot convention for magnetic cores, 129
Double-rank shift register, 158
Drum, magnetic, 211, 286
Duodecimal notation, 29
Duplex, 301
Duplication, checking by, 67
Dynamic flip-flop, 133
Dynamic storage, 133

Emitter follower, 120
Encoder, decimal-to-binary-coded decimal, 149
definition, 145
diode matrix, 149
mechanical, 146
relay, 146

End-around carry, 52, 63
End of block (EOB), 297
End of text, (EOT), 302
Excess-3 code, 434
Excess-6 code, 434
Exclusive OR, definition, 76, 80
logical block diagram, 93
truth table, 83
Execute phase, 353
Exponential numbers, 25
Extended Binary Coded Decimal Interchange Code, EBCDIC, 45
External storage, 295
Extract, 347

Fetch phase, 353
Firmware, 390
Fixed-point computer, 252
Fixed word, 253
Flip-flop, dynamic, 133
NAND, 232
NOR, 230

J–K, 96
R–S, 96
T, 98
Transistor, 123
Floating point representation, 252
Forbidden combination check, 141
Formal logic, 74
Fractional computer, 251
Functional building blocks, adder, 184
comparison circuit, 176
counter, 164
detector, 140, 178
gate, 140
generator, 178
register, 152
selector, 144
Functional organization of digital computer, 12

Gates, 140
Generator, clock pulse, 167
timing pulse, 167
two's complement, 182
Graphical logic, 74

Half adder, expression, 95
logical block diagram, 95
truth table, 83
Half-current pulses, coincidence with, 217
Half duplex, 301
Halt instruction, 364
Head, magnetic, 208
Hexadecimal notation, 29
High-speed printer, 295
Horizontal parity, 180
Hysteresis loop, definition, 126
magnetic core, 126
nonsquare, 128
square, 128

Inclusive OR, 77
Indexing, 365
Indirect addressing, 371
Inhibit, electromagnetic, 131
inverted, 81
logical block, 93
relationship, 80
truth table, 82
Input-output, of specimen computer, 406
Input device, 294
Input register, 306
Instruction Counter, (IC), 353
Instruction modification, 365
in specimen computer, 418
Instruction sequencing, 1-address, 353
2-address, 355
3-address, 353
4-address, 355
in specimen computer, 415
Instruction types, add, 325, 362
branch, 362
comparison, 363
conditional halt, 364
conditional jump, 362
editing and formatting, 318
grouping of, 247
halt, 364
implied address, 361, 415
input, 317
jump, 362
left shift, 361
memory, 415
multiply, 413
nonmemory, 415
punch, 407
read, 282, 289
right shift, 361, 413
sampling, 312
set NR, 367, 418
for specimen computer, 398
store, 414
subtract, 412
test, 365, 418
transfer, 318, 410
unconditional jump, 362
write, 282, 289
Instruction word, 1-address, 249
2-address, 249
3-address, 250
4-address, 250
indirect address, 250
Integral computer, 251
Integrated circuit arrays, 227
Interleaving, 376
Interrupt, 312
Inverse arithmetic, 67
Inverted AND, element, 81
expression, 81
logical block, 93
transistor, 120
Inverted INHIBIT, element, 81

expression, 81
logical block, 93
Inverted OR, element, 81
expression, 81
logical block, 93
transistor, 120
Inverter, amplifier, 120
Iteration, square root, 61

Jump, unconditional, 362, 418
Jump-no-jump switch, 420
Jump table, 372
Junction transistor, n–p–n, 115
p–n–p, 115

Keyboard, 298
Key-to-tape units, 319

Language, ALGOL, 273
assembly, 268
compiler, 271
FORTRAN, 271
machine, 13
word and number, 20, 23
Latency, 199
Least significant digit (LSD), 26
Left shift, 335
List processing, 379
Loading program for specimen computer, 425
Location address selection, 201
Logic, basic elements of, 74
blocks, 93
classes, 74
connectives, 75
electromagnetic, 125
formal, 74
graphical, 74
identities, 79
laws, 79
math, 78
relay elements, 106
semiconductor elements, 114
simplification, 80
Logical albegra, 78
Logical block diagram, 93
Logical building blocks, 105
Logical comparisons, 348
Look-ahead processor, 387

Machine cycle, 352
language, 13
Magnetic card, 215
disc, 214
drum, 211, 286
recirculating register, 213
ink character reader (MICR), 294
tape controller, 297
tape recording, 209
tape storage, 208
Magnetization curve, 126
Maintenance of specimen computer, 429
Man-machine communication, 16
Mantissa, 253
Manual control, for specimen computer, 418
Mathematical logic, 78
Memory of specimen computer, 402
coincident current magnetic core, 279
content addressable, 290
cyclic access, 286
Message formatting, 299
Metal Oxide Silicon (MOS), 228
Microcommands, 255, 353
Modified bi-quinary code, 435
Modified qui-binary code, 435
Modulation, 300
Modulus, 29, 41
Modulus counter, 164
Most significant digit (MSD), 26
Multi-computer, 389
Multiple processors, 389
Multiplexor, communication, 302
Multiplication, binary table, 33
circuit, for binary, 336
for decimal, 340
method of repeated addition, 54
pencil and paper method, 53
right- and left-hand component method, 54
by shifting, 335
Multi-processor, 388
Multiprogramming, 376
Multivibrator, one shot, 124
Mylar tape, 208

N-type crystal, 110
NAND, 81, 93
Negative numbers, 40
Nesting of subroutines, 386
Nonmemory instruction, 415
Nonreturn to zero recording, 213
Nonsquare hysteresis loop, 128

Nonweighted 4-bit code, 434
NOR, 81, 93
NOR flip-flop, 230
NOT, element, 78
  expression, 78
Notation, binary, 31
  binary-coded decimal, 39
Number comparison program, 421
Numbers, additive, 23
  ancient systems of, 24
  binary, 31
  coded-decimal, 39
  decimal, 26
  duodecimal, 29
  exponential, 25
  hexadecimal, 29
  octal, 29
  positional, 29
  precision of, 251
  reflected, 436
  Roman, 23
  ternary, 29

Octal-binary equivalents, 40
Off-line operation, 319
One-instruction switch, 419
One-shot multivibrator, 124
On-line operation, 294
Operation, of specimen computer, 429
Operational controls, 419
Optical character reader, (OCR), 294
OR, electromagnetic, 131
  element, 77
  exclusive, 77
  expression, 79
  inclusive, 77
  inverted, 81
Order, 40
Organization of specimen computer, 399
Output devices, 295
Overflow, exceed capacity, 329
  in division process, 342

P-type crystal, 110
Paging, 381
Paper tape perforator, 295
Paper tape reader, 294
Parallel transmission, 255
Parity bit detector for specimen computer, 404
Parity bit generator for specimen computer, 404
Parity checking, 45
Parity detector, 178
Parity generator, 178
Pascal, Blaise, 4
Peripheral equipment, 294
Phase shift modulation, 300
Plotter, 295
Polling, 305
Positional number systems, 23, 28
Printed document reader, 294
Printing devices, 234
Program debugging, 427
  examples, 261, 263, 266, 267, 289, 270, 272
  loop, 261, 365
  number comparison, 421
  preparation, 258
  test, 419
Programming, 13, 258, 421
Punched cards, 206
Punched-card-to-magnetic-tape converter, 320
Punched paper tape, 206
  in specimen computer, 406
Push-down stack, 384

Quantitative comparisons, 334
Quarter adder, 83, 95

Radix, 27
Random access, 201
Read-only storage, 233
Read-write cycle, of specimen computer, 402
Recirculating register, drum, 213
Record, continuous, 209
  unit, 207
Recording, magnetic, 213
Rectangular diode decoding network, 142
Rectangular matrix decoder, 142
Rectangular storage array, 217, 279
Redundancy, 22
Reflected numbers, 436
Register, arithmetic, 326, 407
  buffer, 157
  definition of, 152
  display, specimen computer, 421
  double rank, 158
  drum recirculating, 213
  index, 365
  input/output, 306
  instruction, 353
  shift, 153

Relative address, 269
Remanence, 127
Remote terminals, 298
Residue modulus nine (RMN), 68
Residue modulus seven (RMS), 69
Restoring method of division, 56
Return to zero recording, 213
Right shift, 342, 399
Roman number system, 23
Row address, 201

Sampling, 312
Saturation, magnetic, 127
Scanning, 305
Sectors, 211, 286
Segmentation, 381
Selector, 144
Self-checking codes, 44
Self-complementing codes, 434
Semiconductors, 110
Sense amplifier, transistor, 217
Sequencing of instructions, 353
Sequential access storage, 198, 205
Serial-parallel transmission, 257
Serial transmission, 255
Set N register instruction, 367, 418
Sign circuit, 177, 411
Significance, 40
Silicon diode, 112
Simplex connection, 301
Space address, 201
Specimen computer, add, transfer and subtract, 398
  address selection, 403
  arithmetic, 407
  characteristics of, 398
  command code, 422
  console, 418
  control, 414
  debugging, 427
  input-output, 406
  instruction sequencing, 415
  loading, 425
  M register, 404
  manual input, 421
  memory, 402
  number comparison routine, 421
  operation and maintenance, 429
  organization, 399
  parity bit detector and generator, 404
  programming, 421
  punch instruction, 407
  read-write cycle, 402
  register display, 421
  right shift and multiply, 410
  store instruction, 414
  use of N register, 418
Speed of computation, 5
Square hysteresis loop, 128
Square root, approximation formula, 61
  pencil and paper method, 58
  subtractive process, 58
Start of Heading (SOH), 302
Storage, access, 198
  characteristics of components for, 197
  coincident current, 217, 279
  controller, 296
  destructive read-out, 197
  dynamic, 133
  erasable, 197
  external, 293
  magnetic cores for, 128
  need for, 96
  nondestructive read-out, 197
  nonerasable, 197
  nonvolatile, 197
  physical units, 246
  read-only, 197, 233
  relay, 109
  static, 197
  volatile, 197
Storage devices, dynamic storage, 133
  electromagnetic, 128
  magnetic card, 215
  magnetic disc, 214, 296
  magnetic drum, 211, 296
  magnetic tape, 208, 296
  relay, 109
  transistor, 123
Subroutines, 264, 313, 365
Subtraction with the aid of complements, 42
Subtractor, binary, 189
Sum, 51
Switching, bulk, 225
Switching circuits, electromagnetic, 105
  electromechanical, 105
  relay, 106
  semiconductor diode, 109, 114
  transistor, 121
Syllogism, 11, 74
Synchronizer, 406

Synchronous operation, 361
Synchronous transmission, 302
Sync pulse, 406

Tape, magnetic, 208
Telephone, 298
Teletype code, 46
  terminal, 298
Ternary, 31
Test N register instruction, 366
Time, access, 199
Time address, 202
Time-sharing, 378
Timing pulse, 153, 167
Toroid, 128
Touch tone telephone, 300
Track, 211
Transcode, 47
Transfer, of block of words, 307
Transfer instruction, 318, 410
Transformer action, 126
Translation, binary to decimal, 34
  binary to octal, 37
  of commands and addresses, 359
  decimal to binary, 32
  write and read circuits, 283
Transmission, parallel, 255
  serial, 255
  serial-parallel, 257
Tree encoder, relay, 146
Trouble-shooting controls, 419
Truth table, binary adder, 84
  binary comparator, 83
  complementer, 5421 code, 85
  exclusive OR, 84
  half-adder, 83
  purpose of, 82
  quarter-adder, 83
Two out of five code, 435
Typewriter, I/O, 294

Unconditional jump, 362, 418
Unit record, 207
United States of America Standard Code for Interchange, 46
Universal class, 75
Use of specimen computer, 421

Variable length block transfer, 309
Variable word, 253
Veitch diagrams, 86
Venn diagrams, *see* Graphical logic
Vertical parity, 179

Waiting time, 199
Weighted 4-bit codes, 39
Weights, octal, 40
  of bit positions, 40
Word, data, 250
  fixed point, 252
  fixed size versus variable size, 253
  floating point, 252
  fractional, 251
  instruction, 247
  integral, 251
  size, 253
  time, 286
Writing, in specimen computer, 402

Zero, 23
Zero suppression, 318